RAYMOND WILLIAMS

A WARRIOR'S TALE

Dai Smith was born in the Rhondda in 1945. He studied History at Balliol College, Oxford, and Literature at Columbia University, New York City. He was awarded a Ph.D. at Swansea University for a thesis on the South Wales Miners' Federation, subsequently the subject of his book, with Hywel Francis, *The Fed*. He was the contributing editor to the series of essays *A People and A Proletariat* and published, with Gareth Williams, the prize-winning Official History of the Welsh Rugby Union, *Fields of Praise*. Through the 1980s and 1990s, he wrote and edited a number of innovative and provocative books and scholarly articles on the social and cultural history of modern Wales: notably, *Lewis Jones*, *Aneurin Bevan and the World of South Wales* and *Wales: A Question for History*. The latter was an extensively revised version of the book associated with six documentary films he wrote and presented under the title *Wales! Wales?* He went on to make a number of other films on the arts and popular culture, including most recently *The Lost Pictures of Eugene Smith*.

He became Editor BBC Radio Wales in 1993, and was Head of Broadcast (English) there from 1994 until 2000 when he was appointed Pro-Vice-Chancellor at the University of Glamorgan. He had held Lectureships since 1969 at the Universities of Lancaster, Swansea and Cardiff, where he was given a Personal Chair of the University of Wales in 1984, and since 2005 has been Research Chair in the Cultural History of Wales at Swansea University.

RAYMOND WILLIAMS

A WARRIOR'S TALE

DAI SMITH

PARTHIAN

Parthian, Cardigan SA43 1ED
www.parthianbooks.com
First published in 2008
Reprinted 2020
© Dai Smith
ISBN 978-1-913640-08-8
The Modern Wales series receives support from the Rhys Davies Trust
Cover design by Marc Jennings
Typeset by logodædaly
Printed by 4edge Limited
Published with the financial support of the Welsh Books Council
British Library Cataloguing in Publication Data
A cataloguing record for this book is available from the British Library.

For
Norette

Preface

The book that follows leaves its subject, Raymond Williams, in 1961 on the threshold of a public career as writer and intellectual which resounded across the world. It was in that year, 1961, that I was first made aware of his name when the shiny blue Pelican paperback of *Culture and Society*, his breakthrough book of 1958, slid across my desk in Barry Grammar School. It came, as did most of my challenging reading matter in those days, courtesy of a history teacher of care and genius, Teifion Phillips. Teifion had firm socialist convictions and an equally firm belief in spotting potential talent wherever he found it, in or out of school, and of whatever kind it was. Mine was deemed to be academic, and a working-class home was to be no barrier to university entry, even to Oxford where Teifion's links, though I scarcely knew it at the time, were to Balliol, forged by the summer schools he had attended there in the early 1950s. A conveyor belt for undergraduate historians from South Wales had been duly installed.

It is entirely possible that Teifion had met Raymond at one of these W.E.A./Extra-Mural summer schools but if he did he never mentioned it to me. The purpose in giving the paperback to the intellectually rapacious sixteen-year-old was to fill out the standard Sixth Form fodder with a richer diet of debate and argument beyond factual retention and the rote imbibing of then-current controversies on the interaction, or not, of Protestantism and Capitalism, or the Rise, or not, of the Gentry in those interminable, or it so seemed to us, sixteenth and seventeenth centuries. Raymond Williams entered my life – well almost so – as light relief.

What, of course, captivated me, and many more like me across Britain in the 1960s, was not, at first, Williams' re-examination of the cultural critique that followed on industrialisation, but his emotional and personal account of what it actually and inwardly, personally and familially, individually and publicly, meant to be a handpicked "Scholarship Boy" and, more, what it implied socially and culturally. I vividly remember being both acutely stimulated and deeply shaken as I read his thunderous "Conclusion" to *Culture and Society*, a book whose specific essays had only clung to my mind like burrs that had floated by and stuck, to be picked off and examined at some later date.

For my generation, subsequently, both the detail of his later work and its ever-widening compass became a constant challenge to grow and, in its shape and focus, a resolute reminder of what was to be valued, but radically so, as root for the keyword and actuality of community. His almost weekly book reviews in *The Guardian* whetted the appetite to see how the journalistically compressed and gnomic might become extended by illustration and explanation into yet another strikingly new direction. The books indeed followed. There is no denying that more than a tinge of hero worship – anathema to him – was directed his way and perhaps to a greater extent by those of us learning from him from afar than by those he was teaching close-up in Cambridge. Sometimes, it seems, that personal acquaintance could be an unhappy one as it became clear that his own priorities and needs were not always, or not often enough, those of some predatory undergraduates. There were numbers more, however, who testify to the care and attention he gave in their undergraduate and graduate years. All who encountered him, in person or in his work, agreed on one thing: that whether you like it or not, that work and his life experience were inseparable.

I first met Raymond Williams in 1976. The circumstances verged on the comic and were quite typical of him. Llafur, the Society for the Study of Welsh Labour History, of whose journal I was then editor, had invited him to speak at a conference on the fiftieth anniversary of the General Strike. It was to be held on the hillside campus of the Polytechnic of Wales, now the University of Glamorgan, at Pontypridd. In those days, in the wake of the 1972 and 1974 miners' strikes, the National Union of Mineworkers, especially in South Wales, was not only militant in action, it was intensely conscious of its own past endeavours over sixty years in the provision of cultural and educational initiatives for its members. A strong revival in those activities in the early 1970s ensured that, in addition to academic and local historians, the conference was attended by a few hundred working miners and union officials. It was exactly the kind of mix and occasion he would relish.

Only, Raymond, who was scheduled to speak after the mid-morning coffee break on the Saturday of a three-day event, had not appeared. We fanned out to man the Poly's scattered entrances, armed only with the vague memory of a dust jacket photograph and the helpful thought offered by some committee member that he would surely be driving "a big car". Two minutes before the appointed hour I returned, disconsolate, to the lecture theatre to be met by Kim Howells, a Warwick PhD student at the time, but one resident in Cambridge and often in attendance at university seminars when Raymond had been present. I glumly gave him the news. Puzzled, he said, "But there he is", and pointed as a man in his mid-50s rose from the middle of the raked and assembled audience to make his way down to the front. He had been there all morning, unobtrusive and unannounced, himself a part of a congregation whose connections, cultural and historical, he so much respected. He spoke, with no discernible notes and the utmost lucidity, for almost an hour, and later, as editor, I received the paper he had written up from his tape-recorded ruminations and published it as *The Social Significance of 1926*.

Thereafter, I lectured on some of his Cambridge courses at his invitation and I chaired him on other occasions or discussed his fiction with him at public meetings on his increasingly frequent visits to Wales. By the time of his early death, in 1988, I could feel myself to be a friend as well as a continuing admirer. So, when Joy Williams, a short time after his funeral, asked me if I would like to consider writing a biography, my instant answer was "Yes", despite other commitments that would require shuffling and the reservation I had about writing a Life that seemed to me, then, to be necessarily a life of the mind more than anything else. But, like so many others then and since, I was naturally enough looking through a telescope that seemed shuttered until the full opening of 1961 and his return to Cambridge as a Don and the notorious author of *The Long Revolution*, a work more startlingly iconoclastic than *Culture and Society*.

What became clear to me, very quickly and very unexpectedly, was how my perspective would need to shift from the somewhat conventional biography I had had in view and how daunting that shift appeared when I first considered the materials which Joy Williams rather hesitantly placed before me. That happened after some preliminary one-to-one interviews with Joy, first in their family home at Craswall and then in the house in Saffron Walden to which she and Raymond had moved upon his retirement from Cambridge. I had kept enquiring about letters, diaries, manuscripts, anything really beyond the published works and the list of people to see which I was already accumulating; it was the historian's desire for what is tangential rather than the critic's need for what is central. Late one afternoon, somewhat reluctantly, Joy took me down into the basement of the house and indicated a large and battered white cabin trunk. She warned me that there was no order to anything and that his normal response over the years had been to throw things away or shuffle them off in piles into some corner or other. The trunk had become the principal depository of all this sloughing off.

I opened the lid, delved in and began to take things out. Over the next two hours or so I saw that I was confronted by exercise books full of juvenilia; reams of pencilled and inked manuscript that seemed to be anything from stories to essays to schemes for writing; carbon flimsies and typed copy of unpublished short fiction; mounds of unpaginated and mixed extracts from lengthier fiction; the titled and bound files of novels he had mentioned in *Politics and Letters* (the interviews of 1979) but had then discarded or failed to publish; plus various and confusing versions, hardly any of them sequential, of what became *Border Country*; the dusty note diaries of his father; a typed-up War Diary or Memoir of his own; single sheets of plots or charts of fictional characters; doodled sketches and passages marked in early books from school; and a couple of pocket maroon-coloured Notebooks with hard covers and with his 1950's address in Hastings inscribed against loss on the inside. And that was only the stuff before the 1960s with other "finds" from Joy – wartime letters, obscure magazine articles, early correspondence with friends and colleagues, photographs – to come over the following months. My research work, soon

x

accelerated by the award of a Simon Senior Fellowship from the University of Manchester for 1992-93, proceeded. I did not, at this stage, decide that a single volume would need to be written just to do justice to this material because I did not then fully understand how vital it was to a complete understanding of Williams' life and work. I did, though, know that it was going to be a long haul.

How long is another matter, and for all involved – but especially for my wife and family – as I sometimes wondered if I would, or could, ever get to a finishing line, I can only hope that the outcome proves worth the long simmer. I was on the boil by 1993 for sure, but unexpected and labour-intensive career shifts in BBC Wales and then at the University of Glamorgan, along with the displacement activity of other writing which required shorter bursts of time and concentration, meant I did not really turn up the heat again until the University of Wales, Swansea appointed me to a Research Chair in the Centre for Research into the English Literature and Language of Wales in March 2005, so allowing me to write this book in the way and in the shape I now envisaged. That is my latest debt and this book is its principal repayment.

My other debts, early and late, are as appreciated and as deeply acknowledged to individuals and to institutions. Amongst the latter, in addition to Swansea University where the Raymond Williams Papers are now deposited and are awaiting a full catalogue for scholarly use, I would like to thank Cardiff University where I held a Chair in the History of Wales from 1985 and which gave me leave to hold the Fellowship granted by the University of Manchester in 1992-93, and where Huw Beynon in Sociology gave me a Welsh welcome. The British Academy assisted me that year, for travel and research purposes, with one of its invaluable Small Grant Awards and I used it to research the Chatto and Windus Archive of the University of Reading; the Imperial War Museum's collection of letters of the Second World War; the Records of the External Studies Department at Oxford; the BBC's Written Archive at Caversham, where Joanne Cayford was particularly helpful; the P.R.O. for War Diaries; and the Old Royal Military Academy at Woolwich, where Brigadier Timbers proved an invaluable and friendly aid to a tyro "military" historian. Andrew Green, Librarian at the National Library of Wales which houses another, smaller but complementary batch of Raymond Williams material, ensured that I was able to piece together a few missing bits of a fictional jigsaw (the parts of the early unpublished novel, *Brynllwyd*), and both Sir Adrian Webb, then Vice-Chancellor at the University of Glamorgan, and Geraint Talfan Davies, Controller BBC Wales, were invariably sympathetic (up to a point, of course!) to my authorial frustrations when I worked in those institutions between 1993 and 2000.

Individuals, in the end as in the beginning, were the real catalysts in the thought and in the writing. My principal debt is to the late Joy Williams who was utterly generous with her own time, unfailingly frank and, with no caveats, willing to give me unfettered access to and use of her husband's papers. It is true of many of his books that they would not have existed in the shape we have them, and some not at all, without Joy Williams' commitment and contribution. I am proud to say that this is now also true of my own present book.

To Merryn Williams, and to Ederyn and Madawc, I am profoundly grateful for their long and understanding patience with me and to Merryn, in particular, for sharing her own researches on her family which I pursued further, in Pandy, with the help of Raymond's sister-in-law, Sylvia Bird. Other family members who helped me with memories of his upbringing, especially of his mother, were Winifred Fawkes and his cousin Ray Fawkes, whose marvellous sketch map adorns the inside covers. Correspondence with Brinley Griffiths and his brother Maelor Griffiths, Raymond's close friend of the pre-war years, was as inspiring as it was revelatory. I owe them deep thanks.

And at Pandy and Abergavenny I garnered a great deal in interviews with Joan Leach, Albert Lyons, Lew Griffiths, Violet James, Bill Berglund, Illtyd Harrington, Dick Merton-Jones and Gwyn Jones. I was delighted to be able to trace and correspond with Raymond's Yorkshire friend of those years, Margaret Davies neé Fallas, who provided insights and photographs. For his early Cambridge years I talked to Lionel Elvin, corresponded with Muriel Bradbrook and interviewed his close friend,

Michael Orrom, whose own film and associated memoir were more than a boon. So too were the memories and diary I was privileged to make use of by Lady Anne Piper neé Richmond.

In the Gower I found and talked to Eddie Gibbs who served under Raymond Williams' command in the War and, for the Cambridge years thereafter, Wolf Mankowitz was forthright, disarming and charming. I spoke with Raymond's Adult Education colleagues in the Oxford Extra-Mural Delegacy, Arthur Marsh and Jack Woolford, as well as with his contemporary and friend, Tom Thomas, a legendary and inspiring Extra-Mural Literature Tutor at Swansea. Annette Lees neé Hughes helped with memories of the newly-married Joy and Raymond, and Eric Hobsbawm shed a direct light on both the Cambridge Left and the post-war settling in of their generation.

For the 1950s, especially concerning the marginality and then the centrality of Raymond Williams first to the Communist left and then to the political culture of the New Left, I am indebted to conversations with E.P. Thompson, Raphael Samuel, Graham Martin and Stuart Hall; and, for some subsequent reflections, to Lawrence Goldman, Terry Eagleton, Robin Blackburn and Robin Gable. Members of Parliament can be hospitable and sometimes good listeners to an obsessed author, as Kim Howells MP and Paul Murphy MP proved to be more than once. Still in a Parliamentary vein, though he had not then been elected as the Member for Aberavon, my oldest friend in all these related endeavours and much else, Hywel Francis, proved as supportive as only he can be when he was Professor of Adult Continuing Education at Swansea University.

More recently at that University support has come in no small measure from its far-seeing Vice-Chancellor, Professor Richard Davies, and from Professor M. Wynn Thomas, Director of CREW, who read and commented with critical attention on early drafts, as did his and my colleague in CREW, Dr Daniel Williams, whose own work will take our understanding of Raymond Williams forward. Other readers who have chivvied, urged and instructed me to put drafts into better shape were my former student Rob Humphreys, now Director of the Open University in Wales; Dr Steve Woodhams of Thames University; Dr Hywel Dix at the University of Glamorgan, and Professor John McIlroy of Keele University. Steve Woodhams deserves a double thanks for his care and his help in locating material, especially pamphlets, and for sharing in and often challenging my wilder speculations.

Along the way it was a pleasure to work with Colin Thomas whose BBC 4 film on Raymond Williams, 'Border Crossing', to which I contributed and acted as consultant, won the Jury Award at the 2005 Celtic Film Festival. It was a pleasure, too, to help Richard Davies of Parthian bring *Border Country* back into print in 2005 as the first volume in the Welsh Assembly Government-inspired Library of Wales Series. At the proof stage the book came into its own as a "Welsh European" – Williams' late and accurate self-description – when Martine Jousset fielded and ferried batches of e-mails to me in the Languedoc, at Nébian.

I am grateful to a brilliant Personal Assistant at BBC Wales, Ann Harris, for typing up early sections of first drafts and, as with so many others, putting up with my discontents. At Parthian, Jasmine Donahaye has proved a masterly and inspiring editor at a late stage and working to impossible deadlines: she combines meticulousness with sensitivity in a way that has vastly improved successive drafts and I owe her a great deal of gratitude. As I do to the proof-reading of Paul Duerden and the typesetting of my friend John Tomlinson who have also ensured that the Index was as meticulous as the rest of their endeavours. Finally, two people alone are responsible for ensuring the book took shape at all. The first is my indefatigable and uncomplaining word processor, as I'm told typists are now known; she is also known as my former and exceptional Personal Assistant at the University of Glamorgan, Gwyneth Speller, and quite how she deciphered, corrected and produced readable typescript from acres of pencilled yellow pad remains a mystery for whose solution I am deeply grateful.

And ultimately there was at the beginning as there is at the end, Norette, without whom there would really have been no book at all.

Dai Smith
Barry Island; Nébian
spring/summer 2007

Contents

Preface   vii

List of illustrations   xvi

Introduction   1

1. A Settlement   16

2. A Schooling   44

3. "Nominally Connected Lives"   80

4. "An Odd Adventure or Two"   145

5. "A Quality Beyond Art"   198

6. "Politics and Letters"   238

7. "A good actor sticks to his own lines"   264

8. "The Line is Crossed"   318

9. "Whether it will... be the kind of book you would really wish to publish"   358

10. "A Decisive Stage..."   396

11. "... but I am Price from Glynmawr"   441

"This actual growth"   470

A Note on Sources   475

Notes   478

Index   507

List of illustrations

1. Joseph and Margaret Williams, his paternal Grandparents, buying fish. 1890s.
2. Harry Williams, seated, France, 1917.
3. Raymond Williams seated on far right, Pandy School, mid 1920s.
4. Harry Williams, Raymond and the bee-hive, the summer of 1926.
5. Harry Williams, late 1920s in Pandy, at his garden gate.
6. Raymond Williams seated on far left, Pandy School, mid 1920s.
7. Raymond and his mother, Gwen, in 1930 on a holiday in Teignmouth.
8. Gwen in the doorway of Llwyn Derw, Pandy late 1930s.
9. Raymond at Pandy station, mid-1930s.
10. Raymond in Harry's vegetable patch, 1936.
11. The train from Abergavenny towards Hereford with Skirrid Fawr in the background, late 1930s.
12. Entrance to King Henry VIII Grammar School, Abergavenny.
13. Raymond Williams and Margaret Fallas on the boat, 'Evian', on Lake Geneva, 1937.
14. Harry Williams in his Sunday best, late 1930s.
15. Raymond in 1939 ready for Cambridge.
16. Joy Dalling, aged 13, Devon 1933.
17. Joy Dalling and her friend Annette Hughes, Cambridge 1940.
18. Joy Dalling, Cambridge winter 1940.
19. Joy Dalling, Cambridge summer of 1940.
20. On the roof above Michael Orrom's rooms in the Turret of Trinity's Great Court, summer 1941. Raymond is on the far left with Anne Richmond between him and Orrom who is flanked by two other friends.

21. Enrolled in Royal Corps of Signals, Prestatyn, summer 1941. Back row, second from the left.
22. Wedding photograph, Salisbury, June 1942.
23. Raymond and Joy Williams in Barnstaple, 21 June 1942. Their wedding day.
24. Raymond in foreground with binoculars, winter manoeuvres Scarborough 1943.
25. Raymond in Holland, autumn 1944. On the back he had written: "These foolish things remind me of you".
26. Anti-tank guns salute the silence of victory, north-west Germany, 1945.
27. Raymond, Joy and Merryn, on leave, 1945.
28. Llwyn Onn, the house in Pandy to which Harry and Gwen moved in 1948 from Llwyn Derw across the way.
29. Raymond in 1951, Chatto and Windus publicity shot.
30. Raymond with Joy and Merryn and Ederyn seated and Madawc between them, Seaford, 1951.
31. Raymond Williams at home, Hastings, 1953.

Front cover: Raymond Williams, Cambridge 1941.
Inside front cover: Raymond Williams, Geneva 1937.
Back cover: Raymond Williams, early 1960s.

Biographies always lie, because they impose a clear pattern of development, whereas, in fact, to any man who watches himself, development goes this way and that, back and forward, almost every day. The biography of an hour of a man's life might have some point; it is always the sweeping line that betrays us.

Raymond Williams, *The Grasshoppers* (1955)

Introduction

Writing the kind of novel in which I was interested was a long process, full of errors, and the delay meant that I became first known as a writer in other fields.

Raymond Williams, 1966[1]

He had not wanted it to be the way he would become known as a writer. From 1946 he had spent more time and expended more energy in writing fiction than anything else. When he retired in 1983 as Professor of Drama at Cambridge University, where he had taught English since 1961 and from where his reputation as an intellectual and academic had been rooted, he was quick to say that he had always considered himself as a writer first and foremost, not an elevated member of a Professoriate he typically disliked and mistrusted. The antipathy was no one-way street. His paradoxes were readily seen as self-willed contradictions.

Here was a man who lived most of his life in England and at the core of a literary establishment but sought to subvert the latter and by-pass the former by thinking of himself as a "Welsh European". His work was inflected with Marxism and its myriad challenges, and though he consistently shied away from being pinned with the label of "Marxist", he never denied its increasing definition of his own direction. He could see no human society of worth that did not cohere to the concept of community; at the same time he welcomed social change as the catalytic agency for a common culture. Undeniably, though, in his own life he lived in a manner which, despite a natural warmth and kindliness, shunned the close company of others, whether as friends, colleagues or students. It was as if the unrelenting pace he set himself in his work needed the self-contained dynamic of a long-distance runner and so the support he needed was that of constancy, not the acclamation for a short burst of success. He said it was a long revolution and he lived it as he meant it.

1

How he dreamed was another matter. That life of the mind took him ever back to the Black Mountains of his birth near Abergavenny, the crucible of his life and of his fiction. With a late exasperation in 1979, he would insist that in England the holistic effort of his work was not readily appreciated and that only in Wales did he have a sense that there was an appreciation of its unity.[2] With a few lone exceptions it has remained true that the fiction – six published novels – has not overtaken his work in "other fields" even for his admirers. That does not alter the significance he gave it both early and late. The tension was there even as he prepared for the belated publication of the first great novel in which he found the form to articulate his case.

He had written to his publishers, Chatto and Windus, in early April 1959 in the wake of the phenomenal reception of his 1958 book *Culture and Society*, to tell them of his future writing plans and notably of that volume's "natural successor", *The Long Revolution*, which was to have "three parts – theoretical, historical, and critical – on the development of English culture", and was "not literary criticism, or only very partly so" but rather "essays on the development of the reading public, the press, the educational system and standard speech forms [taking]... certain key ideas – class, mobility, exile –... in both literary and sociological terms, in what amounts to an attempt at a synoptic analysis of contemporary society". With the appearance of *The Long Revolution* in 1961 his impact on contemporary British life, over the almost three decades that remained of his life's span, was assured. Yet in the 1959 letter, this future is firmly prefaced by a past that was, for him, both adjunct and anticipatory:

> To me the first and most important thing is that I have finished a novel that I have been working on for several years. I sent you some time ago a draft of part of this, but the finished work is quite different. It is now being typed, and perhaps the main thing I want to know from you is whether you really want me to submit it to you. In one way all my plans hinge around it, because, having considered the problem very carefully, I am certain that it is the next

thing of mine I want to appear, to fit into the development of my writing as I see it... in a way my writing is held up until something is settled about this.[3]

The draft had been of *Border Village*, his re-working of 1957, in which the narrative moves chronologically forward from the arrival of the railway signalman, Harry Price, and his new bride, Ellen, to the village of Glynmawr where their son Matthew will be born. From here we follow their lives, through the 1926 General Strike and its fallout, to the son's departure for university as the Second World War begins. This is the linear narrative that would largely hold steady. What was being typed in 1959, however, was the complication of the story that the death of Williams' father in 1958 had impelled him to write: the return of Matthew, now a university lecturer in London, to the village and his father's sick bed. This version had been called *A Common Theme* and it took the autobiographical traces even further away by building the story of Matthew, and his estranged wife Susan, into a parallel account that was spelled out in such detail that it threatened to overwhelm the primary relationships with its gloss. So it was not "finished work" even yet. In November 1959 he wrote again, this time to his long-term contact at Chatto, Ian Parsons, to say how delighted he was that both Norah Smallwood and Cecil Day Lewis at the firm liked what he now referred to as *Border Country*: "I shall be very willing to revise... It means too much to me to have any feeling of holding back from all necessary work on it... [and]... it would be preferable... to bring the novel out first".[4] The revisions removed lengthy passages of dialogue and the extended Matthew Price story.[5] What was left was a family-at-a-distance of wife and children to which Matthew would return and, crucially, a new beginning to the novel, which would place Matthew amongst them, and sketch his intellectual quest as a professional historian. Only then do we plunge into the novel of generations, notably of *Sons and Fathers*, which *Border Country* had, at long last, become. The burden of that intricate novel, and of this present book, is that if Raymond Williams' meaning for us

3

is to deepen we will need to be clear about his resolute attempt to keep his work, all of it, both as part of a "whole way of life" and integral to it. It has always been more convenient to do the opposite. But, then, that was another manifestation of the division of "Culture" in society against which he mounted his life-long struggle. He knew the irony of himself being parcelled out and packaged up.

Those "other fields" of literary criticism, cultural theory, social commentary and media analysis – all bundled together as the influential corpus of Cultural Studies for whose origins he was, alternately, as a key figure cursed and blessed – were still the fields for which he was singled out in the heavyweight obituaries that followed on his early death in 1988. Yet as soon as his work had come, from the late 1950s, to receive wider notice he had insisted that his imaginative work, and his novels most notably, were all of a piece with his intellectual intentions. He had already clearly spelled it out in the mid-1960s when his status, middle aged guru of a Cambridge don to a whimsically self-absorbed generation, was already distorting his underlying meaning:

> I am mainly interested in the realist tradition in the novel, and especially in the unique combination of that change in experience and in ideas which has been both my personal history and a general history of my generation. I have been glad to be able to write about this change in critical and historical ways, for the cultural tradition I encountered in Cambridge seems to me deeply inadequate and needing challenge in its own terms. At the same time, the whole point of these general arguments was a stress on a new kind of connection between social, personal and intellectual experience (which have all been diminished by being separated), and I am still excited by the challenge of learning to express this connection in novels, difficult as this continues to be. I see this as my main work in the future.[6]

When he died, unexpectedly and unpreventably, of a ruptured aortic aneurism from a valvular disease of the heart in January 1988 at his home in Saffron Walden, he was only sixty six and, true to his word, was deeply engaged in writing fiction. After his death, Joy Williams collated that episodic novel of time and place and published *People of the Black Mountains* in two volumes in 1989 and 1990. Although his former student and Cambridge colleague, Terry Eagleton, hailed it in *The Observer* as "Williams' major literary achievement", and others claimed it for innovation in the style and form of the historical novel, it divided critical opinion in the manner of all his fiction. Its detailed attention to what he understood as "realism", a connection between the circumstances of people's material lives and their awareness of both their own fate and their own possibilities, had been meticulously researched by Joy Williams.[7] But it was all fed into the hopper of an imagination that was resolutely and deliberately not attuned to current literary fashion and the flotsam of 1980's taste. Worse than that, here was a writer who was viewed – even by those sympathetic to the confrontational stance and somewhat detached personality he could affect – through the teleology of a distinguished Cambridge career even as Williams himself steadily denounced significant aspects of the place, its academic inhabitants, its intellectual pretension and its social snobbery. The Left could be as disenchanted with him as the Right. And it was in the novel form, again, that he chose to do the damage, immediately upon leaving the University in 1983, by writing *Loyalties* (1985), a fictional work impelled forward by the Miners' Strike of 1984-85 but tenaciously grounded in the touchstones of experience that he dated episodically as "1936-37", "1944-47", "1955-56", "1968" and "1984". It was scathing in its denunciation of blind faith, misplaced loyalty and straightforward betrayal as exemplified by successive generations. It pivots around what for Williams remained the crucial and irreducible experience of class formation in British life.

He puts it most succinctly and angrily through Gwyn Lewis, the "natural son" of ex-Cambridge and ex-communist, Sir Norman Braose, who has been left by his father to be brought up in a working-class home in South Wales. Lewis is fully aware of the "general solidity of the argument" that must not allow a collapse from politics into mere parochial feeling, yet, in 1984, he is still uneasy about the easy assumptions:

> ... the Braoses were often quicker than his own people to talk the hard general language of class. Where Bert or Dic would say "our people" or "our community" the Braoses would say with a broader lucidity, "the organised working class", even still "the proletariat" and "the masses" [and] – he had been told, kindly enough, that the shift to generality was necessary. What could otherwise happen was an arrest or a relapse to merely tribal feeling. And he had wanted even then to object: "But I am of my tribe."[8]

It was not that Williams had not been saying this, in his own voice, elsewhere and in different forms. Indeed, that insistence, egotistical or self-obsessed some thought, was exactly what for such critics marred his finest critical works. From *Culture and Society* in 1958 to *The Country and The City* in 1973, he at times placed himself – squarely as an individual – within his dissection of the social distortion and cultural morass of modern Britain; all too much in your face if the cool disinterested scholar was the required model. It was certainly something that was inescapable about him. He felt the sting of ad hominem attacks in his own lifetime, and notably on the publication of *The Long Revolution* in 1961. After his death the personal opprobrium sometimes went far beyond his opinions to caricature his personality and even sneer at his upbringing. In 1990 R.W. Johnson in a wide-ranging review-article latched onto Williams' Welshness as a catch-all explanation for what Johnson saw as unwarranted fame and bewildering respect for a "repetitive" and "empty" thinker. The metropolitan disdain – or is it the howl of the colonial confronted by a native disrespect for the former's spiritual centre – is exquisitely, if unintentionally, a late Victorian pastiche in its dripping prejudice. Thus, the resolutely prosaic Williams is said to possess "a sort of lilting Welsh lamentation"; Williams, non-Welsh speaking and scarcely a chapel-goer, had "the style... of the Welsh nonconformist chapel... a quality of cadence and incantation"; to hear properly one of Williams' written perorations "one should inwardly listen to it in its original Welsh accent". That would be the one Williams did not have then since he spoke, as many others have commented, very deliberately and with the slight but distinctive burr of his native border country. Nor could Johnson resist (as he called for "a whole new intellectual beginning" for which the "greatest danger... will be to get trapped within the rhetoric of an exhausted tradition") a passing double-handed swipe against the Welsh working-class Williams who, apparently, "as a young working-class scholarship boy up at Cambridge seems to have decided, like not a few Welshmen before and after him, that the way to storm this alien citadel, was to overwhelm it with a tide of wordy socialism". A typically laconic Welsh reply, if it could be heard above the laughter, might be that this is more fictive than the fictional works Johnson ignores. But he was right, in principle if not in fact, about the biographical drivers to all of Williams' work as this book will, in different mode, reveal.[9]

John Higgins, though in a dissimilar vein, also recognised that Williams' life was "a central and defining characteristic of his work: its unusual biographical impetus, its powerful sense of an integrity and focus located in the personal voicing of the academic"[10]; whilst John McIlroy, noting the sympathetic welcome but relative lack of emphasis in Williams' thought in the 1980s to "the new movements of women and black people and... the environment", was sure that it all lay in "a continuing commitment to the working class, remarkable in its intensity... the values of his youth".[11] What follows will underline, in particular, the truth of both these insightful observations. Yet that is not to say there were no variations in the Williams persona or contradictions in his work. He would characterise them as explorations and accommodations within a framework of personality and principles that he had created, in struggle, between 1939 and 1958. The achieved self-assurance accommodated flexibility and change.

Williams returned to Cambridge, and as in 1939 by invitation, without any formal application, to a Fellowship at Jesus College, 1961, just a year after he had re-located himself and his family to

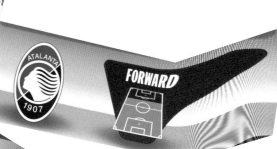

Staff Tutor for Oxford's Extra-Mural Delegacy within Oxford itself, rather than in its outreach areas of Sussex where he had taught in Adult Education since 1946. So far as he was concerned, he was taking on an official English culture in its most important bastion; yet he had been appointed to a University Lectureship in the Facultyfor his contribution to that cultural tradition. By the time he arrived he had published *The Long Revolution*, a work that melded literary, cultural and sociological analysis as nothing else had done. It gave offence for its iconoclasm. Its best-seller status infuriated even more. By the middle of the 1970s his London publishers alone had sold over three quarter of a million copies of his books. The pattern continued. In his lifetime, his critical works were translated into Catalan, Danish, German, Italian, Portuguese, Spanish and Japanese.

He wrote novels – *Second Generation* (1964) and *The Fight for Manod* (1979) – which dealt with Welsh society and Welsh working-class experience. They were unremittingly rooted in his past and on the way in which, on a wider generational front, he saw that developing. He wrote in a vein that he had secured finally for his own voice and never wavered from its unfashionable tone; and even when he wrote a political thriller – *The Volunteers* (1978) – it was with the preoccupations of his marginal country that he grappled. They were his own. He had joined and worked for the Labour Party between 1961 and 1966 but had left, in despair at Wilsonian tacking at home and abroad. He took out a Plaid Cymru party card for 1969 and, though he did not keep up membership beyond that year, he was, as he put it, a "Welsh European" by the mid-1970s with a belief that reformist politics and a rigid "Yookay" Unionist stance were inseparable.[12]

Early alliances between the late 1950s New Left and former Communist Party dissidents had promised a route back into formal political engagement for a very detached Williams, and he was soon a Board member of the magazine *New Left Review*. When the "old" New Left, principally represented by Edward Thompson and the "new" New Left, spearheaded by Perry Anderson, split and quarrelled acrimoniously and entertainingly by the mid-1960s, Raymond Williams remained

8

valued, if not always liked, by both sides. By then he seemed to embody, perhaps because of his earlier and chosen isolation, a "Negative Capability" that could tease impetus from despondency. Edward Thompson, who had in 1965 left Adult Education to become Director of the Centre for the study of Social History at the new University of Warwick, wrote to him in February 1967 just after the first stirrings of the impulse to write a new Manifesto for the Left had begun:

> Dear Raymond,
>
> May I express to you my unreserved admiration for the way in which you have pulled us round and given us a new opportunity? You must have sensed you alone could have performed this role, uncongenial as it may be. I will confess that 3 or 4 years ago when the new left was collapsing at all sides, I deeply wished you to make an active intervention, and I felt a shade of resentment that this did not happen. Now I feel that I – and all of us – are wholly in your debt. I confess my political – not my ultimate – morale has been low (and Stuart's also), and you found the language and the arguments I needed.
>
> ....We should be looking for men and women in their late twenties and thirties who must take the thing on and make it their own.
>
> Thank you: that was the first political meeting I have attended for 4 years and not come back from in a state of depression. Can I say fraternally?
>
> Edward

It was subsequently in Williams' rooms in Jesus College that Edward Thompson, Stuart Hall, Bob Rowthorn and others devised and wrote *The May Day Manifesto* in 1967, and it was Williams who is largely credited with holding it all together and then editing it for Penguin in 1968. If that was a shift leftwards from his only slightly earlier commitment to a Labour Party for whom Joy Williams had stood unsuccessfully for the Council in Cambridge, it was still a distance from the stern programmed Marxism of *New Left Review*. Even so it was Raymond Williams who was accorded their highest accolade as Britain's most significant socialist intellectual when that extraordinary compendium – a new kind of book – of interviews, *Politics and Letters*, appeared in 1979, after his inquisition by Anderson, Barnett and Mulhern. The influential portrait that emerged through the mirror of selected questions and reflected answers is, to be sure, a likeness but it is one of its own moment of capture not of the unfolding and sometimes disguised life he had led.

At Cambridge he continued to write on drama and on the novel – *Modern Tragedy* (1966); *The English Novel from Dickens to Lawrence* (1971) – and to build his reputation with almost weekly reviews in *The Guardian* solicited by its dynamic Literary Editor, Bill Webb. He now eclipsed Leavis as the Cambridge name, and students vied to become his pupils or just to attend his packed, inevitably ruminative, lectures. If he failed to pay sufficient attention to their needs – as David Hare once resentfully alleged – or did not advance quickly enough towards the ideological bun party – Terry Eagleton later retracted his serpent's tooth – he could be, and was, depicted as self-serving or even timid. Fame brought such demands without a concomitant understanding of how stretched he was or, more pointedly, of how much less he thought of those teaching obligations, undergraduate and graduate both, than he had of his adult educational ones. Yet, for every disgruntled encounter, there were, from those Joy referred to as "Raymond's young men", friendships, debts, obligations and acknowledgements that bore different testimony to his gifts of patience and interest. It was it seems – for Bob Woodings, Patrick Parrinder, Ian Wright, Stephen Heath and Lisa Jardine – how you chose to encounter him that brought the most lasting rewards.[13] Certainly, many of those meetings with Raymond Williams, both with the man and his mind, during his life and after his death, seem freighted with the burden of expectation: especially over his total integrity as if he must be blameless in all things personal since he was so demanding of the behaviour of societies; over his lack of sociability to those who did not, perhaps, appreciate or admire the depth of his domesticity and the kind of partnership he had formed with Joy Williams. What holds true for the known life of Raymond Williams after 1961 is its assured position in the cultural history of twentieth-century Britain – "we have lost our best man", Edward Thompson generously wrote of him on his death – and, as a socialist intellectual and writer, a figure of significance across the globe. From all that published work, we can measure him and mark his life as a public figure against it. What has not been seen is how the earlier making of Raymond Williams, unknown or misunderstood in detail, contributed to that full measure. The intention of this book is to show that his meaning – the very thing he meant by Culture as a "whole way of life" – lies in his own making through the struggles of his first forty years from 1921 to 1961.

I have tried to tell this story, where possible, so that the voice of Raymond Williams, in his own words, can be heard; to let the reader see the makings or the drafts that became published works and to read the work – fiction and otherwise – that has never before reached the printed page. It is all of a piece with the direction of an inner life which was, though definitely focused, never straightforward and so allows me to hope I can counter, by ranging backwards and forwards over the area of his life even as its line moved inexorably on, his own anti-biographical dictum from the manuscript of his 1955 novel *The Grasshoppers*: "Only the line of a life, hardly anything of its area, can be articulated, and reduced to grammar".

I hope readers can now see for themselves the circumferences of his life and how he moved within and across its boundaries before he became the public figure from the late 1950s whose difficulty, in one sense, became what not to publish, since everything he said and wrote from then on was liable to find itself in print. His life story thereafter moves along the lines of familiarity that the obituarists and analysts could readily follow or choose to unravel after the event. There are few unexpected biographical revelations from the 1960s, beyond the work itself. He had begun the plotting of another novel, *The Brothers*, on which, as was his custom, he worked intermittently, alongside other projects, from the early 1980s. That would have been another tale of exile and return, and of rediscovery of the past and a possible future, set inevitably on the Welsh Border Country which was always the territory of his imagination.

For this present book, however, it is possible to range further and deeper into the area beyond the border lines because of the astonishing volume and richness of the papers I have been allowed, unreservedly, to use. Not only do they give us, in my view, a new Raymond Williams, a "Jim" you might say, but they also incisively confirm the core values of the one who addressed many issues, from the 1960s, with his sense of himself and his beliefs stubbornly present.

The tantalising and occasionally misleading references to early work as mentioned in the interviews he gave in *Politics and Letters* (1979) are, in this book, present in the actual detail of early stories, essays and plays from the Pandy schoolboy to the Cambridge undergraduate. Here, too, are the guideline diaries of Harry Williams, the father whose story parallels and, in the end, profoundly shapes that of the son. There are also his war-time letters to his wife, a war diary and occasional letters to and from early acquaintances – though he was not a regular correspondent beyond brief notes, either during the War or later.

I have interviewed many who knew him, young and old, and thanked them in the Preface. Extensive taped and untaped conversations with Joy Williams took me down many unexpected directions and to other documented sources. I travelled after Williams from Pandy to Cambridge, across the battlefields of Normandy to Brussels and on to the suburbs of Hamburg. I came to understand the war period as the most crucial, and still puzzling, piece in his mental make-up. A trickle of papers, some in manuscript, some typed, became a dauntingly incessant flow after 1945: successive drafts of novels, fragmentary and near complete, enough short stories for two volumes, film scripts, documentary and dream-like, radio talks, submitted and unpublished novels, work drafts for adult education classes and essays, the first scribbled stirrings of thought for his cultural and historical papers, hares set running and half pursued for new drama or fictional concepts, and above all from the mid-1950s, squat notebooks in which

Culture and Society and *Border Country*, his twinned lodestars, are conceived and born.

The book has grown to accommodate all this and more because I also came to understand that we cannot grasp the Raymond Williams whose work has so reverberated across the world, to the frustration of many he once annoyed and would still be delighted to annoy, until we saw close-up the immense creative and psychological effort of his first forty years. This is a biographical study whose impulse is to reject any overt disjunction between the life and the mind, not least because it was a separating out Raymond Williams resented, as description, for himself and others.

Using the papers that lie behind both the period of relative obscurity and his subsequent success I have tried to reveal the importance, as I see it, of his personal and intellectual conflicts in the context of twentieth-century British history. He was against much of the grain of it when alive and always for the reason that he saw, having experienced it directly, that individual empowerment, material betterment or even the acquisition of knowledge, is another form of disempowerment if there is no common culture, no collective gain, no full recognition of the social implications of human equality. For him, both in his own time and as he later affirmed, "in different places and in different ways", the social formation of class, the negative divisiveness as well as the positives of communities made and renewed, lay at the centre of this civilisation and our ongoing discontents. The novel was his way of appropriating these general arguments in order to make them, as they were experienced, individual dilemmas and individual solutions within the given framework of a binding social and material history.[14]

We might almost say that his work, all of it, was written only because he had lived it, and that though it may indeed be studied without knowing his life, it cannot be fully comprehended without the texture of that life being known. It was what, conceptually, he felt he was distilling as the knowledge of experience into recoverable form in his novels, most notably in *Border Country*, where the main and fictive story is, finally, that of the signalman Harry Price and his growth, through crisis and settlement, to his end. Matthew, the son, ends the novel on its last page by telling his wife, Susan:

> "I remember when I first left... , and watched the valley from the train. In a way I've only just finished that journey."
>
> "It was bound to be a difficult journey."
>
> "Yes, certainly, only now it seems like the end of exile. Not going back, but the feeling of exile ending. For the distance is measured, and that is what matters. By measuring the distance we come home."

Border Country is not autobiographical except through its place and its time. Its own measured end is Williams' final and intended summation of its meaning. But for his life, and so for the biographer, the clues from what is discarded can, and should, speak more insistently of the rawness of a life as it was being lived and experienced.

A few pages before the end of the published version of *Border Country* Matthew tells Susan that he had always thought his father "was good, my whole sense of value has been that. And since I've left home I've watched other people living, and I've become more certain"; and she replies, "You don't have to prove it... If you believe it, you'll live by it". But what was crossed out and excised between that and the final published version is the following passage, something maybe too explicit for the novel, certainly for his publishers, yet a statement from Matthew which clarified the personal endeavour Raymond Williams had, by 1958, made abstract in his critical work:

> "... and I've become more certain. I even see the thing socially: that his class is good; that it is better, in human terms, than the class I'm invited into. And then again, they wait in the margin, with the obvious comment. That I am idealising his class, and that I do this to hide my aggression: that basically I hate him, and despise the people I came from."

14

"Yes, they're very smart," Susan said smiling. "And of course they resist the idea that the people they despise are as good as themselves."

"I said better," Matthew insisted.

"That would be utterly ludicrous," Susan laughed.

"Yes, but I'm saying it. Not in personal virtue, but in the ways they live."

"You don't have to prove it," Susan said. "If you believe it you'll live by it."

"And the idealising it?"

"If it is that even, you can make it real."

"You think it is that, then?"

"No, I've never thought so."

"It all fits, you know," Matthew said.

"Any system fits, that is what it is for. And what this is for, in the end, is to dismiss other people. It's a way of seeing people, that has become established, so that almost every human effort is, in the end, degraded."

"This is to find out the lies," Matthew said.

"You can't live a lie, in the end. What you do will be the truth."

"Well, what am I doing?"

"What you wanted to do. What he wanted you to do."

"Both?"

"Yes, both."

"Except that I've done very little. Anybody can plan things."

"You complicated what you'd started with."

"Exactly. Perhaps as a way of preventing it."

"Does it feel like it? Yes, the thing could have been finished, but is it a loss to be driven back down?"

"In this society it is. One is valued on production."

"But that is the whole crisis. That's what you've been watching, in him."

"I've been watching death."

"Yes, that is part of it."[15]

15

Chapter 1

A Settlement

Eighteen-year-old Harry Williams, dressed in the navy blue serge porter's uniform and cap of the Great Western Railway, carried the lady's cases across the platform as he had habitually done since joining the Company in the early summer of 1913. He had left school aged twelve to work as a boy labourer on first one and then another of the big estates near Hereford. He kept his first employers' hand-written testimonials all his life. George Roper of Tyberton had employed him for two years (from 1910) and had "always found him a respectable, honest, quick boy and his personal character very good", whilst J. Farr of Arkstone Court, Hereford wrote: "to certify that Harry J. Williams has lived with me since Sept 30th last [1912] and I have always found him honest, sober and obliging."[1] The young man, for all that, undoubtedly saw a lifetime's work on the railways as more alluring and more congenial despite the strict discipline and long hours enforced by the railway companies. And then, in the summer of 1914 there were ladies who pressed white feathers into your hand instead of tips.

Harry Williams recounted that story to his grandchildren and he told his son that he was "very unwillingly conscripted into the First World War".[2] In a sense he was, but the force behind the conscription would be as much social and cultural as it was political and legal. Anger and resentment towards the givers of feathers was a more likely response than any embarrassment. Besides, he was already aware of the whims of the more powerful. His own father, an agricultural labourer, had been evicted from their tied cottage in his late forties, when Harry was ten, when his Liberal-voting employer sacked him after a dispute. Inadvertently, though quite typically, for the time, this helped orientate the Williams clan of farm labourers to the cause of trades unionism and that of the infant Labour Party. Harry's father, Joseph Williams, had been born in 1862 in Wormsley, himself the son of a farm worker, and had married Margaret Williams, daughter of a shepherd at Madley and his older wife, Sarah, in 1886. Before marriage, Joseph and Margaret, whose distinctive craggy features foreshadowed that of her son and grandson, worked as farm servants. Harry, the sixth of seven children and the third boy, was born on 30 November 1896 in Pear Tree Cottage, Kingstone. After eviction Joseph lived and worked as a roadman in Moorfields near Ocle Pychard on the opposite, and eastern, side of Hereford.[3]

Harry, thickset and robust, was both adept and clever. He had transferred easily to the railways from work on the land. Before his nineteenth birthday he had become a shunter on a rail network choked with rolling stock in use for coal trains and troop trains. It was proving difficult to fill the latter with enough volunteers. After much political manoeuvring, compulsory and universal conscription was made law by Parliament in 1916 but for almost a year before that there had been a mixture of cajolery, exhortation and registration intended to sweep up single men in non-skilled work. The GWR offered employment on "return to civil life" to those of their employees who joined the Army. Whatever public pressure may have been put upon him it was technically as a volunteer that Harry Williams joined the Royal Welsh Fusiliers on 26 May 1915.[4]

The children who grew up in the village of Pandy in the 1920s would remember him as a gentle, easy-going man who would address each of them in turn with a "Hello, Young Shaver" and would, in their turn, call their friend, his own son, "Shaver Williams". They would also recall the chill Harry could cause them by telling stories of the Great War; stories not meant to impress but rather to horrify. He, himself, had had to grow up quickly. At the end of December 1915 he had passed through a course of instruction in the Signalling School and emerged as an Assistant Instructor. This would serve him well at the end of the war; everything else was a hell he never forgot. Short of death in combat, only injury offered any respite.

In June 1917 he suffered a gunshot wound to the left forearm, just above the wrist, and was hospitalised in France. No. 54249 went home on sick leave as soon as the wound had healed. He now met Esther

Gwendoline Bird, the third daughter of Mary Ann Lewis, dairymaid, and of James Bird, a native of Lincolnshire and a Farm Bailiff of Winnings Farm, Colwall, near Great Malvern. That town, and Hereford itself, was a near enough attraction for the young people of both families. Gwen was quite tall and fair. As a girl she had worked on a dairy farm but thereafter only in the family house. However quickly their relationship and a mutual attraction developed, it is unlikely that she would have immediately revealed all her secrets to this young man. When they married in 1919 she gave her age as twenty-five to Harry's twenty-two. Born on 2 November 1890, she was in fact twenty-nine and the mother of an illegitimate child, Herbert, who was born in 1908 and who was later presented to the world as her younger brother and registered as the son of James Bird. The real father was a groom, a married man in his forties and already with a number of children, who worked on the same estate as Gwen's father. After her seduction there appears to have been no formal acknowledgement of the child by the father. Harry, it seems, was never told of this secret. If he ever was or ever guessed there is little doubt that nevertheless it would not have affected his life-long commitment to his wife.

As the War drew to a close neither Harry nor Gwen could have been confident of their future together. On 26 October 1918 Harry Williams, now a Lance Corporal, was gassed at Poix du Nord and after treatment in field hospitals sent to Cambrai to recover, and then on, via stretcher and ambulance, to the military hospital on the coast at Le Tréport where eleven days in bed followed. He had been gassed less than three weeks before hostilities finally ceased. He recorded in a pocket book the desultory days of convalescence and the poor rations to be endured, but makes more insistent mention of the news he hears from Gwen and that his response was to write to "Gwen every day".[5] It was a month before he was moved out, via Dieppe and Rouen, to rejoin his Battalion on 14 December at Aulnoye. Colliers were, he noted, already being sent home but Christmas, despite a welcome parcel from Gwen, still had to be endured in France. On 25 December 1918 Harry wrote:

Good Xmas dinner and plenty to spare. Plenty of Beer (French)… letter and card from G. Feeling OK and quite sober, worse luck.[6]

Days of cold and rain, of marches and church parades followed. Harry's mind was on civilian life. He wrote to the GWR at Abergavenny, a major rail junction, to seek employment. Gwen was now writing to him twice a day. Then, on Saturday 11 January, he heard that because of long service he was to be demobilised – "All smiles. Wrote home and to G." Normandy was a chaotic traffic jam of buses, trains and marching men. It took another week to end up in Le Havre and sail overnight for Southampton on a "Yankee troopship". On Sunday 19 January he was discharged at a dispersal unit in Chiseldon and caught the first available train: "Arrived Gloster 12.45 am, dead tired but anxious to get home, jumped on goods train to H/ford, arr'd 4.45. Walked home, reached there 6.30am." The next day he simply remarks – "Enjoyable day with G." There was no doubt how he envisaged spending the rest of life.

If the War was one shaping experience, employment on the railways in the immediate post-war period was to be another, and just as vital in underpinning the sturdy independence Harry Williams would exhibit from then on. There was only a fortnight's hiatus before his working life resumed. He filled it with bicycle rides, buying new clothes in Hereford – "Felt 10 years younger in civvies again" – and by spending time in Gwen's company. They visited each other's homes and spent time with his brothers – Charley and Fred – and her sisters and younger brother – Sarah, Lily and William. Gwen's son, Herbert, now eleven years old, had been adopted by the grandparents and was taken for their youngest child. Harry was not without money since his army back pay came in regularly over these weeks, and weekly sums of between £3 and £5 were recorded, not inconsiderable amounts for a working man in 1919. His training in signals in the Army had given him a technical skill he could now exploit. In early February he spent some time as a relief worker in signal boxes, in Pontypool and then in

Resolven, much further to the west and very much part of the booming South Wales coalfield. The work seems to have been irregular but much of his free time was passed in the very heart of the highly militant, socially volatile coal-mining valleys, the Rhondda itself, where he sporadically lived as a typical young male worker – in lodgings, attending Music Halls, listening to political speeches. The names he jotted down in his diary appear to be army friends who eased his way into the craft of signalling and, maybe, the politics of the coalfield.

Letters continued to pass daily between the lovers. By mid-March 1919 he had been formally and successfully inspected in his signalling duties. He was now mostly based in Resolven, a mining village near Neath and quite different territory from the market towns, scattered villages and farms of rural Herefordshire to which he returned on weekends. If his heart and his love were in the latter his still young head was now being much influenced by the former. His Union, the National Union of Railwaymen, was anxious not only to maintain the "war bonus" they had achieved to combat inflation but also to standardise wage rates in an upward direction. Negotiations between their leaders and the Lloyd George coalition government would proceed, hesitantly, all through the summer of 1919. At the same time the even more fraught situation between masters and men in the coal industry had begun its immensely damaging post-war relationship. A threatened national coal strike had only been averted by the establishment of a Coal Industry Commission under the chairmanship of Mr Justice Sankey. It found in favour of the nationalisation of the coal industry. The government, time now on its side, evaded the commitment. In South Wales, the leading export coalfield in Britain, with over 250,000 men employed in the industry, the threat of social rebellion was taken seriously by men and masters. The onset of economic slump in the 1920s did not lessen that tension but it did, as the 1930s would prove, effectively undercut it. For almost two years, Harry Williams lived more or less permanently in this maelstrom, where syndicalists and communists were the kind of minority activists that supporters of the Labour Party were elsewhere in Britain. When he finally moved away from its hot-house atmosphere Harry Williams had undergone some forced growth of his own.

Some 100 miles away he might succumb to the influenza epidemic of 1919, visit international matches in bustling Swansea and, uncharacteristically, after an Easter Bank Holiday dinner at the Colliers' Arms become "properly gassed" and have to sleep "under bed dressed". Yet it was neither politics nor popular culture which obsessed him. On 3 May 1919 he went home for the weekend – "G. met me at Station. Nice ride out. Very enjoyable evening. G. and I engaged, very happy." In the autumn they would marry. Before then the time spent away working occasioned more and more misery. Gwen, in particular, keenly resented the enforced absence. After their move to Pandy in late 1920 they would never live apart again. Until then Harry was to work in Aberdare, a town of some 50,000 people and the chief centre of the Cynon Valley, a classic Victorian product of iron and coal with mining townships strung out, almost indistinguishably, down its length. This was a proletarian world almost out of a text book. Its strength and its power would be acknowledged later by the son who would both theorise about its potential and imagine its distinctiveness in his fiction, but only the father would ever have personal knowledge of one of the great European bastions of an industrial working class at its zenith.

He worked long days in the box, usually in eight hour stints, for pay of around £3 a week. If he remained in Aberdare over a weekend he became part of the crowd. He joined a vast throng in Aberdare Park on Peace Day, 19 July, and two days later wrote of "Lively scenes in Aberdare, at Socialist meeting". Keir Hardie had been elected for the joint constituency with Merthyr in 1900, as Wales' first Socialist MP but, after his death in 1915, a pro-war candidate had succeeded him. In the wake of the patriotic coupon election of 1918, Harry Williams was witnessing the real beginning of a Labour hegemony that would take over the local government and the parliamentary constituencies in both Aberdare and the rest of the South Wales coalfield. Raymond Williams, recalling that his father's first job after the Great War had been "right down in the mining valleys which were very political, with a fairly advanced Socialist culture", added that when "he moved home to the border again, he had acquired its perspectives."[7]

And, his son might have added, its commitment to a wider solidarity. His blooding in that, the railwaymen's sudden and effective national strike of September 1919, fortuitously occurred just at the end of Harry's brief honeymoon, stranding him at home and prolonging the holiday by ten days. That event had begun on Saturday 20 September when he had returned home feeling "ever so happy". He and Gwen had spent Sunday together "bagging hops at Ocle" and had married, quietly, on Monday in St. James' Parish Church at Ocle Pychard. Harry gave his address as Aberdare. Gwendoline Bird was married from Harry's parents' cottage. They travelled to Malvern for the week and went from there on excursions to Tewkesbury and to Birmingham for the theatre. The strike started at the end of the week. It finished, with a compromise seemingly in the NUR's favour, on 6 October, and Harry, at last, had to return to South Wales. There he mostly stayed, apart from a Christmas break, until the year ended. He was determined to build a secure life in which they would both feel comfortable but to do that he would need a permanent position in a busy signal box on the border. The obvious place, if a vacancy for a signalman occurred, was in or around Abergavenny. The young man and his wife who moved there, and would remain until they died, had already seen how the rhythm of their private, intimate lives moved to the beat of circumstances and forces that paid little notice to their individual wills. They had understood too what connected them to others like them without ever wishing that their own particularity be submerged. They would make their particular mark on the village where their first and only son would be born on 31 August 1921.

* * * * * *

Raymond Williams imagined the arrival of his parents at Pandy in such graphic detail that we can assume it was a story told over and over to a child anxious to know what preceded him. In *Border Country* (1960) Harry Price and his wife, Ellen, arrive at Glynmawr station late one

October afternoon in 1920. We see her long, sandy yellow hair and light blue eyes, his broad jaw, wide mouth and "ugly, irregular teeth". Harry's "solidity of face and body" and "withdrawn heaviness" are noted as is Ellen's blue coat and hat, and her "easy walk". They set out, with Harry carrying a large leather box, to walk to their lodgings in Glynmawr which, "to a stranger... would seem not a village, but just thinly populated farming country". Only, to Harry and Ellen, this was not a strange country and, in their son's imagined remembrance, they merge into it physically and emotionally:

> Walking the road in the October evening, they felt on their faces their own country: the huddled farmhouses, with their dirty yards; the dogs under the weed-growing walls; the cattle-marked crossing from the sloping field under the orchard; the long fields, in the line of the valley, where the cattle pastured; the turned red earth of the small, thickly-hedged ploughland; the brooks, alder-lined, curving and meeting; the bracken-heaped tussocky fields up the mountain, where the sheep were scattered under the wood-shaded barns; the occasional white wall, direct towards the sun, standing out where its windows caught the light across the valley; the high black line of the mountains, and the ring of the sheep wall.[8]

The first words Raymond Williams said to his interviewers in his oral autobiography, *Politics and Letters* (1979), were "I come from Pandy." Those words, as he well knew, defined his life and offered a framework for a large part of his work. He was conceived shortly after Harry and Gwen came to live there and, in that sense, for the two decades to follow, all three lives were coterminous with the place. It was, of course, the railway, running north from Abergavenny, taking the coal of South Wales to the Midlands and beyond, which had allowed Harry Williams to find a settlement here, just as it would be the leading edge of the railwaymen's community in nearby Abergavenny which would shape the Williams family's social and political life. Nonetheless, Pandy was also a more poised existence, barely six miles inside Wales, bisected by Offa's Dyke, divided between chapel and church, and more occupationally diverse than it appeared at first sight. Since the 1960s a "new", or by-pass road, the A465, has taken the traveller zooming past Pandy en route for Hereford and up the border to the north-west of England, whilst housing developments just to the south have come to dwarf the huddle of homes which once served as the village's main marker. There was scarcely ever a focus as such because Pandy largely consisted of a scatter of small farms on the hills on either side of the old road, with groups of houses here and there. The landscape was more of a definition than the buildings. On the south-eastern side the Holy Mountain, Skirrid Fawr, rose to almost 1,600 feet against the skyline – a jagged hump with its distinctive cleft – and to the south the conical Sugar Loaf dominated Abergavenny, "Gateway to Wales", on its north-eastern side whilst the Blorenge extended its ridge across the south-western side, beyond which lay the iron and coal towns on the rim of the coalfield. Directly across from Pandy the brown river Honddu tumbled down from the Vale of Ewyas in whose steep wooded gulch are the ruins of Llanthony Abbey. Flanking the Honddu's course were the other valleys which gashed a way through the Black Mountains. This was a dramatic, natural world from whose high vantage points Raymond Williams' fictional characters would gaze down to muse upon the communities which had been created in these folds of mountain and valley. His last novel, *People of the Black Mountains* (1989), no less than his first, was precise about the special beauty of its changing colours:

> From a distance, in a good light, the long whaleback ridges are blue. Under cloud they are grey cloudbanks. But from within they are many colours: olive green under sunlight, darker green with the patches of summer bracken; green with a pink tinge when there are young leaves on the whinberries; dark with the heather out of flower, purple briefly in late summer; russet with autumn bracken, when at dawn after rain the eastern slopes can be red; pale gold

in dead winter bracken, against the white of snow. Yet black, a cellular black, under storm cloud: a pitted honeycomb of darkness within darkness.[9]

"The only landscape I ever see, in dreams", he confessed in his major critical work of the 1970s, *The Country and The City* (1973), "is the Black Mountain village in which I was born." This was a neat, if unconscious, marrying of the small scale society in which he first observed human interrelationships and the somewhat forbidding, yet enticing, tableau of hill and moorland plateau which framed that life. By the early 1920s the latest phase of human settlement, the developments dependent on the industrial growth of South Wales in the nineteenth century, had reached a peak and it was into an established, if still somewhat poised, community that Raymond was born.

He was registered as Raymond Henry Williams by Harry whilst Gwen was still bed-ridden, recovering from the birth. He thus secretly overrode Gwen's wish that their son should have the name of her own father, James. After he left for Cambridge in 1939 he would always use Raymond, his given and kingly name, but his mother called him "Jim" from the start, and Jim or Jimmy Williams was how Pandy always knew him. The Pandy that is transmuted into his fiction as first Brynllwyd and eventually Glynmawr could serve as a map for the real place between the wars. Here, on the western side of the old dividing road was the small general shop; the two grey stone chapels erected in 1837 and 1866, Zoar (Baptist) and Hope (Presbyterian), with attached graveyards, and three pubs, separated by a few hundred yards: the Rising Sun nearer to Abergavenny, the Pandy Hotel and The Lancaster Arms. All were just inside the Welsh border with England, which was marked by the interchangeably named river Monnow or Afon Mynwy, and so, after the 1881 Welsh Sunday Closing Act that closed all public houses in Wales was extended to Monmouthshire in 1921, on a Sunday they were as dry as the river was wet. The village was in the parish of Llanfihangel Crucorney, the larger settlement half a mile to its south, where the sixteenth-century towered church of St Michael and the even older Skirrid Inn echoed a pre-industrial world through whose still discernible contours steamed the Great Western Railway. The population of the district in the early 1920s was around 400, now augmented by one who would become its most famous son.

There were a few large homes, with small estates attached, in the vicinity but the proprietors did not dominate socially. The farmers and their families made up the bulk of the population along with their labourers, themselves often close relatives. A few men had found jobs with the Abertillery Water Works whose large scale excavations and construction from 1911 to 1928 in the Grwyne Fawr valley, quite a distance away, created a reservoir to supply water to the industrialised valleys to the south, but not, until 1938, to the nearer rural villages like Pandy.[10] Others worked as rural craftsmen or jobbing builders. Women before marriage might be in domestic service locally, in Abergavenny or even further afield. The railwaymen, the two stationmasters, platelayers, porters and six signalmen servicing the line and the two stations, at Llanfihangel and Pandy, stood slightly apart, linked by the very nature of their occupation to a wider, modern world. Even so the farmers would spend time talking in the signalboxes, a gathering point, warmed by a coal-filled boiler and mugs of tea, where signalmen played the role of agitator and disseminator filled elsewhere by cobblers, tailors and barbers. Railwaymen, and certainly Harry Williams, worked on neighbouring farms at key times in the year and, between shifts, tended their gardens and allotments. To the outside eye it may have seemed idyllic. *The Hereford Journal* in 1926 put it into a picture postcard world:

> Though the village is situated almost at the foot of the Black Mountains, the scenery of the vale is not worked by grand and sublime prospects, though the range towers on one side, but rather by little home scenes of rural repose and sheltered quiet. Every antique farm house and garden and cottage presents a picture, and as the roads are continually winding the eye is pleased by a continuous succession of small landscapes, the beauties of which are enhanced by the tumbling and sparkling waters of the river.[11]

26

The war had brought a measure of prosperity to the farmers, some of whom even employed maids in the immediate post-war period. Yet the wages of labourers were low and would diminish as the economic misery of the 1920s affected the farmers who employed them. Behind the idyll was real poverty, albeit alleviated by a countryman's ability to "acquire" produce from the fields or engage in a spot of poaching. Those who, one way or the other, could not manage had little in the way of formal support services as Brinley Griffiths recalled: "One family (the Hybarts) lived in an earth floor cottage near to the footbridge which carries the Offa's Dyke footpath over the river Honddu, and up to the railway crossing. I forget how many children there were, but they were very poor. Another case was a middle aged/elderly man who lived in a hut about six foot square and about eight foot high on the edge of one of the Werngifford Farm fields."[12] Charity sustained them: clothes and food parcels sent by London Baptist churches and distributed by Brinley's father, the Reverend Griffiths.

The Griffiths family would play an important part in both the life of Jimmy Williams and interwar Pandy. The family were from the coalfield area of north-east Wales and both the mother and father spoke Welsh. Isaac Griffiths, a Baptist minister, was moved from his first church in Buckley, Flintshire, in 1917. Their first son, Brinley, had been born there and Maelor, their second son, was born in Pandy in 1917 in Llwyn Onn, the house in which the fictional Harry Price and his wife would first lodge on their arrival three years later. Both brothers lost the Welsh language spoken by their parents as they merged into the overwhelmingly English-speaking population of eastern Monmouthshire. Nonetheless, they were the kind of incomers who were providing the grit of Welsh nonconformist radicalism.

Mostly, there was little overt conflict between church and chapel. The predominance of the former lay in its ancient foundation and its control of the primary school. All the children of Pandy attended this school and all learned the catechism, though the Griffiths boys were withdrawn on the annual diocesan inspection of Religious Knowledge.

Tension arose only when the Church or its rate-paying supporters tried to quash wider social developments and, notably, to stop a small rise in the rates to build a Parish Hall. The argument against such a move was that the school could be used for any village function. The counter to this was that the authority of the Church had to be sought for any usage, and usage could be restricted. In fact the Hall, erected in 1929, became the available forum for both the politics and the amateur drama in which a teenage Raymond Williams would participate. The victory, once achieved, caused no sectarian split, yet, undoubtedly, it was a secular outcome of a religious divide on the Parish council: "Chapel won, and the hall was built by James Parry (a Presbyterian) on land owned by Joseph Griffiths (Baptist)."[13]

Inasmuch as the taste of a particular place is dependent on its interaction with a particular time, contemporary witness alone can recapture the conjunction of the two. This is Maelor Griffiths' testimony six decades after he once lived there:

> Since the post war alterations to the road, anyone passing through Pandy or visiting it for just a short while will probably not recognise it to be a place at all. Yet it once had a definite and separate identity, at least in the minds of the inhabitants. There may not have been any natural landmark, no village square, or manorial estate with some substantial employer able to exercise due or undue influences. Gone were the days when the Church could do with the village hall what it had once done with the primary school – unwarrantably claim it as its own, determine its curriculum and deny its use to whomsoever the vicar cared to choose. Unlike many of the surrounding villages the Parish Hall was built by the Parish Council and controlled by it. Allied with the sense of independence which achieved this were the numerous annual events, mainly organised by the chapels and the Farmers' Union, the Harvest Festival, the Sunday School Anniversary, the Eisteddfod, the Annual Outing (invariably to Barry Island!),

the Xmas Parties, the Ploughing and Hedging Matches, the Sheep Dog Trials, the Shearing Matches. Also, the concerts and social evenings to raise funds for these and other causes. And not simply the events themselves: there was the preparation and organisation. Together these things generated a feeling, a sense of belonging.[14]

It was knowing the meaning of the concatenation of such things which made Williams bridle in a Cambridge seminar in 1946 when L.C. Knights, talking on the meaning of "neighbour" in Shakespeare, said no one now could understand the term since a corrupt mechanical civilisation had forever ended the concept. The twenty-five-year-old ex-Army officer stood up to tell the Leavisite lecturer that he knew "perfectly well", from Wales, "what neighbour meant".[15] His own experience grew from the close, interdependent life Harry and Gwen led from the beginning in Pandy. In a sense it literally started in the small, rather inadequate building into which they had moved from lodgings just before his birth.

Llwyn Derw was the name given to two semi-detached red-bricked cottages owned and rented by a builder, Thomas Parry. They were joined end-to-end rather than side-by-side and had originally been Parry's workshop, with the upper floor used for carpentry. The cluster of homes, eight in all, was very much his creation. He had begun, just as Hybart does in *Border Country*, by marrying a local farmer's daughter and being given a couple of bracken and bramble fields down the hillside from the farm. He acquired more land. On and around it he erected well-built stone houses. They were recognisable by the yellow brick trim he put around the windows. In the 1890s he built, for himself, a larger, rather superior building and called it Glannant House. It still stands, much as it was, fronting the old road. It is a detached house, double fronted, in stone, brick and slate, with three windows across the front upstairs, and a few shrubs and trees inside its front garden. On its side, just separate, and elsewhere on "the patch", are smaller, but still substantial houses, some detached and others not, all with gardens, and a feel of solidity. Llwyn Onn was the one Harry Williams yearned for and tried to buy throughout the inter-war years. He finally succeeded, and moved in with Gwen in 1948. Facing the rear of Llwyn Onn and almost backing onto Glannant House was the cottage, rented from Parry, which Raymond would know as home and accurately describe, room by room, in his early fiction.

Their half of the building was on the right-hand side. There was a gate into a small garden, then two front doors almost exactly adjacent and sharing a roof porch. The one on the right opened straight into a kitchen and walk-in larder. There was no connection with the main part of the cottage so all food and drink had to be carried in and out of the other front door or consumed in the kitchen. There was no gas at this stage and electricity only came to Pandy in the early 1950s. Cooking was done on either an open range or on a small oil-run stove. The other door led into a narrow hall entrance which had, at its end, wooden stairs on the left-hand side. Immediately on entering, a door to the left opened into a long, narrow living room, no more than eight feet wide and ten feet long. There were two windows. Light for reading was provided by oil lamps. At the far end another door led into a dark pantry. Upstairs a small landing had a door leading off into Harry and Gwen's bedroom, the largest; then came a small bedroom through which you had to pass to reach the end bedroom (Raymond's) which was situated over next door's kitchen, occupied by Mr Beech, a roadman, with his wife and three daughters. When Gwen's mother and Herbert came to stay after the death of Gwen's father, or younger family members arrived with their children on holiday visits, it must have seemed more than full. It certainly felt that way to Harry. Still, it was common for working-class people to share a bed, let alone a bedroom, with relatives of the same sex and Llwyn Derw, despite its awkward proportions and Harry's frustration – he tried to rent or buy other houses in Pandy or nearby all through Raymond's upbringing – always impressed others by its quality as a home.

Much of the credit lay with Gwen who, as her son would correctly recall in his first novel, brightened up the house with fresh curtains, linoleum and furniture, from chairs to tables and beds, some carefully selected from local auctions along with a few ornaments. The garden had the usual array of sweet williams, lupins and wall-flowers. So, whatever the inconvenience of an outside w.c. with only a bucket toilet until 1934, and with water piped, sometimes intermittently, from a mountain spring, the brick workshop converted into a dwelling was a comfortable home. To the right-hand side of the path that led up a slope to grazing fields for sheep and cattle was a drying green and a small orchard where Harry kept bees and worked his allotment. Like most railwaymen, with time to spend in the day after night shifts, he was a keen and expert gardener. Later he kept more hives on a mountain farm and Gwen tended chickens near the house. Raymond's London cousin, Ray Fawkes, who spent childhood summers there and visited in the war, remembered Pandy as "Shangri La" whilst "Llwyn Derw always seemed a bright cheerful place and was filled with the delicious aroma of honey... because we saw the cottage mainly in the summer we thought it was heaven".[16] In this heaven the young family had quickly found a niche. They were clearly a respectable, well-organised couple who initially tended to keep to themselves in what was still a new environment. Like others they found that a wider social intercourse was dependent upon the pulling power of Abergavenny.

Abergavenny is the Gwenton of Raymond Williams' published novels. It is the first of those geographical staging posts which mark the way out of, and maybe promise the way back to, the original locus. Certainly this is how it would seem to Raymond Williams during and after his grammar school days in the town. In the 1920s, for his parents and others like them in the surrounding countryside, it had a more primary purpose. It was where they could meet people, even people from their own village, in a way not possible elsewhere. The big market on Tuesdays and the smaller one on Fridays were the kind of face-to-face street experiences available to inhabitants of the bustling South Wales valleys on a daily basis, but were here a weekly congress, to be treasured all the more for that comparative rarity.

Abergavenny market was the largest in Monmouthshire. Farmers and their wives arrived by horse and trap in the 1920s. Private buses, essentially lorries with a tarpaulin supported by hoops and with wooden benches down each side, at this time and for the 1930s, shuttled in from outlying villages like Crickhowell, Longtown and Pandy. The pubs and hotels kept special "market rooms" to which purchases could be delivered and collected at the end of the day. In the morning, and after the auction was concluded, the main streets were crowded with sheep and cattle driven to and from the pens.[17] The appeal was as much social as economic. Maelor Griffiths recalled that "prior to the mid-1930s very few people owned cars and even fewer had ready access to a telephone [so] we can... appreciate just how important these market days were as occasions and opportunities for friends and relatives to meet and discuss many things as well as for the farmers and their wives selling or buying the produce."[18]

The town to which Harry and Gwen brought their honey, their preserved fruits and eggs for sale was an old one but their own settled presence, along with the bulk of the town's population, was more dependent on Victorian industry than on rural-urban barter. The latter tradition, though, was a long one and the site, in the Usk river valley at the confluence with the Gavenny, surrounded on three sides by its distinctive mountains, was one that had appealed both to Roman and Norman invaders. Abergavenny was where the Romans had erected their fortress, Gobannium, and the Normans had built a castle whose remains can still be seen: Owain Glyndŵr, in his early fifteenth-century revolt against the English crown came south to besiege it in 1404. Thereafter, though it saw further military to-and-fro on the troubled Welsh March and served as a Royalist stronghold in the Civil War, the walled town existed for the most part without difficulty as a regional commercial centre. Market activity was to be supplemented by rural crafts and shoemaking whilst, by the eighteenth century, it had become a centre for Welsh white flannel and for the manufacture of periwigs. Its genteel decline in the early nineteenth century, bypassed as Bristol and London merchants ventured further into a Wales better served by new turnpike roads, was dramatically reversed by the growth of iron and coal townships along the heads of the valleys directly to the south and west. Their product required an outlet to the manufactories of northern England and the Midlands. Abergavenny now became a junction of another kind.

First, a series of tramroads led from the ironworks around Merthyr, Blaenavon and Tredegar to Abergavenny and then on, after 1829, to Hereford. By the 1850s, rail track had begun to replace the tramroad and in 1854 the first train came into Abergavenny from Hereford. In 1859 the day of steam arrived definitively in the locality, with the incorporation of the Merthyr, Tredegar and Abergavenny railway company. The man behind this development, and after whom the town's Bailey Park was named (though it was actually the public provision of the Boards of Guardians), was the nephew of Richard Crawshay, pioneering Yorkshire ironmaster of Cyfarthfa Castle in Merthyr Tydfil, one Crawshay Bailey (1789-1872). The railway finally connected with Merthyr, then Wales' largest town with near 50,000 inhabitants, in 1873. By then the age of iron, though not of inland steelmaking, was over, but the era of coal had only just begun to transform South Wales into an economic hub of the British Empire. This branch line was not seeking direct connection with the great mercantile argosies that were making Newport, Cardiff and, soon, Barry huge coal-exporting ports, but with the railway networks which could do so, notably those of the London and North Western Railways (LNWR). When the town had its borough charter restored by Queen Victoria in 1899 – it had been removed when earlier notables had refused allegiance to William and Mary after the Glorious Revolution of 1688 – it was, therefore, natural that its first Mayor should be Joseph Bishop, the LNWR's District Traffic Superintendent since 1864. He was chief citizen of a town which then had three railway stations: the LNWR's Junction station which was run by them on a Great Western Railway line, the LNWR's Brecon Road station on the Merthyr and Tredegar line, and the GWR's Monmouth Road station to the south. The latter, in local red sandstone and cream fretwork, is the only station now left in operation. At its heyday the railway system in Abergavenny, in addition to its stations and signal boxes, had locomotive sheds at Brecon Road which could accommodate a hundred tank engines, with twelve roads and appropriate turntables, as well as railway barracks to accommodate overnight train crews.[19]

When the First World War ended, the physical lineaments of the modern town had been laid out around the antique traces of a medieval stone arched bridge, meandering red-brown river, crumbling castle ruins, a medieval gateway and overhanging seventeenth-century streets which the mid-twentieth century would condemn and remove as slums. At the western end of the town, Frogmore Street ran up from its new War Memorial – passed daily in the 1930s as Raymond made his way from Monmouth Road, a mile or so to the school in Pen-y-Pound to the north – until High Street merged into Cross Street. This ran on down past the Town Hall and Market, built in the early 1870s to a Gothic and Hanseatic beat and rounded off by a handsome tower with copper green pyramidal top and clock, courtesy of Crawshay Bailey whose own time was up just before it started to tick. This was the town – of butchers and bakers and provision merchants of all kinds, of tea shops and banks and drapers, of tanneries and brewery and local millers, of tobacconists and dentists and barbers, of jewellery stores and shoe shops and hotels of substance to many bars of dark, sweet solitude – which Raymond Williams would observe through his schooldays in the 1930s and, outwardly, see no substantial change in until the clearances of the 1950s, and the subsequent road schemes, pedestrianisation and larger shopping schemes of the seventies and eighties. It was the kind of border market town whose history of ethnic conflict between native Welsh and ruling Normans, notably the de Braoses who held lordship over Abergavenny in the twelfth century, offered him, perhaps to his later surprise, a rift of local heritage to work as metaphor for conflict in his later fiction. It also wryly allowed him to respond to the boast of the Cambridge undergraduate who claimed that his family came over with the Normans, with the rejoinder "Are you liking it here?"[20] The reality, as he well knew, was that ancient Abergavenny was, for his formative life, essentially a railway town. For, if Abergavenny could indeed be said to be locationally balanced between the "black" of the coal and the "green" of the encircling countryside (the population of the municipal borough, outside

34

the town, was about 8,000 in the 1930s) it was, in its economic existence and its social concerns, tied firmly to that South Wales to the west which fed it coal and consumed its produce. This, above all, was the connection he would later choose to emphasise and value most.

The population of Abergavenny town itself peaked at nearly 12,000 in 1921 and, thereafter, declined by a thousand a decade to just over 10,000 in 1941. In the 1920s over one thousand men were directly employed on the railways. These then, with their families, can be estimated at around one third of the whole population. Even those who had no working involvement with the railways found their lives filled with the sights and sounds of steam. The railway lines enclosed the town as surely as the walls held in the medieval settlement. Almost nothing was built outside its tracks. The noise of express trains and shunting engines was constant night and day – "and nothing was more emphatic than the shrill whistle and frantic puffing of the banking engines which helped to haul long trains up the gradient from Monmouth Road station to the Junction and on to Llanvihangel".[21] This was the line the schoolboy would take home every day, first up then on down the steep incline to Pandy, where the trains passed through on the authority of his father's signal box. Before wireless sets came the villagers set their clocks by the trains puffing up the embankment from Pandy to Llanvihangel or by those skating down the other way. It was a railway enthusiast's paradise, especially in retrospect. GWR carriages were cream and brown with green and brass fittings. The LNWR, originally black and red with gold bands, merged with the London, Midland and Scottish railways whose colours were chocolate brown in the 1930s. Most fondly remembered is the old M T and A line:

> The carriages themselves were gorgeous. They were rich maroon with gold lining, outward opening doors which seemed to be set back into the doorway, shiny brass handrails and handles. They were all of the open-type carriage. You could walk between the seats and the luggage racks would be up over each seat, again in brass, the whole thing very ornately done.[22]

The local impact of the railways, however, went much further than what nostalgia for sulphurous smoke and smart paint can convey. There were railway streets and railway houses. It was a way of life for two or three generations. Boys would leave school to begin work on the railways, maybe first as a "caller-up" knocking on the doors of footplate-men's houses at various times from 10 pm to 6 am. The network which sent them out and brought them home was complex. The GWR ran from Newport to Hereford and Shrewsbury but the LMS had running powers over the GWR from Abergavenny to Shrewsbury and then controlled the lines into the eastern valleys of Monmouthshire. Coal was the mainstay. Passenger trains and excursions followed on from that traffic. The signalman making sense of movement on this cross-hatched map of railway lines held the most vital job. They booked in and passed on every train, using Morse code to communicate with other boxes, those brick and timber sheds on stilts outside every station, and pulling their heavy levers with the metronomic precision required to work the thick cables attached to their distant signals. Each station had its station-master, its booking clerks and porters. There were the locomotive men, the drivers and firemen to fuel the boilers. In the locomotive depots there were storemen and shedsmen for the turntables. There were sandmen to dig up the sand from a mountainous pile in one of the sheds to fill the locomotives' sand boxes. The trains had to be coaled by men who shovelled up to thirty tons a day and watered from the great water towers with their swinging funnels. There were workers in the wheel shops and paint shops, and firedroppers whose hot and dirty work was to rake the fires of the engines and clean out the heavy ash-pans. Behind the locomotive sheds were railway barracks for crews on an overnight stop. This work force was a small, interdependent army. It could not normally congregate in one place as other industrial workers could, so they all assembled for an Annual Dinner at the Swan Hotel on Good Fridays, the only time all these railworkers were on holiday together, and when a football match would be played. It had a clear notion of itself as a distinct community of interest.[23]

This was the culture, with its benefit and sickness societies and sports teams, to which Harry Williams now belonged. The Labour Party and most other progressive movements in interwar Abergavenny depended upon the organisation and the support of these people. This was what allowed his son to say, forty years on, "as an adolescent I remember looking at these men... with a certain resentment – they seemed so absolutely confident. I have never seen such self-confident people since."[24] Undoubtedly this was the source of that supply of calm decisiveness with which railwaymen accepted their involvement in the 1926 General Strike. The unity of moral certainty and collective action, self-justifying and self-sustaining even in defeat, was what made that episode such a crucial one for Raymond. He was only five at the time but its implications rolled on into his youth and its significance, not as event but as epiphany, was one of which he never lost sight. For Abergavenny railwaymen the future would be one of reduced employment in the Depression years of the 1930s, as the coal trains rattled through much less often, and then of redundancies and eventually the disappearance of their rail hub in the wake of post-war nationalisation, rail cuts and regional mergers. In 1926, however, the links with the miners as co-servitors of the capitalist world in Britain were very much in place and ready to be memorably expressed in an industrial fashion that was, in essence, a political challenge. To come out in sympathy with the miners in their rumbling dispute of 1925 and 1926 was to act outside the normal or accepted boundaries of industrial relations. It was, as the dialectic in *Border Country* between signalmen Harry Price and Morgan Rosser would make clear, a confrontation with the state.

A popular guide book to South Wales introduced interwar Abergavenny to its visitors as a "clean, well-lighted, healthy, flourishing market town, charmingly situated, well-drained, and having a good supply of pure water... one of the best starting-points for excursions into the Black Mountains". It could not then avoid including the wrinkle-nosed observation that the "prosperity of the town now largely depends upon the collieries and steel works in its vicinity" but quickly added:

"Fortunately, the sites of these are concealed by the mountains."[25] In 1926 to be out of sight was not to be out of mind. For the nine days of the General Strike, supported by the NUR and called by the TUC from 3 May to 12 May, the solidarity shown all over Britain for the miners' cause by industrial workers was astonishing. Abergavenny was no exception. Councils of Action had been established in the South Wales Valleys to control or prevent the movement of essential supplies, from coal to foodstuffs, and to act as authorising body for those wishing or needing to travel. Those going to Abergavenny market were required to have permits issued. In the town, NUR officials scrutinised such permits or questioned those without them to the indignant horror of the town's elite who "thought that such a thing could not happen outside Russia".[26]

The feeling that there were alternatives available to those who customarily ran things was exhilarating and was made all the more so by the quiet discipline with which strikers maintained their loyalty. The NUR had two branches in the area: Abergavenny No. 1 and Abergavenny No. 2, which covered the Pandy men. The latter were relatively isolated in a small country station with, at first glance, no obvious leadership and yet with their livelihoods put at risk by this tangential action. There were rallies and demonstrations in Abergavenny – even the Borough Band played "The Red Flag" as the NUR and Trades Council celebrated May Day in the Castle grounds – and speeches were made under lofted banners.[27] Still, the decisions on the ground, in spots like Pandy, were the hard ones to take. All around them the Government's supporters, long gathered together by local gentry in the name of the Organisation for Maintenance of Supplies (OMS), were quick and ready to volunteer to break the strike. The Town Clerk acted as Emergency Food Officer and the Mayor as Assistant Road Officer to maintain transport links. When the General Strike was finished, though the agony of the miners' lock out until the winter and the year's end had just begun, the Mayor even thanked "all sections of the community, strikers, and non-strikers and volunteers for the conduct they exhibited during that time".[28] Yet this was to mistake the unflinching determination quietly undertaken for quiescence. In *Border Country* the consciousness of the meaning of their action becomes, in defeat, a more vital component of their lives than the sporadic act of rebellion itself.

Of the three signalmen in the Pandy box only Harry Williams was overtly Labour in politics. Hubert Preedy and Davy Richards were, if anything, Liberals. However, the Station Masters at Llanfihangel, Pandy and Pontrilas were all known Labour supporters. The Station Masters as such had most to lose: a position of authority and a detached red brick house near the box and its station where they were supposed to be on duty all the time. Under him, at Pandy, was the porter/ticket collector and a ganger with his six men working the "Pandy length", which was some three and a half miles. A similar situation existed down the line at Llanfihangel and further up at Pontrilas but the individual signal boxes were the key elements. This brief yet intensely charged scenario was the most overt form of class conflict to occur in Raymond Williams' growing up. It became for him a lode star: "A child of five, as I was then, can gain from a father who had experienced that complex struggle for consciousness a spirit and a perspective that have lasted under pressure, in the radically different places, where I have since lived and worked."[29]

As he wrote and re-wrote the early attempts at *Border Country*, he quizzed his father about the detail and the feel of that time. Most of the material was worked into his novel. Harry wrote some of it out, on an undated sheet in the early 1950s, as an aide-memoire for his son. He headed it "May 1926":

Weather. Fine and very hot.

We used to meet at Branch room each morning to hear latest news and were several times addressed by the Pontrilas Stn. Master, Robert F Thurtle, who was on strike and who was afterwards Editor of the "Great Western Railway" magazine (His brother Ernest Thurtle M.P. died recently).

We had very little money coming in and I well remember going to pay the rent (£1 a month) to Mrs Parry who disapproved of the strike but she said "Put it in your pocket my boy, you need it more than I do." She also arranged for me to work in her garden to earn a little money when the strike was over and I was kept out of work as the youngest member of the staff.

The 2 senior signalmen were taken back to work and I was not required, but one evening the D.S.O. staff asked my mate, David Richards to work about ½ hours overtime to deal with an express train requiring a Bank Engine detached at Pandy. I always feel grateful that he told them, "There's a signalman at home who should be here after me and I'm going on my 8 hours" and he point blank refused to work overtime while I was kept out of work.
My other mate at Pontrilas Arthur Jones also did all he could to get me back to work.

The resulting delays forced the railway company to take me back sooner than they would have done.

I remember going to meetings at Hereford addressed by R.F. Thurtle, Ellen Wilkinson MP and J.F. Horrabin the *News Chronicle* cartoonist urging everybody to stand solid. I believe the only train on this line was driven by Lord Raglan...[30]

Border Country, though decidedly located in its evocation of both place and family, is not a strict or actual chronicle. The signalman who, in the book, refuses overtime is Jack Meredith, stubborn and apolitical but cussedly loyal to a friend rather than a cause. He replicates the actual behaviour of Davy Richards who, a rather self-assured smallholder in life selling his produce in the towns and valleys, is in other respects more like the entrepreneurial socialist, Morgan Rosser.[31] Rosser's other characteristics in turn resembled the railwayman, Cyril Keddle, who was an ardent internationalist and peace campaigner in the late 1930s, a close working companion of Harry, and later well-known to his son. At the same time the final characterisation of Harry Price is a novelist's device more than a portrait of his father:

40

> The normal sense of a son getting his notion of identity and
> life from a father is [in the novel's end with Harry's decline
> and death] here intensified by the sight of an unusual kind
> of self-sufficiency which in the end had proved insufficient.
> The decision to treat the character of Harry Price in this
> way was one I took after several re-writings, and was not
> based on my own experiences. Harry is not my own father,
> because a lot of him went into Morgan too. It would have
> been possible to combine his contradictory impulses in the
> same character; I tried that but in the end decided to
> separate them out by creating another figure who
> represented the much more restless, critical and self-critical
> side of my father's nature.[32]

What had unfolded in Pandy before the child could have any real
knowledge of it not only served to focus autobiographical data in his
novel, it also provided him with the material that allowed him to show
a working class world, albeit small scale and literally on the fringe, as
self-acting and self-aware. There could be no question, here, of
sentimentality or a patronising removal of the observer from the past.
He took a long time to write *Border Country* because he had to discover
a form which would let him present his parents' lives whole, and from
inside their perspective, whilst connecting their lived experience to his
own, necessarily uncoupled existence. The General Strike was the
historical catalyst for the discovery of that form. He came to realise
that right at the start of his life he had been amongst people who were
caught up in the very epicentre of the triumph *and* the problematic of
the twentieth-century working class in Britain.

Fifty years later he told an assembled audience of coalminers, trade
unionists and labour historians, in Pontypridd at the heart of the South
Wales coalfield, how acknowledgement of their centrality to the
struggle, then and in the present, should not hide the significance of less
heralded moments, for, in late twentieth-century Britain, the diffuse, the
fragmented, the socially uncertain, the economically diverse and the

culturally ambivalent was becoming more and more the norm. The problem of human control over human destiny had also been raised and seemingly answered in Pandy in 1926:

I came down this morning from a village above Abergavenny: travelling the quite short distance to this centre of the mining valleys, and travelling also, in memories, the connections and the distance between one kind of country and another. In 1926, in that village, my father was one of three signalmen in the old Great Western Railway box. He was an ardent participant in the General Strike; so was one of the other two signalmen, and the stationmaster, who was subsequently victimised; so too were the platelayers. One of the signalmen was not. In the discussion and arguments that took place during those critical days, among a small group of men in a very specific social situation, some of the most important themes of the general social significance of 1926 became apparent. They were often recalled, in later years. I heard them throughout my childhood, and I went through them again, consciously, with my father, when I was preparing to write the General Strike sequence in *Border Country*...

Consider first that specific situation. These men at that country station were industrial workers, trade unionists, in a small group within a primarily rural and agricultural economy. All of them, like my father, still had close connections with that agricultural life. One of them ran a smallholding in addition to his job on the railway. Most of them had relatives in farm work. All of them had gardens and pigs or bees or ponies which were an important part of their work and income. At the same time, by the very fact of the railway, with the trains passing through from the cities, from the factories, from the ports, from the collieries, and by the fact of the telephone and the telegraph, which was especially important for the signalmen, who through it had a community with other signalmen over a wide social network, talking beyond their work with men they might never actually meet but whom they knew very well through voice and opinion and story, they were part of a modern, industrial working class. It is a special case, of course, but a significant one in the context of the General Strike, which is still too loosely assimilated to strikes of a different kind, with which it, of course, has connections but from which in crucial ways, it has extensions – extensions that raise quite central problems of consciousness...

What remains of decisive importance from the events of 1926 is the achievement of that consciousness [where] real men, under difficulty have to struggle to make their own effective choices.[33]

To that, he concluded, had to be added the perspective of complexity or difficulty in a differential, even fragmented society which "was then and is now, increasingly, our world".[34] He found first, in his own life, that the perspective of acquired knowledge, of school learning, so ardently desired for him by his father was not one designed to let him see this clearly. At least, not from the start and, thereafter, he would always remain sceptical about the education of any society which could exclude the culture of such as his father.

Chapter 2

A Schooling

Pandy School had been built at a cost of £1,000, a considerable sum in 1876. It was a Church of England Primary School (Non Provided) established to replace a Dame School, and initially the local clergymen and local gentry seem to have guided its somewhat shaky fortunes. The school could accommodate around one hundred children although attendance was often sporadic and numbers never quite reached capacity.[1] It was a grey stone building fronted by an unpaved yard, hard and dry in summer, churned up and muddy in a wet winter. It stood adjoining the main road and just a few fields towards Abergavenny from Llwyn Derw. A three-bedroomed cottage for the Head Teacher was attached. The usual grandiose Victorian arch and porch, with carved cross and the scrolled legends, *Laborare est orare* and *Benedicite omnia opera*, was the entrance to the customary inadequate accommodation. There were two classrooms, one large and the other about half its size. The smaller room normally had up to thirty children aged from five to seven whilst the bigger room was subdivided by an old green curtain so as to accommodate two classes, one for pupils aged seven to ten and the senior class for those of ten and above. The oldest children could be fourteen. A few might leave, aged eleven, to take up scholarships for secondary education in Abergavenny. The senior classes were, in turn, subdivided by age and graded ability into sub groups or three standards per class. Floor space was limited, the desks packed together and cupboards for school material squashed into the tiny cloakroom where the children hung their bags containing paper-wrapped lunches. Heating was by open coal fires until the mid 1930s. Sanitation was an ash or cesspit system, alongside a flush toilet, until the late 1940s when the buildings were still described as "obsolete by modern standards". No school meals were provided. The only light came from central windows.[2]

The Victorian fabric of the school did not alter in the seven years Jimmy Williams was a pupil. He was, however, fortunate in his date of entry, 28 September 1925, since as recorded in the school's Log Book on 22 June of that year: "Thomas Davies commenced duties as Head Teacher. The Rev. J.A. Hughes was present at the opening of the morning session."[3] Both men, but particularly the latter, would prove influential figures in his early years. Before their time the school, under successive Heads and with the long-serving oversight of the Rev. A.R. Blundell who was the Vicar at Llanfihangel Crucorney from 1874 to 1921, had delivered a stodgy diet of patriotic history and basic, vocational learning. The curriculum took children from Hereward the Wake to the Princes in the Tower before climaxing with "British Colonies"; the infants were led through knowledge of "Bees, Butterfly, Fox, Horse, Sheep [and] Dog [to] Ploughing, Harvest... Railway Train, A House, Post Office, Money, Wool, Coal [and] Iron".[4] It was almost an encoding of the lines of force in late-nineteenth-century, British and Imperial Pandy.

Tom Davies and the Rev. Hughes were, however, patriots of an emerging kind and the Wales they served was one that set out to re-orientate the direction of the mind in places like Pandy. Despite his later protestations – "What history we were taught in the elementary school was a poisonous brand of romantic and medieval Welsh chauvinism given us by the schoolmaster" – Raymond Williams' later consciousness of difference, of a specifically Welsh identity, probably had its root here for, apart from that schooling, it existed neither in the family, in linguistic circumstances, political allegiance or in subsequent education. It may have festered – "The reading was dreadful – nothing but how such and such a medieval Welsh prince defeated the Saxons, and took from them great quantities of cattle and gold. I threw up on that. It wasn't only that it didn't connect. It was absolutely contradicted by how we were" – but it also fermented.[5]

From 1907 there had been a separate Welsh Department of the Board of Education whose chief inspector was that populariser and proselytiser of Welsh historical continuity, the scholar and patriotic historian, O.M. Edwards. He was one of a generation of liberal and professional

Welshmen who were instrumental, despite, or in part because of, in-migration and increasing cultural change, in emphasising the primacy of language (Welsh) where possible and the necessity of national pride (Wales) where it was not. Since 1914, following a circular from the Director of Education in Monmouthshire, the time-table was to be abandoned on St David's Day, March 1, and a half-day holiday given in the afternoon. This was the flourishing, self-confident Wales whose patriotism was matched by its British and Imperial allegiance: very much the Wales of David Lloyd George, the Welsh-speaking nonconformist radical Prime Minister of Britain and its Empire from 1916 to 1922. The Log Book for 1 March 1921 records: "In the morning lessons given on Patriotism, St. David etc. [sic] instead of the usual lessons. The Portrait of Sir O.M. Edwards was unveiled by the Rev. J.A. Hughes MA. The children sang Welsh airs, and the older children gave a historical sketch – Owain Glyndŵr." Such celebration continued, with the Rev. Hughes making an annual address, through the interwar years.

The contradictions were internalised rather than disputed. The School celebrated Empire Day at the end of the month of May as readily as it did "Labour Day", on the instruction of the Director of Education of the Labour-controlled County Council at the start of the month. It closed for polling in a General Election and for the autumn Horse Fair or the October Ploughing competition or the period of the General Strike in 1926. By 1927 there were seventy-nine children registered at school. On 11 November, Remembrance Day, they were given a talk by the Head Teacher on the work of the League of Nations, and in December eleven of the older boys were taken by him to Swindon to visit the GWR workshops. It was a generation, it seems, being prepared for any eventuality. Each year saw a diocesan visit to test pupils' knowledge of the Catechism, learned and repeated despite the nonconformist faith of the majority of the children.[7]

Tom Davies was a burly man, over six feet tall and with the build of a policeman or rugby player. He came originally from Carmarthen in West Wales. He was a man more respected as a teacher than liked; too free, perhaps, in his use of the cane and addicted to heavy sarcasm to convey his authority. Raymond Williams never referred back to him with any affection though other contemporaries assert that he "brought kids on" and provided tuition for "the scholarship class" after school and at weekends.[8] Certainly, in his time improvements occurred – and he was not above the self-improvement of attendance at summer school in Jesus College, Oxford. In his very first full term, which was also to be that of Pandy school's most famous product, he organised an appeal for subscriptions to start a Library – "Today, thirty new books were introduced into the School and these will form the nucleus of a School Library".[9] The number of volumes increased to ninety-six within a month and he then introduced a gramophone and collection of five records. Pictures and illustrations began to fill the walls. A piano was used and new furniture bought. "Dramatic sketches" became popular in the younger classes. By 1926 he had instituted, for the top group or Standard VI, work "according to the individual method" and found pupils to be "keen on completing the week's contract". On average two pupils a year passed the Scholarship examination, a necessary feat if fees were to be avoided as they had to be.[10] In 1932 seven children from Pandy went into Abergavenny to sit the exam and in July the Head proudly wrote: "The results this year have created a new record for the school." Six girls succeeded, as did one boy who was entered as: "Raymond Williams 1st on the List of boys."

It was a County-wide accolade the boy would take with him to King Henry VIII Grammar School in Abergavenny, and more than improve on there. His father noted in his diary, "Everybody proud of Jim" and, not long thereafter, "Jim's bike arrived". Here was the prize and the "ladder out of the class" which Raymond Williams would describe as a social route for so many subsequent "Scholarship Boys" in *The Long Revolution* (1961). It was not, though, he felt, accurate as a description of his particular adolescent move or of his mature intent. To begin with "there was no sense of isolation from the village. The grammar school was intellectually deracinating… But I was not conscious of it at the time, because in everything that was not schoolwork there was no sense of separation."[11]

There is no strong recollection of him at the time that suggests anything different. It was an easy, gregarious childhood with only a few, though sternly maintained, restrictions placed on him. Within safe and easy reach were all the elements for play any child could want: rivers, streams and pools, fields and trees and mountains. Boys trapped moles and rabbits; on the farms they observed bulls "servicing" cows and the visits of the occasional stallion transported to similarly oblige. Itinerant butchers killed pigs, with the chitterlings or entrails given to the really poor. Watercress was picked from the spring and edible chestnuts gathered to the south of Llanvihangel Court in Chestnut Avenue. Even the railway, exciting in itself no doubt, added to the natural delights. The rail embankments and cuttings were cleared every year by a scythe – or "hook" as Jim would know it – and in the spring the sides were smothered by banks of wild flowers, a pointillist network of colour: wild strawberries, the vivid pink flowers of ragged robins, the softer pink and white of campions, the yellow of oxlips, cowslips and primrose and the creamy pallor of the flowers they called milkmaids. Bunches would be gathered for mothers and schoolteachers. Sometimes the school was closed to allow older children to help with the corn harvest or even just because the "children were black-berrying" or in the lane near the school gathering hazelnuts from the trees that were also used to provide hazel sticks for Tom Davies' too frequent, irate outbursts.[12]

Even that rage was deflated when the pupil delegated to fetch such a stick notched it so that it would split when put to use. Such incidents, along with the personal characteristics of some friends, were incorporated into *Border Country*. Apart from a few surprised grumbles no-one, later, seemed to mind. It remains about the only one of his books read by those with whom he grew up, closely and cooperatively. His cousin, Ray Fawkes, loved his own holiday visits:

> What always amazed me was that in summer time all front
> doors would be open and people would wander in and out
> without question... On occasion we would go on
> expeditions up the Skirrid, the Black Mountains or the

Sugar Loaf. All the neighbours would go. On the way we would gather wood for a fire and Harry always knew where to find a spring to fill the kettle for a brew up.

As children we had our favourite spots around Pandy. There was paddling in the "stubbs" across the field from the Lancaster Inn, hide and seek around the "tumps" up the back field by the old tram road. We even smoked the odd illicit "fag" under the trout bridge close by the Pandy Inn.

Life in Pandy was very much as described in Jim's book, *Border Country*.[13]

A constant visitor to the house was Gladys Sylvia Williams, one of six children of the farm manager and his wife who tended the Homestead Farm of the Manor House. By the early 1930s, Sylvia was Herbert Bird's sweetheart and they would marry in 1934. She was born in 1912 and so has a view of the Jim she knew that is half-way between the perspective of an adult and a child. She remembers him as a "placid, sweet tempered, nice boy" who, though "not shy", was something of "a loner, always studying or walking".[14] The trait would become more apparent, and almost, to some in his later life, a distinguishing mark of aloofness. It did not seem so to those who knew him well. Maelor Griffiths was four years his senior. In a small place like Pandy the age difference was immaterial to friendship:

Williams and I had [in 1939] lived within 200 yards of each other all our lives. Between Zoar Baptist Chapel and the then primary school there resided for most of the inter war years a dozen or so youngsters of near compatible ages. We went to school together. Ten of us went to the grammar schools in Abergavenny. We played together: in winter soccer at home and rugby at school. In summer we camped beside the Honddu and swam in its numerous pools. Many times we climbed the Skirrid. One of the last walks which RHW and I did together was in the Whit Monday of 1937 when along with the son of A. L. Ralphs (Assistant Head of

49

the Grammar School) we cycled to Talgarth and walked over the Black Mountains to the summit of Pen y Fan. Also, as soon as we could hold a racquet most of us started playing tennis in the summer on the courts attached to the village hall... Occasionally we organised a match against a nearby club but we never took the game itself very seriously.

In all of the above activities Raymond was as active as any of us. He was also an avid reader who read everything which had words in or on it. And if a liking for Gorgonzola cheese can be termed idiosyncratic that was about the only one he appeared to have. Mr and Mrs Williams gave us every encouragement and often appreciable help in our activities. They really were a remarkable couple.[15]

Llwyn Derw was home for five for a time. Jim's grandmother Bird and Herbert came to live in Pandy in 1927 after James Bird's death from pneumonia. Herbert shared a bed with the boy who was his half-brother in the end room. After their marriage Herbert and Gladys settled in the Mardy, on the outskirts of Abergavenny, and he worked for a local haulage firm as a lorry driver on long distance journeys, carrying bricks and steel. He remained a countryman in every other respect, possessed of a deep knowledge of wildlife, one readily shared with the young. Herbert, who died in 1984, was a large, amiable man whom Raymond would seek out for long fireside chats whenever he returned home. Their blood relationship was never discussed but much in his later fiction suggests Raymond's knowledge of and, perhaps, obsession with the facts. Grandmother Bird was "strongly chapel" and ensured that Jim went to Zoar whilst she was alive and that when she died she would be buried in its graveyard. She must have seemed a throwback to an earlier time by the 1930s, dressed as she habitually was in a long black dress and white pinafore, with black lace-up boots on her feet and her hair tied back in a bun. She was noticeably "soft" on children and once, when Jim skipped homework to run off to play only to be dragged back by the ear by Harry, she remonstrated fiercely with her son-in-law: "If I had a gun I'd shoot that man."[16]

"That man" clearly did have soaring ambitions for the only child his wife had decided they would have. At school Tom Davies believed in a deal of homework and ladled it out to the scholarship prospects. The Rev. Hughes might speak to the children on "the reward of unselfishness" but the Headmaster was forever "emphasising the need for hard work by every child".[17] Harry Williams approved and lived by both precepts himself. Through these years he conveyed, in his life *and* in the memory others had of it, an extraordinary, self-sufficient strength. The regular visits to Withington outside Hereford to see his own parents (they had moved the short distance from Ocle Pychard) were a part of his own supportive "unselfishness" – he wrote on the death of his mother in April 1936 how it was the "end of a home"; his father, in the care of a sister near Gloucester, died in October and was also buried in Withington – but, naturally his real "hard work" was saved for life in Pandy. There was the long and responsible work in the box to begin with – he worked eight hour shifts, from 6pm to 2am or 2am to 10am or 10am to 6pm – followed by a snatched sleep and then the tending of his allotment and chickens and bees whose swarms were written of with excitement in Harry's diary and memorably transposed into the imagination by his son. Shoes were soled, dandelion and parsnip wine made. Peas, beans and shallots, potatoes, parsnips, cabbages and all manner of other vegetables and arrays of flowers were planted in their season and carefully noted.[18]

If it was a close family life the couple led it was not a confined one. The Women's Institute movement with an emphasis on practical crafts had continued to act as a focus for women in rural areas after the Great War in which it was founded. Pandy was no exception, and having been a leading member for many years, Gwen, eventually, to her intense pride, was appointed the local President. She had been pretty, even coquettish in her early years; now, in her thirties she was a self-assured woman, content in a "very loving" marriage and much respected within the village for home-making qualities and her firm, sensible opinions. Her lighter side seemed to be kept back, as she grew older, for those inside the family circle where stories and secrets were revealed but she enjoyed, at this time of her life, dressing up for amateur theatricals in which she encouraged her somewhat reserved son.

Harry, regarded as kindly but sometimes cruelly blunt, had a more public persona. As with his alter ego, Harry Price, he acted for years as the groundsman of the bowling green he helped lay down and played on, following its opening in August 1929. In that busy spring the work he also undertook with others on the tennis courts attached to the Village Hall was completed. A Recreation Club had been established. Harry, attending book-keeping classes in the evening, served for a time as its Secretary. The village was developing a social life and by the early 1930s ran a regular fête and dance. Since 1919 there had been an annual "Pandy Eisteddfod" – originally organised by the Pandy United Literary Society under the inspiration and leadership of the Rev. Isaac Griffiths – in which both children and adults would compete, learning pieces of verse or passages from the Bible; an almost perfect example of the unselfconscious use by these "border people" of an "invented" Welsh cultural tradition. Augusta Hall or Lady Llanover had been instrumental, in the 1840s and 1850s, in encouraging interest in "traditional" Welsh costume and in propagating Welsh culture. As a result a celebrated Eisteddfod was established in the late 1840s along with a reverberating local tradition of Welsh patriotism. The American consul at Cardiff, Wirt Sykes, in his book *Rambles and Studies in Old South Wales* (1881) caught Abergavenny as it entered the modern world of industrial Wales still festooned in its early Victorian resurrection as a very Welsh town:

> A clean, quaint collection of stone houses is Abergavenny, with half a dozen comely churches and chapels, and a ruined castle. Modern map-makers have had the effrontery to tell us that Abergavenny is not in Wales, but in England – a statement which would be disproved, one would suppose, by the Welsh name of the town, its Welsh customs, Welsh history and Welsh people; but if any obstinate person should side with the aforesaid map-makers in spite of these, let him be crushed by an invitation to a concert at the

Cymreigyddion Hall, in Tudor Street, Abergavenny. It must be a bold spirit which would make Cymreigyddion Hall an English place of entertainment.

The value of the Pandy Eisteddfod was signalled by the presence, as adjudicator, of the ballad-singer, dramatist and harpist, John Owen or "Owen y Fenni", the twentieth-century bearer of Abergavenny's nineteenth-century glory as a centre for the resurgence of an eisteddfodic tradition.[19] Raymond Williams would capture him as the "I. Morgan, Watch Repairer" of Gwenton who is bardically transposed into "Illtyd Morgan y Darren". By his early teenage years Jim appears to have been less than enchanted by the annual eisteddfod and not least because of the rivalry for excellence it zealously, if somewhat innocently, promoted. If the young boy found this to be a stultifying occasion the adult writer had time to reflect on its deeper significance. In *Border Country* his set-piece on Glynmawr's Eisteddfod is ushered in by a brief vignette on Alun Hybart, the local boy who, in 1934, plays professional soccer as a centre-forward with Cardiff City. In the novel Alun disputes with Will the latter's contention that performance in the eisteddfod is about participation, not winning. The footballer thinks that only those who cannot win believe that "playing is for music, not prizes". Williams uses the episode to contrast the ephemeral and distancing popular culture to which Alun is now committed with the continuing and connecting ritual that, more than at any other time in the novel or in Pandy's history, brought the entire community, across generations and occupations and gender and belief, within a single ambit.

He would invest the occasion with a significance more social than symbolic in the fiction he drafted in the 1950s. In the version he finished in 1957 under the title *Border Village*, his account, though broadly the same thematically as the one published in 1960, is slightly longer, more intense in its detail and, if less finally shaped and resonant as a fictive emblem, rings precise and true as a memory of social history and culture within this, his first, society:

The afternoon session of the Eisteddfod was so much less emotionally charged than the evening session that it seemed, in comparison, almost tame... Charm, of the evening session, was the last word you would use: you were either moved and enthralled, or simply stifled... In the afternoon session [Illtyd Morgan y Darren]... was prominent, but as yet contained. His gleaming wing collar stood sharply up under his prominent chin, his long fine nose, his dark eyes caverned under jutting white eyebrows. The sleeves of his black coat were pulled back to reveal several inches of gleaming white cuffs, and from these, sudden as a snake emerged thin wrists and long chalk-white hands, which seemed always in a position to clap... As each child came up, the conductor would identify her family, and would recall, in detail, older members of the same family who he remembered coming as children to the same platform.

"Elinor Watkins. Come up Elinor. Elinor Watkins Elinor Watkins Tremaen. Tremaen, yes. Where the *white* barn, the white barn, stands by the bend of the river. Elinor, yes. Elinor daughter of Mary who was Mary Rees when she went to marry John Watkins, the son of my very old friend John Watkins the Bridge. Mary herself I remember, Mary with red hair, red to her shoulders, singing here where I am standing, eleven years old... And this is Elinor, her daughter. Mary Rees, Mary Watkins, Elinor Watkins Tremaen. Come up Elinor. Come up by this old man who remembers your mother coming to him."... this ritual of identification and memory meant almost everything to the silent and apparently unresponsive listeners. There was the meaning of life, every time: Mary had sung and her daughter Elinor was singing, Elinor with red hair to her shoulders, standing by the extraordinary Illtyd Morgan y Darren. The conductor, Will had also learned, never in the least detail erred in these recollections. Will felt ashamed at his own half-expressed wish that there might be some extraordinary blunder: the child given to the wrong mother;

54

the parents mixed up; bastardy and illegitimacy flung across the valley by that compelling voice. But always... he was right, and a stranger coming into the room would learn, in the course of the day, the greater part of the complicated family relationships through which Brynllwyd lived, and even the geography and the appearance of the place, and something of its economy...

Soon after half past five the afternoon session ended. The evening session, announced for seven-thirty sharp, would begin as usual soon after eight... At last Illtyd Morgan y Darren was on the platform again, and now, in the closer atmosphere of the oil-lit crowded room, the tension rose at once. Everyone stood to sing the English national anthem, put at the beginning so that at the end, when they were really involved, they could sing the Welsh... Tenors, baritones, sopranos, came and went, all practised, polished people, from distant villages and as far as the mining valleys... On into the recitations, and here there were more people from Brynllwyd itself. Many of the farmers of the valley, ordinarily slow inarticulate men, recited regularly and became on the platform, under the single oil lamp, intent and strange in the practised formal eloquence, which was warmer, more deliberately pressing on the heart, than even the singing...

[Then]... the choirs... were moving into position, in their dark rows, and the set, dedicated faces were turning to the conductor, the eyes widened, the lips poised, surrendered, begging for movement and control. The fall of the uplifted hand, and then not the explosion of sound that you half expected, but a low distant sound, a sound like the sea, yet human, insistently human, a long hoarse caressing whisper of sound... a dance of life in sound, holding, moving. You have to talk about this to get it wrong, not listen to it, Will thought, still fighting his excitement. For what was final was the response, the simple collective intentness, a hushed silence that yet held all the potency of these

sounds: so that you listening were the singing, and there
was no room for detachment... [and]... everyone getting
up, standing together, and singing the anthem. Then,
within this, it seemed no longer a matter of the ordinary
senses, but of direct impact on the body – on the skin, on
the hair, on the hands. What would anyone make of this,
Will wondered, anyone looking down on it all amused, if
such a one could be found? Sweat is distasteful or even
amusing on a stranger...
The turn to go, when the anthem ended, was slow but
willing: the limits had been achieved.[20]

This half-fascinated, half-repelled, and surely almost literal account,
of a collective immersion in sound and togetherness stands almost
alone in Williams' carefully modulated fiction. His listener, Will, tries
to hold himself apart in observation, but admits the uselessness of
paraphrase or mere rational response. The particular conditions which
allowed this organised unity to have an organic root were dissipating
even as the participants brought them to a pitch. At the time it was not
this urgent projection of a common life which impressed Raymond
Williams. Like his father he found it, if powerful, overbearing and
maybe a drag anchor. Despite the relative isolation of Pandy he was
more attuned to and involved with that other popular culture of the
1930s: mass entertainment.

It was an effortless transition. Two British worlds touch, page by
page, in his childhood as his father's diaries reveal – Friday 23 August
1929: "Hauling barley at Penbiddle." Monday 26 August: "Trip to
London and ordered 3 valve set complete. £9-11-0." Thursday 5
September: "Fixed up Wireless set." On that radio they listened to
Harry Lauder, international rugby matches, election news, football
results and, on 11 December 1936: "the last broadcast of Edward 8th
listened to by the whole world. He showed strength of will to the end
and we wish him well." The world had entered their living room. Harry
and Jim "rose early to listen to fight Tommy Farr v. J. Louis" on 31
August 1937 and, doubtless contemplating the gallant defeat of the

Welsh champion from Tonypandy, spent all of the following morning together working hard "sawing sleepers" for winter firewood. As he grew through his teenage years "Jim" features more and more insistently in his father's self-recorded life. What is separate about it, the academic prowess and success, is proudly set down but he is clearly attached by and to Harry's ongoing life. They work on farms together at harvest time. They attend Labour party committee meetings and discuss the hopes for peace.[21]

Harry Williams' wages hovered between £2-10-0 and £3-10-0 throughout the 1930s and were supplemented by his stints on the bowling green and the other country work, including his own, which he fitted in. It was scarcely a life without monetary cares but there do not seem to have been deep financial worries either. In a decade of mass unemployment Harry was never out of work. Clothes, for himself and Gwen, were bought periodically, along with furniture, in Hereford. On rail passes holidays were taken regularly: day trips to Barry Island or a week away in Totnes and Dartmouth or Teignmouth. Gwen and Jim often went away on their own. His cousins Ray and "Punch" visited from London and Jim returned with them to the Fawkes home. In 1936 he went to Stratford-on-Avon for the first time, on a school trip, though the Midlands was not strange to him since he had stayed with the family branch there for short visits. Photographs, from age five to fifteen, show a well-scrubbed, well-dressed boy who, from bicycle to dog, was not denied if it were at all possible. Each week Harry put aside 2/6d in pocket money for his son and met any other expenses as they occurred. Before the decade was out the country boy, by train or bike or in Herbert's lorry, would have seen much of England and Wales and stayed in the cities of London, Geneva and Paris. For a working-class childhood this was, by the standard of his Welsh contemporaries, remarkable.

As for books, the evidence is a trifle contradictory although at first books were indeed a rarity. There was no readily accessible library until he went to the grammar school. In Abergavenny a Carnegie Free Library had been opened in 1906 but it was not frequented by the

Williams family. Mostly, books were not bought unless required for school and it was there Raymond was confronted by the "set books" of the English classics:

> There were very few books in our house when I was a child: all I remember are the Bible, the *Beekeeper's Manual*, *Hours with English Authors* (an anthology of extracts used in the evening class which my father attended), *The Wonder Book of Why and What* and a translation of Euripides' *The Trojan Women* which my mother gave me for my birthday. Later, after I went to grammar school there was a one-volume Shakespeare and a set of Dickens bought through a newspaper subscription (I think the *Daily Herald*)... I remember reading all these, with the kind of over-and-over reading I have never, with certain books, lost as a habit.[22]

If the books at home were few, though significantly eclectic, he is nonetheless remembered as forever having his nose in one or other of them. And one that survives is not a book normally given as a birthday present to an eleven year old. Gilbert Murray's 1905 translation of *The Trojan Women* (reprinted for the thirteenth time in the summer of 1929) was one which had enjoyed theatrical acclaim at the beginning of the century: Euripides' passion and sympathy for the plight of ordinary people, and especially women, had seen him reclaimed in a more humanistic age as a writer of tragic relevance. The play unveils the fate of the Trojan women made captive by the Greeks. Raymond's copy, kept among his papers, is inscribed

From Mama)   Xmas 1931
To Jim)

It is perhaps over-fanciful to think that the misery of these "shamed" women chimed with Gwen's hidden past so much that she could be moved to buy it for him by lines such as Hecuba's:

"... And my daughters, virgins of the fold,
Meet to be brides of mighty kings, behold,
'Twas for the Greek I bred them."

Or Andromache's lament:

"One night,
One night... aye, men have said it... maketh tame
A woman in a man's arms... O shame, shame!"

Yet it remains a startlingly untoward gift, with no father's name upon it, from a woman whose interest in literature was only ever expressed in this gesture. Or in amateur theatricals – "The first venture of the 'Amateur Dramatics' quite successful" noted Harry in 1936 in which Gwen, then forty-six, excelled. Raymond's knowledge of or interest in contemporary fiction or poetry seems to have been slight. The prizes he received from school ranged from *Macklin of the Loyals: A War Story of the Western Front* in 1932 to *Sherlock Holmes: The Complete Long Stories* in 1934 and *Erewhon* in 1937.[23] And, though his father was reading and enjoying J.B. Priestley's *The Good Companions* (published in 1930) in 1937, it was film which served as the staple of Raymond Williams' imaginative diet. The Coliseum Cinema in Abergavenny opened just before the Great War: in 1931 Gwen and Jim saw there R.C. Sheriff's anti-war play of 1928 *Journey's End* in its 1930 cinematic version, and in 1936 Jim went to see H.G. Wells' *The Shape of Things to Come* in its startling and futuristic movie form, *Things to Come*. His early championing of film studies owed almost as much to this early impact of the medium as it did to the deeper discovery of film at Cambridge; and drama, one way or the other, was central to his thought all through his life.

Politics and religion were the other providers of drama in Pandy. Both were rather muted there despite the passions they could arouse. Harry was a parish councillor, re-elected for Labour in 1934, willing to travel to hear Lloyd George in Abergavenny in 1929 or in 1932 to go to Pontypool to listen to J.H. Thomas, NUR leader and one of the renegade Labour ministers then serving in Ramsay MacDonald's National Government. Raymond Williams reveals that he remembers as an eight year old "a euphoric atmosphere in the home when Labour won the elections... we greeted the results with jubilation" and, since his father was "running the Labour Party branch in the village", no doubt they did.[24] Yet his father's diary is as silent on these events as it is about the 1935 general election, contested for Labour in Monmouth by Michael Foot. Despite his feeling of unease when confronted in Pandy village hall by the rather patrician young Foot, then aged twenty-two and fresh out of Oxford, he did, at fourteen, work for the Labour Party in that election.

Politics did become more intense in Abergavenny in the late 1930s but, mostly, over wider international issues in which a local "popular front" of Labour socialists and middle-class liberals could genuinely unite. Until then Labour's incursion into politics was blunted, both on the town's borough council and on the rural district council, by solid Tory majorities. Abergavenny Trades Council was quite strong; Labour Party organisation remained weak. Hope lay elsewhere, at a far remove in a national election victory like that of 1924 and 1929, and, nearer to the point, in Labour's complete domination of Monmouthshire County Council from the 1920s. That, of course, was the political by-product of industrial Newport and its valleys' hinterland. In Pandy self-confident socialists, notably the railwaymen, could feel in touch with all of this without having a direct bond. Harry Williams' position as a parish councillor owed more to his standing in the community than it did to his openly professed politics. Conflict, then, was not avoided but, by the nature of things, was found to be avoidable. Through the successive versions of his first novel Raymond rehearsed his characters in this dialogue of conviction and circumspection: the dialectic of a real life experience which others, he discovered, would, if they could, short circuit with orders, telegrams, certainties and slogans.

Decisions were also taken over religion. Firmly, it seems, but without any anguish or hurt. "My father was very hostile to religion", his son declared in 1979 and added that he, himself, refused confirmation in the Church.[25] However, far from a fierce and forthright dismissal or denunciation of all religiosity marking either of their lives, both Harry and his son maintained a close relationship with the Rev. Hughes whose church *both* of them attended during the late 1930s whilst Jim had, in his grandmother's lifetime, attended chapel. The link seems to have been Gwen, who continued regular Church-going after the men went only intermittently, and the school where the vicar was early apprised of the promise of the signalman's son. J.A. Hughes became vicar of Llanfihangel Crucorny in 1920, the year when the Church in Wales was formally disestablished. He had been Chaplain and then sub-warden at St Michael's College in northern Cardiff, in the shadow of the Cathedral itself at Llandaff, from 1913 to 1920, also serving as curate in the mining town of Maesteg in mid-Glamorgan. In 1920 he was thirty-six, a dark, curly-haired man with a strong, prominent nose and wide mouth. He stayed in Llanfihangel until his retirement in 1958.[26] He had been educated at Jesus College Oxford and, if the portrait of the rather wistful clergyman in *Border Country* is near accurate, felt himself to be a scholarly misfit in a Church whose spiritual force could not counter the social organisation of the nonconformist chapels. Raymond Williams came to respect this man as his father had done; he took his own children to hear him preach in the 1950s. Both in the work of the school and in the community, Hughes' integrity and humanity affected the Williams family. Hughes visited them when the boy was sick with the usual run of feverish complaints. His gentle manner and undogmatic influence was appreciated. When a university scholarship began to be a real possibility, he offered his intellectual guidance to the precocious schoolboy. Paths were opened for Raymond. No one, it seems, made him feel that this meant closing his options or being forced to take one or other route. The Rev. Hughes, like Mr Pugh, *Border Country*'s vicar, who shows Will Price the stars and the world from his church tower, was a resident, other dimension; perhaps, in another guise, Will or Jim or Raymond himself:

He knew very well the village opinion of Pugh. He seemed a man isolated from them, sad and indifferent, with few of their interests. But where at one extreme this was contempt, Will had taken from Harry a different opinion: Pugh was withdrawn, but for reasons that ought to be respected... There was never any talk of religion, and very little of books... And at no time was there any kind of personal demand in the growing relationship. Pugh's very withdrawal, which made him so strange and unliked in the villages, served now as a virtually impersonal medium through which Will passed to new bearings and new interests...

"Formerly, you know, Matthew, I should have been educating you, and then sending you on, later, to the cathedral... [here]... I'm just a sort of outpost."

"Outpost of what, sir?"

"There are ways of thinking," Pugh said, "ways that have no roots here, but are nevertheless alive. Religion, I would say, is one of them."

Will hesitated, looking across at this sad, awkward man with something of the excitement of when he had first, from the tower, been shown the figure of Orion...

"... your choice was made, years ago. I don't need to advise you."

"My father asked you to, sir."

"You don't need another father, Matthew. He asked me not for the way, but for the start."

"But it's outside his experience, sir, isn't it? This sort of going away?"

"You could say that. But experience isn't only what's happened to us. It's also what we wanted to happen..."

Will did not answer. They were standing together near the door. "I think it's for him as much as for you," Pugh said. "And I want you to see that, as I saw it in him. That a life lasts longer than the actual body through which it moves."[27]

* * * * * *

On Tuesday 13 September 1932 the "going away" really began. Raymond Henry Williams became a pupil at King Henry VIII Grammar School in Pen-y-Pound; just up the hill from the War memorial, in distant Abergavenny. The school was a prestigious one, though that was owed less to its sixteenth-century lineage than to its later educational reform as, first, a regional grammar school and then a more locally-based one. The first intent was to serve, from the 1890s, as a classical grammar school for a wide catchment area in Monmouthshire. This, by 1914, proved to be somewhat anachronistic since the Welsh Intermediate Education Act of 1889, rather in advance of English provision, had facilitated the creation of grammar schools in the populous industrial areas of northern Monmouthshire. From 1910, when the county council assumed control of the governing body, the Abergavenny school fell into line with a modern pattern and even the Headmaster no longer had to be in Holy Orders.[28] Nonetheless, the establishment Raymond entered had about it the architectural air of a miniaturised public school.

The single-storey building to which the school moved from the town centre in 1898 was constructed, at a cost of nearly £7,000, on a nine acre site on the old Hereford Road. It was built with local dressed stone with windows and doors trimmed in a smoother honey-coloured stone and hints everywhere of pointed arches, stained glass and pillars. The slate roof had thrusting gables at either end. There was a school hall, four classrooms, a library and rooms for the Head and his Assistant. School gates, between stone pillars and a spiked iron fence, opened into a playground with some surrounding shrubbery in front of the main entrance to this ill-proportioned academic simulacrum of a Victorian railway station. Inside, a long, quarry-tiled dividing corridor, with doors off, ran the length of the building. The Hall, sub-divided into two teaching rooms by a partition, had an imitation hammer-beam roof. Before the 1914-18 War the total complement of boys had been as low as fifty. This had trebled by 1930, and four new teaching rooms, a gymnasium and a handicrafts room were added.[29] The driving force was the Headmaster, H. J. Newcombe, appointed in 1919 to both run and change the school.

The new Head was a mathematician and graduate of the University of Wales and although the ethos of the school was, over his thirty-five-year tenure of office, traditionalist, even non-Welsh, in many respects it was decidedly progressive and well-managed. His staff doubled, to six, from its pre-war complement, and a further three were added by the end of the 1920s. The curriculum retained its solid core of English, History, Latin, French, Geography and Mathematics, but developed specialist strains in Chemistry and Physics, and later Biology, with woodwork and metalwork rooms added to the growing building. The school now developed extra-mural traits to round off its growing self-confidence; an Old Boys Association, from 1923, whose patronage supported a school magazine, *The Gobannian*, the library and a sports fund. Rugby, a linking activity between the English tone of the school and its Welsh hinterland duly followed in 1928. Raymond Williams would be one of the stalwarts of the team in a successful playing decade.

School entry was single form, between thirty-four and forty boys being admitted year by year in the 1930s. The entrance class was designated as Form Two and then continued on to Form Five. Fathers' occupations were duly noted. In Raymond's entrance year, 1932-33, of thirty-nine pupils 21% were sons of skilled workers and 8% from unskilled or semi-skilled working backgrounds. It was not an untypical entry and was, more or less, in proportion with the whole school during his time there when some 11% were from professional families, 14% from farming families and 14% from trading families. Others were described as having a commercial or clerical or public service background. Notably, a proportion of 27% classed in 1929-30 as having a parental occupation as domestic service had crashed to 3% within three years, as the affordable status symbol of a servant almost vanished and with it the welcome work. There was unemployment in the area but, compared to any other South Wales grammar school of the era, boys from unemployed homes were an astonishingly low percentage of around 3%. There were no boarders, although, in the 1930s, attracted by the school's growing scholastic reputation, a regular 10% of the pupils travelled from outside the school district.

Raymond came from inside that area but was denoted as a "rustican" rather than an "oppidan", a town/country distinction which caused minor friction. Each year about a third of the intake was excused any fee payment by winning an entrance scholarship, as did Raymond, or through the award of a free place by the County. He entered a school about to enjoy some glory days and one relatively well-equipped to offer a range of teaching and training to a socially mixed intake, whilst small enough to be a cohesive community.

Initially, Raymond went to school by train, later by bicycle. A school cap and tie were obligatory but uniforms were not. It would be a long day however he travelled. Perhaps because so many came distances of ten miles and more there were no after-school activities and rugby was confined to Saturday mornings, travelling by bus to neighbouring towns and valleys. The nickname of "Ginger" was occasionally added to the one, "Shaver", which he brought with him and which older pupils, like Maelor Griffiths from Pandy, would know. From the beginning he was marked out as "highbrow" and a winner of prizes but, also, as approachable and friendly.

Much later he voiced resentment over the competitiveness he felt he had to show in school. If so, it was his father's intense ambition for him as much as the spirit of the school which instilled it in him. He was taught Latin by a Cardiffian, Harold Sharpe, and French by a Cornishman, Basil Mawer, continuing both subjects beyond Form Five into the Sixth where he took his Higher Certificate at the early age of sixteen. The most influential figure in these years was, however, the man who would not only teach him English and History but also direct his political path.

Arnold L. Ralphs had joined the school in 1913 just before the Great War in which he subsequently served.[30] He was in his forties, mature both in years and in conviction, when his greatest pupil arrived in 1932. He had an impact on the town as well as the school: during the inter-war period he selected books for the town library and keenly advocated support for the League of Nations, even to the extent of enrolling every pupil in the school in the League of Nations Union.

Through the 1930s he taught a weekly literature class for the W.E.A. in stricken Brynmawr on the north east rim of the coalfield. A graduate of Manchester University, his politics were certainly liberal, veering after the Second World War to admiration of Attlee's government. He taught an orthodox syllabus of British and Empire history, with a trawl through Shakespeare and Milton to fulfil the requirement of the examining Central Welsh Board. It was his method and his rigour that marked him out. In 1960, a year before Ralphs died, Raymond Williams addressed his old school at Speech Day and, as he recollected a year later, he felt he had not, adequately and face to face, told how much the teacher had been an exemplar. He regretted that he had made only "an incomplete statement of thanks... cut off by death", since Ralphs' interest in the books his pupil had published was always expressed "as if he were part of them, as indeed he was and is." There could be no doubt, by the tone of his memorial, how warm that affection for the man and his values remained.

> In the bewildering world of a new boy's first weeks at school, the masters are strange figures... I can remember clearly my first identification of Ralphs with the neat, small determined figure, turning through the front gates with a practised intentness that made it hardly necessary for him to look up from his copy of the *Manchester Guardian*. For two years he did not teach me in class, but then in the Fourth Form I remember him as a clear and stern critic of our methods in the debates he arranged; half English, half History and International Affairs, in his own characteristic combination of interests... he began a process of critical training which has always remained as a true centre in my own life and in that of many others. He taught English with a genuine passion which his control and quietness only threw into relief. He taught history as an immensely serious and continuing process which was so close to our lives as to be inevitably a moral concern. He extended this work into his devoted care of the school branch of the League of

Nations Union. As the 1930s, my years in school, darkened towards war, the firmness and clarity of his own beliefs in law, in justice and in peace gave me and others the bearings which overcame despair, and the convictions which could survive even failure, when war at last broke out.

I remember him with devotion and infinite respect, for his careful teaching of History and English for the Higher Certificate, but his influence was always more than that of an exceptionally able and conscientious master. In his quiet but articulate witness, he embodied a civilisation; the liberal seriousness of the North. This was unforgettable and is unforgotten.[31]

In turn, A.L. Ralphs, just before he died, had spoken to his long-time colleague, Harold Sharpe, "of many old boys and in particular Raymond Williams and his work and growing reputation as a thinker and writer".[32] Under Ralphs' guidance the pupil had taken the School Certificate of the Central Welsh Board in 1936 – an equivalent of 'O' Levels – and passed in English, History, Geography, Latin, French and Chemistry. His success in the Higher Certificate which he sat in July 1938 was quite outstanding: English (with Distinction), Latin (with Distinction) and French (with Conversational Power).[33] Harry Williams had been noting in his diary for April how hard his son was studying and, in late July, how he, Harry, "confidently awaits the result as Jim has worked like a Trojan". Then, on 27 August: "We get the very good news of Jim's remarkable success and are proud of him indeed." More was to follow in September: "I get the letter offering Jim the County Exhibition of £10 and placing him First in results", and the following day, after haymaking and spud gathering, "Jim gets State Scholarship" of £100 a year and "I go to see Mr Newcombe who is very pleased about him".

The Headmaster had, after his initial degree, taken an MA at Cambridge and now urged Harry to let him propose the school's star pupil for admission to that university. "My father said afterwards 'we didn't tell you in case you'd be disappointed if they'd not taken you'.

The Headmaster wrote to Trinity asking them to accept me... Why didn't my headmaster send me to a university in Wales? That would have... suited my life much better."[34] But those were the later thoughts of hindsight. At the time he seems to have taken it all as passively as if he had been groomed and could now be paraded almost without reference to himself. On 20 February 1939 Harry could write, "Jim gets news of his acceptance for Trinity College, Cambs." Without admission exam or interview, this was the first but not the last occasion Raymond Williams would simply materialise at Cambridge. His fees were paid by his exam success and, with a further School Foundation Scholarship of £25 per annum, he would be reasonably secure financially. It all seems to have been planned to go like clockwork, yet Raymond Williams' recollection of it all as "a surprise" since "I wasn't thinking of further education" has a ring of truth to it that is borne out by the other side to him at that time. Or, more accurately, "the university professor" who emerged was not the persona the adolescent imagined himself as becoming any more than he could be "the booking clerk" his father had once proposed. As he claimed in 1979: "I had a definite view of what I wanted to be, in which the university was not primary, but which it did not contradict... I think I can honestly say that it was very much what I am now... a writer."[35]

The ambition may have been the projected wish-fulfilment of any young man whose bookishness was so apparent. The energy with which he was already, secretly, pursuing the dream was very much his own. Just a trace survives of the novel, *Mountain Sunset* – about a British revolution marked by battle on his own border country – which he sent to Gollancz in 1938 or 1939 (a kindly rejection slip followed). Other juvenilia, however, three stories and a play, confirm his sense of himself and, intriguingly, already indicate a few obsessive themes.[36] Amongst the fragments, surprisingly perhaps for a boy in his late teenage years, there is no poetry.

In the mid to late 1940s when he had written and indeed published a few stories, he revised some of his earlier efforts and placed them together with new stories in a putative collection which would never appear. Some of the material he excised almost immediately to cannibalise for the version of the novel, then *Brynllwyd*, that he was currently writing. What survived from the Thirties were two stories of rather too-knowing observation and "Sugar", written in 1937 but published in the Cambridge student magazine *Outlook* in 1941. "Sugar" is a bold attempt to move away from the local colour he knew at first-hand to the connected wider world he had yet to experience. It begins with the daily papers being thrown off the train at Pentre for distribution by the paperboy:

> The porter smiled. The boy crossed the lines and took the bundle from him. He unknotted the string and drew out three papers to give back to the porter. He went back to his bicycle and put the bundle into the big front carrier. The train was now out of sight, and was only traced by a small white cloud of steam moving above dark trees. The porter went up into the signalbox for breakfast complaining that he had nothing to sweeten his tea with. He was lighting an oil stove as the boy pedalled away.
>
> The morning news had come to Pentre.

The news, as we immediately learn, is the repression of "disturbances in the sugar plantations of the Indies" where the "authorities had the situation well in hand. And, of course, the sugar." The rest of the story ties in petty theft by a passing tramp with his appearance before the local bench where he is to be dressed down and then sent down by the indignant local J.P. Miss Lilley, who is the daughter of one of the heads of the great sugar firm of Lilley and White. With a telling accuracy, the young author had tied in the "great homes" of Abergavenny and its rural hinterland to the fruits of colonial service and the profits of Empire. His own direct connection with this world remained slight, although his father had undertaken work for a Colonel Woodhouse on whose land he had an allotment garden in 1938; yet it clearly fascinated him as an undiscovered terrain and one whose secrets needed to be uncovered.

His first crack at this alien world, not too surprisingly, emerged as melodrama allied to farce. It was also a considerable success when performed in the Pandy Village Hall in April and May 1939. This was the play, *Silent Motive*, written with Maelor Griffiths to raise money for the Tennis Club in the Autumn of 1938.[37] The script, in a hardback exercise book in Raymond's hand, has a rather grand title page:

"Silent Motive"

A Two Act

Mystery Play

By Raymond Williams

AND

Maelor Griffiths

Copyright reserved

Reproduction strictly forbidden

A W – G Composition in Autumn 1938

On the inside cover is a pencilled sketch Plan of Stage and a list headed *Dramatis Personae* of the eleven characters. The period was "The Present Day" and the location the "Library of Rushden Manor". The authors anticipated a playing length of 100 minutes and carefully noted the stage properties and effects – "door bell, two revolver shots, telephone etc." – that were "essential". The plot was less complicated than some of the speeches, and the motive for murder, if clear, did not seem too convincing. Still, it rattles along, tries some low-life comedy with "the domestics" and is a creditable imitation of the kind of drawing-room "thrillers" made by English film-makers of the 1930s. Authors and audience seem to have been happy enough to follow the allotted lines of class hierarchies and accents, although Terrence Duncan, one of the sharper characters who pushes the investigation along, gives us a glimpse of a more radical agenda. He is a youthful

County Police surgeon, friend to Betty Howard, niece of Leicester Howard the politician and owner of Rushden Manor. Duncan's forthright, sententious views on women, experience, careerism and D. H. Lawrence scarcely moved the story along. They were, however, little platforms of monologue delivered by Raymond with the gusto of one who could speak out to his own people from behind that mask in a way the boy, as himself, might not have managed. Maelor Griffiths took the other main part, that of fellow MP Allan Murdoch who, second-bested all through his life (in Oxford, in Parliament and, fatally, in love) by his old friend, Leicester Howard, finally squares the circle of fate by shooting Leicester, but making it look like suicide. Tormented by his act he exonerates the young suspected lover of Jean Howard by shooting himself after quoting copiously from the Bible – specifically the indictment by Nathan of King David for stealing Bathsheba, which ends, as does the play, with the words "Thou art the man". Whereupon the second revolver shot comes, followed by applause from those who had bought the tickets at one shilling a time. It was a head-spinning triumph.

That summer before the War was one in which, for the future Cambridge entrant and State Scholar, there seemed no end to success. Privately engaged with his own writing and reading, attending school intermittently, playing in rugby and cricket fixtures, increasingly involved in political activity, he was a minor celebrity. In May, Harry had attended school speech day in Gwen's absence because of illness. Raymond scooped up the prizes. Harry wrote: "Jim very popular with all there and I enjoy myself meeting different people." In early June the golden boy won the School Sports 440 yards and 100 yards and, overall, was runner up to the Victor Ludorum. He walked away with a camera, a watch and a set of tennis balls. Social assurance, at least in Abergavenny terms, had been honed by the poise which achievement allows an adolescent at home. Yet, some of his self-confidence must have come from the opportunity he had to travel away from that home's confines.

Between sixteen and eighteen, by road as well as by rail, he saw a great deal of the British Isles haphazardly emerging from the Depression years. On a holiday in London in September 1938 he had watched

71

Chelsea play Leeds, visited Regents Park Zoo and took in Selfridges and the Holborn Empire; sport was a keen pursuit – Aston Villa against Birmingham at Villa Park was only matched in January 1938 by Wales' 14-8 victory at rugby over England at Cardiff Arms Park, and the proudly obtained autograph in the street of the former British heavyweight champion, Jack Petersen. Trips in Herbert's lorry took him to North Wales and Scotland, and overnight stays in the company of drivers which his father recorded as "an adventure" and "having added to his experiences". More than this his success in May 1937 along with a fellow pupil, Peter Laycock, in winning an essay prize sponsored by the League of Nations Union, meant a two-week summer school to study International Affairs in Geneva in August of that year. Raymond had been placed second amongst all the entries for his essay entitled "If I Was Foreign Secretary"; the first prize had been awarded to the future novelist, Iris Murdoch. Following the trip he wrote a wide-eyed, excited report for the school magazine on the glories of the Alps and Lake Geneva, as exotic and foreign to him as the "two dusky negresses" he noted as fellow delegates.[38] A stop-over in France on their way home enabled him to visit the great Paris Expo of 1937 and the famous Soviet Pavillion where the purchase of *The Communist Manifesto* gave him his first taste of Marx.[39] Over 300 young people from all over the British Isles, the USA, Germany and France attended the summer school and on the final day he was chosen to read the report of his working group (or "Commission") on the Reform of the League before "the full Assembly of the School, with Sir Norman Angell in the chair". Not yet seventeen, the sober phrases detailing "alterations" to the Covenant of the League and apportioning blame to "the members which should apply it", ran along with a young idealist's hope that "this education" would allow him to "go out into a world torn by hatred and strife... to pass on my experiences so that I may help a little in the spread of knowledge which will lead to the end of war".[40]

It was indeed the politics of peace which, along with his writing and his sport, took up his time away from study. He attended the regular League of Nations meetings in the town, and those of the Left Book Club which virtually merged with it in concentrating on topics of international interest.[41] In January 1938, during the Christmas holidays, three days were spent in London at Queen Mary's Hall, Great Russell Street, listening to lectures arranged by the L.N.U. Amongst others Raymond heard the celebrated Commander Stephen King Hall, as well as Harold Nicolson, Wickham Steed and Douglas Jay. His notes were dutifully transcribed but accompanied by tart pen portraits: King Hall was a "precise idealist who will not translate his beliefs into drastic action", a man who reviewed "the year in politics with an undertone of the old school tie always present", whilst Douglas Jay, the Chief Editor of the *Daily Herald*, was "a handsome youthful figure… seemingly more at home behind the journalist's desk than on the orator's rostrum".[42]

His friend Maelor took the lead in forming a local group of the Peace Pledge Union and advocating, in public meetings and through leaflets, pacifism as the solution to the drive to war. At the time of the Munich crisis, in September 1938, the Left Book Club organised a Saturday night rally in Abergavenny Town Hall for "Peace and Democracy", where Kingsley Martin, the revered editor of the *New Statesman*, was the principal speaker. Into 1939, in letters to the press Maelor continued to urge that pacifism "does not mean defeatism it means working for peace". L.N.U. luminaries such as Konni Zilliacus, the future Labour MP, "the first wholly cosmopolitan man I had met",[43] and the former Labour Leader and disarmament advocate George Lansbury, came to support a campaign against arms races and the doctrine of collective security. For the Griffiths family this was a socialist extension of their Christianity. The two brothers and Raymond distributed and collected the Peace Pledge opinion poll forms. It would all reach a peak in July 1939 when the Quaker pacifist Frank Hancock, who had moved to live in Cwmyoy on his adoption as candidate, stood in a by-election as Labour's nominee for the Monmouth seat.[44] "It was virtually inevitable," wrote Maelor, "that Williams and I should become involved in his campaign."[45]

There is no doubt that Raymond, impressed by his older friend and deeply influenced by A.L. Ralphs, thought of himself at this time as a committed pacifist. The most heavily annotated of the few books he owned was one of the school prizes he had been awarded in 1937: an Everyman edition of *Stories, Essays and Poems* by Aldous Huxley.[46] One essay, written from an explicitly mystical though not Christian position, was "What are you going to do about it? The Case for Constructive Peace". It ended, after a long forensic demolition of counter arguments, all set in a contemporary context, with advocacy of Meditation as a psychological technique to prepare "Constructive Pacifists" for "an exercise of the soul in training for an event of much more than Olympic importance". Almost every page was underlined or comments added and on 29 April 1937, at the top of the chapter, he found space to pencil in: "Began this work and ended it as a convinced Pacifist; with the youthful hope that the people of our noble democracy will one day be converted to the same views and ideals; those views and ideals which alone can save our world from murdering itself in the bloody sweat of War's inferno." As he read accounts of imperialism and colonialism and of the ongoing conflict in Spain he clearly yearned, as did others of his own generation, for a wider consciousness of their outcome. Local political conflict seemed increasingly petty. He had refused confirmation into the Church in 1935; in 1936 he declined membership of the Labour Party. In November 1937, he wrote to himself:

> I find that the world has forced a new opinion on me. Everywhere the forces of Fascism are crushing Liberty and all it means to so many. It is my belief that we can best show our Christianity by becoming soldiers of Christ in the immortal cause of true Brotherhood. There must be a revolution of Civilisation.[47]

And so he and Maelor Griffiths worked full-time on the Hancock by-election from the Trades Council base in Neville Street. They were branded "those reds from Pandy" as the elder brother Brinley recalled. They faced down the jeers and heckles and spoke at public meetings, on door steps, in village halls and market squares. Hancock lost, as would all Labour candidates in Monmouth until 1966, but he reduced the majority in a lower turnout which saw Labour uphold its vote. His youthful supporters took his message to heart. In June 1939 another note appeared in Raymond's copy of the Huxley Everyman – "War never achieved anything; it is in every sense a denial of all that life means. Morally it is entirely inadmissible."

1939 had already been a busy, almost feverish year for him: a Cambridge University acceptance; performed plays; the esteem of all those he respected in the community of family, friends and mentors; a school-leaving process, and wholehearted, day by day, political activism. It had not been quite the free and easy summer he had enjoyed after his examination stress in 1938 when, by train and by bike, he travelled for a month through Wales, its mountains and villages, and into the industrial conurbations of South Lancashire and Yorkshire. It was another rapid transition into a self-sufficient life and, this time, partly undertaken with a romantic intent. His essay in the school magazine, "Round Britain on £5", was a jocular, breezy travelogue apart from one sentence: "After the Pennines I stayed with friends in Wakefield. For a week I relaxed seeing Yorkshire by the energy of petrol and enjoying the change."[48] As Maelor recalled, the time in Geneva in 1937, had "brought him... his first romance... the daughter of a senior official of Wakefield Council. This did not last long. Distance was all against it."[49]

If so it was a distance he had physically covered a year later and which, in 1939, was still bridged by a holiday visit and gifts. His cycling trip to Yorkshire in 1938 was followed by a return visit from the girl he had met in Geneva and with whom he corresponded for over two years. Margaret Fallas, along with a fellow pupil from Wakefield secondary grammar school, had attended the League of Nations Conference and formed there a "boy/girl friendship" with Raymond which began to take a more serious turn as they grew to know each other. Harry and Gwen wrote formally to her parents to invite her to Pandy. In April 1939 Margaret arrived at Hereford by train to be met by the boy she knew as Jim. That second Saturday in April Harry wrote: "Margaret comes and we like her very much." She stayed ten days, explored the countryside and found "his Mum and Dad... lovely people – so friendly and welcoming – and [Jim] so obviously... their son". For a time the young couple, at least in the eyes of both sets of parents, seemed destined for marriage: "Then Sept. 1939 – the war started and from then fate stepped in."[50] It was all a heady mix. And there seemed no time to be steady and secure in it. The family in Pandy tried to reassure each other as the coming war threatened its public mockery of their future hope. Harry's diary entries railed and despaired:

31 August 1939	The news seems to indicate that all my worst fears are about to be well founded.
3 September (Sunday)	War officially declared and I'm afraid the times are going to be bitter for millions. What madness it all is.
5 September (Tuesday)	I try to face up to things but have a heavy heart. Sympathise very deeply with Jim as I know he is worried.
6 September (Wednesday)	Jim and I cycle to town to Labour Exchange but they can tell us nothing. He seems more content after visiting Cwmyoy.
7 September (Thursday)	Mam not very well and the strain is telling on everybody.
8 September (Friday)	Still unable to concentrate.
9 September (Saturday)	Letter from Cambridge tells us that Jim will be able to go up. News still very depressing as the Cabinet expects at least 3 years War.

In that same week Harry's son was writing, in red ink on six pages torn from a school exercise book, a piece curiously in the form of a short story, but too close to the surface of a passing autobiography not to have that raw, abrupt taste. He called it *I Live Through the War*.[51] It began:

It's my eighteenth birthday. August 31st, 1939. A dull day, full of grey leaden skies. As I looked at the blank mass of cloud I thought a storm was coming. A storm came.

He goes to Abergavenny on an errand. He meets

a pacifist friend of mine, a small fellow, a very conscientious worker. He was talking to an ex-Scout commissioner whom I had been very friendly with in my Boy Scout days. We smiled, and started bantering of course. They had been talking about the 'international situation' which seemed to be rather important. I airily answered them it was all capitalist scare stuff and rather paradoxically in the same breath said I doubted if I would ever see Cambridge – where I was going to the University in the autumn.

Nonetheless he is invited to meet a relative of the Scout leader who happens to be in the town. He moves from one acquaintance to another, still clinging to a hope for peace. Perhaps, as he wryly affirms, because it was his only future, and deserved:

We couldn't afford Cambridge... but unlike most of the people who criticise our educational system, I had worked at school and won a few scholarships. Going to Cambridge gave me some social status among the town's elite. Even my politics were forgotten. Before I had been just 'one of them Labour kids from Pandy', but now, now, I was a young Cambridge socialist. What promotion.

Everywhere the older people he meets sense war is inevitable. He refutes them with "wish fulfilment" and talk of "the Russian pact". "What a laugh I shall have when the tension dissolves, I told myself" but a "History master at school [who] had taught me all the world politics I ever knew" confirmed the grounds for pessimism and so, at the last, he concedes: "Aye I can't see much hope." He cycles home in the dark:

I was thinking of love affairs all the way home. For the last two years a girl and I had been dreaming of life together in the dim years of the future. Potentially that girl is the finest human being I know. But I was worried about her at the time. She had developed rather a liking for another fellow she had met in Southport. I told myself I was quite certain she would come back to me but I was worried – insecure.

When I got home my father had gone to work. He was a signalman on the railway and was working nights that week. He had not seen me all day and as it was my birthday Mother and I decided to walk down to see him. He was very worried by all this war talk. I suppose both of them were thinking of me. I told them it wouldn't be war.

We came back up and to bed. I forgot to pray for peace or my love affair that night. It was my first night in my own bed for a month and more.

I had a birthday present by the next morning's post – Winifred Holtby's "South Riding". I had got well into it when my mother came into the room for the news bulletin at half past ten.

We tuned in, but kept the sound low for fear of waking Dad.

The announcer sounded cheerful but the news meant war.

Whether or not the final reality of the war brought a sharper focus to their thinking immediately, both Harry and his son would be "among the first to join" when the Local Voluntary Defence Force (forerunner of the Home Guard) was formed.[52] And Raymond's own confusion came to an early head that September when he re-visited his Huxley Everyman. At the end of Huxley's essay, in May that year, he had already scribbled an N.B. which told of the tugs in his mind: "Reflection some year or two [sic] shows my marginal notes a little inexperienced and confused. Conversely and paradoxically pulled by my adoration of the League and of Bolshevism I deplored all reference to the violence which is an essential part of the two regimes as now constituted. Both systems, however, offer the highest hope of mankind." Now, in extremes, the Popular Front line hardened, with a little help from Clausewitz, and he temporarily concluded this particular debate with himself by dating his final thoughts, September 1939, and placing them, at the front of this much-thumbed volume:

> War is a continuation of politics by other means. We share its burdens as social burdens. But we fight in it for our own socialist objectives.

But that was still two years away for him. First, there was Cambridge.

* * * * * *

Harry and Gwen had been there before him. When Raymond was on holiday, in late July 1939, they used Harry's rail privilege card and, via two overnight stays with London relatives, they visited the lodgings he had been assigned in Maid's Causeway. Harry wrote in his Diary: "A most tiring but interesting day. We climbed stairs till we were tired out. A very nice day indeed in Cambridge. Jim should be very happy here." A box of marmalade, ham and honey were sent ahead with his trunk when the day finally came to leave home in October.

The leave-taking is rendered with care and poignancy in *Border Country*, with Matthew moving from one end of the carriage to another to take in all the sights of home whilst his father passes the train through the signals: "When you go out first on your own. When you marry and settle. When your father dies. When your son leaves home."[53] Reality was more prosaic but just as meaningful for the participant. Harry, carrying a new, initialled leather suitcase, the gift of Colonel Woodhouse, went with his son to the connecting train at Newport, and then went home alone that Monday morning: "On a pouring wet morning Jim sets out on his University career and may good luck go with him. I have a miserable time in Newport waiting to return."

Chapter 3

"Nominally Connected Lives"

The moment of departure which would become a life process of arrival was first re-imagined by Raymond Williams in the immediate post-war years. In the early drafts of an unrolling novel sequence that would later be pared down in both size and intent the fictional mirror has an undeniable autobiographical reflection. The personal chronology cannot yet encompass Matthew/Will of *Border Country* and is here a more spun fiction of Paul/Jack, but the portrait is still drawn from the life of Raymond/Jim as is the uncertainty that unfolds both in his Cambridge years and in this unpublished account of them:

> At a little past seven on a bright morning in April, 1939, Paul Ramsay was walking to Brynllwyd station to go up to Cambridge for his final university term. He was tall and slim, with an unusually long waist; his hands and feet were small, almost delicate, but his face was large-featured and strong. He had the colouring which is common in that part of the Welsh border country: reddish-fair hair, which he wore rather long and brushed straight back from his high forehead, and which grew thickly over his wrists... and skin of an unusual pallor, into which the heavy freckles of his boyhood were at last fading... In the freshness of the morning his expression was lively and open: the rather sunken green eyes looked quickly around, the heavy nostrils were widened, and the very long upper lip was drawn slightly back from the large, uneven teeth. His head was tilted back, and the heavy oval line of the jaw, and the firm chin, stood out clearly.[1]

What immediately follows in the novel will become familiar to later readers of Williams as the known and rooted "Jack" walks his countryside, meditating on the contrast between "dark mountain" and the scattered habitations of his inwardly absorbed landscape, until the hurried farewell from the railway carriage:

> His father put up his hand, and Ramsay took it quickly and pressed. He saw that his father had turned away his face, and now there was the loud burst of steam as the engine prepared to start, and as he released the hand the carriage was moving under him, and his father was running slowly alongside it, and waving up to him. Ramsay remained standing at the window, looking back. He saw his father turn, and go back up the narrow steps to the signal box, and then the train was gathering speed, and behind the diminishing square of the box he could see the dark slopes of the mountain, and then, as the line curved, that too was gone.

It is now that Paul emerges. In the novel the writer's actual Cambridge experience from 1939 to the summer of 1941 is compressed for his fictional protagonist into a final term of feverish activity. Here, all the themes that he would allude to later in interview and essay – the sense of being outside any official university system, the conflict between perceived political duty and his own tendency to prefer aesthetic interests, of being accepted as an insider by force of intellect and through an aloof personality yet feeling remote in an altogether more visceral sense, personal tensions and intellectual inadequacy – are detailed in the dialogue and narrative that centres obsessively on the figure of Paul Ramsay. The measured writing, of course, had been done by a Raymond who had indeed emerged physically intact from both Cambridge and the War but the painfulness of its depiction of a life not quite holding together would prove too raw to incorporate in any subsequent work. "The truth is," he recalled in 1979, "that for the first time in my life... I looked at myself with a radical doubt... Nobody could construe from reading my published works the sort of person I then was... it was a time of quite extraordinary personal and emotional disorder. The last term of that year [1941] was really pretty horrible in a way... the situation was more than I could handle."[2] Cambridge brought both his private life and his intellectual direction to an early crisis which only the release of marriage and the removal to war service would temporarily end. In a sense he kept returning to both the inner and the physical site of that struggle for the rest of his life.

* * * * * *

There were two essential aspects of Cambridge which did not hold him in their grasp at all – and the former of these never would: college life and academic work. Trinity was one of Cambridge's pre-eminent colleges, both socially grand and academically distinguished, yet it seemed neither to attract nor faze him. The foundation of the College, in 1546 by a dying Henry VIII from the amalgamation of two smaller colleges on the same site, owed its provenance to the same royal flush of charitable work that had, a decade earlier in that century, given Abergavenny its grammar school. Through the Great Gate off Trinity Street into the Great Court and on through Neville's Court past Wren's Library, behind which the Cam ran, and across to a great avenue of lime trees was an architectural progress that took two centuries to bring to an exquisite, planted and tree-lined, head.[3] It did not, ever, seem to turn Raymond's head even to the uncomprehending horror of those otherwise fixated.[4] The shades of Trinity men, of Isaac Newton, Tennyson, Thackeray and even Byron, did not whisper to him.

The College had scarcely bothered to make his induction easy. He had no friends or even acquaintances to second him for membership to the Cambridge Union, the debating society where he would quickly make a (black) mark. He never lived in the College, exchanging in his second year the room on Maid's Causeway, which was, then, despite the Georgian façade, a rather disreputable, down-at-heel broad thoroughfare to the east of the College clustered centre, for a ground floor room at No. 11 in the more central yellow-and-brown-brick early Victorian terrace of Malcolm Street.[5] He was never taught in College since, as he discovered after a perfunctory welcoming speech to the new undergraduates, Trinity had no provision for the teaching of Cambridge's new-found academic glory, English literature, whose direction since its foundation as a subject in 1920 was hotly disputed between those who valued it for sensibility and those who argued its values could be based in rational even scientific discourse. "Cambridge English", an appellation that would come to signify an approach to living appropriately and with moral sensitivity in a "mechanical age", emerged from the study of English language and literature at Cambridge. Between 1919-20, when the English Tripos for separate examinations in the subject was instituted, and 1926, when English as a subject came under its own Faculty Board, its study was already suggesting how critical analysis might replace the dead-handed grip of both the academicist concentration on language and the belle-lettrist approach of the late Victorian age. F.R. Leavis (1895 – 1978), himself a Cambridge undergraduate in History and English, became one of the first of a new breed of doctoral students – he received his PhD in 1924 and became a probationary lecturer in 1927 – but it was the startling lecture series which I.A. Richards (1893 – 1979) first gave to undergraduates in 1925 that signalled the future rigour on which a Leavisite moralism could begin to base itself.

I.A. Richards had read Moral Sciences but was about to take up medicine and psychoanalysis when, somewhat unexpectedly, he was appointed to a Lectureship in English. He moved the Practice of Literary Criticism, in a short span of years, from praise to process. His pedagogic technique was the basis of his written analyses, so much so that his standing as lecturer and guru were, for that first generation of acolytes and imitators, as one. In packed lecture halls, with both faculty members and undergraduates present, he would hand out sections of poetry or prose, without any indication of author or context, and then elicit the written responses which would, in turn, allow him to explicate the extracts and judge the value of literary opinion. Without bearings or directions most of the respondents floundered. What was conditioned taste and what was prejudice, what was rational and what was instinctive, what was demonstrable and what was opinionated, all this was opened up for cold examination and

modern literary criticism as a discipline was ushered in. Richards'
Principles of Literary Criticism (1924) and his *Science and Poetry*
(1926) were quickly the guide books that supported the wider claims
which Leavis, in particular, would make for the supremacy of English
at the core of humanistic study and at the cusp of modern life. For a
time the standard bearer would be the phenomenally gifted William
Empson (1906 – 1984), a talented mathematician turned brilliant
poet whom Leavis, the older man, deeply admired for his verse and his
criticism. Empson's pathbreaking *Seven Types of Ambiguity* (1930), as
much the godchild of I.A. Richards' original theories as Empson
himself was Richards' favoured protégé, declared the new Cambridge
English to the world. Both Richards and Empson would leave
Cambridge in the 1930s to teach in the Far East and never, formally,
returned. Leavis' own bravely combative career would, in turn, make
his own name synonymous with Cambridge English. Yet it would be to
the increasing annoyance of other long-term colleagues, appointed, as
he was, in the 1920s but who shared neither the sense of self-esteem
with which he comforted himself for promotional slights, both
imagined and real, nor the intensity of his critical vision for English
literature. Leavis rapidly sloughed off both Richards and Empson as
mere technicians of cleverness.[6]

It was a conflict which, at a remove, Raymond Williams would find
echoing in his own life, but, at this point, the Cambridge of I.A.
Richards and even F.R. Leavis was as distant to him as if he had gone
to any redbrick university. He was, in Oxbridge parlance, "sent out" to
the Classics-trained E.M.W. Tillyard (1889-1962), at Jesus College,
who promptly passed him on to a younger don, the thirty-two year-old
Lionel Elvin, of Trinity Hall, who was a prominent member of the
Cambridge University Labour Party; he had been elected to the Council
as its first avowed socialist member in 1936.

In this first year the expected work, from Shakespeare's sonnets up
to the poetry of Pope, was read for and completed as essays in the
manner he had worked at in school. Elvin was a sympathetic first
encounter – much more so than the High Tory Tillyard to whom he

would return in his second year – though he was keen to steer his charge onto orthodox critical paths. The tutor remembered weekly encounters with a young man who would noticeably "brook before saying something" and about whom he thought there was "nothing special".[7] But if Williams barely cut his teeth on Elvin's teaching, with Tillyard over 1940-41 the encounter was barbed. He seems, however, to have had no sense that Tillyard, Master of Jesus College from 1945 and at the heart of the dominant forces within the English Faculty, was already Leavis' nemesis, one quick to thwart the career and dispute the influence of Cambridge's most significant post-war teacher.

At the time an assertive but intellectually isolated Williams felt inadequately knowledgeable and deeply frustrated as his bare assertions about literary purpose in society were effectively countered by a disdainfully puzzled Tillyard. "All I can remember about you, Williams, is boots," Tillyard told him in 1960 and meant not the abrasive stance of a confrontational pupil but the army footwear Williams had to wear as an officer cadet enrolled for military training, hurrying to a tutorial after a weekly Bren-gun session. The enrolment was compulsory for men finishing a complete year's course in 1941 and, in that particular confusion of shifting politics and enforced action, symptomatic of the swirling time into which he was plunged. For the most salient feature of this first time at Cambridge was that the War, distant and constant, permeated all their lives.

At first it was the distance which seemed most marked, allowing the politics of the 1930s, at least in Cambridge, one last, forlorn hurrah. It was this Cambridge ambience which Raymond found most congenial and which, assured in its own sub-culture, embraced him. In particular, the Cambridge University Socialist Club framed his interests and directed his social activities. It had already proved itself to be the most dynamic section of 1930's student life, drawing to Cambridge in 1938 the Labour Party's leader Clement Attlee; the Communist Party's General Secretary, Harry Pollitt; the South Wales Miners' President, Arthur Horner, and writers such as Naomi Mitchison and W. H. Auden. The Club's rooms – where study groups in various specialisms, from politics to drama, met, wrote and performed – were situated behind Petty Cury, a cross street of old established shops and inns with a lively, slightly raffish air.[8] "The Clubroom" in 1938 ran an appeal for more members emphasising that it was "not an organisation for convinced Socialists and Communists alone, but [was] trying to become the general broad organisation of all progressive students in [the] University".[9] The drive was towards an inclusive "Popular Front" of undergraduate life and, at its peak in 1939, it had over a thousand members amongst a total undergraduate population of less than five thousand. Yet it was, in the memory of Eric Hobsbawm, at King's from 1936 to 1939, and then a Research Scholar until Army call-up in early 1940, "run, de facto, by the Communist Party".[10]

Hobsbawm, made the Communist Party's secretary in June 1938, was a central figure in all the Party's student activities. He was a Marshal for the Cambridge students' section on the No Conscription March on May Day 1939 in London, when bus-loads of CUSC members marched behind their banner, with its Star insignia, and called for a Pact with Russia.[11] Then, in that last pre-war summer, CUSC, still afloat on a sea of fellowship and optimism, held Summer Schools to which the scientist J.B.S. Haldane came, along with *New Statesman* editor Kingsley Martin and the MP Konni Zilliacus. On through the "phoney war" and even in the wake of the Nazi-Soviet Pact that particular culture of the 1930s survived briefly here, as in a cocoon, and Raymond, calling for "social revolution in England" in order to prosecute the war that had indeed begun, subscribed to it in all its confidence, and its naïvete.

His memory was that there was no debate within CUSC circles over the switch-back policy adopted by the national leadership since the "dominant opinion in the Club was very much that this was an imperialist war... Any fight in common with this ruling class would not be a war against fascism." Opponents of this dictum, chiefly mainstream Labour Party supporters, were in a minority:

> I know people now who I don't think had anything more than
> a pretty marginal commitment but who at the time would

have said they were Communists. The main cultural pattern
of the thirties still held, at least until the spring of 1940.[12]

The permeation of that student culture, from film to poetry to formal
political affiliation, by Communist Party allegiance to the Soviet Union
was, publicly, unquestioned. For Eric Hobsbawm, more seasoned in his
allegiances than his younger friend, there was no question but that the
essence of "democratic centralism" was to accept the Party's new line
that the War was no longer an anti-fascist one.[13] Collective discipline was
all. Any private intellectual reservations were suppressed and when, in
November 1939, the Finnish-Soviet war broke out, the argument that the
Imperialist powers might contrive to attack the Soviet Union took on
some weight. Soon Williams would collaborate with Hobsbawm on a
pamphlet defending the USSR's actions in attacking Finland. The ongoing
stance of disassociation from the British government's war efforts
coloured student activism within CUSC throughout that year. The reality
was that events had torn apart that particular late-thirties web and
Raymond's student generation was left at a stumbling pace behind.
Harry Fearns, a Canadian student who was an eager acolyte of
Cambridge communism in the 1930s and, as a distinguished academic,
a withering apostate of that faith thereafter, sensed the mood had
changed more quickly than minds could adjust:

> After the war broke out in September 1939, the political
> movement in Cambridge seemed to fragment. It was not a
> matter of great arguments among people of different values
> and points of view. The great calamity all of us had
> concerned ourselves with since coming to Cambridge was
> now on us, and I think it silenced us.[14]

Increasingly, then, Raymond and the incoming generation would
prove to be more attracted to life – in film, theatre and party going –
beyond immediate politics. He was drawn to the circle of literary lions
and film enthusiasts around Michael Orrom, the man who worked
closely with him, as friend and collaborator, until their abrupt split in

1957. For a year or so, in this Cambridge, Raymond balanced, and lost balance, in two, or even three, lives.

The tensions surfaced in his first fictive account of them through the story of Paul Ramsay and then with Paul's reappearance, as Paul Bergel from Austria, in the fragmented sequence *A Map of Treason*; their traces would continue but would widen out, in his later fiction, through conflicts which marked out both the generational and social class positions of his protagonists. However, in the early "Paul Ramsay" pages, we are given an autobiographical work-out that only takes off into a completely imagined world when the later Paul is removed from Cambridge via wartime service into a world of deceit and usage of others. The boy from Brynllwyd will be betrayed twice in this connected work of the early 1950s; the fiction, somewhat exotically but accusingly too, marries Paul's uneasy adjustments to pre-war Cambridge life with the Cold War re-adjustments made by some formerly Communist, abidingly bourgeois, friends in post-war England. *A Map of Treason* is part *noir* thriller and part political meditation as it runs on from its longer and earlier Ramsay prequel. Williams eventually finished the work, in a different form, but with a still rankling hostility in 1985 as *Loyalties*. In strict chronological terms, the quite explicit autobiography within this early and ambitious fiction opens up Williams' dazed response to his early Cambridge years with a startling, flash-gun clarity as he exposed it, still raw in his mind, in 1953.[15]

Paul will go down from Cambridge, and to his fictional fate, in the summer of 1940 with a First in English. Before joining the RAF he will continue in London with his love affair with Sally Nicoll, the undergraduate he has met at Cambridge. That is fiction. Elsewhere the slight displacement of fact reveals the mirroring of Jim/Raymond by Jack/Paul. In life, Raymond was recruited into the Communist Party after some speeches of his in the Cambridge Union had attracted attention. He said that he then made "the extraordinarily crass reply 'how much does it cost?' " because he was querying "a financial commitment rather than a programmatic leap"; whilst, for him, "there wasn't a real opposition between [Labour politics and becoming a Communist]... in my background".[16] In the novel the gloss on Paul's elision is more fully put:

Sidney Phillips, whom he had known for the past two years… was a small, dark Londoner, sallow-faced and wearing thick-lensed spectacles. He was not a friend of Ramsay's but they had met often in the university communist party, of which they were both members. It had actually been Phillips who had originally asked Ramsay to join the party. When Ramsay had come up to Cambridge, he had had behind him some years of adolescent work in his local Labour party, of which his father was a keen member. In his first year he had spoken several times in political debates, and towards the end of the year Phillips had approached him and suggested that he should join the communist party. Ramsay's answer had been characteristic, although it had surprised Phillips. He had not asked anything about the principles of the party, or what obligations membership would carry. He had said simply: "How much will it cost?", and when a low minimum figure had been quoted, had at once agreed. It was not that the principles were indifferent to him, but he had at once assumed that he would share them, since the communist party was an active part of the working-class movement to which his loyalty was automatic. And indeed so had he found it; it was not that he accepted Marxism, for he knew little of it, but he found the actual policies of the party sensible, and was satisfied with the allegiance to the working class on which the policies were based. Indeed, there had seemed no problem, and it had been with genuine surprise, a few months before this present meeting with Phillips, that he had found that he was subject to a good deal of criticism within the Party. He had still not read any of the main books of Marxism, mainly because it was not the kind of reading that he liked. And it was on this matter that he first got into trouble, because he had consistently failed to attend a study-group which he was now told was obligatory.[17]

Worse is to follow as "the secretariat" chastises Paul for his lack of co-operation and indicts his behaviour, with its lack of social "theoretical understanding", as "mere opportunism". The cause of this maverick stance is discerned to be personal. Paul associates too freely with "a minority in the party... primarily interested in the arts". These are the "culture boys" against which the "Org gang; the secretariats, the organ-grinders, the job lot" rail. Paul is valued for his drafting skills to enable party literature to lose its leaden prose but, much more, for who he was:

> Hardly any of the other members of the party who had come from working class homes were to be found among this minority, and this, too, told against Ramsay. It was pointed out to him that his profession of communism, which he did nothing to understand more fully, was in danger of becoming a mere cover for his actual drift away from working-class allegiance. The politics would become a mere salve to his conscience, assuring him that he was still on his natural side, but in fact the working class origin would soon become a mere romanticism, unless he took his political obligations seriously.[18]

So, Paul, divided in allegiance, moves between these polarities. He attends study-group meetings, does the necessary reading and makes prominent interventions and speeches. In an episode that moves the actual writing of a pamphlet on the Finnish-Soviet war to the crisis over German demands on Poland, he works hard to translate the Party line into effective journalism. Yet, "he did not give up his former circle of friends, whom he naturally liked and had much in common with". These were, in Raymond's actual encounter, the "Aesthetes", caught up, socially, "in an upper class style... prevalent in Cambridge Communism at the time... the makings of a neo-Bloomsbury atmosphere". His sympathies waned somewhat for this group of people as the years passed and, as with so much in his thinking and action, became personalised. Even so, there is no doubt that his young life moved, from

1939 to 1941, through bouts of what he considered duty to be undertaken in an organised way, and pursuits, mostly cultural, to be experienced because they were as potentially fruitful as they were enjoyable. His intellectual split was lived as a personal divide.

A Map of Treason simmers with resentment. Too much is expected, too much is misunderstood, too much proves rootless. Raymond Williams cannot, yet, in this work quite draw out the personal interaction of characters in ways that allow wider meaning to be suggested rather than told. Yet the lack of subtlety in this striving also manages to dispense with the oblique in a manner which takes him directly to the awkwardness of Paul's (and his own) unwanted predicament: having to be and to act and even to believe in a fashion that is exactly that, an acceptable mode of being but one put on and ill-fitting. One long, entangled episode which takes Paul, Sally and their friends for a long walk by the Cam ends with Paul "stealing" and eating a packet of sandwiches left in a punt. This horrifies his companions and when they are discovered, the leading Party member, Owen Iverson, a Spanish Civil War veteran who will figure in the sequel, insists on paying for them. The money is refused. Paul furiously and stubbornly continues to eat. It is both a trivial moment and one freighted for Williams with all of the nuance, and the exposure, of easily professed opinions and stubborn class division. Paul behaves badly because it is his only way to confront assumptions that never concretely disturb the placidity of these other lives.

More to the liking of Paul's circle is the song, to the tune of "The Lincolnshire Poacher", which, a drink or two to the good, he sings on request to another kind of party. For former comrades – Williams' party membership lapsed in his last year at Cambridge and was not taken up again after 1945 – the irreverence, even as Stalin's life petered out in 1953, would have surprised, if they had read it then, as much as it would have shocked, if they had heard it, in 1940. It finally surfaced in 1985, in a different context in the "1968" section of *Loyalties*. It also puts one more piece of kindling on the slow-burning fire of Raymond Williams: his Welshness abroad.

Ramsay heard Merrick calling to him across the room.

"Paul, we want your anti-Secretariat song."

"No," Ramsay called back.

"... What is this song?" Dawson asked.

"It's a thing he began to sing after little Phillips had him up to the Secretariat," Merrick said, coming over and standing above them. "Come along Paul, sing."

"I sing very badly," Ramsay protested.

"Nonsense. That's just a bit of Welsh apostacy. I tell you I have never met so much concentrated inferiority feeling until I met you, and realised that it was because you're Welsh."

... "You're making too much of an issue of it," Ramsay said. "The song won't bear it."

"Drink," Merrick repeated.

Ramsay lifted the glass to his mouth, and drank it off quickly... [then]... he began to sing, hurrying the words.

"Now... when Trotsky trotted his droshky down
the Kingsky Prospekt wide,
The Party had a heart attack, and ran to the Whim to hide.
They called the Secretariat to consider what to do,
But... first they ordered a Moka and a chocolate sponge for two.

One very vulgar frachs-i-on proposed to throw a bomb,
But the party was out of dynamite, and the shock troops lacked aplomb.
The Secretariat argued on, their mouths were full of cake,
They... said "we must make our attitude clear, for the Revolution's sake".

Some said: "well just ignore him, the fellow must be cut,
He's down in the dustbin of history, the lid must be quietly shut,"
But others were all for acsh-i-on, their faces were raw and red,
They... said "we must not only cut him, we must cut the bastard dead."

... and now, at the long laugh which had followed the first verse, he felt suddenly in command.

> "As Trotsky trotted nearer the glass in the windows shook,
> A Party girl got under a couch, and burned her Party book,
> Then up stood Comrade Chamberlayne, and showed them the way to go,
> They... must all go out in the street and cheer, and pretend it was Uncle Joe"...
>
> As Ramsay finished, and turned quickly away, several people shouted approval, and Merrick and Dawson leaned on his shoulders and laughed with him...
> "One thing, Paul," Dawson asked. "Why Chamberlain? Why not Phillips or Iverson or any of the actual boys?"
> "It's written Chamberlayne", Ramsay said. "With a 'y' and an 'e'. I think it makes my point."
> "You know I smell a heresy here," said Willis, who had been standing on the edge of the group. "I think it isn't only the Secretariat that Paul's hitting at, but us." Ramsay smiled.[19]

This first Cambridge period would not be the first or last time that inscrutability allied to ambiguity would give offence to those who wished to see Raymond Williams plain. What is clear is that he recognised that need, and his turning away from its fulfilment, in the fiction he wrote of this time. Nor did he ever forget the tightrope he was then, by choice or by compulsion, walking publicly. In the essay he ironically entitled "My Cambridge" – though indeed it was his more deeply than irony allowed – he reflected of his younger self: "There is an infinite capacity, at that age and especially in certain conditions, to live several merely nominally connected lives."[20]

* * * * * *

The three he led over those two years to the summer of 1941 were that of an intermittently conscientious but academically blocked student, that of a full time political activist cum student journalist and, no less deeply, for he was scarcely twenty, that of an incomplete personality yearning for a more defined expression in art and in love. It was, at the end, the personality which came through strongest. In part this was because the contrast with Pandy was constant and, as it turned out, disconcertingly continuous as his career proceeded:

> "If I... say that what I found was an extraordinarily coarse, pushing, name-ridden group, I shall be told that I am showing class-feeling, class-envy, class-resentment. That I showed class-feeling is not in any doubt. All I would insist on is that nobody fortunate enough to grow up in a good home, in a genuinely well-mannered and sensitive community, could for a moment envy these loud, competitive and deprived people. All I did not know then was how cold that class is. That comes with experience.[21]

And it was also in part because, in his very first term, he met the woman he was to marry in 1942 and with whom he created a lasting and interdependent partnership of life and work.

Joy Dalling, an undergraduate at the London School of Economics, was in her final year when the LSE was evacuated to Cambridge as the largest of the "guest colleges" at the beginning of the war. They were housed for teaching purposes in rambling, overcrowded but "elegant" Grove Lodge just beyond the Fitzwilliam Museum. Here they helped install the sense of a London university presence in alien Cambridge – around two thousand London students overall had been moved there – with their own lecture room, library and café: "From the beginning of the war to the end... Grove Lodge lobby was decorated with signs and slogans like a float in a May Day Parade... you could scarcely push your way through without being sold or given homiletic literature", recalled one dazzled evacuee, Norman Mackenzie. Crucially the LSE student union ran the college, with men acting as porters and women washing dishes. If the gender roles were still so readily adopted in 1939 the rest of the LSE cultural climate took Cambridge by surprise. Not least in the gender balance of the student body where half of the 450 evacuees were women (the normal total complement of LSE students would have been around three thousand, half of them part-time). Lectures, unlike the Cambridge practice of take-it-or-leave-it, were packed, and for the Labour Party guru, Professor Harold Laski, they overflowed onto the damp lawns outside. The expected political balance of the host university was not disturbed since the largely male undergraduate body of around four and a half thousand was, active or not, to the right; but, on the left, the Communist predominance was now shaded by more straightforward Labour Party allegiances. As the Communist Party continued through the "Phoney War" period, down to May 1940, and even beyond that with its anti-war opposition to an "Imperialist War", so a Labour breakaway from the Popular Front of CUSC became inevitable (it happened in February 1940). CUSC maintained its social predominance but some of the LSE jibes undoubtedly struck home – "You belong to a University and yet you have no say in the way it is run. With us the Union is not simply a boy's club with good debates; it is the government of the students, by the students, for the students... With luck we shall pep you up, or at least not let you demoralise us."[22]

This example was enough, at least, to pep up student organisation within the Colleges. At Trinity Raymond Williams later helped found a Trinity Union against senior college opposition – largely to protest against college dining regulations and the rations of wartime – and he consistently argued that the Undergraduate Council, formed in late 1939, could transform itself into a "representative student body". Certainly it would have been one in which women could not be barred from membership as they were in the so-called Cambridge Union itself.[23] It was in that cause that Raymond Williams first attracted attention speaking from the floor in the Debate: That women should have the same rights as men. He called his opponent, the curator of the Fitzwilliam Museum, an "exhibit" more than a curator and, ticked off by the Debate's reporter – "Mr Williams (Trinity) might use his abilities to better advantage if he learnt some elements of manners" – he was suspended for good measure.[24]

The LSE atmosphere, whether experienced in pre-war vacation time in London by Eric Hobsbawm, or in its translated and truncated form in the Fens by war-time Cambridge, was undoubtedly different. But perhaps, the journalist Norman Mackenzie reflected later, it was the catalytic mix of old place and new people which made the difference count both ways:

> The Cambridge life-style soon rubbed off on us; it is harder to say what rubbed off LSE onto Cambridge. From the outset dances were common ground; so were the flickering film shows in the basement off Petty Cury where the Cambridge University Socialist Club ran *We from Kronstadt*, *The Last Days of St. Petersburg* and Fritz Kortner's endless *Warning Shadows*... You could get into anything except the Union Society, the Pitt Club and the Apostles. There was all Cambridge as a context... in a Cambridge where women were still in a minority the more genteel members... got taken up and out to the Copper Kettle, the Whim... or Toni's for a posh meal. The Blue Barn, perched above the Red commune [three houses where Communist Party policy was argued out by day and night] of Round Church Street, was cheap Chinese for the evening out, with *Duck Soup* or *Dr Mabuse* at the Cosmo to top off the chop suey... [and] the dark streets seemed full of people going somewhere, for there was always somewhere to go... big meetings at the Dorothy, or the Co-op Hall, little meetings in Round Church Hall, or college JCR's, or in someone's room, plays at the Arts or the ADC, dancing out at the Rex. In winter there were walks to Grantchester, in summer the Backs and punts on the river.

And not least there was the welcome numbers of women suddenly introduced into the public-school and largely male world of Cambridge. Many were keen to defend from attack "These Londoners" as their denigrators in the student newspaper labelled them for reasons less political than personal. An anonymous "Green Knight" wrote in the winter of 1940:

> I feel that at least feminine Londoners leave nothing to be desired. With Newnham and Girton this is not the case. These fair Londoners, moreover, have made the Guest House a scene of revelry by night on many an occasion, and there has been no stint of invitations for Cambridge men. Regard the poets of Cambridge. Are they not all ensnared (or about to be) by visiting sirens? The USC committee too? Those desolate organisations where a herd of males clustered around some mediocre Girton beauty, are now alive with the fair nurses of Bedford and sex life in Cambridge is now on a basis of equality and opportunity. Who are the reigning social beauties? Bedford students. Who is the most striking blonde in Cambridge? A girl from the London School of Economics.

To which the laconic editor's note was "You're right about the LSE blonde". The blonde continued to attract some badinage and passing comment in the editorial columns of the *Cambridge University Journal*, not least when Raymond Williams, under the Party's direction, became its editor in his third term, in the summer of 1940. Some comment was hostile – a Girton student, suggesting a beauty contest to settle the Girton/LSE rivalry with funds raised to go to the Red Cross, concluded: "Modesty is all very well in peace time but to kill such birds as the LSE blonde by aiding a good cause is well worth a stone or two."[25] The blonde in question was clearly ahead in the popularity stakes and quite capable of looking after herself. Only, a determined Raymond had no intention of letting her do so.

They had met on Bonfire Night, 1939, Joy's twenty-first birthday. She had gone to a CUSC-organised dance in the Dorothy Ballroom, upstairs from the café, with a group of friends, notably her closest, Annette Hughes, a small dark Welsh girl, who had been born in Aberystwyth.

They had shared lodgings in London and now lived above a photographer's shop on King's Parade. They were interested in but scarcely overawed by Cambridge. Annette recalled that most of the men they encountered seemed "young" in comparison with the more cosmopolitan mix of company they had known in their London days at LSE. Besides they were both in their third year and, inevitably, more mature in outlook. So it must have seemed at the beginning of that night when they bought tickets at the door from the sandy-haired eighteen year old boy from Abergavenny who was, inexplicably as they thought, talking incessantly in an assumed American accent and only in phrases culled from the movies and popular music. Joy was three years older and generally pursued by men she had to "push off". Annette remembered that at that time her "very light hair" was cut short, enhancing her attractiveness, and that she was invariably dressed extremely smartly in clothes made for her by her talented seamstress mother. She and Raymond danced together and later, finding him "lots of fun" and somehow "older" too, a small group continued the party in their lodgings above the shop. Then a scene occurred which later friends would experience in different ways – when a bunch of LSE students "talked their way in", Joy, not wishing to upset a resident landlady, grew furious and chucked them all out. Except for Raymond who, in the weeks and months that followed, visited and sat in their room as the two young women began to work for their final examinations.[26]

Joyce Mary Dalling, always known as Joy since the War ended in the month of her birth, was born on 5 November 1918 in Yard House on Rolle Quay, Pilton East, at the head of the estuary of the river Taw. It was a residential and industrial area on the north Devon coast about a mile and a half from Barnstaple into whose ancient borough it had been incorporated since 1894. Barnstaple, situated on an angle of land between the Taw and its tributary, the Yeo, which surrounded Pilton to the east, had thrived as a woollen town, greatly helped by an influx of Huguenots escaping France after 1685 and bringing their weaving skills. It had a population of around 15,000 in the year of Joy's birth and would for another decade or so bustle with small-town prosperity from its sawmills, tanneries, glove-making, flour mills, potteries and cattle marts. The busy Friday market for local produce and the great September Fair, a horse and pleasure fair combined, marked Barnstaple as the focal point in its sub-region. Traditionally it had looked down the Bristol Channel to the open sea and if maritime commerce was never large scale, though its merchants had grown rich on trade with Virginia since the seventeenth century, it was constantly busy. "The trade of the port" said *Kelly's Directory* by 1919 "is very small, the principal import being timber from Norway, Sweden, Canada and the United States of America. There is a coasting trade in coal from South Wales and a little general merchandise from Ireland."[27] It was in this business of carting and bartering and building that the Dalling family had established themselves at the time of Joy's birth.

Rolle Quay had been developed to take account of the expansion of the South Wales coalfield from the 1840s. From there, timber for pit props could be shipped across and cargoes of steam coal, for the mills and for domestic use, could return. William Dalling and Son, Joy's grandfather and her father Charles, were the Coal Factors and Shippers who dominated the Quay with their yards, work buildings, weighing machines and tramp steamers.[28] The family were prosperous without being wealthy.

In an attempt to cure what may have been incipient tuberculosis, Joy's father Charles had lived and cowboyed on a relative's ranch in Canada before the First World War but had returned to Barnstaple to work in the furniture department of the store to which his mother had sold her business. There, this tall, fair and handsome man, tanned and seemingly full of all things American, met twenty-four-year-old Amy Horwill of Exeter who had moved to work in the shop as a dress cutter. They became engaged; but it was 1914 and so marriage had to wait until Charles' release from military service in 1916. Joy was the second child in a family of three brothers and four sisters born between 1917 and 1928.

Such a large young family meant hard work, at home and in the workplace, if they were to prosper, and Charles Dalling, though physically damaged, set about establishing his father's business on a sounder footing. He concentrated on coal, diversifying in Barnstaple into property for lease and rent, travelling by sea to South Wales but by road and rail to Yorkshire to ensure his supplies. The family lived well, not lacking in necessities for comfort, but carefully, even frugally. As his father weakened, Charles ran the Dalling business, and the extended family, mainly in trade as butchers or milliners, meant the name was known in the town and further afield. Charles took his boys fishing and shooting, a particular hobby, but his daughters were not neglected. They all enjoyed long summer holidays in their family chalet on the sands at Saunton and frequent countryside trips in Charles' motor car. By 1929 the Dallings had moved into Barnstaple proper, onto the High Street itself, into Northgate House, a substantial property which stood in its own walled garden of front lawn and flowering trees with a backyard of pear trees. They were able, at this time, to afford a live-in maid who cooked, cleaned and polished boots, and for help to come to chop wood and make fires. Yet Joy thought Raymond's upbringing, when she sensed it at second hand from early visits to Pandy, was "pampered" compared to her own far from prissy and quite boisterous upbringing in a large household. Perhaps he was sheltered, other than being an only child, in a different way, too.

The Dalling idyll, already somewhat marred by the deepening economic depression which saw unemployed Welsh miners crossing on the pleasure steamers to Ilfracombe to sing for coppers in the streets of Barnstaple, came to a tragic finality when their active and cheerful father became increasingly bed-ridden with the return of his TB. Four days before Christmas 1934 he died suddenly, aged forty-eight, leaving Amy a widow with seven young children. Joy was just sixteen.

The family had many readjustments to make. The eldest, George, at seventeen, began to help with the business and the older girls would rise earlier to clean and tidy up but there were still three others under ten and scarcer resources all round. However, despite the fact that in this family of doers and goers education as such had never been highly rated, the notion of Joy continuing at school, Barnstaple Grammar, and, as she now hoped, going to university was not questioned. Other than in Latin, a tedious set of exercises in grammar which she detested, she was a star pupil; but she knew that without Latin she would not be able to read an Arts subject, even English which she favoured, at university. As for place, it was likely to be Exeter until, in a somewhat unlikely fashion, the Workers' Educational Association intervened.

Joy's widowed mother had a friend whose husband was a schoolteacher and he encouraged her to attend, for therapeutic reasons, the various lectures held by the local branch of the W.E.A., which happened to meet in an adjacent building. Joy went with her mother and sat, silently, as visiting lecturers from Exeter University expounded on Keynes and the ills of modern capitalism. For Joy this was a welcome revelation of the possibility of making structural changes to a world whose ills she could, even if at a distance, see all around her. The family were not driven by politics – Liberal voting in a largely Liberal constituency but conservative in manners and attitude – but their charitable gestures were, to this bright schoolgirl, little more than that. The schoolteacher friend told her that if it was economic analysis and insight she wanted she should go to the London School of Economics. Knowing very little else about it, she agreed and after a successful Higher School Certificate she was confirmed as an accepted entrant for 1937.

In that summer she went abroad for the first time on a school trip to France. She returned to more tragedy. Her youngest sister, the eight-year-old Elizabeth had appendicitis and, perhaps not diagnosed soon enough, she died suddenly in hospital. Joy had not been told but was allowed to continue her holiday. No homecoming could have been worse. Since her father's death she had acted increasingly as a mother figure in the household to her younger siblings. For a sensitive teenager this second death was almost intolerable. Throughout the rest of her life it was translated into a cosseting, occasionally over-protective response to the lives of her own close family. At a personal level Joy found inner resilience in being resolute. She was never, in later life, overbearing but she was firm and determined over what she felt to be right for her family and dismissive of silliness or frippery in others.

At the LSE, Joy, though obviously from a middle class home, was, equally obviously, a provincial in this most cosmopolitan of British universities in the 1930s. She found the "foreignness" of it all somewhat disturbing. She positively disliked most of her fellow women students whom she thought resembled, on a small but similar scale, the public school element she would soon detest in Cambridge. She formed a two-person alliance with Annette Hughes and in her second year found lodgings with her in a nearby club. There were some men, mostly older, on whom she had the occasional crush but no one serious intervened to stop the conscientious attendance at lectures, libraries and note-taking. Joy, in this most politicised of undergraduate atmospheres, joined nothing and, at the time, did not consider herself in any way politically defined. Except that, when pressed for views or opinions she found herself, more and more, saying things that seemed to align her with a socialist stance. If so it was all in the head at this stage. When Joy finally and irretrievably embraced left-wing politics it was because of a direct, and first time, experience of working-class life in the War. She put herself, in an emotional commitment, firmly on one side and, for her, that ruled out wavering. That rectitude would almost end her relationship with Raymond within a year of their first meeting.[29]

There is no doubt that for his part he had no wish for that to happen. He had fallen in love and there were consequences for others. Margaret Fallas, with whom he had been in constant correspondence since 1937 and whom he had visited in 1938 and 1939, thought she was to be evacuated to Cambridge with the Yorkshire Training College in Housecraft. But her College remained unexpectedly in Leeds. For both sets of parents the assumption had grown into firm belief that, one day, Margaret and Raymond would marry, and it "was a great shock" when Raymond wrote that he had met a girl from the LSE and they had become friends.

> So our affair ended. Of course I thought the world had come to an end. Quite dramatically I had a bonfire and to my parents' amazement (they really thought Ray and I would marry!) I burnt all his letters![30]

Of course that hurt young love would heal and Margaret went on to have her own lasting and happy marriage, but though she and Raymond never met again their friendship did have repercussions. In particular his mother, Gwen, had convinced herself that Margaret was not only to have been but should have been her daughter-in-law. She continued to write to Margaret throughout her life. Between herself and Joy the hostility would deepen but from the start it was an open conflict.

In Cambridge Gwen Williams would have found strange allies in those who, equally openly, deemed Annette and Joy to be "politically unconscious" when they accompanied Raymond to CUSC discussions. He was, after all, a coming man and, for some, all of his relationships required alignment with the attitudes a young working-class communist needed to espouse. His friends knew considerably less about the working class than he did – even Eric Hobsbawm only came face-to-face with the British working class after call-up in February 1940 in the Army – but they could spot gradations in the middle classes with the ease of the trained and aspirational eye. Their logic was to unite extremes of social polarity through the mere act of political commitment. Raymond would be, for a time, pulled into a bewildering orbit where allegiances and loyalties spun disconcertingly.

His first year, though he prepared and wrote his tutorial essays with all the habitual discipline of a grammar school-trained scholarship boy, and would repeat the trick in his exams, ended by signalling the full-time student activist he would become when both the grip of Pandy and of Joy temporarily loosened. He took over the *Cambridge University Journal* as its editor in his third term. He had already become a regular contributor under the pseudonym of Michael Pope, who first surfaced in its pages in the letter columns in the winter of 1940. Pope put the official Party line comparing lack of support for Chinese resistance to Japanese aggression with "well-meaning" support for Finland against the attack launched by the USSR in November 1939. But he did not sound entirely convinced:

> The facts of the case in Finland are not clear. We do not yet know whether the USSR cannot make out a pretty good

case… I am as yet not entirely persuaded that Russia is a bad place… I would suggest that for every shilling they give to the Finland Fund they should give ten to the China Fund.[31]

He was now speaking regularly at the Union and made his maiden speech as a Proposer in March 1940 to the motion "That the Freedom of the Press has diminished, is diminishing and ought to be increased".[32] The motion was defeated but his view that advertisement, ownership and fear of the libel laws meant the Press was not free was one to which he would return, after actual experience as an editor, in a talk he gave to a Labour discussion group in Abergavenny in December 1940. That talk opened with an admission that "the war in its movements and results is the ultimate and deciding factor in our lives" but then insisted that "no people can be asked to suffer what the British people is suffering now without an excellent prospect of a better world when the war is won".[33]

It was a sentiment which, as the war unfolded, would prove unexceptionable. Not so clear-cut was the hot-house student politicking on the left which, Hobsbawm later reflected, "made neither emotional nor intellectual sense".[34] Yet "Hands off Russia" sat easily alongside "No Student Conscription" and both were taken up by the students who remained across British universities. In Cambridge students from the Conservative Association and those from CUSC clashed in a "free-for-all" in the streets. But this was little more than previous set-to's between Boat Club hearties and eggheads. Until May 1940 unequivocally slammed the door on any lingering illusion of the "phoney War" period, the atmosphere was of an uncanny continuity. Cynicism about the anti-fascist motives of both the British and French governments pushed away any deeper reflections on the Nazi-Soviet Pact. And the way the Finnish-Soviet Winter War unfolded, with the Germans giving the Soviet Union a free hand whilst Britain and France contemplated sending an expeditionary force to aid the beleaguered Finns, seemed to confirm Hobsbawm's contention that there was more desire to defeat Communists than fight Nazis. The distant events in Finland were seen as a lifeline out of the political morass to which Communist intellectuals had been wilfully, and too willingly, consigned by their Party leadership.[35]

Paradoxically, the Finnish War which caused wider public sympathy for the Soviet Union to plummet, was such a lifeline precisely because the matter was not quite as it was idealised at the time in the press nor as simplistic as the depiction of some later press commentators would have it. Notwithstanding the courageous resistance of a small country of some four million people to the brutal aggression of their large and contiguous neighbour, Finland in 1939 was, in the context of the wider world war, a somewhat ambiguous case. It had ceased being a dependency of Tsarist Russia in 1917 only to suffer a savage civil war between "Whites" and "Reds" in which the former were, in 1919, brutally triumphant under the future Marshal of Finland, the "strong man" of the 1930s, General Mannerheim. Thereafter, with left and especially Communist opposition crushed, Finland's stance was both resolutely anti-Soviet and pro-German. Soviet observation of this was more pragmatic than paranoid as they probed, through the interwar years, for a diplomatic agreement over territorial guarantees of the security of Soviet ports, and especially of Leningrad, across the Gulf of Finland. They were consistently rebuffed by a Finnish obduracy which subsequent historians consider to be misguided, even foolish, in the light of the Great Power realities of the late 1930s. The cynical alignment of Hitler and Stalin in late 1939 ended any Soviet reluctance to take by force what they had not managed by other means.[36]

The sixteen page pamphlet which Hobsbawm and Williams produced in February 1940 was issued by CUSC under the title "War on the USSR?" and duly ended with the exhortation:

> No Volunteers for Finland.
> Hands Off Russia![37]

But, although it briefly alluded to Mannerheim and Finland's key strategic position in any possible military thrust against the Soviet Union, it is mostly concerned to use the actual, not theoretically projected, intervention against the early Bolshevik state to justify its own call. Events from 1919 and 1920, from the Baltic to the Black

Sea, are presented as precursors of developing allied aggression. The authors then cite chapter and verse from January and February 1940 to strengthen their contemporary reading of the trend from past history to present politics. Other events could not be tidied up quite so briskly by such grand geo-political surveys. They say nothing of the despised puppet government imposed on the Finns by the Soviet invader nor of the popular national unity which, to Soviet surprise and consternation, had abruptly emerged in this conflicted Finland to oppose the Russian juggernaut. By the time peace, entirely on Soviet terms, had been accepted by a defeated Finland in March 1940, the defence of the Soviet invasion as mounted by the two pamphleteering students would already have seemed to most observers as contorted as it was undoubtedly derivative. The time had passed.

Yet there had indeed been seriously contemplated British and French proposals to intervene with a force of one hundred thousand men even if, by some, this was also widely considered to verge on military lunacy. In the Commons, Hugh Dalton and Aneurin Bevan led other MPs in saying so if it meant, as it clearly would have done, waging war against both Russia and Germany. In the Cambridge Union they disapproved sending any military aid, and with "Mr Williams (Trinity) attacking the Labour Party leaders" for pusillanimous behaviour, such a motion was passed. The final twist, not entirely unanticipated if a wider historical viewfinder than one merely focused on the climacteric of 1939/40 was used, came with the enthusiastic alliance with Hitler made by the Finnish government in June 1941, when Nazi Germany turned its war to the east. The German invasion of the Soviet Union was, for the Finns, an opportunity to reclaim the territorial losses of the Winter War and consolidate a national status within the New Order of continental Europe. In December 1941, Great Britain reluctantly declared war on Finland as a co-belligerent of the Nazi regime.

The official Communist Party line on the war from 1939 to 1941, for all that, had neither principle nor logic, given its past betrayals and future shifts and was impossible to disentangle from its primary defence of the Soviet position on all matters. Support of this position was the

106

least expected of its satellite parties abroad. Nonetheless, in its vaguer anticipation of a People's peace to match the war which the people were now being asked to fight, the British Communist Party tapped into a wider unease. In Cambridge the young debater who had assumed no real differences on the Left, turned and twisted, but with hairsplitting enthusiasm, to riddle the conundrum, accusing the Labour leaders of "keeping up the old tradition of opportunism and working class betrayal; they had evacuated socialism for the duration... [socialism was] the only way to peace, meant the end of Imperialism and the profit system... Anti-War activity [was not] defeatism... it was victory for the working classes they were aiming at."[38]

The life of a student politician was made more piquant by the thunder off stage of all these momentous events, but the churn of meetings – the Easter national congress in Leeds, May Day high jinks in Oxford and trades council marches – made their unreal waiting room bearable. Student life, in any case, bustled along through a flurry of personality – John Maynard Smith, tall, Etonian and President of CUSC; John Donaldson, future Attorney General and present President of the Conservative Association; Jimmy Edwards, Footlights Secretary, trombonist and wit not yet whacko-ed! into 1950's television-box size, and Hamish Henderson, of the left and of the Gaels, poet and future folklorist supreme; George Scurfield, then a "Philistine with a difference, for the Red Flag serves as his loin cloth", and the visiting troupes of ballet dancers, the entrancing Margot Fonteyn amongst them, who had visited with Sadlers Wells, and lovely Sally Gilmour of the Ballet Rambert, who broke hearts each May, and especially in 1940 at the Arts Theatre. The Editor was now writing a weekly Commentary on matters Cambridge, large and small; the gossip and clues could be tart: "The Girton challenge to London for a beauty contest has not been taken up. The LSE blonde, anyway, says people who make generalisations are fools. Which is exactly what I think of the LSE blonde."[39]

In the early summer of 1940 the Nazis rolled across Belgium and Luxembourg. The Fall of France was weeks away. The University newspaper was as subject to censorship as any other section of the press though its editor had been running lively cross-party discussion columns. As the British Expeditionary Force was pushed back to the beaches and eventual evacuation from Dunkirk in early June, the newspaper announced the forthcoming debate in the Union: "That this House welcomes the imminent collapse of Western Civilisation." Hamish Henderson and Jimmy Edwards were to have spoken, emphasising the "Humorous" nature of the occasion as the Editor noted, but higher authorities advised that this "lack of patriotism" would bring "a most undesirable notoriety". The Debate was cancelled. The editor printed the humorous views of Edwards and Henderson anyway and wistfully reflected that the comparison with the infamous Oxford Union motion of 1933, "that I will not fight for King and Country, made at a Cambridge Rotary luncheon was misguided even if the speaker there had added that the Oxford motion [compared with the Cambridge one] was just typically English... All the Oxford boys were just foxing." "Ah," said the editor, "we subtle Englishers... But then, I'm Welsh and wouldn't understand." It all seemed to be winding up anyway, "the way of life just now. Half of our staff casting their fate in the exam rooms, the other half glancing wistfully at the sunshine through a medley of clocks, old copy... Everyone wanting time to talk of the war. Time to work, time to write, time to go on the river, time to sleep. And no Union debate to report, no play at the Arts to review; no printing pictures; no night climbers... Such is an editor's life."[40]

But not for much longer that surreal term. The following week the *Journal* carried a front cover Stop Press. All the Colleges had "unanimously decided that all undergraduates should go down from Cambridge as soon as possible... in order that they would be available to undertake work of National Importance". The Union closed down further debates. Invasion seemed imminent. The fiercest discussion in the *Journal* that week was over the merits of Lubitsch's *Ninotchcka* which was reviewed, indubitably with a straight face by the resident film critic, Michael Orrom, whose comment could be taken as the last inane echo of the 30s in Cambridge:

A witty and on the whole well made satire on the Soviet Union and its bureaucrats. At a few times, when he degenerates into an anti-Soviet propagandist, the film becomes irritating to anyone knowing anything about the USSR. For instance, Garbo, as a young Russian is represented as tasting champagne for the first time in Paris, and saying "wonderful, wonderful." In reality of course the USSR is the largest producer of champagne in the world. Again, silk underclothes are certainly not the prerogative of the Parisienne bourgeoise. And so on.

The editor noted elsewhere that when he went "there was no audience reaction. Most people were listening to the thunderstorm outside."[41]

At home, in Pandy, his father was alternating reports of the hot sticky weather that brought "heavy storms" at the end of May with news of the war in June: "France ask for terms and it's a shock to all wondering what the next move will be." Letters were common property:

21 June   We wonder where Jim has got to as letters are being sent on. One from his professor tells us he has got a first class.

22 June   Letter from Jim at Barnstaple and also letter from Cambridge tells him he is elected an exhibitioner of his College. We are very proud of him.[42]

On 6 July Raymond, "looking well", arrived home. His first year at Cambridge had ended. He had not yet introduced Joy to Harry and Gwen. His academic success continued. He would return as a noted figure in his university. He had published his first stories.

* * * * * *

"Red Earth" was a fragment really, a satirical sketch that ended on a tinny up-beat note. It was a way, unconvincingly perhaps, of distancing himself from his new world, looking askance at "avant garde students" whose interests he nonetheless shared.[43] "Red Earth", the soil to which he returned in the summer of 1940, not expecting to go back to Cambridge that year, was more scenario than narrative. Its protagonists, the novelist, the journalist, the "boswell... who rinsed the milk bottles and knocked the food tins flat for a little path up from the stream", and the poets (for "All but one of them wrote" revolutionary poems and fiction about factories), live together in a wooden hut beneath a hill. The milkman who on one occasion calls not, as they assume, for money but for direct help in the struggle of the striking miners over the hill, is a better poet than they are. He leaves an example with his daily delivery – "It told of ideas in furrows breaking the breast of the uplands and of curlews rising black against the morning sky and the endless lines of roots... and the toil to pull them and scatter the red earth on the straddled gaping boots of the labourer." He asks for professional help from "the good sympathisers" but it seems they had already "written this before" – the solidarity of farm-workers and miners and strikes – so they offer to send "one or two [such pieces] over to the local paper". He leaves. They put the gramophone back on and turn to books – "Marvellous, that first sentence... Don't know how he does it, quite frankly" – while the man tramps back slowly, the gramophone insistent in his ears until, from the mining valley, he hears shouting and singing: "He could hear the words of the song they had been singing as he ran along... He wanted to shout to the world that Spring had come, and the time for sowing. The red earth was scattering on the pale worn furrows as the land was prepared."[44]

Another story, "Mother Chapel", written in 1938/9, had been published in his college magazine at Easter in 1940. Somehow, he recalled, it was seen more widely at home and caused some family embarrassment because of the local recognition factor of knowable places and faces to put to names. The story is, despite a few filmic intercuts, a straightforwardly told tale in which two young women are married, hurriedly and with hypocrisy on all sides, to avoid the scandal of being an unmarried mother. Its indictment of a repressive non-conformity is as conventionally done as the by then outmoded cliché itself though the story registers strongly enough in its dialogue and scene setting. Its author would not have understood, perhaps, that the tongues that wagged and the fingers that pointed at home would not have been at him for his fearless denunciation of the souring of a charitable religion, but at his mother, Gwen, who, in another life, had been such a girl.[45]

The summer itself, though full of the uncertainties of the war and Jim's future, passed at Pandy as previous summers. He went on long bike rides – to the Brecon Beacons to the west and around the Black Mountains – and, with his father, on six-hour walking hikes. The bees swarmed and were fetched. The garden was dug and tied to "look more like it used" and, to no avail, the student looked for a promised holiday job as a clerk for the railway. Harry took in the last of a "very satisfactory… honey crop" in a hot August. As occasional German planes dropped sticks of bombs, far enough away but "too near to be comfortable", he joined the Local Defence Volunteers and Jim accompanied him. There were more and more planes flying overhead at night. Potatoes were pulled up from the field and the plum picking finished for sale as fruit and as jam. Jim began another play for local performance – a "comedy" or "modern morality play" – which would be put on in the village hall over Christmas. At the end of September he visited Barnstaple again and from there went to Cambridge for term in early October.[46] It was already an even more emptied and changed place.

He was now living in 11 Malcolm Place, an address from which arts publications would emanate, and as the elected Secretary of the Cambridge Union he was at the heart of what remained of its open forum. Only, that term there were no debates, and after Christmas, with paper shortage everywhere, no paper to edit. Energy was instead directed into organising the Cambridge section of the People's Convention. This was the outcome of the Communist Party's drive to square the circle of the dilemma it faced since the Molotov-Ribbentrop non-aggression pact of 23 August 1939. How could opposition to the waging of war against Nazi Germany be reconciled with anti-fascism? For some, like the CPGB's

General Secretary, Harry Pollitt, it could not. After a furious inner-party debate he had resigned his post – though not the Party – and picked up his former trade as a boilermaker. In South Wales, the Communist leader of the miners, Arthur Horner, was secretly agreeing to assist resistance in case of invasion. Across the working-class cadres of the Party, in London and in Manchester, in Scotland and in Wales, there was profound disquiet that a decade of frontline opposition to European fascism had come to this pass. Party discipline held under the Jesuitical rationale of its most intellectual leading figure, the Cambridge-educated Rajani Palme Dutt. The paradox remained that throughout 1940 membership increased as the Party sought, not unsuccessfully, to rationalise support of the declared neutrality of the Soviet Union – not against any war, not for this particular one in this specific way, willing to lead a social revolution in the heart of the Imperial lair – with a steady stream of demands for a more democratic agenda and social gains. Some historians have speculated that if the Communist Party had taken the nearly identical line of Bevan and Cripps, and unequivocally supported the war against Nazi Germany whilst simultaneously denouncing the failure to widen the scope for change on the Home Front, then it would have been an attractive outlet for many. As indeed it turned out to be, with Pollitt restored, when Hitler finally turned on the Soviet Union on 22 June 1941, ensuring that the denounced Imperialist War could again be primarily an anti-fascist one.[47] A fortnight later, Raymond Williams received his call-up papers. From the autumn of 1940 to the summer of 1941 his life had been as topsy-turvy as the Party itself.

The "People's Vigilance Committees", established in the wake of the Party's appeal for a "People's Government" following the fall of France, had broadened by September 1940 into a "People's Convention" under the chairmanship of D.N. Pritt MP, who had been expelled by the Labour Party for defending the Soviet invasion of Finland. The Convention issued a Manifesto with six aims – defence of living standards, trade union and democratic rights, improved Air Raid Precautions, friendship with the Soviet Union, a "People's Government" and "a people's peace that gets rid of war". Over 250,000 copies went out and the trawl they brought back – actors, scientists, writers, politicians, and clergymen – was, on the surface, impressive. In Cambridge a student Convention was arranged to build support and to elect delegates for the major national Convention to be held in London in the New Year.

The Student Convention ran over the last weekend in November and opened with a rousing address from the Rev. Mervyn Stockwood, future Bishop of Southwark, then a charismatic Anglican vicar in a poor district of Bristol. The Convention consisted of five "commission" or discussion groups – on the Standard of Living, ARP, Education, Colonial Policy and Foreign Policy – with a plenary to bring them together. The Foreign Policy group was chaired by Cambridge's leading Communist don, the economist Maurice Dobb, and Raymond Williams was its Secretary, or rapporteur. On the Sunday, with a long list of educational demands for "equality of opportunity for all" and a maintenance system stripped of "local anomalies", he was elected as one of the three student delegates (the others were John Maynard Smith, CUSC President, and Martin Lytt, President of the Liberal Club). The editor of the much-reduced, and censored, *Cambridge University Journal* wrote his last defiant Editorial of the term in an exhortatory mood before the Christmas break:

> The only policy in wartime art is to have no policy. Emotions can be roused, purged, repeated; you can have tragedy, courage and hope. But never reason. Official wartime politics are the same.
>
> This is something that we at Cambridge cannot disregard. Students of science, of the arts, must all if they value their work consider the future. Our training is part of a policy. But if the other part is not there, the genuine desire not for a brave new world but for planned social change, our training now will never have full effect. In this war we are a privileged class. Not, we genuinely believe because we are at Cambridge or Oxford, but because the completion of our training can benefit the whole community. The Government does not seem to be thinking of the future. But if there is not

even an outline of a better future there can be no excuse for accepting the hateful present. Students are ready to serve the people. They will accept no other use of their privilege.[48]

A great deal of brave rhetoric mingled with the winds blowing over the Fens that Michaelmas term. In the cinema they were enjoying the "masterly" John Ford's *Grapes of Wrath* and noting "the importance of the individual in the face of large scale inhumanity", and on the stage Robert Ardrey's *Thunder Rock*, a "smash hit" American play transferring from the West End, with Alec Guinness and Bernard Miles following on Michael Redgrave's war-time success as the man who gives up his intellectual isolation to face the world with a typewriter and a gun. Raymond Williams saw it and wondered if it was not "a way out" rather than "a way in", presented as a solution in a play that did not, however, "provoke constructive thought". Not that a viable future was easy to locate in that frozen time of "the still peaceful atmosphere of Cambridge... Here the Latin grace is still read before meals; here proctors and bullers still watch for smoking or unacademic dress in the street and impose the fine of 6/8; here on Saturday the new Master of Trinity [the sixty-four-year-old historian G.M. Trevelyan whose *English Social History* (1944) would be a war-time best seller] will be installed with all the old, and to the layman, meaningless ceremony; here each Friday is published the 'Cambridge Review' resolutely turning its back on the future, hopefully looking forward to the past."[49]

Nor was the present any great comfort to a student population dwindling in numbers as men joined up or were called up, with no warning, in mid-term. Raymond discussed by letter with Joy who had taken on a management training course with Woolworths in Barnstaple, whether he would go or not if called up. Her two adult brothers, on Christian grounds, had decided that they were conscientious objectors and Joy offered him support if that was to be his decision. Inwardly, he was not clear that as 1940 came to an end he would fight in the forces when the time came.[50]

Meanwhile he drifted through academic work, not able or knowledgeable enough to develop his creative desire to make a "new" literature alongside his critical need to challenge the dessication of the entrenched modes of teaching and writing. Or so he felt later when he reviewed in his mind the limited texts of a sympathetic kind then available to him – Ralph Fox's *The Novel and the People* but not the pioneering Marxist critique of Christopher Caudwell or even the passionate life-enhancing views of literature being determined by F.R. Leavis, of whom the undergraduate remained unaware. Tillyard, published scholar on Shakespeare and Milton, was just fifty-one when he encountered and often derailed his young tutee. Like Trevelyan he would find war-time fame with his succinct *The Elizabethan World Picture* (1943) which dissected the mind-set and the mind-furniture used and available to the first Elizabethan Age. In the second Elizabethan Age Raymond Williams would effectively challenge the thinness of an approach that did not even nod to material explanation for thought. At the time, he considered in retrospect, he was rude to the point of brusqueness, covering by anger his inadequacy of response to questioning. Maybe so; but even then he posed the questions to himself and confronted the intellectual abyss which, in his own mind, he wanted to bridge, as one surviving undergraduate essay from November 1940 astonishingly reveals. Entitled "Experience and the creative process" it mounts a solid, if unremarkable, analysis of the poetry of Wordsworth as triumphant exemplar of the association of emotion and thought; yet this is a connection which, in the student's view, falls from grace as revolutionary hope is replaced by conservatism when Wordsworth relinquishes reason as the core of his work. It is the essay's wider opening, however, which remarkably heralds the later Williams. What Tillyard made of it, unfailingly courteous, personally and coldly distant from his student's aspirations, is not clear. It was the start of a never-ending bout with "Cambridge English":

> The history of the materialist criticism of literature, which seems to offer the best hope of a general literary under-standing, is so short and so small in range that many serious errors have been made.

Most leading critics of today do not accept the materialist standpoint. Their success rests on their personal sensibility of approach, and the result is that we have much criticism of individual poets and novelists, and even of special literary periods, but we have no solid heritage of explanation of the whole creative process. A new technique, or combination of techniques, is necessary for this: to ally the knowledge of the economist, the psychologist, the student of language, and the sociologist. There has been no planned approach to this, and certainly no one critic has combined more than two of the qualities. The new criticism, [he cites Edgell Rickword (1898-1982) who had edited *Calendar of Modern Letters*, the 1920s literary journal which was so much admired by Leavis as the precursor of his own *Scrutiny*, founded in 1932. Rickford, in typical 1930s fashion, moved leftward to edit the Communist Party's intellectual house journal *Left Review*], grounded on economics and sociology, has made enough mistakes to discredit entirely any movement with less intrinsic merit... But the main lesson to be drawn from such work... is that knowledge of biography is not enough; that the complex relation between experience and creation must be unravelled before we can get anywhere with literature; and that we must study the active mind alongside the active life. ... The poet or novelist must be considered as a man among other men in a real world of economic forces. That is our first principle, and the best understanding of economics will be the best understanding of the life and society of the poet, since economic factors are finally decisive. But we must not stop there: we must also consider why the writer is a writer; that is, consider the quality which makes him, if not distinct, at least different, from other men. We must provide an adequate explanation of the creative process that lies between experience and expression.[51]

If the pendulum there swung more ponderously to the first principles of economics than it would as his life and thought matured, still we can

116

detect, a trifle solipsistically perhaps, his counter-balance of the qualities, !undefined as yet, that makes a writer write in a particular way. For a nineteen-year-old it was a long-sighted overview. He remained frustrated that, up close, he could not marshall the necessary detail. Besides, preparation for the forthcoming People's Convention in January seemed more immediately vital than for essays, week by week, to be "properly prepared and referenced". In the long view, of course, the time seemed to be shortening rather abruptly. In early December the *Cambridge University Journal* signed off, for the duration of the war as it turned out, with a front page ditty entitled "Buy Us to Read in the Train":

> Christmas again; before we've time to stop
> And think, it's caught us on the hop;
> The old year is but folly, looking ahead
> Imagination sees the star turn red.
> So now – for on the primrose path we dwell –
> The Journal bids its readers "Fare you well."[52]

Christmas at home meant more speculative scribbling and constant thoughts of Joy Dalling. He planned his trip to London around seeing her, writing just before the New Year to tell her that after the "People's Convention on Sunday, January 12" he would "travel back that night to wherever you may be" and "stay until the Wednesday morning". Joy could read "I want you terribly" alongside the more teasing "I went to a party on Friday night and only just remembered myself, or rather yourself" and that "the plays are not going too badly". There had been some drunken revelry at home in Llwyn Derw, too; so Joy, it seems from a wistful remark in a letter from a suitably repentant Raymond, had won a bet. His cousin, Ray Fawkes, on embarkation leave from the Royal Marines, had turned up unexpectedly to visit his mother Lily, Gwen's sister, who had been bombed out of their Birmingham home and was staying in Pandy for several weeks. Then "my lorry-driver friend Herbert also turned up" and after a night in the Lancaster pub all three men repaired, drunk, to sleep "in our huge bed". Jim wrote to Joy to picture his cousin being sick through a window; his cousin recalls Jim shouting "Put that light out" between alternative bouts of vomiting and "Herbert chasing rabbits in the bottom of the bed". Gwen hid the remaining whisky.[53]

Just before Christmas he gave a lecture to a local Working Men's group on the function and limitations of the Press; limited because controlled and homogenised by financial and political interest. He ended a dense talk by revealing how, as editor for the past seven months of the "largest University newspaper in Great Britain", its proprietor *The News Chronicle* via the *Cambridge Daily News*, he had been hemmed in and had editorial wishes curtailed when he had sought to be critical of the press, and of the power of placed or withheld advertisement. As for "opinion in wartime", his attempt to run a three-column "Political Forum" was ended when only articles uncritical of the Government were allowed to appear "in blind support". To this audience of working men he proposed a functionary link out of their class and his:

> Some of us are inclined to shelve the problem of the world after the war; but enormous financial, social and material problems are picking up, and if we have no plan to meet them, the sacrifice of war will once more have been in vain. The government is doing something to meet the need. For instance I, in common with other students at the universities, am being allowed to postpone my service in the army until I have taken the examinations for my degree. This keeping the universities open means that there will be after the war a nucleus, unfortunately very small, of people who have the training to overcome these inevitable problems. But as a whole the government is not doing the job properly.[54]

If this was doing one part of the role that his worker-poet had requested, in vain, of intellectuals in the story "Red Earth", the other was telling stories in different ways. "Clear as Crystal" was a one-act play written for his own and known community. It is scattered with local reference to place or accent or event or custom designed to make that audience smile. And listen. The action was perfunctory – a widowed gentry lady plays at spiritualism and fortune telling, annoying and upsetting her sketchy and unruly wartime staff. Into this farce steps the Tramp, arrested by the Home Guard as a suspicious stranger but quickly established as a local Glamorgan-Monmouthshire man. He uncovers the deception of the crystal ball and, in turn, exposes the social trickery that allows some to be served and makes others into servants. Harry Williams was its only reviewer at its only performance: "Play's a great success and a full house."[55] The next day "Jim to London" for the People's Convention, having wisely excised the one lengthy speech in the play. But the Tramp's words were the most succinct statement of what the young playwright really thought and truly believed as he rushed to join the other two thousand to be gathered together in the Royal Hotel, Woburn Place.

Celia Fremlin, a reporter for the Mass Observation Project and herself a former Communist was there and wrote of how, some committed left-wingers aside, the majority were "of the rank and file", overwhelmingly female and aged twenty-five to thirty-five with a small number of "student and intellectual types". If they were, as Orwell sharply alleged at the time, foolishly duped or naively misguided by the Communist Party, it was, Fremlin considered, because of the "overwhelming feeling... of hope... that somehow a way would be found out of the present mess."[56] If the Tramp had spoken there, his soaring rhetoric would have received the applause which might have eluded it in more earthbound Pandy:

> There's some of us can plough meadows, and some of us can mend roads and build houses, and others can drive lorries and buses. And there's some of us can take the post round, and some the newspapers. And of course there's some who have to write the newspapers and a few others who have to learn a lot of things so that they can teach them back to the children... Of course there's lots of different jobs. There's those that raise the sweat on your brow and make your back ache and your feet tired – them's the heavy

jobs that is the real substance of life like. And there's writing jobs and counters and classrooms and all sorts... There's some as just make medicine... some that make engines to make work a bit easier, some as make guns to fire straighter and cars to run faster, some that make music and books and pictures for those that like 'em... There's some as spend all their time making the plans that others'll do something with. But you got to have the plans. The main thing is that them as does the work gets the fruits of their labours. Them as sweats and aches in the fields and the mines and the factories, them as fights when the time comes on the battlefields, they're the real people in the country and it's them as have got to be looked after. And if them as can write a lot, and know a lot, an' speak a lot, 'll only speak out for those people, if they'll only use their own kind of bent to make the working people happier, to make 'em stronger and healthier, and to give 'em pleasure when the day's work is over, then I say they're doing their duty, and they're being fair to the people who really matter... [57]

Joy would increasingly have agreed. Wartime work was proving a revelation to her. She moved to live in Birmingham with her friend Annette, and there found a job working in Personnel for Vickers Armstrong, dealing with the welfare of disabled women workers. She voluntarily spent time, to the management's surprise, working on the assembly line for aircraft. It was arduous and stressful work. Her eyes were opened to the skill and speed it entailed. She grew to admire these women she represented here and the others she met later in the war as she took various factory jobs around the British Isles.[58]

The contrast with the life she considered Raymond to be leading in the first half of 1941 could not have been starker. If her politics were still not as overt as his, she felt that her own instincts were moving towards the close identification with "working people" he was professing, even as his life, outwardly, was moving startlingly further from them. This was the first crisis of their proposed partnership and though he worked in Cambridge in January to bring out an edition of *The Daily Worker* after the Home Secretary, Labour's Herbert Morrison, had banned it, even those instinctually reactive politics were slipping away in a murk of isolation and ambiguity. Quite soon not having access to "ordinary news sources" became the same as not having anything new to impart. The whole sub-culture of CUSC which, appropriately enough perhaps, now moved to one of the extensive basements beneath Peas Hill that served as air raid shelters, was atrophying. Debates in the Union were, by order, strictly on non-political topics and though he still spoke and became Chairman of Debates, the wartime equivalent of President, in Easter 1941, it was now strictly oration to a diminished student world in which traditional complaints about food, the infamous Bitok rissole, were what made the news. Later he could not remember how or when he had ceased to be a Party member, only that he had, without consciously deciding to leave, "lapsed", and that he was no longer a member by the time he left in the summer of 1941. What had filled the vacuum was Culture with a capital "C", and one that pirouetted, always from the Left, around film and performance.

Film had been at the core of the Cambridge he liked from the very start. As early as 1936, in commercial terms the town could boast of ten cinemas showing the latest British offering and Hollywood releases.[59] They were all reviewed and discussed in a weekly full page in the *Cambridge University Journal*. What would have been new for him, apart from this feast of celluloid which was often tasted two or three times a day, was the chance to see European and especially Russian films. The chief attraction of CUSC, company and canteen and wall newspapers notwithstanding, lay in its screening of Vigo and Eisenstein and Pudovkin. He was reading Joyce now rather than Shaw or Wells and writing spoofy word games for fun.[60] But if there was a juvenile re-orientation, in formal terms, from realism to surrealism the underlying and lasting pull was that of expressionism, of cut and montage and image, on the screen. It was his most significant encounter with an art form whose modernism offered the chance of a popular audience and a challenging poetic essence. Or, at least, so he would think and work towards for a decade after the war ended.

At the heart of Cambridge film culture, and soon Raymond's closest adviser and ally in all this, was Michael Orrom (1920-1997).[61] He had arrived in Cambridge in 1938, from Bristol Grammar School and a well-to-do family, as an extremely bright scientist set to read Mathematics in Part I and Physics in Part II. He avoided a profound row with his barrister father by sticking to those subjects although his heart was not in that study. Since he was fifteen, when he had purchased a remaindered camera-projector for £3, he had been "making films", both home movies about family and dogs and "a story film" which had its climax, helped by a "lot of friends", in a pothole in Somerset. He had already saturated himself in whatever reading about film he could find and as a schoolboy in Bristol discovered or met, through screenings and lectures organised by Bristol University, the documentary makers John Grierson, Stuart Legg and Basil Wright. At Cambridge, however, amongst dozens of non-political associations, there was no semblance of a Film Society. He quickly found the loud, confident, public school-dominated Trinity dispiriting. He was directed to the rooms of the editor of *Granta*, a man known to be an enthusiastic "cineaste". But Eric Hobsbawm was unable to think of anyone "making films" in Cambridge so Orrom concluded he was on his own, at least so far as his aesthetic passion was concerned.

But then there was the comradeship of left-wing Cambridge. Clement Attlee, the Labour Party leader with a battalion in the International Brigade in Spain named after him, spoke in the Corn Market on the dangers confronting the world from fascism. Orrom signed a petition that was circulating. After that he was asked to attend "a meeting for a selected audience". The Chair was John Maynard Smith, former Etonian and current Party recruiter; Orrom was soon in the Socialist Club and then the Communist Party itself. He had found a use for his camera, and for his study of Pudovkin's "Film Technique", after all: it would be to record the great 1939 May Day demonstration in London, and particularly, the Cambridge section of it. He was swept along on a wave of "incurable" optimism and across to Paris for the huge 14 July rally of the French Left, and all on funds supplied by his *Daily Telegraph*-reading and very conservative father, who was persuaded it was a "cultural trip". In a sense it was because, for Orrom, left-wing politics and the avant-garde in film were inseparable. Together with Patricia Elliott, a *Granta* film critic, he began to set up a Cambridge University Film Society. They overcame logistical problems, caused by none of the big cinema chains allowing any outside organisation to show films, and by the law forbidding Sunday openings, by discovering a loophole which allowed a "cinema" to have a limited Sunday opening if no money was taken. However, their proposed society was initially a victim of the declaration of war.

Michael Orrom now made his crucial intervention. He persuaded some "better-off CUSC members" to contribute to a fund to raise £30 for a 16mm sound projector which he had seen advertised. The bait was that a CUSC Film Group – to go with the Writers' Group and other grandly titled sub-sections – would be able to show Soviet classics in the clubroom. So *Potemkin*, *Storm over Asia* and *October* and the German expressionist masterpieces *Caligari*, *The Last Laugh*, *Waxworks* and Pabst's *Kameradschaft* flickered onto the minds of a Cambridge intelligentsia more familiar, like everyone else to that point, with Cagney and Capra and Busby Berkeley. It did more than help pass a damp East Anglian Sunday; it seemed to offer a glimpse of a different artistic future.

At the end of 1940 Raymond Williams was sure that this new era would not come yet, not in this war where contemporary invocation of the vigorous language of confident Elizabethan England against Philip II's effete Spain was not convincing enough. Still, he felt that "the cinema will undoubtedly have a great future... because with the cinema freed from its present restrictions, all the scientific force and frustrated art of this century will be turned to the making of real films for the people". [62]

Raymond Williams had met Michael Orrom in the course of his first year and they grew closer over 1940/41 when Orrom, then in his final year, lived in an envied room in the Turret of Trinity's Great Court. Through this year, working on film and politics projects, they began to complement distinctive thought and personalities. Orrom was not one for public speaking, Williams was; Williams was self-contained with an evidently strong sense of himself that attracted others to him, while Orrom sought out company and found solace in the reverberation of others; Orrom assisted Williams in editing and writing the much reduced *Cambridge University Journal*, Williams backed Orrom as he helped found a Cambridge University Film Society in November 1940. Raymond was then still toeing a Party line but Michael was drifting away in front of him:

> For many of us attitudes [after summer 1940] were difficult and political conviction harder to maintain. Instead poetry and art, allied to the People's cause, became the growing enthusiasm.[63]

The new party, almost a continuous one it seems, was mostly held in the rooms of Nicholas Moore, poet and son of the philosopher G.E. Moore. The music was jazz and the voice of Billie Holliday. The drinks were gin and cider mixed in frosted glasses, and wine. The younger Moore's heroes were Henry Miller and Dylan Thomas; he published them, along with Anaïs Nin and Lawrence Durrell in *Seven*, the magazine he produced. It had a starry cast list. George Scurfield plunged all his legacy into the literary collection, *Cambridge Front*. Mark Holloway sent in poems. Scurfield and Williams submitted stories. Conversation was quietly insistent, a murmur of conviction and a milieu that resembled pre-war Bloomsbury more than wartime in the provinces. John Lehmann, then in his early thirties, who had been at Trinity in the 1920s, returned to meet and recruit young writers. He had been, since 1938, a partner in the Woolfs' Hogarth Press and editor of *New Writing* (1936-40), an influential bi-annual book/periodical which he re-launched as *Penguin New Writing* for the rest of the war.[64] Lehmann had a room in the Arts Passage where acolytes and wannabes could gather round him. A divergence was occurring, and not just the increasingly acrimomious one between the

Socialist Club and the Labour Club in which all pre-war political unity had split apart: "We consumed a lot of wine," recorded Michael Orrom "and were accused of having 'bourgeois parties'. We were dubbed the 'Culture Group' – and got looked on with great suspicion by the Communist establishment." George Scurfield added: "We were supposed to be running away from reality, escaping from our responsibilities by plunging into poetry, films, jazz, wine. More likely we were escaping from some of the political half-truths which surrounded us, and from our comrades' somewhat dessicated and humourless approach to the arts. And escaping too from all our futures."

By the winter of 1940 they had all seen friends move off and into that uncertain future. Those who returned to Cambridge felt themselves to be in "another world: time suddenly seemed very short, and could only be measured in months. In face of the all-embracing cataclysm which had now started, we felt more than ever the need to assert our identity." And if that meant writing and performing, it also meant consumption and enjoyment. London theatrical life de-camped to Cambridge. Plays were full. So was the Arts Theatre when ballet companies arrived. They welcomed, more than any other, the Ballet Rambert whose dance "reflected somehow the whirl into which our lives had developed, and at the same time gave it a reassuring formality".[65] Not to mention the "fleeting contact with living art and desirable girls" – both commodities still in short supply beside the Cam. Parties for the dancers were welcome diversions and some undergraduates made the journey the other way to mingle with the enchanting Peggy van Praagh and the enticing Sally Gilmour in their London dressing rooms. Raymond Williams was easily and quickly converted to being a balletomane but still enough of a Cromwell amongst these cavaliers to chide his fellow students over their less than "conscientious" treatment of the ordinary Londoners evacuated to Cambridge:

Undergraduates who are only too keen to meet the delightful Ballet Rambert company must remember that many hundreds of other London people have sought refuge in Cambridge. The hospitality we offer to culture must be extended to those people who by their work on the essentials of life alone make everything else possible.[66]

* * * * * *

Michael Orrom pieced together the film he took over his time at Cambridge between 1938 and 1941, and made it into a haunting, often poignant, documentary for television that was broadcast in 1984.[67] Raymond Williams had been pulled, almost decisively, into the world Orrom relinquished so reluctantly in the summer of 1941 and never forgot to mourn. The film recounts the little magazines they brought out through the first half of 1941 as if nothing was more important to them than their, perhaps final, signature. The journal *Cambridge Front* No. 2 appeared after interminable delays in the spring.[68] Its fourteen stapled pages edited by Michael Orrom and Lionel Cole cost sixpence and it promoted itself as the successor to George Scurfield's similarly titled but purely literary magazine of the previous summer: "We appear at a time when all other undergraduate publications in Cambridge have ended... to fill the gap existing in Cambridge journalism by coming out every fortnight during term." But there were no further numbers. Raymond Williams, from whose address the paper emanated, was one of a four-man Editorial Board and he contributed a two page story, *"Frontier"*, in which "Jim" and an older man on Home Guard patrol on the Welsh border stumble across and rescue a German survivor of a plane crash. Jim and the Nazi officer, a former student of English, fleetingly exchange sympathies over the irony of their encounter: "A hero in my own country. You should see me when I'm on leave, the time they give me. But, over here, the symbol of everything to be hated... Because I cross a frontier... I change from a hero to a devil. And the strangest part is that in the air you never know where the frontiers are."

Cambridge Front printed notes on its list of contributors – Alex Comfort, poet and "Christian Pacifist, reads medicine"; Maurice James Craig, "Irish poet and critic. At Magdalene; reads English"; Mark

Holloway, "was in Navy after getting degree in English; now working on the land"; Nicholas Moore, "Contributor to nearly every literary magazine in the country. Has worked on a land drainage scheme since getting his degree last summer"; and "Raymond Williams: Editor for last two terms of University Journal. Has written several plays which have been acted in South Wales. Now Secretary of the Union. Goes into the Army in June." Variously waiting and choosing then. Exaggerating, understandably, and hoping there were threads of connection to be held in lives coming apart.

Cambridge Front advertised its next and never-to-appear number as having articles by Bernard Miles, their favoured thespian, and Raymond Williams' review of the Workers' Library edition of Lewis Jones' 1939 Welsh industrial epic, *We Live*, the relished antidote to Richard Llewellyn's *How Green Was My Valley*, which John Ford was about to turn into an Oscar-gathering movie, a clichéd imprint of Welsh history for generations to come. The review would have been worth having. Though it would be the 1970s before he would turn explicitly to write about Welsh fiction and his own place within it, there is no doubt of his early awareness. His commentary on "Modern Writing" in this second and last issue of the magazine reflected on how "progressive politics of the giddy popular thirties are a different matter from progressive politics in the present advanced social crisis", of which the war was only the most destructive symbol. However, towards the end of the thirties there was "something more in the progressive political movements than specific political issues... a general popular emotion, a vague dynamic urge forward, an association with physical power. In the present situation only the specific issues are left; many of the previous associations have gone over to the other side in politics, the others have disappeared." He lamented the way the gap was filled, for public literary expectation, by "the poetry of older generations" whilst "the majority of the population: the writers and the reading public" were left dissatisfied and yearning.

At Cambridge the evanescent literary coterie sighed and struggled on. Raymond, as always, found his own specificities through imagining life on the border. Sometime over that summer he finished the story

"Sack Labourer", a vignette told in the first person by a man whose labour over fourteen years of loading sacks and bundles onto lorries is hesitatingly questioned by him as wartime and new mates bring perspectives that irritate and intrigue him. The question would fester and, perhaps, germinate new action. Woodrow Wyatt took it for *English Story* later in the year. He was, in and out of Cambridge, a published writer and one convinced of his path.

In the summer of 1941 *Outlook* came out, edited by Williams, Orrom and Maurice Craig. Raymond's story "Sugar" was included in a rich array of offerings, a "selection of stories, verse and articles by past and present members of Cambridge University... issued... at a time when university education, as we know it, seems likely to be closing down indefinitely". The elegiac tone melded into one last lingering summer on the river and at play, with a passing glance at the work for exams. Michael Orrom remembers his friend as distracted, often moodily silent and, despite his unsevered attachment to Joy, "footloose". She did more than sense this – she was convinced, and remained so, that the distancing was more problematic in being more rounded and social than fleeting and personal. For her the talk of ballet and the implicit emphasis on superior taste, somehow innately possessed and which he appeared to share and endorse, was close to insufferable. She felt that she did not like him, at this time, at all. Others did and she would have felt even more removed from him if she had been in closer contact. Some of the tensions, notably in the work-relationship he clung to with Orrom, would linger and deepen in the post-war years when he did not readily relinquish one sense of Cambridge life which Joy hardly experienced at all. A sympathetic but puzzled observer of the enigma was Anne Richmond, then a second year English student at Newnham and a film critic for the *Cambridge Review*.

Anne Richmond, already acquainted with Orrom, became a close friend of Raymond Williams over the weeks from April to June 1941. They had been introduced in March by Mark Holloway who had read a poem she had published in *Cambridge Front*. He was, she remembered, "at the top of the Cambridge hierarchy" in the term she knew him and she was "flattered that he wanted to spend any time with me and take me to the pictures and to the Marxist English Group. He never mentioned his background – no one did, we all lived in the here and now at that bad time of the war. All I really knew about his past was that he was promised to Joy from the LSE, who indeed arrived to claim him at the end of term as I was promised to David Piper whom I was to marry in 1945".[69] There was no deceit on either side and, as both Anne and Joy separately made plain later, neither of them had contemplated sleeping with anyone before marriage. Even, it seems, in that bad time.

Anne's friendship with Raymond is traced in a daily diary she kept.[70] It covers a host of friends, retails parties, meals and gossip, and notes her work habits. And, for this time, all connected to the man she knew was "Welsh from his name" but who never talked of home.

> *April*: Friday 25. 3 hr essay on Nature. Did lots of work. Called on Peter Price [Editor of *Cambridge Review*] at 7pm. Gave me neat whiskey for my cold. Supper at [Blue] Barn with Raymond and evening in his room. Showed him poems... I want to send some to "Poetry". He seems to have decided to see more of me. I like it because he is getting married in Summer and... is unlikely to fall in love and become a responsibility – in the meantime he is a good companion, pleasant and intelligent – so this should be a much better term than I imagined it would be.

Then, through May, after daily work sessions, she spent most of her leisure time with him. They go out to the Unity Theatre's political pantomime "Jack and the Giant Killer" or hear Bernard Miles speak in Trinity or rub shoulders with Robert Helpmann and Frederick Ashton at yet another ballet party. The strain of the coming exams and the troublesome love affairs of others come and go amidst coffee and cider and gin and "the eternal wind up gramophone". Then

> *May*: Thursday 29.... Beastly day. R. had telegram from Joy saying she mightn't come on Sunday, was v.

disappointed... realised he is still in love with her. Round to Michael and gloom all the morning. Systematic banishment of gloom at lunch. R. and I out to Venetian + Anthony [Huxley].

There was no doubt now why for some days "R" is "furious", the cause of "irritation", drinking and "in filthy temper". On Sunday, 1 June, Joy did, after all, arrive. By Tuesday Anne was clear:

June: Tues 3. Still cold and grey... To No 11 by 6pm. To Ballet Rambert with Raymond, Joy and Michael. I like Joy and think she and R. obviously fit which is somehow rather depressing at the moment.

Weds. 4. Hot day. In room all a.m. Raymond turned up at 1pm to ask me to go on river with them. He is definitely in love with Joy.

At the end of the week, Saturday 7 June, they all began to say their goodbyes at yet one more party. Joy was to leave Cambridge in the morning and Anne reflected: "No longer sad about R. That was all last week. Now I've seen Joy I'm sure it's OK his marrying her."

A week later Anne Richmond left Cambridge for London, and Michael Orrom, ending his academic time at Cambridge with a Third, lingered in limbo: "One by one my friends went down, but I could not bear to leave. I stayed on and on in my rooms until the end of June. On the 21st Hitler attacked Russia. Overnight Britain and the Soviet Union became allies – at last. The left became respectable again."[71]

For Raymond Williams, home in Pandy on 14 June, the general disarray of the life of this "impossible young man" as he later labelled himself was over. Never again would he feel quite so imbalanced or his personality quite so divided. For the short term, though, things were not as settled as he might have wished. He, too, had plummeted in his exams, taking a II.II in the First Part of the Tripos. Harry wrote both of their concern for him and their disappointment at the exam result.

The worry was deeper than academic. Joy had arrived for a brief visit the day after Raymond but whatever plans the couple may have made were to be put on hold as both his future wife and his mother, for very different reasons, stalled. Joy wanted to be sure of him again and to see him away from what she never ceased to think was the corrupting influence of Cambridge and the set he had chosen most, and freely, as his friends. Gwen still wished Margaret Fallas had been Raymond's choice and always did, making this unpleasantly plain to Joy throughout her life. Now, stubbornly, she would object to any marriage since Raymond, at twenty, was still a minor in need of parental permission. Then, on 5 July 1941, Jim "gets his call up" and the worry wormed even deeper into Harry Williams.[72]

* * * * * *

Three days later Raymond Williams joined the Army at Prestatyn in North Wales. Number 2373418 was enlisted, in common with most undergraduates, as a Signalman into the Royal Signals, No. 2 Battalion. It was intended to be a quick training in a skilled section of the Army and appropriate enough perhaps for the son of a railway signalman. Half his fellow trainees were former students, for whom the summer passed drilling on the seafront, idling on the golf links and absorbing signal codes in wooden huts. Harry and Gwen took a September holiday in Rhyl and went to nearby Prestatyn whenever Jim could "get out". Joy made the longer journey from Devon and accompanied him on his brief leave to Pandy in October. By mid-November he was a Lance Corporal but the Army had other ideas for his future service.[73]

For Raymond, these months of basic induction seem to have passed in a mind-numbing blur which, happily perhaps, left the hot-house discomfort of Cambridge days far behind. As the year turned and the British Army reassessed its future fighting requirements he was transferred to an anti-tank Regiment, No. 50, within the Royal Artillery and stationed at Church Stretton, scarcely an hour's journey north of Pandy. Within the month, however, he had been posted to No.

122 Officer Cadet Training Unit at Larkhill, near Salisbury, and five months of intense preparation followed as the Army turned its civilian intake into war-time regulars able to lead men in battle. In early 1942, the imminent threat of invasion had passed but it was clear that the world conflict, with the United States now also at war with both Japan and Germany, would need to be fought on many fronts, not all of them locational, and in new ways (so far as armour and personnel were concerned) if a People's War was to deliver a People's Victory.

After the defeats of 1940, military thinking was clear about the next development in tank warfare: the need in the Artillery for anti-tank guns that were self-propelled. Tanks, in fact, by another name but tanks specifically for destruction of enemy armour. As Major General Sir Campbell Clarke put it in 1950: "The anti-tank gun was the only new type of artillery in the field army throughout the war." In turn the no longer static Artillery officer had to be as mobile in his thinking: "the whole outlook of training changed in an anti-tank regiment; instead of the steadily increasing demand for centralised control that was taking place in the field artillery, the exact opposite had to be instilled into all ranks down to the most junior NCOs... All ranks had to know a great deal more about the activities of the 'other arms'."[74]

In Pandy, Harry Williams' ritual of pig slaughtering and beehive-making in the time away from his signal box and Home Guard duty continued through the bitter winds and heavy snows of January and February 1942, but his diary's list of essentials to be stored away moved beyond seeds and potatoes now to note "830 rounds Ammunition. 1 Lewis Gun. 2 Magazines. 7 Rifles. 3 Grenades." And in March "Plane crash on Skirrid. A Ghastly sight."[75] It was by such an incursion of the twentieth century, albeit in this form of modern savagery, that his son intended to unite immemorial rooted landscape and emigrant history in the concluding volume of *People of the Black Mountains*, his last posthumously published fiction: an American airman, connected by family to that ancestral place, crashes his plane into the hills. Even as he was being shaped to be fit for military purpose, a tale with this detail was being lodged in Raymond's mind, with always the forceful need to make a meaningful connection. It would take forty years to surface in that way in his imagination. Yet nothing else from these "missing" war years of training and waiting engaged his imagination again. It was a time, after all, just to get through. At least for individuals. In every other sense time was short.

At Larkhill instructors took five months to take officer cadets through two years of peacetime training. Now corners were cut at will as D.H. Macindoe, M.C., recalled with some pride:

> 122 OCTU was formed at Larkhill by a handful of officers with the minimum of material. A CO without a uniform, an adjutant without a staff and a quartermaster with no stores... accomplished miracles. Blackboards, paper, books, transport (mostly civilian) were collected somehow; dilapidated huts were made into miniature ranges, sleeping quarters and dining rooms; new huts and a gymnasium sprang up on the slopes above Hamilton Battery. Almost at once the first two courses arrived, both consisting of cadets from the Royal Military Academy, soon to be followed by the first of the civilian intake.[76]

And here the cadets tramped on duckboards above mud between their huts and their classrooms, learning tangents and cosines, moving between playing-fields for rugby to fields where they simulated battles to come. Cadet Williams was, throughout his life, not gifted with any great technical competence but he was capable of rote learning and imitative mechanics. Nor was he overwhelmed, in this novel anti-tank section, by the stultification of hidebound army traditions. On the contrary there was an insistence that these officers should not only be taught "to fight efficiently" but also to know "for what" and "against what" they were fighting, whilst "elements of a civilised life" were not to be forgotten even in wartime. Sadlers Wells Opera Company, their full company and theatre closed down by the Blitz, re-grouped in the minor key: with a reduced cast and an orchestra of four they performed *The Barber of Seville* for fifty-three troops at the Larkhill Garrison

Theatre. The units with which he was fortuitously caught up could not have been more open to the spirit of a citizen army even if the full substance did not always match the democratic wish. The watchwords drilled into these young officers were "Thought, progress, initiative and vitality", and their most hateful traits were underlined as "Lethargy, mediocrity and obscurantism".[77]

He can have had no argument with any of that. On 19 June he was discharged to a Commission and on 20 June appointed to an Emergency Commission as a Second Lieutenant with the Royal Artillery Regular Army, posted to No. 21 Anti-Tank Regiment. He joined his Regiment at Okehampton in Devon on 28 June. There had just been enough time for a honeymoon. His father had recorded, calmly and simply, on the day of his son's discharge as an officer, Friday 19 June: "Jim's Wedding day", though there had been nothing calm about it in Harry's household, where Gwen had long refused to countenance the marriage until, in the end, her husband brought her to a reluctant acceptance of the inevitable. The marriage had taken place in a Registry Office in Salisbury, witnessed by an army friend and the taxi driver who took them to a hotel near the railway station. On 23 June they went to Pandy as husband and wife and then it was back to the Army.

During the two years he served before the allied invasion of Europe finally began, Joy followed him, whenever possible, as the Regiment's duties and manoeuvres pulled it to the west and north and south of England, and back again. Working on factory floors and assembly lines to learn her business as a personnel officer deepened her political convictions profoundly. She went home to Barnstaple to live in her mother's house in the spring of 1944. Their daughter Merryn was born on 9 July, just over a fortnight after her young husband had landed in Normandy.[78]

What remained of 1942 was taken up with military exercises, in preparation for Normandy, and snatched periods of leave. The 21st Anti-Tank Regiment remained at the Royal Artillery Practice Camp at Okehampton where they could train with tank guns but deployed widely, sometimes in concert with the 5th Coldstream Guards, across the south

134

west of England in exercises gently named "Lilo" (at Weymouth) or "Cheddar" (at Weston Super Mare) but rising to "Pegasus" and "Normandy" itself, with clearly no aim to disguise possible future strategic intentions on the Salisbury Plain in October 1942. They dug gun pits, fired their guns and maintained their somewhat obsolete vehicles. They also listened to lectures on International Affairs, on Poland, and, with tank veterans returning from North Africa, on anti-tank tactics in Libya. There was still talk of a German invasion or raids into Dorset – at least to the point of drawing up plans to combat them – in which the 21st would have supported counter-attacks by Guards Armoured Division from Black Down Hills, to the west of Dorchester. Raymond Williams, like all officers on three hours' notice to move at all times and attached to a telephone number if they left their billets on leave of absence, had been absorbed by the Army. On 20 December 1942 he was promoted to War Substantive Lieutenant.[79]

Or almost absorbed. If his short story "This Time" indicates something of his state of mind, it was one of confusion allayed by grim acceptance. The story was a definite advance on his previous writing; it is sparse and poised, not quite willing to settle for any assurance, of any kind, in "this time". It was published in Lehmann's *New Writing and Daylight* for 1942-3 with a bare, and slightly erroneous, biographical three liner: "Raymond Williams was born at the end of the last war in South Wales. He has written four plays which were produced there, and in Cambridge helped to edit two magazines. He is now in the R.A."[80] So, too, is Thomas, his officer trainee in the story, who has sneaked back into his barrack room billet after a night of gin and rough cider ("his favourite drink") and music ("Mood Indigo" and "swing music too, 'the songs of a people' ") with Anna. For everything that might unfold, these two have a "definite attitude" for they had seen through the illusions: if the war came they would understand it perfectly, as they understood themselves and the political struggle and the god fallacy. Munich, Danzig, Warsaw, Paris: "This time we understand."

The rest of the story, in Thomas' dreams and in his recollections, questions that assumed understanding – how American "negro soldiers" are turned away from the bar of the "Dolphin... a good hotel", how dancing drunkenly to the insistent rhythms of the "Okey Pokey", in line with others and their girls, sounds a discord to the memory of the "Unity record" he and Anna had played "incessantly":

> Once before
> We were unaware the chance we were waiting
> Was close at hand
> This time we understand:

We were right, said the dreamer. It happened as we said. Now we shall see history work itself out to the end we wait for and welcome.

The chance we were waiting is close at hand.

A sudden discord blurred the rest of the song. It was a little frightening, the break of the rhythm. Remember how we laughed at anarchy and feared it. We are in it now... War is tearing out our vitals. Bombs are splintering our reason. We are improvising, madly. Learning how to cook in fields, and make sanitary ditches. Starting from nothing, moving on to nothing again. Here is this field, make it your home for tonight. Now it is morning, move on to that one. And get your guard posted. It is anarchy, it is anarchy, anarchy.

If so it is also a well-directed anarchy. Thomas awakes to the diurnal duties of the Army – spit and polish, shaved the night before, quick march to breakfast and attention on parade. He decides, in a world lost to ideals of beauty and reason, that only "Speed and power" in an embrace of action to "lose our standards to win them more completely" can now suffice. Somehow, that too has a hollow echo as he envisages the roar of actual battle and the flash of guns:

> From the red glare his eyes fell back suddenly to normal focus. He looked around. He was alone on the ashpath, and the colour was spreading in the sky and over the sea. He suddenly became more aware of that momentary quiet which

precedes a day's work in the army. He realised he would be late. He broke into a run and as he rounded the buildings saw them forming up on the square. He increased his speed and slipped into the blank file of his squad. Almost immediately they came to attention and they were moving. The rhythm began again. His mind went blank. Suddenly he realised that they were marching. His body moved now with deadly precision, turning about with high steps and about again so he was marching the same way as at first. His boots trod firmly into the ashes. Dust covered the shine.

I don't suppose it can last long.

The firing of the guns intensified for Lt. Williams in January and February 1943 as the Regiment, now in Dorset, practised small-arms firing, bren-gun firing attached to tanks, firing six-pounder guns, exercising on "Spartan" with 5 Guards Armoured Brigade and attending tank recognition lectures. In March the Regiment had moved to Kimberley Park, Norfolk, still in association with the Guards with whom they put on a "Demonstration for their Majesties" in April. Raymond was now established as C Troop Commander within Q Battery, itself a renowned part of his Regiment under its nickname of "Sanna's Post", so called from a Boer War action fought at Sanna's Post in March 1900 when four Victoria Crosses were won. Its history was a long one – raised at Poona in 1824, active in the Afghan and Persian campaigns of the 1850s and 1860s and from South African glory to First World War entrenchment, with recent service in France from 1939 to 1940 and attachment to Guards Armoured Division from October 1941. The manoeuvres with which they were now engaged – "Border" under Northern Command in May and June – were, however, about changing entirely the fighting capacities of the anti-tank regiments. The key to that change was, as ever, armour and personnel: "The M10s (destined to make history in Normandy) came to us at Birdsall in July 43. So did Lt. Col. (then Major) R.I.G. Taylor DSO, MC."[81]

British tanks, the fast Cromwells and more heavily armoured Churchills, were designed either to exploit breakthroughs or support infantry units. What became clear was that towing guns into position to bombard large enemy tank forces was cumbersome and, if static, invited counter-fire. The concept of an anti-tank gun that was self-propelled now came into its own. Opponents of this idea alleged – accurately enough – that it was just a tank by another name, but the American Army in its creation of Tank Destroyer Units to become "tank killers", or destroyers of enemy armour, made the design fit the intention as their Field Manual of 1942 explained:

> For individual tank destroyers, offensive action consists of vigorous reconnaissance to locate hostile tanks and movement to advantageous positions from which to attack the enemy by fire. Tank destroyers avoid "slugging matches" with tanks, but compensate for their light armour and difficulty of concealment by exploiting their mobility and superior observation... The characteristics of tank destroyer units are mobility and a high degree of armour-piercing firepower, combined with light armour protection; strong defensive capacity against attacks of combat aviation; and flexibility of action permitted by generous endowment of means of communication.[82]

The relative lightness of armour plating allowed for speed in manoeuvre, and the heftier the gun the more likely a hit would be effective. In fact in the Normandy countryside where hedgerows made open tank warfare impossible most hits would be made at 500 yards and even then the Allied forces would be underpowered in comparison with the Tigers and Panthers of the Wehrmacht. The British compensated to an extent by mounting 17-pounder British guns onto the Sherman M4 tanks and its variants that were shipped over in ever-increasing numbers after 1943 – these were christened "Fireflies" – and also onto the first M10s to arrive, whose motor-gun carriage had been constructed on the lines of the Sherman chassis. Twin diesel engines powered them and a crew of five manned them. The British model would prove a more effective tank destroyer than the American original.[83] In Normandy, reliability, mobility, efficiency, manoeuvrability, general firepower capacity and, above all, numerical superiority was what would overwhelm the German opposition, not one-to-one killing capacity.[84] For the crews themselves team-work was essential, their true life saver.

As the M10s arrived in July 1943, so the 21st Anti Tank Regiment was moved to Scarborough in north Yorkshire for the last bout of their intensive training. "Q" Battery was stationed at Birdsall near Malton but Lt. Williams was immediately dispatched to the Royal Artillery Military Training School in Rhyl to attend a special Self-Propelled Anti-Tank course. The armoured vehicle now became another essential body part – to respect and maintain. Amongst the papers he kept – indiscriminately and haphazardly but, importantly, of fiction and ideas and agendas for work – is also a single scrappy notepad sheet with a pencilled-in rota:

M10 Troop class: *1 week*

Monday:	am	Crew Maintenance
		(demonstration and practical)
	pm	Gun and Bren attachment
		1 hour Gas (after tea)
Tuesday:	am	Driving
	pm	Weekly Task 1
		Last Parade (after tea)
Wednesday:	am	Breech (2 hours)
		Weekly Task 2
	pm	Minelaying
		P.T.
Thursday:	am	Bren attachment
		Weekly Task 3
	pm	Driving
		Last Parade (after tea)
Friday:	am	Driving
	pm	Gun
		Weekly Task 4
		Last Parade (after tea)

Saturday: am   Driving

                 pm   Weekly Task 5

                            Last Parade

                            Inspection

Realisation of what they were doing all this for and with what possible personal consequences lived with them all the time. Only it was not yet happening, perhaps not ever, for them. Raymond Williams penned, literally so, in a school exercise book a story that both imagined a destructive death and displaced it by exposing the unimaginative, callow response of a civilian. "Isn't it a scream" is set in Italy, which the Allies had just invaded, through Sicily in July 1943, and where an advance troop of self-propelled guns is seen fanning through a town above the coast.[85] He dated the story, precisely, as "25.7.43", and there appears to be a distinct spin-off from an actual news item, which may explain why the story's instant contemporary feel in turn seems, in our own contemporary context, an uneasy curiosity from its opening sentences:

> The official photographer was a dark little Jew who perspired from his upper lip under provocation. He wore a blue beret and smoked incessantly.

The photographer is after an action shot. Accompanying the infantry troops in their carriers, he finds three dead Italians beneath a fountain bedecked by three naked cupids. He takes his picture with a driver, from Merthyr, self-consciously posed in the frame. It is this picture which will appear in a newspaper, but the driver dies immediately after it has been taken when he takes a booby-trapped helmet as a souvenir. In England a woman picks up the paper in a hot and crowded railway carriage:

> She opened it and read the headlines. "Our advance continues. More coastal towns taken." Underneath was a picture. One of our soldiers standing in front of a fountain

in a white walled square. Around him lay the bodies of three Italian soldiers. She seemed pleased. She smiled. She looked at it again and then passed it over to the soldier opposite. "Look at this" she said. "Isn't it a scream."
The soldier grinned faintly, and looked out of the window.
She settled back into her seat again.

In September, they began to put the mechanics of all they had been learning into motion, conscious of the test that would come overseas, as they took to battle formation tactics on the Yorkshire wolds. It was a winter of Exercises – notably "Rhine" with the 5 Guards Armoured in snowy February 1944 – and of Lectures, Training Films and Firing ranges, trips to town to see Betty Grable films, and as much time with Joy as he could manage and a few snatched days in Pandy before Christmas. They remained in Scarborough through the winter and early spring, Joy in lodgings in the town until, on 1 May, the Regiment packed up again, clutched their "Top Secret" orders and in long columns took to the road. They slept under the stars and ended up at Vine Hall, Mountfield in East Sussex, where they waterproofed and modified their vehicles and steadied for the complete mobilisation that was coming. Under the valued leadership of Dick Taylor they had, they all felt, come together at the last of this pre-battle period.

On paper Q Battery now sounded to be a formidable force. It consisted of eleven officers and 169 other ranks. Major Taylor was Battery Commander, with Captains Beaty and Smith beneath him; and under them there came a Liaison Officer – Lt. Hardy – and the three Troops (A, B, C) led by their Troop Commanders, Lieutenants Porter, Handford and Williams. Battery strength, as at 1 May 1944, included eleven Self-Propelled M10s, five other armoured vehicles, motor cycles and jeeps and the back-up of lorries and trucks for Signals, General Stores and Water.[86] They were, along with Y, Z and 2nd Batteries, self-contained and self-sustaining. Now they waited.

The opening chapter of a post-war novel that Williams did not complete placed his bored fellow officers on the requisitioned lawns of

Vinehall. We can take the unforced incongruity of these descriptive passages as witness to their documentary accuracy:

> Martin Squire, frowning, walked back along the path through the trees to the brisk edge of the lawn... Before him, around the low west wing of the house, the lawn stretched away towards the high rhododendrons. The grass was level, but not recently cut, patches of daisies and of white clover lay over it in many places, in a spreading pattern.
> The lawn was normally reserved for officers; the mess occupied the two large rooms which opened on to the terrace. Squire wondered now if he could risk going into the anteroom for a quarter of an hour, to rest and read. He was bored with the clatter of the tank park, and would have welcomed any alternative activity. But the anteroom at nine thirty five was too great a risk...
> Squire looked back through the trees at the tank park. The M10s, self-propelled seventeen pounder anti-tank guns, mounted on Sherman tank chassis, lay scattered over what had been a paddock, in various stages of dismantling. Three general operations were being carried out on them: the old rubber tracks were being wound off, and new steel tracks being laid; the Browning machine-guns which had been mounted in the rear of the turret were being transferred to a new mounting... above the main gun; and the two diesel engines in the rear of each tank, and their wide exhausts, were being waterproofed. Men swarmed everywhere over the blue-gray hulls, working bare-headed in loose denim overalls...
> Squire... walked on into the stable yard. Here, on the uneven cobbles, was the wheeled transport of the battery: eight three ton lorries, eleven fifteen hundred weight trucks, a water truck, half a dozen jeeps. These, also, were being waterproofed. Men bent inside the open bonnets, their hands working red plasticine over distributors and leads.[87]

The inner workings were what would take them through the surf of the Normandy beaches, and off them, rather more than any outward show of paint and polish. Yet there was, too, the need, and the excuse, for showier emblems like regimental pennants. Lt. Williams was sent to London to procure them. He took the opportunity to re-acquaint himself with the memories of a Cambridge now transplanted to actual Bloomsbury, and to say a silent goodbye to it. He met Anne Richmond there, on D Day 6 June, and Michael Orrom came to make a party of it with a friend of Anne's in Clifton Hill. The summer of 1941 briefly re-surfaced. Anne Richmond, living in a one-room flat five minutes' walk away from the University of London where she was working for the Ministry of Information, took Raymond and Michael with her to spend the night in the large and open house of her hospitable friend. She wrote up her diary:

D Day
Tuesday June 6

Usual crowd of planes went over from early morning – thought nothing of it so didn't know till in office that we landed between 6 – 8.30am on Normandy coast... Met Raymond Williams... at 6pm. He had won £9 for getting D-Day right. At 7pm we went down to Pillars of Hercules. Mike Orrom turned up about 7.30pm. Eventually v. gay supper at Chez Filet plus wine. Back to my house to pick up luggage and then all in taxi (found by Raymond) in rain to 105 Clifton Hill... Raymond took me a cold walk round block when rain stopped... I liked him again this time because he was funny. All stayed up to hear midnight news. Talking for hours. Didn't go to sleep till about 4am and then up 7.30am.

Weds. June 7

Raymond came with me at 9am. (Orrom had gone at 8am). Got a lift in lorry from Maida Vale to Goodge St. Terrifying experience – nearly ran down a bus and two children.

143

R. stayed in my room to telephone and later went off to fetch the flags for his tank which were nominal reason for his appearance. Gave him lunch there. And he went off again to see Ginger Rogers. Beastly day in office, practically no work to do. Very tired and desperate. In mood to cut down trees. So went back very early. Gave Raymond and Orrom tea in my room about 5.30 and we stayed there till 7pm. Funny to hear booksy talk again. Nearly went to sleep. All down to Charing X to see R. off by 7.40. Drink with Mike, then supper with J at Viarni's. Gloom by this time overwhelming – all my own fault, hangover, and exhaustion.[88]

Raymond Williams had clearly made a conscious decision to pick up the threads of that other, previous life. Yet he had had no connection with those friends during the war and answered no letters Michael Orrom sent to him.[89] The need for some contact was not to be denied for all that. Having made it he let it go again. In the post-war years it was a path, social and professional, that he would still stray towards though with less and less conviction or need. Back with his Regiment he learned that their orders were to move to France on 18 June. He had a forty hour pass to see Joy in Barnstaple and then travelled to the Marshalling Area at Tilbury where tedium settled over the massed tanks, waiting again and unable to leave their vehicles, swilling tea and using steel helmets for purposes necessary but not authorised. It was certainly not the case that he had resolved the direction his various started lives would take, but what awaited him, and the others, was the strong possibility of no life to take forward at all.

Harry Williams filled his diary with thoughts about the lives at risk and the lives to be lived:

6 June	-	D Day and our hopes and fears are with the Boys
21 June	-	Letter from Joy tells us that Jim has sailed
8 July	-	Letter from Jim in France and we are glad of it
9 July	-	We get the grand news that we are now grandparents and will Jim be proud of his daughter

Chapter 4

"An Odd Adventure or Two"

When Raymond Williams disembarked with his regiment onto Juno Beach, at Courseilles just east of Bayeux on 23 June 1944, he embarked on that intense period of his life in which he would be most isolated from the diverse currents of wider and formative social experience. This would not just be the necessary condition of a civilian combat solider. He discovered a detachment in himself that made him an exemplary officer in the Army's own terms: "army discipline and the extraordinary sense it instils that the rest of the world outside your unit ceases to exist."[1] It was an experience of conditioning which he later resented greatly and which he used, ahead of political disquiet, as his principal defence in 1950 before the Tribunal deciding on his refusal, at the outbreak of the Korean War, to be called up as a Reserve Officer with special expertise. The resentment was, in part, fuelled by a moral revulsion at the psychological disarmament that he now felt Army discipline forcibly entailed – "a strong existentialist sub-note to it, the idea of a total retention of autonomy"[2] – but more so by a conviction, one upheld thereafter, that submission to a military organisation meant relinquishing any kind of personal or political judgement irrespective of original intent. By 1950 this was a prospect he found intolerable.

This was not the case five years previously when the reasons for which he felt he had fought were being ferociously delineated by him from within an Army about which his emotional feelings of attachment were running high, even as he prepared to leave it. In July 1945, in an almost incandescent Leader for the army newspaper he was editing, he railed against a memorial service, held "to our British dead in a German church" and intermingling German civilian and British Army personnel, as a mock sentimental occasion that "seemed a parallel tribute to the fallen that disregarded nationality". This, the twenty-four-year-old officer thought, was "fascinating and fatal" in its mindless echo of anti-war films from the 1930s with their unifying message of "universal love".

The Tank Commander who confessed that "it [once] inspired me, as it inspired millions" dismissed the "day dreaming" as "pernicious nonsense" before the overwhelming issue of power and who wields it, and for what purpose:

> For we must have power to destroy the things that make war, and we must hate those things with all our souls. The cutting edge of our reasoning power to hate must never be dulled by cloying dreams of universal love. That is why those red wreaths in Pinneberg church, the two nations seemingly united in mourning those who had fallen to the last enemy, made no impression on me. I would tear them down for the false gods they are; the memory of a man who died for Fascism should be guarded only in contempt and hate, and never in reverence. For Fascism is the first thing we must utterly destroy, and love can't help us.[3]

Here and elsewhere at this time there is clear indication that within that Army he did not always feel singular or entirely helpless. On 14 October 1945 he left military life for good, sailing from Ostend to take up where he had left off in Cambridge. His valedictory column was for service colleagues, present and past, but also for an institution:

> I suppose the reprieved murderer, looking out at the free and lively street, would say the condemned cell was an experience he wouldn't have missed. Yet, without chicanery, I can say that of the Army.
> In the going down of the sun and in the morning I shall remember the thrill and high endeavour of Normandy, the wild excitement of Brussels, the privilege, however unpleasant, of having seen war ravaged Europe for myself, the host of good friends, the jeep and M10, mixed fruit puddings, and the smell of derv smoke in an evening harbour.
> Yet from haversack rations, from Sunday-afternoon barrackrooms, from the smell of dead cows and the pity of broken bodies, from the obsequious bows of defeated Nazis and from

146

the Wilster marshes, I thank the good lord for delivering me. One thing a near-civilian must say. As a wartime soldier I have learned to respect the regular army. Its traditions, its experience and its sacrifices were the leaven that saved England. I am glad that I shall never want to mock at them again. The country should realise their worth.[4]

With a related measure of consistency he would, over thirty years on, express annoyance that "the Left", particularly self-styled revolutionary elements, could so readily live in ignorance of "what a modern army can do".[5] But, equally, by then, in what amounted to rare reflection on that experience, he would also express the suppressed rage at what he was carrying with him from that experience, the ever-raw emotions which kept welling up:

> It was appalling. I don't think anybody really ever gets over it... there is the guilt: about moments of cowardice, but also about moments of pure aggression and brutality... what you lose is the most significant dimension to humanity – it is a commonplace about war, but is an absolute truth. You do function on a fighting animal level. I do not think that you ever sort it out afterwards.[6]

In the conflict itself as well as in its immediate aftermath he stuck to the tactic of writing, both for publication and in private, in a prose quite blanched of colour. It was almost as if any other tone would betray him. To his wife he scribbled a po-faced note towards the end of 1944:

> Everyone is well, with the exception that Bill Palin blew himself up on a booby-trap the other day, and injured his leg and face. I don't know how serious it is.
> That reminds me, I think I should now tell you, in instalments, of an odd adventure or two of my own. I didn't dare tell you at the time that on my second day in France I blew myself up on a mine, with only very slight

effect. I'll let you know more sometime. It's not that I'm concealing the truth, but I know you, like myself six months ago, have no idea of what war is like, and only long after should these incidental discomforts be related and laughed at.

Nothing more, Darling, except my love and longing to be with you again. Maybe we'll pick strawberries together.

Yours with all my love,
Raymond[7]

* * * * * *

The 21st Anti-Tank Regiment of the Royal Artillery left Scarborough, and training, for Sussex, and the real thing, as April turned to May in 1944. The men and their armour would be part of the support waves bound for Normandy after the beaches had first been held on 6 June, D-Day, and then bridgeheads established as the British Army moved inland to its first major destination, Caen. That progress over the following weeks would be initially stuttering, then increasingly slow and painful. In England the Thames, from Tilbury to the sea, was choked with landing craft, guns, tanks and men in waiting. LST [Landing Ship, Tank] 199 had threaded its way down river with the rest of the craft bound for France after the successful breaching of the Nazis' "Atlantic Wall" but then, both for the unblooded Lieutenant Williams and the veteran Desert Rats of his regiment, the "tempo slowed... and for three days we lay off Southend, passing our time drinking port in the wardroom... losing slightly at gin rummy... and heavily at bridge to the captain". LST 199 was the flotilla leader and when the great storm which had blown up over the Channel on 19 June finally ended the loaded craft pushed to the front of the queue, sailing beyond choppy inshore waters, and finally on to a calm sea:

The sea was beautifully and mercifully still, the weather fine and warm. Pontoon and port persisted, relieved by three minor incidents; hectic firing by the whole convoy at an object thought to be a U-boat periscope but in reality a sunken wreck, the passage of a flying-bomb, still a novelty then; and the laying of a smoke screen in the Straits by a flotilla of MTBs [Motor Torpedo Boats].

Boredom punctuated by edgy nerves was ended with entry into a theatre of operations designed to support the largest amphibious invasion ever devised:

On the morning of the 23rd we woke to see the unforgettable array of shipping off the Arromanches beaches and there was Normandy, a quiet yellow slope, and around us [HMS Flagship] Rodney firing inland, the big ships moving in to the beaches, the DUKWs [amphibious trucks] and landing craft scuttling around between. We grounded at high tide, and were dried out by noon. We unloaded with very little trouble. Major Dick in Bahrain, flying the new Sanna's Post pennant, I had been to London to fetch, was determined to be first off, but lost one of his crew and was beaten by Corsair, first M10 to arrive in the regiment back in August 43, first fighting vehicle of the Guards Armoured Division to land, eventually honourably exchanged after being the first British tank in Germany, still in the very best of order.
Along dirty roads, with flabby-breasted Frenchwomen waving, and small boys saluting us with what seemed to us all to be the Hitler flip, we made our way to a concentration area near Bayeux.
We put up our beds in an orchard and watched an air raid on the beaches. We felt we had arrived.[8]

The diary that he kept of service in action from June 1944 to the breakthrough into Germany in February 1945, was begun in the winter lull of late 1944 and was possibly intended as a later aide-memoire for fictional writing. Or he may have thought it might stand

149

on its own as a direct account.[9] He wrote to his wife on 30 November 1944: "Only other item of possible interest is that I'm writing a personal history of the Battery from Scarborough on: I've done the first chapter which gets us to Normandie. It might turn out well"; and on 8 February 1945, knowing since the weather had improved that he would soon see action again, he ended a letter by asking Joy, "Darling one, lift up your head and smile at me", then added, "PS. I have finished the diary – or rather I have brought it right up to date. Will bring it home with me – you may like it".[10]

It is an account written by a serving officer in the midst of an ongoing war, though with eventual victory by that point assured. This may explain the briskness of description and even the laconic dismissiveness of brutality that he had already experienced. The jaunty tone seems, on the other hand, to come directly from that absorption into the domesticity of military life, even or perhaps especially in wartime, which carried him and his closest comrades through the battles that awaited him in late June and which he recalls with trance-like precision a few short, intense months later. We can place his diary amongst those personal accounts of tank warfare in Normandy that return insistently to the carnage and confusion to which their lives were driven by the imperatives of the "bigger picture", only ever glimpsed.

Lieutenant R.H. Williams would be directly involved in the major military offensives undertaken by Montgomery's 21st British and Canadian Army from late June, until the Germans, caught in the Falaise pocket of encirclement, were finally captured or driven out of Normandy in August. By then he, along with so many other young citizen soldiers, was already a veteran for whom the subsequent race into Belgium and Holland, on through the 1945 campaigns to Hamburg, had put his individual personality on ice:

> ... an army functions so much as a true machine – the whole point of the training, although you don't realise it, is precisely to be able to do all these actions without being immediately motivated. You do in battle what you did in an

exercise, with of course much more chaos. What you lose is the most significant dimension to humanity... By that time [1945], quite honestly, we had been brutalised – you cannot fight for nine months through strange country without acquiring a totally different attitude to human suffering. The front line unit does not feel, it cannot have humane responses.[11]

Other than fear perhaps; constant fear within the shell of a tank, ears both battered by the high pitched revving of the engines and attuned to barked instructions; intermittent fear in the lulls of battle as the stop-start nature of the Normandy campaign drew the regiment in and out of their support role to the infantry. His diary records that the day after embarkation they were pulled straight in: "we were wakened at 7 am by an LO [Liaison Officer] who told us we were off on a private party with 15th (Scottish) Division to make bridgeheads over the Odon and Orne."[12] This was to be the Epsom offensive.

In the three weeks that had followed D-Day the British and Canadian forces, attacking from bridgeheads to the east and west of their objective, the linchpin city of Caen, had taken losses of nearly 24,000 men or 1,000 a day. The city had been, perhaps still was, the hinge on which rested Montgomery's strategy to swing south and east onto the open plains beyond Caen. Nonetheless, German resistance, as fiercely professional as it was last ditch, prevented any easy resolution. Caen would be flattened but it would not be taken until 8-9 July and even then the enemy remained entrenched in its eastern suburbs and outlying villages. It would be Montgomery's later contentious argument that the objective was not, in fact, Caen, but tying in German divisions, particularly Panzer regiments called up from the south and east, in order to enable the Americans to mass to the west, break out of the Cotentin peninsula and, eventually, effect an allied pincer movement to squeeze out German forces. Insofar as Epsom was concerned this objective, if such it was, was successful in that it pinned down the enemy and made the British-Canadian Army pivot south-east to Caumont. Yet the stated intention for Epsom was bolder: to cross the Odon via a narrow salient

– the so-called "Scottish corridor" – move south to the Orne and over it to the plain to the east. This was an infantry battle, preceded by heavy artillery bombardment and then supported by armoured brigades. It began in rain and mist on 24 June with preliminary attacks, ending, with withdrawal from muddy potholes akin to World War One and after heavy losses, on 29 June. The Orne was not crossed and the Caen-Falaise plain was still beyond allied reach.[13]

If that was the "Big Picture", the close-up was the detail of fighting in this part of Normandy where the "Bocage" began. To the south of Bayeux and just west of Caen the cornfields gave way to thick clumps of wood and to fields cleared for cattle outside the small villages clustered around a church, a cross roads, a chateau, a small open space, a few solid stone houses, a farm. In 1944, down to the Odon the roads were often no more than ancient sunken lanes topped by thick hedgerows, and around these, in barns or in ditches, in orchards or small woods crossed by streams, the Germans had dug in and fortified; from here they were able to pull out and retreat and return as the battle lines shifted, not in the connected trench warfare of 1914-18 but along routes and paths they had reconnoitred and networked. From these positions machine gun nests and snipers could open up, often after the enemy had passed through. The Germans placed auxiliary but fighting forces, often engineers or enlisted Ukrainians, in the advance lines, but then brought up front-line troops, SS Divisions and Hitler Youth, to counter-attack with venom. Tanks had to move slowly in this terrain, roads were easily and often choked by burned-out vehicles or too much armour, and German infantry could, and did, suddenly appear with deadly hand-held Panzerfausts to fire their rockets directly. Nor, by common consent, were Allied Tanks the match of the more heavily armoured 88 mm German Tigers and Panthers which, though slower to manoeuvre than Churchills or Shermans, generally outgunned them. Only the British 17 pounder guns mounted onto 75 mm Shermans which made them "Fireflies", along with the M10 17-pounders, allowed parity of fire power. Advantage of numbers lay entirely with the Allies but inexpertise at the ground level, and defensive bloody-mindedness with the Germans ordered to yield nothing, meant the German forces were more than a match.[14]

The first thing Lieutenant Williams hit, as Q Battery moved beyond the start line for Epsom, was a Teller mine – all the verges were mined – from which, thanks to sandbagging, they escaped with minor injuries. They were moving towards the tiny village of Cheux, already in ruins through bombardment by shell and mortar fire; it was a crucial junction for seven roads in this section of the front and the site of constant attack and counter-attack. A little way beyond Cheux the first onslaught had stalled short of the Odon by the evening of 26 June. Q Battery, variously attached to the 91st Anti-Tank Regiment and 44 Infantry Brigade in support of mopping up operations as the advance continued from 27 to 29 June, now encountered the enemy directly. The retrospective account in the Regimental Newspaper in July 1945 was resolutely brief:

> At 0930 hours on June 29 the Battery commenced an action which went on throughout the day. It was a bloody and bitter battle and was the first action seen by any Battery of the Regiment in this campaign. When the fighting ceased, one Panther, one Tiger, one 88mm A-tk gun had been definitely destroyed and hits scored on one other Panther and Tiger. Approximately fifty enemy infantry were killed or wounded by small arms fire. Our losses were not light. The SPs [self-propelled guns] Avalanche, Condor II, and Cossack II were knocked out and our casualties included Lt. Desmond Porter (severely wounded) and Sgt. Stone and L/Bdr. Tomkinson killed.[15]

As they had deployed in and around Cheux, Q Battery's Order of Battle had been Battery Commander Major Dick Taylor, regular army and strict in battle, with a Group Captain and Liaison Officer directly acting to him and then the "Q Captain, Bill Beaty" in charge of the three troops of four tanks each. Lieut. R H Williams, RA was leading "C Troop" of Cormorant, Condor, Centaur and Cossack. There were five men in each of the vehicles – a driver, a wireless operator, a loader who pushed in the shell and a layer who scoped for the required range and fired. The officer would direct operations from an open turret. Major Taylor, remembered warmly as "wonderful" and with an intriguing mismatch of "one blue and one brown eye", sharply advised his young officers, at risk to snipers, to keep their heads up nonetheless in order to observe enemy movements.[16]

This, in cold but graphic detail, is what the twenty-three-year-old student officer saw and did after they had descended the gentle slope to the narrow trickle of the Odon at Grainville where they "leaguered" for the night:

> Early next morning [June 29] a Panther flushed out by the sweep [by a battalion of Churchill tanks and infantry] moved hull down across my front. When it stopped we fired, and got several hits, but it didn't brew. It didn't move on either. Meanwhile, a black pile of smoke was rising over to the West, and Sgt. Woolley was being congratulated on the first kill, a Panther at 200 yards which went straight up. A few minutes later, after much excited talk of big friends and "Fire if you can see it", Sgt. Forder brewed up another Panther at a thousand yards, and we began thinking it was too easy. Unfortunately, Desmond Porter, in "Avalanche", just looking around the corner of a hedge for another enemy tank, was shot up at long range by an anti-tank gun from a flank. All the crew got out, but Desmond was wounded and was taken away, grinning, on top of a jeep, saying "Why the hell didn't I remember there were four tanks in a German troop." But it was a gun that had hit him, and Sgt. Woolley, some while later, had the pleasure of hitting it right out of its pit with a few rounds of HE [high explosive]. Shortly afterwards, Sgt. Marks knocked out a mortar post.
>
> By this time the force was on its objective, although tanks and infantry had quite heavy casualties. Tony Handford (Lieutenant "B" Troop) took a composite troop into the

wood, with five Churchills, and a company of infantry. My sector having gone quiet, I was brought over to relieve him. We were played in to a sweet salvo which was more frightening than damaging, but when we got into the wood, an unfortunate mistake brought seventy-two of our guns down on to us for a while, which was really frightening and damaging. The Boche added a few mortars to the general noise, and then counter attacked. We learned later that it was the extreme flank of a division counter-attack by 12 SS Panzer (Hitler Jugend). In the close country they got right among us, and Sgt. Stone, in "Condor" was killed when his tank was hit by a bazooka. Two of his crew got back, Dvr/Op. Lancashire (wounded), and Gnr. Clingo. L/Bdr Tomkinson and Dvr. Frame have not been traced – it seems very likely that they were made prisoner. As we were engaging a house where a few infantry had lodged themselves, Sgt. Sherlock, in "Cossack" was hit, but all his crew got out and made our own lines. Eventually our infantry withdrew, and as the Churchills went out, Major Dick brought the rest of the battery up on the right, about three hundred yards back from the wood. I looked where one of the Churchills had been and saw two Germans lying in the undergrowth, about five yards away. I threw a grenade and backed out. I joined up with the remainder of the battery and we fired point blank HE at the infantry coming through the wood. It stopped them, and eventually turned them back. Then a Panther poked its nose round a corner of the wood, but retired hastily on being shot at. We held that line until dark, shooting some field guns to fill in the time, and then leaguered two fields back. The night was noisy with tracer zipping through the trees, but it was all high, and we got some sleep, in spite of a stand-to on a reported attack which didn't materialise.

Next day we remained concentrated. The infantry reformed and patrolled, and in the afternoon we were relieved by a Crusader-towed battery of 17-prs from the 91st A-tk Regt.

We moved back through our lines, covered in yellow recognition panels, an odd pennant flying. We got a great reception back at regiment [HQ], and talked and drank till the small hours. It was a short action, and a very minor battle, but the orchard at Granville-sur-Odon is still spoken of with respect by those who were there.[17]

The official War Diary of the 21st Anti-Tank Regiment recorded how, after a German attack on an axis from Granville-sur-Odon to Cheux with both tanks and infantry, Q Battery had given support to the allied infantry by fire from their Browning guns "accounting for many Germans who were held up and turned back". According to the War Diary of Q Battery itself, C Troop's Commander Lt. R. Williams "fired at German Infantry with sten gun at a range of five yards". Heavy infantry losses dictated later withdrawal but the raw recruits, officers and other ranks, like Eddie Gibbs, Cormorant's nineteen-year-old wireless operator, had been blooded and bonded.[18]

* * * * * *

Former tank crew members stressed the unity and the inter-reliance that they found from necessity as well as choice. Crews often slept under or near their tanks, reasoning that prime targets were still safer than being out in the open. A direct hit, though, from an armour-piercing Tiger or an anti-tank gun or a close-up Panzerfaust meant almost certain destruction for both tank and crew. A shell amongst the high explosive they carried along with their fuel of diesel or petrol meant a "brew up". The Shermans were notoriously known as "Ronsons", after the cigarette lighters, and, invariably, those who could not scramble clear were incinerated as the smoke and fire rushed to escape through the turret. Ricocheting shells inside the tank, splintering off deadly shards of metal, brought instant terror and disfigurement or worse. Crews who ate and slept together, "in harbour", soon knew that cresting a rise in the Suisse Normande of undulating slopes and wooded valleys, or turning a corner in a square, or leaving the cover of a hedge, exposed all of them to such danger. Fear and psychological burn-out and, of course, turn-over of crews through death or even fatigue as much as any other cause, were the quickly-learnt facts of existence. Officers mixed with men in such direct ways that some military customs were set aside and first-name terms often established between officers and other ranks. Lieutenant Stuart Hills, twenty-year-old tank commander in the Sherwood Rangers, fought close to the same actions as Lieutenant Williams from late June 1944:

> On a rail alongside the skirt of the tank above the tracks was fitted a tarpaulin which could either be folded over the top of the turret as camouflage or pulled out sideways, supported by sticks at the corners, to make a bivouac under which we could sleep. There was just room for five to lie side by side, the commander always at one end of the row so that he would be immediately available if called for. We always remained fully dressed except for our boots, although in freezing conditions we had to rely on our mutual body heat to keep us warm. We wore belted grey denim overalls, with plenty of pockets, and the black beret, and we only shaved when it was possible to do so...
>
> As far as food was concerned, we were supplied with rations we could eat while in action: small cardboard boxes filled with biscuits, chocolate and oatmeal slabs, together with pills to keep us awake. We had a Primus stove we could use outside the tank when things were quieter and on which we heated up tins of meat and vegetables, bully beef, soup and so on. If we needed to cook on something bigger, we would fill a large tin with earth and diesel oil, set light to it and use a frying pan. Drink was supplied in tins of tea, sugar and powdered milk all mixed together: you simply added boiling water. We also tried to live off the land when we could and in Normandy our chocolate and cigarettes could be bartered for eggs, butter, cheese, chickens and calvados. Not surprisingly after days in action the stench inside the tank became almost unbearable, and the fact we

157

often could not get out for long periods of time resulted in regular bouts of severe constipation... Living so close to each other, we tended to drop all formality and the crew called me by my Christian name, yet in action very strict discipline prevailed over the intercom and they answered every order immediately.[19]

Eddie Gibbs remembered his own Commander as "caring and competent... not a soldier officer... not death or glory... [who]... didn't like killing".[20] It was Lieutenant Williams' batman, the Londoner Vic Polhill, who foraged, rather recklessly at times, for artichokes and camembert and calvados and tried, sometimes unavailingly, to keep his officer's dress code up to standard as testified to by a rather less-than deferential note to Lieutenant Williams which he sent on to his wife in bemused admiration:

My Dear and exalted *Sir*,

I humbly beg you on bended knees (my permanent position through hard work) to add an afternote, or afterthought to your very next letter to Mrs Williams to the effect that your very tired (or tiresome) batman has no –

	Brown Boot Polish
or	Brown Boot laces
or	Washing Powder or soap (for clothing)
or	Khaki Darning wool

If you are not fatigued by so much, will you please ask for a couple of new Neckties and back-to-front collar studs.

If, Sir, you will so oblige I promise to wash a shirt for you. Or I might even make your bed!

Your Most Dis-obedient
V Polhill[21]

This gently-mocked but well-respected officer struck the men in his immediate command as "deep" and "a bit of a loner" who was compassionate enough to "fix" leave passes for family or for romantic reasons and who did not, though "educated", seem distant. By choice, though, he "spent his time writing".[22] And all the rest was not from choice but circumstance – "in our self-propelled tank guns, you were not a traditional officer commanding thirty people, but one of a crew of five in a tank with three other tanks under your control. You all had technical jobs to do. So the immediate social relations were not so hierarchical. Relations with the Guards officers themselves [as an artillery regiment within the Guards Armoured Division] were much more difficult."[23]

He seems to have been fortunate that the officers with whom he most closely served, notwithstanding gradation of age and class and indeed considerable gaps of any common experience, were men whose personal characters, beyond outward characteristics and foibles, he came to admire, and even to like. He provided quick sketches, retrospective and so perhaps more astute than if he had penned them at the time, of those who had readied for battle in Scarborough and then waited on Vinehall lawn in Sussex for the invasion to commence:

> We had managed to live very much our own lives in Scarborough, but here, with a battle obviously ahead, we began to wonder how we could ever manage to live with each other.
> Dick Taylor the highly respected Battery Commander, was, perhaps a little reluctant to be leaving the England he had so recently rediscovered. But he knew what he was fighting for, and his frequent trips to Windsor and Ascot amounted in reality to a restatement of his war aims before battle.
> Bill Beaty, "G" Captain, began in Sussex to take an interest in the war for the first time since Dunkirk, and armed himself with nails of varying length to stick in booby traps (the obvious joke was made). In addition he managed several motorcycle trips to see his wife in Portsmouth, on

all of which he contrived to break down and eventually came home on everything but a Mulberry (his breakdown on leave became a classic tradition later in Belgium).

Donald Smith "Q" Captain, recently married and behaving very "miel de lune", wrote letters to his wife half the day, and wrapped plasticine around distributors the other half.

Desmond Porter, "A" Troop Commander, dropped nectarine wit with a touch of strychnine in the most unlikely places, and wrote lyrics for the Battery Concert, "Q UP", which was so successful on the eve of "D" Day.

Tony Handford, new "B" Troop Commander, casual as ever, made the grounds echo with unauthorised explosions, and just failed to make a big score at cricket under the Robertsbridge willows.

John Hardy, L.O., maintained enough licit liaison to keep us fairly misinformed, in the manner of "I" staffs, on the prospect before us, and enough illicit liaison to make the room I shared with him a very attractive single residence.

What I did myself I cannot remember, except that I had forty eight hours with my wife... and once found a stinkhorn on the treasure hunt with which we whiled away most afternoons (oh yes : and I had dinner in Soho on "D" Day – a longstanding ambition of mine).[24]

These men, some to be replaced, some wounded, some decorated, some killed, are the close companions, a number to his surprise becoming friends, whose doings and welfare are constantly mentioned in his letters home. They would be transmuted into the choral, slightly mythical, re-named companions Major Hunter, Lieutenants Strong and Squire to his own Captain Knight, in the ambitious novel of his war experience which he will plot and begin and never finish in the early 1950s. *Our Lords The Moon and The Sun* probably shattered under the weight of his attempt to find its appropriate form. He did not disguise his contempt for others of the officer class who attracted neither friendship nor respect. When Dick Taylor was appointed as Second-in-Command of the Regiment in August 1944, Major S.A. Wilson-Brown arrived to take command of the

160

Battery.[25] He did not endear himself to a subordinate who found enforced company in the officers' Mess over the winter of 1944-45 re-inforcing the feelings that bubbled up whenever close combat receded: "I am of course in my permanent state of anger at these bloody people I have to live with. I realise this is unreasonable, but it is just unending pomp and stupidity, and in a period of relative inactivity it is difficult to bear."[26] Wilson-Brown became, in the projected novel, Tiger Duckless-Hale or, more directly when he replaced the now promoted Colonel Taylor entirely: "an awful little bastard who is ineffectual and pimpish to a degree and a social climber of the purest water. He is thoroughly ignored by us all, and is fortunately in England at the moment on a course. His name is Stewart Arthur Wilson-Brown ("call me Buster"). Christ! The rest of the boys are in good form and much as you knew them".[27]

As he remembered them after the War it was the systematic irreverence within the system of authority which he found hopeful and which, in a handwritten page fragment of *Our Lords The Moon and The Sun*, he highlighted in a sketch of a Battery concert:

> There was one item left before the singing of the National Anthem. It was a song of the Gunners – which the middle ranks of the Battery knew well. Sergeant Long, flushed with beer and yet nevertheless very shy and a little embarrassed, came to stand in the centre of the stage, extended his hands and began the verse:
>
> > Now gather round, my comrades,
> > And hark to what I say,
> > My tale is of those gallant men
> > The gunners of today
> >
> > For till the sun and moon go down
> > And stars shall cease to shine
> > There's one brave band shall always stand
> > On the righthand of the line

You know their name, you know it well
Their fame shall never cease,
The gallant British gunners, lads
Defenders of the peace.

The officers in the front rows and some of the younger gunners looked pleased at the verse; some of them from foreknowledge. The Colonel, who was new to the regiment, seemed especially delighted, and looked round approvingly. Sergeant Long, staring out over the rows of heads, seemed again embarrassed, but suddenly, with a lunge of his hands, he shouted into the chorus, which was immediately taken up from the body of the hall.

Ohhhh...
Ubiquitous
Iniquitous
The darling of the halls
The solid British gunner,
With his solid British balls
He plugs the breach
He rams it home, and then
The solid British gunner
Is away on top again

Sergeant Long's embarrassment had disappeared; he was now very well pleased with himself and as the swell of the chorus dissolved into a cheer, he swung his arms, and began it again.

Ohhhhhh...
Ubiquitous
Iniquitous
The darling of the halls
The solid British gunner
With his solid British balls
He calculates

He elevates
He lays for line and then
The solid British gunner
The gallant British gunner
The fiery British gunner
Is away on top again.

As the cheer rose again, with an expression of calculated dolefulness, Long raised his hands for silence, and moved into the slow march of the finale:

And when the fighting's over
The battle lost and won
You will find the British gunner
The solid British gunner
The gallant British gunner
The fiery British gunner...
Looking after Number One.

As the last phrase lurched into sudden speed, the captain moved swiftly and jerkily across the tiny stage. The Colonel was still left wondering what to do, looking rather ruefully at Hunter, when a note from the piano announced the National Anthem, and everyone in the room stiffened at once into a firm military attention.

* * * * * *

That summer of 1944 in Normandy there were no safe havens. After their first tank battle at the Odon and a night of carousing away from the front line at RHQ, the intermeshing of the fighting became all too apparent. In the morning they were shelled from a distance and counted three dead and eight wounded as casualties. The crunch of shellfire was now a constant as was the whine of the multi-barrelled "Nebelwerfer" and the machine gun rattle of Spandau fire against tanks, "like peas hitting a canister".[28] The role of the Battery was set as a counter-attacking or support force and around the environs of Caen they were moved as battle strategies dictated. For five days they sat from 5 in the morning to 11 at night on the runway at Carpiquet Airport to the east of the city, sniping at enemies seen and imagined. Then, the next phase began.

> On Sunday July 16th all officers went to Divisional HQ for the GOCs briefing for the breakthrough into the Caen plain. We were thoroughly glad to be properly back with the Division again.[29]

This was the start of Operation Goodwood, a battle that would rage from 18 July to 21 July and prove even more controversial in its execution and outcome than Epsom. Defenders of Montgomery's strategy believe that its consistency was clear and did not entail any "breakout" through hotly contested enemy lines until all other objectives had been secured. And these were to engage as much of the available German armour in a battle that would "write it down to such an extent that it is of no further value", towards the preliminary destruction of all German fighting capacity in Normandy. With Caen in British hands and St Lô to the west now taken by the Americans the task was to clean up the defences still heavily mustered south and east of Caen and to clear out the pockets of resistance still ensconced in suburbs and villages to the north and north west of the blitzed city. The Germans had anticipated an allied thrust to the east, though this would only finally come in July-August, to the south and west before swinging on the hinge of a turning door eastwards. That is what eventually happened. The problem was that even at the time, it was not entirely understood in such sophisticated holding terms – the 21st Anti-Tank's historical notes of 1946 recorded "on the 11th July the regiment concentrated near Bayeux to prepare for the Division's first complete operation, the armoured break-out in the Caen plain"[30] – and the operation itself would not go smoothly to any plan, actual or projected.

Apart from the formidable enemy strength – seven strong Panzer divisions and five infantry divisions, half of these armoured – they were on this front also entrenched in the southern mess of industrial Caen, "a little Stalingrad of factory suburbs" in John Keegan's evocative phrase,[31] and in the string of small villages and orchards, outposts of the plain, beyond the criss-crossing railway lines and undulating country marked by the commanding Bourgébus Ridge which the Germans still held. Allied forces, infantry first and then armoured divisions, were required to march into a corridor six miles long by three miles wide, starting from the north east of Caen and heading south west, constantly overlooked or flanked, and with all the advantages of long distance range for their anti-tank guns lying with the Germans. Goodwood began with an attack on German positions at 5.30am on 18 July with a thousand RAF bombers. Successive attacks from thousands more aircraft and a gun bombardment of 250,000 rounds followed. It seemed as if nothing could survive this three-hour maelstrom. The front lines were cleared but as infantry advanced the in-depth German defences surfaced relatively intact. Objectives were met but territorial gains, deceptive in extent at first, were small.[32]

The British Armoured Divisions had moved across the Caen canal and the Orne to the north and east to be at the "start line". The 21st Anti-Tank Regiment found the roads choked, and their role as separate units confined to support in fierce mop-up actions in the southern suburbs, in which Tigers and Panthers were "bagged" and flushed-out German troops corralled. When torrential rain fell on 20 July they were withdrawn, north again, to the Orne until, on 21 July, they were concentrated together as a reserve to the Canadian Corps' attack along the western end of the Bourgébus Ridge.[33]

Raymond Williams, now an Acting Captain, was to be at this point more observer than participant:

> Once you've recovered a full perspective the whole thing seems unbelievably bloody. This was a time when I was reading Tolstoy and he was absolutely right about what fighting is like, how unlike the military history of battles it is. There was also a dreadful sense of loss. If you have seen

a tank with people you know in it go up, you never forget it. The Normandy battlefield was... for some weeks relatively static, so that there were dead men and animals all over it. It was frightful. After we broke out from Normandy there were some bad times, but never again the same peculiar oppression and confusion... Throughout, there was the difficulty of sustaining a perspective.[34]

In late July, with four hundred British tanks, a third of the total available, already lost assaulting the high ground, the armoured attack had been withdrawn and, with constant rain churning roads and fields to mud, the High Command decided that only infantry, the 2nd Canadian Corps specifically, would first attack the Bourgébus Ridge under constant bombardment and machine gun fire. If their sacrifice was not entirely futile (a foothold was taken and secured) it still remained a sacrifice. One Canadian participant recalled: "No one has succeeded in accurately describing the ferocity of [that] battle... And perhaps no one ever will for few who served with the rifle companies of the infantry battalions, including artillery... managed to survive more than a few days."[35] Goodwood had ended two days after it began even if the fighting had not. In his diary the Q Battery tank commander recalled:

We and "Y" Battery sat in a wrecked football stadium just below the horribly bombed Colombelles steel factory. There was more dirt, decay and flies in that stadium than we now care to remember. The only distinction was the nightly air raid, with the whistling butter-fly bombs, and the incredible firework display, it was nothing more, of the AA Barrage... During the day, from the tops of our tanks, we could watch the battle on the ridge ahead. It was very clear, and we looked a little wonderingly at the obvious OPs [observation posts] beyond the enemy ground.

The division was never used, and I marked up my map with a thick chinagraph instead of a thin one to show the current advance. During these days we also looked frequently at my map of the world, on which the bridgehead seemed still insignificant.[36]

The short account of these few "demoralising" days which he wrote up for *Twentyone* in July 1945 reeks of the futility of lives so expended amongst dust and mosquitoes, by moonlight and in the early hours of day, as the 2nd and 3rd Canadian Infantry Divisions to the south along Bourgébus Ridge mounted the attack after which Q and Y Batteries were to move up after dawn:

> At first light "Q" and "Y" had a grandstand view of the battle; looking out over the ridge the tanks could be seen as tiny objects crawling through yellow cornfields, 2 little moving specks of infantry rushed in and out of villages; a merciless carpet of shells fell continuously in the battle area. The main objectives were not gained; very bitter infantry fighting developed, and we sat on our start line with nothing to exploit.[37]

Seven miles were eventually gained at the expense of six thousand allied casualties. To the immediate west, however, where the Americans faced German forces that were weaker in both number and quality, the cessation of rain opened up the next phase: the American break out from St Lô southwards into the Bocage. British troops and armour eased westwards to begin their own drive south of Caumont into the difficult terrain of "la Suisse Normande" and directly against crack Panzer divisions as the Germans made one final effort to hold their fortified lines south of Caen. This was Operation Bluecoat, a see-sawing battle of attrition and micro-encounters with infantry and tanks now combining in action rather than acting in isolated thrusts. The 21st Anti-Tank had marched west day and night "through the wreck of Caen" then south beyond Caumont "to join 2nd Irish and 5th Coldstreams". On their right flank VIII Corps were attacking to prevent any German disengagement whilst the Americans continued to advance on the west and to the south. In essence, overwhelming superiority in the air and on the ground was inexorably crushing German forces that could not be replaced or re-supplied. Piece by piece, though, nothing in Normandy was an easy gain.

The Battery rolled forward at a pace on the first two days of August down roads dominated by steep slopes covered with pinetrees. If the trees stirred in the hot wind they were shot at, for any advance that was made still left enemy troops behind, and particularly snipers ready for any incautious tank commander surveying the way forward. Proferred flowers and even cider now from more welcoming, perhaps more assured, local people did not ease feelings about the somewhat forbidding scenery of wooded gorges and overhanging branches. They were heading south east through the village of St Charles de Percy towards Estry, which was to the south and still strongly in enemy hands, and they had orders to by-pass opposition and, if possible, to move on to Vassy, almost half-way between the towns of Vire to the west and Falaise to the east. The country north east of Vire was typical of the Bocage – small fields, thick uncared-for hedge-fences growing above banks that formed natural obstacles to tanks, studded as they were with tall oaks and ancient elms.

Squadrons of infantry probed their way; communication by wireless was difficult; German infantry was known to be in the vicinity of a crossroads known on the map as Point 176 just east of the tiny hamlet of Le Désert. At 9am on the morning of 3 August after an uncomfort-able night of watching and waiting they all moved out, with C troop leading, and motored easily for a mile or so until they reached the dominating crest which carried the main Estry-Vire road on a south east axis. Two Panthers were spotted on the other side. Whoever showed on either side was shot at, so a stand-off ensued, with the infantry preparing "to go in… supported by a stand from a Battery of Leicester-shire Yeomanry who were in position back in the area of Point 176."

Then, "another historic day for the Battery" began. At Point 176 at least eight Panthers had suddenly appeared with a large force of infantry to attack the Field Guns. Q Battery was, except for Williams' troop of four, ordered back and into action as fast as they could travel the short distance. C Troop was left to maintain the forward impasse whilst the rest of the Battery once again deployed around the cross-roads. Tanks manoeuvred around hedgerows or waited as silent assassins on that hot August day in fruiting orchards surrounded by hayfields dotted with stooks. For these men, if they momentarily turned their eyes away from danger, the countryside was fresh and green and "distractingly beautiful".[38]

At Point 176, under mortar and machine-gun fire, the Battery claimed three Panthers destroyed to one M.10. Five men were dead and several wounded. When evening came C Troop was ordered back with its accompanying infantry and arrived unscathed:

> At 176 itself it was dark, but the enemy had just fired a burst of Spandau into a thatched roof nearby, and the flames lit up the whole area. We passed through the orchards and harboured in the hayfield...
>
> There was a close, cold early morning mist as the Battery reoccupied its positions of the previous day. I went out with Tony Handford ['B' Troop], and below us Bert Stott's "A" Troop was lining the edge of the orchard, all of us facing East towards our targets of the previous day. So many curious shapes appear in the mist at that hour that we all imagined things. Tony shot a cow with his 17-pr., and enemy was reported on all sides. But stray shots, and a burst of machine-gun fire that ripped the seat of Bert Stott's trousers as he dived to the ground on hearing German voices, soon made us realise that the enemy had in fact infiltrated into our orchard. Sgt. Pollard's tank, very shortly afterwards, was hit by what we thought was a mortar. Sgt. Farrow, however, claimed he could hear a tank engine, and opened fire in the direction of the noise. He fired eight or nine shots in very rapid fire, and to our surprise and his own, the unmistakeable brew-up of a tank resulted. This was followed by an exchange of machine-gun fire; some 3rd Irish infantry tried to get into the orchard, but were in too little strength.

All day we watched the orchard intently. In the early afternoon two figures emerged from its western end, and were about to be fired on when we saw they were civilians. They were in fact the farmer and his wife who lived in the orchard, and they came to us and told us there were three ("Non, non, deux seulement" – "Mais non, trois"), three, perhaps, German tanks and infantry with machine guns. A little later Sgt. Farrow saw a crouching figure, dressed in dark green clothing and carrying a German sniper's rifle, move under a hedge. He aimed his Bren but it failed to fire, and as he recocked it the bland, bespectacled face of Gunner Polhill was turned towards him. Farrow exclaimed "My God", and I think Polhill still remembers the click of the Bren as it failed to fire. The object of his lone patrol was as mysterious as all his excursions, but the load of his jeep is a good index to their results.

About teatime we were enlivened by a visit from a loud-hailer van which exhorted the enemy to surrender, in German and Ukrainian. It then played "Lili Marlene", and we were sitting on our counterweights enjoying the music in the warm sun when a burst of machine-gun fire in the direction of the noise reminded us that the war was still on. One wretched little Ukrainian, in S.S. uniform (they were 9 SS Pz Div. "Hohenstaufen"), came in as a result; a farmboy of about nineteen who did not even know he was in France. "They" had come along to ask him to join the army; his enemies wore khaki uniforms, and he could use his rifle and shoot them. "Young barbarians all at play", but this was no Roman holiday. The enemy pulled out in the night. We entered the orchard, de-fused some mines and found the brewed-up Panther Sgt. Pollard thought he had hit. As indeed he had with a shot that penetrated two thick farm walls and the tank itself as its crew was breakfasting.

The farmer and his wife came back, and told us the story. Their servant girl had been very friendly with the English when some of our tanks first occupied the place. Having gone to bed with the English in possession the place had changed hands, without fighting, in the night, and she had gone out the next morning to see a tank standing where one had been the night before, and had shouted "Allo, Tommy" to a figure standing in it. From the turret of his Panther, a lugubrious SS lieutenant had leaned over and said "Nichts Tommy". The girl was not amused.

The battery concentrated in the hayfield and started showing visitors round the battlefield. All four Panthers were inspected again and again... We buried our dead at Point 176 – BSM Woolley (later awarded the MM), L/Bdr Sowerby, Gnr. "Yorky" Holmes, Gnr. Campbell and Gnr. Biddlestone. The insignificant crossroads, the orchard and the hayfield must for ever be a proud and sacred place in the history of the Battery.[39]

In his imagination he will return to it, early and late, and let it become the essence, human and therefore irreducible, of a battle campaign which kept sweeping men along on its unforeseeable tides as mere flotsam. The Battle for Normandy was closing and over the next few days, after the Orchard fight, they were informed by wireless that "the big picture is tremendous. The enemy are withdrawing everywhere, and the Americans are closing on Argentan." Yet the Division had merely sidestepped to the right to attack south over the Vire-Vassy road with troops of the Irish Guards and two Grenadier battalions who were locked in combat with "determined paratroopers". And the German barrage of 88 mm fire was continuously knocking Thunderbolts out of the sky. The exhausted Lieutenant Williams listened to the good news but wrote "I confess I was sceptical".[40]

And then it was, for the 21st Anti-Tank Regiment at least, temporarily over. The enemy was caught in a six by ten-mile loop or bag – the Falaise "pocket" – as all four allied Armies pincered them from west, south and north. By 20 August the German Army had crumbled, with twenty to forty thousand squeezing an escape route to the east, leaving behind a vast array of armoured vehicles, 50,000 captive troops and over 10,000 dead in the biggest set-back to German arms since Stalingrad itself. Q Battery, under command of the 5th Brigade of Guards Armoured Division had been held in reserve on the Estry-Vire road as to the south and east of it resistance ended with an Allied turkey-shoot.

Q Battery recuperated. The War Diary recorded that "maintenance of vehicles, guns and personnel was the order of the day".[41] Major Dick Taylor was promoted to Colonel and 2nd-in-Command of the Regiment – "It was a wrench for him and for us, for Dick Taylor's Q Battery was a very happy and confident concern"[42] – and Acting Captain Williams, as he had been since 19 July, was put in charge of "A" Echelon as "Q" Captain. Echelon duties involved locating and mapping the movement of the Battery troops to ensure supply and re-fit of vehicles as action was co-ordinated by the Battery Commander. He had his own jeep and driver for these duties, which involved both HQ and front line activity. When Major Wilson-Brown arrived to take command on 22 August Captain Williams was not there – he had been sent to Bayeux to run a course for Self-Propelled guns. With the Allies advancing on all fronts in late August, by the time he rejoined the Regiment it had uneventfully crossed the Seine and the Somme. On 1 September, Q Battery took the lead as part of 5th Guards Brigade and with "movement unchecked by night" the "Great Swan" began. The breakneck push to Brussels covered over three hundred miles with no mechanical breakdowns though the tank troops, no longer confined by the countryside, "burnt out the bogey wheels of their vehicles".[43] The first ordeal had been met and left behind.

* * * * * *

The only fictional reference to the Normandy campaign published by Williams is in his novel of 1985, *Loyalties*, a key text in establishing the personal divergence that he felt necessary to establish between himself and some actors and actions of the "British Left" from the 1930s. At that late stage in his life, the continuing rawness of the

Normandy experience could be folded into a more panoramic social experience from the Spanish Civil War to the 84 – 85 Miners' Strike, in which Bert Lewis, collier, International Brigader, Normandy veteran and life-long socialist, serves as his emblematic lodestar of ultimate class loyalty. It is Bert Lewis, a sergeant in command of one of the tanks in the troop of new Lieutenant Angell, who features in the fire-fight in the orchard in the novel. The chapter is brief but vivid ("a bit of an error in an orchard... this black line on the Vire-Vassy road") and, despite drawing on a compound memory of any action undertaken, the fictional purpose overrides the documentary recall of "radio crackle... the sudden shattering roar of the big diesel engine... the cloud of foul smoke... the unmistakeable sound of tank tracks moving... a shell whistling above... and the crump of high explosive somewhere beyond the farmhouse". The underlying purpose in the novel is emblematically served by Bert's severe facial injury (a mutilation to be captured in an oil painting by his wife, Nesta, for whom it acts as a record of other sacrifices and betrayals) and by his assumption in battle of the command of a working-class troop (Paddy, Dai, Sam, Harry and Tom). First Conqueror and then Cossack are hit by two German Tigers. Only Bert, personally attempting to locate and then effect a rescue of Conqueror, which is lost and unseen in the confused and blind fighting behind hedges, walls and orchard, manages to survive. In the novel the significant factor is the removal of the officer class, both from the action and from any pretence that control is being exerted at their level in this kind of warfare. It is the only time Raymond Williams described, in fact or fiction, things of whose like, as he had written home at the end of 1944, he had had "no idea":

> Bert ducked round the back of the tank. A corpse burned to an almost shapeless blackness lay under the engine cowling. Another body, still retaining some of its shape, hung halfway out of the turret, overcome there while trying to escape. He looked quickly around and even called, quietly, "Dai". But he was almost sure that Dai was the shapeless body under the engine, and there was no other human

173

sound or sight. The driver and the radio operator must have been trapped inside; there could be no hope for them.[44]

Bert Lewis' courage, and inevitable wounding, have only one direct relation to Raymond Williams' life. Notwithstanding his own undoubted bravery at Grainville-sur-Odon (on which the fictional conflict is based rather more than on the Vire-Vassy engagements), Williams carried with him a sense of the unfulfilled duty to fallen comrades which Bert Lewis, leaving his tank in his quest, carried out. On the actual day in June 1944, Lieutenant Williams, commanding C Troop in that shelled wood, saw two tanks, Condor and Cossack, hit and lost, but all of the latter's crew escaped, as did two from Condor. It was Sergeant Stone who died, and two others, later presumed captured, who did not return. Yet the driving force shaping Raymond Williams' recollection in *Politics and Letters* is so strong that he mentions no survivors at all and, though sure that nothing could have been done differently by himself, he concludes in a fashion that underlines why, in *Loyalties*, it was done differently by others:

> I lost two [tanks] in that particular battle against the SS. I was actually overruled. I was told that I must occupy a wood which had a small railway line going through it, which I said was ludicrous because in a wood you can't see any more... When we were ordered into the wood I divided the unit into two pairs, my pair going to one end and the other to the other end of the wood – that was the only way to do it. They never came back. Since we were subsequently withdrawn and put somewhere else, I never knew what happened to them. We went on calling and calling on the wireless trying to establish contact and not getting it. There was an extraordinary temptation to get out and look, but the entire wood was being shelled and there was no chance of that. Meanwhile we had destroyed... two SS tanks.[45]

Normandy had disrupted so many certainties in the personality and psychology of Raymond Williams that the rationalised justification he had for war service – ultimate opposition to fascism in the guise of Nazis – played thereafter around the existence of and physical encounter with identifiable SS troops. The Manichean picture could then be resolved. What beat beneath the skin was altogether different. He approached it directly only once, in a complete but unpublished story he entitled "The Traitor".[46] Written in pencil on eight foolscap pages, in late 1944, we can detect in it such a forceful, near clarity about the changes he had undergone that even their displacement into fiction was, perhaps, too close to bear further scrutiny. He put it away.

From its very title on, "The Traitor" is impregnated with the smell of betrayal: but of what and by whom will hang in the air. It begins with a tank troop at rest in a Normandy wheatfield on a hot, windless afternoon. Its main protagonist, the tank commander Peter Bridson, idly smokes a cigarette, scanning the horizon through binoculars as his exhausted crew sleeps amongst the tanks, their long guns sticking through the foliage that lines the hedgerows on three sides of the field. It is a bucolic pastoral, silent, with a "solitary peasant" scything his corn in the next field. The idyll is first breached by the delivery of a letter to Bridson by Redman, his batman, "a shambling be-spectacled boy with long untidy fair hair... So young and irresponsible, so assertive and egoist that he forced himself into... crazy displays of courage, it seemed impossible that he should have two lives depending on him, should be a breadwinner, head of a family". It is Redman who will cause the first betrayal when he goes off, recklessly, to a nearby farmhouse in search of eggs. When not seen for some hours, he is searched for, only to be found dead, probably shot by a sniper. Whilst that begins to unfold, off stage, Bridson reads the letter from his wife:

> "So now it's the Liberation Army," his wife had written. "That helps a good deal. It brings some sense of purpose, some idealism into a war in which otherwise neither you nor I could have seen any point. It's easier for me here.

175

Watching our child grow up I feel I'm still working for the good things in life. But for you, among ruins and fighting, it's so much harder. Hold on to the things which mean so much to us, my love. Hold on to life and progress. When liberation really starts it will be easier. But even now when it's going so slowly – don't lose faith. You said long ago the war was a fraud unless it was a fight of the peoples of the world against fascism. Forgive me, dearest, for this kind of letter, but you'll see there's nothing left for us unless we go on believing that."

As he pockets the letter Bridson muses on pre-war anti-fascist rallies – "that sunny market-place in 1938 a day much like this and how he'd spoken to those farmers and shopping women – told them Munich meant war" – and then, to the distant sound of heavy shelling and "the chilling shriek of a nebelwerfer", he wonders idly who was getting it:

Another SS Divison had moved into the line against them. He wished he could tell his wife that – it made the anti-fascist war she talked about seem real. "Hold on to life and progress." Most people here were more concerned with just holding on to life. "If you can live through Normandie," someone said, "you'll die old in your bed." Progress here meant something different, meant small bitter advances against a fanatical enemy, progress meant death. On the map of Europe liberation looked like a practical joke.

His reverie is interrupted by the arrival of a loudspeaker van designed for propaganda warfare: "He talked to the thick-lipped little German Jew who was to broadcast." The betrayals are already mounting. The playing of "Lili Marlene" and the promise of amnesty is directed to Russians and Jugoslavs mixed up in that section of the front line. At the afternoon's end Bridson takes two tanks to the farm to look for Redman. They find him, face down, on the farmyard's cobbles and no Germans in sight. A frightened farmer, just returned home, is flushed from hiding and accused of the killing.

"… I have told the truth. I just came back and find him already dead."

Bridson stamped angrily.

"It's all the same with you lousy Normans. You all did too bloody well out of the Boches. I've seen you with your sullen eyes and your greedy faces. You're hating us for coming."

"Sir, we all hated the Boches. I am a good Frenchman, I fight in fourteen-eighteen with the Tommies. Now I am glad for the liberation…"

The sergeant swung him off his feet.

"Liberation! You dirty little rat. Money's all you bloody Normans care about. You don't give a damn for liberation…."

"All right sergeant" said Bridson. "Take him back to the tanks."

The farmer is marched away. Redman taken to be buried in the wheatfield and the farmhouse roof set alight with incendiaries. Bridson is then called to interrogate a prisoner who has come in after the propaganda appeal. He is a young boy, smooth skinned, fair haired, trembling and Ukrainian. He is dressed in SS field overalls. His story is that he joined up to fight the Bolsheviks. He is uncertain which country he is now in; he simply wishes not to be shot. Bridson rejects his story. He strikes him across the face. The boy covers his face and weeps.

Bridson turned back to the boy.

"Listen, you frightened little wretch. You're lying, and if you lie you'll be shot, whatever the voice said. You're a traitor, a filthy greedy traitor, d'you understand. And now you're frightened. Well, you ought to be. There's only one way with traitors."

Bridson pushed the boy back into the wheat, and he lay where he fell, his head resting on his arms, his shoulders heaving. The mottled daub camouflage of his SS uniform stretched right across his back.

177

"Lennox you make me some tea, will you? I'm starving."

"Very good, sir."

"And bring it across to my tank. I'm starving."

"Right sir. Right away."

As Bridson walked back across the field his wife's letter fell from an unbuttoned pocket into the wheat. He walked on without noticing.

Williams' notes to himself on the manuscript remind us not to read actuality off the pages of this fiction. He names the real Redman – "wounded, not killed"; adds "Farmer bandaging him" and, as far as revenge and destruction is concerned, "Fire at sniper; burn farm by accident". No letters from his wife to him survive to compare the political sentiments, if any, expressed by her. Nonetheless, and despite the halting dialogue and contrived plot, the felt power of despair at the crookedness of the reality war visited upon idealists is clearly no mere imaginative invention. It is, in a distilled essence here, what had happened to him. Traitors cast off loyalties, usually for the best of all conceivable motives. It was another theme he would work at over and over again.

* * * * * *

His personal diary breaks off after the Normandy break-out, only to pick up again on 6 September as they, and the Grenadier Group they were now complementing, reached Louvain. Before that the drive to the Belgian Capital had been, if not a joyride, certainly joyous. They left behind the landscape that had entrapped them for three months; the terrain of killing, of mis-shapen bodies burned and twisted, of dead bloated cows their legs stiff in the air, the roads strewn with knocked-out cars, jeeps and tanks, the villages blitzed, the people more shocked than jubilant, more resentful than relieved. The weather, hot sunshine and blue skies, seemed made for young men who were now, as they crossed the river systems into Belgium, suddenly cheered and greeted all the way by men, women and children who showered them with flowers, smothered them with kisses and plied them at every stop, through night and day as the cafés stayed open, with alcohol. The girls came out in clothes that had been mothballed for the duration of the war. Homes of collaborators were burned and looted. The cities were in a delirium of celebration.[47]

The excited absentee officer rushed to join his comrades:

> I was still in Bayeux when the Battery started the advance. I was thoroughly bored with giving lectures on Bocage tactics when all signs seemed to show that the Normandy fighting was over... I heard on the BBC news that British tanks had reached Beauvais. With the jeep still piled high with booty, and my map of the world folded to show Northern France I set out after them.

It was an "exhilarating" personal drive from Bayeux through Caen and down to Falaise, re-tracing the roads and battles and memories of the previous two months until he made Beauvais at dusk, only to find the Regiment had moved on. The Guards Armoured Division's personal route marker was a "77" road sign. It took him to Amiens – "where the world and his wife were carrying banners and I tasted the first fruit of liberation by being kissed by two very pretty girls simultaneously" – and on via crowds beyond Arras until "within a very short time I saw the battery of M10s drawn up on Douai Aerodrome, and the officers in a Hangar, drinking a toast in rum. It was the 2nd of September".[48]

The troops entered Brussels on 3 September. Q Battery, with the 5th Armoured Brigade Group, and with Acting Captain Williams now returned to command of A Troop, arrived at the outskirts at ten-fifteen that night. Half an hour after midnight on 4 September they were drawn up near the great cathedral, the Basilique. The official War Diary records: "Cheering crowds would not let us sleep until 0400 hours. They came back at 0700 hours and started all over again. The tanks by this time were completely covered with flowers."[49] Brussels would remain in the memory of these men and be, through the winter and beyond, the desired destination for 48-hour leave passes.

Never has any of us seen or believed in such wild joy and enthusiasm. The roar of the cheering, the huge crowds leaving such a narrow passage for the tanks to pass, all stretching out their hands to touch us as we went by, children in jeeps, tanks laden with flowers, girls riding on the back of motorcycles looking divinely pretty with their hair streaming in the wind.[50]

In the very first number of *Twentyone*, the Army newspaper he would edit in Germany from June 1945, Raymond Williams recounted the grimmer reality of the Brussels he had revisited about a year later – the return of the King and the Flemish demonstrations against him, the obvious economic crisis beneath "the gaiety we loved in the Belgians", the widespread Black Market. Amidst the tasted joys of new found horse-racing and old style cabarets, he advised his comrades:

The famous Brussels girls are still around but in very diminished numbers. More and more troops are seen with service girls, and perhaps because of the recent return of the DPs [deportees], many more Belgian men are seen with girls and incidentally with nearly all the attractive ones. In spite of all this it is still not safe to walk through the Place de Bronckere at dusk, unless you are strong minded and sober, or take a prophylactic station with you.[51]

So armed or not, the Acting Captain clearly cherished Brussels as much as anyone after surviving Normandy. In the same number of that newspaper he published a short story – "The Girl Who Couldn't Say Robert" – whose fictional twist returned to betrayal as the "quite irresistible... small blonde", Annette Vanderkindere, with whom the tank officer will dance and spend the night in the open, is revealed, a month later, as a collaborator, along with her brother Robert, who had betrayed Resistance members to the Gestapo. She had been sentenced to death. That was, at least directly, all fiction. The story's opening is pure re-call:

As we entered Brussels in September '44, the delirious welcome of the people seemed to become more feverish in every street. Thus while in Chaussée Ninove they had been content to throw lilac blooms, in the Boulevard Nord they began to throw bottles. There were bottles of champagne, straw flasks of chianti, flagons of beer and long tapering decanters of Benedictine. But the glories that lay inside them were not so readily appreciated as the patent fact that when they hit you on the head they hurt. My left eye was already showing signs of the bruise it had received back in Tournai from an underipe pear, and when I received a stinging blow from a champagne bottle just behind my left ear I decided that liberation was too rough a game, and got down inside the turret of my tank. I stayed there for a while, dividing my attention between the roar of the engine behind me and the boots of the wireless operator, who was hanging almost completely out through his hatch, when I saw thru [sic] the driver's periscope a pair of dangling female legs.[52]

All such encounters were, at this stage, brief ones for most of the Battery who were, after noon on 4 September. "with considerable difficulty extricated from its crowd of admirers". Williams had, however, again taken over A echelon from Captain Beaty, who had returned to HQ troop, and so he remained a while longer until they were moved to Schoot beyond the Albert Canal which had been seized and crossed with little enemy resistance on 6 September. Q Battery was now, with intermittent enemy contact, protecting the rear of 5 Guards Armoured Brigade, one of the divisions thrusting north to the Dutch frontier as the Allies stretched their lines to make the war shorter.

For a while there was a pause. On the wider front the 11th Armoured had taken the great port of Antwerp, which, undamaged, was a huge prize. Yet the British and Canadians did not sweep in to clear the Scheldt estuary, which was the key to using the port and, with the Germans moving to nullify the advantage, the delay would return to haunt them. The 21st Anti-Tank Regiment concentrated together again around Bourg-Leopold, resting in the sand-dunes between Hechtel and the Meuse-Escaut Canal just south of Holland, where they undertook serious maintenance work of their vehicles and enjoyed ENSA concerts.[53] Tactical errors over consolidating the possession of north-east Belgium and Holland seemed minor, at the time, compared with the strategic push that was about to occur.

> The detail of operation "Market Garden" came out early and the battery was addressed by Colonel Hulbert who said "it was going to be a great adventure and he wouldn't miss it for worlds"... The only immediate difficulty was breaking out of the Meuse-Escaut bridgehead and then, "See you by the Zuyder Zee..."[54]

This daring plan was the combination of airborne landings behind enemy lines and the near simultaneous seizure of the bridges at Eindhoven, Grave, Nijmegen and Arnhem which would pave the way along that direct road for an airborne "carpet" ride of sixty-five miles by armoured troops into North Holland and Germany itself: "We [had] stayed there ten days, well aware that something big was brewing, getting our tanks in good order again, and getting our first trips on leave to Brussels... with the champagne we had found in the Brussels custom-house flowing like water, it was a most pleasant interlude, and in the warm mid-September weather all our prospects seemed good."[55]
Operation Market Garden began at 1400 hours on Sunday 17 September. They stood in the dunes on their tanks and any other vehicles and watched the long lines of aircraft from south-east England flying over into the drop zones between Eindhoven and Grave, between Grave and Nijmegen and at Arnhem on the lower Rhine. The Irish Guards led the break out of the Meuse-Escaut bridgehead after an opening barrage and attacked straight up the main road to Eindhoven, whilst a "cabrank of Typhoons flew over the breakout area, diving with

rockets and machine guns". Speed of support for the airborne troops was essential to the fruition of Montgomery's bold plan whose prospects on paper seemed so good. On the ground the pattern of enforced delay and cautious follow-through quickly became evident and, ultimately, daunting.

The Irish Guards under Lieutenant Colonel J.O. Vandeleur were spearheading XXX Corps. They hit an ambush by a tough paratroop training unit armed with hand-held Panzerfausts who destroyed nine tanks in two minutes. Advance was halted until infantry came up to clear strong enemy forces packed around the bridgehead. It was after five that afternoon that Q Battery's M10s crossed "Joe's Bridge" and as "they halted, and were pulling to the side of the road for the night, Tony Handford [Lt. in Troop B], who was seeing his troop in, was killed instantly by a shell". The Regiment had "made little progress before halting for the night".[56]

When, four days later, after enormous sacrifice and gallantry the resistance of 1st Airborne Division at Arnhem was crushed and only the evacuation of survivors was left of the ground plan, both the strategic and the tactical recriminations began. The latter was directed at the pace and failure of the armoured units to get up. They had been stopped south of Eindhoven at the first serious encounter: they had hoped to reach that town within two hours.[57] Instead, conscious of the difficulties of travelling by night on a raised single road front, they waited. It was a slog the next day, too, with resistance at Aelst and Valkenswaard, before advance troops found a path to by-pass the defenders and charge them from the rear, until the road to Eindhoven was opened. Q Battery, its M10s abreast of the Grenadier tanks, dashed into the town as evening came. At the time it felt like a triumph: "Eindhoven was a wonderful sight; from somewhere or other orange cloth had been obtained sufficient to dress most of the small girls in frocks of the national colour, great orange flags hung from all the windows, and the genuine joy of all the inhabitants was very touching".[58]

The following morning, the 19th, it was on to the bridge at Sou, and from there to the Grave bridge over the Meuse held by American paratroopers. Behind the advance troops was a narrow fifty-mile salient choked with armour and infantry, subject to sniping attack and heavy counter-attack. Williams' A Echelon was "shot up badly by machine gunners along [this] road, every truck being hit". Their night march to reach Malden just south of Nijmegen was "slow and anxious". They harboured in a pine wood three miles south of the bridge. The fields all round were littered with parachutes and gliders. When dawn broke it would be Wednesday 20 September and the Guards were still six miles from Arnhem. Only six or so miles it would be said later. That is not how it seemed to the troops with whom Raymond Williams was serving.[59]

The vital bridge at Nijmegen had not been taken. US 82nd Airborne troops had, as planned, been dropped short rather than risk more casualties by dropping directly, even in small parties, onto the target. So, with heavy losses anyway, they had to fight in and through the suburbs of the town. When the Generals Horrocks and Adair of XXX Corps met with the American Brigadier General Jim Gavin they could still see Germans unconcernedly crossing the distant road of the steel arched bridge. They feared the bridge would be blown. Frontal assaults having failed, the objective was finally achieved by an outflanking manoeuvre by American troops who crossed the Waal downstream in inflatable boats. The atttackers lost half their force, 134 men, in this fierce assault but took the railway bridge and reached the northern end of the road bridge. What has remained so contentious is the failure of Guards Armoured to race on to Arnhem after a similarly courageous storming of the southern end by four tanks of the Grenadier Guards.[60] This attack had been supported by B and C Troops of Q Battery whilst the rest had been engaged throughout the day in support of American troops holding high ground in the Reichswald forest to the south east of Nijmegen. During that operation a Q Battery troop under Captain Beaty became the first British soldiers to cross the German frontier in a foray that returned thirty-five prisoners.[61] It was because of this kind of constant and brave action that so much resentment remained amongst these support troops at their alleged lack of vigour.

Williams' personal diary records, from his own and other eye-witness accounts, how these Battery troops rattled across in the dark, houses burning at the bridge's end, just after the "historic attack" of the Grenadiers: "No infantry could be contacted on the other side, and only four tanks, of which one had just been hit. It was a very anxious vigil until some American paratroops, who had crossed the Waal in assault boats, came in from the north, silently approaching through the darkness, each party, after the first suspicion, being very glad to see the other." The following day they secured the area, frightened off German tanks in a nearby wood from engaging with American infantry and harboured, with 5th Brigade Headquarters, "in a market garden under the railway embankment about four hundred yards over the bridge. A miserably wet period followed, during which the garden turned into a mud bath." Heavy mortar fire and shelling continued all day along with air raids on the Bridge and fighting from pockets of resistance.[62] No further advance, from the Irish Guards, was under-taken until 21 September at 11am on the road to Arnhem and stiff opposition from 10 SS Panzer was waiting. What remained of the airborne troops in that vicinity was brought out by 25 September and Arnhem largely remained in German hands until the end of the war. Allied losses were severe and the population of Arnhem, 100,000 and more, were expelled to face, under continuing German rule, a winter of severe hardship and deprivation for all of Holland.

For some analysts, even at the time, it was a cusp point of a war that was already won but was now prolonged by this failure. For others it remains a "rotten plan, poorly executed".[63] For those, like the gunners of Q Battery at Nijmegen, there was a need, still, for resolute defence of the tactical decisions they took on the ground. In September 1945, a year on, Captain Williams provided them with one in a short riposte called "Arnhem and the War Correspondents". The crux of the matter remained the road itself, "Hell's Highway", from Eindhoven onwards, so stuffed with troops and armour that delay was a fact of life, and then, beyond Nijmegen, so elevated and exposed that any mad dash would have been precisely that. This British Army fought with tanks supported by infantry but at Nijmegen there was no "bloody infantry". The road south was cut twice by counter attacks during these crucial days. Q Battery, "by this time operating more as an armoured squadron than an anti-tank battery, got rather widely deployed" from 20 September, and on 22 September two of their batteries "had to turn back with 32 Guards Brigade Group to restore the Centre-line which had been cut behind us", only returning to the Nijmegen area on 30 September.[64] Williams, seeing all this, was scathing about the flattening of perspective in tailor-managed journalese:

> I am commenting... because the general public, in my experience, has not been given any accurate picture of the battle which has become famous as "Arnhem". We constantly read of the gallant band of paratroops fighting in their desperate perimeter, waiting for the Second Army to link up with them and relieve them. Always the phrase is the "Second Army". Automatically the reader pictures a tiny, gallant band fighting tremendous odds while a few miles away all the might and power of a great army fails to reach them [but] the facts were quite otherwise.

The facts that he tells of the advance to Nijmegen are of the tough fighting and casualties that took the Guards on from the Albert Canal and across the narrow bridgehead, which was supposed to allow "a drive on more or less through a carpet of paratroops to beyond Arnhem [to] start fighting again to reach the Zuyder Zee". This was "not an army trying to reach one airborne division. It was an armoured division, with two infantry divisions following more slowly, trying to link up three airborne divisions." And in his view it was the forty-eight hours needed to capture the bridge at Nijmegen rather than driving across "an already captured bridge" that scuppered the possibility of progress. There is no apology from this officer over what happened, or did not happen, next:

> Then came the attempt to get north to Arnhem. But the mighty Second Army which the Arnhem war correspondents talk so backhandedly about consisted of the division

advancing in a one-tank front along raised roads, providing targets no anti-tank gunner could miss. Meanwhile the centre-line was cut behind us, and half the division had to turn back to re-open it. At one time both the Nijmegen bridges were unusable. These are the facts of the picture and they are rarely acknowledged. After all the delay, caused in the main, but not by lack of skill or courage, by the paratroops' failure to secure the vital points for the armoured division to traverse, the Germans had brought up too many reserves to allow the swift, clean, demoralising breakthroughs that had been planned.

... This is not a mean debunking of the First Airborne Division, whose courage and endurance were of the very highest order... [but]... but for the equally heroic battles of the Irish Guards in the initial breakthrough, the speed and initiative of the Household Cavalry, and finally the magnificent Grenadier victory at Nijmegen, supported throughout by the Divisional gunners and sappers, not a man of the First Airborne Division would have got away at all. If Nijmegen bridge had not been crossed and saved from destruction, there would have been no... survivors of the heroes of Arnhem.[65]

Q Battery was finally withdrawn south from the Nijmegen bridgehead and from fending off counter attacks in the second week of October, for "maintenance and rest" at Alverna between Grave and Nijmegen: "The winter lull had started for us."[66]

* * * * * *

For the three months that followed until this Army moved back onto the offensive Q Battery not only "lived in peace" but also through the "Second, Third and Fourth Champagne Ages".[67] There were occasional support expeditions as mopping-up operations continued to the east and north but first in Alverna in October, where they resorted to rum only when champagne ran out, the Battery put its feet up:

In Alverna we had a mess in a café fronting the main road, with white cane chairs on the verandah from which we watched the army go by. We were glanced at very superciliously by all the passing traffic. The Battery flag flew outside, adorned with its eleven swastikas for the tanks knocked out and its small German flag to celebrate HQ troop being first into Germany. We were photographed in front of it as King George and the Field Marshal passed, in the photograph too being an array of signs saying "Salvage", "POW Cage" and "No Right Turn".

The tanks were parked in the pinetrees, and the crews built log huts, some of them very elaborate, to live in. Sgt. Prosser's crew burned one down. A gaggle of officers and NCOs came up from the RHU again, and I ran another course for them.

There were frequent trips to Brussels where "the beautiful girls who had waved us in... were now purplefaced and chewed gum", and lunchtime drinking in the Corps Club at Grave. They moved in November to Sittard and settled in Born, a "little Limbourg village with very hospitable inhabitants". When the unexpected German counter-offensive started to the south east in the Ardennes in mid December they were put on stand-by, but nothing happened in their sector. Nearer to Christmas they were moved to Velm, south of St Trond, to oppose any German action across the Meuse and subsequent threats to Antwerp itself. None materialised. They did small-arms-fire training and maintenance and repair of their vehicles. They went out on armoured patrols or stood ready for support calls. Their woollen battledresses soaked up the dripping rain and, drenched to the bone, they snuffled through constant colds and influenza. Route marches and educational courses added to the tedium. The frantic yearly calendar of festive events was marked punctiliously but perfunctorily by these men waiting at this sinister border edge of their lives. A New Year's Eve dinner was held in the Goffin family farm house where the officers' mess was sited, and leave to England started after a great ceremonial draw for officers and men. Williams had grown a moustache and filled out. He was twenty-three and, despite the tone of jollity in his diary, was often miserable through a cold, sodden winter. But he was alive and, at home, in Pandy and Barnstaple, that was everything. For a prolonged period he could communicate with them again.

The only personal letters between Raymond and his family which seem to remain are those from him to Joy. There are twenty-seven of them, the first sent in October 1944 and the last in February 1945. Others written prior to that, as his father's notes for 1944 testify, gave in short missives the bare facts of his sailing and his surviving. Then, after the fighting had momentarily passed, in October, the letter about Brussels is "cheerful" and presents sent home to his family, a fountain pen and a box of powder, followed. Harry and Gwen spent Christmas in front of the fireside quietly: "but our thoughts are faraway".[68] To Joy he writes frequently, sometimes scribbled notes, requesting information, gossiping, reassuring, confessing despair but mostly full of yearning and love.

Enforced close proximity to Guards officers did not help the mood swings of the letter-writer. Letters arrived regularly if necessarily confined to a flimsy page or two and sometimes in batches as delays or troop movements backed them up. But what he was mostly doing as the Allies amassed their forces for the final assault was routine, whilst waiting for his personal liberation from the social and military carapace that trapped him:

> This regular letter-writing is all very well for your morale, but it's damned hard on my imagination. You see, nothing at all happens that would really interest you.
> I might even do as my dull friends around me – and pop your letter in front of me to answer. "Well, dear, I see you had a nice evening at the pictures – I wish I was there with you, dear. Yes, dear, the news does look good now – maybe you're right and we shall all be home for Christmas."
> And yet I love writing to you. For I can be frank at last. I am not by nature rude, although occasionally an odd barb will poke through my somnolent politeness, but, god,

189

Lenin, or the pound sterling, how bloody stupid these people are. And they have a veneer; they know exactly how dry sherry should be, and the difference between loot and booty, and just why England must maintain a standing army in post-war Europe to underline the edicts of the Foreign Secretary.

My only intellectual delight [other than reading] is a study of tangents as evinced by amateur billiard play on a decrepit Dutch table... But tonight I know for a certainty that the world is mine, for my mind is working again, and the razor edge is well ground on the sandstone of my nonsensical fellow-liberators.

And there is a moon through the light rain, and the windmill sails heave slowly, just tipping the golden spire of the monastery. And tonight I had your letter, and later I will dream of my head on your breast.[69]

He could dream of such a future as the first rains turned to hail and frost, followed by hard deep snowfalls, but immobility bred lassitude and misery in him. What remained unspoken between them was that he might, still, not yet return at all. He barely suppressed how downcast he was as he tardily responded to Joy's views:

Excuse... the dearth of letters. Apart from rather mixed circumstances, I have been feeling unsettled and unduly intolerant of the nonsense I hear talked around me. If I could strike an odd flash of sense it would settle me, but I have to wait for your letters for that.

You have twice asked for my opinions of the Greek situation... of course you know my views. I have forecast this suppression of any revolutionary forces in liberated Europe by British arms many times already. I only dread being personally involved in it, as I would quite definitely face court-martial rather than serve in such circumstances. It's a tragic business, which underlines how much of the real war has yet to be fought, indeed is only just beginning.[70]

As the personal and the public meshed here in profound psychological disengagement, Joy – real, longed-for and unattainable – was the life-line he had left even if he had to deepen her concerns for his state. At the end of the year, on 30 December he wrote:

> I am sorry to say I am still utterly depressed, and contemplating the most nonsensical things. I can't remember being so acutely and hopelessly miserable since some of the worst pangs of adolescence. I think it is mainly frustration. Apart from a certain revenge feeling for the Nazis (which in any case is utterly foreign to me) all the interest I had in the war has gone – and the power politics in its wake have just made me too cynical to want or believe or work for anything. I'm afraid this is colonising my whole life, and I can think of very little else. I am frankly desperate, as there is no-one but you who would even partially understand.[71]

The Army had been told that the first rota of home leaves would take some officers and other ranks home early in the New Year, but he drew the short straw, sixth out of six, and only came home, to Barnstaple and to Pandy, for brief leave in early May 1945.[72] That first personal liberation allowed him to see his daughter, now almost a year old; her picture, he told a startled Joy, reminded him strongly of Roosevelt's presidential opponent, Wendell Wilkie.[73] For the two of them it marked the beginning of a truly inseparable lifetime, one he had been sure of as he contemplated the future through the longest and wettest winter in the Low Countries since 1864.[74] He had scribbled impatiently just after the "lonely" Christmas of 1944 from his "large bedroom in a small village" that despite his continuing emotional dislocation he was "physically well – enjoying the hard cold weather" and that "Christmas was lovely with a full moon and hard-gleaming stars and a white frost-mantle on everything", but that:

I longed for you darling... Christ, how I long for you. To be able to get outside myself, to talk to someone sane, to rediscover each other, and make our wonderful love again. I'm told re-adjustment for husband and wife is difficult when a child arrives. We shall see, but equally certainly we shall adjust.

Goodnight, precious. Kiss my darling daughter for me, give my love to the family, and save yourself for me.[75]

The physical circumstances of these months, apart from rain and mud and snow, were, initially anyway, the best they had had "since the Campaign started". There were white-walled bedrooms, sprung beds, bathrooms to wash in and dining rooms to eat in, with cherry flan and champagne to enjoy – "Of course life isn't all like that." For entertainment there were the latest Hollywood movies – *Cover Girl* and even *Kansas City Kitty* – and American swing bands. He went on forty-eight hour leave to Antwerp for an "orgy of cinemas" and returned "feeling very mellow" but with a scarred nose and forehead, having gone through a windscreen when the car crashed. He asked for histories of Holland and "any changes in the German-Dutch frontier in the last hundred years" and "the rather older history of the Saar and Alsace-Lorraine. Please, it all fascinates me".[76]

For the first, and indeed only, time in his life he drank whatever, wherever and whenever he could, mostly gin and champagne, and spectacularly so in Brussels: "we drank in about twenty places, running the whole tariff from Benedictine to beer." Hangovers became constants along with tedious exercises and educational courses – "I'm still engaged in teaching presentable young men the facts of life. Frankly, at times, the deadly dullness of this... makes me want to do the same with some presentable young women. Of course there are none, so fidelity romps home unopposed" – all of whose residue of frustration led to the "Main outlet [which], as I told you before, is alcohol, of which we all drink too much".[77]

Through January 1945, his windcheater lined with locally acquired cat and rabbit fur, he continued to be-moan the biting cold, hard frosts and no coal. He was almost groaning too with the physical lack of Joy, as others went on and returned from leave:

> I'm so starved of love and, in spite of Merryn I'm sure you must be, that I fear we shall be quite immoderate when we have overcome the initial strangeness... We shall have that wonderful leave, precious, and I do remember the Foley Arms – Bearskin or no bearskin, you'll learn that the spiritual and intellectual love which keeps us close at this distance has its logical completion, and the whole love, and everything between us, will be lovelier than it's ever been.[78]

The absent father, who decidedly did not wish to be called "Dada" but "Raymond" whether he was there or not, was reaching out for a future life in any way he could – "The photograph of you and Merryn is daily gazed at and cherished. How lovely you both are" – even down to lessons in pronunciation of the name he had chosen for their daughter. It was to be said as "Maireen" in which the "err" was not as in "ferret" and the "e" as in "ai" or "ay". The insistence was because "my pronunciation of Merryn... is based on its origin which is as you well know Anglo-Saxon – in which the e is as I described it. The fact that the BBC pronounces an obscure Cornish village (where the Merryn is doubtless, being Celtic locality, of different origin) in the obvious way is no need for us to ignore the pronunciation that in our language gave birth to the word".[79] He was a long way here from his own "Celtic locality" whether as birthplace or later, much deeper, self-identification. It was as if the Cambridge of his heady time was bubbling up before the final trial of arms. As indeed it actually had.

The spring, Dutch sunshine and Dutch crocuses in thawing woods, had cheered his spirits. In Brussels in February he had seen the Sadlers Wells Ballet once more, four productions, with Ninette de Valois, and Robert Helpmann's *Miracle in the Gorbals* – "terribly exciting". For a wife to whom he confessed: "I regret that I failed to get your stockings. All I could find were artificial silk, which I presume you don't want", when she certainly did, his rapture may have sounded as off-key as his earlier misery was distressing:

I also met the company afterwards, and went to one of their rehearsals, of "Dante Sonata". Margot Fonteyn is really a lovely dancer, and such a funny little thing, dark and pretty in a Jewish sort of way, with lovely dark eyes. Dear Bobby Helpmann is much as ever. Alexis Rassine is their second male dancer – and is apparently John Lehmann's new boyfriend. Christ, how faraway all that clique seems. But I was glad to see the ballet, and it refreshed me thoroughly.[80]

That letter ended with the perhaps more reassuring postscript that he had finished his diary – "or rather I have brought it up to date" – and that he would "bring it home with me – you may like it". As he wrote that, he knew the War had started up again for the 21st Anti-Tank Regiment.

In fact the period of stasis had ended the previous day:

> ... in the early days of February, with the Russians reaching the Oder, rumours of an impending battle began to spread. The American band of the AEF drank a highball to those all-out fighting men in the East, and the local inhabitants of Velm watched our packing, were more than ever kind to us, and murmured to each other "Berlin".
> The roar of tanks passing the office window drowned the rattle of the typewriter. It was February 6th and we were moving to Tilburg in the morning.[81]

* * * * * *

The Regiment was concentrated at Tilburg, north east of Antwerp, and kept on one hour's notice to move out for over two weeks. Their role, from here to the end of the war, was to support the attacks on successive military objectives as the 21st Army advanced, finally and cautiously, into Germany. The Americans, to the south and east of the British, rolled over the remnants of major resistance after their bloody repulse, in the Battle of the Bulge, of the final serious German counter-offensives in the Ardennes in December and January. To the east two juggernaut Soviet armies were set to crush the remnants of Third Reich military power in months of savage fighting and butchery. The Allies had in effect won but there was still opposition along the frontiers of the Rhine and casualties to suffer in the sleet and rain which shrouded the hard slog of Operation Veritable in the Reichswald and beyond.

The 21st Anti-Tank Regiment had moved up, once more, to the Nijmegen area on 22 February and the next day followed the advance into Germany itself. Battery HQ – whose HQ Troop Captain Williams was temporarily commanding – was established, to some grim satisfaction, in the former residence of the local Hitler Jugend leader at "38 Adolph Hitler Straat" in Pfalzdorf. In early March, with Captain Williams having once more rejoined A Echelon as its commander, they advanced to a position between Winnekdonk and Kapellen, linking up with the Irish Guards Group prior to an attack on Hamb which the Guards took. Their role was as a counter-attacking formation guarding the rear of the Irish Guards by preventing any enemy thrust down lateral roads. At this point, so superior were the Allies in armour and equipment that the men in towed batteries were retrained as mobile infantry. The Army's tactics remained the same: use of overwhelming superiority to dictate the pace of battle and preserve its soldiers' lives. By the end of March, after more intensive gun barrages and smokescreens, Montgomery's Army crossed the Rhine, now virtually undefended on its western side and with scant opposition on the further bank. From here on the nature of this anti-tank regiment changed to reflect the paucity of tanks the Allies now faced in general, and so the self-propelled guns of the Battery became armoured squadrons. As such they would see their last action in the last few weeks of the War in the company of 5th Guards Armoured Brigade.[82]

Their primary task now was to cover the roads around the main advance and to go out on armoured patrols on the flanks of the advance when it became static. Resistance could still be stiff, especially in the wooded country they traversed, but the Battery had no casualties and, increasingly, were used to round up POWs or prevent Dutch civilians crossing the borders "to loot German homes". Q Battery was now, from

9 April, part of the so-called "Busterforce" (after the Battery Commander's personally chosen nickname), operating as spare Armoured squadrons "as the prospects of our employment in an ordinary anti-tank role were becoming remote".[83] Intermittent shelling and mortaring of troops by day and night made for continued discomfort and trepidation, since the end, and personal safety, was now so near. A Echelon was at Vechtel by 11 April and on to Elsdorf on 20 April. Some sections of the Battery were now straightforwardly acting as auxiliary infantry as the last redoubts of small villages and townships fell on the north-eastern plain of a devastated Germany. The Regiment's Historical Notes concluded its war with matter-of-fact satisfaction:

> Operations came to a close with the relief of [the POW and Concentration Camp] Sandbostel by the Grenadier Group of 5 Guards Brigade Group with Busterforce on 28 April. "Y" Battery got two enemy SP guns on the Westertinke road, the last blood to the regiment in the campaign.[84]

In the afternoon, the next day, 29 April, Hitler took his own life. On 4 May, as the Regiment closely guarded SS and Paratroops now rounded up at Sandbostel, all offensive action ceased. On 5 May the enemy surrendered on the 21st Army Group Front and on 8 May the war in the west was formally ended. And Captain Raymond Williams had, at last, been granted leave. His father recorded the joy:

4 May, Friday –   We are thrilled to have the phone call from Barnstaple telling us Jim is safely home.

6 May, Sunday –   At 6.45pm we are excited to welcome Jim and Joy and dear little Merryn. They all look extremely well and we are proud.

8 May, Tuesday – VE day and the realisation is received by us with quiet thankfulness.[85]

By the weekend Jim was back with his Regiment. Harry Williams remarked to himself how the weather, close and stormy, had given way to brilliant sunshine and that although it was "extremely hot and an effort to do any work" he had used Saturday to make "a start in the Station Wilderness" by planting "Wallflowers and Sweet Williams at Station". This was all duly recorded in the separate note book he meticulously kept for his plants, vegetables and seeds.

Chapter 5

"A Quality Beyond Art"

In northern Germany the rhythm of life and of growth was not so easily resumed. The immediate horror for the Regiment was the nature of the typhus-infested Sandbostel Concentration Camp where both political and military prisoners had been held. The dead, the dying and the barely existing were found, ankle deep in their own excrement, in the same huts. Two thousand out of the twenty two thousand inmates had died in the ten days before liberation. For the troops burial parties and medical relief now replaced the urgency of killing and advancing; and all the while sporadic mortar fire and sniping continued.[1] Those who had known Hamburg before the war quailed at the immense destruction they now witnessed; in a single night over forty thousand had perished in the fire storms wrought by the air raids of July 1943.[2] Quartermaster clerk, G.C. Miller who was a journalist by profession, wrote home on 8 May:

> The Hamburg we knew is a thing of the past. It is just a corpse of a city now and not a pleasant sight to see. The damage is appalling. Miles and miles of shells of buildings. As we approached the centre of the city... the damage seemed to grow less and the place became more or less recognisable. There wasn't a piece of glass left in the roof of the Central Station, but the big swastika above the entrance was still there... There is running water and electric light though the latter is rather dim... The streets of Hamburg are thronged with people all day until 7 in the evening, when everyone except us and the civil police have to be indoors.[3]

The British Liberation Army – soon to be renamed, again, as the British Army of the Rhine – ringed and penetrated the city and its out-

198

lying areas, holding and freeing up the Kiel Canal especially, in a mode of occupation that was rapidly transformed into another military way of life. Here, too, cafés and beer cellars became their haunts and, initially with great discretion, the victors strolled in a May heatwave down bombed and burned out avenues under chestnut trees in bloom and past municipal gardens in incongruous flower. What impressed British observers was the speed and resolution with which German civilians – the contrast with the Belgians was unfavourable – set to work to rebuild and reconstruct. Shop fronts were restored in the main shopping streets. Lorries took four-wheeled trailer carts out of the city with rubble and returned with rhubarb, lettuce and whatever else could be foraged from the countryside. The cinemas were quickly up and running with the latest British and American movies for the troops, as well as theatre from the Old Vic Company with Laurence Olivier, Sybil Thorndike, Ralph Richardson and Joyce Redman in *Arms and the Man* and *Richard III* and for two weeks in June, productions of *Richard II* and *Peer Gynt*.

The 21st Anti-Tank Regiment were informed of all this, and much more, by their new regimental newspaper, *Twentyone*.[4] It first appeared on 29 June and thereafter every Saturday in its eight page format, largely thanks "to the enormous amount of hard work put into it by its first Editor, Captain Raymond Williams". It was indeed a full week's work from editorial conferences on Sunday with representatives of all the Batteries, through to collation of material to printing by the press at Pinneberg by German linotype operators, proof-reading, and then distribution for each Saturday, with the crucial Entertainment Guide only set and inserted as late as the Friday afternoon. The Army hierarchy kept a watching brief on editorial policy and contents but in the format and content of the first seventeen numbers of *Twentyone* we can distinctly detect the voice of its pseudonymous editor, Michael Pope.

The Regiment had finally left the 5 Guards Armoured Brigade of which it had formed a part since the Normandy landings to concentrate with the 7th Armoured Divison of the Royal Artillery south of Cuxhaven near Pinneberg, then at Wister in the marshlands in a blustery cold August, until finally they settled at Brunsbütell. This latter town on the north bank of the canal was formerly a ship-building area, its yards claimed back from the sea. The pre-war population, now swollen by evacuees, had doubled to ten thousand. To the south of the canal was Koog, the town's other quarter and site of the Regimental Headquarters. Apparently anything was an improvement on Wister but this was still dreary and soul-sapping countryside even for the leisure of amateur sailors. The original inhabitants claimed to be old English stock but they really meant, and were right, that it was from an earlier Brunsbüttel that Angles had sailed to England. So, it was under the slightly ironical headline "Land of Our Fathers" that Michael Pope told his readers: "We should feel that we are coming home to Brunsbüttel. It has been a trading and fishing port for more than seven hundred years and even before that it was from this coastline that the early English settlers sailed to Britain".[5]

Brunsbüttel's new occupants were scarcely less anxious to leave. It was the primary task of *Twentyone* to lift morale in a civilian army wearied of fighting and, perhaps, to suggest multiple futures. Its prime weapon was a lively format and readability. In its eight pages were packed cartoons, some quite risqué, gossip, sporting news, lots of photographs of their mates and themselves, crossword puzzles, reminiscence and narrative of the past war, occasional stories, weekly back-page pin-ups and vigorous discussion. This was largely undertaken in Pope's Editorials and, though the paper kept up a running mystery about Pope's real identity, he made no effort to disguise his past or present opinions. The very first number of *Twentyone* claimed a free press as "the best sign of a healthy community" and pointedly added: "A paper based on the partiality of merit alone, and not on rank or prejudice, would be the sign of a good regiment. This is a good regiment, and it is up to you, its members, to see that our paper becomes truly representative of the best that's in us".[6]

The first troublesome question for the Army in occupied Germany was the non-fraternisation order placed on the troops. The immediate and more pressing news, however, concerning echoes of the British General Election of 5 July 1945, was reported with a whimsical fairness, just short of outright partiality. The day after the poll the paper published a forthright article, "Let the People Govern".[7] When the results became known on 26 July, Labour had 393 seats to the Conservatives' 213 and almost 50% of all votes cast. The services had voted overwhelmingly for Labour and, perhaps even more than those at home, for a new country. *Twentyone*'s editorial stood as "amazed" as everyone else, but quickly moved on to declare Harold Laski (1893-1950), Labour's troublesome Chairman and still left-wing academic, "the most honest and farseeing man in the Labour Party during the election" for facing the future (Labour's Election slogan) with realism at the inevitable "showdown between the Labour Government and the present leaders of industry and finance". Pope concluded that Laski was "a political thinker and not an electioneering politician".[8] He might have concluded the same about himself.

Michael Pope continued to express his political views – on the situation in Indonesia, in Poland, in Palestine – but briefly and despairing of any sense of lasting international co-operation. Nearer to home he had scorned the reconciliation that moved so quickly as the fraternisation ban was lifted in early July. Scorn is too mild a word, perhaps, for the mood that made him refer to himself as "an unrepenting apostle of righteous hatred". And this was because, he believed, to stop "day-dreaming" of an end to the "age-old nightmares of war and squalor" it was necessary to "go beyond [the] airy politics: who will run the mines; who will own the land; who will own transport? All these are as nothing beside the vital question – who will own power?"[9] To that end he had railed against the common mourning for soldiers on both sides in Pinneberg Church. He, in turn, was sharply rebuked in a number of letters for his attitudes, which were seen as at once un-Christian and insufficiently sensitive to genuine patriotism as opposed to political fanaticism. He was told by his correspondents that no new world could grow in the soil of hatred. It only caused him to re-iterate his views and to review his personal war:

I have heard so many voices raised in mock horror at my suggestion that the memory of a fascist soldier should be guarded in contempt and hate, and never reverence, that I am wondering if I have been asleep these last five years, and the war has just been something I dreamed up. [But] I am not mocking the heart that mourns the loss of a loved one. What I am attacking is national mourning. Those red wreaths in Pinneberg church made me furious because they were so obviously a corporate tribute. These were not the silent offerings of a bereaved parent, the little bunches of wildflowers... we see and respect on so many quiet graves. No. Red scrolls, red scrolls, red scrolls all alike devoid of personality – a corporate tribute, something symbolic and collective – with the flamboyancy of a people that has embodied fascism. The banners of the swastika, that waved at Nuremburg, that carried death, lying, torture and famine to Guernica, Rotterdam, Lidice, Rostov and Coventry, are still waving, disguised as mourning wreaths, in the chancel of Pinneberg church.

Nor did his defence stop at emotional revulsion; "righteous hatred", he insisted, was a synonym for "just war". To attack him, then, was to attack "all of us, this great army, for supporting a just war":

Three years before the war I was a Christian pacifist. The Sermon on the Mount was for me the final embodiment of truth. Faced with war, with fascism, having seen what was happening to a Europe that was turning to Hitler its other cheek, I found it no longer satisfied me. I may have been wrong. But the only people who attempt to translate the great principles of the Sermon on the Mount into political belief are the Christian pacifists. I respect them. The people I don't respect are the sitters on the fence who claim to accept Christian doctrine... yet accepted and supported the war. Read the Sermon on the Mount, as I have just re-read it. Ask yourself if there can be anyone so purblind as to accept that and accept war in one and the same breath. If we were willing to kill, we are hypocrites or mercenaries if we

are not willing to hate… Let us with a purpose unclouded by
sentimentality get down to the job of re-building peace in
Europe, the greatest of all memorials to our own dead, and
from which a refusal to think straight has kept us so long.
Let us go on hating fascism which caused this destruction,
and go on working for all that is true, all that is noble, all
that is human, all that is opposed to the horror we hated,
and which at least I still hate.[10]

Most of his strongest opinions, love or hate, were reserved for his
persona of Michael Pope. Articles, by "RW", on reform of the Lords or
voting systems were measured undergraduate reflections and the one
story using Joy's maiden name was a piece of melodrama ready for the
screen. Deeper passions were reserved for Pope who could be ebullient
about Lauren Bacall and *The Cabinet of Dr Caligari* but positively lyrical
about Capra's *Mr Deedes Goes to Town*. The favoured word from that
Thirties' social comedy was "pixillated" and it crops up over and over
in Pope's editorial pronouncements to express his bemusement at the
indecipherability of the world and its ways. Film, almost reverentially
so, is mentioned more than any other art form and he begins to muse
on its social effects as well as on structural support for the still young
industry. On the latter he was unequivocally committed to developing
quality in British films as against the commercial drive to make enough
to export to the American market by deliberately sacrificing "our film
style". This is what had happened when Quota requirements were
introduced to prevent American films swamping Britain, and the US
companies had simply created subsidiary companies to "make enough"
that was home produced, but that was not home grown. Pope's view
was that the talent that had gone, in the war, into the documentary
units' brilliant war-time shorts should be nurtured now to overcome the
prejudice against short features being shown in cinemas. He was not
hopeful that quality in post-war Britain could long prevail against "the
noise and variable quality of Hollywood because J.A. Rank, who now
has virtual control of the industry seems to envy American methods…
His own taste in films are religious shorts".

Michael Pope's proposal, one that he would pursue ardently in the immediate post-war years, was to convince audiences that short, possibly poetic films, might be added to that regular and commercial "Full Supporting Progamme" which he saw as the cynical add-on to the full social whirl of lights, rich curtains, Persian carpets and ice creams.

> But must good short films always be cartoons or docu-mentaries? Is there to be no cinema counterpart to the short story? It is obviously possible from a technical and artistic viewpoint; at the moment it is impossible commercially... [the short] is thrown in free, no great trouble or expense is incurred in making it. The horrible results we know.
>
> The majority don't really want all this; it's taken regularly because it is offered regularly, and offered as a monopoly. Producers, directors, authors, editors invariably under-estimate their audiences. But audiences are inarticulate...[11]

Which was, maybe, another way of saying that he thought they might need their very own champions, those working-class audiences, to better articulate their underestimated cultural needs. His instinct already was to identify the cultural process which lay behind overt political change and which, he felt, could move society on to fuller demands or subvert popular taste by pixillation.

Editing *Twentyone* was another Army job he had performed efficiently. At times it seems it was a labour of love, but mostly so when he broke the bounds of army decorum. From the ashes of his combat bitterness there had come a cold tempering of his intellect, almost all of it directed towards finding a future of permanent personal freedom to express his vision. That, too, would broaden as it sharpened but, indisputably, it was bound by the tensions and duty held within a skein of human relationships. He could sound, at times, quite priggish about this but since he lived it he spoke it; or rather, he wrote it, spinning off his larger distaste for fraternisation to a running disdain for any closer contacts. At first the latter is seen as presenting no difference from being in any "port town" where prostitutes are "the most fervent internationalists" in the world, but when the cinema for the 3,000 troops at Wilster is closed for lack of films (all the best ones were being shown in Hamburg) he widens his lens: "Entertainment must be local to provide an adequate alternative to the streets. The English newspapers scream about fraternisation; why don't they scream to give us some alternative? Let us be quite frank. The VD rate is steadily rising. Good entertainment facilities can check it, although they will never stop it. But for the clean-living majority of this Army, it is not too much to say that on a good entertainment programme depends both moral and physical health."

He had assured *Twentyone* readers that he had personally been "strong-minded" on leave in Brussels. His night forays into Hamburg almost persuaded him that the street lamps and the unscreened lights of hotels and apartment blocks could soften the evidence of its physical destruction into a cinematic glamour that could conceal "the evil that none can be blamed for thinking is the heart of Germany." The personification of that was a figure "with obvious evil intent" who moved mysteriously towards him from a doorway. He feared the worst – "I stiffened. It was within two yards... And then came the sickening international "Good evening, darling" of the prostitute. In a German accent! 'Gut abening, tarlein'. "[12]

His meanderings on the subject had been heightened by a brief leave he took in Copenhagen in early September. He saw Denmark as everything that Germany was not and had not been – "... a smiling country. The Danes are a laughing people. The colour and freshness of the land after an ashen-grey Germany is immediately exhilarating." His praise for a nation that had resisted was unstinting. The ubiquity of English speakers, English books and English-language films all helped, of course, but so did the well-laid out flats, the lack of pretension – "The Danes have little imperial tradition, and so have very little room for ceremony" – and the acceptance of planning, of towns and taxes, as civic goods. He was no kill-joy in Copenhagen where "it is difficult to stop life becoming one long succession of parties" and "monumental meals" are washed down with schnapps, beer and gin before "dancing either at the public balls (rather dull) or at the Bellevue which is excellent". There is more than a hint that he had glimpsed a society he would like to see replicated: "Politically, Denmark is a practising democracy, and the effects of planned government is everywhere apparent. The real reason for the abundance of food is the existence of the efficient cooperative movement: the way price controls are observed shows that they not only preach democracy but are fit to live under it." But he knows, too, what his comrades also want to hear, and what he needs to tell them.

> ... so much of the royal time there is because you are an English soldier. The occupying Germans had a joke about the Danes all having English sickness (VD). They have certainly never wavered in their faith in England, and their spontaneous kindness to an Englishman is remarkable. The women? There seems to be a rather smart divorce set, very international types. There is a great percentage of natural blondes; many pretty little dark girls who look very French. There is a sort of English average standard of morals; the worst types of women seemed to me to gather in the officers' club; the respectable ones are the very great majority everywhere else. The Danes used to call the cheap women who went with the Germans "field mattresses". They call the same women who cavort the midnight streets with Englishmen "channel featherbeds". It's revealing that! To me it indicates a morally healthy country... they are a sane people, they celebrate their freedom, and entertain their allies, without casting overboard all the moral values which are the structure of their social life. Most Englishmen, after so much different experience in other liberated countries, will, as I did, prefer it that way.[13]

Clearly, he was more than ready to come home. There was a brief trip home in mid September, and then a month later his father writes: "I read 'Michael Pope' and wonder what it means. Is it goodbye to the Army? I phone Joy and we get the grand news of Jim's demob and return to Cambridge. Both very very glad."[14]

Michael Pope had written his last Editorial on the previous Saturday. It had begun, wistfully enough, with praise "even in Schleswig Holstein" for the russet colour of autumn and "the sheer beauty and awe of Brunsbüttel locks at night", where "As you enter from the north bank, and pass the guard, there is a wall and a flight of steps whose contrast in symmetry and shadow with the viscous water lapping at the quay has a quality beyond art. A ship hoots in the estuary, a red lamp swings forlornly over the lapping debris-edge of the water. The trees on the island wrinkle in the north sea wind." He was scripting his way out of Army mentality and editing his mind for an artist's future: "I don't know whether there is any precedent for a Pope to abdicate. But I'm putting my mitre into stores, and sailing from Ostend in the morning. Thank you all for listening."[15]

The next time Raymond Williams appeared on the pages of *Twentyone* it was as himself, photographed with his "eldest unmarried daughter", and from Cambridge. Only the weather on the other side of the North Sea was unchanged. Both Cambridge and its returning student were very different from the place and the man of 1941.

* * * * * *

Returning servicemen made the immediate post-war years at university distinctive ones, for both teachers and taught. Old certainties had become, for some, new habits. At Cambridge, former party loyalties could not be taken for granted. Stellar figures of the 1930's undergraduate courses, such as Williams and Eric Hobsbawm, the first person he encountered in the winter of 1946, detected a religiosity that was as novel as it was apparent; both agreed that the world of the university was quite different now. Flatness, confusion and relief were the emotions which predominated, along with an unremitting seriousness of purpose for those, with academic ambition, who had seen their twenties slip by without personal achievements to register.[16] Or almost so, for Williams had left the Army with an encomium in print, "R.H.W. An appreciation":

A change of Editor is an event in the life of any publication. The departure of the first Editor is even more important. He it is who has the task of bringing a paper to life. A first issue is very much of a gamble. Is it what is wanted? Will its standard be too high to maintain? Too low to interest? As a Service paper will it offend unless subject to strict censorship? Will censorship strangle it at birth?

Successfully to steer the correct course through all these possible snags was no mean feat... Captain Williams has returned to Trinity College, Cambridge as a research student in English... although no longer on our staff he, together with his shadows Michael Pope and Peter Dalling, will continue to make occasional appearances in our columns.[17]

Twentyone had been his first solid creation as writer/editor and he deeply valued it for its insistent seriousness of tone and its popular reach. He had actually given his full-time occupation on his wedding certificate as "Journalist" and the wish had been fulfilled in wartime necessity. Now, in the months of re-adjustment down to Christmas 1945, as a third-year undergraduate and a family man rather than a free-wheeling "research student", he did not find it easy, or even desirable, to cut the emotional ties along with the more readily relinquished physical ones of an Army existence. The play he completed before the year's end was ironically entitled 'Liberation'. He was anything but liberated as he tried to make wider sense of the moral impact of the war. He sent a paper-bound copy of 'Liberation', dated December 1945, to his pre-war acquaintance, Bernard Miles (1907-91), whose war-time fame in Noel Coward's film *In Which We Serve* (1942) and then work as actor-director for the Old Vic Company now made him an important name for Raymond to be able to contact directly. The response was a warm one and must have kindled further his sense of himself as a possible playwright since Miles offered more than praise:

My Dear Raymond,

I have greatly read and enjoyed your play. I think it has a lot of magnificent stuff in it and I think that you will, if you set your mind to it, *be a fine playwright*. The play has a lot of wit and a lot of lovely things in the way of memorable lines – and some fine situations. A few technical awkwardnesses could easily be remedied...

And if it could be managed – if I am free and so on – I should greatly like to do the production for you, and I feel I could make something very moving out of it...

Let me see you when you are in Town

very many congratulations

As ever

Bernard

You can tell any of the people you send it to that I would like to be associated with it either as actor or producer.[18]

He had listed four "small ventures" as theatres that might take it on but warned "I don't know whether you'd have the least hope of getting it produced just yet – probably the moment for war plays is not yet". Clearly Miles was right about that though there is no extant evidence that the play did make the suggested rounds. Like almost all of his direct wartime writing, Raymond Williams let it lie. It may be, too, that the rather arch naturalistic conventions of this three-act play quickly fell out of favour with a writer whose interest in the poetic verse dramas of the late 1940s was about to take off. Either way it is difficult to read it today without a sense of the over-theatricality of its thuddingly coincidental plotting and the centre-stage rhetoric of both dialogue and monologue. What remains, bearing in mind the time of its writing, is the startling unwillingness to place blame or shame on a medley cast of collaborators (bureaucratic and horizontal), soldiers

(German and English), resisters (proletarian militants, thoughtful compromisers, drunken revengers) and, too, the suggestion of a war that would have disturbing personal effects beyond its formal ending.[19]

The scene is a street café near a bridge over a canal at the western end of a Belgian village in September 1944. That remains static. What changes is the retreat of the Germans, the coming of the English and the return, into conflict, of the Germans. Whilst this happens those who had befriended the Germans, from female café owner to Burgomaster, defend their actions as legal or natural (what else to do?) and are, in turn, quizzed and berated by shades of friend and foe. The sub-plot concerns the secret marriage of the Burgomaster's daughter to Max Rolland, the "Fascist" schoolteacher who had worked, in uniform, with the Gestapo. In fact they are both resistance fighters.

Inevitably the husband, spotted in uniform as he flees from the Germans who have finally understood (and wounded him), is killed along with the Burgomaster by avenging villagers emboldened by British Liberation. Others in that local Resistance – Antoine Vogel, unsure of the turncoat's real allegiance, or Paul Maassen, in love with Sonya, the Burgomaster's daughter – now hail Max as a Hero and Martyr and lament their own complicity. Paul mocks the Communist Vogel for talking of a fight when only managing an incident of church-burning and revenge killing:

> Maassen: So you were sorry you had no chance to fight them before they left. And in your disappointment you arranged a little excitement of your own.
>
> Vogel: I won't take that from you, Maassen.
>
> Maassen: Don't be a fool, Vogel. We'll all have to take worse. The fire and killing of those two men last night has burned its way into all our histories. If we are ever again to be rational, let us be honest about our motives.

Vogel: They're not exactly Christian virtues.

Maassen: I'm no religious opium-smoker, whatever your
           jargon might call me... But all civilised
           experience has shown us that violence is evil
           both in itself and in its issue. You'll try to
           minimise the incident, I know. Two lives
           destroyed during a war which has so
           destroyed so many millions may seem trivial.
           One of them a traitor, stupid but still a villain,
           the other at least wearing the uniform of
           treachery. A burned house can be rebuilt. All
           this you can say, but I know, and you know,
           that those excuses are only soothing ointment
           for our hands and can never touch the heart of
           the thing which is happening to us.

Vogel: What is this thing? The enemy tanks, perhaps
           coming this way?

Maassen: The tanks are nothing to it. It is our liberation,
           our gateway to the new life, being fouled in its
           first hours by all the filthy horrors of the old.

But none of it ends there as watery theoretical hopes are countered
by the circumstances of actual lives and by Sonya's determination not
to let her unborn child's future be sullied by either Maassen's lack of
optimistic will or Vogel's blind wilfulness. Besides, as the play ends,
the war continues.

If, in his confrontation of the demons he had taken with him in and
out of the war Raymond Williams paused here, at the year's end in
1945, in a more consciously multi-faceted fashion than he had brought
to the early pages of *Twentyone*, there was nonetheless no ambiguity
about his disdain for those who commented on the conduct of war and
its aftermath from the security of home and newspapers. As he went

through his academic paces in 1945/6 his memory still kept taking him back. The last published sign of this, until *Loyalties* in 1985, came in a bravura piece of writing, more prose effect than prose narrative, in April 1946, when he placed "Nijmegen Bridge"[20] in the Cambridge journal, appropriately also named, *The Bridge*. It is just four pages long. There is a page of overheard snatched dialogue between husband, wife and news vendor either side of a staccato burst of men and tanks in action. Then a middle section which ends with "the sound of marching men. The irregular clatter of nailed boots of British infantry moving up… [passing the tanks] in staggered lines… on each side of the roadway. A section of guns moves silently past and on. And still come infantry, marching stolidly, awkwardly. A firm bridgehead is held. When it is light they will boil tea and gather in the dead." And finally, as a counterpoint, the newspaper buyer and reader, for whom the war was not going fast enough at Arnhem, is placed, on a train, in post-war Holland:

> "Is this Nijmegen bridge?"
> "We're on the rail bridge. That's the road bridge."
> "Wonder it didn't get blown in the war."
> "This one did, by some divers. Didn't get the road bridge, though."
> "That's why the train is going slow."
> "Yes, not as fast as I'd like to see it."
> "God, look at those kids."
> "Always run by the train for food."
> "Throw 'em that bun I couldn't eat."
>
> …
>
> "Surely the train'll go faster now."
> "All the engines got shot up in the war."
> "And the stations."
> "And the ports."
> "And the lorries."
> "That's better."
> "Last of those kids."
> "Going quite fast now."

The whole experience of war had, perhaps, gone too fast for Williams to absorb with any facility more than anger or loyalty in play. His wife's memory of him at this abrupt time of return was as someone suddenly matured[21] but also gravely reserved. He was back but not quite, and for a while to come, fully present in his new life of partial liberation. He had kept his promise, for the first few months, to keep in touch with those now out of sight, through the newspaper he had run. It was the early and immediate Class B release of undergraduates with incomplete degrees that had given him his exit. He wrote to those who still waited of the anti-climactic journey of re-entry:

> I left Brunsbüttel on Saturday. Michael Pope came with me, not feeling too well. So many goodbyes, and so many unsuspected emotions at leaving the regiment and the army, were not good for his constitution. He'll get over it, but not quickly.

The actual journey home was not quick either. Transport difficulties kept him in Hamburg over the weekend until he took a train to Ostend on Monday (time, at least, to see the brilliant *Double Indemnity*) and then by tank-landing ship ("The craft was LST 198, a very near relation to 199 on which half the regiment, including myself, originally travelled to Normandy... a nice symmetry to my exit from Europe") to Tilbury by Wednesday morning. Then it was travel to Woolwich and the Royal Artillery Depot where officers in transit and on release mingled in great and bewildered number. The divesting of the uniform was for him as so many others a generalised rite of passage but one alleviated by small personal touches. After a night "with friends in town" he proceeded to Olympia and the selection of clothes, thanks to a "rather superior sausage machine":

> After a certain amount of rummaging and polite refusals on my part I got the suit I wanted, and was pleased beyond my dreams. I also got a good Burberry. Then the snags

came up. The suit was grey, and there were only blue shirts; only green or blue ties; only green or brown hats. None of these items was at all up to the quality of the suit… But the shoes are good, and the socks have the right colour range, if they are rather short in the leg… A most impressive service on the whole. And so I was out. [But]… "Twentyone" will always retain a very high priority of interest for me. Sitting now over tea and toast in The Union, I realise that I left so much of my heart with the regiment that only continued contact through "Twentyone" with you all can satisfy my strange loneliness.[22]

He was now lodging in a house at the top of Victoria Road, a curving thoroughfare just north of Trinity College at the centre of Cambridge; Joy and Merryn were with Joy's mother in Barnstaple; and Pandy, where he sent long weekly letters, would not see him until term ended in December.[23] It was already very cold. Coal was rationed and whisky in short supply. He exhausted his cheap Naafi cigarettes and discovered the variety but "fantastic civilian prices" of all others. He ate in restaurants to eke out his rations. He studied the "Seventeenth-century moralists"; worked alone and enjoyed the solitude; he started "a book called 'Alice in Zombieland' which should be published in late spring" and avoided "dreary and deserted pubs full of platinum blondes".[24] A zombie, he added, as explanation of his projected book's title is "a body that looks alive, and goes through all the motions but is dead, quite dead".[25]

His last appearance in *Twentyone* was adjacent to the back page pin-up, as a snapshot of a newly be-suited, moustachioed, "lean and sallow", old young man in Trinity's Great Quad. He stands sideways on and looks back wistfully. Time, even more than distance, was moving him away, even as he expressed guilt at the lessening of his contact. So many other things were now happening. There was a filmscript to write on an ex-serviceman's response to university life, with commentary and dialogue easy to do but hard to match to "visuals", and "the nightmare sequence too arty" for the technicians;

and plays and films to see: "two Shaw plays, an Oscar Wilde in French, two German films, a Russian film, five French films, eight American films". It has the whirling feel of a 1930s which, at least culturally, has not entirely disappeared: "On the strength of a lingering reputation as a red, I'm asked to debate [in the Union] against Quintin Hogg. We have a pleasant evening and talk some sense over coffee afterwards. Kingsley Martin drops in between Norway [1940] and Jugoslavia [1945] and prints a mutilated version of my views on the delay in the mobilisation of officers." He laments, but clearly enjoys, being treated as someone "back from Europe", as "an Authority". He goes into the Fens for the Workers Educational Association to run a course on "Problems of Modern Europe" at twenty five shillings a lecture. Almost casually he jots down: "Then writing. I sell a few stories… I sketch a theme for a novel, and I know I shan't have time to work on it, for years yet. I potter away at 'Alice in Zombieland' "; and he signs off poetically with the inevitable bow to the all-encompassing influence on that post-war Cambridge of T.S. Eliot: "My pencil nods. Thoughts of a dry brain in a dry season. And tomorrow it will rain." More prosaically, and more accurately since the key factor in this re-emergence was a determination above all else to succeed at the work he had hitherto neglected: "My own reading I enjoy".[26]

He worked, as he later recalled, with a Stakhanovite fury which became an academic obsession, as if all could be, this way, both revealed intellectually and, as a way of proving his own worth, delivered personally. As an ex-serviceman he was able to substitute for one paper in the final Tripos a fifteen-thousand word thesis on a subject of his choice. He decided on Ibsen and chose to see his own mirror image in the socially and psychologically hemmed-in tensions of the great dramas where individual break-out was essential for well-being. His interest became all-consuming until he forced himself to relinquish the subject to cover other things. Even so the thesis would serve as the keystone to all his published writing on drama in the 1950s. In his first published volume on close reading, *Reading and Criticism* (1950), he also made use of the intensity he had poured into a special paper on George Eliot.

The rest, for preparation on Tragedy and Criticism, as well as sixteenth and seventeenth-century French writing – Montaigne, Corneille, Racine, Molière – he mopped up in a deliberate frenzy in the second term. His calendar of work was organised and implacable; he wrote it out in columns to split his days into "a.m.", "p.m." and "evening" and moved from George Eliot to Criticism or French on a Monday or Marlowe and Greeks and Tragedy on a Saturday. The weekend would normally take him to Devon on a Friday, returning on a Sunday. One by one he ticked off the allotted topics and piece by piece he practised in his notebook by writing paragraphs of practical criticism on metaphor, conceit and symbolism in Shakespeare, Donne, Wordsworth and Blake. Apart from an absorption in Strindberg and Ibsen which crucially allowed him a personal focus – he carefully copied out Strindberg's credo of 1888: "I find the joy of life in its violent and cruel struggles, and my pleasure lies in knowing something and learning something" – his intellectual ballast in the hot-house world of Cambridge English had been dramatically restored by the emphasis on textual criticism which he now embraced with the fervour of the convert. The revelation had been as sudden as it was unexpected.[27] It took a full decade before he felt he had absorbed it and then that it was not sufficient. In 1958 he drafted as a sketchy fragment in one of his occasional notebooks the beginning of a review piece on E.M.W. Tillyard's *The Muse Unchained*, itself a lament for what had happened in English Studies at Cambridge. The review was subsequently subtitled "Revolution in Cambridge" when it appeared in complete form in print. The heading was both as descriptive and as ironic as the Oxbridge demotic he here deployed:

When I went up to Cambridge, in 1939, there was no one to teach me English in my own college, Trinity, which seemed large enough in other ways, and so I was sent out, as a day-boy, to other establishments, ending up, in my second year, with Dr. Tillyard at Jesus. I confess that I did not realise, in those years, that there had been a revolution in English studies: this is perhaps the usual state of mind of a post-revolutionary generation. Indeed it was only after the

216

war, when I went back to Cambridge and met some of Dr. Leavis' students, that I encountered the recognisably revolutionary atmosphere – the excitements, the key documents ["feuds" crossed out], the struggle against the old Gang ["continuing gang warfare" crossed out]. I recall these things now... to make it clear that I cannot possibly be Olympian about it: I was only a day boy, and cannot write with authority; I have become a partisan, and bring to the book guilts, passions and memories... Yet the changes in English teaching at Cambridge are of public importance, and need public assessment. Only this, ultimately, is relevant....

If there had been a revolution, I understood ["was told" crossed out] it was only the March and Kerensky; the October was still to come.[28]

If in 1958, with *Culture and Society*, the heavyweight publishing sensation of the year, he saw himself as one of the harbingers of a deeper revolutionary moment he still contemplated the resolution of that crisis as unfolding outside the walls. His move from extra-mural dedicatee to inter-muros maverick would come about, partly by chance, in 1961. Yet only partly so. The concerns of "Cambridge English" – close textual reading of both passages and whole works, an educated reading public, those life values which the best literature defined and the worst desecrated, a stubborn morality that was neither moralising nor socially hollow, in short a credo for individual life that F.R. Leavis both exemplified and documented – became his concerns. They offered a way of seeing literature as intrinsically whole rather than demoted to a lame echo of more profound social and economic forces, or merely trotted out as background or foreground in orthodox histories. In the immediate post-war years what came to be seen as "Left-Leavisism" was a niche where Williams, and some others, felt able to hold on to their progressive politics without relinquishing the cultural high ground of Leavisite criticism.

An era appeared to pass at Cambridge in 1944 when Sir Arthur Quiller-Couch ("Q" as his literary pseudonym since his days at Oxford in the 1880s had it) died and the King Edward VII Chair in English Literature which he had held since 1912 became vacant. The appointment was made on Prime Ministerial suggestion, after advice. The Chair was filled in 1946, not by F.R. Leavis but by the solid, conventional figure of Basil Willey, another near contemporary, who specialised in a long-standing Cambridge speciality, English moralists of the seventeenth and nineteenth centuries. Leavis, the champion of T.S. Eliot and D.H. Lawrence in the 1930s and the man whose conviction about poetry and prose in the English tradition was a constant confrontation of Bloomsbury sensibility and the "higher" journalism of London magazines, glowered and skulked in the fastness of Downing College. His pique did no favours to either his case or his embittered personality. Nor did it stem his certainty. These years, from 1948 with his re-assessment of the novel in *The Great Tradition* to the fuller argument in 1955 for Lawrence in *D. H. Lawrence: Novelist*, saw Leavis in his pomp, not as teacher and educationalist, but as a critic committed to his practice and its impact on society. The parallels with Raymond Williams would become obvious; less so, perhaps, the early and lasting divergence even in the face of Leavis' 1940's intellectual magnetism.

Raymond Williams' introduction to Leavis was a second-hand one, via post-war discovery of *Scrutiny* as a significant intellectual under-taking and by word-of-mouth. At Trinity, through B. Rajan, a young research fellow who published in *Scrutiny*, Williams now encountered a new intellectual sub-culture and, consequently, some of Leavis' pupils, notably Wolf Mankowitz, a lively charismatic figure with his origins in London's East End and war-service as a Bevin Boy in the coal mines. Mankowitz was taught by Leavis at Downing and, along with Clifford Collins (a personality fragile with enthusiasm, an English student at King's but also a pupil of Leavis) set out to organise the next generation's next step. Williams, shaky and still traumatised by the war, found himself, in late 1945, through the force of meeting Mankowitz, to be part of a congenial and vitalised Cambridge trinity. These three envisaged themselves, and the little magazines they aspired and plotted to create, as the coming October wave of Leavis' revolution.

Leavis proved sympathetic to both the three men and their project, but decidedly at a distance. Williams was in his presence only twice at this time. Once to attend a talk by Leavis and, again, in an incident Williams thought significant enough to return to on more than one occasion, when Leavis vigorously nodded agreement to Mankowitz's forensic dissection of "sentimental" nonsense. The nonsense in question was that of his friend, Raymond, who had asserted at a seminar given by L.C. Knights, then an up and coming Leavisite scholar, that he, "coming from Wales", in contradistinction to Knights' view of the word's practical disappearance in the modern world's vocabulary, did know, still, what "neighbour" meant. This would be registered as a personal splintering away from the firm Leavisite conviction that only an élite could now carry forward and embody older values of civilised thought in "a mass culture", including those of civilised manners. This ran counter to Williams' instincts and to his growing conviction. Over and again, in detailed ways, by precedent recalled and through fresh example, he would refute the critical accusation – variously couched as idealism, nostalgia or romanticism – that would be made throughout his life's work, as he continued to advance concepts of place, culture or community as intertwined and necessarily actual. For then, in 1945, it was an intervention, bare and dismissed as gauche, that he had felt bound to make. In 1958 the incident was pinpointed, in the intensely personal statement that was his explanatory essay "Culture Is Ordinary", as the moment he had had to take "away" such argument in order to think it through for himself, in despite of all that Leavis had made compellingly explicit about the "real relations between art and experience":

> We have all learned from him in this, and we have also learned his version of what is wrong with English culture. The diagnosis is radical, and is rapidly becoming orthodox. There was an old, mainly agricultural England, with a traditional culture of great value. This has been replaced by a modern, organised industrial state, whose characteristic institutions deliberately cheapen our natural human

responses, making art and literature into survivors and witnesses, while a new mechanised vulgarity sweeps into the centres of power. The only defence is in education, which will at least keep certain things alive, and which will also, at least in a minority, develop ways of thinking and feeling which... maintain the finest individual values.... For my own part, I was deeply impressed... enough for my ultimate rejection of [the diagnosis]... to be a personal crisis lasting several years.

For, obviously, it seemed to fit a good deal of my experience. It did not tell me that my father and grandfather were ignorant wage-slaves; it did not tell me that the smart, busy, commercial culture... was the thing I had to catch up with. I even made a fool of myself, or was made to think so, when after a lecture in which the usual point was made that "neighbour" now does not mean what it did to Shakespeare, I said – imagine! – that to me it did. (When my father was dying, this year, one man came in and dug his garden; another loaded and delivered a lorry of sleepers for firewood; another came and chopped the sleepers into blocks; another – I don't know who, it was never said – left a sack of potatoes at the back door; a woman came in and took away a bit of washing). But even this was explicable; I came from a bit of the old society, but my future was Surbiton (... it's served a good many as a symbol – without having lived there I couldn't say whether rightly). So there I was, and it all seemed to fit.

Yet not all. Once I got away, and thought about it, it didn't really fit properly. For one thing I knew this: at home we were glad of the Industrial Revolution and of its consequent social and political changes.[29]

At home, that peace-time winter of 1945/6, Harry Williams began the last decade of an active working life by greeting "more normal times" in his diary. His hopes, as ever, were for his son – "Looking forward to… Jim settling down in a Civvy job" – and for a communal reward for communal effort in the first year of his Labour Government – "A year of great promise if we all work hard and play fair."[30] It would also be a decade in which his son would, at first slowly and then with deepening insight comprehend the interaction of his parents' lives with social shifts that did not necessarily undermine Leavis' "finest individual values". He would learn harsh lessons about himself in the process. The outcome would be his first fiction and his most innovative critical thinking. All these factors had to come together in his life to let him pick them out intellectually, one by one, and then re-bind them imaginatively.

* * * * * *

But first there was the almost ceremonial settling of an academic account. Always, for Williams, there was the looking back as well as going on and so, as he crossed Jesus Green on his way to his final Tripos examinations in the early summer of 1946, he said of himself that "all I saw was my home village, which in a strange way now seemed at stake".[31] He sat the exams in an intense passion far removed from examination nerves. He believed in what he was doing and saying in that place and at that time even if, in memory, the formality of the testing seemed absurd. When it was over, a burst of three-hour examinations done in his small short-stroked hand, he left Cambridge abruptly. Enjoying his first summer freed from pressing obligations since 1939 he contemplated, with Joy, a future direction; that he would try to make a living through writing or find a way of life that would allow him to write was clear to both of them. Much would depend on his examination results but not all since he had decided to avoid the life of a career or orthodox academic. The firmest idea was to rent a cottage in Devon, to write and to find occasional teaching in W.E.A. classes. He had already been given some classes with farm-workers in the Fens and now more were to be arranged. However, he saw an advertisement in *The New Statesman* for a post with the Oxford

Extra-Mural Delegacy in conjunction with the W.E.A.. Based in the south east of England, it paid over £300 a year. Another child was due in the autumn. He applied, was offered the post and took it. One journey had ended. "We get the good news", wrote his father on 8 August, "that Jim has fixed up a job and hope he will be able to fix up for the family. Also he has First Class Honours".[32] That had led to an offer from Trinity of £200 a year as a Senior Scholar. But he wanted to move on: there was a projected novel, a magazine in prospect with Mankowitz and Collins, and a film script in collaboration with Orrom who was now an assistant director to the outstanding documentary film maker and historian, Paul Rotha.[33] It all promised to be rather more fulfilling to an ex-army officer aged almost twenty five than any conventional academic work, even a research degree under the admired Leavis. In late August he took his new friend Clifford Collins to Pandy where he celebrated his birthday and explained his plans. By mid-September he had managed to rent a large flat in Seaford, East Sussex and, at a base level of adult education teaching and of domestic life, the pattern of his regular work was set for the next fourteen years.[34]

This first settlement of the new family was their home until 1952. They moved in before the bitter winter of 1947 froze the entire country. Their first son, Ederyn, or Eddie as he would be called, had been born on 21 September 1946 at Braunton in Devon. Joy had had a difficult first birth with Merryn and a severe haemorrhage had then caused grave concern. In Pandy and Barnstaple there was now pleasure and relief, though in Gwen's case, there was also a deepening of disaffection with the woman who had taken her son away and now given him a boy. Harry bought a carpet and books for Jim at his request and sent them down by train. He followed alone in mid-October and stayed, putting up curtain rails and generally working to settle the young family in and "am indeed pleased to see that Jim and Joy have such a nice home".[35]

The home in Seaford, called "Betton", was in Southdown Road, over-looking the gorse-covered Downs running down to the sea with, in the distance, the white-chalked Seven Sisters cliffs. The Williams family had all of the lower floor as a spacious flat: a large sitting room, dining room, kitchen, bathroom and two bedrooms, with a small glass conservatory where Raymond worked, typing and preparing his teaching. There was a sizeable, overgrown garden for which Harry supplied plants and advice, though the self-absorbed young father tended to neglect both. He wrote incessantly: in 1947, a restrained, if slightly sinister short story, "A Fine Room To Be Ill In"[36] which Woodrow Wyatt took for *English Story* in 1948. The narrative revolves around the tension between the peace the academic Mr Peters has discovered in renting a place and staying there before the arrival of his young family – mother and baby – and the neighbours who, he feels, tend their gardens and little else. If it was a self-rebuke it was a quietly effective fictional one, leading to the Dahl-esque dénouement of a pram, left by Peters in the garden, which tumbles and spills the baby out. The family leave; the idyll of the nest finished for them.

Joy Williams remembered a "very cold winter with ice and snow for six weeks, shortages, rationing, two small babies and little money". They were visited by Annette Lees, her close friend whose scientist husband had died from a viral infection in the war. They were poor, Annette thought, with Harry's home-made wine a rare treat, and Raymond locked away, writing, his clattering typewriter echoing in the barely furnished flat. Whatever displacement occurred in his story, (and clearly the "pram in the hall" did not stem *his* creative juices), the elliptical biographical detail is as strong as the merely descriptive, confirming Joy's view that the story was indeed about that place, but also his adjustment within it. The fastidious Mr Peters scorns his neighbours who separate out flowers from weeds and festoon their crazy-paved gardens with ornamental tat. But in his amused view of how cool colours and general good taste were "nowadays... written down as indigence", he mirrors them, and, in his bookcase, prunes, weeds and arranges with as much dessicated denial of nature, or culture, as they do. There was:

> ... the fine dark oak cupboard, with its glass doors, behind which could be seen the carefully arranged relics of Mr Peters' travels in Sicily and Mexico. Then the matching

bookcase with its titles arranged according to branches of literature, for as Mr Peters so often said to his students, there is really very little point in a kind of inclusive chronology of literature: it is the development of work in specific media which it is so important to emphasise. So there was drama, from the fine old calf-bound Greek texts, through the red texts of the Romans, on to the green collections of the miracles and moralities, the uniform saffron editions of the Elizabethans, the patterned green covers of Racine and Corneille, the blue omnibus texts of Restoration tragedy and comedy, right down to the cherry collected works of Ibsen, the poison-bottle-green of Strindberg, and the tall black and pastel volumes of the modern verse dramatists. It was the same with novels, with poetry, with essays, with biographies and with criticism.

If this was a different kind of floral dictation it was one to whose pattern-making, accepted so glibly by Mr Peters, Raymond Williams' own clear response, immersed as he was in writing about drama specifically within such an intellectual categorisation, was as yet unformed. He could and did, however, gently satirise the Leavisite tendency to dismiss the ordinary, in the guise of the suburban, or even the vulgar, as the Lawrentian spirit supposedly did on behalf of those who truly possessed "living experience":

> "The point is", he said to his wife, "that these people are really dead. Their daily actions are just like the routine visitations of a ghost... They just clank on regardless, up and down their crazy paving, hoping their tended vegetation will do their living for them."
> "Nonsense," his wife answered. "They have their habits and their pleasures, just as you do. They're just not your habits, that's all."
> "They've got no contact with living experience, that's the point," said Mr Peters.
> "Oh, experience. That."

But if the eventual thrust of the story, and the wife's practical wisdom, is one thing, the story's poised ambivalence over the circumstances of such "living experience" is another, and one which he found hard, in life, to accept. Seaford, itself, was no isolated west country inlet designed for the brooding writer and a carefree brood. In reality[37] it was a former medieval seaport become, by the 1920s, a small genteel seaside settlement where the Sussex Downs meet the Channel between Brighton and Eastbourne. Just west of Beachy Head its most beguiling aspects were cliff top walks and rambles; it boasted of having neither pier nor amusement arcade. The war had seen Canadian troops and Commando units billeted in its villas and sprawled in tents along its heights. In 1946 the fabric of the township was dilapidated and careworn. There was the air of the place, and then again it was the place for the air, as he mordantly sketched in the background town in the novel, *The Art of the Actor*[38], which he began in Seaford in 1947:

> Grant had reached the level of the group of houses where he lived. He held his bicycle behind him and turned to look at the beach and the town. The sea in the bay was bright green, with a heavy swell... The beach, naturally, was deserted. The shingle had been piled steeply by the heavy sea, and the breakwaters... were almost submerged. Grant watched a taxi moving slowly over the shingle-covered track which was marked in the official guide as the esplanade. It stopped as he watched, and the driver went round to open the passenger doors. Three old ladies, dressed in gray, with furs high round their necks, stepped out, took a few paces, and stared at the sea.
>
> "Come to Seadown to die," Grant muttered. His eyes moved away to the unusual aspect of the town. What was remarkable about Seadown, seen from the south, was its lack of normal houses. The buildings which predominated were large, red-brick institutions, variously scattered along the wooded slopes at the foot of the downs. One was a

hospital; five were convalescent homes...; the rest were schools. Seadown was a place of some eight thousand people, but it had forty eight schools. Some... were called colleges, but were none the less schools...

The reason for this concentration of institutions for the old, the very young and the infirm was, of course, the air. Grant inhaled it now, deeply, and observed that everything that had been said about its freshness and purity was undoubtedly true. The institutions were well placed; and along with them, according to custom, had come the villas of retired officers, moderately successful civil servants, spinster ladies with foreign investments and a few fortunate seamen. At a close view these villas were sufficiently remarkable; but now Grant merely observed their splashes of red and green among the trees and turned with a sigh to his own house. He lived in one half of a gray house among a group of some dozen gabled villas. The house next to his was yellow-brick with a heavy, low, thatched roof, from which rose a television aerial. Another arrival.

This England, compared with the fertile adult education territory of the industrial north, was not promising soil in which to root the banner of a life-changing process through education. But it was, however, where he had been planted by the Oxford Delegacy and the base from which he now began to find both his students and, as he would later insist, his own way.

The interviewing panel for new tutor appointments in the Extra-Mural Delegacy of Oxford University had been chaired in 1946 by the formidable A.D. Lindsay, Master of Balliol, the Oxford College long at the centre of the university's academic and social progressivism. Under "Sandy" Lindsay, Master from 1935 to 1952, and his predecessor, A.L. Smith, Balliol had pioneered the development of adult education classes, especially in the North Staffordshire Potteries. Balliol's involvement in the extra-mural world would continue through Lindsay's chairmanship of the Delegacy, especially with the vibrant and well-attended summer schools the College hosted in the 1940s and on into the 1950s, but its missionary drive for adult education was long associated with its former Fellow, the economic historian R.H. Tawney (1880-1962), whose genius inflected socialist thought with moral integrity and whose physical presence in the classes of the Workers Educational Association in north Staffordshire since before the First World War had become legendary both for his practice and his inspiration. Indeed the extra-mural work of Oxford was inseparable from the W.E.A. which had been founded at the University in 1903 and this, in turn, led to the rather confusing structural organisation that had subsequently evolved for adult education. The Tutorial Classes Committee (T.C.C.) was formed as a joint venture with the W.E.A. in 1908 to supplement the Extension Lecture system of one-off and occasional lectures to large audiences outside the University. Through local W.E.A. organisers the T.C.C. was "intended to provide an opportunity for more concentrated study by a limited number of students [since] Resident tutors and more concentrated study groups increased understanding between the university T.C.C. and those wishing to experience university education".[39]

Then, in 1924, the Delegacy for Extra-Mural Studies had been formally constituted with two standing committees – for Extension Lectures and Tutorial Classes – of equal validity. By 1945 the Delegacy, with many individual success stories behind it and a record of liberating the education of adults beyond any narrow, and patronising, training, had a vibrant past. For the leading figures in its ranks its future, as a vital force for facilitating in post-war Britain an informed and active citizenship, was even more vital. Raymond Williams was more than willing to become a young acolyte of this important and extensive organisation.

Extensive because the Delegacy's geographical remit at this time went beyond its three encompassing counties of Oxfordshire, Buckinghamshire and Berkshire to take in Kent, East Sussex and the jewel-in-its-crown of north Staffordshire. In 1945-6 the Delegacy, buoyed up by its war-time success and growing recruitment figures, moved to appoint several new staff tutors who would be resident in the various areas. These tutors would report to the T.C.C. in Oxford but, locally, work together with the W.E.A. branches and local education authorities. They were expected to teach one-year preparatory classes to prepare students for the rigours of the three-year tutorial classes that could follow and to present material, lectures and seminars, at one-day and weekend schools across the year. Traditionally, study of economics, philosophy and political theory, with more tailored work for trade unionists and other activists on public expression, had been the mainstay of the teaching, but a broad liberal education in the "social sciences" remained an ideal even where, as in the 1940s, internal political divisiveness over ideological positions caused deep and bitter rifts. Literature was by no means ruled out but it was a subject some felt needed justification in this context. Initially, tutors might well teach across disciplines and, indeed, Williams offered, in his application in 1946, expertise in politics and international relations as well as the expected literature and drama.

Appearing before the Appointments Committee in July 1946, Williams was well armed with the first-rate distinction of academic achievement, a varied and educationally slanted army career as organiser and editor and a flurry of publications and proposals. In addition to the testimonials he received from W.E.A. organisers for the classes he had taken on post-war problems in international relations in the Cambridgeshire Fens – "a natural... interesting all his students and gaining their confidence and affection"[40] – there was, as there would be throughout his life, the matter of his direct presence, an apparent inner certainty that impressed at once.

He was appointed on £400 per annum on a three-year contract with probation waived because of his cited W.E.A. experience.[41] For that autumn he took over four one-year courses on the post-war settlement and its problems but within the year began his preparatory tutorials in literature. Perhaps because of proximity to London and the direction of his other plans, he had not applied for the posts available in North Staffordshire. This would, as it turned out, much reduce his opportunity to teach industrial working-class students within an embedded tradition

– which he would somewhat regret – and keep him distant from the Cold War politics that had destroyed any consensual amity on a broad left front in that area by the early 1950s. By choice and by chance he would be removed from such tensions until their separate and painful resolution, in the late 1950s, still found him standing and waiting to be involved. None of this was apparent at first. In particular, his sense of support, over this time, from his two most important seniors was acute. H.P. Smith had been long involved in adult education – he had been assistant secretary to the T.C.C. since 1926 and was its organising secretary when Williams joined – and provided both an encouraging voice and a loose administrative hand. He was succeeded, due to reasons of ill health, in 1949 by his former assistant, Frank Pickstock, brought in upon his army demobilisation by A.D. Lindsay, Chair of the Delegacy. To that point, however, the ideal of adult education as Williams expressed it forty years later seemed straightforwardly assured: "This was the social and cultural form in which they [the Tutors] saw the possibility of reuniting what had been in their personal histories disrupting: the value of higher education and the persistent educational deprivation of the majority of their own originary or affiliated class".[42] As a member of that "originary class" he was certainly thinking of himself; so far as affiliation was concerned he would have had in mind the Delegacy's Secretary between 1945 and 1952, his other great support, Thomas Hodgkin.

Tommy Hodgkin was about as well-connected an Oxonian as could be: his father was Provost of Queen's College when Hodgkin was born in 1910, whilst his mother was a daughter of Balliol's Master, the historian and social activist, A.L. Smith. After a First in Greats at Balliol, colonial service in Palestine and then work organising classes for the unemployed in the north east of England, Hodgkin became a Staff Tutor in North Staffordshire and, being unfit for military service, spent the war years there. He was seen as tireless and driven in all he did. In 1945 A.D. Lindsay brought him back to Oxford as Secretary of the Delegacy and a Professorial Fellow of Balliol.[43] He was also, from 1938 to 1949, a member of the Communist Party.[44]

The contrast between him and Frank Pickstock could not have been more marked. They only shared their year of birth and an Oxford education though that had come to Pickstock via a Delegacy Scholarship to Queen's College where he went in 1934 to take a degree in PPE. Before that this son of a miner from Staffordshire had worked as a railway booking clerk who became deeply involved in both the W.E.A. and the Labour Party. When the war began in 1939 he had become a stationmaster near Wigan. At its end he was a Major in Transport Intelligence in the Far East.[45] Pickstock, though another summonsed by Lindsay, was Hodgkin's polar opposite, in both tastes and outlook. Only Adult Education united them.

Raymond Williams, not for the first or last time, made no easy alliances. If Pickstock, from a similar background, was someone with whom he could work through the 1950s with a mutual, if guarded, respect, it was Hodgkin, with his balder belief that working class education needed to be rooted in wider working class institutions and taught by "committed socialists", who touched Williams' instincts for education as a process of social change, not just the purveying of training skills and intellectual objectivity. Not that these tensions only surfaced in Williams; there was a long history of conflict between the explicitly Marxist National Council of Labour Colleges established in 1921 to provide independent working class education, and the W.E.A., thought by many to offer a route to incorporation rather than release for working class students.[46] In practice, even where the divisions were most sharply articulated, as in South Wales, students did not always make such a clear distinction and were inclined to sample or even sate themselves on the wares of both. Nor, in 1945, is there any evidence that Willliams would have been more than mildly aware of this past history. But there was, indeed, the rub for those on the Left, not all Communists, who set out to claim a part of the W.E.A. tradition for explicit political ends and, in savage fashion, were rebuffed. Where Williams fitted in to all that puzzled some at the time; always, it seemed, there was the difficulty, in any context of relationships that were both political and personal, of elucidating his exact position.

Colleagues who now came across him in summer schools, tutor meetings and conferences reveal a remarkably wide range of views. Jack Woolford, appointed to Kent by the Delegacy in 1946, and another whose background, in the north east of England and then Cambridge before the Army, was not dissimilar to Williams, described him as "a good guy" and "warmly supportive" but could still add that many colleagues, and there were eleven staff tutors in the Sussex and Kent areas by the late 1940s, thought him a "prima donna" who set out to "plot a career". That he was "benevolent... courteous... helpful" – particularly in pleading the cases of other tutors as their staff representative – was not in doubt, but he was palpably "detached" and "distant". Most startling of all, perhaps, is Jack Woolford's only properly understanding his colleague to be Welsh and working class when he read *Border Country* on its publication in 1960. Either, he thought, Raymond Williams simply did not want to "share his background" or, more wonderingly, said he "concealed his Welshness and working class origins" for fifteen years.

Jack Woolford would have reason to think of such matters in this way when it became apparent that whatever "career" Raymond Williams had been "plotting" turned and turned unendingly on the meaning of such things in his own life and their sudden public revelation in Williams' work at the end of the 1950s. It may have been that the shock was not in the uncovering of detail but the intellectual and imaginative use he was making of it. Evidently it was not the unvarnished facts that were in question, for Woolford also recalled, with a deal of pleasure, Balliol summer schools ending with a kind of Tutors' end-of-pier party, one of which had Raymond as a "Welsh yokel" talking of his "life in the fields" and miraculously, by "native wit", refuting the higher wisdom of a tape-recorded lesson on Economics (the voice being that of the historian Henry Collins) to hilarious effect. On other such occasions, he would sing, in a terrible "tone deaf" fashion, the "left wing working class song", 'They're digging up Father's grave to build a sewer'.

At the outset of his years in the Delegacy, with fiction running through his head and plans for the magazine with Mankowitz and

Clifford Collins afoot, the young family man seems, most, to have appreciated the relative autonomy of his job. This, and the miles he had to travel to do it, seems the most obvious, though perhaps not the most telling, explanation for his air of being slightly at a remove in the late 1940s. Much of this perspective comes from the way the light has been cast backwards by friends and colleagues who, like Lionel Elvin and Tillyard earlier, had not anticipated his stellar fame, some even resenting the leapfrogging of others whose degrees were as good and whose teaching as committed. So the man they glimpsed as just another contemporary remained just that, a friend and colleague, not "a guru" to quote Jack Woolford; or, for Eric Bellchambers, W.E.A. South East District Secretary, "a good teacher and valuable colleague" but not in "the same class as G.D.H. Cole and Tawney", and becoming "a preacher rather than a teacher". Arthur Marsh, appointed by Hodgkin to teach Economics in Berkshire and then Kent for the Delegacy in 1948, thought Williams had a "portentous air... always detached... subject obsessed" with an irritating "sense of superior wisdom" as "a contemplative" who was "in a way, not of this world". As for politics, Marsh felt that Williams, at this time, did not "stand up" and say what "he was politically in the extra mural world". Woolford dismissed the idea of his friend being a "Marxist", or of any "crypto" variety, merely asserting that "Raymond was always independent" but influenced by his father's "uncompromising trade union socialism". Testimony of this came, perhaps, most tellingly in the role he took representing tutors, in all aspects, before their employers. He was, by general assertion, outstanding: well briefed, courteous, forensically sharp and firm in the employment interests of all and sundry. Yet even in this role he was perceived slightly askance, as if all was too good to be true. Eric Bellchambers appears to encapsulate these puzzled views:

It has to be said that there was something of the prima donna about him; that he was preparing himself for the role of savant or guru. He was not exactly a loner but he did not appear to have any close friends – at the same time he was friendly and courteous when he was being the wise man, or the tutors' representative. In his early days in Sussex, Clifford Collins and Wolf Mankowitz, friends from his Cambridge years, seemed still very close but they soon drifted apart and all went widely different ways. Raymond was a complex character. One other point needs to be made, Oxford had at least two other outstanding literature tutors contemporary with him; Pat Roberts and Cecil Scrimgeour.[47]

No one doubted the hard work he put into his classes. The irritation, and some confessed to finding it vast, was in the late discovery that so much else had gone on beneath the placid surface. Even when he had just left Adult Education the compliment, from Frank Pickstock, was of the place-putting kind:

> Williams is more inspiring as a teacher and as a person than he is as a writer…. Amongst his colleagues both his thought and teaching had great influence…. In later years some of Raymond's colleagues were better than him as a tutorial class teacher in the sense of drawing out individuals. Still, he had something else… not just an academic brain, but the personality and purpose of an inspired educator.[48]

Naturally, then, the years of his adult education teaching were, in due course, sieved for clues to all that was subsequent to it, though not necessarily consequent upon it, and clues or traces spotted to find threads that might serve as intellectual lineaments. Indeed they are to be readily found, and early on, but what they signify often goes back to what he had been taught as much as they may be said to suggest his future, more original thought. The tutor who set out on an adult education career did so convinced by the weaponry of Cambridge English and the serious moral purposes of its favoured writers.

Williams' pedagogic intentions were made clear after he had finished the 1946-7 preparatory classes on "peace-making" at Bexhill-on-Sea,

Eastbourne and Robertsbridge, all of which he had inherited.[49] From then on, all roads would lead to Literature and how the method of practical criticism would prove the best vehicle in all and any contingent study. The following year he had established four "Preparatory Tutorial Classes" – two on Literature at Brighton and Cuckfield – and two on "Culture and Environment" at Bexhill and Eastbourne (the latter had also been the title of a one-off short course the previous year). What he meant by "Culture and Environment", at this stage, derived from Leavis and Denys Thompson, not only in its direct echo of the title of their 1933 book, *Culture and Environment*, but also since it proposed, as they had earlier sketched, a sociological examination of the cultural signs of modern life – advertisements, cinema, the Press, popular fiction, commercialisation of the theatre – through the analytical lenses of close-up literary criticism. Words and their changing usage could be a key but so could the loss of community living if it succumbed to the inorganic factors of imposed or commercial leisure and the trumpeted necessity of more and more material consumption. To Leavis' stringent diagnosis of distaste he was adding his own disquiet though he did not register this as despair. At the Balliol summer school of July 1948, where his old tutor Lionel Elvin gave a general lecture on the "Culture of Popular Politics", Elvin's former pupil spoke on "The Politics of Popular Culture". These concerns bubbled away. But he did not, despite his hammering on with such courses, including one in Hastings in 1949 called "Culture and Society" (mostly on film), make a consolidated breakthrough with them into mainstream and established Tutorial Classes. In essence they remained preparatory, both for his students of literature and for his own thinking. He began to read himself into the subject until he could confront the issues on his own grounds.[50]

On the other hand, his teaching methods were quickly fashioned to meet head-on what he regarded as some of the absurdities of the literature sessions he was employed to teach. His concern, after all, was with equipping his students with skills, not stuffing them with knowledge. This led, on occasion, to a questioning of both his methods and his attenuated syllabi. Insofar as he was concerned, the only way forward for adults was by "Discussion" and in 1950 he contributed a defiant note on what he had learned and what he did to a Bureau of Current Affairs volume on Discussion Method.[51]

> The good tutorial class is... not just the bad extension lecture stood on its head. The authority it creates is not that of the students or of the tutor, but of the embodied class – the group. The process of his authority and the manner of tutorial class education is what I call discussion....
>
> I began tutorial-class teaching in literature when I already had reservations about the value of lectures on literature. Most academic work in literature, it seemed to me, was concentrated on secondary material. It was easier, tidier and much safer to work on literary history, bibliography, biography, background, correlation and so on, than to read and judge actual poems, plays and novels. The overwhelming majority of lectures on literature were lectures about the literature, and often at two or three removes. Because such material is easier to handle, courses of study habitually covered very large areas, frequently having relation to an enormous number of texts, many more than in the time one could read intelligently or with interest... To make students proficient in literary history seemed to me a poor substitute for making them able to read literature with intelligence and insight.

Instead he reduced drastically the number of texts or extracts to be read over the customary twenty four meetings of two hours per session and he ensured the texts were read, often in class, with the tutor silent, and remaining so, until discussion was instigated by the students. Many found this disconcerting and there were complaints made to the centre at Oxford. Still he persevered and introduced no extraneous information until its need rose from the discussion, and this particular tutor, "embodied in the group", never ever lectured. By the late 1950s he had tempered the rigours of his prescription, not least because of a

235

growing frustration with the stubborn passivity of his students. In 1950, however, the preparation, the method and the desired outcome – to make others as familiar as himself with the techniques of reading literature in order to make valid wider judgement – was still crystalline:

> It is, as I have said, a method of teaching literature, but it can be extended at least to critical sociology. I have taken tutorial classes which spend their first session on the study of newspapers, advertisements, propaganda, magazine and best-selling fiction, films, broadcasting, etc. Extracts are used in exactly the same way for discussion. Information about the Press, advertising and so on, is reserved until the need for it arises from discussion of a response to a particular newspaper or advertisement. For classes which are shy of literature, this kind of course is often a good introduction to critical reading.

The break with convention had come soon. It probably had to do so. A surviving copy of his syllabus for "Literature and Society since 1800"[52] (undated but probably for 1947-8), is five pages long and lists authors from Austen to Greene, via Dickens, Hardy, Lawrence, Woolf and Joyce, some twenty six novels, and poetry from Blake to Eliot, touching all the major bases in between, not forgetting stops for historical survey and methods of both literary criticism and sociological evidence. He omitted the (secondary) booklist on the grounds that it was "too long to be quoted". His "Assessment" of the direction and purpose of the course could leave no potential student in doubt of the serious import of their study.

> The issue of "minority culture and mass civilisation".
> The present balance of forces.
> The responsibility of literature.

In his preamble he was even more forthright about the sanctity of Literature and the individual vessels its light alone illuminated:

236

The literature chosen for study has been included on literary grounds: it is a critical estimate of the most important literature of the period. It will be read as literature: as the record, that is, of detailed individual experience.

The social history will be studied as such; but perhaps with particular references to problems of community and relationships and similar complexes which radically affect individual experience.

It is realised that there is danger alike of simplification and of distortion or omission. But such risks... must be taken in the attempt to chart the immediate hinterland of our own literature and society, and so of our consciousness.

This capaciousness he had rapidly found was a recipe for a discussion only with himself, and he had quickly dismantled the tower of knowledge from which he could only look down. Nonetheless, for a few years as he journeyed, laden with book-boxes, by bus and steam train from one East Sussex town to another, his educational spirit was almost sacerdotal as he sought to make the world he encountered, night by night, the springboard for a wider and diurnal consciousness. The theme was consistently, if hesitantly, the unity of his letters with his politics.

Chapter 6

"Politics and Letters"

The world of Adult Education was one which would afford him more than a safe haven; it would prove to be the space he required to form and test his independence of mind and outlook. But that was to be in the decade of retreat and re-grouping down to 1958. First there would be the more immediate dashing of post-war hopes for a central role in the breakthrough politics of culture. The disillusion when it came, abruptly and decisively in 1948, seemed to him to come on all fronts. There was the growing conviction that the timidity of the Labour Government in charting its own distinctive course based on an established working class culture was all too apparent – the resignation from 1946 onwards to economic dependency on the USA, the exhortations to work harder and produce more rather than redistribute and equalise consumption in the great fuel crisis of 1947, the recognisable swing to the right in attitudes towards strikes in 1948 – and for him the Communist Party's mechanistic, even antagonistically wrong-headed response, could not satisfy the complex needs in cultural and educational activity amongst the adult working class population. Feeling these bitter failures three decades later he still defended the utopian, perhaps wish-fulfilling stance, he had espoused then as, at least, unproven in its outcome. For that brief time, 1946 to 1948, he and a few others genuinely thought that a cultural intervention, grouped around the intellectual forum of a magazine, could influence a significant sector of opinion, and especially in the burgeoning world of adult education. Some of their valued precepts came directly from Leavis' insistence on "the standard of living", the phrase he and his student, Denys Thompson, had employed in their 1933 book, *Culture and Environment*, to mean, in every sense, a rejection of falsity of tone and action in all human relationships. But Leavis' examples, other than in the full revelation of a chosen canon of literature, were impossibly remote from the actual lives of an industrialised working class for whom the fustian antiquity of a non-technological future was as unimaginable as its opposite was desirable. In some of the techniques Williams employed at this time to rid himself and others of the suffocation of cliché, in thought and behaviour, the echo of Leavisite criticism – close reading for practical purposes, pricking of lazy populism and sentiment, insistence on felt experience as prior, even superior, to abstract thought – is self-evident. Stronger, though, is the use to which these insights were to be put. For Williams there could be no worthwhile "politics" without the depth of hinterland behind "letters" but there was no achievable "individual" sensibility in the present without a linked "collective" future of potential. At this point he tried to keep a balance but it was a pose in which his future tilt was plain to see; he concluded his first major published article, in 1947, in this way:

> We must, then, retain the right to judge a civilisation by its culture. For culture is the embodiment of the quality of living of a society; it is this "standard of living" with which the critic is concerned. Assessment of it is the social function of the critic and the creative writer. And the function is surely so important that in its valid exercise the writer is entitled to practice in the teeth of economic crisis, and without being overawed by the claims of that narrower section of politics which is both the total preoccupation of the professionals and the average man's major intellectual distraction...

> Our precept is clear: we must, negatively, by the application of the strictest critical standards ensure that inwardness is neither abused (becoming "profitable introspection") nor set up for sale in the commercial market; and positively, we must attempt, however often we fail, to ensure that in our own inevitable development towards a planned, rational society, the distinctive values of living embodied in our literary tradition are preserved, re-created, expanded, so that ultimately, with material may grow human richness.[1]

A decade on he will not confine those "distinctive values" to so narrow a front and in the 1970s he was adamant that it was a hopeless venture since any Leavisite direction was towards an opposite pole from any conceivable socialist position. Besides, the weaponry to hand, Leavisite criticism, was all technique and no profundity, and left the deeper structural issues which lay outside the text beyond available analysis. In the mid 1940s, though, for the new graduate in English and Drama the "immense attraction of Leavis lay in his cultural radicalism... the range of Leavis' attacks on academicism, on Bloomsbury, on metropolitan literary culture, on the commercial press, on advertising... took me."[2]

Sufficiently so for him to want to collaborate with others of like mind. He had made an unlikely third member of an ambitious Cambridge triumvirate, alongside his new Cambridge friends, Wolf Mankowitz and Clifford Collins; of like mind, for a time, but with distinctive personality differences that made holding things together a fraught process. At first sheer energy drove them, most of it supplied by Mankowitz whose quick sketch of their characteristics points up the strengths and the discernible flaws of the partnership. Of himself he wryly observed that he was as "evanescent as he was effervescent", lacking patience for the long haul but, with "enormous energy" at his disposal, capable of operating on a number of fronts – as academic critic for *Scrutiny*, fiction writer and business manager of the magazine he, largely, would front. Yet Mankowitz (1924-1998) was a doppelganger for Williams in some respects; from London's East End, the son of a Russian emigré market trader, he had been the first boy to "go to Oxbridge" from East Ham Grammar School and had been "very active" at Cambridge in the Communist Party. He was there, initially, as an Exhibitioner at Downing where Leavis was his Director of Studies. He had parted with the Communists when he was "thrown out for cultural deviationism" and with the University when called up to the Army and as a "Bevin boy" did wartime service in the pits of Durham. He had returned to finish his degree but, in effect, to launch a career as man-of-letters that would, soon, take him into the different orbit of successful 1950s novelist and scriptwriter whilst his Welsh friend, that "earnest intellectual cooker of ideas", was apparently becalmed. Mankowitz thought that Williams was actually more bothered or "tested" by the class structure represented by Cambridge than himself because he was not, in Mankowitz's somewhat awry but interesting sense, "very working class" at all. But Mankowitz's sense of this seems to have just as much to do with finding Williams rather "genteel" for not swearing, allied to being "very single-minded" as he "drove a particular furrow". As for Clifford Collins, Mankowitz had known him from the end of the war when Collins went up to King's College to read medicine before deciding to switch to English. Collins, too, wanted to write, poetry as well as fiction, and impressed acquaintances by somehow having an access to things which seemed to give him knowledge, about Jung's theories, "in advance" of others. His was an "exploratory mind" though a brittle personality: neither schoolteaching nor bouts as an adult education tutor settled Collins into a routine. His later life was marred by breakdown and isolation.[3]

Raymond Williams was closer to Collins, despite the bitter quarrel to come between them. He acknowledged how Collins' commitment to the magazine was the binding factor and the twinned presence of "old friends", Mankowitz and Collins, "the editorial dynamic". His admiration for Mankowitz was tinged with envy: "He was already in effect a professional writer; I used to think he could write virtually anything. Beginning with that talent, he took his own material into the most popular forms: by the end of the fifties a film and a musical". Eventually, his later feelings for Collins, who taught sporadically on courses with him to the mid 1950s and who was one of a small number specifically thanked in the Foreword to *Culture and Society*, were suffused with regret, if not quite guilt. His own rhetorical question of 1979 hung in the air: "Who can say, who can ever say whether these differences were always there between these three people?"[4]

The magazine's files of correspondence, along with accounts and subscriptions, have been lost but it was, in any case, a creative undertaking in more ways than one. In the summer of 1946 Williams was in Barnstaple and Mankowitz in a farm labourer's cottage at Mistley Heath,

Essex with use of a gypsy caravan for his office. From here he set up the Critic Press as a company and drummed up a list of potential subscribers for the companion journals they had discussed: *The Critic* to demonstrate the importance of a serious critical review of the arts and *Politics and Letters* to establish how the health of the former was inseparable from the latter. There were severe practical problems to overcome, not least the paper shortage imposed by government quota on publishers. They worked around that by using a paper allocation to which Williams, as an ex-serviceman, was entitled. Mankowitz raised some finance by selling some paper, on the black market, to other publishers. They even thought about a gamble at Newmarket. They were in a determined hurry.

On 19 June 1946, Clifford Collins wrote from King's College to his older friend, Raymond, in a bantering mode which seems to capture, inadvertently, the closeness and the confusion of their friendship:

> Though I am in no position to be self-righteous about it – why haven't you sent my trunk back, you bastard? I have to move out of college next year and I have nothing to send my books home in. Have you no sense of moral responsibility – and about property, too.
>
> When you want your loan back say so, don't hint. You shall have it in September if that will be alright, otherwise I shall have to start paying you back in monthly amounts. Perhaps you didn't mean this, or perhaps you just find the question of tone difficult to manage in letters. Or perhaps I just find it difficult to recognise real forethought when I see it.
>
> Jack, Wolf and I are meeting in London on Monday. I will be able to let you know after that whether it will be necessary for you to come up the following Thursday... so far there is nothing new, though we are thinking in terms of starting with a smaller circulation but no other alterations. This will considerably decrease our liability and the circulation ought to be up to 5,000 by the end of the first year.

Of course I want to come to see you, and I should like to go to Wales…

Clifford[5]

He did go, to Pandy in August, and, meanwhile Mankowitz was picking up the threads, cajoling promised articles, using the contacts they thought could supply a base line of subscribers. In July he wrote from London:

Dear Raymond,

Thanks for your letter and list. Clifford told me he had heard from you, and that you were having difficulties. I was sorry to hear it, particularly as you seemed to have been getting on so well with the novel. But since I too have been rather nervy and irritable and bored as well, I feel it might very well be an effect of pregnancy in the family.… What is more, I do not think that it is a possible or even desirable function for a woman to "sympathise" with the artist to whose sympathies she feels committed. I don't think we require sympathy or understanding from women, and I don't think it's possible on a sustained level even if we do demand it. What DHL said about "don't touch me" is true for the artist absorbed in his art – and he isn't this very often. Personally I really don't like Ann to talk about what I am writing – because I want her admiration and so on all the time, she is not in a position to be a critic. Anyhow, you'll know what I am getting at. We should really all be living in the same village. We are, I'm afraid, for some time, our own audiences.

Concerning *The Critic*. Some headed paper will be sent to you as soon as Metcalfe gets it through. I assume that the list you send me is a copy of the list you will be canvassing

243

yourself.... We are all designing a prospectus as bases for discussion. You do so as well, let us have a copy and we'll collate all four and send you a copy of the finally decided one... I don't know whether Clifford told you – we are seeing a solicitor Monday re. forming a company etc. Will report back.

Love to you all from us both, and let's hear from you.

Wolf.[6]

The twenty-one-year-old Mankowitz's notion of the Lawrentian male idyll seems to have been shared by the twenty-four-year-old Williams in one respect: he proposed to Joy that she move with two-year-old Merryn and her unborn child to share the house and caravan in the country with the Mankowitzes. She reacted with a cold disdain to the idea let alone its possible reality. What her reaction would have been to Mankowitz's other epistolary thoughts is not recorded. She showed little sympathy, however, for the principals in this publishing venture, a possible part-explanation for her memory of Raymond's secretiveness over the whole affair.

Mankowitz thought Raymond Williams was "averse to business" and so reluctant to take up any formal position connected to a magazine with no capital and no credit when he was himself in search of employment. But the last came quickly and he was soon named as one of the six Directors of "The Critic Press Limited : Publishers of *The Quarterly Review*, *The Critic* and *Politics and Letters*"; the other three were the Cambridge acquaintances, John Metcalfe, B. Rajan and George Scurfield. Offices were found in "a garret" at 7 Noel Street in central London and printers and distribution outlets were pursued by the indefatigable Mankowitz. In the early autumn term Collins wrote from Cambridge: "Thank you [for] the information about paper – I hope something happens soon. A *Critic* that is the same size as *Horizon* would not be very distinctive and the review would lose a lot by not being able to apply the line on a broad front."[7]

There would be an initial print run of around two thousand and two editions of *The Critic* (Spring and Autumn of 1947) before it was incorporated in 1948 into *Politics and Letters*, which itself began in the summer of 1947 and ended, with its fourth number, in the summer of 1948. They retailed for 2/6d, carried scant advertising and despite being sold on W. H. Smith's railway bookstalls foundered in that "very bad, breaking year" of 1948.[8] Maybe "the line" was on too broad a front. Collins clung to his ideal amalgam of T.S. Eliot and Lawrence as psychic healers in a de-humanised world; Mankowitz felt that his own major impulse, and to that extent with Leavis, was that he was just "fucking irritated" by the "bullshit going on in literary circles – by *Horizon* and the Sitwells" and wanted a "battle against the literary establishment... as a projection of the class it represented in society"[9]. Though he later conceded that the illusion of Collins and Mankowitz was that such a battle could be fought within the terms of a literary argument or culture discourse, Williams likewise invested a deal of hope that such a coming together, in an open magazine, with sensitivity to individual life and belief in social equality, could stand as a banner against the closing cultural walls of the Cold War. Their list of contributors is a solid indication that others shared the thought if not the resolution of it.

Leavis was never far from the editors' thoughts. What would he think of it? Would he approve? Would he contribute? Mankowitz, his pupil, had written a confrontational, even abusive, review of Dylan Thomas' *Deaths and Entrances* for *Scrutiny* in the summer of 1946 and would contribute an essay on T.S. Eliot in an edited collection of 1947. *Scrutiny* writers, notably recruited by Mankowitz, filled the pages of *Politics and Letters* and *The Critic* as the debate was tweaked. Williams wrote to Leavis, whose reputation as the most significant cultural critic of his day was about to be cemented by the publication of *The Great Tradition* in 1948, to ask if he could acquire a particular back copy of *Scrutiny* he required for his own forthcoming article. Leavis replied courteously but firmly to say "No", he needed it himself, its rarity was not to be risked even via a 'diplomatic bag'.[10] As to the venture, Mankowitz had no real doubt that Leavis "did not like it" but that his reasoning was personalised, that he "objected to anybody else doing it".[11]

Possibly so, though even a cursory reading of the first Editorial of *Politics and Letters* ("For Continuity in Change") would reveal not only that a seasoned Scrutineer, R.O.C. Winkler, was contributing a piece on the relationship of politics and the arts ("Critic and Leviathan", with a follow-up billed as a "Marxist comment" by the Balliol historian Christopher Hill who was then an active member of the Communist Party), but also that : "In our second number there will be a comment by Dr. F.R. Leavis." He had, in effect, chosen the battleground for them even if he was not dictating the detail of tactics. His foes were theirs as well. The Editorial damns the polarities as directly as *Scrutiny* had in the 1930s: affirming neither the personal introspection of literary coteries masquerading as the keepers of the highest values of society (aka Bloomsbury) nor the political name-calling of the cultural traditions embedded in literature as hopeless "idealism" by "the English Marxists". Instead it insisted upon the assessment of "the structure of society, its institutions and directions" by "standards resting on certain immediate qualities of living, qualities which social history scarcely records", but which "for continuity, our cultural tradition embodies". The only qualm their mentor might have felt was on their emphasis, though politically non-specific, on the change in social formation that was inevitable in a new "planned society". We can then straighforwardly locate Mankowitz and Collins, and an assenting Williams, in the Leavisite stress on literary criticism as the supreme diagnostic tool, and its "continuity" through education as its evangelic platform; and, beyond these positives, even in the Leavisite plea for extension of such analysis into cinema and popular literature, those bearers of negative qualities within civilisation. In their fourth and concluding point for intellectual action we can sense Williams tentatively probing further than the priestly certainties allowed:

> Fourth: though it seems to be impossible directly to relate
> the highly specific experiences of a work of art to any more
> general qualities of living in the society in which it is

produced, we must attempt to plot the social and intellectual background of the present time. And to this end, the most satisfactory means (failing the direct relation of literature and social events) would seem to be the enlistment of specialists to assess evidence provided by their own fields of enquiry, and to revalue the conclusions arrived at by other disciplines.[12]

He would come to recoil from the anodyne anathema of "background" and the compartmentalisation of "disciplines" but only when he had quizzed that "impossible" task and penetrated the smokescreens which, as he would detect, conveniently veiled things actually connected. The doomed attempt of 1947 and 1948, however, was to try to unite what was, on many fronts, splintering apart. There was no chance of any pre-war reconciling of progressive cultural views under the aegis of the post-war Communist Party though that is where most of those to the left of the Labour Party and with whom Raymond agreed still belonged. Nor could he find himself at ease with a stern aesthetic moralising against the fripperies of a self-serving metropolitan élite so long as the former clung to social views that easily shaded into an objective reaction. Still, the two magazines were genuinely open to a broad range of views and engagingly lively, with a mix of writers from younger critics and historians like D.J. Enright and Henry Collins to the major figures, George Orwell and Sartre.

Raymond Williams' own contributions of short notes and reviews were eclectic: a smack against the cheery de-historicisation of Noel Coward's stagecraft and the popular journalism of Rebecca West's dissection of treason; reflections on the unwillingness of the State, here personified by the youthful Board of Trade Minister, Harold Wilson, to "lose money" in the cause of a Film Industry, especially for documentaries, "as museums or libraries lose money"; and passing glances at Joyce, Ibsen, Dali, P.H. Newby, American radio and Cyril Connolly.[13]

He wrote three more substantial articles. The last to appear[14] was on Joyce's play "The Exiles" and was billed as "A section from a forth-coming book: Studies in Modern Drama : Ibsen to Eliot." The book, finished in that year, failed to attract a publisher and would wait another four years for complete publication. The most substantial article[15] was a look at the unwarranted censoring of style and content underway in the Soviet Union, under the philistine direction of the literary commissar Zhdanov in 1946, and at the perspectives taken on this in Britain both by "popular Marxist writing on culture" and those who "sneer at all things Soviet" and merely "cry culture". Williams' claim that a commercial populism can be, in market conditions, also antagonistic to "depth of response" should not, however, be seen as any kind of excusing of state interference. On the contrary, though Soviet society is seen "on all the accessible evidence" as suggesting "socially desirable attributes of width", and struggles, both material and military, are presented as mitigating factors, the judgement he arrives at could not, at that time, come from any intellectual within the British Communist Party, a fact that gave him no personal satisfaction when, a decade later, all that was to be much and belatedly changed:

> What now we have a right to deplore is the active influence of the State – towards stabilising the quality of their civilisation at its present level [To do so]... is... to condemn Soviet literature to superficiality, to the replacement of the individual by the unreal composite, "Soviet Man". So mechanical a figure is as far from any kind of realism as the "Average Man", the "Little Man", the "Successful Man" which have been created by the press-peers and advertisers of the West.... Only a writer like Mr Priestley, whose literary productions display the same qualities, and who, significantly, appears to be highly esteemed in Russia, can feel happy about that.

J.B. Priestley (1894-1984) was, in 1947, still basking in the afterglow of his immensely popular "common man" (and somewhat anti-Churchill) wartime radio broadcasts. At first sight he seems an unlikely target but Williams hit out at him on more than one occasion, even seeing him as an extension of the Labour government's failure to make cultural issues central and about value, rather than organisation:[16]

Democracy does not demand a cultural levelling-down and the general record of the Labour movement, with the example of the Workers' Educational Association before them, ought to lead to sensible discriminating aid. But so far there has been too much evidence of a stand on the untenable principles of cultural demagogy: the indeterminacy of taste; the proof of value in commercial success; and the sticky populism which was given title by Mr Priestley's *Let the People Sing*.

If this was, all told, a scattergun delivery, it was a bold series of attacks for all that and one whose self-belief rested on the sureness of its own ground: win the cultural arguments, diffuse them widely and see how new art formations would grow to reflect and shape evolved social expectations. It was, for sure, Leavis in new left clothes. It did not seem to Williams either utopian or even wrong-headed at that time. Consequently his most characteristic piece for the magazines was his first, his oddest and the one that drew most attention: "A Dialogue on Actors".[17] The article consists of seven closely-printed pages in which "L", "M", "N" and "O" debate, paragraph by paragraph, the state of English theatre. Along the way such describable outcomes as the growth of popular interest in drama and the broadening of its themes are welcomed only to be dismissed if quantity were to be thought more important than quality and if naturalism as either "a slice of life" or "Soviet realism" were to be considered seriously: "The whole danger of naturalism today is that the strong socio-political case for it obscures its dramatic poverty." If the Dialogue is lively, the discussion enters dense thickets where the young critic is keen to reveal how he is up-to-date with the academic jousting. Reference after reference to contemporary staging of West End plays – Gielgud and Ustinov in a barebones *Crime and Punishment*, Flora Robson in a James Parish vehicle and O'Casey's overhyped *Red Roses For Me* – shows, however, that not all his time in the spring of 1947 was being spent poring over text. Yet it is text along with imaginative staging that emerges as the chosen saviour of contemporary drama from mediocrity. The play will embrace poetry or rather a speech convention that will break with naturalism and the staging will be symbolic and balletic. T.S. Eliot's *Murder in the Cathedral* is the only modern English drama that, in the final paragraph, he admires.

It was the journalist in Mankowitz who had spotted that amidst this heavy swell of critical thought there were sharp smacks at individual actors who, it was alleged, filled the emptiness of their parts with overweening tricks of personality and interpretation. These stars were, by their craft skill, corrupting what was potentially good, and underlining what was ineffably hopeless. Raymond Williams named names. They ranged from his friendly mentor, Bernard Miles, to his bouncy Welsh namesake, Emlyn Williams. It was the kind of crossover that Mankowitz, who would later take such a step himself, relished. He suggested that they circulate the piece to actual theatrical practitioners in advance. They replied in character.[18] Donald Wolfit, the fruity-voiced flamboyant Actor-Manager who had long barnstormed his Shakespeare showcases–for–one across Britain, was amazed that there was no reference whatsoever to himself, whilst the "far too erudite" tone of the dialogue hid personal prejudice and political slant. The British theatre, he concluded, would have been lost without the great professional actors for it was "the leading actors in any country that keep the great drama alive". He remained a pioneer and a revolutionary and Mankowitz's obedient servant. Ralph Richardson, writing from The Old Vic, found it "extremely interesting" but did not feel he had anything to say on the subject. E. Martin Browne of the more experimental Mercury Theatre, was more encouraging; he looked for an end to the "picture frame" and new "speech convention" to "allow adequate expression on all planes of thought" but he thought the "Arts Council... and real lovers of the theatre" needed to join "actors and dramatists in blazing a trail". The most vituperative reply came in a "dictated but not signed" burst from Emlyn Williams, who found the whole thing "juvenile – pretentious, muddle-headed, soaked in inverted snobbery, and betraying woeful ignorance of the psychology both of acting and playwriting". He hoped they were "sending both letter and article to Mr Priestley asking for his friendly collaboration in a worthy cause".

Raymond Williams might well have taken all that as mere confirmation and may also have seen Nevill Coghill's measured two-page letter from Exeter College, Oxford – where the dramatic and poetic Richard Burton had so recently come briefly under his tutelage – as a compromised, yet sensitive, defence of the actor as instrument of both (readable) text and (adaptable) convention. One letter, addressed directly as "Dear Raymond", was, at the length of four pages, the longest and the most show-stopping. It was from Bernard Miles and even as it expressed a polite admiration so it stung with practicalities. The question was one of bringing an audience inside and if the "star-actor" did that, then fine, so long as something followed from it. To say actors swing performances through personality was "moonshine" since good plays were always being altered in tonality even as they were indestructible in essence. Besides, an actor had as much right to interpretation as a literary critic, the difference being that "the poor performance of one was ephemeral but that of the other continued to stink in print". Actors, too, wanted to "form a new drama" but they were "helpless to bring such drama about by a stroke of magic". Finally, Miles slammed a "ponderous style" and the use of "semi-cliché conventional literary phrases". He ended:

> In fact a literary criticism I believe suffers just as acutely from our present-day malaise as does the theatre itself, and one of its chief weaknesses is that it cannot find any fresh or simple or vivid way of saying things (apart from the fact that it has very little say)... I certainly think you ought to re-write your Dialogue six or seven times before you let it be printed.

There is no evidence Williams did anything of the kind. He was ruffling sensibilities from the left to the right, from state-supported arts to commercial theatre, from the self-perpetuating reviewers and critics of metropolitan London to the academic and the populist. For a while in 1948 it seemed as if he was succeeding: a quarterly that was making waves, a backlog of fiction writing that was moving on, a book on drama just about complete, a work of practical criticism commissioned and begun, and, through his friend Orrom, a definite entrance into the world of film. Then it all fell apart, starting with the documentary film he had worked so hard on.

Raymond had urged that Michael Orrom[19] write film criticism for *The Critic* and arranged for his friend to meet up with Collins and Mankowitz in the "Swiss pub in Soho", where what Orrom took to be a "couple of mafiosi-looking chaps (typical Soho...)... over in a dark corner" turned out to be the formidable literary lions. When he asked what their "overall aim was" he received the reply: "Clear the critical scene and then get down to the creative writing... Shouldn't take more than a couple of years!" That accorded well with Orrom who was convinced that the development of film theory, or rather technique, was a pre-requisite of the "new film" about which he dreamed. He wrote on Film and Art, dutifully echoing his mentor Paul Rotha's influential and early *The Film Till Now* (1930), for the short-lived *Critic*. More importantly, his re-awakened friendship, with a man whose own "working class background" Orrom felt offered him "contact with another part of society... [he] had missed... coming from a middle class family", seemed to presage a working partnership that might unite theory and practice.

Orrom, living in Finchley and working in Soho around those documentary film-makers still buoyant from war-time success through the Ministry of Information, was a satellite in the orbit of Rotha, then at the peak of his own powers. Paul Rotha (1907-1984), just forty, had enjoyed a spectacular career as film critic and pioneer documentary-maker, and had lived down his temporary demise as a 1930s leading advocate of pacifism to emerge as cultural adviser to the Labour Government. His own socialist beliefs and internationalist views were ardently promoted in his didactic films. Orrom took great pleasure in introducing him to Raymond Williams whose own visits to Soho for editorial discussions increased through 1947 into 1948.

So, when the Central Office of Information asked for a film on the history and achievements of British agriculture, Orrom immediately suggested himself as director with a treatment and subsequent script by Williams, who produced a fifty-two page typescript[20] (rather more essay of analysis than shooting script) entitled *Effect of Machine on the Countryman's Work, Life and Community*, as the basis for a three-to-four-reel film. The idea, however, foundered on the COI's scaling down of the project to a much shorter version of machinery in the agricultural industry, as a preface to a film on post-war reconstruction. At the meeting to discuss the matter Rotha walked out in contempt and the Orrom-Williams collaboration collapsed. For the scriptwriter it was, in retrospect, yet another example of the dessicated cultural thinking affecting the embattled Labour Government. But at least some of the effort he had put into its writing would not be wasted.

On the surface the film treatment is straightforward enough, moving through in-depth accounts of the enclosure movement to the rural depression of the late nineteenth century and on to the interwar years. But it was precisely the insistence on a long historical perspective allied to a linking of the lives of landworkers to wider social relationships which took the film way beyond the COI's required propaganda snapshot. After the history was established and the contemporary economic and technological outcome assessed the film was to turn to a present-day sample village:

> Opportunity is given for comparing the old peasant community, with its settled, integrated system, with a contemporary village where there is no real economic centre, and where utility services, leisure, and even work, are to varying degrees dependent on geographical relations to the nearest urban centre. Various social activities of the village are described: on the principle that the only available way to assess human change is to assess the culture (in the broadest sense) of human communities.

> The general conclusion is that there has been no settled organic community life in the villages since they were

radically altered by the various phases of industrial expansion; that life and work were altered directly by industry...

The first two parts of the film would show how and why late eighteenth-century industrialisation altered everything and so, "against a short-term account confined to techniques", was key to understanding all development on the land to the present. The second half was to provide the larger setting which puts the "problem of the countryside" into perspective: "since most of the sentimentality about rural problems is due to an artificial separation of them from those of the urban districts". This was an insider's view and one he did not hesitate to proclaim as such.

The "organic" village does not survive his relentless description of unalterable change: the myth of seasonal patterns of work for most of its inhabitants; the end of an inter-relationship of goods and services; the effect on patterns of distribution of trade and labour of new road systems; the appearance of the greengrocer's van as emblematic of the demise of self sufficiency. It had become, he argued, "something between a small town and a residential suburb". All of this would lead to the real burden of the un-made film, and the root of his own nagging interest confronted by what he knew by upbringing, and now by research, as against what he detected in the simplistic writing and thinking of others: that the problem was either entirely caused by outside mechanical agencies or that there was no problem at all because modernity was a welcome mechanisation of both material and emotional life.

It was a common theme that he subsequently never let go. This was his first and prescient statement of why he rejected these received opinions, and why, to give respect back both to lives that had been lived and were now being lived, their complexity as agents of change as well as recipients of it had to be registered. But how?

We are getting nearer to a position where it may be possible to estimate the human changes. The field as yet uncovered is what may be described as the general quality of living in

254

the village. Human change is recorded in community change, and most tangibly this change is recorded in types of community activity, in what may really be called the culture of the village.

Here, specifically, the incorporation of village life into overarching patterns, a "general process" of government and administration and indeed national leisure habits, meant any previous sense of community was at an end: "sentimentalism of rural life, arguing stability, wisdom, virtue and so on as qualities that living in the village or by the land automatically creates, is pernicious... [for]... it is not the work that determines a man's living; but the community, the capacity for human relationships, which matters. And the village community, in that sense, has gone".

There is little trace, in any of this, of the "nostalgia" for which he was later berated in the 1970s and his "idealism", though certainly there, is narrowly confined. On one side he flays concepts of "closer personal relationships" in village rather than town with personal observation of hypocrisy and interference in the lives of others. *Mother Chapel* is never far away and nor is it uniformly beneficent. Only in "small local ways" are people "good neighbours", but: "Close personal relationships within a community are only good if the community has a centre which gives them meaning." Instead of despairing he concludes that "new methods of production demand a new community" so the "solution can only be forward". The film would have surveyed the existing forms of community life, from the W.I. to the W.E.A. via drama and local eisteddfodau, in ways that strongly suggest he had Pandy in mind as his "sample village", even down to the way tennis clubs are said to "organise social dances, even dramatic performances". Affection for the positive is not, however, swamped by misty-eyed praise. Such features, in the absence of new socio-economic unifying factors such as light industry and co-operatives, are all as nothing compared to the urban "centres of gravity" that draw in energy from all that surrounds them.

Raymond had gone, via a socio-historical route studded with statistics and data, into his own past and into the industrial-rural bifurcation he could see in his own father, whose post-war activities, as a small itinerant retailer of produce, would take off with post-war road building. He had, for the first time in his thought, linked this up to a concept of "culture" as the indicator of social change and of "industry" as the undeniable, even desirable, driver of that change. He found, in his last, vague but hopeful paragraphs, his trinity of keywords; if there was to be human meaning that could still inflect community life, whether in villages or towns, then culture and industry would both require democracy:

> The infusion of light industries can solve the problem of the degradation of the village into a dormitory suburb. But a mechanised industry too often means mechanical living. In this sense, the wage-earning farmworker, who rushes to mechanical occupations and amusements, to fill his leisure house, is very like his brother in the towns... Better machines, better transport, will only emphasise this.

> Yet increased production of food will increase the national wealth, and with the increased chances of capacity for democracy, the labourer can actively participate in building a new community... which is a social and personal matter.

> The effects of mechanisation and science should not be overestimated in human terms; all they offer, and then only under social control, is a skilled job and adequate material conditions, in a process of gradual betterment.

> So far as human development goes, the real effects of the present mechanical increase will begin to be felt when it is settled in which way the economic structure, and so the social structure, moves in response to the changed methods of production. As yet, no significant change in the personal, as opposed to the working, lives of the men who live by the land can be recorded.

* * * * * *

No audience was ever found for a film of this challenging dimension. His own words were filed away. 1948 certainly delivered the significant progress of Bevan's National Health Service but *Politics and Letters* – off sight, he would later reflect, from the real need for the building of strong "popular cultural mobilisation… inside the Labour movement"[21] – took loftier aim than the grind of politics required and, in its own cultural drive, simply ran out of steam. Or rather out of the force of tripled energies. In particular, Williams wanted something solid to show for his own labours, a book with purpose in the adult educational sphere, and in frustration and with increasing anger he turned in that direction. Its production marked a crisis in his personal relationship with Clifford Collins and the effective end of his working association with Mankowitz.

None of this is straightforwardly evident from either the 1950 published text of *Reading and Criticism* or the respectful Preface[22] of its young author in which thanks are bestowed to Mankowitz and Denys Thompson, bouquets are delivered in acknowledgement of "a long standing debt to Mr A.L. Ralphs" and a "personal indebtedness" is noted "to Mr Clifford Collins, who helped to plan this book in its early stages" and with whom "many of the matters treated" were discussed. It is dated and signed off at "Oxford, 1948" and is indeed attached to the work of "Oxford University Tutorial Classes committee" for whom he had been teaching for two years. Nonetheless, its origins go further back, as the roll call of honoured intellectual debts is unveiled, to include "Mr T.S. Eliot, Mr J.M. Murry, Mr I.A. Richards, Mr William Empson… Mr L.C. Knights" and, especially, "Mr F.R. Leavis… largely responsible for the intelligent development of critical analysis as an educational discipline". Not unexpectedly, then, the emphasis of its nine chapters as they move from analysis of short pieces to complete works, from verse to prose, from literature to society, is on close textual reading and the view that literature, read and comprehended in and for itself, is the best guide to human living as experienced and as to be desired. Further, its appearance as one of the short volumes in the "Man and Society Series" designed for "use of students in adult classes.... Such as those [of] the W.E.A. and University Extra Mural Departments" gives the book the shape, replete with bibliographical notes, exercises and syllabi, of a work intent on proving that there is no such thing as "a born reader" anymore than the "fantasy" of a born writer. We are, instead, shown, or even instructed, how and why to appreciate Joyce but not Priestley, Eliot or Lawrence but not Greene. The proselytising tone is kept up to the very end of its one hundred and seven pages of text:

> Every improvement in reading – the growth of awareness and flexibility and honesty – represents an advance similar, in its smaller degree, to the advance made by the work of a creative artist. For it, too, extends the boundaries of human consciousness and creates again the most permanent of human values. That is why it is a task important in itself, just as literature is important for its own sake. It is an importance that needs no apology, but rather allegiance and application.

He wrote that in July 1948 and then dedicated the book, his first, "To My Parents". It should have been a satisfying moment but was not. Beneath the mantra there was an uneasier beat. Even in his rather fulsome Preface he had immediately registered himself as part of no "school of criticism", especially not as a "partisan" of *Scrutiny*. He was, instead, and despite being entramelled with all these debts, an "independent student". Only hints as to how he would, in practice, differentiate himself then emerge but they sound, if not a dissident then, at least, a dissonant note. For him the literature he is about to discuss in such necessary, awed detail also exists in an "environment", that of modern social development since the 1870s, which here has to be "assumed without detailed demonstration" though it must be insisted upon since "any enquiry into the reading of literature, or into the present position of any of the arts, had a danger of becoming no more than marginal, unless the cultural atmosphere in which all the arts exist is recognised…"

Already then he is moving, if not directly, to a sense that a cultural without an historical or sociological perspective is as potentially misleading as it is palpably incomplete. He states but moves on. Not far, however, from other formulations which will become key concepts in his work on culture and society. So, in a rather high-handed dismissal of an extract by Julian Maclaren-Ross as of the "popular kind", we read that its only value is in demonstrating "the structure of personal feelings of many writers and readers" through its clichéd language. But if "feelings" can have "a structure" so too can an industrial society have a "largely impersonal structure" which might cause "dissociation of feeling". And, underlining the extraordinary weight he places on "criticism" in restoring or creating a sense of "continuity in change", he advocates "groups, as centres to which individuals are drawn by the quality of their personal responses… built into a clear critical responsibility". "Good reading", an individual concern, then becomes "criticism", which is "a community concern".

The scale of the ambition, and it was re-formulated in his unpublished novel of social action *The Grasshoppers* in 1955, is immense and perhaps hopeless – "The ability to create these groups… may or may not be present in our own community. Discussion of their practical growth is outside my present scope" – but it is thereafter, in various manifestations, ever-present in his depiction of the consciousness required for meaningful social change. At this fevered level, gesture more than demonstration, we can detect the fervour with which he had discussed the idea of the book with Collins and how both saw it as a vital tool in adult education classes. Its original title was to have been *English for Adults* and it was, at the outset, the brainchild of Mankowitz and Collins, as an extraordinarily forensic letter from Williams to Collins on 29 September 1948[23], just as he had finished the book, reveals:

The first I heard of a collaboration in a Literature book for adult classes was of one between you and Wolf. This was in Cambridge between November 1945 and May 1946. I assume this collaboration came to nothing.

The cause of the letter, five closely typed pages, was a correspondence between the three of them (the rest is now lost) in which Wolf attacked Raymond, "on my conduct in the affair", and Clifford contradicted Raymond's version of the events and conversations that had led to single authorship of a smaller than envisaged book. What we have, now, is an account from just one side though the facts up to the summer of 1948 seem incontestable. Thus, the matter had progressed to a discussion between Collins and Williams in the winter of 1946-7 and had led to the latter producing an outline of the book by March 1947. At that time, the letter-writer recalled, he had already decided to prepare a shorter book since he doubted Collins' "adequate intention". Yet, after meetings in July and August 1947, and at Collins' expressed desire they went back to the original scheme and by October found a publisher in Muller (the "Man and Society" series emanating from the W.E.A.) for whom Thomas Hodgkin was then one of the editors. They agreed to complete by the summer of 1948 and, as late as March 1948, a joint book under the original title was still expected.

Then it fell apart. Williams was roundly accused of acting in bad faith for not only appropriating the original idea but also for signing, alone, the contract for delivery of a forty-thousand word book; a much reduced length. Williams' anger was directed against Collins for failing to keep a series of arranged appointments in Seaford in June and for not delivering anything agreed (though there were several nominated extract and chapter schemes which Williams felt duty-bound to scrap); he affirmed that he still saw the book, in June, as a jointly-authored one, with "moneys" to be shared, despite Collins not having seen the contract. "It did not work out that way", he wrote, "because you broke your agreement". He was off to Oxford for the annual summer school in mid-July when he, finally, contacted Collins by phone "in the afternoon of July 10 at Critic Press". The break-down is swift and irreparable as Williams traces its path:

Your letter disputes my account of that [phone] conversation. Clearly a verbal transcript is not available, but I will record in detail my memory of it. You just rest on an assertion that you did not say what I absolutely believe you to have said. When I asked if it was you speaking you said yes. I assumed that you would know what I was ringing about, since rightly or wrongly I was expecting you that weekend or at least some word from you about the book. But you appeared not to know what I was ringing about, for your next remark was "Well?" I said I was ringing about the book. Your words, as I remember them, were: "It's no good my coming down. I've not done any of it." I must have expressed some surprise and you then said: "It's no good, Raymond. There it is. It's just an occupational disease"... "You'd better go on with it on your own if you want to"... I said I would like to think what I should do.

What he did, angry and appalled, over-worked and over-stretched, was discuss it with Joy and decide to do it alone:

The personal situation had come to a crisis in which I could no longer respect myself if I submitted to your behaviour, and the fact that I made the demarche I have not, as an issue of relationship, regretted...

I do not say that I regret none of my actions, although I reject categorically your own somewhat bland simplifications of motive – But I may say that I do not at all regret an action which made an end of a mode of relationship which had become intolerable.

Communication,[24] of a fleeting kind, was restored over the next few years but a close working partnership had been closed down. Mankowitz remembered the Raymond Williams of that time as "secretive" with compartments to his life, though neither pompous nor dull, and with a lively sense of fun. Orrom, too, recalled the amusement of his mimicry, a sardonic wit and a man at ease with a range of people. Yet, in these contradictions of character there is, perhaps, a turning inward towards self-sufficiency of spirit and a ruthless removal from his life of anything that might stand as an obstacle to that. It was what would happen to Michael Orrom, to Orrom's lifelong hurt, after years more collaboration on joint film work. In 1948 Raymond Williams wrote a stand-alone oddity which appears to cast its self-reflecting light back on to its author. He called it *Interlude*:[25]

> He was always a man who found it difficult to know persons adequately. In a host of cases he was unaware of the facts of crucial personal relationships in which he was involved. It was always a shock to realise the truth of this, for he seemed a person of striking alertness, and even in certain matters the possessor of a remarkable insight. His perception, however, rarely extended to persons with whom he was in any close degree of relationship. In affairs of personality, one might say, he was exceptionally, and to his own and others' harm, longsighted.
>
> It was not that getting to know people, in the usual fashion, did not come easily to him. On the contrary, he was a most fluent person socially, and never lacked friends. For people were impressed by him at first meeting. There was his evident vigour, and then his quick movement to informality, which supported his constant affability in an assurance that one was being granted a specially privileged relationship. And then there was the variety of his talk, which most people found attractive.
>
> [But]... the event of all his early relationships was so similar, the pattern of development so persistent in its detailed course, that continually his motives came to be suspected. For it invariably came to pass that some person to whom he had been attracted, and who had been encouraged by his intimacy to place some reliance in his friendship, found sooner or later that he was likely to perform a series of actions which seemed entirely

incompatible with the terms of the assumed relationship; and moreover that protests and remonstrations about such actions were habitually received as acts of enmity, usually leading to some quite violent and ruthless act of exclusion. As a boy he had been told by a girl whom he had promised, lightly, to marry, that it was next to impossible to dislike him in early acquaintance, but that fuller knowledge led quite inevitably to disillusion and contempt. He was inordinately proud of this dictum...

Such proud confirmation of identity, whether liked by others or not, always exacts a price. Raymond Williams took on the disappointments and the personality clashes of 1948 and dealt with them by concentrating almost exclusively on his own innermost life. There was the career in adult education to pursue, of course, and he tried for a wider purchase through the impact of drama and film studies but, in essence, he did indeed pull back "to do my own work... in nearly complete isolation".[26]

The most vital segment of that work, at least so far as he was concerned, had been, all along, more creative than critical.

Chapter 7

"A good actor sticks to his own lines"

Raymond Williams completed *Reading and Criticism* over the summer of 1948, though the book would not be published until 1950. He had pointed out that its material was, in places, drawn from his few published articles and the "introductory chapters of my *Studies in Modern Drama: Ibsen to Eliot*", which, in turn, did not appear in print until 1952. All in all, this was, from 1946 to 1952, a creditable work-load for a fully-stretched adult-education tutor. If it had been all he had produced it would have stood comparison with the output of contemporaries inside or outside the university; and there was, in the few stories he had successfully submitted, occasional fiction, too. Yet, the astonishing reality was that his major creative engagement through all these years was with forms of fiction, and it stood no comparison because no general reader ever saw it. In his work memorandum, written to himself on 26 October 1948 the emphasis and the effort is clear. The balance, at this stage of his writing life, was in practice as well as intention, all one way.[1]

Between 1948 and 1955 he worked at six separate projected novels, fully completing three of them and writing lengthy drafts of others. The one to which he would return from its early, ambitious scope in 1946 to its fullest re-working in 1949, then referred to as "Brynllwyd", was broken down in 1948 to make "a short novel" and to use it as additional material for the eleven completed stories he felt could go into the "complete Welsh volume" which in shuffled and re-shuffled guise, *Mother Chapel* was meant to be.[2] He had typed out a book title and a table of contents sometime in 1948. The length was to be seventy thousand words and its coherence was entirely one of location so that the two "War Stories" he had considered in a similar list, along with post-war tales of uneasy marriages and chance encounters, were relegated to a second volume of stories to be provisionally entitled *The Art of the Actor*. He carefully copied out, then typed and assembled the fiction he hoped would float his name at a time when appetite for short stories, increased by war-time reading habits, was high.

Hopeful or not, there is no evidence that he sent them out for consideration as a book, and within a few months was tinkering to remove the last three sections – drawn from the extended narrative "Black Water" (1946) – to use for "Brynllwyd". He turned to his projected second volume of stories, all written between 1944 and 1948, and decided there were at least twelve here, with only "A Fine Room to be Ill In" previously in print. They were constantly changed in name, and some, as with the story "Liberation", in shape and content, but he finally settled on the generic title *Stories*[3] and opened it with "The Claustrophile", a grim descriptor for the whole intense collection. The atmosphere of the stories reeks of post-war Britain: chilly rooms and ill-lit streets, fuggy and over-heated trains, everywhere the slogans and detritus of wartime, bunting in the streets but slates missing and gables cracked. The external mood of the times is mirrored by the disturbed sense of self of each of his protagonists. Frenzied flight is never far away as in "After the Game" (1947) in which two former tank commanders meet by chance at a cricket match and, later, over beer and cigarettes, re-visit their war and the imposed memory of the war that has been manufactured for public consumption:

> ... this was... the first time [Edwards] had met or talked with any of the men he had known in the army, the first time in more than three years. Yet the immediately revived memories of persons and places and events were so fresh as to be startling. It really seemed that this whole other life had been continuing in perfect order beneath the apparent intermission.... They talked of men and of places, particularly of places; of small towns and villages in Belgium – Velm, St. Trond, Jodoigne; of the floods in Limburg, and the Christmas morning above Namur; of the mud of the Reichswald and the Rhine crossing at Rees; of Enschede and Hengele and Cuxhaven; and then, swinging back, of Nijmegen and Tilburg and Louvain; of Brussels – this with

265

a wealth of detail; of Douai aerodrome, of Falaise, of the factory at Caen, of the Vire-Vassy road and Point 176.

> ... The places and people came out in a steady stream... as if these memories had been dammed intolerably over the last years, and were now re-asserting their course.... While they ate, they talked of meals, then. Of green Camembert and the immature Calvados which burned the throat as it washed down a tinned steak pudding; of Cointreau and corned beef and hard biscuits eaten in the trucks in the dark streets of Louvain; of crème caramel in the farm at Velm; of a breakfast of raw marmalade pudding on that cold morning under Point 176.

They feel that the official memorialising of the "capital letter War", by politicians and professionals, has made the war "all lovely common knowledge" designed to deceive by helping "us to forget". But then their shared reminiscence amounts to "much the same; a campaign history, a tour of the battlefields" and "hardly ever a living moment of real memory". The memory which is triggered is of death and the nightmares inflicted on those guilty enough to live. The story ends with Edwards frantic to escape the encounter, certain he will never, by choice, meet his old comrade again. Nothing is what it seems in a Britain where normal men and women walk and talk and carry their secrets with them.

In "Mr Dearman Goes Home"[4] the smugness of knowledge is exposed over a short train journey as a lapse into ignorance but, first, there was the more confident reading of signs from a railway poster of a shepherd with crook and dog with grouped sheep and purple hills beneath the sun:

> Mr Dearman smiled. He could place this sort of thing. He could never, he told himself, be tricked by a railway poster into buying a ticket for an Arcadia, which he knew, when he arrived, would be dull and damp, like most of the English countryside. He noticed with interest, an obscene

scrawl across the shepherd's face. He wondered if the expletive was a comment on the art – Mr Dearman lectured to adult evening classes on modern art and felt he had a vested interest in popular taste. But he reminded himself it might be merely a specimen of the strange self-expression found in such places, of a kind with those which he now saw at the bottom of the poster: Kill all Jews (except Issy Bonn); What a Dump – no fags, no beer, no women; and Charley Buddle, Station Road, Thame, slept here 9/9/46, missed the connection. Mr Dearman always read these signs with great care, on the assumption that as an adult lecturer sociology was his business. "And of course, the killing need for self-expression," Mr Dearman said to himself. "If these people would only understand."

That is precisely what "these people" wish to avoid. "Understanding" ushers in the hidden vermin that kills a baby in a tale of sexual betrayal in wartime, "The Rat", and it brings on the sense of exclusion the man of "Fragment" experiences when he returns from the war to his wife and their now year-old child. This "Fragment" is so-called both because it leads to nowhere complete – a second pregnancy, his fevered anguish over sanity, their sticking together through the tensions of a present existence – and because it is torn from the earlier pages that led to the novel sequence "Brynllwyd", stripped of its earlier specificities. What had been written there was too raw to let surface in public. In life, though a sort of neutral stand-off was later reached in the 1950s, antagonism between Joy and his mother severely worsened, first with Merryn's birth and then Ederyn's in 1946. Joy was given to understand that, somehow, two children were, indeed, twice as bad as one; whilst the one Gwen had not wished to let go was pulled further and further away from her influence. There had been no girlfriend at home of any consequence before Joy; but there had been an alternative and Joy was to suffer from the dangled comparison.[5] In these fiction passages, excised from "Fragment", the unbearable pressures of these relationships found a temporary sublimation:

Mrs West's disapproval of the marriage – Tom West never gave his own opinion – appeared no more once David had made his definite intention clear. When David had gone on foreign service, and their first child had been born, Mrs West travelled to meet Mary for the first time. She was delighted with the child [and] in her letters to David she told him about this child and all she was making for her, but said nothing about Mary.

As Mary lies pregnant with David's second child and he prepares to visit his mother with Megan, the first born, the wife bursts into prolonged uncontrollable laughter that he finds "unforgivable" and "incredibly vulgar and obscene". The laughter follows David's statement that "I have some duty. The ties of home, what was my home, can't be broken completely."

Mary's objections are to deceit and hypocrisy; Raymond Williams here wrote dialogue he had heard more than created:

> ... her voice was broken "... you refuse to be honest about things which concern me. Why don't you tell your mother honestly what you think of her behaviour? You must be kind to her, I suppose. But I have to suffer it, take the insults and pretend to wink at the deception. How can you stand it?"
> "I don't know what you mean."
> His voice was rational, the accent careful.
> "Don't lie," she burst out. "You know well your mother has that girl in her house every minute she can. Can't you see why? It's just something to use against me, to keep you attached. Any weapons against a stranger, that's your border morality. I am the stranger; I married you, took you. You're mine now and she's lost you. But she thinks she'll get you back. She'll use everything – this girl is only a start – to get you away from me. I'd have thought that now, with your child inside me, your allegiance was pretty clear. But you're stupid, stupid. You play into her hands, because you won't let yourself see what she's doing."

The stories piled up and went nowhere. He was still revising pieces like "Fragment" in the early 1950s when the two earlier volumes had been pushed aside as separate entities and he was now envisaging a mixed collection, taken from both sets. The attached pseudonym of R.W. Ridyear seems a slight distancing of name and time, and, in reality, the stories were increasingly used more as quarry for the novels which were welling up. Yet, in two senses this heavy commitment to the shorter form was vital to him – first, because, for all their fictive integrity and fictional flight, they were too entwined with his own persona and life not to have been, in some measure at least, therapeutic; and, secondly, they were exercises in experimentation in that genre which Williams carried over and built on further in those other novels of the late 1940s and early 1950s which were a decided and deliberate turning away from any sense of autobiography-as-fiction. There is a palpable sense of relief in the way, in late 1948, he turns to adventure and a world he could *only* enter through imagination, and appropriation.

The original idea had come from Michael Orrom with whom he was still briskly collaborating.[6] Orrom, working daily in Soho, would spend hours browsing the shelves of secondhand bookstalls for "early writing about films". On one occasion, at Foyles on Charing Cross Road, he stumbled across something else, a book called *My Years in the Klondyke*, written in 1899. It told of a man who found a fortune in the Alaskan gold rush of 1898. Orrom saw it as an adventure that seemed to fast forward the hazards of life by increasing its usual pressures "ten thousand fold". He read more widely and thought of a film. Working for Rotha he had come across Arthur Calder-Marshall[7], a novelist of left-wing persuasion in the 1930s who had become a documentary scriptwriter and made *The World is Rich*, an award-winning film, with Rotha in 1946. Calder-Marshall suggested a radio documentary and introduced Orrom to the BBC's head of radio documentary, Lawrence Gilliam. A fiftieth anniversary was coming up, always a green light for broadcasting commissions, and one duly followed for a drama-documentary. Orrom, a little nervous of his own writing ability, asked his friend to write the dialogue; it was a "trouble-free collaboration". The script was accepted but never transmitted as slots and series came and went.[8] Orrom later agreed that Raymond could "borrow the material"[9] and the work first called "Brandon" and then "Ridyear" became his major writing project through the late summer of 1948 to its completion in the winter of 1949.

What survives – a number of fragmented versions of over a hundred pages, an almost complete typescript of over four hundred pages presented as a straight memoir, various pencilled synopses – is the major oddity in all of Williams' work and something he recalled as "a curious attempt" to marry an adventure story with "a sort of parable" about "contemporary and social experience". The latter, or what is left of it, emerges in the parallel story of Edward Rider, a writer who is introduced to the elderly and reclusive John Ridyear to hear, and perhaps write, his story. The novel, as complex form, begins by telling us, in its very first sentence, that: "This is the story of two adventures separated by more than fifty years in time, but connected in other ways, and particularly in my own life". That is, the life of Rider who speculates, Marlowe-like, at the moment of his entry into Ridyear's story on how "adventure can happen to anybody" and may not be defined in action terms alone but also through character and outcome. We have, then, two protagonists and twinned narratives which mesh only through Rider's role in both.

The pace is leisurely at first, almost a pastiche of Victorian tales of Empire and dark deeds in faraway places. Ridyear lives deep in the Sussex countryside in a mansion, The Stone House, set on high ground outside a village and approached by a long driveway. Leather, shaded lamps, oak, polish, grey stone and a black-dressed housekeeper set the tone. Ridyear lives in a room of white and gold which is reached by means of a long corridor with a "perfect curve" of a wall. The two come to an agreement that Rider will read Ridyear's half-begun account, listen to his story, research a chronology, question and collate. Rider insists on being able to go to his own home in the Welsh countryside to write it all up before returning. What is then introduced is a multiple-layer of narratives – Rider's introduction to the story, Ridyear's own first person account of his early life and the start of his adventure, Rider's narrative of the story – all of which do not tell the complete Ridyear saga which Williams only finishes, in the longest extant typescript, in the third person.

The outline of the Ridyear story is that of a young man pushed out of England in the mid-1890s by a combination of impoverished family circumstances and restless ambition. He sails from Liverpool for America and some three years later, with his new friends Winthrop and Roche, sets out for the fortune-making gold fields. There are fights, fallings-out and Roche's seemingly accidental death from drowning as the three make their ladened way across lake, river and mountain to the Yukon. They stake a claim. All around them the mushrooming settlements – overpopulated and under-resourced – parody the purposes of community by making self-aggrandisement and vigilante law their bedrock. Ridyear leaves for San Francisco only to return twelve months later to find the claim has yielded gold; but Winthrop, married to a schoolteacher of evangelising intent, tells him that his share is lapsed. Along with thousands of others who cannot, penniless, survive the winter isolation, he treks out. Winthrop, we learn, is later found shot dead in his cabin. Ridyear makes it back to London and a life of poverty from which he is mysteriously rescued by Winthrop's widow who has sold the claim and made a fortune. It is she who sets Ridyear up in Stone House, and she, or so it seems, who is the housekeeper who first takes Edward Rider to hear the story. It is clouded with the uncertainty memory lends to motivation. Perhaps, on the raft in the river, it was Ridyear who allowed Roche to die; perhaps it is Ridyear, or perhaps the schoolteacher, who has killed the parasitic Winthrop. We are left to surmise. Before Rider can probe his informant further Ridyear suddenly dies.

The narratives of the Ridyear story, first or third person accounts, are a heady mix of Boys' Own adventures – back-alley knife-fights, prostitutes with less than golden hearts, raft building and running the rapids, snowy passes and roaring gold towns – told in fast-moving, short-sentenced prose held up from time to time by more ponderous reflections on the

271

shifting nature of human relationships in adversity. Underlying it is the troubled mind of a man whose direction in life has been contorted by actions he may, at fatal cost to others, have taken to save his own life. The detail of life in the mining camps and the mass exodus of the miners on marches up and down the passes to Eldorado, Alaska's actual Sageaway, is riveting and clearly derived from first-hand accounts; but the attempt to write American accented dialogue only makes the historical background more authentic and the foreground of activity less so, rather like the magnificent scenery in a rollicking Hollywood 'B' movie.

So why did he write it at this time and against the grain of his direction? One answer is: Mankowitz. Envying the facility of the future novelist and scriptwriter, Williams may have hoped to emulate it. Certainly the ambition of "Ridyear" was Conradian in scope if not in execution and an indicator of how confined he felt he had become by the small change of academic articles, little magazines, pedagogy and the daily compromises of a domestic life. However, the reason for a biographical enquiry to pause over it as a link to Williams' life is found in the parallel adventure story of the "other" narrator, Edward Rider.

Most obviously, Rider is from the Black Mountains. His parents who had kept a small farm above "Dilwyn" are dead. Having sold the land and stock, Rider retains his boyhood home to which he retreats to write. The generalised detail of place for this fictional character then becomes more insistently autobiographical in its location as Raymond Williams turns to a room-by-room inventory of the house and the back-kitchen which only allowed entry into the house proper by going outside and in through another door so that, as in life: "When my mother and father were alive, we ate in the back-kitchen, to save carrying round the food." But, if place survives the parents do not. They are dead and their son has killed them, in his fiction, in order, it seems, to roam imaginatively over a world which, yearningly, could have been his own. Before the war there had been a farm and a second cousin, Eira, to whom he could have been married. Now, Rider feels almost, but not quite, "a stranger... in a village which was formerly one's own essential world, but in which one no longer plays any real part". It is through Eira, who had married another farmer, had a son, Maelor, and was widowed, that Rider seeks to re-connect with the world from which he has been displaced. The connections to Ridyear are heavily flagged in the joined symbols of Ogof Celyn, a cave found by chance before the war and entered by Rider and Eira, and by the mining underground in Alaska, whose results will see Ridyear end up in his own gold and white cave. The Dilwyn cavern is called The White Cave and, post-war, is to be further explored as a network of caverns under Eira's land. Williams drew up a single page for another novel in which he seemed to suggest the projected interplay. He headed it *The White Cave* and it combines, in alternate chapters, the stories of the separate quests of Ridyear and Rider, ending the fifteen chapters with these headings:

12.	Into Ogof Gwyn. The way back
13.	Eira and Dilwyn
14.	The steamer out, and home
15.	Eira and Maelor

He never managed to turn the digression of "Ridyear" into the more rounded satisfaction of *The White Cave*. That he thought to try is what is intriguing. He could not, in any possible reality, go home again as he once was. He could not, by extension, write a fiction in which, even if only imaginatively he could re-find a niche. Only when he had worked through the deeper structures of a place and time in which his own individual psychological concerns were not paramount, would he be able to see how to re-present those individual ties, broken but never discarded at either end, as the relationships which made his mature fiction into a realised history of lives lived socially.

Just as he later suppressed the unresolved nature of *Ridyear*, so he omitted completely, in his answers and chronology in *Politics and Letters* in 1979, both any reference to the contemporary stories he was writing at great speed in the late 1940s, and his Seaford-located novel about performance and identity. He worked on that, *The Art of the Actor* from the autumn of 1948 to the summer of 1951, after which he finally moved it down the list of his priorities. What survives indicates that he wrote, in the most sequential fragment, some 150 pages of typescript to which other work-in-progress was appended. In one version the second-hand bookseller is Arthur Wellman, in another it is Zeff and his wife Meg but, mostly, it is the more grounded Grant and Jane with their young daughter Sally. In the different attempts, all these characters live on the south-coast in a ground floor flat beneath the difficult and belittled landlady Mrs Natterden who, for her nocturnal noises, is re-christened Natty Bumpo. The surface is that of Williams' actual life in the late 1940s. The rest is inverted Williams, almost down to Grant's discourse on naturalism in acting in his acclaimed work *A History of the Art of Acting*. Grant wishes to follow this up with an illustrated historical account of *The Rise of the Actress* to indicate female influence on the spread of "naturalism" in the theatre. Grant, it seems, is at the polar end of any "academic" dismissal of the malign influence of the star actor on the text.

The novel is a pot-pourri of ideas through dialogue – Grant with his assistant, the donnish Bill Stephens who has been wounded in Spain and written a book on Expressionism; Grant with Dr Harris, retired G.P. and social theorist of a cranky exactitude; Grant with the long-suffering Jane who leaves him when his benign neglect extends to the illness of their child; Grant with Rawlinson, a friend who takes him through current theories of Time and Space; Grant with his friends in the metropolitan world, critics and actors, by whom he was introduced to Yvonne Marshall, the young actress with whom he begins an uncertain affair. As such, the novel sustains an interest which its limping shifts of scene from Flat to Bookshop to Theatre to Beach, as backdrop for all the conversations on life chances and the obligation to duty, threaten to halt at every step. Grant is not a wholly unsympathetic character; his pivotal position being that, a dissembler to himself, he can only argue that simulation of feeling, as in an actor's role or in a relationship, is not really deception but a compact, if successful, between performer and audience.

In this five finger exercise, full of hints of possible activity and desired freedoms, Raymond Williams again finally ran into the ground, all too well reflecting the frustration of his life in his art. But in the conversation between Grant and Rawlinson on the origins of human life and its contemporary effect on living, Williams wrote a dialogue which echoed his own wider needs and suggested a more limited place from which to kick on to reach them:

"I often think, you know," Rawlinson went on, "especially lying like this, just near the edge of the sea: it was really here, in a place like this, that the whole business began."

"What whole business?" Grant said, looking over the calm, bright sea, at the very distant edge of which a steamer was moving down-channel.

"The whole business of life," Rawlinson said. "It's a fact you know. It was just on the border between sea and land that it all started."

"You mean jellyfish?" Grant said yawning. He was very sleepy after the morning and the contact with the water.

"Yes, jellyfish," Rawlinson said seriously. "And all the other early creatures: the zoophytes, the seaweeds, the smaller crustacea and the algae."

"It's all a shade remote," Grant said.

"No," Rawlinson said. "No, not at all. I often feel when I'm lying here, that one can know again exactly those first stirrings of life; feel, as it were, the quick of it."

"I don't really think so," Grant said, turning on his stomach. "We lie on the pebbles, as we lie on history; both obstinately hard and angular."

"Yes, but in imagination," Rawlinson said. He was speaking very earnestly. "What I mean is, Edward, one looks out at the sea, at all that alien element, and it makes one feel, don't you think, very small and insignificant and accidental?"

"...I somehow never feel like that," Grant said. "Perhaps I've not read enough."

"It isn't a case of reading; there the things are," Rawlinson insisted. "I mean just think of the distances...

the earth is here, the size of a pebble and on that scale the nearest star is fifty thousand miles away."

"… This is the new religion, perhaps," Grant said. "Every galaxy a deity and the dinosaurs the founding fathers. I don't object to the calculation of these things, but I feel quite disinclined to worship them."

"If it is the reality, if this is our universe, surely it's necessary to take account of it," Rawlinson said steadily.

"I'll start a new table on astronomy, if you like," Grant said, smiling. "But apart from that, it'll keep, and can, as far as I'm concerned."

"It's no use blinking realities, Edward."

"No", Grant said, again yawning. "But you'll be telling me next how Melanesian women leave their gardening and rape every passing man. So they may and good luck to them, but Melanesia is a long way away."

"It's a distortion of a complicated bit of evidence," Rawlinson said. "But again, it's a part of the human reality."

"A good actor," Grant said, "sticks to his own lines."

* * * * * *

"After the War," Joy Williams emphasised after her husband's death, "all he wanted to do was write."[10] In 1946, he had instinctively turned to a form of writing through which he could make sense of himself and twenty years later, in 1966, he wrote an autobiographical sketch for a proposed American volume, *Mid Century Authors*, in which he noted the salience of the year: "In 1946 I started again on the unpublished novel, and it went through about seven re-writings until it was finally published, now in a wholly different form, as *Border Country* in 1960…"[11]

In this sense, *Border Country* (1960) was the begetter of *Culture and Society* (1958), or rather that, in 1946, his imagination was the facility he most trusted. That summer of graduation and limitless ambition had begun as if, since he was intimate with it all, he already knew it all. The surviving typescript of 1946, fragmented and muddled in places, runs to around two hundred and fifty pages and, though untitled, is the clear precursor to the versions that would follow for over a decade.[12] This is the story of David West, the University-bound son of Tom West and his wife Sarah; of his friends the preacher's son and platform orator, Gwilym Rees and the local girl, variously Glynis or Gladys; of growing up to be educated out; and, in this version, of actually returning with his English wife, Mary. The novel begins in the late 1930s and, skipping the war, takes us into the post-war world in a chronologically straightforward manner. Its actual locational cradle is changed in name but, as it will be consistently thereafter, is easily placed from its opening words: "The village of Bwlch lies across the mouth of the Mandry valley where the western plain wrinkles into the foothills of the Black Range".

This continues for four pages as a bird's-eye-view of physical features and field patterns, swooping down to take in church and pub and school as landmarks before landing us in the Wests' kitchen for tea and talk. The mapping is rather antiseptic, even sour in tone:

> Above this string of public buildings, which only the extremely tortuous road could connect, the homes of the villagers rise, in scattered groups, towards the hills. Some abstract description might convey an impression of a lovely terraced village but in the particular, Bwlch is very far from that. No single mind or collective consciousness has imposed its pattern on the village, so that there is no tradition of building, and no unity.

What follows is relentless description of what is other to David West from the outside and what is inner to him presented as the necessary focus around which life and relationships must flow. There are events – political meetings in the by-election, public meetings to discuss and argue the benefits of a new water scheme, mountain walks and family quarrels – and there are story lines: David's gradual turning away from the local girl Glynis/Gladys who is favoured and selected by his mother for him whilst, in the Army, he meets Mary, schoolteacher daughter of a Sussex doctor, and marries her; but nothing that suggests they are much more than a frame for David's sentimental journey. At times the prose lurches into quasi-biblical cadence as a deeper unsettled history of Abbeys and Warriors is interwoven with the stolidity of work and settlement. Nothing quite convinces in depth or roundness of appreciation except, perhaps, for the rushing hysteria of the post-war passages where the underlying conflict between Mary and his mother, doting on the replacement child they have provided, emerges as argument and denunciation. It is when David spends hours away from Mary with Gladys that the crisis breaks.

The only sensible biographical speculation is why Williams chose to re-imagine the tensions in his own life in this fashion, for he did not return to Pandy, Joy decidedly did not ever live there, and nor was Gladys any physical embodiment of earlier attachments. Yet, in 1946, a looming detachment from Pandy was about to break in his life directly, caused by the dislike of mother for daughter-in-law, and vice-versa, which would never be properly healed. The use of his own background to create this solipsistic fiction places it not further from observable fact, but closer to the unbearable personal isolation he was carrying around with him. The coiled prose emits a scream:

> "Well?" she asked.
>
> "Nothing happened," he said.
>
> "You've told one lie. Not for the first time. Can you ask me to believe you now?"
>
> "Well perhaps we don't mean the same thing by 'nothing'."
>
> "You put your own construction on everything you take part in."
>
> "How can you know what happened?" he asked. "It's hidden."
>
> "Not very efficiently."
>
> "You doubt my capacity?"
>
> "My dear David, your capacity was always your own illusion. Capacity was just part of the mother's boy

atmosphere. For her you had to be something. And you had sufficient talent for cheating to fool her, and some of the others."

"But not you."

"Me for a long while."

"But no longer."

"No."

In the novel-fragment the ensuing row degenerates into vicious name-calling and separation and, though we are given to understand by an anonymous third person that David changes, the verdict is still damning: "I found him, as his maturity took shape, always exciting, although at times his instant percipience, based as it was on an almost total destruction of all he had been, a ghastly self-annihilation, amounted, in its effect practically to terror."

The after-shock of changed circumstances was all around the tyro writer and teacher. In a new job, in a new house, in a new country, with a new baby, he lived for the first time in any settled sense with his wife in a new domesticity where routine could be arranged but goals and targets were by no means fixed. Even at home, as Pandy would essentially remain for him, he saw different patterns emerge, but now without him. Between October 1946 when Harry Williams travelled to Seaford to help set up their first house, taking with him cans of fruit, plants and seeds and his inexhaustible expertise as a handyman, and until May 1947 he did not see his parents at all. Harry's diary records the depth of that winter, from January to March, with the hard frosts and snow that then turned into February's deep drifts, with ice and frost following on to make roads impassable for cars and buses on glassy surfaces. In March, as winter seemed to return, snow blizzards buried whole trains and it only departed with gales and incessant rain. When the storms began Harry had slipped and broken his leg and was not able to return to work until mid-March. The winter only finally ended when a curtailed spring arrived and mountain thaws made swollen rivers flood. Letters took the details to Seaford where Harry and Gwen visited briefly in May.

For Joy this brought ample confirmation that both the Williams men were controlled by Gwen, the "dominant character" of a "domineering home. They had to do what she decided and, if not, she could be sulking, difficult, bad tempered". Quarrels between Joy and Raymond, both acutely conscious of the Lawrence "model", took off when son defended mother to whom, Joy felt, his "loyalties as a child" still lay. Gwen encapsulated the certainty from which education – "the whole thing... plotted" by the father – had removed him. For his wife, a mother-in-law who was "horrified" at the arrival of other children and "played up" in hurtful scenes about dealing with the children was increasingly insupportable.[13] Joy Williams did not visit Pandy from the spring of 1946 to the Indian summer of 1950, when the open quarrel of November 1947 flared again. On that occasion Gwen had accompanied Harry by train for a weekend in Seaford. For Raymond, the injured party was clearly his wife to whom, no scintilla of doubt now intervening, he committed himself, even against his mother, in a letter written to his parents on their return home:[14]

16 December	We have a letter from Jim that gives us a great shock and wrote back trying to straighten things out.
17 December	A miserable day for both of us worrying about yesterday's letter.
18 December	Mam is completely knocked out. I write another sharp letter seeking explanations.
20 December	We get a letter from Jim which does not yet clear things up.
23 December	A further letter from Jim and we fail to understand what they can find wrong.
25 December	Mild and we spend a very quiet day with very many disturbing thoughts.

Harry started the New Year, 1948, as a new employee of the national-ised railways as "the great experiment of Nationalisation begins" and thirty five years as a member of the GWR staff ended. Peace with his son only came at the end of the month at his own initiative:

> 25 January   I call up Jim and have a straight talk to him and hope to straighten it out for everybody's sake.

> 30 January   It is good to see a letter from Jim and we will try to have no further cause for misunderstanding.

That was to prove a forlorn hope: 1950 brought "a really agonising day for all of us" when "more words" didn't improve matters so "must keep silent". These rifts were not only happening at a distance; they were occurring when Pandy itself was being pulled into that "inorganic" post-war world Raymond Williams was confronting in his reading and thinking; and his father was soon a busy part of it. From early 1947 Harry was anxiously looking to buy a car and travelling to Hereford in search of one. In August 1947, post-war shortages notwithstanding, Harry's extended family in Birmingham found a suitable car for him and with £300 removed from his Bank saving account ("I feel quite rich"), he brought it home. Harry finally passed his driving test in January 1948 and for him and Gwen more frequent short trips and holidays followed. However, the car's main role was as the essential vehicle for transport for the produce of the growing business in honey, fruit and flowers, to market towns on the Border, in which he was increasingly engaged. He was, in terms of *Border Country*, becoming the entrepreneurial Morgan Rosser whose commercial exploits Raymond Williams rightly stressed were aspects of Harry Williams, but separated out in that novel's father figure, from the signalman Harry Price.

Harry Williams was fulfilling his life's dreams quickly in post-war Britain. He had long yearned to leave the cramped Llwyn Derw, whose interior would figure so much in his son's fiction, and move across "the Patch" into Llwyn Onn, a more substantial stone-faced, bay-windowed semi-detached house with three bedrooms where the Griffiths family had once lived. For some it was a gloomier dwelling. For Harry it was a proper home, not a cottage knocked into shape from former workshop buildings. In April 1948 the agreement to take the property was reached and buyers for Jim's childhood home also found. Harry's diary swells with domestic activity as he visits sales in the "Big House", Glanhonndu, to buy china and glass, to Hereford for a glass table and to Abergavenny for curtains and new linoleum. By November they had moved in furniture, employed plumbers and electricians and plasterers, and put up wallpaper. Harry and Gwen slept "in an empty Llwyn Derw" for the last time on 16 December 1948 and on the 17th, with their "very own bathroom" to wonder at, "go to bed at Llwyn Onn for the first time, very tired". The work on the house was finished before Christmas Day which they spent in their new home, alone. For Jim, who was to imagine their first arrival in Pandy in such vibrant detail in his novel, there would be no emotional attachment to the new house. It would never be home again. Harry notes a "letter from Jim" in February 1949 and in that same month in Seaford his exiled son dreams of an unwritten novel to be called "Brynderw".

He played with a series of titles for the novel he now picked up again in 1949, filling scraps of paper in pencil with names, ideas, isolated passages, chapter contents, topic lists, word counts, symbolic schemes and even a sketchmap of the village's location and lay-out marked by the Honddu, the river of black water. It was after the latter that he had named the long opening tale of his planned volume of "First Stories", at over twenty thousand words, but by 1948 this had been taken out of the list completely for use again in a longer work, a novel of self and home. When he finally turned to it again by name, in the spring of 1949, it was no longer the "distant prospect" of "Brynderw" but the more definite "Brynllwyd", which he now scribbled across the tops of flimsy paper.[15]

Brynllwyd was, from its opening pages, more assured than anything he had written before, as if he had accepted the end of a process and was now more genuinely intent on envisaging its meaning than in telescoping it into more current concerns. The focus was shifted from the adult son to the parents, including their individual difficulties of personality and relationship, as he thickened the layers of detailed living and layered in a much broader social canvas. Even so, this novel, his first major completed work, begins with a birth. That of a son. It was, again, to be the son's story but, we soon learn, a story only to be understood through its connections, until they fray and snap.

The diagrammatic structure he had pencilled in before he proceeded was turned when he had finished, sometime in 1950, into a typed single page or "Scheme". He had written over seven hundred typed pages and seven chapters in which, for the first time in any extended fashion, he had attempted to tie together the lives of his parents, his own upbringing and the social and psychological pressures caused by his departure. Or rather the departure of the boy registered as "Martin George" by an insistent father, George Price, the railway signalman, and universally called "Jim" through the practice of a determined mother, Ellen. The first four chapters, two thirds of the completed typescript, are the most resolutely autobiographical, at least in the sense that they stick to known incidents and a traceable history, and in their vivid re-telling have a fresh, page-turning vivacity. Until, that is, he flounders again into the morass of Martin's sexual awakening and social displacement. The concentration on a child's-eye view in alliance with an empathetic, though not entirely sympathetic, account of George and Ellen, produces a convincingly powerful narrative which only falls apart when he resorts to an embroidered plot of social inter-stitching that leaves the world of Brynllwyd behind. It was one solution, of course, but, for him, as writer and man, it would not suffice.

This time he begins the novel not as an omniscient surveyor of a map but by plunging us right into the middle of a storm that is wracking the village of Brynllwyd. The mountains, lashed by high winds and rain, spill their waters into the swollen Honddu. It is autumn. A sole yellow light burns in the scattered group of houses near the grass covered tumps of an old stone quarry. A woman is giving birth. A man is out in the rain unblocking the culvert. The birth is a hard one. The midwife is an older neighbour. The man, soaked to the skin, is kept away. The boy is born and then it is morning. All this is told at a relentless pace, not stopping to inform us who these people are or what they do. Throughout the novel the reader is made aware of the power of water, even down to its social ordering or denial, and of the enticing threat of fire, and the release of air. Liberated by his use of symbols for the passage of human existence which are yet specific enough to be given actual, mundane forms in the burning of a hayrick, the dangers of swampy bogs, the perspectives gained from mountain tops, Williams eases himself into a confidently full-hearted description of what passes for ordinary life.

Here, more so than in later re-tellings, we learn of the background of George and Ellen, of her father's sudden death and the eviction of herself and her mother from a tied cottage; we meet, with the boy Martin, George's father and mother in their own cottage home. Both George Price and Ellen Shepherd are seen in the round. They have met and married in the war, in 1917, when he was on leave after being wounded and hospitalised. George finds work as a railway signalman "at the little station of Llanverthine" and they find lodgings, in a dwelling converted by the local builder from his workshop, in Brynllwyd. We are in familiar territory, though in this accurate snapshot Raymond Williams reverses the image and gives the name Llwyn Derw, his boyhood home, to the actual house that stood opposite and into which his father had just moved:

> The Brynllwyd houses were seven in number, strung out along the banks of the brook. Nearest the road, and on the north bank, was the largest house, Brynllwyd itself, a square red house of eight main rooms, in which the builder, Mr Evans and his wife lived childless. Upstream on the same bank, was a smaller version of the same house, thirty years older,... where Mr Evans had himself grown up.... Behind this house – of which the name was Llwyn Celyn – was the old building workshop, now divided into two

cottages. In the nearer of these to Llwyn Celyn lived the Prices; next door were an old couple, a retired police sergeant and his wife, the Duggans. The lane to all these houses ran between them and the brook.

Opposite Brynllwyd house was a high wooden footbridge, which led to the other houses. There was a block of two near the bridge; new, rough-cast houses, built on the urban biretta pattern, with through corridors from the adjacent front doors.... The last house of the group stood near the brook opposite the Prices', facing east, and with a blank side wall nearest the brook. It was named Llwyn Derw, from the nearby oak. The tree was, in fact, on the other side of the brook, but it had not originally been thought necessary to give the workshop a name. Its cottages were now known, simply, as Brynllwyd Cottages, 1 and 2. Llwyn Derw was occupied by a bachelor, the minister of the local Baptist chapel, the Rev. T.H. Rees-Jones.

The focus is then widened to spot the landscape with the public buildings of Brynllwyd and to populate its adjacent villages with those who "lived" as opposed to those who merely "resided" there; the latter is presented "in the class sense of the term" and takes in a small group of retired colonial officials and businessmen, notably the Claverley family of Llangattock House, a tree-screened large Victorian residence. Their appearance in the novel, intermittent and in episodes of conflict with George, is sketchy, since for this fiction they will only serve as a trapdoor for Martin's dilemma; his early dislike of Jane Claverley ends, for him and the novel, in a love match away from Brynllwyd and the nearby town of Abergrwyne. Having then established these social and historical settings, down to pinpoint detailing of the interior of the cottage, with its separate back-room kitchen and the "Room" which you could only enter by an outside door, he elaborates his twinned themes: how does a man live a life of meaning and integrity within given circumstances and bounded horizons without the weakening of despair, and how can other lives be made more equal and fulfilling without betraying that hard-won meaning and integrity?

George is shaded with unexpected complexity. He is absorbed in his work, respectable and mostly teetotal, yet obsessive about money, especially any debts loosely incurred by Ellen. When charity is offered by Captain Hannon, a family friend of the Claverleys, it is bitterly spurned, and in his temper George hits out at Ellen. In all things George wants his due worth, and no more than that, to be acknowledged. An episode Raymond Williams retained for subsequent versions sums up his stubborn integrity: when his son is sent on an errand by the elderly neighbours and loses the pound note with which he has been entrusted, George, furious with the boy, insists on paying it back despite having no leeway to do so. Then when the money is discovered not to have been in Mrs Duggan's purse at all, he stifles his rage at the way in which emotions can be so stirred and distorted by trivial materiality and a whim of fate. This George Price accepts his own fate but more resentfully than his fictional successors. In *Brynllwyd*, when he meets his social superiors he is gruff, even surly; he addresses them as "Sir" but in a resentful tone of subservience. George is set to be acculturated when he decides to attend "a course of lectures in the Assembly Hall, on *Great Figures in English Literature*" at the suggestion of "the local schoolmaster".

> At first he had been shy of the idea, but eventually he agreed to attend whenever he was not on the turn from two till ten. Not the least person pleased at his decision was Ellen. She had been disturbed by the fact that George was taking an increasing interest in politics. It was not that she disagreed with his views – indeed she was willing to support them in the secret ballot – but she feared the effect of aggressive politics in a village where conservative and religious temper was so marked. The village men who thought of themselves, in the new phrase, as workers were in a tiny minority. The small farmers worked to pay the interest on their mortgages, rather than for wages; and so

placed themselves as if by natural right on the side of the masters and the owners of property. The farm labourers, who in most minds were obviously workers knew well – and if they forgot were quickly reminded – that their job was to work, as such, rather than to be a worker in the political sense of that term. The few railwaymen, and some of the roadmen, were the only men to belong to a trade union. George, as one of the most active of these – he had arranged meetings at the time of the General Strike, and a few political meetings, in the Labour cause, in succeeding years – was in a fair way to become notorious in the village, and of all things Ellen did not want that. It made it difficult with Mrs Evans who had been very kind to them and in other ways it would bring harm. The idea of taking an interest in Literature seemed a good way for him to occupy his mind.

Direct politics for the father-character is always at one remove in *Brynllwyd*. The General Strike is just a part episode rather than the defining moment it will prove to be in *Border Country*. And it is, piece by piece, the education of Martin that divorces him from the "children's books" his father is given to study in a reversal of actual life growth. For, as yet, in Williams' fiction, though aspects of George's work are dealt with lovingly through the eyes of a child invading the adult world of the signal box, there is no full recognition of the independent, indeed self-sufficient, state that the father has, in fact, attained.

The centre of attention, in the novel, switches to Ellen's Jim who is only slowly transformed into George's Martin. The book lingers over boyhood games and adventures and circles of friends in a recall of memory clearly as affectionate as it is deep. It gives the novel, in places, a lyricism more sparingly present in *Border Country*. When Williams tries his hand at a broader comedy – the Hardyesque capers of country people at the village Eisteddfod and a close-up replay of the drama Martin and Gwilym write to raise money for village amenities – it is done with a subtle understanding of how conscious the community is of the role it chooses, in public view, to perform: "The distinction between the acting of country people and the characters of country sketches was less a distinction between illusion and reality than one between varying degrees of illusion. The primary interest was in antics. Acting was fooling about. At moments the actors took themselves seriously, but in fact they knew that they were there to make fools of themselves, and it was this the audience had come to see."

By the time Martin has reached this understanding in his own late adolescence he has also learned how to generalise his growing knowledge beyond a country experience. It is Ellen, not George, who gives Jim two books for Christmas – Euripides' *Trojan Women* and a *Book of Flowers*. It is Ellen who shampoos his hair with egg to make it shine and then takes Jim to sit his Scholarship Exam in Abergrwyne where he comes top of all the district. It is Ellen who, more quickly than George, recognises a distancing of love in the boy and reconciles herself to his growing difference. All this is effected with a telling economy of language, as shown in Jim's immersion in the trial of examinations and the disdain of village schoolmasters at his groping, ambitious will to succeed against their definition of him as little "Jimmy Price". Over several pages of immense passion, though just in the pinging of one word against another, Raymond Williams found a poetry to show what his future paraphrasing would spell out elsewhere in his critical works:

> ... they would go to play along the brook, or in the fields up to the quarry and the tumps. Every detail of these fields became known to them: the small island in the brook, with the wild rhubarb of which they could pick the broad leaves to send sailing on the water... the tumps themselves where they rolled on the yielding turf; and the quarry in which grew blackberries and dog-roses. This was their actual learning of the country: an intimate discovery and handling of natural objects, only a few of which they could name. There were primrose, bluebell, cowslip, foxglove, violet, honeysuckle, dogrose, daisy, hen-and-chickens, anemone; oak, ash, birch, beech, elm, hazel, alder, willow, hawthorn, blackthorn, mountain-ash, holly, yew, larch and pine. There were the

eggs and nest of blackbird, thrush, hedge-sparrow, starling, swift, robin, peewit, rook, wren, lark and moorhen.

These were actual, assumed knowledge; experience that was taken for granted. But this experience came increasingly to be set alongside a different kind of knowledge of the countryside: the books of what was usually described as nature lore, which Jim, in particular, read assiduously. At the beginning there was no conflict between the two varieties of learning, but as the reading became wider, there were the beginnings of conflict. He had begun with a book on fungi his father had once bought.

And from unfamiliarity with a plethora of mushrooms, he graduates to beetles, birds, eggs and flowers, to be bewildered by their variety and a nomenclature which leads him to a dictionary and the further discovery that much of the naming his family did was, well, just "Vulg.":

Ox-slip, which he often picked on the field up to the tumps, was only to be found in East Anglia. The commonly-called ox-slip was a large cowslip, or a cross-breed of the several kinds of cow-slip. Only commonly called; Vulg.

... The wild rhubarb on the island was butterbur... Hen-and-chickens was called Birds'-Foot Trefoil (Hen-and-chickens Vulg.)... Hardheads were knapweed; Birds'-eye was the Germander Speedwell. The moon-daisy which grew on the railway bank below the box was not called that, it was dog-daisy or ox-eye. The leaves of the mullein and the foxglove were easily confused. The bog cotton on the mountain was called Bog Myrtle... The Spotted Lily was called Lords and Ladies and the name he knew for it must be Vulg.

...

Spring came towards the end of March, with long, warm days. The books for a time were put away, for there was hard work at school; in April there would be a Scholarship. Nature Lore. These vivid glimpses of Nature Lore. Earned good marks.

289

He tried, for a time to relate the names he had learned to their birds, beetles, fungi and flowers. There were so few that could be identified that he gave it up. He sensed the direction himself, and this was passively agreed. The two faculties, of naming and experiencing, grew ever more distinct and separate.

There would, of course, be no turning back for Jim. There would even be a personal and parental satisfaction to take from Jim's ability to become that other son, Martin. And part of this shape-shifting is just about growing up. Still, a part of it, too, is about not wanting to lose hold of something just in order to grasp something else, something alien to what, say, a family had had together. *Brynllwyd* reaches to a number of crescendos across its sprawling length but one comes relatively early on and is the most poignant:

> A few oak leaves floated over the reflected scene [in the water butt], and he shifted so that they would pass over his eyes and mouth.
> A shout came from the lane, and, letting his feet drop to the ground he turned in its direction. It was George, already half off his bicycle, waving a newspaper in his hand.
> – Mam, Jim, he's through.
> – What is he then, she asked gently.
> – He's first. Top of the county. 143 marks.
> Out of 150 I expect. First anyway.
> Jim was still standing on the crown of the little path. The bitter smell of the water butt remained in his nostrils, and it seemed that the reflection on the iridescent pool of his own face and shoulders, with the hair falling downwards, was still the scene at which he gazed. The dance of tiny waves of light and water remained like a gauze over his eyes. George and Ellen at the low door of the back-kitchen; the square red posts of the porch; the piled sleepers at the end of the house under the apple tree: all were seen through

this net of iridescence. His eyes dropped as he heard George's words. *First anyway*. The sheen net tightened, and the objects behind it trembled slightly. *First anyway*.

– Come here, Jim, his father said, holding out his arms.

He walked slowly forward, and George took him under the arms and swung him up towards the roof of the porch.

– Not up there, Dad, said Ellen.

– No, Mam, no. I was just giving him a lift.

Jim looked up to see his mother's eyes fixed on him. He smiled at her, a gratified, confidential smile.... He felt suddenly secure again.... When his father had called him to his arms he had thought for a moment that he would be gathered close to his body, that the strong arms would press him closer inwards to the rough coat and the firm shoulder. When, instead, he had been swung in the air... he had felt suddenly frantic, and was prepared to kick to stop himself being put up there. His mother's intervention had come just in time.

Williams had found a part of his major theme and, for most of this novel, a form to give it an effective shape. The second thread of the novel sticks almost as closely to the life he had lived in Pandy and, with the emergence of Martin into self-awareness, is as engrossing as a narrative. It falters, as a novel, precisely where it strives towards the entirely fictitious and to assume a fictive form that can make Martin's life more vitally interesting than the staider one his creator had pursued. If this seems a paradox it is so only insofar as he had not yet taken the further imaginative step of perceiving that the portrayal of a mature consciousness of those earlier lives would allow for the more profound illumination to come.

Whatever ultimate resolution Raymond Williams may have been seeking, here the overall direction appears, still, to be more outward than not. We know that few of his close colleagues at the time of writing knew him to be Welsh and in this they echoed earlier Cambridge acquaintances. He remained ambivalent about what exactly he was, in those kinds of terms, until he was in his middle age. What lurks in the fiction that was relative to himself, however, is an obsessive prodding of this whole more generalised question. *Brynllwyd* refers constantly to Welshness, and the Welsh language, as class definers against others. It is another colour of saying which people recognise as their own. It is the English gentry who have mangled and mis-pronounced and made official the very places in which the people live and the gentry merely reside. Of the Minister, Rees-Jones, we read: "As minister, he was required to preach in English, although most of his congregation spoke Welsh. It was held that to the bi-lingual it was only a partial loss to have the sermon in the alien language, while to the few who did not speak Welsh the loss in a Welsh sermon might be almost total. The Rev. Rees-Jones, however, regularly practised in Welsh. He thought in Welsh. His speaking voice was Welsh. It was difficult, he explained, to *pitch* a sermon in English. The English sacred manner was merely solemn."

He could scarcely leave it there, however, for most of the "Welshness" that he, without the language, was forced to imbibe was a hodge-podge of sentimentality and patriotic trumpeting. The future self-titled "Welsh European", remarkably enough, pondered on all this, too, as early as 1949. He gives Martin the best of the argument against Gwilym as they look at and think of "the border castles – to keep the English out or the Welsh in?" – and Martin insists the Welsh fought as mercenaries with the invaders:

> And I for one don't blame them. I am very glad of what the English did to the Welsh, as well as what the Welsh did to the English. You won't find me in any little Welsh gang, thanking God for my Welshness. Pure latter-day Welshness has only one real talent: cant. They might even have caught it from the English, and worked it up from a stiff upper lip mumble to full male voice choir.
> – It's wrong to speak bad of your own people, Martin.
> – It's wrong to speak bad of your own intelligence.
> Anyway, what's it to me. Let them go on with their Druids, who were never Welsh anyway, and their lovely

Eisteddfod mummery, which was faked up for them about the time of Ossian...

– The Welsh have an ear, said Gwilym.

– Welsh rhythms, of course. In English, taking their place in that whole complex of speech, the Welsh rhythms are important. On their own I think they are decadent: poetry mechanised to demagogy.

– You don't think much of your own people, then?

– They are good and bad, more good than bad on the whole. But whenever a people becomes as conscious of its difference from others as the Welsh have – and the Irish more than the Scots – then the way is open for every kind of cant and posturing. If I am made to choose between the European tradition and the Welsh, no Celtic tourism will bring me here. The Welsh is a major part of the English tradition, not a cut-price privacy behind a string of castles.

If this extraordinary novel, so much more dangerous in its cool dissection, so much more moving in its array of dilemmas, than the cleverness of *The Art of the Actor* or the dogged fabulousness of *Ridyear*, holds one further, unexpected surprise, it is the chance encounter on Black Darren, Brynllwyd's looming mountain, which Williams engineers between Martin, in his final school year, and an English writer, James Franken, who has come to live in Priests' Valley in the old Abbey. Franken, a friend of the Claverleys, has seen and admired Martin's play. He tells him that he farms the land, though not personally of course, and tries to write accurately of the countryside and those who live and work in it. They talk of the history of that landscape and the relation between mountain, plain and valley. Franken speaks of a "rich tradition" and of the nature of "everyday... neighbourliness". Martin is more sceptical. Franken recommends he read Lawrence and George Bourne and that he should come for tea and further conversation at the Abbey. So, the Friday after Easter with his final examinations confidently in sight, Martin takes a "small market bus" to the top of Priests' Valley.

The next episode is without precedent in anything else Williams ever wrote. It remains a fiction, of course, but it is another possible exit out for the fictional Martin, one as socially as it is sexually other, which reveals graphically that the writer had considered, for Martin, this changed boy, many possible futures other than settlement of any kind.

They sit for tea and talk of books "and the past of the valley", when suddenly Martin looks up from a book to see Franken across from him in a deep armchair:

> The event was a matter of seconds. A third person in the room, perhaps even Franken himself, could not have been aware of it. Martin sat forward, tightening his fingers on the book. He was suddenly aware of an intense physical excitement, a physical desire of a kind wholly new in his remembered experience. He made to move forward, to touch the man's body, but he remained, as he knew he must remain, perfectly still…. He felt his cheeks burning, and was aware, although it was only a matter of seconds, that he was staring at the other. Unobtrusively, he looked back down at his book, and the event had ended.
>
> …
>
> When he was alone again, he considered the experience and attempted to account for it or explain it. He was perfectly aware of its nature, at least insofar as the desire itself was concerned. He was aware, also, of the stated general disapproval of desires of the kind. But he did not feel any need to disapprove the feeling he had. He was aware suddenly, and the knowledge seemed to him significant, that this was the first moment of physical desire about which he felt no admitted guilt…. Yet he was, in spite of this, deeply disturbed… the reason was not the direction of his desire, but the sudden, almost blinding, irruption into consciousness of a force of which he had not been aware…. It seemed incredible, and certainly contradictory to all his ideas of the nature of feeling, that a moment in a casual, even an emotionless relationship, should have become, in

silence and stillness, while he stared through a writhe of ascending smoke, passionate.

The remaining third of the novel lurches just as unexpectedly in style as in subject matter although the tensions that have been called into play through the driven life of Martin remain at its core. First, and inevitably, Martin leaves his village for Cambridge but he also does not quite leave behind two romantic, unconsummated attachments. He hovers between the schoolfriend, Glynis, who wishes to have his child, and Margiad, a farmer's daughter, to whom he is increasingly attracted but with whom he fails to make love. In stages the novel becomes epistolary: letters home to the girlfriend, to his parents, to the local newspaper; or pieces of prose, like "Red Earth", his undergraduate satire of undergraduate writing, are slotted in alongside a sub-Joycean phantasmagoria of nocturnal big city life in search of drink (found) and sex (a prostitute rejected). Page after page floats free of what appeared to be the grounded main text as Martin slips his moorings. When we return to Cambridge it is to an account of those years that is less like the politics-soaked years of Williams' fictional Paul Ramsay and rather more concentrated on the relationship Martin strikes up with the slim, fair-haired Jane Claverley, whose gentry links from home are resented but who, encountered at a Cambridge party, begins to move to the centre of Martin's life.

If the fictional Jane is neither Joy nor Anne Richmond any more than Martin is Raymond she is, nonetheless, in the location of her room where they sit and talk or silently work no less than in her utility as a sounding board for Martin's sometimes cold insults and gauche posturing, a facsimile of the situation of his fraught years in war-time Cambridge. In the novel they become, touchingly and guiltily, lovers, and begin to commit their lives to each other. The writing is stiffly done as it attempts a sketch of undergraduate wits and acquaintances beyond Martin's social circle. It reads somewhat as an exploratory probing of feelings whose motives the author still suspects. Possibilities are stretched in this fiction. The protagonist does not merely let go of the expectations of home and upbringing, he positively subverts them by teetering on the edge of a union which would indeed be one of marrying out of his confines. Perhaps not surprisingly, even in this fiction, it is not quite tested to the full. Much is left unresolved. Though not before, more fully here than elsewhere, Raymond Williams forces a direct confrontation between, first, the Son and the Father and then, even more tellingly, between Mother and Son.

This all occurs in his last chapter, "Chapter Seven" or "Three Encounters", where the third confrontation will be between Martin and existence itself. The first, between George and Martin in the former's signalbox, occurs when a newly graduated Martin returns home. His degree is completed and he has been called up: "First signals and then a fighting job." His secret, however, is the classification of his degree. He will not tell and George, until he can bear it no longer, will not ask. The stand-off has been deliberately provoked by a son who will not readily give the satisfaction of pride in his achievement to a father who, he now thinks, has not understood how both have been duped into the betrayal of self-deception by a competitive system which should have been anathema to all their professed beliefs. Worse, for the quarrel that is to ensue, Martin has been awarded a First. His father angrily rehearses the life chances that he has never had and which his arrogant son appears to spurn, even to the point of throwing them back in the face of family aspiration:

> – What we've said is that the best places in education shouldn't simply follow the money. That everybody should have an opportunity, and money should not count either way. Then if he's good enough...
> –... But isn't that capitalism to the very core? Isn't it all the narrowness of a society that has lost so much of life that it can only think in terms of winning or getting on?
> – Yes, but a poor boy never used to have the chance. What happened to me? I left school at thirteen and went crow-scaring. Would it have been wrong for me to have a chance?
> – Yes.

– Well, I don't agree.

– It is wrong for you or me or anyone to have a chance of winning over other people. It is a miserable kind of thing to use your life for.

– It's not so much that we want to win, mun. For most of us it's just been a case of keeping up.

– [But]... what happens to the promising boy – the boy who promises to go on? An egg is broken over his head, and he is marched in knickerbockers to be questioned by the priests. He says to them that the spring is dewy, fragrant, balmy in fact... and then if they can number him in the thirty out of seventy three, they stick a pen in his ear and say Go on, little man; go thou onward and upward, little climber;... and whatsoever things thou canst repeat the answers of, think on these things.

– Yes.

George laughed, and Martin, smiling, walked across the box to the long black bench, and sat down there. He glanced nervously at the space under the flap table below the window where he had hidden from the inspector. He looked up and away, letting the memory take charge, to the notice board above the fireplace, with its duplicated lists and circulars, most of them yellow and curling with age, with the specks of coal dust strewn on the papers.

– I didn't hide well enough, did I?

– How do you mean?

– I sat there waiting for it all.

– It was what you said you wanted... It's come as a bit of a surprise to hear you say all this.

– Has it? And I suppose you think it's easy for me to say it now that I could be said to have won. A kind of upside-down bragging.

– I don't think that.

– No? Then perhaps I think it myself. But I know for certain that I am tired of it all, tired to death. It seems almost that I have been uprooted, graded away, sent off to be finished. Well, I am nearly finished... taken out of a community, to be separated once and for all. The cream, as they call it. What matters is the fact of separation.

The father clings to his pride in his son. The son sticks to the irrefutable emotion of his argument. Now, with the mother the deeper secret is revealed, the outcome of their pride. And that is that "Jim" no longer exists for them. Martin taunts his mother with her connivance, worse still her knowledge:

–... You just let yourself be sent.
– Let you send me, do you mean.
– I didn't send you. It was what had to be done. I didn't interfere.
– Interfere? No, you were far more active than that. The real will, the real drive always came from you. Dad only said what you had told him.
– He wanted it to happen.
– And didn't you?
– I tell you, I knew it had to be done.
– And what it meant?
– Yes, I think so.
– From the very beginning?
– From very early anyway.
– And you didn't mind?
– I minded, and I was proud. Both too much.

The conversation grows more bitter. They confess there is no love between them that is not complicated by hurt and impossible demands. The son implicates the mother and the girl in hopeless possessiveness: "She wants Jim, that's it. And you wanted her to have him. But it can't be done. Jim isn't here any longer, he's gone. And you and Margiad will spend your lives wanting him back, to share between you. Whatever I do, what I'm doing now, well, you'll say, it's not like Jim. Jim wouldn't do that".

It is, therefore, Martin who goes on to tell his mother of his love for Jane Claverley and that they have spent time together in her uncle's seaside cottage. Ellen takes this in her stride and it is she, no airbrushed-into-the-shadows figure in this version, who surprises him by her own revelation that she had met Jane Claverley's uncle, Captain Hannon, just after Martin was born and that he had come to see her in their house in George's absence and to his later great anger. Martin can only speculate at where attraction began and flirtation ended. He prepares to go out, on Home Guard duty, and for his final encounter. He pulls on a greatcoat and shoulders a rifle:

> – You look like George in the coat.
> – Do I?
> She had come to the doorway, and was standing looking at him.
> – I was wondering if you'd say that, Mam.
> – Well, Jim, I've said it.
> – Yes. You've committed yourself, haven't you?
> – I suppose I have.

Over the twenty or so pages of typescript that he tapped out to end the novel Williams has Martin walk the lanes and riverbanks of his youth and lets a stream of consciousness – of duty, desire, conscience, impotence – flow. Martin is attracted back, time and again, to the "deep, still pool which extended in the shadow of the bridge to the right bank... this black water", into which, as a boy, he had once thrown his prize book. He contemplates his own immersion: "To go down, to go down into the water. Here, in silence. And the water would flow over hands and temples, flow quickly through the outspread fingers". He recollects the misery he has induced in his father and mother for which, he decided, the logic of his argument or the sincerity of his sentiment is, in fact, an irrelevance. He contemplates the actual fact of failure to respond to the need of others: "He took up the rifle, and walked quickly back to the Honddu bridge. He had reached a clear understanding, the limit of his present understanding. It was time now to do what he understood to be necessary".

Slowly he wades into the river and falls face down into the water and drifts, arms extended, with the current towards the bridge. Then he kicks hard and reaches to the bank, pulling himself clear. This has not been suicide after all. It is a kind of baptism, a rebirth that echoes the water and light of the novel's opening:

> He shivered... in the cold air and, at the involuntary movement, stood again, and looked out over the dark valley. He could see the screened lights of the station, and the line of the hill above Llanvetherine. He could see the line of peak and rockfall of the Holy Mountain, and, westward, the dark scarp of Black Darren. He looked lower, over the road from Priests' Valley, over the darkness where the culvert stood, over the faint line of trees, following the lane. There were early lights in the Brynllwyd houses, under the silence of the gray ridge.

Yet if, in the fiction, we are meant to see this as an affirmation, it is not clear what, beyond living, it is affirming. The burden of explanation falls squarely on Martin but he is not prepared, in both senses, to take that on. Or, at least, the detail of the significance of other lives, even those close to him, remains elusive as the novel remains an impressive but tellingly incomplete structure. In an extended sub-section of Chapter Five, "Watershed", Williams seems to recognise this by writing of another, and final, meeting between Martin, now at Cambridge but not yet Jane's lover, and Franken who has invited Martin to his home "overlooking the estuary". It is only an opportunity for Martin to reflect, in an astonishing prose-poetry synopsis of the landscape and history that will mark much of Williams' later thinking, on the people between mountain, valley and plain. Franken's role, no longer book-learned mentor, is only to listen and, maybe, comprehend. The episode goes strictly nowhere but Martin is made to reverse his earlier insistence that the "valley" was "the first penetration of the plain into the border mountains". On the contrary, he now begins, since it is "a part of the mountains, containing all their nature... as much opposed to plain as the mountains themselves. The valley is the last essence of the mountains, at the edge of contact with the plain. That is the fact, as I see it, and there lies the whole issue". The issue, of course, is one of commitment. But, in human terms, to what? The idea of commitment leads Martin, in a graphic historical encapsulation of the clash of priests, warriors and peasants in this landscape of valley, mountains and plain, to consider isolation, independence and the myth of self-sufficiency:

> But the measure of the history depends on what you take the valley to be. Consider its formulation, outlining a mask of shape.
> From the interior, from the frontier, attack.
> Violence stored in the heart of the countryside, the damp green countryside. Damp in the hayrick, mouldering to fire.
> Violence and fire on the frontiers; choosing of sides. *For us or against us. Hammer and anvil.*

* * * * * *

If you chose not to choose you could be damned, or at least resented, for that too. When the Extra-Mural Delegacy in 1948-9 shuddered with the crisis that would see many of its tutors put under close watch because of their Communist Party affiliation, Raymond Williams remained to one side. Since the concentration of the crisis, a "witch hunt" in the view of its historian,[16] was in North Staffordshire not East Sussex that has seemed, to many, sufficient reason. Further, the direct involvement of most of these committed tutors was in Trade Union schools as well as in forays to Nigeria and the Gold Coast to establish extra-mural work in universities, all of which riled the political sensitivities of the Labour Government and its civil service.[17] Of course Williams' own subject area and the social composition of his classes were as far removed from all this as he was himself geographically distant. The complaints, and the investigations, were often no more specific than to warn of too much overt expression of opinion being the enemy of good teaching and learning. But beneath that genteel pedagogic warning and the echo of it in debates in *Highway*, the W.E.A.'s magazine for tutors, action was, in this climate, rather more brutal. Some tutors were not reinstated and, with Frank Pickstock prominent, others were freshly appointed whose "social-democratic" credentials were rather more evident. Thomas Hodgkin, who had taken more and more interest in west Africa, as both historian and educator, found his attempts to extend the work into east and central Africa blocked by the suspicions of the Colonial office. In 1952 he resigned as Secretary of the Delegacy to escape curtailment of his activities on behalf of nascent African nationalism and to pursue the scholarship that had made him pre-eminent in his field by the time of his death in 1982.[18] His leaving the Delegacy was a blow to Williams largely because his successor, Frank Jessup (1909-1990), the Deputy County Education Officer of Kent, and an administrator above all, was so singularly not to his liking. The modernisation that Jessup undertook would eventually lead to further incorporation of extra-mural activities into the University and, along with education for leisure came training for graduates. The dream of adults entering into education to equip themselves as citizens of a participatory democracy was allowed to recede.

This was a shift which would, by the end of the 1950s, convince Williams that he had personally come to the end of that route. In 1948 and 1949, however, it was not so much that he was apolitical or disengaged or indifferent to the fate of tutors whose espousal of Communist Party politics was deemed to be a barrier to objectivity, more that he would not choose between those dubious certainties and the unadventurous pragmatic purposes of social democracy. Between that hammer and this anvil he was, defiantly, a dragon-fly who would not settle. His colleague, Jack Woolford, considered, in any case, that he was comparatively junior at the time and unlikely to be involved in the defence of those dismissed. The case echoes because of Williams' later prominence and friendship, then and certainly later, with Communist Party members. Associated slightly with the Communist Party Historians' Group when it convened in 1954 at Netherwood House, a conference centre near Hastings, he was also attached, personally and intellectually, to Tony McLean (1911-1982), the Spanish Civil War veteran who, following the lead of Francis Klingender's work was another pioneer of "cultural studies" whom Williams later properly acknowledged. Klingender (1907-1955) lectured in Sociology for the W.E.A. at Hull and was a Communist Party member from the early 1930s. His adjunct work, notably on a subtle Marxist interpretation of fine art, gave him influence beyond the Historians' Group. He and McLean are warmly acknowledged in *Culture and Society*. But, and it is worth stressing in this context, not only did colleagues like McLean and Hodgkin give up their Party cards in the late 1940s in the wake of events in eastern Europe, Williams himself was never tempted back into the disciplines of a Party he had tasted and let go in Cambridge. His own struggle, one which he would come to see as political in itself, was with thinking through the intermeshing boundaries which, negatively or positively, he felt defined actual life experience – and so could not simply be ignored or by-passed – in order to find antecedent cultural re-definitions which might be worked through to deliver related social and individual empowerment. In 1968, reviewing a work on Sartre's philosophy, he put it as plainly as he ever did. But by then, of course, he had come through:

> I do not mean at all that he [Sartre] is a thinker who has also taken part in current politics. That is a description within an inert and orthodox version of intellectuals, in our kinds of society. He is not a writer and thinker who takes time off for politics and journalism: that familiar English accent in which thinking is a professional activity, a job, and politics is another professional activity, on which amateurs may sometimes intrude...

> As one who accepts neither that Marxist thesis [of individual identity arising from the "relations of production to the structures of groups"] nor that Sartrean antithesis [of the individual reaching out to explain identity through activity first and thereby consciousness of a totality of

303

"practical links"] but the quite different starting point of lived relationships through which the abstraction of "individual" and "society" are both made and known.[19]

To say that he did not know these things in this way in 1948 is to say, too, that he did not know himself. Silence, wrongly interpreted as a knowing one, and personal aloofness, felt as coldness towards others, were traits of a personality and a mind still in formation. He did not, in these years, choose clear-cut positions intellectually or politically because the dilemma of irresolution lay within his own personality. This is why the outward signs were so difficult to read and so rarely replaced by any overt response: "I think Raymond was the most courteous man I ever knew", wrote Jack Woolford to Joy Williams, "I only once succeeded in riling him (in 1949) and that was certainly all my fault." He also remarked: "Even a rebuke [over Woolford's "illiberal" behaviour as a "social democrat" in the "North Staffs. Controversy"] was offered in a friendly way, almost as an aside, and was not accompanied by any physical expression of distaste."[20]

Then, again, the sheer material circumstances of his work patterns at home in Seaford, and later in Hastings, meant that even if not in splendid isolation, he was, at the very least, remote from the gossip and personalising of issues that most academic figures took on as the added flavouring of their profession. Whether by luck or by design, and certainly this latter in part, it suited him to work at his writing each and every morning, to read and prepare work in the afternoons and to teach in the evenings. It was a strict regime and one that was only relieved of being solitary by the presence in the house of his young family. Holidays and wider social contact was mostly reserved for an annual exchange of houses when they went to Oxford in July and August for summer schools and the tutors' conference. There is no doubt that he was conscientious both as an organiser-cum-administrator of his classes and as their driving force. In the winter of 1949 and into 1950 he had two three-year tutorial classes running in Literature at Bexhill-on-Sea and Brighton with twenty one in the former and fifteen in the latter, with the customary average ratio of three women to one man, whilst in Battle and Hastings his Preparatory Tutorial Classes on Culture and Environment and, again, Literature attracted sixteen and twelve respectively. No matter what the numbers he had to be there and this meant leaving early for and coming home late from meetings that typically began at 7.30 or 7.15 and lasted two hours. So, on Mondays that winter he left the flat in Seaford to catch the 5.24 afternoon train to change at Lewes to arrive in Hastings at 7.00 in time to reach Battle by 7.30 for the class which he finished at 9.30 in order to be back in Seaford at 11.20 for the dark walk home. That was, in essence, a seven-hour shift. On Wednesdays, leaving slightly earlier, he was home at 11.00 and similar stop-start journeys took him over similar time spans to Bexhill and Brighton on Thursday and Fridays. Sometimes the teaching was in a private home, sometimes in the Reference Library in Bexhill or the Friends Centre in Brighton, and rarely in conditions of any comfort.[21]

Theirs was a vocation not a profession. Out of their moral engage-ment with how and what to teach to adults in ways that derived meaning from the life experience of students as well as from the trained observations of tutors, they began to build arguments for inter-disciplinary studies that could reflect the nature of lifelong learning outside the Academy. In particular, their emphasis on literature beyond any narrow confinement to the "practical" subjects of Economics or Politics sparked lively debate between and across generations of Adult Educators and, by its eventual outcome through example, led from English to Cultural Studies. It was an intellectual network akin to collegial fellow feeling between some Adult Education tutors across Britain: almost a freemasonry of dedicated endeavour. If they met infrequently they shared ideas and news of each other on the grapevine of conferences and through the vehicle of occasional papers. They wanted to share the outcome of their best work. They wanted to learn from each other.[22] The two most important figures in the whole movement that would, later and haphazardly, be called Cultural Studies, first hesitantly contacted each other in 1948.

Richard Hoggart (b.1918) was teaching in English in the Department of Adult Education at Hull where he had been, since de-mob, in 1946: "We wrote about aims and first principles, and about the details of methods of teaching those kinds of subjects to those kinds of students. An exchange of this kind first put me in contact with Raymond Williams, who was then based on the south coast".[23] Hoggart had written "Some Notes on Aim and Method in University Tutorial Classes" for the journal *Adult Education* to set out the case for discriminatory reading and thinking over the false expectation of "magisterial indoctrination" by the tutor. In the next number, Williams responded to "Mr Hoggart's Appendices" warmly and supportively, but with reservations about any literary analysis that concentrates on technical process to the exclusion of "value-judgements". It was a debate typical of the passionate enthusiasms of those years in Adult Education and one which would echo: should there be a concentration on manageable extracts or was the reading of a complete work necessary? If Adult Education was not about the creation of intellectual elites could it, nonetheless, work on more than one level to encompass the intellectually gifted and the intellectually stretched? When was the silence of a tutor as intimidating as the overbearing knowledge of a lecturer? They felt themselves, from Hull to Swansea, from Leeds to Sussex, at a cutting edge.[24]

That Williams was making a mark was scarcely in doubt. His editorial involvement in *Politics and Letters* had made his name known, especially to Adult Educators whose numbers were increasing steadily as post-war British universities tended these external offshoots, in collaboration with the W.E.A., more tenderly than they had done before the war. What is most striking, though, is the assurance of his tone when he enters this public arena, immediately declaring in his 1948-9 Rewley House Paper on "Some Experiments in Literature Teaching" that "the teaching of Literature to adults has... been both battlefield and laboratory" with the "guilt" accorded to, and felt by, tutors for teaching such an "escapist" subject the first thing that needs to be eschewed. His dismissal of guilt is propelled by the indignation of his attack. Literature is not only central to any "coherent record of human experience" it is one of the "permanently valuable disciplines of any education".[25]

The ire and the self-confidence are even more marked in his reflections on a special course held for tutors, with himself as Director of Studies, at Hertford College in the first week of July 1950.[26] It was on the subject of "Literature in relation to History", with special attention to the years 1850 to 1875, and it attracted thirty one adult education tutors of whom nineteen "tutor-students" were History specialists and twelve in Literature. This is how, for the Rewley House Papers, he began his "Formal Report", though the statistics rapidly gave way to the dazzle of names that were eminent, or soon to be so, in their fields. Humphrey House from Oxford on Dickens, Raymond Williams himself on George Eliot, G.M. Young on "Mid Victorianism", Isaiah Berlin on "Scientific and Philosophic Thought", Asa Briggs on "Religion in England", Raymond Postgate on "English Political and Social History 1850-75" and Sir F.M. Powicke on "The Study of Writing of History 1850-75".

These topics were variously covered in seminars and lectures with cross-disciplinary work expected. But instead, as he ruefully reported, over and over again literary study was seen as a handmaiden to historical analysis: to be used as inspiration or to be corrected for fact and detail. He was, accurately enough, describing the general use of literature by most academic historians of the time. His reaction was scathing: what was needed was not a "corrective to literary study" but "a corrective to the non-literary study of literature". Literature could not sensibly be reduced to the status of a document. It required its own nature to be understood in order for any analysis, literary or historical, to be of use. Worse, he could see little merit in the historical approaches that were adopted if only documented evidence was thought to be of worth. As was his custom when necessary, as it evidently was now, he placed himself personally, as well as his considered views, centre circle:

> For my own part I know very little about history (I was brought up on Welsh history only, out of little books with the Welsh dragon sticking its tongue out on the cover, and learned all about the predatory and perfidious English in a manner which I am assured by my English historian friends

307

was quite unsatisfactory). But I had thought that the study of dates and treaties and constitutions was now more widely recognised as only a part... of the general study of human actions in time.

I had assumed that historians would be naturally interested in an account of the nature and quality, at any given time, of specific, though unpolitical, human experience; or of the particular workings of social institutions; or of the effect of economic change upon differentiated individual persons, as well as upon a class. I had assumed this because it did not seem to me that the nature of the lives of the people I now know (the thirty people on the course for example) could be adequately understood by a study of their personal incomes, their occupations, their expectations of life, and their opinions on the Atlantic Pact. The fact that experience, including social experience, had been shaped and assessed by the workings of an imaginative consciousness did not seem to me to make it any less important than experience which had passed through the statistical or generalising process of the historical record.

His animadversion against the history being professed in Britain in the late 1940s and early 50s was both instinctive and prescient. It would be another two years, 1952, before the journal *Past and Present* was founded to bring an equivalent to the French Annales School of social and cultural history from the 1930s to bear on the direction of historical analysis in English. Many of its leading contributors, Rodney Hilton, Eric Hobsbawm and Christopher Hill amongst them, were also prominent in the Communist Party Historians' Group who were beginning to produce the kind of intermeshed study for which Williams yearned. This group of intellectuals would also be at the heart of inner-party dissidence by 1956. Only at the end of the 1950s and early 1960s with the first collected volumes of *Essays in Labour History* edited by Asa Briggs and John Saville, along with the stunning impact, in 1963, of Edward Thompson's *The Making of the English Working*

Class, would Williams' 1950 diatribe seem otiose. But by then, with the new Social History beginning to sweep all before it, especially in the newer universities, alongside Labour and Local History, Williams had been a part of a revolution inside and outside the walls of the Academy. In 1950, in Oxford, very much extra mural inter muros, he had then boldly breached academic defences in a Report, of limited circulation, that was, in fact, a Manifesto ahead of its time, one which startlingly prefigures the full panoply of critical work ahead of him. And, typically, for him, it had welled up from within more than being stimulated from without. That literature was a key he had no doubt, but locks were subtle and doors double-barred. His emphasis was merely on the necessity of opening things up for:

> One is concerned with society as a whole, including the social activity which is literature. One needs an insistence on disciplines of economic analysis, political analysis, social analysis, analysis of the religion and philosophy and science of the period, as satisfactory as one can achieve. One needs also, with reference to the literature, an attention to it as a thing in itself, as the only way of drawing from it full and adequate evidence, to be set alongside the evidence of other activities... something of what this kind of response involves... is the study of language... changes in the use of language... not changes in spelling or grammar or pronunciation, but rather the changes in language as a medium of expression, changes which reflect subtle and often unconscious changes of assumption and mental and emotional process. The change and continuity of a language, often seen most clearly in its use in literature, forms a record of vitally important changes and developments in human personality. It is as much the record of a history of a people as political institutions and religions and philosophical modes. Of all the evidence which literature can contribute to the study of human affairs, this evidence of language is perhaps the most important.

By no means did he now restrict his energies or his ambitions to the shaping and outcomes of Tutorial Classes but nor did he neglect the primary work in and for itself for which he was employed. The proof of which is the rise and rise of both classes in Literature and in the methods of practical criticism so that by the end of the 1950s no one now questioned the centrality of Literature studies in any extra-mural teaching body.[27]

His work-rate and the growth of his classes had been noted and appreciated early on by Frank Pickstock. When his initial three-year contract was renewed from the autumn of 1949 – as it was periodically thereafter to 1961 – he felt more secure and began to consider buying a house.[28] That would not happen for another three years. But a car was a priority. It was Harry Williams who set about arranging it as son followed father onto the roads. First he went "to town for Jim's £50" to put towards the secondhand car the extended family found, again, in Birmingham and travelled there to buy it in late January 1950. Two days later, on 24 January, he hears that "Jim passes test" and Harry with Herbert Bird work on the vehicle. Harry's son came home on 4 February and the next day at dawn the two men drove to Guildford where Harry took the train back to Waterloo, and from there to Paddington, to arrive home in Pandy at 9 pm.[29] Harry continued to loan his son sums of money at intervals of need over the next few years and to pay repair bills on the car that turned out not to be so reliable as hoped. The loans were repaid, and noted, whilst the car made life considerably easier for the itinerant teacher's growing family: the third and final child, Madawc, was born in Seaford on 31 December 1950 whilst, to Harry and Gwen's unconcealed delight, the six-year-old Merryn stayed with them in Pandy from the end of November to mid-January 1951.

Family hurts were, through all this activity, mended to the extent of an accommodation of neutrality between Gwen and Joy. Harry relished the times they managed to visit Oxford and stay, as in July 1949 and in August 1953, in "Jim's Oxford house". They took a deep satisfaction on the appearance of his first books, in 1950 and 1952, but pride swelled in December 1949: "Jim's Broadcast 7-15 and we are both very thrilled to hear his voice over the radio. A splendid job."

The talk was on the Third Programme which the BBC had begun broadcasting in September 1946, to meet the heightened demand for programming of the arts and cultural discussion which war-time had revealed. From the outset the Third took itself and its audience seriously. It could be, and was, accused of being elitist; it certainly saw itself as a centre for excellence in the broadcasting of music, drama and literature.[30] Raymond Williams' first effort for them was, in a sense, a programme note to their short "Ibsen Festival" which was to feature *Brand* and *Peer Gynt*. He had been approached, in October 1949, by a new Producer of Talks, R.E. ("Dick") Keen, a post-war Cambridge acquaintance. Williams responded enthusiastically to the notion of "Ibsen – Poet or Realist":

> Dear Dick,
> Thank you for your letter. I would very much like to do a talk on Ibsen. I have, to my cost and some profit, virtually lived with that impossible old man for the last three and a half years. I have a book, *Drama from Ibsen to Eliot*, ready to be published, which has a 30,000 word essay on Ibsen; I have two tutorials on Brand and Peer Gynt now running; and I have lectured on him for the past three years at the American post-graduate literature school in Oxford. So at least I have the stuff in my mind.

The script, now focussing on "Ibsen's non-theatrical plays", was to home in on the discrepancy between the widespread belief that Ibsen was only a "social" writer of causes and purpose to highlight instead the non-representational "dramatic poems" to which he had turned in his maturity. Keen had the proposal accepted and the date for a rehearsal and live twenty-minute broadcast was set for the evening of 9 December 1949. The talk went well, particularly in Pandy, though its reader, frozen to the marrow, arrived back in Sussex at 2.30am after a crash at Victoria had delayed the trains; he then had a three mile walk home. They repaid his 16/3 train fare and gave him twenty guineas for Christmas.[31]

311

Not surprisingly he was eager to do more. Indeed he had been in discussion about contributions to the Third since its inception, responding eagerly, in 1946, to the idea of his sending in a short story, and in 1948, after he had submitted a script, to possible talk with them on aspects of Strindberg for a proposed series. Nothing came of this, however, until Dick Keen had re-contacted him in 1949.[32] After the Ibsen broadcast Williams sent in a synopsis for a treatment, part biographical and part critical, of the First World War poet, Isaac Rosenberg (1890-1918) whom he claimed to be overdue for "reconsideration" not only for his sensitive documenting of "the experience of war" but even more for Rosenberg's concern with "permanent and fundamental human themes [and] his striking technical originality". He notes, wistfully, that the "work of a man killed in his 28th year is bound to seem incomplete". Williams, always conscious of individual chronologies, was himself twenty eight and, in his own mind, himself, too, on "the lonely personal search for a technique revitalised by contemporary speech".[33]

But they had clearly marked him out as their "Ibsen person"[34] and it was in speaking of "Ibsen's Last Plays" that he went on air again in May 1950, with a further twenty guineas to bank and the thought that everyone told him "the Ibsen sounded quite well".[35] Dick Keen had been supportive even if he had expressed some reservations on Williams' earlier broadcast. In a "special report", for management, 30 December 1949, he had written: "I considered this a very competent but not particularly outstanding first broadcast. The script was rather heavily loaded... and it probably accounts for the appreciation index for the talk being four below average. I thought Williams' performance entirely satisfactory. He has a pleasant, quiet voice with a trace of Welsh in it; is certainly interested in speaking as well as just writing a talk and should improve with practice."[36]

The reservations, however, did not recede. The Rosenberg idea died because it was thought poems were "bad in broadcasting", and lengthy proposals and counter-proposals for a series on crime for Forces Educational Broadcasting, which Keen oversaw, finally fell, partly because his scripts were "too allusive" and partly because "his sermonising manner" did not, they felt, lend itself to a "talk down" approach. The Forces Educational Unit, from 1945, had been given a remit for talks of no more than twenty minutes directed at men and women serving in the armed forces. Some of the service listeners resented this kind of enforced education in social history, music or science; for others in the BBC it was another example pointing towards the dwindling enthusiasm for popular education that seemed to follow on the end of the war, and by 1952, with listeners so few, the specialist nature of this unit was finally phased out.[37] In June 1950, Keen wrote to the Supervisor for Educational Talks: "I have now had to turn Williams down, as after a voice test [we] found he was unable to achieve quite the right manner of address for a Forces audience".[38]

This time, after outline specimens of six talks and two fifteen-minute specimen scripts, Williams was paid off with ten guineas and his clearly innovative series on the writing-up of crime in fact and fiction was never used to leaven the stodgy content more conventionally assured of a broadcast on this wave-length.

Almost the same thing happened as, from March 1950, he simultaneously pursued the concept of a series for Forces Educational Broadcasting on the process of practical criticism. Here he wanted, along with making extract material available on paper, to "bring together discussion of newspapers, advertising etc., with discussions of literature, and the integrated Culture and Environment approach... seen in practice." He had stressed: "In this way one can get right into a working discussion of language, and indicate some preliminary judgements of value.... I don't think myself that the most down-to-earth kind of general discussion of "good and bad" provides anything very useful." Dick Keen's internally expressed view was that, again, Williams was underestimating "the reluctance of the audience" and "the problem" which was "to devise varied and persuasive presentation."[39] Somewhat disingenuously Keen pointed him towards approaches and techniques designed to deliver the message without, it seems, any serious contemplation of how effective those BBC methods really were. In reality Keen was concluding that "it would be useless to have broadcasts tied too closely to a sheet of this sort

["Use of English Practical Criticism Sheets"] since instructors/teachers could not be relied upon to be either willing or sympathetic, or even able. He was inclined to think of "broadcasts which discuss different sorts of literature fairly generally (as we often do already)".[40] None of this was conveyed to Williams. Instead he was told by Keen that "they would probably be interested in one or two talks dwelling on the method rather than the results – the challenging account of your approach to the problem of teaching literature to adults" since "the bogey is not so much the approach to education as the approach of education – that is, they don't mind discussing adult education, but they don't want talks to sound like adult education".[41.]

If Williams writhed at all this inwardly, outwardly he stuck to the task of compliance which, it seemed, broadcasting demanded. The audience, after all, was a potential one beyond any other reach. In telling Keen, now pushing for a one-off talk, that he found it "very difficult to judge what kind of thing and what level", he added, ruefully, "Then again, as you say, one has to assume one is talking to the enlightened; and yet, at the same time, it seems, to me, not to assume it. Perhaps that is the secret of the Third Programme".[42]

Either way, his first experience with broadcasting was almost at an end for some years to come. This last broadcast, before a degree of fame ushered him back on air, was requested as "a purely personal statement of your teaching method and your experiences".[43]

In January 1951 Keen billed the talk as "Reading and Criticism: An experiment in the teaching of Literature", and, for the now customary twenty guineas, on 26 February the twenty-nine-year-old Staff Tutor sat before the microphone and, almost inadvertently, summed up the impasse – how culture as a body of values could be continuous in a mechanical civilisation – at which his practice had actually arrived. Though he felt, still optimistically that if culture was a tradition embodied, as Leavis had taught, in literature, then its worth could indeed be salvaged for a bemused contemporary society. He, therefore, still envisaged the study of English as an exit route from the impasse, provided standards of appreciation were maintained. The purpose of his "experimentation" in adult education teaching was, then, to ensure the widest transmission of the values wrapped up in this knowledge of literature. He was no heretic yet within the hieratic church of Cambridge English.

The argument was straightforwardly put in this way by him at this time because the later ambiguities he will so painstakingly pick over in the word and conceptualisation of "culture" were overridden by the drive to insist that even in the agreed traditional sense of the meaning of Culture in 1951, it need not be confined to a university, and that it could, through internal university validation of the standards prevalent in adult education, be successfully taught on a wide front.

Even when he stumbled across the phrase "a whole way of Life" – which he would come to turn into a synonym for culture itself – he used it in a more confined sense than he would later, limiting it to a slap at dessicated scholarship or flighty surveys:

> It is said, very rightly, that standards in literature are inevitably a part of a whole way of life; that they cannot be simply uprooted and transferred. Look, we are told, at the results of trying to do just that: scholarship is divorced from sensibility; and literary professionals, with no established canon of taste behind them, settle down to producing graphs of the emotional development of Hamlet... or genealogical trees from the Father of the English novel to the latest contemporary small boys.

However, free from the dead weight of an examination system, he went on to argue, Adult Education allows the insights and findings of I.A. Richards to be given free experimental rein in the context of an unexpectedly wider society:

> In my own classes I begin by choosing, with the students, a small number of works for close reading. Then we go on to the discussion of short poems, paragraphs of prose, scenes of drama and similar extracts. This method is part of the practical criticism teaching which was developed in Cambridge by Richards and F.R. Leavis.

315

Williams then stressed what he regarded as the novel addition he had pioneered – the absolute silence of the teacher until the group finally contributed and the subsequent creativity of "group criticism", here meant as an opinion, beyond personal taste, that clearly arose from structured argument and commonly accepted standards. He was keen to emphasise how the technique could be applied to "films and... propaganda" all "within the context of our actual living".

Actual living was his vernacular for environment, but it was an environment that was still being described passively rather than with the active additional dynamic of a culture that was itself the shaper of any given environment. Instead, he was still defining Culture as achieved accomplishment but one that could, and in the face of T.S. Eliot's strictures, be both taught and appreciated. This explains the ferocity with which he expounded on the inherent properties of literature: merely using them as descriptive props to historical or social analyses diminished the life-revealing qualities of the texts themselves, and it was that flash or revelation which alone could cause a reader to participate in cultural development rather than stay stranded as a consumer of other people's knowledge. Raymond Williams definitely saw himself as a cleric back among his people, not a preacher in a pulpit. He understood, from within, the barriers to full access put up by an adult educational system merely imitative of what existed for conventional higher education. His frustration with the three-year Tutorial Class lay, precisely, in its origins as a mirror to the University – "a certain mystical equivalence with the three years of a university degree course" – which he considered "a dangerous sentimentality" in which, at summer schools, even adult students sometimes "enjoy pretending to be undergraduates". Ahead of his time he pushed for a more effective and sensitive overcoming of "the practical difficulties" put in the way of "parents with young children" and others with "family responsibilities". Three years was "an arbitrary period" and not reasonable "in the context of adult living". And his cool rationale could explode into a controlled anger which, so right in itself, was a release of deeper doubts about the potency of his practice:

There are several objections, I suppose [to his pleas for flexibility]... First, I suspect it is a feeling that this would be making things too easy. I confess that I can find nothing more substantial in this objection than a remnant of the sensibility which produced the phrase "deserving poor". It is to be related to very many similar attitudes, the old demand for hard practice as a toughening process of character. "A lecture of one hour, followed by one hour's discussion": most of us have discarded this routine, but sometimes we are not too well liked for it. I have heard tutors criticised as being "too entertaining"; I have heard superior comments about "a rambling discussion" (as if one had not learned as much, in one's own life, from just such casual discussions; idle conversations even, as from all the clocked-on lectures one has ever attended).[44]

For all the honesty and effort of his practice, for all the dogged idealism as he operated within frameworks and structures that could be unconducive, he was not able yet to wholly reconcile the several intellectual lives he was living – scholar, critic, sociologist, scriptwriter, educationalist, novelist, dramatist – by finding a breakthrough that might make sense of this scattered patterning. Little wonder that, towards the end of 1950, contemplating his over-worked and under-paid life, he wrote to Frank Pickstock that "my work as a whole is getting too much for me... I don't want to get out of anything, but the real question, every time, seems to be whether my own academic work can in fact be carried on in my conditions as an adult tutor. I would very much like this to be discussed and some decision made as to what in fact my function is".[45]

Chapter 8

"The Line is Crossed"

"To turn suddenly; to extend a hand; to await the stillness
                                    that the movement planned;
To command the voice; to speak and to move to the answer;
to commit to the public view the personal choice.
These are the beginnings of action, and the line is crossed
That lies at our feet always: in the centre of a room; at
the edge of a pavement; at the foot of a stair;
And the line is drawn and extends, is knotted in action,
A setting of voice and hand that contains the choice,
And across the line is action, that the sudden hand designed."

(Untitled poem by Raymond Williams, probably 1950)[1]

It is a late afternoon in the first month of the year in England in the early 1950s. A man walks to a headland above white chalk cliffs just beyond a seaside town on the south-eastern coast, itself "a finely drawn articulation of down and ridge and combe, edged by the tiny nesses of the cliff". The mild light of the closing day sweeps over olive slopes of grassland and turned-over fields of brown earth: "The hachured lines of the ridges leaped into sharp relief, black against the warm bronze light which moved over scarp and hollow… the grass seemed alive with light, and the earth itself seemed warm and living, a single presence that moved against and dominated the pale sky and the mild gray-blue sea." In his memory he revisits the different shapes and colours of summer foliage, dry and white with the chalk dust of the quarries. He lingers as others retreat to their cars and dusk falls on a landscape that "cancelled people". Except for a figure, hitherto concealed from view, which moves below him along the ridge across the rough grass to the cliff. It is a man, tall like himself, wearing a dark hat and overcoat. Almost instantaneously, the observer realises the walker intends to throw himself over

318

the cliff and watches, intently, as the man sits with his legs dangling over the edge. He is, he feels, witnessing but also participating in the event of the fall itself as a common fantasy, the compulsion and the desire to fall: "It seemed to have been always there, in his life, the fall. It existed not only as a finished event, the newspaper account, the legal verdict, the end of biography. It existed also as something that happens many times in each life."

He contemplates possible action. A sudden lunge. A stealthy, calm approach, then a physical restraint. The decision to act at all. And save him. But for how long and for what? He moves, knowing there is no real question but only the act to perform. The stranger turns as the man, Adamson, walks swiftly through a gathering dark. He shouts "One moment! Wait!" but the words are a surprise and, startled, the man, in the same movement with a single loud cry, goes over the edge through the darkness towards the sea.

That, in spare and swift prose, is the opening of the metaphysical mystery story *Adamson* which Raymond Williams was writing from the summer of 1950 to the summer of 1951.[2] Its central concern is the nature of identity: lived, lost, retrieved, inescapable. Its hues are the grey and wintry ones, outer landscape and inner mindscape, of post-war Britain. This is Williams' existential take on the impossibility of stasis and the ludicrousness of action. Its only counter to the act of disappearance is resignation or resilience. The writing says of itself that it spins around "Consciousness. Autonomy. Responsibility." If the story is recounted in a traditional narrative form it is not done so straightforwardly in either its plotting or its characterisation. The mood is conveyed by lengthy digressive dialogue that quizzes motivation and meaning. The feel is intensely visual, slow cinematic pans over landscape or quick filmic inter-cutting of places and people. At once static, then, in its obsessiveness with the manacles of lives that cannot find simple release, not even physically, and fluid in its use of genres – detective interrogation, flawed romance, friendships betrayed, pasts hidden, psychologies uncovered. It is a long way in style from his near contemporary writing of adventurous trekking in *Ridyear* in the Yukon or the discoveries of multiple selves in *Brynllwyd* or the domestic and social adjustments required for personal contentment by *The Art of the Actor*. It is another, often impressive if often off-key experiment in finding an appropriate form to hold the quest for self-worth through action, which all his fiction had so far lingered over.

He would return to it a few years later to consider, with Michael Orrom, if it could be re-written as a script for a commercial film. Instead, and with a grim appropriateness, this account of suicide and salvation turned out to be the occasion for a final break with his old friend, although the plot outline, suitably streamlined for the screen with police car chases and the love interests more central to the dénouement, had certainly appealed to the film-maker who envisaged "fresh ways of expression... [and] interior monologues, counterpointing the dialogue, to take the psychology deeper and heighten the drama".[3] Orrom was under the impression that they were blocking out a story which had, for Williams, stuck after the first few chapters. In fact he had completed, and discarded, over three hundred typescript pages of the incident which he had used to open up a life closed down.

In the novel Henry Adamson finds the car of the dead man and decides to assume his identity. His own wife has died in a bombing raid during the war and we see Adamson, a composer, as reclusive and melancholy. The dead man is Peter Corbyn, a shadowy figure whose wife, Freda, has been left to cope with the financial difficulties Corbyn was seeking to avoid. Adamson, in leaving his own home and tracing Corbyn's through hotel receipts and train ticket stubs, becomes a second missing person for the police after a body is found. Into this steps Robert Hearsey, a Cambridge friend, who comes to visit Adamson only to find him, by chance, in his guise as Corbyn. The police seek to unravel the mystery of death by accident, suicide or foul play but Adamson, who now returns home, will not, at first, assist them. Through Freda he finds another possibility of love though this, too, remains enigmatic as he destroys some evidence that was faked – for insurance purposes to make the incident appear an accident – and that may have implicated her in Corbyn's death. Freda, in turn, manufactures a fake suicide note, thereby losing the needed insurance money in order to clear Adamson of any possibility of guilty practice. At the end Adamson walks to the cliffs. He is observed silently by Hearsey whose own connection to Freda, and perhaps to the Corbyn act, is hinted at but not revealed. Aware he is being watched Adamson pauses at the edge before walking "alone, against the final condemnation, towards the road back to his house".

Adamson has three parts – "Event", "Investigation" and "Guilt" – of which the happening and its subsequent unfolding are related in a gripping enough fashion. The novel's failure is at a deeper level in which neither the actors' actions nor their relationships are ever brought to a focus that causes us to see what moves them to act or think. But this does not seem to be the interest the story held for Raymond Williams. He wants to find an exemplification of wider doubts and of the conditional responses that a culture can impose on those who, otherwise, live and act consciously within it. The most interesting passages in the novel are those that made it unpublishable and they occur in Adamson's written account for the police investigation. The question is, as he poses it, how response – sincerely and significantly meant – might differ from responsibility – what is obligatory either morally or legally – and how personal autonomy does not signify being a law unto oneself but being the law of oneself in which response can override responsibility and induce a destructive guilt.

> My actual response [when I saw Corbyn preparing to take his life]... was not to intervene, but rather to remain still, to observe and to describe... I found that I was analysing the society in which I lived in terms of the same non-intervention... the basic pattern of our kind of society... indifference that could well be called non-intervention.... And we had all constructed an habitual indifference: a keeping-away from crime, from deformity, from violence; an acquiescence in pain and hunger. There was only a little we could do, we said, and in the meantime we had our own lives to live. The events themselves we reduced to stories, or to statistics, or to spectacles according to taste. In these

ways nothing active was required of us; we remained, for it all, ourselves.

He finished the novel at the end of August 1951 before the family left for a three-week break in Barnstaple. Naturally, he took some work with him – an article on Film within Adult Education to write – since it seemed the only thing keeping his growing sense of hopelessness at bay. At the start of the grim twelve months that had led to the completion of *Adamson* he had written to Mankowitz to enlist him for a new journal, *Essays in Criticism*, which an older and socialist English Don in Oxford, F.W. Bateson, was about to launch. Mankowitz's reply, from his Piccadilly address as Gered (Antiques) Ltd appears to echo Williams' own expressed mood:

> I know how you feel. I am nearly 26 and have been promising myself and everyone else so much for so long. Not a decently sustained piece of work finished – but two sons and a business and a lot of good openings and endings. But on the whole I am content.... The past year has been fairly abortive from the writing point of view... several interesting shorter things, but never the elusive novel.[4]

Raymond Williams was anything but content. And he was not only thirty in the August of 1951: he had been under threat of imprisonment since refusing a military service recall in August 1950 as a reserve officer for the Korean War, which had broken out in June 1950. It had been a difficult year to find authentic responses to civic responsibilities. In February 1950 Attlee's riven and creaking reform government had been returned to power, but with a greatly reduced parliamentary majority and with incipient civil war amongst its leading figures virtually impossible to allay. In April 1951 when the new Chancellor of the Exchequer, Hugh Gaitskell, responded to the American drive to re-armament by designing a British budget to follow suit, with not entirely incidental damage to the finances and principles of the infant National Health Service, Aneurin Bevan, the NHS' architect in 1948, resigned from the government. The Labour government fell in the General

Election of October despite winning popular majorities in both 1950 and 1951, and thirteen years of Conservative rule began.[5] Raymond Williams worked locally for the Labour cause in their 1950 re-election but not in the autumn of 1951. He made no pronouncements on these events that were recorded at the time. His public energy was directed at avoiding war service and as he fought that he thought about, wrote and finally abandoned his plans to write a war novel.

The intention had been there since the end of the war. As was his life-long practice he worked on it, intermittently but intensely, alongside the plethora of other projects that engaged him in those immediate post-war years. Sometimes it would be a version of "Liberation", the play that was also a story and a political romance spanning wartime and post-war Brussels, and sometimes jottings about incorporating his war-time diary into fiction. He had even set out, in 1946, to sketch a kind of displaced fiction entitled "Flag into Whip"[6] in which "the village atmosphere" would be Pandy, but only as the virtual setting for the first half of the twentieth century in Germany. His protagonist, aged twenty in 1945, was to have been Anna Muller, the daughter of Johann Muller, railway worker and trade unionist. Raymond gave the projected protagonists characteristics of Pandy people even to the bracketing of "HJW", his father's initials, after Johann Muller's name. Anna becomes a nurse and, via various love tangles, takes her faith in National Socialism to the final logic of becoming a Concentration Camp guard where those "too weak or too vicious to co-operate" were, rightly she feels, eliminated. What survives is Anna's "Statement of Arrest" and a further two pages of plotting. What tingles is his willingness to see Pandy and its religious and educational certainties as, in other circumstances, a closed community capable of evil expressed as justly held belief. Already this was somewhat at odds with the righteous indignation that the editor of *Twentyone* had been dispensing in the summer of 1945.

And steadily the gap was widening. What had been lived through was, to his dismay, being re-packaged for other use. He thrashed around in an undergrowth of expressionist poeticism that flailed out in June 1947 into this draft opening of his novel *Bocage*:

Unaccoutred as I am for public puking... Stars! I could scream at the bombust... My Lords, Ladies, and Gentlemen. The Lieu... – the Captain... Two stars, three stars... rank may be polished for ceremonial occasions, duraglitter a while... Is too modest... Is too great a hero... Oh Hero! What a Hero hadst thou been... Gripped in muchdoing, bravenesses, corrige... Of action not of words... Will address you. Approximation in the usual way. Thunderclaps.

My Peers (That Gyntish self. A great collector of decorations, that old Norsey skold). Out there, well over there, in the, well, the bocage. You understand bocage? Well, woody, orchardy, close fields. Well, the hedges have high banks at their roots. Difficult for our armoured vehicles to transverse. Well, nothing really. All my men. Your lads. Your boys. I should have recollected baokage. Did every bit as much as myself. Mucker. One for one and each for each. Fought.[7]

He tried to see how the actual events of his war experience could be slowly explained, as to their individual and group effect, through the developing consciousness of participants. He devised a verse drama "Black and White"[8] in which "the mad lyricism of war" in Normandy would be both shown and noted by a choral presence. Each chorus was to link back to the end of the previous one, each constituting an underlined comment on action which had already been foreshadowed before the move on to its next delineation. It was to end with "Nijmegen, the bridge. Over it – to death" whilst "The different planes on which the chorus abstractions become real is represented in the different levels of consciousness of the group". The scope changed but his ambition for a form to hold the individual and group life enforced by war stayed with him. Nor, when these dramatic approaches proved unsustainable did he abandon a quest for a novel that could match the prosaic, almost blanked out, account of the mechanics of the military action with the nightmare consciousness of inner personal adjustment and outward public lies. This, worked over in 1947 and 1948, periodically put to one side, then revised and typed up, became, though only shards of ideas and a mishmash of pages remain, a work that suggested significant promise. It was still very much in his mind in 1951. He called it *Our Lords the Moon and The Sun*.[9]

This time, instead of leaping straight in with prose poems sublet from Joyce and contracted through Eliot, he plotted a more careful passage. He envisaged a novel of around 75,000 words with seven chapters, taking an anti-tank regiment from England in the summer of 1944 to north eastern Germany in 1945. Each chapter was to have contained the episodes of his war-time diary. The officers he served with were precisely, according to rank and personality, renamed and assigned to their troops. The writing, though satirically cast in places to mock the hapless Wilson-Brown aka Buster who here was to be known as Duckless-Hale aka Tiger, was doggedly exact, but its framing was of the high endeavour of men impelled into a horror, barely alleviated by ideals, only to be left bewildered, even betrayed. The name he gave himself was Captain Edward Knight. And Hunter was the name for Major Dick Taylor, who also led Lieutenants Squire, Gentle and Strong. He intended it to progress from the confident gentility of pre-invasion freedom and troop games to the mayhem, masked by the coded falsity of military language, of invasion and beyond. The "Epilogue" was to be called "*Vendu*. And who and by whom?" Sold. Sold out. Six years after the war had ended his conclusion was that it was he, himself, who had been betrayed, by himself. Maybe he just lost interest in the novel which he now decided, in the autumn of 1951, to pursue no longer. It is likely, too, that the things which had been alive with immediacy from the war no longer pursued him. What is certain is that he chose to represent them in a distinctively reworked version in his own appeal to be released from any future National Service.

His appeal to be released from call-up for military service was not made on political grounds though he was clear, then and later, that the Korean War was an extension of the conflict that followed the Chinese revolution of 1948/9. At the same time he did not believe the straight Communist Party line that in Korea the south had invaded the north;

yet nor did he sympathise with the alliance of British and American forces to support the south. In the 1970s recalled memory of his objection was that it was not so much political, amidst so much confusion, as a moral one based on his army experience of losing all personal autonomy within a military machine.[10] But his memory or slant on his action was markedly different from the out-and-out pacifist case he had actually made at the time.

He had replied to the War Office, refusing their request for information about his "present position", in a letter of explicit statement in August 1950, "for the following reason":

> ... before 1939, as a schoolboy, I held strong pacifist views, and from 1939 onwards I held that the war was a profound mistake. After much debate of conscience, I decided in 1941 to accept military service, and I served from 1941 to 1945, as you will be aware. Since my demobilisation, I have held with increasing conviction the view that my service was incompatible with my moral and religious principles, and I have determined never to serve in or support any other war. I have given this determination formal status by signing the pledge-card of the Peace Pledge Union.[11]

This had been followed by a similar letter to the Under Secretary of State affirming that his decision to join up in 1941 was "based on specious reasoning". Now it became serious. He was informed that not only was he not at liberty to resign his commission, but his failure to comply with a recall made him "liable to arrest and trial by Court Martial." Letters and notices were batted to and fro. The erstwhile officer informed his military superiors that if they were indeed threatening him they had mistaken their man and that he would not be moved whatever the consequences. He had already been informed by the Board for Conscientious Objectors that the likely result, in the event of re-mobilisation for war, would be court martial and imprisonment before being allowed to appeal to a Tribunal.[12] Williams did later discuss possible imprisonment and attendant disruption of his tutorial classes with the sympathetic, if rather facetious, Thomas Hodgkin whose crabbed and business-like note ended in a way that only a patrician "child of nature" or a Balliol grandee could devise:

> I'm sorry you are having this bother – but I hope it doesn't turn out that they gaol you. Though even that may have some advantages, I expect. I always feel at a disadvantage myself through never having been to gaol.[13]

The threat hung over him into the winter of 1951 and was made clearer in the dated call-up for training as a reservist in July 1951 which he received in February. It was only in March that he learned they would allow appeal to a Tribunal to be held in Fulham in May of that year.[14] He prepared his case carefully and added to his written submission a letter from Frank Hancock on whose behalf he had worked in the by-election of 1939.

Hancock first testified to the nearly two years he had spent in prison in the First World War and to his continuing work both for the Society of Friends and the Peace Pledge Union, before he turned to his younger friend's beliefs:

> I first met Raymond Williams in Monmouthshire in 1938. I had just come to live there, having been chosen as prospective Labour candidate for that division. Raymond had just won a County Scholarship and was waiting to go up to Oxford [sic in original]. We lived in adjacent villages and were soon good friends. A by-election became necessary in July 1939. War was imminent. Transport House [Labour Party HQ] did not want a contest; particularly they did not want me, a pacifist, to fight it. Without any assistance, and against the wishes of Transport House, I was nominated and the seat contested. (Result of poll was that Conservative majority was reduced from 10,000 to 5/6,000). I was free to contest it on anti-war issues, and did so almost exclusively. My chief supporter on the platform was young Raymond Williams, years too young to vote, but so much

wiser and abler than his years. He defended my pacifism, in town and village, indoors and in the open air. I have always regarded my fine poll for peace, a few weeks before war broke out, as largely due to the sincerity and sustained efforts of Raymond Williams. There is no question but that at the time he was against war, body, mind and soul. Otherwise he could never have faced the massed opposition that gathers for a by-election. It was a great surprise and a great sorrow to me when I heard that he eventually joined the army... and I was glad to find that he had regretted two years ago or more having been in the forces.[15]

The Tribunal was to be chaired by a Judge, Sir G.P. Hargreaves, and had on its panel of four worthy men, Sir Arthur Pickard-Cambridge, whose academic work on ancient Greek theatre would be used in some of Williams' future work, notably *Drama in Performance* (1954). Harry Williams waited at home, and indignantly so, for their verdict on a son who had already served through the War. Raymond Williams later considered that his judges, as non-combatants themselves, had taken the "pragmatic line" of enough was enough.[16] Or they might have been over-whelmed by the manichaean passion with which he imbued his closely-typed three-page statement sent on official paper in March 1951.[17]

In this he surveyed the years up to and after 1941 as they had unfolded for him. Yet it was his opening remarks that rolled back those years to earlier positions which had then been fervently held. He declared that, without any exception, war was "an absolute evil... a calculated denial of man's brotherhood" which destroyed "the creative impulses of man – love, tolerance, sympathy, imaginative effort" in its "socially barren" progress. War begets only war, he argued, and cannot defend either "peace or security or freedom or human dignity". To accede to war service would be to "destroy [his] conscience of moral existence". On the contrary, to deny war would be to act for the community against violence even when "a majority of the community decides... otherwise... and that even in the extreme case of armed attack against one's own community I believe the right course of action to be one of positive non-violence".

That said, he turned to a summation of his "similarly complex... personal development towards these views". His narrative clung to a truthful version of events, though if they had wished to probe, they could have uncovered equally valid other such versions. He saw his life through the telescope end he chose to emphasise:

> I was born in 1921 and grew up in an atmosphere of Christian instruction, left wing politics and opposition to war. In my adolescence I did much active work for the peace movement, but the apparent unity of this movement in the 1930s concealed for me conflicts of principle which I could not then perceive or resolve... but the real difference between a belief in collective security and in pacifism became sharply apparent on the outbreak of war. I opposed the war and I spoke and wrote in public on several occasions, principally in Cambridge, against the war's continuation. I never shifted from this opposition to the war, even throughout my subsequent military service.

Taking this last as an accurate account of what he felt to be the case in 1950, with not only the hot war of Korea but, increasingly, the Cold War of nuclear stand-off as a further shaper of violence without end, the turmoil for him of the years since 1945 becomes clearer. He turned the magnifying glass on himself:

> In 1941, after much debate of conscience, I registered for military service. The main ground for this decision, which went so much against my previous record, was that I then believed that I had no right, whatever my personal views, to cut myself off from the experience of my generation. Put more formally, I believed that I was equally guilty with my fellows that the crime of war had been allowed to develop and that I must now accept with them the consequences of that guilt and its retribution. That decision, once taken, distinctions between types of service seemed to me to be sophistry.

329

He ended by asserting that henceforth through his writings and all available political opportunities he would work for peace and that was why he had refused service and had already offered to resign his commission. What seeps through everything, however, beyond any sophistry of judgement or sophistication of argument, is the guilt, deeply felt, and bitterness:

> My experience of fighting war (I was a front-line officer in an armoured division) confirmed my belief that war was an absolute evil, and I have often felt particularly bitter that the courage and loyalty of my army comrades were exploited to such ends. As to the futility of war, my experience of Germany in 1945 and of the war mentality and worsening situation in the subsequent years of "peace" seemed to confirm my views absolutely. Twice in the war, in the liberation of N.W. Europe (in which I took part) and in the burning down of a typhus-infested compound in a concentration camp, I was forced to ask myself again whether something of value was not being achieved. But even within these events, I saw within the rejoicing there elements of violence which have since grown and threaten to over-whelm us... I came to the conclusion that I must renounce war absolutely: that, although I must bear my portion of the guilt of war and violence, I must not again allow this to involve me in action which would intensify that guilt.

The Tribunal was convened by the Ministry of Labour and National Service in Fulham Town Hall, London, on 7 May 1951. It was a short hearing in which Williams' only added information was that "It's a very complex matter and life can never be morally taken". They found that "the applicant should be regarded as conscientiously objecting to performing Military Service" and he was duly informed two days later. On 19 May 1951 he was able to write, again, to the War Office, now duly registered as a C.O., to resign his Army Commission.[18]

It was a summer in which many things in his life had come to a head. Very little appeared to offer openings. No books of short stories had appeared or were ever thought of again by him. He had sent a version of *Brynllwyd* to a literary agent, but now, with *Adamson* nearing its conclusion, decided to retrieve and reshape the former over the autumn. He put a trio of started projects on to his memorandum for thinking about from "Mid October on", and added that he would make a decision on the next novel to be tackled from a list of three: "*The Art of the Actor*, *Our Lords the Moon and the Sun*, *The Medwyn Project*".[19]

All three were to be written under the name "R.W. Ridyear", a quasi-pseudonym that would also not see out the year. The first two novels were stuffed unceremoniously into paper files and discarded. The third never went beyond five pages and his usual detailed listing of chapters. It would have been another sideways approach to Pandy and its changing history, taking the ostensible form of a Report, commissioned by "the trustees of the Fraser Foundation", as a "social research project, centred on a village in the United Kingdom, with particular reference to the effect on village life of contemporary economic conditions and developments of wider social changes". The Report was to be compiled and written by a team of academic sociologists, statisticians and historians who were to descend on and live in Medwyn, "at the eastern edge of the Black Mountains... eight miles north east of the market town of Abergavenny, on the main road to Hereford".

What they were to discover professionally and what they were to experience personally was the motif around which the fiction would have spun. It was another angle of approach into that conjunction in his own life and, as an effective entry, another dead end. He would have to find a different fictional route back that would allow him to marry consciousness of the process of social change with representation of its experience. He was not, in 1951, sufficiently aware that he was himself both the problem and the key. Nor was his other kind of intellectual work transparently clear to him. The critical work on drama was in the offing, though in its major formulations it already felt out-dated to him, and his vaguer attempts at a broader sociological approach to cultural questions remained just that, vague. Still, the typed memorandum to himself, right at the bottom of the note, pointed to the real and effective direction of the next few years. Beyond an accepted sense of a subject framed and closed around the twin poles of "culture" and "environment" he had come to recognise the need for a quizzing of concepts and theories through an historical overview. He had had to gear up more, in his reading, for his tutorial classes. The more he read the more the questions were posed.

In the laboratory of his Preparatory Tutorial Classes he had been extending the analytical skills of practical criticism from literary texts to all those more environmental "texts" – advertisements, radio, pamphlets, speech, cinema – which, he thought, constituted a passively accepted or unquestioned cultural atmosphere. The separation of its individual elements, however, avoided the issue of their compound origins and of their combined overall power. He was not yet ready for that task. He began, in the classes, to first strip down further constituent parts. For a class in Battle for the 1949-50 session he drew up a simple one-page syllabus and headed it: "What is Culture?"[20] He continued through fifteen questions which would be answered, for him, only when *Culture and Society* and *The Long Revolution* were finished.

What is Culture?

1 Why is Culture a word we prefer not to use?
2 Is there a "Problem of Leisure"?
3 What is relaxation?
4 Is there a difference between art and entertainment?
5 What is a highbrow?
6 Who are the masses?
7 Is "I know what I like" the last word?
8 Why do we read newspapers?
9 Why we "never read" advertisements.
10 Is the cinema an art?
11 Why is the radio an authority?
12 Why do we believe propaganda?

13   Are best sellers born or made?

14   Why is modern art "difficult"?

15   Is the artist one of the "useful people"?

But if this was a catechism for beginners, including the quizzer himself, it could not elicit meaningful response if it lacked historical depth. His first tentative attempt to provide such depth also seems to have been in 1949 when he sketched out the structure of a book to be entitled *Culture and Work*.[21] The striking thing about this proposal is the bringing together of the contemporary and the historical. He imagined *Culture and Work* in three sections: Book One was to be a "Statement", only to be written on completion of Book Two, with Book Three finally addressing "Policies". Book Two would also have three parts and would make up, at 180,000 words, the bulk of the work. Part one of that central text was, simply, "the History" but he fleshed out the other sections in a manner that would germinate:

Part Two: the Analysis:	the town; the house; the newspaper; advertisements; radio; cinema; fiction; sport; politics; propaganda; education; criticism; industry; government.
Part Three: the Theories:	Marx; W. Morris; Arnold; Eliot; Dawson; Leavis; Social Democratic; Mumford; D.H. Lawrence; Caudwell.

It was a list (at least of thinkers) as odd, in retrospect, for its omissions as for its inclusions – Christopher Dawson was the author of *Progress and Religion*, (1929) – but it was, also, a breakthrough in juxtaposition of themes, even if the cart (of outcome) was still being placed before the horse (of origins). We can see how deeply and steadily he now read into the subject from the bibliography for "Culture and Environment" studies which he drew up in 1949 and provided for an article in *The Use of English* journal in 1950.[22] The reading list was both long and eclectic, with works on logic and "straight" thinking bumping into official Reports on the Press and the "Economics of Advertising", as well as the usual suspects from Leavis to Eliot and Orwell's "Critical Essays" of 1948. Most of the seventy books and journals dated from the 1930s and 1940s, brought up to date with 1949 works topically cited. Once again it looked back – to the practice he had envisaged in contemplating an essay on "Culture and Education" in 1948 – by considering the purpose of such study to be about "training of awareness and judgement" of the "forms of expression" used in contemporary society, rather than to the way that society had itself been shaped by culture that was prior to such individuated expression.[23] Fortuitously his bibliography ended with reference to a 1947 inquiry into *Democracy in Industry* and to Ruth Benedict's 1934 work of comparative anthropology, *Patterns of Culture*.[24] Fortuitous and significant since those three abstractions of culture, industry and democracy would, with art, be the poles around which *Culture and Society* would turn. As for Ruth Benedict, this was the book which had been on Joy Williams' LSE reading list and to which she had referred her husband as he grappled, haphazardly, with the terminology of culture.[25] He ended his note of suggested reading, in 1950, with a paean of praise to Benedict's "comparative social evaluation... necessary both to give the work of cultural analysis full scope and to keep it relevant".[26] It was undoubtedly a "distinguished" work and the American anthropologist's book, comparing customs and traditions of "three very different primitive peoples", had been re-printed twice in Britain since the war. Its interest for Williams, however, surely lay in the lucidity with which she generalised about the relationship of individuals to their society.

"No man" she wrote, "ever looks at the world with pristine eyes. He sees it edited by a definite set of customs and institutions and ways of thinking... The life-history of the individual is first and foremost an accommodation to the patterns and standards traditionally handed down in his community". Not only did Benedict emphasise the relative and diverse nature of all cultures but she also highlighted the inadequacy of any "analysis of culture traits" rather than "the study of cultures as articulated wholes... all the aspects of cultural integration". This was a direct lead into Williams' investigations into the forces (such

334

as industrialisation) that changed a culture (a way of life) and into discovery (in theories of the time) of how culture re-formed itself to direct society through compartmentalised interests. Benedict wrote: "If we are interested in cultural process, the only way in which we can know the significance of the selected detail of behaviour is against the background of the motives and emotions and values that are institutionalised in that culture". Above all Williams would have read these sentences as a legitimising endorsement of his own enquiry: "... society and the individual are not antagonists... culture provides the raw material of which the individual makes his life.... No individual can arrive even at the threshold of his potentialities without a culture in which he participates. Conversely, no civilisation has in it any element which in the last analysis is not the contribution of an individual.... It is largely because of the traditional acceptance of a conflict between society and the individual, that emphasis upon cultural behaviour is so often interpreted as a denial of the autonomy of the individual".[27]

Those views and insights would be echoed indirectly in *Culture and Society* and very directly, on the page, in *The Long Revolution*; the fact that they were related by Benedict to the vastly different cultures and societies she had studied was a key trigger that allowed him to question, beyond "What is Culture?", how any culture could, more than as a trait of behaviour, be itself the articulator of social being. His later recollection of the gestation period, initially from 1949 to 1951, as one of "constant redefinition and reformulation" pulled hither and thither by new thoughts and new revelations was surely accurate, since, at each step, he was now uncovering the patchwork evidence of the historian, not the mosaic of the literary critic:

> I first started to look at the idea of culture in an adult education class, and it is very significant that the writers I discussed then were Eliot, Leavis, Clive Bell and Matthew Arnold. They were all I knew. The realisation that the notion actually extended down from the industrial revolution was the result of a process of rather haphazard and accidental discoveries in the period... in '49 [to] about '51. By then I

335

was clear that since the term had emerged in the course of the industrial revolution, it was a very key moment in the interpretation of that experience and indeed in all the social thought that had accompanied it. But as can be seen from "The Idea of Culture" [his essay of 1953] my awareness of the history of the concept was far from supported by knowledge of all the particular writers I eventually studied.[28]

Nevertheless, he had been sure enough of the notion of an Ideas of Culture, in the plural, to discuss a synopsis of a possible book of that title with Thomas Hodgkin in January 1951,[29] and to keep it in his sights in August of that year when, with so much else written and unpublished, he reminded himself

> – begin note-taking and preparation on
> *Ideas of Culture*
> order dependent on book supply, but preferably:
>
> (a) Chapter 4 –   Marxists
> (b) Chapter 3 –   Arnold
>   Leavis
>   Bell
>   Eliot
> (c) Chapter 5 – parts
>   Lifted Veil
>   Mother
> and see from there –[30]

* * * * * *

"Whenever I went to his house in that period," Michael Orrom remembered, "there would be a new tea chest full of books from the.... University Library, through which he was impressively working."[31] The books were read as they arrived, setting him off in different, sometimes unexpected directions. The house to which Orrom now went to visit and work until the mid-1950s was 44 St Helen's Road in Hastings, the larger seaside town further east along the south coast where the

Williams family went to live in the early spring of 1952. It was the first house Raymond and Joy had bought. They had been looking for a "cheap house" since 1949 when the Delegacy agreed, as they renewed his contract in that year, that he should stay as a resident tutor in East Sussex until at least the mid 1950s, and so approaches for a mortgage were then made to Building Societies.[32] Instead, with his father's help, they bought a troublesome car and stayed in the flat for another three years. The move only finally became more pressing when the grounds and house in Seaford were bought by a woman who "started to run the place as a market garden", and a third child, born in 1950, made them more cramped for space.

They found a three-storey Victorian house whose terraced neighbours stood on a hillside above the town and the sea, both less than a mile away. There was only a small garden to the front with higher terraced levels behind but it was right opposite Alexandra Park, an 1870s confection of a valley's running water, ornate boating ponds, rockeries, woods and bushes, flowers and lawns – "a lovely green place" remembered Merryn, who was then eight – into which the children and their newly acquired dog, Sirius, could vanish daily. From the beginning they all seemed pleased to settle in their own home even though its cost, with frequent loans of around £65 from Harry keeping them afloat, meant that the car had to go. Harry and Gwen visited Seaford in mid February to see the possible purchase in Hastings – "they'll be pleased if they buy it" noted Harry[33] – which was complete at the end of the month. They moved in as March 1952 began.

Hastings was still recovering from war damage as it would be throughout the 1950s.[34] A sudden day-time air raid in 1943 had killed twenty five people and devastated parts of the old town in the eastern sector. As a front-line channel town it had seen a good deal of collateral damage and, of course, occupation of its boarding houses and the surrounding downs by the allied military forces. It still boasted its cliff-top castle, its medieval glory as the premier of the Cinque Ports and the date of 1066. In the 1950s its role as a fishing port had long succumbed to silt in the harbour and as a resort it was now decidedly secondary to the follies and grandeurs of Brighton or the refinements of Eastbourne and Folkestone. Its population had, with fluctuations, stuck at around fifty five thousand since the 1880s, the heyday of its Victorian expansion and, when a direct railway line to London did not bring the visitors and upper-class incomers for whom its Victorian worthies hoped, its Edwardian leaders, devoid of ideas and of commitment to any new amenities, saw steep economic decline accompany a bemoaned lack of gentility. As Robert Tressell would make pikestaff plain in *The Ragged Trousered Philanthropists* (1914) Mugsborough, his fictional Hastings, was class-divided and class-exploited.

The town to which Raymond Williams brought his young family had, nonetheless, some natural advantages – sheltered by cliffs it had a balmy climate and an inviting shingle beach – and a liveliness lacking in Seaford. Notably, the White Rock Pavilion, to house its Winter Garden attraction, had been built in 1926 and the succeeding decade, albeit a reinforced concrete one, brought on promenades, concert halls, indoor swimming and outdoor bathing pools and even a pier as Hastings tried to recover its Victorian pole position on the south coast. Harry and Gwen would now spend a week or so each year on holiday in the town, walking the length of Alexandra Park, two and a half miles right through the town centre, and 110 acres of greenery in all, to take a trolley bus back up the hill to 44 St Helen's Road. The children went to nearby Silverhill Primary School. Each morning their father would turn to his unbending routine of writing. Each evening when he left to teach, Joy would type and work on his page proofs. Each summer they would de-camp in an exchange of houses for a month to Oxford for summer schools and conferences, and his parents would, as in 1953, arrive there to see their successful son in his, albeit temporary, "comfortable house" in Merton Street. In 1954 they travelled to the south east in May to "go to Methodist Church for Merryn's christening" and later that day, after a long walk in the glorious park they could almost call their own, Harry and Jim sat and sat to "talk about Education etc. till 11 pm". The outwardly gentle ease of Raymond Williams' life in Hastings concealed the continuities of ambition and frustration. With his father he was, perhaps, most probing of all. The relationship was often severely tested. Harry Williams yearned for a placid one. His son had to provoke before he could pacify.

In January 1957, six months after his first heart attack, Harry was, once more, delighting in his son's company back in Pandy and, especially delighting, as he wrote, that they can, again, "have a good talk together". The father's illness would hasten the resolution of passing difficulties even if, in that year before Raymond Williams found a lasting public fame, it did not, as yet, eclipse the son's recurring depressive moods of the early 1950s.[35] These occurred despite the constant hard work which, Joy believed, he used to drive them away. In extremis, he would take to his bed for days. The mood swings were often close to racking him with despair. It may have been sheer exhaustion, for in the five years from 1952 he had been even more demanding of his stamina than ever. Yet it was also a tension in himself, both what he had become and what he had once been, which was being felt as much as a personal crisis as it was a quest for a wider, more public analysis. He was coming to realise that the two were inseparable for him. Resentment against the pushy father for making the gifted son the exiled one who had to confront such challenges slowly gave way to a son's abiding love and respect for the nature of his father's life and the choices he had made. Nonetheless, in these quite crucial years in his development, Raymond Williams had to articulate the resentment and then understand how, for his father too, life had not left him frozen in a childhood time. There was, for Raymond, a terrible realisation that being an expert did not signify for others the validity of hard-won expertise. It might even mean a betrayal.

The questions bubbled up in the fiction that he used to bring to his surface the issues that festered deep in him. He wrote, rapidly and obsessed, his "alternative" Brynllwyd novel over 1952 and into 1953.[36] This was the long, untitled, narrative, in two parts and over two hundred pages of typescript, which took Paul Ramsay through Cambridge and the War to Soviet incarceration and a new identity as Paul Bergel, an Austrian Communist Party activist. The follow-up, *A*

Map of Treason, has Paul return, quietly, to England to take up the threads of pre-war acquaintances, including that with the former International Brigader, Owen Iverson, whose loyalties have, one way or the other, shifted politically even as they have reverted in social class terms. The novel, composed with the brouhaha surrounding the defection of Burgess and Maclean to the Soviet Union in 1951 still resonant, reads like a dialectical rehearsal for the debates Williams would, more sure-footedly and soon, make explicit in both his critical and fictional work. The stuff of spies is less prominent; his large themes are the multiplicities of betrayal and commitment that individuals are required to meet and assess. Ramsay, and we can be sure Raymond Williams, adopts an unremittingly accusatory tone. First, towards erstwhile comrades but, with startling painfulness, against his father, also, since the shared dilemma is a continuity.

With what ultimate purpose is not made clear, Ramsay visits Benson, an Oxford don and pre-war recruit for espionage who chooses to be vague about his past. He tells Ramsay that Europe is no longer "the centre – the real issues are in Africa and Asia" and they agree that, at least, those matters, "simpler" or "clearer", are "the kind of issue around which one's political consciousness grew up". Ramsay pushes the point home:

> "One can feel towards native peoples," Ramsay said…
> "as it was possible to feel towards the working-class, if one was from outside it. The traditional feelings, and one takes part with the weak and oppressed."
>
> "Yes," Benson said, looking away.
>
> "But in fact, surely," Ramsay said, "the same complications follow. One finds that they are not only weak but that in radical ways they are different, and intend to go their own way. Disillusion can be at the limit of charity."
>
> "Hardly charity, surely? Although I agree with the implications of what you say."
>
> "Unfortunately," Ramsay went on, "there are always other candidates for charity, or at least for the traditional feelings. One moves on, taking part with the weak and oppressed."

"And you think that is wrong?" Benson asked, looking across at him.

"It is dishonest," Ramsay said, "if only in effect."

...

"But... surely one has to distinguish between the centres that will be decisive, and those that are less so. All kinds of bourgeois feelings may go into one's attitude, but objectively one's analysis may still be right."

He smiled, and handed across Ramsay's tea, and the plate of sandwiches.

"A bourgeois feeling remains itself," Ramsay said... "whereas in Europe... the dishonesty is no longer possible. The decisive stage has in fact been reached, and one has to choose one's side. The traditional feelings, at the moment, are quite likely to land you on the wrong one."

Benson smiled.

"What does Owen think about all this?" he asked.

"Owen? Owen is a Marxist in Africa and Asia, and a liberal in Europe. It is a common enough condition."

The condition of Paul Ramsay who has become Paul Bergel is one of a commitment which, in its murkiness, has its own fraught implications to consider. In a three-page note – "Outline of continuation of *A Map of Treason*" – Williams sketched the corkscrew twists that would come when the novel was complete. Ramsay has been working for the British Government to investigate "scientific leaks" from Barfield. A former friend, Naylor, is arrested and confesses to passing information to an "agent in London" as well as being a secret member of the Communist Party. Ramsay, in turn and possibly as a double or perhaps triple agent, secretly assists Naylor to commit suicide. Then, amnesiac it seems, he disappears with crucial evidence. Later he is dismissed from government service and removes to Cornwall "to start writing again". A year later a boating accident occurs. Suicide is presumed.

Raymond Williams reminded himself: "Everything turns, of course, on understanding Ramsay's character and motives; but these must be left for the actual writing." Through a narrative labyrinth, for himself and for others induced into their once unravelling lives by the glimpse of a once true path, Ramsay, in word and in act, seeks to inspect the meaning of treason as it has been mapped out for his generation.

The woman he has loved in pre-war England and will love again, the former comrade, Yvonne Marshall, insists on telling him that "Treason... is an obsolete, emotive word [for what is in practice]... a going across, a move from this allegiance to that [and so]... one could only speak of it, now, if the units were clear and separate; one's own place all this, another place all that, and then one could speak of crossing the lines. But as it is, with every line confused, treason means no more than your opponent's reason." Ramsay, however, will not blur the lines anymore.

> "If one could believe that," Ramsay said, looking down and smiling. "But rebellion is not treason, opposition is treason. Treason is the covert, the secret, the underhand; breeds, as I say, wherever the hand is turned. When the break in continuity comes, and only a few may have perceived it, the issues of treason and allegiance are conscious, and the few know what they are doing.... Treason, ultimately, is the perception of allegiance; although those who commit it may have to be discarded as merely negative examples."

The implication seems to be that the man, even the traitorous one, who sticks tight in a tight place, is preferable to those who cease to oppose what no longer appears to them continuous in their lives. A few years later in his chapter on "Marxism and Culture" in *Culture and Society* he puts it more coldly:

> Much of the "Marxist" writing of the thirties was in fact the old Romantic protest that there was no place in contemporary society for the artist and the intellectual, with the new subsidiary clause that the workers were about to end the old system and establish Socialism, which would then provide such a place. The correlative protests against

342

unemployment, poverty, and Fascism were genuine; but the making-over of the workers' cause into the intellectuals' cause was always likely to collapse: either as the intellectuals found a place in different ways, or as the workers' cause asserted its primacy and moved in directions not so immediately acceptable or favourable... I have of course the advantage of hindsight: it is a characteristic of [such]... negative identification that it breaks up at points of real social crisis and reacts into an indifference to politics, recantation, or sometimes violent assault on the cause that has been abandoned. Because I believe this to be a law, its actions subject to the immense pressures of society, I have no desire to rehearse personalities. I note only the fact that "culture" was not so far ahead, not so firmly affiliated to the future, as was then [in the 1930s] thought.[37]

Those "immense pressures", however, are presented as having worked on Ramsay as well; perhaps forcing his ultimate formulation as one outside his native pale, certainly as instrumental factors in causing his exile or removal in the first place. By the time he finishes *Border Country* after his father's death in 1958, Williams has reconciled himself to the outcome of the force of all those decisions and presents them in that novel as matters that need to be accepted emotionally and resolved intellectually. Not so in the fierce pages in which Paul/Jack is Matthew/Will or Raymond/Jim. In a number of passages quite harrowing in their indictment, we can taste the resentment and sense the mutual bewilderment that underlay the conversations "about education" that he and his father had between 1954 and 1957. He set it down with an unflagging ferocity which, in life, was scarring them both.

He placed the moment of crisis back where it might, fictionally, have been seen to begin. Ramsay, having graduated from Cambridge with a First returns home to Brynllwyd in the late summer of 1939 to await his army call up. First the idyll:

When tea was over, Ramsay went out with his father into the garden and was shown around. The plums were ripe, and the crop was so heavy that several branches were supported by stakes. The apples were ripening and under the trees there was the constant hum of the bees going out from and returning to their hives. Ramsay turned away and looked at the onions… and the high screen of the runner beans, and the row of tall late peas, on which the pods were almost ready to pick. Beyond the currant bushes the hens were scratching the earth of their narrow wire enclosure and his father's black and white dog was lying sleepily in the shade… Ramsay reached up and picked a handful of plums. He began to eat them, walking quietly around and looking at every detail of the garden.

… For a while he was a child again, and the concentration of memory and desire was overwhelming in its intensity and pressure.

The reverie slows time down for only a few days. The letter which arrives to offer Paul a three-year research scholarship is seen by him as only a vague possibility to consider after the War, which appears unstoppable, an endnote. His father urges a more open-ended, optimistic view after what might be only "an interruption". The two men begin to spar verbally with each other and an irritable jumbling of the coming war with Paul's finished education – how can they be connected – leads to dialogue which, generalised and empowered, will give *Culture and Society* the provocative impact of its parallel conclusion but here, specific and embodied, was unpublished though certainly not unspoken:

Ramsay persisted. "What has all this scholarship business been…? Work and push, and may the best man win."

"That's for education, because education is right. It hasn't been for war."

"Yes," Ramsay said, slowly looking down at his hands. "But have we thought where the ladder gets us? Have we thought, ever, what's at the top of it? For me, I know, it used to be a good job, at five pounds a week. That's the sort of blindness that shames one."

"It's twice the wage I'm getting," his father answered slowly. "What's there to be ashamed of in that?"

"Because it's blood money, that's why. And you know it."

The father replaced the key on the mantelpiece, and turned slightly away.

"It's no use talking like that," he said quietly, after a pause.

"I think it is," Ramsay said. "Where does the ladder get you, in the end of it? I feel myself that it's been the kind of thing firemen use... wheeled about and ends in the air. What do I do when I get to the top of that? Vanish like the boy in the rope trick?"

Ramsay sweeps aside this father's view that he is overly upset by the military registration papers he has received and insists that he is now "well trained" to vanish anyway, without the call of war, because the "priests" – teachers and examiners – spotted him and remade him, a "cream" that is separated from the rest.

"Don't take pride, that's all," he said, "for steering your son to something they will tell you is better than yourself. Don't talk about my better chances, because what does better mean between you and me? Nothing that I am is better than you; nothing that I do is better than you have done. I wouldn't want you to have had what they call a better chance, because then you would be different, and I want you as you are."

The father turns away in embarrassment and weariness. The son feels that, in his own bitter intransigence, he has been confused and somehow false, that it is not education that has distanced them but a deeper "personal division" in which the work of one has sustained the being of the other and, to the detriment of both, has to be repaid, and, inevitably almost, in the language of "cash terms". Much of the imagery Williams employs will be startlingly transposed to the ostensibly more objective pages of *Culture and Society*, where the fate of "the scholarship boy" is placed within the structural imperatives of society to the detriment of the class from which he comes. Ladders are rejected there as well though with more positive alternatives offered than were available in Paul Ramsay's vision. It is clear Raymond Williams himself felt, and in his familial bond too, a line had been crossed and left behind a long time ago. His only way back to it, though not to recross its boundary, was to think, and finally write, with a deep yet critical empathy, of his father's life from within his father's character, rather than as a mirror or sounding board for himself. The 1950s gradually forced this on him more and more for neither Pandy nor the idyll had stayed as they once, in memory, were. Quarrels and disagreements aside, Harry and Gwen remained supportive of their son; for themselves they thrived and this aspect of their life, when understood more fully, enriched immeasurably the profundity of their son's most important novel.

The paradox of the last decade of Harry Williams' working life can be summed up by the twinned events of January 1948, when he simultaneously ceased to be a servant of the GWR and rejoiced in the newly nationalised status of the British railways, and, within days, passed his driving test. Though neither father nor son would have quite seen it like that, he had been doubly liberated.[38] Through a decade of greater personal freedom, materially and spatially mobile, he consolidated his political and social beliefs whilst, literally, enjoying the fruits of his and Gwen's labour. Throughout the 1950s sociologists and other commentators agonised or rejoiced over what they saw as the demise of a "traditional" working class as levels of prosperity spread. At the decade's end Raymond Williams supplied the most subtle riposte yet to those who would assume that collective values of community and citizenship, all wrapped up in working class historical experience, could not survive individual betterment. In truth he had seen his father's unfolding life testifying to the opposite.

When Harry Williams died he left £1,570, a sum substantial enough to be noted in the local newspaper, along with his new and paid-for house. Harry and Gwen had always been careful with and sometimes necessarily anxious about money, but it was not the signalman's wage that had seen them able to buy new "consumer durables", unaffordable to them in the 1930s, and to take holidays, notably by car, to west and north Wales resorts. Harry had become an entrepreneur, a small but successful trader in country produce. It was the car which allowed all this to happen for him as he and Gwen struck out beyond Abergavenny to reach the towns and markets of Hereford and Shrewsbury and Ludlow, their own border country.

Meticulous as ever, he had noted, in April 1949, a record honey "harvest" of some 2,205 pounds. It was hard work to collect, prepare and pour into glass jars. Year by year Harry and Gwen sat up late into the night when the time came to make their pounds of honey saleable. It was worth it. By 1952 they had contacts for bulk sale in Monmouth as well as Hereford which meant seventeen dozen honey jars selling for seventeen guineas and on a harvest average of 2,000 pounds a year, annual sales of around £200 and a high profit margin, one nearly half his income as a senior signalman.

But it did not begin and end with honey. The pigs he kept nearby were killed, two a year, and their bacon salted for use and sale. Yellow plums and damsons and Bramley apples and gooseberries found their way to market along with vegetables and flowers from his constantly tended garden allotment. Gallons of wine, potato or elderflower, barley and wheat or parsnip, were for both convivial use and bottling for sale. He sawed wood, mended fences, acted as green-keeper and grounds-man and laid paths around semi-detached Llwyn Onn. It was all of a piece. On 7 February 1950, in the middle of that second Labour victory, he noted: "I decide to go to Hereford with honey and am hopeful of a contract for the rest of it. Went Tory heckling in evening", and the next day: "Had an afternoon's wood chopping of old plum trees, then thrilled to listen to Jim Griffiths at 9.15." In 1951, in the middle of an election, with Labour losing, despite a popular majority and an increased number of voters for Labour for the third successive time, he wrote on 19 October how the electricity supply for Pandy was switched on, at last; "A day we shall always remember", and one that prompted the purchase of "a Hoover; an electric fire" and an electricity boiler for the water. Then, less than a week later, on the day of the General Election, 25 October: "Before we go to bed at 4 am I feel we have lost *our* Labour Government."

Raymond Williams was telling a straightforward truth when he claimed that in *Border Country*, the signalman, Harry Price, steady and clear in his living and his beliefs, and the businessman, Morgan Rosser, quick and excitable, were both aspects of his father and, in essence, pre- and post-war in their embodiment. In this working-class world, driving to Stratford in 1955 to see *All's Well That Ends Well* or returning in 1956 to catch a fiery Emlyn Williams as Shylock in *The Merchant of Venice*, were the extension of minority tastes that had no "social correlative", as their son had earlier written. It was a natural thing for them to do when it became possible to do it.

* * * * * *

In 1952, as Harry and Gwen's life was changing in ways unforeseen by Raymond, so the life of Raymond Williams the writer was finally taking off. Although he was certainly not seeing it that way himself, the key breakthrough was not, finally, the publication of *Drama From Ibsen to Eliot* but long term contact with a publisher who would, patiently, invest in his ambition.[39] He had written to Chatto and Windus for the first time in November 1950 to ask if they would like to read, with a view to publication, a book on drama which he had "just finished revising". The greater part of Raymond Williams' book *From Ibsen to Eliot* was, as he noted in the Preface of its 1952 publication, "written between September 1947 and April 1948". Other chapters were revised or slotted in before its final form took shape and was offered to Chatto and Windus in November 1950. "It seems to me", he had written in an accompanying letter, "the kind of book which might command some interest, and I do not know of anything that has been published in the same field. There have been histories of the drama of the period, but there is no general work of criticism." That, indeed, was the burden of the book's proving: that drama required the kind of serious literary criticism which other literature had received, and that this criticism was a requirement, for drama as well as literature, of any sustainable standard in contemporary practice. He was not about to alter his robust views on acting as, much too often, a creative interpretation beyond the given words, though nor was he in any real sense being dogmatic against character and action unfolding in performance. Some early critics would think otherwise. It was certainly a book which would prove malleable in form as it later extended itself from Ibsen to Brecht with, in 1968, a clutch of "more recent" dramatists to round it off. Such extension was counterpointed by excision, notably of the influence of T.S. Eliot, whose contemporary influence and dramatic practice run through the earlier volume.

The thrust of the succeeding chapters – the charge heavily led by Ibsen and on through Strindberg and Chekhov to Shaw and Synge, then via Pirandello and Anouilh to Yeats and Eliot himself – is that the back of Naturalism had to be broken and that out of the break would come, amongst other less welcome things, the possibility of verse drama whose complexity and richness of language might, yet, be able to compensate for what had been a loss of common sensibility and a fatigue of common language. The "embodiment of experience" is all, and the means to achieve this was not the simulation of naturalism but the effect of reality achieved by the evident truthfulness of aspects of experience. What is startling in an otherwise competent but conventional analysis of plays and playwrights is the pessimism which he hauls behind him from Leavis and Eliot, with only a bare disavowal of "the social correlative":

> The pressure of a mechanical environment has [today] dictated mechanical ways of thought, feeling, and conjunction, which artists, and a few of like temper, reject only by conscious resistance and great labour. That is why all serious literature, in our own period, tends to become

minority literature (although the minority is capable of extension and in my view has no social correlative)... The artist is no longer the spokesman of the whole society, and he suffers by that fact. But it is not the lack of common beliefs in society which restricts his communication. It is rather the lack of certain qualities of living, certain capacities for experience... But [minority drama's] communication may be extended, and its writing made more possible, if developments in society (the sum of individual developments) make possible the re-creation of certain modes of living and of language against which such complexes as industrialism have militated.

He concluded this almost impeccably "organicist" view with the half-promise that "on the chances of such development this is not the place to comment".[40] Chatto were however interested in the substance they already had before them.

In the spring of 1951 he worked on it again, under the editorial guidance of Cecil Day Lewis, taking out a further 30,000 words and offering to pare back even more if necessary. He was anxious to publish. In April, Chatto finally accepted the book for publication at the cover price of fifteen shillings and an advance, half on signature, of £75 to the author. He agreed and met Ian Parsons, a Chatto Partner, for the first time at a handshake celebratory lunch at The Garrick Club at the end of May. By this time, Ian Parsons was acknowledged as the leading publisher of literary criticism just as Chatto and Windus was the most prestigious firm. Raymond Williams might not have been aware that the publisher was also an English graduate from Trinity, with a First Class Honours in 1927, and, before that, a friend and contemporary of Empson's at Winchester, but he would certainly have known that it was Chatto that first published Empson's *Seven Types of Ambiguity* in 1930, Q.D. Leavis' *Fiction and the Reading Public* in 1932, and her husband's breakthrough book on the English novel, *The Great Tradition* in 1948. This was a stable in which, understandably, Raymond Williams would very much wish to find himself. In the autumn of 1951 he had reiterated, in the absence even of a date for proofs, that he was "too glad that the book is being done to want to complain about anything. Even apart from this, I am not at all impatient".[41] By now he was, however, in correspondence with "Mr Parsons" – who would, as familiarity and confidence grew as the decade went on, transmute from "Parsons" to "Ian" – and quick to characterise himself as more than a plodding academic.

As early as October 1951 he had alerted "Mr Parsons" to the new book on which he was working, "enclosing a list of contents and part of a draft preface". He said he had "got about two thirds of the book to the stage of full notes before writing" and wanted to keep the publisher "informed". This was his "next book of criticism" (*The Idea of Culture*) and they did, indeed, express a mild interest. The burden of his letters, at this time, was, for all that, about work completed:

> My main writing interest is fiction, and in the last few years I have written three novels. I am not very satisfied with any of them, but I am now revising them in turn, and hope that I can make something of them. Before you had accepted *Drama From Ibsen to Eliot*, I had already given one of the novels to an agent, although I have now taken it back. But he has seen my most recent novel, and believes he can sell it after a few revisions that I am now making.

The ostensible purpose of this information was to clarify his future obligations under his contract, though he understood that that would refer to works of a similar genre, and his scarcely hidden intent was to wonder "whether you would be at all interested in the novels yourself... [and]... while I don't want to appear to misinterpret the contract to my own advantage, equally I don't want to try to involve you in the novel on the basis of the other book". The logic was a trifle muddy but the hope was crystalline. He even expressed his wish to be known as R.W. Ridyear.[42]

If early publication of one of the novels – *Ridyear*, *Brynllwyd*, *Adamson* – had occurred, perhaps the subsequent pattern of his writing life would have been different. As it was, the fiction would, though never to his mind, appear to come after the "works of criticism". His agent, the firm E.P.S. Lewin, as instructed, sent *Adamson* to Chatto at the very end of November 1951. Sight of Lewin's letter and Parsons' reply, in January 1952, would scarcely have cheered the novelist. John Johnson from E.P.S. Lewin wrote:

> Williams has written three novels, all of them with unusual themes. The first two were not wholly satisfactory in our opinion but Adamson showed very much more promise. He finished it some months ago...

> Williams has undoubted promise as a novelist and I believe he might well have an important future. His style is always rather obtuse but I feel that, with maturity, this will smooth itself out. At any rate one can always be sure of original work by this writer.[43]

And Ian Parsons from Chatto replied to the agency, citing production costs and the difficulty of even recovering the outlay on a first novel as prime reasons for rejection, but also to say:

> Although *Adamson* is a most unusual book, and clearly the work of a highly intelligent writer, we feel that it suffers from some major defects which would militate strongly against its success with the general public. It is... difficult to follow the psychological trail in places; the descriptive passages, admirable as they are, do not seem to tie up quite closely enough with the outer and inner actions of the characters. The result is that the theme does not really come through clearly enough, and this makes me wonder whether Williams, despite his undoubted ability to write and make one think, is really a novelist.[44]

Whatever the soundness of this as a publisher's judgement on *Adamson*, it was the precursor to a determined compartmentalisation of his work against which Raymond Williams would always struggle.

Chatto could look to the reception of his book on drama to confirm their estimate. It was widely reviewed, in the London and the provincial press, from December 1952 on, with heavier notices in the weeklies and periodicals following up into the spring of 1953.[45] There were complaints from Shavians and the more recent acolytes of Christopher Fry, that their chosen dramatists were, rather differently, slighted, and also from some who saw Williams as one of "the solemn school of contemporary criticism, the literary puritan" too willing to cite Eliot on every other page. With that last view he would later concur. Still, for the most part his championing of critical analysis of drama in order to restore the primacy of language had a respectful press whose unease lay more with the firmness of Williams' stated position than its sense. The two most probing notices appeared in the *Times Literary Supplement* and the *New Statesman*. The anonymous *TLS* reviewer, in two columns of praise for Williams' cogency and substance, wondered whether the emphasis on the dramatist's ascendancy over producer and actor could, away from paper and back on stage, satisfy the emotional need for something more than "arrangements of words". Again it would be a point he felt he had made himself already in the book in his attempt to unite language shifts with a community's needed commonality of culture. The gap between 1950's British society and the potential he glimpsed in contemporary verse drama did not, however, convince. For the *New Statesman* (whose back half was the most influential literary review of that decade and the next), Montagu Slater, a prominent Communist Party commentator in the 1930s, concluded that "Mr Williams is right in his discussion of Synge, and Mr O'Casey – and, elsewhere, of the Elizabethans – in looking for active community as the source of richness in language", but he hit a note which Williams' future readers would have found unexpected: "How shall we get it? Not by 'minority culture' which is Mr Williams' only proposal. The theatre does not become literature by moving up to the top shelf. This is where Mr Williams' argument leads – and where it breaks down."

He defended his book twice – once publicly, because of an intemperate peer review by an Adult Education tutor, and once privately, because of a forthright claim of plagiarism. The first defence was occasioned by J.R. Williams, an extra-mural literature tutor of the University of London, who told readers of *The Tutors' Bulletin of Adult Education* that his namesake was a clear illustration of the "way the wind of fanaticism blows". Application of so-called "Practical Criticism" to drama, where non-verbal elements were so much a part of the play, was, he claimed, "what we knew to expect from Mr Williams". It was the undercurrent of bitterness – as to "how to treat drama in our classes" in J.R. Williams' formulation – that elicited a reply, mild enough by contemporary academic standards, pointing up the reviewer's inaccuracies. But it was the ongoing tremor of further accusation – "Mr Williams is frankly of the nose-to-the-words-on-the-page-school" – which led Raymond Williams to what would prove to be his last real deep concern with arguing for the primacy of text. He does it with a reasonableness that makes it hard to deny the logic of only realising context from text in order to elucidate the latter when, first, the text has been read in and for itself and as its own matter: "But it is also necessary to recognise that one is never, finally, alone with the text; nor is the text alone, but is always in relation with other texts and other facts... The difficulty, in practice, is both to recognise this and yet to maintain the essential discipline. It is, in fact, finding what other facts are relevant". Yet his instinctive drive remained: to go to the wider context – "society, belief, conditions of publication or performance, biography... language" – because and only after "the text sends one there". The literary critic, as such, had, in 1953, not yet crossed the line entirely.[46]

His reputation as a scholar was assailed more directly by a letter to Ian Parsons at Chatto claiming that the plan of *Drama From Ibsen to Eliot*, the writers selected, and the emphasis on "texture of language", all derived from Muriel Bradbrook's lectures at Cambridge in the immediate post-war years, whilst the central section on Ibsen was also closely derivative, in argument and quotation, from Bradbrook's own 1948 publication with Chatto and Windus, *Ibsen: The Norwegian*. Williams' response in February 1953, as his own book was receiving wide attention and had sold well over a thousand copies, was to refute the implications, chapter and verse, and to threaten action against his accuser if his explanation was not accepted. For a young scholar, whose first important work this was, probity was crucial. Besides, Muriel Bradbrook (1909-1993), an Elizabethan scholar, who had lectured at Cambridge before the war and had post-war made herself the pre-eminent Ibsenite scholar of the day, was a figure of some weight. He needed to reply. He began:

> In the first place, and this point seems rather important, I did not attend Miss Bradbrook's lectures on Tragedy while I was at Cambridge. This may have been very remiss of me, and I am sure I should have learned a great deal, but I had just come out of the Army, was right out of touch, and preferred to spend most of my time working in Libraries. I think I attended four or five lectures all that year, and so far as I can remember none of them [sic] was Miss Bradbrook. Nor did I see any syllabus, outline or notes of her course.[47]

Any similarities in comparative explanation or comment on individual playwrights lay in the general familiarity of scholars with the writers who had been chosen for discussion.

> Since I did not hear Miss Bradbrook's lectures, and they have not, I believe, appeared anywhere in print, there is clearly no other explanation: not even unconscious reminiscence, which as you know is always possible, but could not be so in this case.

For the rest, he acknowledged his indebtedness to her book on Ibsen, but as much for the way it allowed him to put a different case as for its own and different judgements. He thought he had made full and proper reference to her book in his own, and emphasised the differences, over Ibsen, that his concerned publisher seemed to "underestimate". It had come as a shock, for all that, and his insistent chronology of the writing, revising from 1947 to 1950, adding some writers (Hauptmann, Toller, Pirandello) "that I hadn't read... at that time" (which is to say in 1946) speaks of his psychological vulnerability even as he asserted his professional behaviour. In all essentials he was right to think himself slurred and, subsequently, vindicated. Comparison of the works yields, at best, echoes and re-used information but there are no direct, unacknowledged traces. The case is perhaps indicative of the way Williams would later disconcert many by the apparent ease, almost as if by osmosis, with which a writer of his originality of mind could absorb the work of others and transmute it into his own purposes without betraying or denying the prior validity of his source. If there was any fault of his that had affected "Miss Bradbrook" he sympathised, "accidental though it clearly is".

His own speculation as to the identity of his assailant was inaccurate and Parsons did not comment further on the actual letter he had received in January 1953 which drew his attention to "remarkable correspondences of matter and treatment in Mr Williams' book" to "a course of lectures delivered by Miss Bradbrook on modern tragedy for the faculty of English in Cambridge". The letter was from Miss K.M. Burton of Newnham College and she continued: "Miss Bradbrook was already giving those lectures in 1945-6 when Mr Williams was in Cambridge reading for the English Tripos. I attended these lectures myself – and as a personal friend of Miss Bradbook's I felt bound to write to you."

Ian Parsons gave Kay Burton a copy of Williams' letter to him. She withdrew her allegations "unreservedly" and gallantly told Muriel Bradbrook so.

What puts this matter to rest is the salient fact that Muriel Bradbrook worked closely with Raymond Williams when he returned to Cambridge as a don in 1961, as she recalled in 1992:

> By 1946 I was back in Cambridge from the Board of Trade,
> but most other people were back too. I got to know

Raymond well when he returned [in the 1960s], and we worked together in the faculty. Especially when I was Chairman and he was Secretary in the mid 1960s when Leavis was at his most virulent... Raymond was a tower of strength in the situation. He was always polite, calm and unruffled... and he remained friends with everyone... I helped to get a Chair for him, and with Marie Axton he edited the festschrift for me... in 1977.

Our work overlapped because both worked on modern tragedy for the English Tripos, Part II. In fact his first book was very much on my territory. But of course he later developed on other lines.[48]

Chapter 9

"Whether it will... be the kind of book you would really wish to publish"

The syllabus for the Preparatory Tutorial Class he taught in Hastings in 1951, under the title *Culture and Society*, asked, rather wistfully of its students, at the end of his scatter gun list of topics and books: "Any common factors?"[1] If there were, the surface flotsam and jetsam of topics – Advertising ("The technique of producing irrational beliefs"), Newspapers ("values in the contemporary newspaper"), Cinema ("special circumstances of film going"), Theatre ("Distinction between drama and acting"), Fiction ("As a business"), Radio ("response to a mechanical institution"), Politics ("Analysis of speeches") – were not easily patterned even when prefaced by his emphasis on "The nature of culture" and "Word functions". Amidst this ferment, in sum the descriptors of contemporary life which he would seek to explicate in *The Long Revolution* and its sequels, he needed an historical anchor and a directional compass. The former he was glimpsing in the course of the reading he was undertaking, reaching out more and more widely as unexpected things came into sight – Coleridge, Carlyle – and here called "Theory and practice in English culture since the Industrial Revolution"; the latter he was beginning to devise as a steady concentration on the analysis of how the idea of Culture both changed itself and influenced a whole set of other social relationships. To see this whole, in its impact, he had first to isolate it and its mutant possibilities.

In the summer of 1952 he sought limited assurance; F.R. Leavis replied to him in early September.[2]

Dear Mr Williams,

I found your letter waiting for me on my return from abroad. That was some time ago, but I've had a lag of correspondence – and other things to deal with. I intend to be at Oxford on Wednesday evening, so I hope we have a chance of meeting. I've merely agreed – having been approached by a nice man after a public castigation (by me) of the Brit. C. – to give one of my routine Practical Criticism performances, as elementary as possible, at Oxford.

I don't suppose I shall be illuminating about Culture. But, as you know, it's not a matter of defining it. Or rather, one's preoccupation with defining it is a matter of defining one's own preoccupation with things – defining, "controlling" and correcting.

A history of the idea in terms of its effects on Criticism sounds promising.

Leavis had airily ended by remarking that as for his own "C. and Environment" of "more than 20 years ago", he was "well aware of questions not answered". But it was the way in which the questions should be put that was now pushing Williams further and further away from the confines of "Criticism" and into territory he, more than any one, would mark out as a border between "ideas and the other products of man's life in society", for the "idea of culture is not to be considered as a process of independent evolution; [it is] shaped and at times directed by the total environment to which it is one kind of response". This was how he put his first major exploration of the theme in the essay he finished in late 1952 and published as "The Idea of Culture" in *Essays in Criticism*.[3]

This journal had been founded in 1951 by F.W. Bateson (1901-78) who was an Oxford Don based in Corpus Christi College from 1946 as a university lecturer in English.[4] "Freddy" Bateson, from an earlier generation, was an interwar activist in the broad socialist cause with a special interest in conditions on the land, and the *New Statesman*'s agricultural correspondent. A widely published scholar, especially in seventeenth and eighteenth century literature, Bateson was someone to whom Williams felt he could turn for guidance. He was one of a number of lively "internal" dons, like the Dickensian scholar with a penchant for

359

social history, Humphrey House (1908-55), with whom the "external" Williams could rub shoulders and ideas at the Delegacy's Summer Schools. Williams was flattered to be asked to join the initial Editorial Board and valued his contacts, peripheral as they were, with what served in the 1950s as a more rounded perspective on literary matters than either the respectfully admired *Scrutiny* (defunct by 1953) or the Bloomsbury world of taste and discriminatory manners still represented by the heartily disliked and then anonymous *Times Literary Supplement*. Bateson wished his own quarterly to range as widely over non-literary matters as had Leavis' *Scrutiny*, but to be more profoundly rooted in unassailable scholarship. Leavis did not return any compliments. He thought Bateson's project was a muddle and asserted, as ever, the necessity of reading the text to determine how a creative mind had plumbed social formations rather than how a context of understanding could reveal the meaning of texts. Raymond Williams' article, for all its careful contextualisation of the changing idea of culture, was still leaning more to a Leavisite position but, increasingly, in order to find how the connections (between "artist" and "society") were, in origins *and* outcome, inseparable: "one did not have to be an artist to feel that society was indifferent or hostile to individual desires.... The pattern of hunger and suffering [after the first phase of industrialisation] was not background, but the mould in which general experience was cast. One does well to remember this in turning to consider those factors which affected artists in the actual exercise of their arts."

His original "Notes" to the article underlined that he was concerned, in an essay that looked at thinking about culture and art from around 1780 to 1880, with moving away from the unhelpful categorisation of either term as "an absolute". But he went on to explain that it was only "a shortened version of the Introduction to a book of the same title" to deal with "theories and ideas of culture... put forward in England since the Industrial Revolution". The projected work had, in its sights, the effects of those things on "literary criticism", "the issue of tradition" and "the standard of perfection". He was still on known intellectual ground, but, as the article's final, tantalising references to "rising working class power" in the late nineteenth century hinted, beginning to stretch across that ground to find himself in another guise. It would take him a further three years and a serious sense of personal crisis before he finally linked up his thought with his own life's pattern.

At the same time as his exploratory article appeared, in the high summer of Coronation Year, he was writing, again, to his publisher, now clubbily addressed as "Dear Parsons", and enclosing the existing manuscript of his new book. In fact it was a general plan and two long chapters with the further explanation that he proposed, bringing "the history of the idea down to our own day; to study its explicit and implicit influence, and to assess its effects on criticism and on more general contemporary social thinking". He wavered on almost all substantive points: the title, "descriptive enough", could be changed "for selling purposes"; the sections of chapters expressed "the real divisions of the subject" but could be modified; it was all "still a draft" and he could "change wherever necessary"; its "attention to detail" meant it had "to be academic"; but the subject was of "such potential interest to many different kinds of people" that he wanted "to try to make the book easy for the general reader, as well as satisfactory for the student".[5]

Parsons had replied in August to say it was "full of interesting possibilities" though difficult to judge "final shape and weight" from "the first 30,000 words". Generalities bothered him, whereas more discussion of individual authors might make it "more flexible and persuasive" for a general list such as theirs. On balance he seemed to be steering its author to "one of the University presses" though Williams answered within a fortnight: "I fight shy of pushing out an idea through a university press."[6] By the autumn Williams himself had become less sure. He would need in fact to dispense with other matters – creative and educational – before he would drive it on to a self-directed completion. He wrote to Parsons in early October 1953 to say that he had been asked to write a short book on *Drama in Performance* for the "Man and Society" series "designed for use in adult education", adding, a trifle dolefully, "which is mainly why I was asked". He was overly polite in worrying about any downside effects on his larger drama book with Chatto but came, inevitably, to the point in his final paragraph, with words which could have become the epitaph for the book that might never have been taken further:

> Perhaps it is unnecessary for me to put [all this] to you, and if so I am sorry to be a nuisance. But I felt I should do so, before I entered into any firm agreement. The effect of agreeing to write the book [on Drama] on my writing *The Idea of Culture* has also to be considered. As you know, I would like to continue with that, as I have been doing since I last wrote; but although I believe in the book wholeheartedly, I confess I have had doubts about whether I can afford to concentrate all my present attention on it, in view of your perfectly reasonable doubts as to whether it will, in the event, be the kind of book you would really want to publish. Forgive me for all this indecision...[7]

He had to wait until Ian Parsons returned from holiday towards the month's end to have a reply. It was amicable enough about the new "Man and Society" book and gently deflating on the main issue: "I appreciate of course that [it] will postpone your work on *The Idea of Culture* but can't help sharing your doubts as to whether you can afford to concentrate all your efforts on the latter in view of its somewhat uncertain sales potentialities. All the same, I very much hope that you will go on with it even if it's only after an interval."[8]

There was a further complication. In April 1953 he had become a Company Director. The company was Film Drama Ltd and its other Director, each with a £1 share, was Michael Orrom[9]. He had not lost touch with Raymond but now, to Joy's growing concern, the two friends grew closer again. They met in Hastings through the summer of 1953 to mull over breakthrough projects in which dialogue became an arm of movement, and movement was stylised by camera and design into all that was not naturalism as they understood it. There were precedents, even in some of the fantasy sequences of *Singing in the Rain*, which they saw, and quarrelled over, that year. In retrospect, their idea of cinema seems as anachronistic for its own time as it seemed to them beyond the current filmic limitations of that time. Either way they worked hard at it. The most worked on piece that survives is Raymond's *A Dance of Seeing* which dates from September 1953: fifteen pages of description in which an artist, Matthew, living at the harbour of a fishing village, surrounded by the life of the quayside, discovers, in a dream, the dance of a lovely young woman whose final frozen immobility is only released for him when he realises that the dance is really the dance of life that he can find with his own love, Anna.[10] Orrom received it by post and commented at once, in detailed camera shot terms, with praise and excitement. He wondered: "Can we discuss it all soon? I don't think we should go on by writing. Shall I come down [from London] this week? For the day that is."[11] Joy did not welcome any of this but Orrom had nursed too long the disappointment that followed from their earlier failure to collaborate on the Rotha-style documentary to let this momentum slip; he had felt all along that the documentary would have allowed for a little success that could have led on to more dazzlingly experimental ideas.

As his friend taught and wrote academic pieces for publication, so Orrom worked for the BBC on documentaries about shipping and refugees, and, as a freelance for Shell and British Transport, on quasi-educational films. Shell had the first zoom lens in the country and, though it took an hour to set up, it excited Orrom with the use to which he could put it if the chance to make a "non-realist" film ever happened. He decided that the only way to bring about the chance was to "publish... what amounted to a manifesto... and have, waiting in the wings, a worked out proposal for a film which would put [their] ideas into practice". The manifesto would be the book they would publish together under the title *Preface to Film* in 1954.[12] Taken alongside *Drama in Performance*, also published in that year by Williams alone, the *Preface* is ample proof of his unwillingness to settle for anything less than the creative shake-out he still felt could come from a full acceptance of the death of Naturalism.

Their company was set up to publish "the Manifesto" and then to produce the films they felt would follow. They wrote their separate sections, exchanged them and finally there was "the pair of essays" they had had in mind for some years. With Introduction and Postscript the book was "Film and the Dramatic Tradition" by Williams, and Orrom's "Film and its Dramatic Techniques": "Its title – *Preface to Film*" said Orrom, "meant on the one hand the whole historical sweep of drama which had been at the preface to film, and on the other the book itself seen as a preface to the films we envisaged." At the least, in their driven energies, the two were an integument; in practice the non-appearance of the films would end a friendship which, for Williams, was dependent on such progress.

His own essay set out the case which became Orrom's task to translate into a technical reproduction on film. For Williams the key point to register was the protean nature of "drama", as convention and as literary work, over different times and in differentiated spaces. The lead-in to contemporary film would argue both the absolute novelty of the cinematic means and the relative conventionality of the "drama" it had, mostly, though not entirely, shown on screen. What he was after was a medium that could bring to bear "a total expression", writing for all that worked in the dramatic film: "the principle of integrated expression and performance, in which each of the elements being used – speech, music, movement, design – bears a controlled, necessary and direct relation, at the moment of expression, to any other that is being then used." If this was an aesthetic concept which would not bear the weight of its ambition it was, nonetheless, now stemming from what he had been grappling to say when he claimed verse-drama as a possible answer to the inadequacies of a naturalist tradition or admired the film of early Soviet Cinema, as movies reaching out, by their "inner, hidden psychological movement", beyond mere "extended details". In a bold flurry of explanation he wrote, in 1954, a page which shows him at the precise turning point that encapsulates the purpose of his co-joined fiction and analysis. It pirouettes around a phrase he would re-cycle over and over, a maddeningly precise and yet indefinable capture of the organic and the constructed, a society's "structure of feeling":

In principle, it seems clear that the dramatic conventions of any given period are fundamentally related to the *structure of feeling* in that period. I use the phrase structure of feeling because it seems to me more accurate, in this context, than *ideas* or *general life*. All the products of a community in a given period are, we now commonly believe, eventually related, although in practice, and in detail, this is not always easy to see. In the study of a period we may be able to reconstruct, with more or less accuracy, the material life, the general social organisation, and, to a large extent, the dominant ideas. It is not necessary to discuss here which, if any, of these aspects is, in the whole complex, determining; an important institution like the drama will, in all probability, take its colour in varying degrees from them all. But while, we may, in the study of a past period, separate out particular aspects of life, and treat them as if they were self-contained, it is obvious that this is only how they were studied, not how they were experienced. We examine each element as a precipitate, but in the living experience of the time every element was in solution, an inescapable part of a complex whole. [13]

And for Raymond Williams this "structure of feeling", or "mentalité" (as British historians had been learning from the Annales School), was palpably present in "the effect of the totality" that could be analysed in art. This was to accept Leavis' point that only in some such representation of experience could you judge an experience of life that was otherwise indeterminate and, at the same time, to make it, more than Leavis would warrant, co-equal in its value with the art it had brought out of its being: "This element, I believe, is what I have named the *structure of feeling* of a period, and it is only realisable through experience of the work of art itself, as a whole."

He was repeating the same mantra in the more orthodox companion volume *Drama in Performance*.[14] In five chapters he took a play – from classical Greece, medieval England, Elizabethan England twice, and Tsarist Russia – and analysed the setting, staging and interpretation of his chosen, classic and representative drama. He illustrated concisely and in detail the issues of chorus, dance, music and gesture before the nineteenth century's abuttment into naturalism, the eventual diminution of which, even with symbolism tacked on, was seen in the heavy-handed onstage paralleling of probability as the touchstone of life. In some senses this was a practical handbook for his earlier arguments about the text being matched by the total performance required in drama. This time, however, he confessed a lack of faith in the further advances of verse drama – Eliot's latest work was lamented as a clear failure – since that technique, too, had now embraced the stifling habits of naturalism in everything other than speech. He urged a rhythm of speech that was integral to movement, not behaviour – and speculated, as wild as it was wide, about song, dance and design. Within a few years of Osborne's *Look Back In Anger* he would appear to be bypassed by a newer orthodoxy, yet some of the critic's thinking anticipates the multi-dimensional work of both Joan Littlewood and Dennis Potter, and his own later unfashionable defence of the similar attempts of Welsh writers like Dylan Thomas in the early 1950s and Gwyn Thomas in the early 1960s to disrupt stifling stagecraft through exuberant expressionism. He trails his own creative intent within the analytical critique, and in a way which most confirms his real mind set in 1954.

The prologue once again bemoans the "disabling" separation of literature and theatre before it mounts the general proposition of the book. Yet here he open-handedly admits that discovery of "the general problem" is nothing like actual demonstration of its creative resolution:

> My own attempts at a general solution have all along been closely related to attempts at particular solutions; but to offer these belongs to another place. What I can hope... to do... is to define an attitude to the solution of the general problem, which can for the time being be considered in its own terms, but which it may be possible later to ratify in particular terms.

His Credo built and built. This generation, here and now, he claimed, could find, through critical understanding of the common terms, a new "common language", and this "common understanding" would "quickly find its counterpart in creative achievement". At the end of this other manifesto of 1954, he reaches a fervent pitch in his call for collaborative activity in the theatre between writers, designers, composers and dancers to replace all that has "made naturalism outmoded", so that "a conscious acceptance of a different dramatic intention can be realised, in practical terms, by the full use and development of skills that already exist in the theatre, but have not yet been integrated into a satisfactory general form". If this was still a comparatively young man's plea – he was thirty three – it was also the cry of someone whose early creative endeavour had gone nowhere. And if there was a way to envisage, in practice, his desired new tradition of drama, he fell back, for illustration, on film – "which indeed, as a new medium of drama, offers exciting possibilities of development that as yet have hardly been explored".

Whilst writing the above, Williams, typically, was making one final push, with Michael Orrom, to prove the point of their theory by actual practice. The book itself had not convinced two veteran film makers. Basil Wright told Orrom that "I got the distinct impression that your colleague doesn't really like films" and Paul Rotha remarked: "I didn't really get what [you] were driving at". Orrom shrugged and concluded, still, that:

> What mattered was a film based on the ideas we had set down... we wanted something which would allow us to develop (and make acceptable) a stylised form of acting; would demand stylised décor; would use a non-realist form of language – probably a kind of poetry, and probably used non-synchronously. It would be a short film of some 20 minutes.[15]

Most weekends Orrom would travel to Hastings and the two would be closeted together. The break, when it finally came, would be impelled by a minor domestic drama – Raymond and Michael returned to St. Helen's Road after a long walk to find the house in disarray, young children running around and a 'flu-stricken Joy in bed. Raymond made some complaint and a very long-suffering Joy finally exploded with rage. Michael Orrom left.[16] The decisiveness of the subsequent rupture between the two friends really stemmed from Raymond Williams' final abandonment of his various forays into mythicising his past in favour of the resolute, dogged realism of the prose fiction for which he would become known. Nevertheless, what is clear is that Raymond Williams was throughout this time stretching himself in two quite different directions and that being taken with Orrom was, prior to the break in relations, by no means the secondary one.

They had toyed with ideas of folk tales and music until a "Welsh" idea emerged. Orrom did not quite seem to understand its haunting provenance for the writer. A young man leaves his village to walk in the hills and, pulled onwards by music and voices, he finds a mysterious house. When he returns home, a vision of a girl in his mind, he finds a whole generation has passed. Orrom remembered that "we changed the village to a small industrial town, and made the young man's going out from it the rejection of a mother relationship and a desire to grow up. The attraction of the music became a discovery of love.... Finally came the return to the town and home, and the fitting of the new love into the old pattern. We called it simply *Legend*".[17]

Legend, eight pages of continuous prose-poetry rather than a shooting script, was completed by Raymond Williams at the end of January 1955.[18] It reads like a description of a contemporary ballet with physical space and movement between people as the shaping elements of the drama. The young man is a maker of vases, one of which, more graceful in design than the rest, he tries to give to his mother. The father, irritated perhaps by the material uselessness of the beautiful object, intervenes. The vase is placed on a ledge. The youth leaves when his approach to the mother is blocked by the father:

"Now there was only a little space
Between the son and his mother, and, holding out his arm,
he made to rush to embrace her.

But he looked suddenly into her face, and saw
That she was telling him not to come. He
Looked at her in bewilderment, and repeated
His appeal, but again, looking towards her
husband, she refused. The son, sadly, put his
hand over his eyes, and turned away."

When he returns, thirty years later (as it turns out to be), he sees his own former self reflected in the window of his old house. The image becomes reality. He is married and the girl who now brings him a drink in the house is the girl with whom he has danced in the past far away. He is now her husband.

Colours and sets were to be designed by Michael Stringer, already with a number of film credits to his name, and John Cranks, Sadler's Wells choreographer, was keen to join, telling Orrom that he and Williams "had proposed more exciting images in the mirror than Cocteau ever had". Music would have been by Malcolm Arnold who had been working with Orrom on recent documentaries. These were not negligible names. Enthused, Williams wrote sections of speech for the Young Man and two girls as dramatic poetry and, Orrom thought, "they would have joined with the music and the action very well, at least to begin to create a new film form". They worked on through 1955 to write a full film screenplay with actions on one page and "the speech words" on a separate page opposite. There were "large colour design sketches,... a skeleton of continuities... a timing breakdown and a detailed budget".[19]

The whole thing was to be proposed – as a "colour and sound development from *Caligari*" – to the British Film Institute's Experimental Film Fund. Basil Wright, on the committee, told Orrom he liked the idea very much and that they should "at least prime the pump". This was, for both men, more than just about the fate of one small film. They had convinced themselves that they might be able to change the shape of cinematic history: that their up-dated use of colour and new techniques, without synchronised sound and with the use of camera movement to suggest flow rather than by the editorial composition of cutting, would make for a "classic" film in the mode of the great silent "classics" of film's pioneering age. Besides, this was a way, without dialogue or subtitles, to create a subjective emotion on film which could, again, have an appeal beyond national boundaries. "In our opinion" they wrote to the BFI, "it is possible to make sound films which make much greater use of all the dramatic possibilities of the medium, and which are capable of being translated into foreign languages with little loss of validity: in other words, regain the place for the film as a truly international art." Experiment, in order to win over public taste, was everything, and would require subsidy to allow for failure before success. They called for the establishment of an Academy of Film to train cinematographers to use all the technical means now available to increase the "dramatic expression" of film. They aimed high, prepared to make a proposed practice the proof of their certainty:

> ... if [an Academy]... had a directed policy of experiment, together with a full and honest approach to the public, we believe that it could effect a great change not only in the artistic qualities of films themselves, and not only in the artistic taste of the general public for the film, but indirectly would also heighten perception and appreciation of art in many other fields, through a general raising of the whole cultural environment.[20]

By the spring of 1956 Raymond Williams had, with that solitary determination that he might well recognise as his true strength after a decade of dedicated work, also come close to fruition with the longer generated *Idea of Culture*. Orrom certainly realised that. And it would be easy to see the film-maker's own wish to see such a film made as a far more overpowering psychological need for him than for the writer. Except for two things. The first being the creative Manifestoes or small books of 1954 on which so much still rested and, secondly, Raymond Williams' own extreme reluctance to let go the dream. So, Joy continued to prepare lunches and teas and usher into her home a man she felt, with increasing certainty, was feeding the dreamer not the doer in her questing husband.

In June 1956 *The Legend*, as documents and sketches, was sent to the BFI with, as Michael Orrom recalled, "a flourish of confidence that something would happen. It did. The project ran head on into formidable realist opposition". It was too expensive. It was too experimental. Or, paradoxically, it might be too commercial. Any and either way it was not to be made.

At first, they did not give up on their huge ambition. They looked for a more accessible or popular story into which they could blend elements of their novel use of voice and image. Raymond suggested an adaptation of his unpublished novel, *A Map of Treason*, with its *doppelgänger* theme or, similarly, his novel *Adamson*. Orrom liked the latter very much. Once more a scenario was prepared; notions of interior monologues to counterpoint dialogue and deepen the psychological drama were sketched out; a high speed police car chase to the cliffs and a last minute dramatic intervention was written in. Orrom remembered that he "left Raymond's house in Hastings one evening in January 1957... feeling confident that we were in sight of a solution... and we would meet again as soon as possible". Weeks passed without him hearing anything, then Orrom sent a letter to his old friend. He recalled:

> I received a three-line note back, which said simply "It doesn't convince any more. I can't go on with it."
> I looked at the words over and over again. I could not believe that they were actually on the paper. Slowly I realised that they signalled a total cutting of ties; the curt dismissal extended to all our recent work. I felt utterly drained. But emptiness turned to anger. How could he write like this after all our years of working together? I could get no explanation. All was silence. For week after week there was no reply to letters, no lifting of the telephone.[21]

Michael Orrom never forgave Williams. Partly because he really believed that "at a different time and in different circumstances" they could have taken on their "original ideas.... We might have done it together." More so perhaps, because he could not fully explain to

371

himself why his friend, working on his own idea after all, could just slide away "demonstrating an absolute ruthlessness at his centre". There had been no "blazing creative row", just the abrupt end of fifteen years of sharing "so many thoughts and feeling on such a wide range of subjects and ideas". Later Orrom wondered if the "energies" of the book he was working on needed to be concentrated by driving all else out. Perhaps a "compromise work of art", like the film *Adamson*, did not fit into this new venture. Perhaps it was a writer's block, but then why turn one's "back on the good as well as the unsuccessful... creatively/dramatically he never seemed to try again".

The brief attempt by Orrom to re-write *Adamson* was vetoed by Williams. The company, Film Drama Ltd, was wound up at his insistence. They met once more only, in 1966, when Orrom, who was filming a documentary in the science laboratories in Cambridge, called on him without warning at his house in the village of Hardwick. Somewhat awkwardly they went to a pub at Raymond's suggestion and chatted like two old friends with nothing much to say anymore until it was time for Michael to leave.[22]

* * * * * *

Joy Williams' sense of the break was sharper.[23] She and Raymond discussed the years of work that had been put in and she told him firmly it was all a dead-end. Wolf Mankowitz had sent a copy of his book – and subsequent film hit – *A Kid for Two Farthings* to his old acquaintance with the inscription "For Raymond who chose the hard way". But the hard way, for Joy, was not less commercial film making, it was the relationship of her husband's wider cultural analyses to his originality of voice. She felt he had to find the latter for himself in order to give his idea of cultural change a personal charge. That was how he was. That was how he worked. The rest was be-dazzlement and purblind foolishness. The word "Fool" was bandied about between them. She wanted no more dead ends, but she saw clearly enough that any success he might achieve as a writer could not, by its and his nature, be a conventional one. He must court difficulty and even opposition because they were things implicit in his most solid stance and his most complex thought. It was another tight place and he must stick fast. At the very time when the tectonic plates of the 1950s' own "structure of feeling" appeared to be moving at last – politically and culturally – he was experiencing a heightened personal crisis. It coincided with the onset of his father's serious illness.

Harry Williams had his first confirmed coronary thrombosis at the end of June 1956.[24] He was confined to bed for several weeks and his son made the first of a number of trips home to see him – "Mam tells me Jim is here, it helps a lot" – through a summer and autumn of weakness and pain. Harry was never again free of sudden chest pains and a physical debility that ruled out the entire pattern of his previous life. In January 1957 he had the first of his periods in hospital in Abergavenny and, again, an urgent telephone call summoned the son – "I feel ever so well today and the talks and understanding between us as a family have most certainly done me good. We stay up till 11." Before spring came he was in and out of hospital and it was clear he would not be able to return to work. Jim and Gwen talked privately with their GP and the hospital doctors. Neither had any doubt that the prognosis was not just about early retirement. In April Harry Williams wrote of Jim: "It does us good to see him. He is kindness itself." Raymond Williams notes of himself, in deep and disquieting privacy in June 1957: "Depression or break up".[25]

In effect it had been bleak since the previous October, with one life in the process of drawing to a close and little sense of any satisfactory completion in his own work and life.

At this time he began keeping two maroon-coloured pocket Notebooks in which he had carefully written his name and address. One was labelled "Daybook". Its second entry on 11 October 1956 recorded a dream he had had after hearing a radio broadcast by the historian Asa Briggs who had had an acclaimed publishing success with his book of essays *Victorian People* in 1954. First, the unconscious: "dream of parcel of writing, arriving for Stanley Williams, or from him;

373

I pass some of it on, and immediately people arrive, reporters etc., asking for Stanley Williams, whom I find I didn't know and couldn't direct them to, but they kept coming and soon I was reading, in some sort of large print, Stanley Williams, the other Great Writer of the First World War (the first it seemed was Hitler!)...". Then, wide awake and conscious, he groaned, perhaps from general frustration as much as from personal conviction:

> Briggs so disgracefully bad that one felt dirty because in a sense involved: it showed the academic method was a trial and found wanting, but the whole point was that Briggs had *none* of the academic virtues: no passion, no substantiation, no flexibility of question. So? Is it sheer pain that makes me ask why this kind of mediocrity is so highly rewarded? Not just by public merchants (*Observer*, BBC) but in a spectacular university career, based on very little. All the m. class guns? The souless, beavers and salesmen triumphant everywhere? Felt like it tonight. But I distrust pain.... And try to read *King Macbeth* tonight.... Then get to work on second writing of it. It is the most immediate thing in feeling and compass. Will she like it?

The last query is the clearest indicator of how central Joy Williams was to the whole of his endeavour from this point onwards. She dispelled his wracking doubts. She scorned his dismay at the spiralling difficulties of his enquiries. She vigorously insisted that his belief in his own intellectual views coincided rather than conflicted with his personal experience of life. She took him out of the wash of those structures of feeling that unavoidably beset him in a culture of contemporaneity to root him in the fixed point of their existence together. But only so that he could continue to glimpse other horizons. She was the most creative critic he ever had because she came before the page and she was there after it was filled. He wanted her to like his work but, more, he needed her to believe in it. She did. More, at this period in his life, than he did himself.

He continued to write of a sequence of disturbing dreams in his notebooks, in a sometimes indecipherable hand, throughout October 1956. He is in a kitchen. It is Day in the Night. He taps repetitively at a window. Somebody's wife has "just slipped out". Or he rings the police. They ask if it is urgent, if it is important. The connection breaks. He is involved in some work with his father but "Me, I can't get the hang of it, get all mixed up". The man who sold him the children's dog, Sirius, returns to take it away "for examination" but returns with a "quite different dog – a ginger spaniel". He pays before the difference is noticed. One longer account is headed "Dream : end October":

> Wake and go to window of my bedroom and look down to find men concreting my garden. I go down and they tell me all the gardens are being concreted, on orders from the Owner Sir Harry Williams. I object that I own this house. They agree to delay, giving me the owner's and contractor's addresses. I ring up but can't get through. I look up the numbers and find myself looking up [indecipherable word] in the dictionary. It has two meanings – one of them 'gyre'. Wake.

It was this prolonged miasma of helplessness, a vortex spiralling away with himself in its centre, which Joy Williams alone was seeing close-up. The break with Michael Orrom was a product of it in early 1957. He had to let go of some things if he was not to fall into a void of hopelessness. The crisis was still with him in June 1957 when his usually careful, somewhat crabbed handwriting filled a page in the Notebook, in a leaping scrawl:

> June 14th 57
> Why does nothing happen out there? It has happened – the book is coming and yet still much the same feeling. Almost frightened at the amount I have to do, the direction in which I am moving. Better experience a break-up. Obviously... I want to think the latter; and the former is flattering – if in

fact I get all this work done, fine. But the priorities matter
– and to what extent will they be dependent on critical
happiness 'and then'? All I must be sure of now is pressing
the possibilities of publishing in particular direction, so that
I can see the choices; but I sometimes feel that the choices
will never be made. Almost any critical work is Mobility and
mobility is both bad and good affect.

These are the inner thoughts of a man still divided between the kinds
of intellectual work before him – critical or creative – and, at this stage,
naturally unknowing of the incredible reception *Culture and Society* will
have in 1958. But he had cast the effort of his work onto the waters
and had to wait. The dreams, or at least his recounting of them,
stopped, with only one last exception in October 1957. This time he
sees new and powerful machinery delivered to his garden. It is in a pen.
Farmers stand around watching it. His *doppelgänger* – here named as
"Matthew and Will" for he is deep into the penultimate stages of his
novel – go to a function of some kind. It is recognisably (orchards, a
distant valley) his native country. But, as full-grown plants and flowers
are put into the earth to wilt in the sun, it is, from gates and fences to
colour and setting, a "theatrical rehearsal". There are two dummies
now, "in working attitudes". Angry "police and officials" arrive, furious
at this discovery. An official figure acts: "Pokes with his stick at each
figure, to topple them over. Expect this to happen. And then the figures
come alive, and go on working. Immense general laughter. Wake."

* * * * * *

The dream that ended with such relief had been a nightmare to live
through. During that time he had, in addition to his teaching and the
exigencies of living with a young family on small money, whittled away
at his own imaginative writing. He had two more novels and plays to
show for his effort – but he was increasingly absorbed, to the point of
obliteration it sometimes felt, by the manner in which the Idea of
Culture had become the explanatory vehicle for his entire self-

376

questioning. Or so it began to seem to him. Michael Orrom and other dreams shared were rudely put aside. Nor is there any doubt that without Joy he would not have carried his work on cultural change through all its difficulties on or forced other issues aside for it. His own recollection of his preparation for the work on *Culture and Society* was one of almost constant panic, as the discovery of one avenue of approach through one or other semi-forgotten piece of writing led him on to another and another. The final list of writers paraded was, as he stressed, neither pre-determined by tradition or exhaustive as a result of his scholarship. He just kept reading and discovering through 1954 and into 1955, and even on, as he wrote more systematically from the early drafts of 1953, until its completion in 1956. The year before he died he put all this succinctly within the generational context of the 1950s but he also sounded the note of personal need, even urgency, as clearly in 1987 as it had been with him a quarter of a century previously:

> It is [still] widely used as a history of the thought and writing of this English tradition, and perhaps that is enough. But I did not write it only as a history, as the Conclusion sufficiently shows. I began it in the post 1945 crisis of belief and affiliation. I used all the work for it as a way of finding a position from which I could hope to understand and act in contemporary society, necessarily, through its history, which had delivered this strange, unsettling and exciting, world to us.[26]

As much as the reading, then, it was the unsettling state of that contemporary world which disturbed him. There was no easy settlement in it for him. He found travelling into London a strain, since the sight and sounds of advertisements everywhere in the new Ad-Mass world made him feel physically sick.[27] From time to time he stopped reading newspapers in a mixture of anger and frustration at how they told the news and how long it took him to compose useless letters of reply. Although, through Henry Collins, he met and socialised with members of the Communist Party in their "house" in Hastings, he felt utterly distanced from Party policies, a stance even more exacerbated by the failed uprising in East Germany in 1953. He was amongst the thirty or so asked to participate in discussion when the Historians' Group of the Communist Party convened at Netherwood House, Hastings in July 1954 for a week of "intensive sessions... on the entire history of British capitalist development". But it was only as one of two 'outside contributors invited along for their expertise'.[28] He remained outside. He canvassed and spoke for the Labour Party in 1955 but with no conviction that such politics, saturated with a culture of limited satisfaction, could effect any likely change.

Nor, by the mid 1950s, did palpable changes in perspective seem to be occurring in his tutorial classes. For a time, as with his notion of a unified dramatic art in film, he had placed his hopes on opening up cinema as a legitimate mode for teaching. A Preparatory Tutorial Class at Battle in 1950 attracted twenty students for "An Introduction to Film" and followed earlier, and later, short courses he devised with the help of Michael Orrom. He had long recognised the potential of film to connect with working class cinemagoers and its innate potential to stretch both its art and its audiences. In 1953, he wrote another report from the front line – "Film as a Tutorial Subject"[29] – and, despite knowing the contemptuous suspicion with which his experiments were viewed inside the academic profession, went straight for the jugular: "The arts are still dangerous in education... the dangerous quickening of experience". He placed the arts, and not just the lately respectable "Literature", firmly amongst the necessities for "adult and workers' education":

> Film appreciation, as it is commonly understood, is certainly not a tutorial subject; but then I would argue that the mere appreciation of literature or of painting, or of music is not tutorial work either. But the cinema has overtones; for reformers and conservatives alike it is conventional shorthand for depravity and cultural decay alike. Many fear that if education touches it the taint will be indelible. It is a pretty fear; but if adult education cannot handle and assess an institution which weekly serves the leisure of twenty-five

million British adults, and which deals well or badly, but at least with great emotive power, with the values of man and society, then adult education deserves to fade. The case for film as a tutorial subject is, first, that it provides opportunities for criticism, and that criticism is a major educational discipline; and, second, that the study of the cinema as an institution is an inevitable part of our sociology.

Here, and with deepening intensity away from more familiar fields, is the combination of critical values and social validation which is the hallmark of his beliefs. He envisaged a criticism of film which would be, by nature of the art, different in kind from the literary or practical criticism which was acknowledged, by the end of the decade, as having swept all before it. Literature classes had become, to all real purpose, "classes in criticism" rather than in learned appreciation. Yet, soon his own classes, as they grew in numbers and popularity, somewhat ironically became more like the lectures and discussion classes he had earlier dismissed as near to useless. There was, in retrospect, a cross pollination at play. The fructifying ability of adult education, freed from the straitjacket of internal university examination in the Humanities to open up new subject matter, would turn out to be the real begetter of Cultural Studies within the new universities of the 1960s. Williams, and others, would in that decade extend their innovative teaching and scholarship inside the very walls against which they had often railed. But it was a creative genesis that had been carried forward after this reluctant exodus for him and others, from Adult Education, that he was never slow to insist upon as the true begetter of the burgeoning industry of Cultural Studies. However, in the early to mid 1950s, this was not the central question; the central question concerned the difficulty of keeping any such liberal adult education as a core part of workers' lives in a culturally fragmenting Britain.

The concern was felt deep within the Delegacy, as the 1953 Annual Report emphasised: "Whilst adult education should serve the whole community and classes usually attain their best standard if they are representative of all walks of life and of a variety of occupations, the

Committee has a special interest in providing facilities for working men and women and their organisations, especially trade unions. A consistent effort has been made during the year to attract working men and women into classes." Two years later, concerns were expressed about the recent "decline" in the number of "manual workers" in adult education. Whether the concern was based on fact or not the Report found "difficult to say". By 1956 the doubts were gone: "An analysis of the occupations of students shows a further increase in housewives and a reduction in manual workers".[30]

Raymond Williams had actively sought some means to affect the trend and, notably, worked hard to introduce classes designed to teach the basics of speech-making and letter-writing as products of clear thinking and structured argument. These were specifically directed towards trade union education with which he had also been involved, particularly in Hastings, since 1951. The fulcrum, he insisted, was "your attitude to the working class". For Williams:

> ... workers often know quite well what they want to say or write, but find too frequently they have not been equipped to express it. All this is a matter of fundamental choice, in which I as a tutor have taken my side. Does one impose on a social class that is growing in power the syllabus of an older culture; or does one seek means of releasing and enriching the life experience which the rising class brings with it?[31]

It was another approach to the questioning of newspapers and the quizzing of advertisements which buttressed his classes on culture and environment, and at no point did he baulk at the elementary logic and literacy issues that had to be faced. For all that, he never deviated from the view that certain tools could only perform certain jobs. The teaching of, as he put it, "Public Expression", would only be an effective tool in trade union education if a workers' educational movement based itself on the hinterland of knowledge that a liberal adult education represented. What has been subsequently overlooked is the way in which his own concurrent searches, at this time, into the dynamics of cultural and social change were derived from a desperation to penetrate the passive acceptance, everywhere evident he felt, of an unchallenged language for society.

After a conference for tutors of Literature, Philosophy and Social Studies in May 1954 Williams wrote a Report[32] which he considered more vital to the growth of adult education than any breakthrough in Film Studies. There was, he argued, in Public Expression a need to provide the skills in "public speaking and writing which members of the working-class movement are increasingly called upon to employ" but that this interacted with "developments within Literary Criticism and Philosophy which have produced a greater emphasis on *Language* than was the case at the beginning of the adult education movement". He proceeded to spell out in detail, a trifle disingenuously perhaps, since it was his own growing practice to which he referred, the move towards a theory of communications derived from linguistic analysis coupled with social questions based on cultural analysis. He set out on four cyclostyled sheets where his own work was taking him:

> Similar extensions [to study] have been made in the relation of kinds of writing, and certain general questions of language, to particular periods of history. Courses in this field have included:
> (i)   The analysis of certain key words and concepts in relation to particular periods, and the development of society;
> (ii) The correlated study of periods and styles;
> (iii) The history of English, usually in particular relation to certain periods in English history.
> It has been the opinion of some observers that in this work, adult education, by its comparative flexibility in matters of the division of academic subjects, has been able to some extent to pioneer in certain experimental fields of great potential academic value.

His concern in 1954 was to maintain "continuity between formal adult education and the educational activities of the rest of the working class movement". It was a practical link between a utilitarian need for language skills ("public expression") and the "important academic work in language studies" (the expression of a society) which he yearned for. This, he asserted, was "difficult but surely... vital, – the satisfactory bringing together of a simple demand and the complexity of the study which must satisfy it". So vital that, as he was increasingly concluding, he could not leave it at that.

He began to plot and sketch a book, separate from "The Idea of Culture", yet clearly umbilically connected even though its eventual progeny, *The Long Revolution* (1961), *Communications* (1962), and *Keywords* (1976) would find their way and be influential in a different climate than that of the mid 1950s when he first conceived them. Four flimsy typed sheets survive as witness to his early intention.[33] The first is just listed as "Memorandum" but states its "Intention" as an examination of Language and Society – to include contemporary writing and reading and on to history and sociology "with a study of structure of instns" – as a dovetail into the "new social demands" of Public Expression. This bare syllabus, on the second sheet, has been fleshed out to "Language and Working Class Education", where the power of knowledge is translated into active knowledge through (trained) expression to allow for "successful" communication and communication analysis. The purpose is succinct: it is to find "The Grounds of Value" under its two heads, the first of which is "Tradition and Popularisation", and "Class Society and a Common Language" being the other. Then came the overall title of *Language and Society*. A third sheet, a mix of type and pencil, had four groups to it: Criticism, Education, History, and Sociology, with some first thoughts for specific examples. Given all the work that was to come later Sheet Four of *Language and Society* is a revelatory precursor which must have startled its author with its demands. It certainly sent him back to more books before he could begin his own:

Language and Society

Introduction
Part One (i) James Joyce – four passages
    (ii) Essays of Lawrence and Eliot

Part Two   (i)   Expositories

(ii)   Political Autobiographies

(iii)   Press Day

(iv)   Pah!

(v)   Er... ah

(vi)   Metaphor, simile and analogy

Part Three   (i)   Keywords (culture, civilisation; art, aesthetic; Ladder-grade-class-degree-levels; standards; organic, values; liberal; conscience)

(ii)   The Press and 1870

Part Four   (i)   Language in Intelligence Testing

(ii)   Plain Words

Conclusion: the teaching of Language and Society.

Always there were in his head such projected books, and planned schemes even as he ground his way through immediate matters of teaching and learning. This period, with plans for film theory and film production with Orrom and the slow burn of his accumulating reading on responses to industrialisation and culture not yet on fire, was no exception. At some point in the autumn of 1955 he would work steadily on the opening chapters of a novel of social antics, *The Grasshoppers*, and, by the spring of 1956, see it as his most hopeful chance yet to make a wider literary mark. He would be wrong about that, too.

The true fate of his fiction lay in the work already behind him. He had tinkered with *Brynllwyd* in 1953 and 1954. Then he wrote it again, yet not exactly so, and finished it in March 1955. This time he called it *Between Two Worlds*.[34] In it he found a way of describing a working class society of integrity but without power, one with an implicit language for its explicit culture but one struggling to express it fully as an agent for change. This time, for the first time, he foregrounded his father rather than himself. He shifted the balance from place to event so that it becomes 1926 itself which forces the consciousness and not the long aftermath of the General Strike.

* * * * * *

Between Two Worlds is, like *Brynllwyd*, a stage towards the final composition of *Border Country* and he presents it as such in his slightly misleading chronology in *Politics and Letters* in 1979. The final telescoping of the material, much changed in detail and in direction, occurred in 1957 and 1958 and created a novel whose pieces, at last, allowed both protagonists onto the same stage. The earlier novels, *Brynllwyd* and *Between Two Worlds*, are entire in themselves. The first presents the sentimental journey from working class cocoon to the chrysalis rebirth of the boy as an intellectual escapee; the second fully-fledged account makes the father's life integral in itself. It is now that he imagines this life from within, not from without. To the sensibility revealed in the first complete work he brings to the second the significance of a history lived, a life experienced. We no longer race through the 1930s to parallel his own life in an autobiographical re-take. In *Between Two Worlds* we feel the solidity of the lives that have made his life by preceding it.

He had asked Harry in 1954 for specific information about the General Strike but the episode is no mere framework: it is the test whose crisis defines a generation. Amidst a widespread sense, in the 1950s, of the diminution or even disappearance of traditional working class culture, it is a resounding affirmation of human values beyond the confines of a time and place-bound culture. *Between Two Worlds* was his first major achievement and it has been unread for over fifty years.

Some elements – places, people, events – are familiar to him and to readers of his published work. What is different is what he introduces afresh and the relationship between classes and within the working class which his compound mixture reveals by placing the one against the other. This time, in the key person of David Mortimer, we will have a non-working-class viewfinder who is not displaced by virtue of education though he is, in some ways, de-natured from his own class by his sympathies. Through Alec Lewis, brother-in-law to the signalman Arthur Meredith, the reader goes directly into the South Wales Valleys themselves instead of only sensing their brooding presence just beyond the mountain plateaux. Crucially the action of the novel begins on 30

April 1926 and takes us, via General Strike and miners' lockout to the end of that year and no further.

We begin with the landscape, this time swooping in over the "rockfall of Black Darren, under the long grey ridge of Brynllwyd" with the "facing rockfall of the Holy Mountain". The geographical detail is accurately local down to the naming of the "isolated hamlets", one of which is clearly Pandy, renamed here as Glynmawr, but Abergavenny is not yet the Gwenton of *Border Country*. Our introduction to this country, seen from the vantage point of the Kestrel, a great stone above Black Darren, is almost in the precise tones of a social historian turning 180 degrees to survey an historical geography and to place men and women within its changing perspective:

> Through the first sixty years of the nineteenth century, [the] iron age flared above the farming country. And then, in the narrow valleys beyond, began the intensive mining of coal, to go down by rail and canal for the new steamships. From Glynmawr and all the farming countryside around, from the Border, from Central Wales, and from the neighbouring English counties, men crowded into the narrow valleys to the southwest: Ebbw, Sirhowy, Rhymney, Taff, Cynon, Rhondda.... And over the face of this apparently integral countryside, a new frontier was drawn, following the hidden line under the hills, the line of the outcrop of the coal measures.... This whole country had known, through centuries, the drawing of frontiers, in the fighting of settler and invader. But now it was in the grip of a different history, and a border was drawn by the hidden rocks, and between different ways of man's using the earth over which he moved. Lying side by side, in this long disputed country, were a past which had been continued into the present, and another present that was wholly new, an unimagined history. In the twentieth century, looking from the Kestrel, the watcher saw, not the three kingdoms of Gwent, Morgannwg and Brycheiniog, but three other kingdoms: the green, quiet land of farms and orchards, stretching east and north; then, to the

385

southwest, the crowded blackening valleys of the mining towns; and finally, to the west, over the Black Mountains, the barren wastes of heather and bracken and whin.

It is not a landscape untouched, either, by more immediate and devastating events from outside its disputed frontiers. David Mortimer, who lives with his five-year-old daughter, Marian, in Kestrel House below the ridge, is a disabled ex-officer whose right arm was amputated after a shell burst in the trenches in 1918 just before the armistice. He limps on a badly damaged right leg. His wife died in childbirth. He has a pension and a small private income. His nearest neighbours are the Naylors: Colonel Naylor, his sister and his daughter, Elaine, who is half in love with the thirty-year-old David and seeks to guide him over his daughter's education. It must be, she thinks, private and away from Glynmawr. Brooding on all this, Mortimer walks at night down into the valley where, seeing a light in the signalman's box, he impulsively climbs its steps to enter.

Arthur Meredith, the signalman, had also been in the "Welch regiment", wounded by a sniper's bullet clean through the wrist in 1917. Taciturn but polite, he calls Meredith "sir". They drink tea and discuss the coming coal industry crisis; the coalowners' notices of final offer are to be posted that very night. Trains rattle by, stockpiling coal as Arthur explains. The signalman has worked in the Rhymney Valley after the War and there met and married the slim, dark-haired Ellen whose brother, Alec, is staying with them as he recovers from an injury sustained underground. The two warily begin a friendship of sorts based on mutual respect and an ability to probe their connection to public affairs without prejudgement.

The pattern set here continues throughout the novel. In the Naylor household it is the Colonel who tries, without real success, to recruit Mortimer to the Organisation for Maintenance of Supplies, the government's locally derived networks that were established to maintain a semblance of order. Mortimer's unwillingness to join appears a form of betrayal to the bewildered Elaine. Similarly, Arthur Meredith and the more militant Tom Rees seek respectively to persuade and intimidate their colleague, Pritchard, of the link between the miners' cause and their own existence as railwaymen, as all but Pritchard come out on strike from 3 May. The arguments echo later in *Border Country* where the blustering Colonel Naylor will become the slightly more emollient Major Blakely, and Arthur the even more stiff-backed Harry Price. In *Between Two Worlds* the encounters across class lines swell and take on the weight of highly charged emotions. Arthur especially finds words less than adequate, and it is almost as an embodiment of convinced rectitude that Raymond Williams brilliantly portrays him.

This is how he is seen by Elaine Naylor when her father peremptorily stops and detains Arthur Meredith to berate him for his foolishness, "good man" as he is, for going on strike:

> Colonel Naylor looked at him sharply, as he spoke, and Elaine, who had been sitting in the car, with her head down, looked up quickly. She remembered Meredith clearly from the episode of the rabbit, when she had been impressed by his quietness. Now, she looked at him again, and seemed to see something different. On the previous occasion he had been better dressed; now, he was in a loose, badly-fitting black uniform, with a collarless shirt gaping at the broad neck; he was unshaven, and the reddish growth of beard seemed to emphasise the roughness of his features. It was around the mouth that the roughness was most apparent: the teeth were big and irregular, and when he opened his mouth he showed a wide area of his upper gum, which gave a sudden shock of rawness. The thick neck was set on heavy shoulders, and the thick reddish hair lay very flat over his head. The eyes, in which the irises were of an unusual green, were curiously alert, and now suspicious. When she had seen him before the eyes had been dull, as if filmed over by some withdrawal of interest into himself. Elaine noticed the quick clenching of the fists, and looked quickly from Meredith to her father. She was suddenly aware of the actual physical contrast between them, and she saw

Meredith, no longer as a name, but as a man; saw him with a quick, yet distasteful, physical recognition, which produced a feeling of confused awareness and alienation that she had never previously experienced.

"And you yourself, Meredith," her father asked.

"Are you one of the strikers?"

In his emphasis of the final word, Colonel Naylor conveyed his whole feelings in the matter; Elaine saw Meredith's quick reaction.

"Yes sir," he said in a slow, hard voice, the slow Welsh accent of this border country. "Yes, I'm on strike."

On his way home to comfort a wife all too familiar with coalmining strikes that have no possible outcome other than defeat, Arthur Meredith becomes "desperate for breath. In the concentrated effort of talking, it seemed almost as if he had forgotten to breathe..." It is this very quality, of slow deliberation but quick responsiveness, which Ellen values in her husband and notes as the strike deepens in its effects:

His eyes were still clouded in their characteristic, hidden enquiry. Ellen looked at him as he sat drinking his tea, his whole posture awkward, his mouth large and coarse over the cup. She had the sense which had first attracted her to him, a sense that in this rough, slow man – so much slower than the laughing quick-talking boys of her own valley – there was yet something she could not grasp, something native to him and beyond her, which he now took good care that nobody should reach.

As he had done before in his exploration of his central theme, Raymond Williams uses that childhood lore of lost money, school beatings, unpaid rent, green-keeping, bee swarming, eisteddfodau and tending allotments. In *Between Two Worlds* they are told at greater length than elsewhere, essential components of the close-up humanity of his characters who might otherwise be swamped by their roles in the enforced narrative of strike and politics. The signalman, anticipating

Harry Williams by twenty years, becomes a trader in flowers and vegetables to supplement his pay. With the strike's sudden end, he too is finally returned to work at the insistence of an a-political work mate. Arthur is liberated by the strike to spend time with and give attention to his young son, John: walks, plays games, sharing his countryman's knowledge. Williams' style is in a spare, stripped-back prose of direct description and taut dialogue with which he replaces some of the rhetorical rodomontades of a more fevered *Brynllwyd*. It is not yet matched by the fine lyricism for the country and the warm description of the Prices' house which gives *Border Country* such light and shade. But, once more, the details of Arthur and Ellen Meredith's house are practically an architect's plan for "Llwyn Derw", his boyhood home.

Three things mark out *Between Two Worlds* as exceptional in Williams' entire body of work. The first is the disentanglement of knowledge and practice in the equal relationship between Arthur Meredith and David Mortimer – so much so that we can almost detect Williams himself present here, not as Matthew the son, but as David the friend. The second is the journey that David and Arthur make to Alec's house in the Rhymney Valley towards the end of the lock-out in the winter of 1926; and, the third, is the way he illustrates the conscious solidarity of purpose across the working class that was the General Strike's true revelation of the commonality he wished to reflect, no matter how many interstices there were between these several worlds.

He does this last by having Alec Lewis, the injured brother of Arthur's wife, Ellen, bring a fundraising choir for the miners' cause to his sister's village. At first the visit of the Fforest Miners' Choir to the Church Hall is forbidden by the trustees, so Arthur goes to David Mortimer, who persuades Colonel Naylor to overturn the decision. Glynmawr turns out for the concert as an occasion in their "common life" more than as a means to raise money for the distress fund. Some things prove to be tangible only without intervening words through a unity of action, music, setting and gesture. Raymond Williams finds here his drama in performance after all:

And now it was again the turn of the choir, and the emphatic intentness returned to performers and audience, but with an obvious heightening of feeling. The sense of commitment to the singing, even above its actual emotional power, was irresistible in its effect, while it lasted, and even beyond. To David, wholly and almost humbly attentive, it seemed less a musical than a social experience; although the singing was the form in which the living relationships expressed themselves. It was not the excitement, edged by hysteria, of a crowd; nor was it merely the exaltation, in a shared feeling, of a simple art. It seemed, in the end, to be more of an answering than an ordinary means of expression; yet an answering to something which could not be separately defined: a sense underlying the familiar categories of thinking; yet not thinking replaced by feeling, as if by an opposite; rather, in the intent and yet delighted commitment to the shared singing, an answering, not solely of pleasure, nor yet of seriousness and conscious responsibility, but an answering to the known singleness of men, in the actual terms of what it was like to live in a community. Because it was so positive, it needed no separable definition; it was less the consciousness of community than its willing, habitual and sustaining practice.

When at last the whole audience stood, with the choir, to sing their own anthem, David, standing among them, and not knowing the Welsh words yet lost, while the singing lasted, his own consciousness of the questions in which he habitually lived; lost it, however, with a sudden accession of shared feeling which seemed wholly positive and reliable: the positiveness of extension into a partly unfamiliar, yet general, kind of living, which he had also felt, at times, in his meetings with Arthur Meredith. The singing excited him, physically, but he felt also that his mind was being changed, the whole basis of his thinking being extended and altered: not, however, with the discovery of new ideas, but with the discovery of the embodiment of ideas and their conversion or reconversion into practice and assent, in the way of common living.

David Mortimer is now introduced to Alec Lewis, still militant despite the slow crumbling of the strike and still spurning all thoughts of charity and sacrifice. David takes him up on his suggestion to come and see for himself the condition of daily life in the coalfield and so with Arthur he takes a train to Alec's township. They are laden with food and clothes, and, at Ellen's insistence, flowers for Sarah, Alec's wife. From the "dirty little Valley train" which they take after Abergavenny Junction and on into the steep terraced streets, Raymond Williams takes them into the territory of a classic proletarian world. Or so it seems in abstraction and to the first sight of an outside eye like Mortimer's, for Williams naturally enough writes like a consummate insider, alert to nuances of working class respectability and rough humour, in a number of vibrant passages which read like a forgotten entry point into the too often clichéd world of the South Wales Valleys. He appears to draw on some perfunctory research into conditions, statistical and impression-istic, of those harrowing months, but the overall effect is, again, of insight into the knitting together of individual identities and social destinies. Arthur Meredith and David Mortimer, carting their heavy parcels up the gradient of unpaved roads, are suddenly stopped by children riding boxes fitted to pram wheels. Mayhem and a fight break out until Arthur stops them. David is, again, the watcher:

> After the burst of noisy vitality, when they had been running down behind the boxes, the children now stood listlessly, and the condition that he had heard of, and feared stood evident in their faces and bodies. A little girl, who could not have been more than five, stood shivering in a thin dress and a brown coat that was much too large for her, almost hiding her body. Her eyes were watering as she stood beside the spinning wheel of the overturned box. Carefully David looked at each of the other children in turn.

...Two or three were ragged, but the others wore clothes that had been patched and darned.... All but two of the children... had facial sores... The raw ugliness of inflammation stood out again and again on the otherwise pale skins.... His eyes moved over the... footwear; among them all there was only one pair of shoes that could be called tolerable and even these were light summer shoes, leaving the tops of the feet exposed and, from the colour of the short, darned stockings, wet.

... The things he was seeing were, he knew, the long-known evidences of poverty and lack of food. They could not even be said to be new to him.... The map of poverty was known in the mind; what had not been known, not seen, was the country to which it referred: the actuality of this child, shivering in the ugly brown coat beside the overturned box; of the boy, drawn back in the shop doorway, hiding his fit of coughing; the older girl, standing aside pale and listless, her fingers moving restlessly over her face and neck. There was nowhere, in any adult mind, in any circumstances, ignorance of these things; but the knowledge had been circumscribed, and chartered; preserved, by many, from the disabling contact with these of the thousands of children, these, now, standing in the bleak street, silent and watching.

No one was writing prose as luminous and as savage as this in 1950s' Britain. Significantly, perhaps, its subject matter had to be historically based. In other hands this could have spilled over into a wallow of righteous nostalgia, redolent of some sentimental parts of a contemporary Labour movement that was already wringing out a dishcloth of tearful piety before denying any relevance of such an actual historical experience to a desired consumerist and managerial future. Williams steadily moves us away from any such false comfort in ignoring the past or speculating all on a deftly conjured future. At the very end of this singular novel he reasserts the present as always the only available human lived time, and its future as the issue of its past.

As he had at the start, David Mortimer visits Arthur Meredith in his box. The signalman is waiting for flares to be detonated on the line so that, in a dense night fog, trains can be passed through. Their conversation, touching on the strike and its manifold meanings, is constantly broken into by Arthur's quick and careful responses to the signals. David Mortimer calls himself an "observer... of the larger movements, the making of contemporary history", whilst, for him, Arthur seems "tied to the present and the short-term, yet in fact... helping to make the thing as a whole." David tells his friend how he has spent the summer reading everything he could "about the industrial history of the last century" and how he has come to realise that nobody "can know the strength of a people like this unless he knows that long endurance and organisation of the working people". What worries him, though, is the failure of this strength and, too of any sympathy for its needs and its ideals, to translate itself beyond being "permanent" into "history". In other words, to win and to effect change. As Arthur insists, "We've got to a different position", and David Mortimer agrees that there is indeed "more power" and that "nothing can stop it finally":

> "But how can I explain it, this other feeling? If I go back to the 1840s – I mean go back to read of them – what do I find? Strikes, demonstrations, long hungry endurance, the usual official answers. I know the balance of power is changing, but I think less of the event than of reactions to them. Then, too, you know one could find men and women who sympathised, who tried to help, who raised the conscience of their own kind, and were determined on change. If that alone were enough, you see, then the last eighty years would not have been what they have."

> ... "History goes too fast," [Arthur] said. "I mean the history you say you've been reading. It's not just an idea we've got to change; and change of any kind is hard to think about, in our own time. There is, in any case, so much else."

"Yes" David said, walking across to the grid. "That is what I've been trying to learn. Not as an excuse for doing nothing; not even to relax into saying that these things take time; but to know, if I can, what the real springs of action are, so that one need not feel inadequate. Anyone is inadequate, measured against history."

"It's the way of putting it," Arthur said. "Men have to live close."

"Yes. By the minute.... The ideas... have to be geared to that."

"We need more thinking," Arthur said. "We're too narrow. I know that."

"Yes. We are too narrow. But what, above all, I have learned from these last months is that the thinking has to be returned, again and again, to what you call living close. When the thinking gets separate, self-deception is very easy, and so is disillusion. What I have learned from watching, is that your way of life is not in those terms, and that is its strength."

"I've not thought enough," Arthur said again, turning away.

"You mean that you have not thought separately. That is what I am trying to say: the ideas will come, will make themselves. The solutions will come, minute by minute. What you think of as the Labour Movement and call political, is not to me political at all. It is what you call living close and slowly finding the institutions that embody that."

"Are we finding them?" Arthur asked, as the bell rang again, and he crossed quickly to the grid.

"You are bound to find them, because you live in a certain way."

They part to go to their separate houses and their sleeping children. The last words of the novel are:

The valley of Glynmawr lay in a dark silence, broken only, at intervals, as the night trains passed through and beyond it, out of the border country over which the Kestrel seemed to watch.

Then he typed "RW. 8 March 1955" and underlined the date. Arguably, almost three decades after the events of the novel, some of those institutions to embody what "living close" signified had, indeed, been formed; and, perhaps, in 1955, were being lost again. There had been a decade's caterwauling about whether or not an historically recognisable working class was disappearing or could yet survive to influence social change, by "living close". Raymond Williams, in this signature work, had, unheralded, penetrated further to show how minute-by-minute events and longer cycles of thinking were not only inseparable factors in human existence but were only how things may be delineated: they were not how they were felt. His own analytical study, two years after he had wondered whether Chatto was ready for a book that could indeed see the things experienced in life as a culture that was "a whole way of life", had reached the point where it would absorb more energy than anything else. To take it forward into 1956 with a sure conviction, however, he had had to give people of his father's generation their own life back. This, in *Between Two Worlds*, he had triumphantly accomplished. At last he could take his own life, personal and intellectual, forward on his own hard-won terms. There would be moments of severe doubt and even despair over the next two years but, in every sense that mattered to him, he had come through.

Chapter 10

"A Decisive Stage..."

Ten years on from the War he seemed to those who knew him well as colleague and teacher the model of a settled family man and a minor academic scholar. Teaching was prepared and taught as conscientiously as ever. Thoughts about, and work on, the epoch-changing possibilities in drama and film continued. And remained as ideas. Little books lay, as proof, in his wake. And not all was serious. At the Oxford Summer School he had led the way in devising and managing tutor entertainment, notably the Programme Notes for the "Ballet Balliol" which had hitherto "performed before crowded and wildly appreciative audiences in Sadler's Wells, Parsons Pleasure, Dames Delight, Vienna, Moscow, Wigan and Mow Cop".[1] The ballerinas – drawn from the Delegacy's ranks – scorn "tuttis" for the simple "sheety" or "nightie". His abilities as a dry wit, an impersonator and an engaging companion were buoyed up on these occasions by his willingness to cast off the air of detachment which was so readily detected and, by some colleagues, resented.[2] In their temporary Oxford home that summer of 1955, the Vicarage at St. Cross, he worked every morning on the current novel, *Between Two Worlds*, and plotted others. He sat and read Victorian sages in the Bodleian by day, and at night he read to Madawc the animal stories he had once written for Merryn and sang the songs he had made up for Ederyn.[3] There was the occasional Oxford party to which he and Joy could go when Harry and Gwen came to babysit. Their lives were in every sense domestic and, it would seem, fulfilled insofar as they and their family were concerned.

This period of Williams' life, however, as ostensibly calm as it was, concealed a continuing insecurity and self-doubt. Joy Williams knew its source and sought its release. It was not, she knew, a mid-life crisis of any conventional kind. Indeed, if Joy was at all concerned that her lively husband spent a great deal of his teaching time in the company of women, there was never, as a none-too-admiring Arthur Marsh insisted, "ever a hint of scandal". Some of the tutors who were envied by

Raymond for their "trade union" students envied him his "middle class ladies" but as one such from his Eastbourne class recalled she was, at thirty three, easily the youngest member of a class largely composed of women over sixty and all dressed in coats, and hats, "not to mention stockings! And only gloves were removed for the class".[4] Ruth Middlemiss remembered him as "tall and broad and pretty slim" with fading ginger hair, worn long and swept back, above "an enormous brow". He would certainly have attracted some attention in clothes of "the most extraordinary colours, with tweedy suits... dark blue shirts, yellow ties, green sweaters... he had piercing blue eyes." At thirty four in 1955, not quite six foot in height, his younger raw-boned and long-faced look was filling out into a robust frame. He had, she thought, the look of "A real professor! Very scholarly!"

In some classes where he had told Orrom the sound of women crossing and uncrossing their nylon stockinged legs was "very distracting" he might have found temptation to stray from the routine of marriage.[5] It was a common enough fate for adult tutors. He wrote, and kept, an odd little note to himself, one scribbled in short lines in ink and folded away, dating, from the handwriting and war reference, from the late 1940s:

> hallmark of the booksy crew
> who populate literature classes
> In the adult educational movement.
>
> The hallmark: as always, the
> mattress. Not the field mattress
> of your licentious soldiery
> but a mattress double sprung, set
> under Spanish walnut – the typical
> bourgeois mattress

and then, ambiguously perhaps,

> In a male, maturity refusing an
> invitation: in a female, surrendering
> to one.[6]

397

There is no reason at all to believe Joy Williams would have been complaisant. However, what would have and indeed did concern her far more was any sign of her husband's wavering from the long engagement with ideas of culture, an engagement she urged him to bring to a conclusion. She was convinced that it was the route out of a professional impasse, and that it was, in the most urgent manner, an important enquiry, and one for which she had no doubt he was uniquely equipped. It was the daunting of his ambition she feared, not any sexual dalliance, real or imagined. Privately, she championed his efforts against the languid disdain of the academically complacent at Oxford, whether inside or outside the University proper.[7]

Stuart Hall, a Rhodes Scholar from Jamaica, who was reading English at Oxford from 1951 and was a central figure in the formation of the first "New Left" at the decade's end, reflected on how seminar groups around the still-grand and independent socialist figure of G.D.H. Cole (1889-1959) opened up an otherwise moribund Oxbridge concept of political study and how Freddy Bateson's literature classes – where he first met Raymond Williams – could bring a welcome whiff of Leavisite seriousness to Oxford's dilletantism.[8] But the predominant tonality was deadening:

> Outsiders like myself found it particularly hard to adjust to being catapulted into the centre of the process by which the English class system reproduced itself, educationally and culturally. The Oxford of the mid-1950s was dominated by the "Hooray Henries" of its time, attempting to relive *Brideshead Revisited*. Its atmosphere was relentlessly masculine, and – though we did not recognise it at the time – sexist. I 'hear' that Oxford now principally as a particular pitch of the voice – the upper-middle-class English male commanding attention to confidently expressed banalities as a sort of seigneurial right.... In fact, Oxford also contained its rebel enclaves: demobbed young veterans and national servicemen, Ruskin College trade unionists, "scholarship boys" and girls from home and abroad.

Although they were unable to refine its dominant culture, these outsiders did come to constitute an alternative – not to say beleaguered – intellectual minority culture.[9]

Within that minority Raymond Williams would finally come into his own; himself of another generation yet attuned to the interest of those now seeking to bypass narrow political attitudes and structures which, especially on the left, were not in correspondence with the "structure of feeling" detectable in contemporary life styles and the wider culture. Alan Hall, a Balliol classicist and close friend of Stuart Hall's, had begun, in the summer of 1956, "to sketch out a book on the new contours of cultural change" within contemporary capitalism, and before the invasion of Hungary and Suez forced the pace dramatically. They went on vacation together with a work load of books – including Crosland's *Future of Socialism*, Leavis' *Culture and Environment*, Angus Maude's "smug little book", *The English Middle Classes*, John Osborne's *Look Back in Anger* – and, Hall added, two typescript chapters of "what was to become Raymond Williams' *Culture and Society*". Joy Williams had been right to think that he could say things in this work that others would find echoing and enlightening about their own predicament. What Williams gave Hall was the product of the winter of 1955/6, work that was still lacking a firm, or indeed any, commitment from a publisher. The "constituency" that would form for him around the magazine *Universities and Left Review* in 1957 would have to wait until the autumn of 1958 to lay hands on the first and soon best-selling edition of *Culture and Society*.

It had been with some excitement that Raymond Williams had written to Chatto and Windus once more, in early January 1956, to re-kindle their interest:

Dear Ian Parsons,
All through the autumn and now into the winter I have been meaning to write... I have delayed, I suppose, because I wanted also to tell you what I have been writing, and only now is this coming to a decisive stage.

You may remember that some time ago I showed you two chapters of a book called *The Idea of Culture*... I am still no nearer a title I really like, but the book is almost finished. I have never in my life worked so hard at anything, but I believe it has been worth it.[10]

He outlined the purpose of the book as "a history and criticism of the ideas which have been concentrated in the modern meanings of 'culture'... being definable as the area of thinking that lies between the experience of society and the experience of art and literature" and presented the new "general plan", in three parts from the 1780s to the end of the nineteenth century, an overlap or "Interregnum" from William Morris to D.H. Lawrence, and the final section from Lawrence to "our own period". He did not name all his chosen thinkers, though Herbert Read was one he would later drop with regret. His earlier mixing in of notes on changes in the meaning of certain keywords was to be relegated to an appendix to meet earlier objections "so that the text now reads as a general work", but that addendum too, would not survive even in this form, and *Keywords* (1976) would have to wait. What Parsons had not heard before, however, was what Williams now mentioned as something that "may or may not be interesting", though, on publication, it would cause most comment, favourable and otherwise: "I have also a concluding essay, putting forward certain ideas of my own, as a continuation of the 'culture' argument; I've found, on going through, that I really had to try to work out a new position..."

He was, for all that, still very much the supplicant: "I hope more than I can easily say that you will like it when you see it, and will publish it.... This coming book is one into which I have put so much that its eventual publication by you had, at times, been the only spur.... I am extended enough to be unashamed to try for a word of encouragement, if I can get one..." There was yet more diffidence – "Having said [all] this, I realise, of course, that you will be entirely free to decide". He only wanted "an expression of continued interest". No typescript accompanied the letter because he felt, "in the last and rather formidable effort to complete *The Idea of Culture*", he would prefer to wait until it was "quite completed" in March.

Ian Parsons gave him the encouragement he requested. When Raymond Williams replied, at the very end of March 1956, the letter was more brisk, more confidently business-like but, nonetheless, heartfelt: "After five years with it, I feel quite unreasonably involved in it, and to send it to you, and then go on holiday seems too good to be true".[11] Chatto was delivered a book of some 125,000 words with reference notes tidied away at the rear to make for easier reading of what its author half apologetically called "a general work, on a really big subject". As for title: "I told you I was not certain what title to adopt. At the moment I think the best, because most accurately descriptive, would be *Culture and Society : 1780 – 1950.*"

Most accurate indeed, and one that lasted beyond that moment. The book, however, was not as complete or, rather, as finished as he thought.[12] Chatto were keen but nervous as to cost at that length; they weighed it in, with the Keywords Appendix, at around 170,000 words. Williams received a final "Yes" in October 1956, conditional on a reduction in size. In November he excised a lot of the bibliographical references he had checked and compiled in the Bodleian over the summer, cutting out a great deal of quotation from the text and losing the Keywords section completely. Smaller sections on Thomas Arnold and on Herbert Read were also removed. On finally signing in December 1956 for an advance of £75, half on signature and the same terms as in 1952, Chatto had a volume of 130,000 words, a book that would become a marker for its generation and a continuous best-seller across the world. He had to wait almost another two years to feel the aftermath of its creation. They remained, as before, years of personal uncertainty.

Not the least of which concerned the continuing limbo into which he felt his imaginative work was unjustly consigned. In the very same letter in which Chatto had finally taken *Culture and Society* they had rejected the novel he had finished and sent them the previous July. *The Grasshoppers*, begun in 1955, was, Williams later wryly commented, the "only one of [the] early novels I tried hard to publish".[13] The reason for showing them such a novel after their earlier rejection of *Adamson* was his strong feeling that he had found a form and a subject which came directly out of the present time: "I have also", he wrote, "been working on a novel, called *The Grasshoppers*. This is a comedy, with what I think is an original contemporary theme... I hope that... you will let me show it to you. I know that a first novel is said to be publisher's poison, but one has to try to start somewhere, and *The Grasshoppers*, so far as I can judge, might easily be quite successful".

The novel is in part intended as a satire on the inefficacy of "direct action", without a political base or a cultural root, undertaken by an intelligent and liberal élite who are self-chosen. In this sense he would neither have written it, nor would have wanted to do so, in the swiftly changing atmosphere of the later 1950s. Its own origins, though, lay in the mood of hopelessness that many felt when faced by the crass commercialism and passive consumerism that took off in that decade. And if those were its antecedents, its heirs would come to be the actual watch-dogs of consumption and quality control, precisely guided and controlled by the kinds of "activists" he had mocked, albeit with some ambivalence, in the fiction. The novel's abiding interest rests here, in its attempt to characterise an inchoate temper of the period which, in time, would be fully fleshed out. For its author, both the 1950s' fictional possibility and the 1960s' actuality seemed inadequate, even though the targets – bad design, inept bureaucracy, dishonest advertising, a misleading newspaper press and all the ills of a "communications" society – were ones which he kept firmly in his sights.

The narrative, moving in and out of differing perspectives, was one he felt confident enough about as a device to think of making it central to his fast changing conceptualisation of *Between Two Worlds* in late 1956. He noted:

> Narrative techniques as developed in *Grasshoppers* i.e. a personal narrator who is not yet the central person of the narrative. Often this will be close personal narration, but at times will move from and to wholly impersonal narration...[14]

The Grasshoppers itself he somewhat bewilderingly, and in any case only for a short time, envisaged as part of a grand and connected sequence of novels. Its time span was to be 1945 to 1955 and its plot the "Study of a group developing: the artificial social group amended as absorbed in real society."[15] On the page the plot lines followed his familiar device of "action – character – meditation", within a genre. He himself saw his characters as a kind of "comic commando", desperate for change in an "inert society".[16] The judgement he clearly reserved for them in the book makes them perhaps beyond our sympathy from the start. The admirable reasons for their motivation are entirely negative.

Prior to 1957, Raymond Williams could see little that was positive in any contemporary political intervention. He prefaced the novel with a pithy Baudelaire quote sucking energy from the nemesis it would, if it could, confront:

> C'est un satirique, un moqueur;
> Mais l'énergiè avec laquelle
> Il peint le Mal et sa séquelle
> Prouve la bonté de son coeur.

We start, and end, with an anonymous narrator/historian whose task is to write up the origins and fates of the group and of the individuals who constituted themselves as the Grasshoppers:

> Everyone, now, seems to be writing about the Grasshoppers, and this is hardly surprising. They are, after all, the only new thing that has happened, or seems likely to happen, in England in the nineteen-fifties. The old things, of course, are still there, as they always rather heavily, are, in England. [But]... The Grasshoppers is the one new thing we have, and we are naturally making the most of them.

Gradually, via unfolding personal histories and chance encounters, we learn that "the groups" – not originally known as "grasshoppers" – came together as a post-war university club, where a high I.Q. was a prerequisite for entry, and that they saw themselves as descendants of the Coleridgean concept of a "clerisy"; this time an "elite against mass

403

society". They are self-named as the General Service Organisation, their secret ranks drawn from artists, academics, civil servants, actors and writers. After a number of actions or incidents that bring them to public and press attention, one of their number, Mark Stanton, a brilliant illustrator and disaffected son of a Labour Minister who has "risen" from working class origins, devises a grasshopper as their calling card logo. Mark Stanton has been at University with the historian/narrator through whose filter the action and interlocking relationships are largely seen. A summation press report of events which the novel recounts in the detail of "low comedy" takes us to the Grasshoppers' first fame:

> In recent weeks, several curious episodes, which seem from internal evidence to be in some way linked have come to the public notice. In Oxford, an empty shop was hired, under a false name, and a display mounted in its window which was, to say the least, embarrassing to a furniture store which was immediately adjacent. At the time the affair was dismissed as an undergraduate "rag", although the perpetrators were not in fact discovered. Within forty eight hours, however, a very large number of advertising hoardings, in London, had been raided, with small numbers marked "Yes, but" which we do not doubt proved, for the time, as embarrassing to the advertisers as the Oxford display had been to the furniture store... the scale and efficiency of the operation... was not easy to ascribe to an *ad hoc* student demonstration... The third and most notorious episode, in which many points are still obscure, is, of course, that of the Bowery New Town, as it is called, which still stands, an entertaining if equivocal protest, in the quiet Cotswold country where, again by persons unknown, it was erected. Finally, on a recent Sunday, there was the affair of the dummy newspapers, with the strange headlines, for which, again, no explanation has so far been forthcoming.

Uncertainty is, in fact, the hallmark of the novel. Or if not uncertainty – for it is plain to see which way its author leans – then shared ambivalences. Our narrator, early on, though fascinated by the group as a phenomenon requiring historical understanding, is clear that they are also, as a symptom, an infection not a cure for ills that cannot be separated out even if – as with "noise...; foul air... the opening of National Parks... river pollution... dirty railway carriages... cracked and dirty crockery in restaurants... dangerous corners and stretches of road... wild life destruction... inaccurate reporting... bad development... petty penury – the closing down of an orchestra or a museum... undisclosed interest" – there is indeed a list which the consumer lobby society of post-1960s' Britain, then and still now, could embrace as an agenda. The Grasshoppers themselves end by losing their "direct action" tricks and transforming themselves into the Society for the Defence of Amenities, not secret but respectable, not devolved to local "Panels" but with a strong central organising body, informing and educating within the existing "networks" of society.

For the idealistic Stanton this is not enough. He retreats to the Black Mountains to practise his art. The Grasshoppers, he decides, were valid when they were subversive of a whole way of life, but not now when they see their principal role as that of a self-elected cultural leadership. At the novel's crux, Williams shows how quickly leaders can betray. The Grasshoppers "create" a West Indian torch singer, "Sadie", from the talent and needs of an actual person, a struggling academic, Dr Anthea Jones. They have stage success for her beyond expectation. The ruse is maintained. Impersonation has become another reality. Deception of the gullible can be endorsed by the better informed:

> Mark went to Constable, and gave him his opinion of Sadie. This, he thought, would make everything clear. But Constable said it was all right, the General Panel had approved...
>
> "I don't believe you," Mark said. "People aren't that low, aren't really low at all."
>
> "I'll give you a badge for that," Constable said. "Though

you don't deserve it; you simply took over this theory of sticking to your own side from your father. It was all very well then: people stuck to their principles; my lord agitator didn't so monotonously become my lord eminence. Anyway, then, there was still a theory of probability in character and one learned it at Sunday School. That's had it, I tell you. You must draw your own conclusions."

Mark did not argue the reference to his father; he had not thought Constable capable of it, although he had watched (and enjoyed) the technique being applied to others. He merely repeated that he had found Sadie degrading; he had seen the performance and drawn his conclusion.

"But that's what we intended, surely," Constable said happily. "We wanted to prove that people will accept indifferent material as art, and unlikely persons as artists, if only the publicity and the atmosphere are right... the rackets really are easy, and why shouldn't they be played? One can know, basically, that admass deserves what it gets, and there will always be a chink, here and there, for something of a different kind."

"I don't believe in admass," Mark said.

"That's why I'm getting out. There are no masses, there is no admass; there are only ways of seeing people in that capacity, and the ways are one's own affair..."

Those "ways of seeing" will be what his raging "Conclusion" to *Culture and Society* will lightning-flash for a readership that worked its way through his moderate text to the raw emotion of its end. He was writing both versions, the fiction and the critical history, at the same time. In his novel, entrancing though clumsily executed in its quest for a fictional capture of ideas, he left his protagonists stranded, unable to make the final connection to a society apparently diminished beyond repair. The phrase "admass" was the invention of J.B. Priestley on a visit to America in 1954. He wrote in 1955 that it stood for "the creation of the mass mind, the mass man" who was dazzled into submission by the cornucopia of a consumer society and its "mass persuaders". Priestley's concern was genuine enough but, for Williams, a mirror not a vision. The consumer-led society was not challenged but only reflected by the new watchdog, the Association for Consumer Research (turning into the Consumers' Association of the 1960s), given its Biblical imprimatur through the Guideline to Living of its 1957 magazine *Which?*[18]

Raymond Williams had anticipated life in his novel but he had not, to his own satisfaction, made a work in which ideas and action could be embodied in character and motives. It had been, again, an ambition too far and one that seemed to label him as a writer of talent who was not, in the understood meaning of the 1950s, a novelist. He would argue against this as a tired convention used to mask difficulties of form. He would, in a number of later works of fiction, offer convincing proof of what he could do when his own intention found its appropriate form. Yet there is no wonder that he wanted to publish *The Grasshoppers* at the moment of its conception because it spoke directly to that precise mid-1950s' mood of despair and resigned confusion. It also, significantly, spoke out beyond that contemporary mood through the authorial voice of its scrupulous narrator-historian:

> I stated at the outset of this narrative that, while I naturally wanted my account of the Grasshoppers to be balanced and accurate and reasonably complete, still, for any final analysis, we should have to wait, until fact and story could be separated, and event had become history. I cannot, therefore, attempt any such analysis, but I can, perhaps, indicate some of the lines along which it may be fruitful to enquire.
>
> It has to be noted above all that, regardless of the merits of those things that the Grasshoppers attacked, the method of attack, which was the real novelty, can be seen to be characteristic of its period. For some time, and particularly since 1945, there has been the paradox of a belief in direct action, for which one can be held personally responsible, alongside an almost total absence of belief in any of the bodies through which action is normally channelled. To this

paradox, we can add another: that a deeply pessimistic view of the condition and prospects of our civilisation and our culture has co-existed with, has even been expressed through, an extraordinary and refreshing gaiety of mood; the autopsy... has been written and played as a farce. These, clearly, are the basic conditions which produced the Grasshoppers, and within which their significance must be studied. The mood, in fact, is one of fundamental social commitment, and the taking of responsibility, in ways which in themselves are anarchic and irresponsible. This is the paradox of the Grasshoppers, and in their own terms their justification. We shall have, clearly, to go on living with them; the Grasshoppers, as Mark has said, are, in whatever form, here to stay. "Just too many people for comfort," he adds, "have been educated, and as the process continues they are going to find, after their own fashion, ways of raising hell. This is excellent, because hell deserves to be raised, and it's our last chance of saving ourselves. Of course it will be very uncomfortable for the old system and the old gang."

I have already confessed my own, very different judgement, and will not now retract it. The Grasshoppers, I would still insist, are an illness, an infectious illness. Their false response to a situation which needs remaking as a whole is to discern all that is false and fragmentary, and to attack it as fragments. I am more at home, I freely confess, with a Robert Owen, or with any all-out radical reformer, than with the new critics of my own generation. It is when I say this that Mark repeats that I am the last of the fanatics.

* * * * * *

He was, at first glance, an unlikely fanatic. For all the moderation of his lifestyle and, broadly, of his opinion, this isolated integrity was nonetheless what in the mid-1950s he had been seeking for over the decade: comfort neither in the "mediocrity" of a "spectacular university career" nor solace in the icy embrace of Communist Party conformity. After 1953 and the crushing of revolt in East Germany he could see no point in clinging to any raft of Soviet illusions and frequently told those he met in the Communist Party Historians' Group in Hastings that he could no longer comprehend their staying inside the Party. Fanatically he worked. Fanatically he looked for historical explanation of the structure of feeling into which his generation was locked. Fanatically he held tight to his position, yet knowing, or at least sensing, that he could neither recoil nor yet move forward from it. The seismic shifts of late 1956 altered all of that and made the fanatic someone who could now be seen to be, in truth, what Eric Hobsbawm, remembering the 1940s, characterised him as: "a man in waiting".

Raymond Williams would, within two years of 1956, be a central figure within the emerging "New Left" but it was more as a self-made pre-fabricated addition than as a participant builder. If he had natural allies on the political left they remained those in the Communist Party he had long since left behind and who now, or soon, appeared to be moving towards him. Yet none were more than friendly acquaintances. His closest friendship, until he foreclosed all options in early 1957, was with Orrom, the committed artistic dreamer he had long ago chosen over the "Party Org". Nor is there any indication that he was torn by the revelations Krushchev had made at the closed session of the Party Congress in Moscow in February 1956, and subsequently leaked to the western Press in June. He had carried no banner for Stalin or his totalitarian personality cult since the 1940s. The agonising of leading Party intellectuals as they struggled to redefine inner democracy within their British branch of Democratic Centralism, was not his agony. He had the role of the perpetual observer and a distant one at that. He would have been aware, largely through his extra-mural colleague Henry Collins, of the deep disquiet being expressed within the Communist Historians' Group – a galaxy of talent about to burst into decades of academic stardom for Christopher Hill, Rodney Hilton, Eric Hobsbawm, Edward and Dorothy Thompson and John Saville – as leading proponents of a reformed Communist Party. One by one, with the exception of Hobsbawm who rationalised his life-long decision to remain as the product of his European origins and early anti-fascism, they would be suspended prior to resigning or being expelled within eighteen months of Krushchev's denunciation of "past errors". But for all these communist intellectuals, the question was how, or to what degree, to respond to these "errors" and not, initially anyway, to question the validity of the Communist Party itself. John Saville, as always, saw and put it with explicit candour:

> ... for Edward and Dorothy Thompson and I... it soon became clear that if the British CP was to recover its self-respect, let alone the respect of the labour movement in general, it must encourage an honesty of discussion that would... be painful to many. By about the beginning of June [1956]... we had agreed first, that the Party leadership was deliberately curbing and confining discussion, and second, that the most obvious way to force an open debate was probably to publish independently of the Party press. The key word was "probably". We were highly committed Party members who had come through the tough and difficult years of the Cold War – more difficult than is often appreciated – and we had personal experiences of those who had left the Party to cultivate their own gardens, or of those who had left to become, in our eyes, renegades.[19]

In 1956, Raymond Williams was widely considered to be one of the former. Saville and Thompson were indefatigable activists in their Party branches in Yorkshire, the former in Hull, where he was a lecturer in Social and Economic History, and the mercurial Thompson as an Extra-Mural Lecturer in Leeds. Williams' acquaintance with both was slight though he knew Saville, who had been a Party member since 1934, through Hobsbawm (within two years the final transformation of Matthew Price in *Border Country* was into the kind of distinguished historian of population movement that Saville would show himself to be in his 1957 book *Rural Depopulation in England and Wales, 1851-1951*).

Edward Thompson both knew of the literary circle at post-war Cambridge – the triumvirate of Raymond Williams, Clifford Collins and Wolf Mankowitz whose particular "flamboyance" Thompson heartily disliked – and of Williams' own early work, including the "primer on literature teaching" for which he also did not care. Yet, though both he and Williams taught literature within Extra-Mural Departments and both were moving towards the centre of an historical enquiry, albeit differently conceived in their work, they had neither met nor corresponded. If anything, the dashing Thompson, a master polemicist and phrasemaker, was more the "known" figure at this time, than the reserved and self-contained Williams. Already, in 1955, Edward Thompson had set out his own stall for a revolutionary intent within the forgotten framework of English socialism, with his dynamic and controversial, *William Morris: Romantic to Revolutionary*.

From a distance then, geographical but also familial, Williams would follow the brave launching by Saville and Thompson of their inner-party dissident magazine *The Reasoner* and their suspension from the Party for it. The rumbling crisis around the July nationalisation of the Suez Canal leading on to collusion between Israel, France and Britain to invade Egypt in late October 1956 was a clumsy act of skulduggery which led on, from public outrage and demonstrations over the summer and until British withdrawal in December, to deeper fissures in both political life and wider society. What compounded this drama into a spiralling tragedy of conscience and action for the Left was the almost simultaneous Soviet invasion of Hungary in early November. Disaffection in Poland with the Soviet Union's control had flash fired during the summer and on into the autumn, but in Hungary a new communist government's decision to declare neutrality as a stance between the two power blocs – as another Yugoslavia in effect – was enough to trigger outright invasion and the crushing of any dissidence. There were arguments raised about the mixing in of "counter-revolutionary" elements in the revolt in order to justify, as the British Party immediately did, the Soviet action. For Thompson and Saville, and many beyond the sneeringly-depicted "intellectuals", this was more than enough.[20] They resigned in November 1956, and in 1957 would bring out *The New Reasoner* to develop "left socialist thinking... theoretical analysis, creative writing, discussion material". Raymond Williams did not contribute to that journal and only made a belated appearance in the second number of the more influential *Universities and Left Review* whose contemporaneous creation inevitably had both sets of editors soon considering merger. All this, for Williams, was, as yet, in the guise of noises off stage.

Typically, he displaced the external political crisis by internalising its long standing tension between intent and outcome in a stand-alone play, *King Macbeth*. He began to write it at the start of that incredible October.[21] It places itself within a contemporary range of "History" plays with a modern flavour and a moral point to make, and is more than a touch strained in its staginess of action and dialogue. It was never produced nor published though it might have been one of the "three or four other plays" along with *Koba*, which in 1979 he proposed to bring out together[22] (*Koba* was his study of the unformed Stalin, begun in 1957 and finally published in 1966 as Part Three of his drama essays on *Modern Tragedy*). Perhaps he thought the moment of his plays had passed or he conceded silently to his critics that his several attempts never quite convinced. The collected plays never appeared. However, in the case of *King Macbeth* the suppressed potential can often be glimpsed. The play teased meaning from the experience of 1956 and, more actively, probed what prefaced such dramas and the uncertain future they could still, even in their catharsis, distort.

The two act play is introduced by a Note:

> The source of Shakespeare's play *Macbeth* is Holinshed's *Chronicles of Scotland*. But Shakespeare, in writing his play, radically altered a number of Holinshed's facts. *King Macbeth* is also based on Holinshed, but with the altered facts restored. It is thus, within its theatrical convention, a radically different reading of the dramatic story of Macbeth.

We are introduced to this radical difference by the device of the ending of a contemporary staging of *Macbeth*, which leads the actor Macbeth to begin to commune with his unease at the portrayal of the king which the play has forced him to give. He discusses with the actor Banquo the myths and superstitions around the "unlucky" play:

> Macbeth: Do I think it is unlucky? Unlucky, perhaps, is hardly the word. Unlucky is easier than haunted, yet perhaps it is haunted that we mean. Murder we watch as a diversion, but here there is something else, more disturbing. A sense, almost a conviction, that it is wrong.
>
> Banquo: Wrong?
>
> Macbeth: It is wrong, and it is haunted. When I say it is wrong, I do not question its greatness. In its own terms it is right, and always magnificent. But to know Macbeth, as I have had to know him, is to move, in the end, into a different dimension, and to know why the play is haunted and unappeased.

They continue, on the empty stage, to probe the "possession" of Macbeth the actor by "wronged" King Macbeth, himself murdered and a better king than the Duncan whom he had killed and replaced. The actors slowly take on their roles again but this time questioning their motives and justifications beyond the "dream" (or is it "the lie"?) of the play. Anger builds between them as Macbeth insists on replaying the "tragedy": "I want only the truth, the heart and truth of all this action. We are not here to blanket evil, but to know evil as it moves."

The new play then begins as the dispersed actors return to play their new parts. We now have, in Duncan, a wise and gentle but weak and vacillating king who does not quite accept that it is the war leadership of Macbeth that keeps the Vikings at bay and his dynasty on the throne. For Duncan, the "old and easy doctrine of the firm hand" squashes a few rebels but does not eradicate the causes of rebellion. Macbeth points to their common grandfather, King Malcolm Duff, also murdered, for proof of the need for vigilance, and proof that indecision in moving against rebels and invaders, combined, would be the cause of further, unnecessary death. The debate gradually causes the Scottish lords, Duncan's thanes, to wish Macbeth to take Duncan's place as king if Scotland's peace and prosperity is to be assured. Slowly, they decide to strike against their king as Macbeth leads the regicides openly to take action – nothing is to be done in the dark. No spirits lead him on or voices chide him. Not only does Lady Macbeth have no children that live, she also becomes her husband's support, rather than his goad. Duncan reluctantly joins Macbeth at the battle; their wives wait and talk:

Queen: I pray my husband will come safely home, to me and to his children.
Lady Macbeth: It is a good prayer, madam, if the safety of Scotland is added.

They return home, and safe. But Duncan who has "tricked" his enemy into a defeat through subterfuge, is the tortured one rather than Macbeth, who has done what military men must do, and killed them.

Ross: Scotland is safe, my lord.
Duncan: Safe, yes, but we have not reckoned the price. I am a king of peace, but I have killed, in my own fashion. I did not kill as Macbeth kills, in anger, in danger, putting his life to risk which arm is the stronger, his own or the maddened enemy who rushes on him. I have killed, for Scotland, in secret; offered food, and given poison; offered comfort, from our natural harvest, and given death.

For Duncan this poisons "the peace" and will inevitably mean the future of Scotland will not be at ease in "blood stained" hands. He tries to pass the right to succession to his son by naming the boy "Prince of Cumberland", and so his heir. Macbeth and Banquo stab him to death and Macbeth claims the crown at the end of Act One:

> Macbeth: Order must be kept, for we live by order. I look to you, my lords for service, as you love your country. The weakness and division of Scotland lie behind us. Our present and our future are peace, order, and calm. The killing of Duncan, as you saw, was necessary; but there will be no more killing. Scotland is strong again and can face the light.

Act Two opens with a speech from King Macbeth, ten years on, in a Scotland where peace and justice have been installed and maintained. What begins to unravel, in speeches amongst and between the co-conspirators, is their agreement that present prosperity can expunge memory of the past. Macbeth insists on truth and honesty even if a king has killed a king. They beg him to forget, but he insists a King must look back as well as beyond the present, that there are "facts" that surmount "loyalties".

> Macbeth: Cannot a man speak honestly among his friends? Is truth an enemy, for I speak only the truth. You move, uneasily, my lords, but let me tell you this. I was Macbeth before I was a King. I was Macbeth, and honoured, because I dealt with real things, in their own terms, and did not turn from what I might be wiser to deny... We are at peace, you say, but peace, as I said to Duncan, a few minutes before I killed him, is not a sentiment, nor a mere absence of trouble, but a continual effort, a whole

admission, a mature balancing of gain and loss. Our gains, my lords, are real, but I as King, must strike the balance. It is not dangerous to mention Duncan, but to forget him. If we have saved our country, we should not fear to recognise the means. Duncan was killed; I killed him: it all starts from that.

It is not the conscience of Macbeth that widens the rift between him and his thanes but his insistence that "treason" might not be traitorous. Seeing a king who chooses not to trust them, they consider the risk of treason again. Malcolm, Duncan's exiled heir, rallies them from England. Macbeth has Banquo killed, and waits his own end at Dunsinane, the castle he has built on a hill to survey all of Scotland. The play scarcely resolves the dilemmas it has set itself, nor does it intend to do so. Malcolm, now king, welcomes a new day for Scotland after "the dark night" of Macbeth's tyranny but sees no "ghosts" lurking behind his own actions. The ghosts of Macbeth and Banquo, spectres of the actors who have just replayed the "true" Macbeth story, return to the stage.

Banquo:	You would have it, you said, without equivocation. You wanted the truth, the heart and truth of action.
Macbeth:	I had to die again, to learn it. Macbeth and Banquo had to die again.
Banquo:	How many more will have to die, till the lie is ended. Guilt upon guilt, cry upon cry, and this, in the end, is the reality… Now, again, the difficult journey begins. We are all reluctant to face the journey, for when we wake, from dreaming, the dream, for a time, is more real than the world we wake to. We have to come back, slowly, with the dream still on us, into the different world.

Macbeth: Into our own world, where the action
                  continues. The peaceful counties, the
                  harvest, the child's cry on the wind.

That autumn, contemplating the difficult journey of the "long" revolution, he wrote his Conclusion to the final draft of *Culture and Society*.[23] It was the most astonishing part of a book of well-wrought and respectfully phrased essays on those thinkers about the "Idea of Culture" whom he had assembled to trace the shift in meaning and relationship between "industry, democracy, class, art and culture" since the "Industrial Revolution". Astonishing because of the emphasis he placed, in his own thinking and at a time of general crisis for "intellectuals" committed to "socialism", on working-class specificities derived from material conditions and transformed, collectively and institutionally, into individual values held in common. He had, for himself, worked it out and never recanted what he now articulated. Whatever else, he was now, amidst the smoke and confusion of changing positions and political retreat, emphatically clear. This was the reality he had repossessed from past evidence and this was the world, separate from dreams, which he felt could control its own fate beyond the rule of any kings. In the published Introduction to his book he described his Conclusion as "an attempt to extend [the tradition of thought] in the direction of certain meanings and values", but in an unpublished "Foreword" he made claim that "An Epilogue... attempts to define a personal view of some of the social problems raised".[24] And not only there. The whole book, he told himself, was a personal response in the face of academicism. He put it with a typical measure of circumspect diffidence and defiant assertion:

> In a period given to specialisation, the attempt which the book represents requires a measure of apology. I do not offer the book as history, although a number of historical judgements are inevitably made. The essay, really, is in criticism, in the wide sense of a judgement of literature which has to be brought into harmony with one's judgements of society and ideas. In my *Drama from Ibsen*

417

to Eliot I was unwilling to enter what I called the "no man's land between literature and belief". I was unwilling because I felt incompetent, but I knew that the attempt would one day have to be made. One's incompetence in a field of study which requires so many kinds of training and discipline, is not easily reducible.... But the attempt is always necessary, if one is to keep terms with one's own experience. Mistakes will be inevitable, but the need in life to correlate and to try to make whole is not to be denied.

Keeping terms with his "own experience" was what mattered to him more than anything of the moment in October 1956. Only he could write at that instant from such a combination of intensity of thinking, lived experience and learned insight. It is what distinguished him, when his book was finally in print, from both the more digestible working class vignettes of Hoggart in *The Uses of Literacy* (1957) and the proletarian heroics so wonderfully induced by the Romantic Edward Thompson. Williams' conclusion in *Culture and Society* was the most startling thing being thought and written in Britain in the autumn of 1956. It was shocking because he said audacious things in such a cold and reasonable voice. Like the book itself those forty or so pages from the middle of the 1950s were rapidly absorbed into the 1960s' structure of feeling as if they were commonplace. Yet reading them in 1958 was, for many, to feel the excitement of discovery and revelation made plain. He wrote with the incandescence of molten metal cooling into hard certainty. This was why the idea of culture had had to be worked through so that, after all the particularities and details of change in the way people had had to live, its general properties as a whole could again be seen, as a whole, in this "slow reach... for control". Not just understanding, then, or even alleviation of circumstances, cultural or social or economic, but "control". This was Culture as Politics of a new kind and his clipped epigrammatic sentences were the building materials of a manifesto. The prose is that of an effective counterpuncher at the end of a long bout, reaching, sinuous, stunning. To comprehend its impact at the time bland summation has to step aside:

The masses are always the others, whom we don't know and can't know... To other people, we are also masses. Masses are other people. There are in fact no masses; there are only ways of seeing people as masses.

Loutishness is always easy, and there can be few things more loutish than to turn, at the end of a long training, and sneer at those who are just entering on it, and who, harassed and insecure, are making the inevitable mistakes.

The only equality that is important, or indeed conceivable, is equality of being. Inequality in the various aspects of man is inevitable and even welcome; it is the basis of any rich and complex life. The inequality that is evil is inequality which denies the essential equality of being. Such inequality, in any of its forms, in practice rejects, depersonalises, degrades in grading, other human beings.

Unequal developments of knowledge, skill, and effort, may not deny essential equality: a physicist will be glad to learn from a better physicist, and will not, because he is a good physicist, think himself a better man than a good composer, a good chess player, a good carpenter, a good runner. Nor, in a common culture, will he think himself a better human being than a child, an old woman, or a cripple, who may lack the criterion (in itself inadequate) of useful service. The kind of respect for oneself and one's work, which is necessary to continue at all, is a different matter from a claim to inequality of being, such as would entitle one to deny or dominate the being of another.

Class feeling is a mode, rather than a uniform possession of all the individuals who might, objectively, be assigned to that class. When we speak, for instance, of a working-class idea, we do not mean that all working people possess it, or

419

even approve of it. We mean, rather, that this is the essential idea embodied in the organisations and institutions which that class creates: the working class movement as a tendency, rather than all working-class people as individuals. It is foolish to interpret individuals in rigid class terms, because class is a collective mode and not a person.... To dismiss an individual because of his class, or to judge a relationship with him solely in class terms, is to reduce humanity to an abstraction. But, also, to pretend that there are no collective modes is to deny the plain facts.

We may now see what is properly meant by "working-class culture". It is not proletarian art, or council houses, or a particular use of language; it is, rather, the basic collective idea, and the institutions, manners, habits of thought, and intentions which proceed from this.... The culture which it has produced, and which it is important to recognise, is the collective democratic institution, whether in the trade unions, the cooperative movement, or a political party. When it is considered in context, it can be seen as a very remarkable creative achievement.

The development of the idea of culture has, throughout, been a criticism of what has been called the bourgeois idea of society.... The stress has fallen on the positive function of society, on the fact that the values of individual men are rooted in society, and in the need to think and feel in these common terms.

I was not trained to this ethic [of service to the public good], and when I encountered it, in late adolescence, I had to spend a lot of time trying to understand it, through men whom I respected and who had been formed by it. The criticism I now make of it is in this kind of good faith. It seems to me inadequate because in practice it serves, at every level, to maintain and confirm the *status quo*. This was wrong, for me, because the *status quo*, in practice, was a denial of equity to the men and women among whom I had grown up, the lower servants, whose lives were governed by the existing distributions of property, remuneration, education and respect. The real personal unselfishness, which ratified the description as a service, seemed to me to exist within a larger selfishness, which was only not seen because it was idealised as the necessary form of a civilisation or rationalised as a natural distribution corresponding to worth, effort, and intelligence. I could not share in these versions, because I thought and still think, that the sense of injustice which the "lower servants" felt was real and justified. One cannot in conscience then become, when invited, an upper servant in an establishment that one thus radically disapproves.

The idea of service, ultimately, is no substitute for the idea of active mutual responsibility, which is the other version of community.... The idea of service to the community has been offered to the working class as an interpretation of solidarity, but it has not, in the circumstances, been fully accepted, for it is, to them, inferior in feeling. Another alternative to solidarity which has had some effect is the idea of individual opportunity – of the ladder... a perfect symbol of the bourgeois idea of society, because, while undoubtedly it offers the opportunity to climb, it is a device which can only be used individually: you go up the ladder alone... [but] the ladder idea has produced a real conflict of values within the working class itself. My own view is that the ladder version of society is objectionable in two related respects: first, that it weakens the principle of common betterment, which ought to be an absolute value; second, that it sweetens the poison of hierarchy, in particular by offering the hierarchy of merit as a thing different in kind from the hierarchy of money or birth. On the educational ladder, the boy who has gone from a council house to

Oxford or Cambridge is of course glad that he has gone, and he sees no need to apologise for it, in either direction. But he cannot then be expected to agree that such an opportunity constitutes a sufficient educational reform. A few voices, softened by the climb, may be found to say this, which they are clearly expected to say. Yet, if he has come from any conscious part of the working class, such a boy will take leave to doubt the proffered version. The education was worth the effort, but he sees no reason why it should be interpreted as a ladder. For the ladder, with all its extra educational implications, is merely an image of a particular version of society; if he rejects the version, he will reject the image. Take the ladder image away, and interest is returned to what is, for him, its proper object: to the making of a common educational provision; to the work for equity in material distribution; to the process of shaping a tradition, a community of experience, which is always a selective organisation of past and present, and which he has been given particular opportunities to understand.

Only quotation at this length can do justice to the force of Williams' expressed thought. The poetry behind that thought lay in his tempered passion and in the shape of the mature personality he had struggled to make true to his individual self and his social origins. Neither prose nor person can be paraphrased if their public effect in 1958 is to be fully understood. He would, literally, be swamped by the volume of response. Much of what he said would be endlessly re-configured, by himself and others, to meet or shape the shifting conditions of the future. Not all of the response, even from those nominally sympathetic, would give the same weight of accord to his social class emphasis as he did, and which, notwithstanding subtle variations of tone, he continued to affirm throughout his life. Few denied the fresh perspective he had found from within the historical record for the main body of his book. Edward Thompson claimed it forcefully in 1961: "With a compromised tradition at his back and with a broken vocabulary in his hand he did the only thing that was left to him: he took over the vocabulary of his opponents, followed them into the heart of their own arguments and fought them to a standstill in their own terms."[25]

The book which he finally put completely into the hands of his publishers, signed and delivered in December 1956 with only the sealing of the proofs to come in the spring of 1957, was more than that however. Edward Thompson characteristically went on to say that Raymond Williams had held open the roads down which the young were "moving... once again". But the military metaphor, apt or exaggerated depending on which 1960s' road was actually taken, was not quite the way, in an equally bold metaphor, with which Williams chose to close the book that ended his relative obscurity and ensured him of a public platform thereafter. The note he sounded, as always, was of the particularities of human experience and on to the meanings they entailed:

> To take a meaning from experience and to try to make it active, is in fact our process of growth. Some of these meanings we receive and re-create. Others we must make for ourselves, and try to communicate. The human crisis is always a crisis of understanding: what we genuinely understand we can do. I have written this book because I believe the tradition it records is a major contribution to our common understanding, and a major incentive to its necessary extensions. There are ideas, and ways of thinking, with the seeds of life in them, and there are others, perhaps deep in our minds, with the seeds of general death. Our measure of success in recognising these kinds, and in naming them making possible their common recognition, may be literally the measure of our future.

* * * * * *

As 1956 ended and he planned for 1957, his own future was decidedly more circumspect. There were classes to prepare, as usual, and reasonable numbers in attendance through an unusually mild winter.

The works he taught included *Hamlet* and *Faustus* in Eastbourne, and Lawrence and Hemingway at Battle; he reserved Greene's *The Quiet American* and Dylan Thomas' *Under Milk Wood* for racier Brighton. He drew up lists of what he called "Future Stories: since 1945" and ranged from Orwell's *1984* through Bradbury's *Fahrenheit 451* to Vonnegut's *Piano Player*. "Earlier Future (Utopian) stories" were also considered, incorporating Mercier's *L'An 2440*, Mary Shelley's *The Last Man*, William Morris' *News from Nowhere*, and Huxley's *Brave New World*. The January/February admonitions to himself of "Full Work to Prepare" led him from *The Great Gatsby* and *Sanctuary* to *A Farewell to Arms* and on to Sartre's *The Age of Reason*, Amis' *That Uncertain Feeling* and the poetry anthology *New Lines*, which had appeared in 1956 and declared itself as part of "the Movement", poetry against the romantic, the emotional and the attitudinising where metaphor and technique had swamped "integrity and judgement".[26] To Williams' mind such plain-dealing words in prose and verse meant rather more than first met the eye. He took the Anthology (edited by Robert Conquest and showcasing Davie, Wain, Larkin, Amis and others) into his classes for dissection, and in his Notebook he scratched out versions of a poetic reply which he finally published, his only poem in print, in 1984. He called it "On First Looking into *New Lines*", and the publicly known four-stanza version is almost identical in its chiding rebuke of "dumb" neutrality and "careful" passion as the original, in which such modes are seen as having "evacuated... All regions of a man but those/That can be smiled at in a casual prose..." However, there is a penultimate stanza in which, in 1956, looking to those contemporaries he was reading and teaching, he struck a note that resonated with a resigned anger against the dismissiveness of the "group" when confronted by those "still learning how to write":

> There is so much here to respect,
> So much intelligence, as well as so much pose.
> The fools are winning, though, by your neglect.
> The attitudes absorb what you connect.

This is just how it happens, with a friend,
And this is what will hurt you in the end.
You have too much, and are afraid, to lose.

Undeniably, in its full form, the poem is expressing as much frustration at as denunciation of the tone and subject matter being adopted in poetry (minimal and wry), in novels (mannered and comedic), or in plays (facile structure to facilitated rant in one easy step from drawing room to attic flat); all far removed from the creative ambition he still nurtured and which his work had fitfully attempted. What did not cease was his effort or his experimentation. From this time we can date another play, called *A Dance of Life*, which he worked on sporadically into late 1957, pitting a scientist against his science-journalist son in a domestic framework of divorce and betrayal. There also emerged the first thoughts for *Koba* and plots for the novels, *Figure of Eight*, about political careers since 1945 and *A Generation in Waiting* which would have centred on journalism and academia. *A Letter from the Country* was another possible novel or as eventually realised, a play.[27] These were speculative hares, though many were later run down, and we can see them form and re-form and evaporate through charts, chronological and general, diagrams and squibbles in the three Notebooks he filled, at will and in chaotic order, from 1956.

He had long been in the habit of jotting down random thoughts or even elaborated ideas on sheets of paper. Paragraphs would start, names of characters appear, numbers would signify the reshuffling of chapters, the rearrangement of pages. Typescript, carbon flimsies, pencilled drafts and inked corrections were discarded from his desk and loosely packed into paper covers for, he noted sometimes, recovery and reuse. The Notebooks, though, are a step change in this creative jumble of an agenda.[28] He kept such pocket books for the rest of his life but the three – two purple and one black – that are inscribed with his Hastings address and which he filled between October 1956 and 1960 are the densest of his work books and the most indicative of his restless pattern of creation. He carried their squat 6-inch by 4-inch bulk in his pockets and opened them, day or night, sedentary or travelling, at will.

The first, "Daybook", begins neatly enough with brief reflections on "Renaissance literature" and "Rhetoric", bouncing almost immediately into the enigmatic "Joyce and Degas?". But then we are off, page by page, into a mix of recounted dreams, personal remarks, dissections of theme and characters in Shakespeare or Lawrence, booklists and lecturing duties, ideas, garnered facts and statistics on the price and circulation of the Press and class profiles of its readership, snatches of dialogue or narrative from projected fiction, quotes culled from his reading and the ticked-off or crossed-out books and references he double-checked for final notation in *Culture and Society*. There is no order, no sequence, no resolution. Just a ceaseless flow that finds shape and outcome in his mind, and on the written page outside the Notebooks.

In addition to this further evidence of his energy to read and absorb unremittingly, they present us with an invaluable understanding of the scaffold of chronology which he increasingly used to frame the order of his work, the lives to be lived in his fiction and, indeed, his own unfolding life. In genealogical relationships and calendar years, fictive and actual, he scrupulously noted the dates down. It is as if he had found, and so wished to record by those selective milestones, the framework and direction of his past and ongoing life. This was a habit from which he never veered thereafter. In the Notebook entries for 1956 and 1957, with the detritus of his research for *Culture and Society* in his wake, he stretches himself finally to bring together the fiction that he could increasingly recognise as paralleling the critical work. On the central pages of the "Daybook" but with the same dating as its opening page – 9/X/56 – he headed a section with the title of his 1955 novel *Between Two Worlds*. The title, or *BTW*, as he often abbreviated it, had become generic in his thinking for the entire clutch of work he had completed or planned since the late 1940s to imagine his own past. He reminded himself of his starting point and the hoped-for arrival:

> Initially planned as three novels.
> 1. *Border Marches*
> 1920-1939.

2. *Our Lords The Moon and The Sun*
1939-45.
3. *The Grasshopers*: 1945-1955
4. *The End of Exile?* 1955 on

Even as he wrote, the "three" had expanded to four, though this seems from the squashed entry to be a late levering in of *The Grasshoppers* for which he clearly still had fond hopes and some of whose protagonists he had "retired" from activity by having them choose "exile" in the Black Mountains. But the inclusion of *The Grasshoppers* would have been a maverick aberration to which he could not have been wedded in the overall scheme whose guiding concept was: "taking continuity as a commonplace idea... and working then back into the actual". He envisaged a "Prelude" in which "familiar" feelings and ideas would appear to be all that was "actuality, yet temporary". Reluctant to lose the effort, perhaps, he placed sections of *A Map of Treason* and *Our Lords The Moon and the Sun* together with pieces of his early stories and of *Brynllwyd* to be made all together into the "novel" that would theoretically preface *The Grasshoppers*. He still had not understood how the imperatives of his story needed to be pared back to a form that could, all at once, hold the dimension of continuity and displacement. As late as 1956 he was separating out the strands as if they were the sequence of lives, not the simultaneity of experience. The first novel, *Border Marches*, was, he scribbled to himself: "Basically, *Brynllwyd* – all early chapters", spliced with "*Between Two Worlds* – all less the big house, though retain some of this", and that the central part, concerning 1926, was already written. Then he set out the segments of narrative, moving chronologically from the parental "Arrival at station; work, lodgings" and on to "House. Birth of child. Christening", then to adolescent self absorption before a growing-up framed by the crisis of 1939. Securing these continuous narrative blocks was the exact socio-geographical locus of "Border country. Black Mountains Village – Patch."

The last projected novel – *The End of Exile?* – was set to take the mature son to a new landscape of sea and mountain and post-war progress or re-encounters with friends from the late 1940s before, from a separate family life and changed professional status, he is returned, as Raymond Williams would be himself in 1957, to pressing, inescapable shifts of experience and expectation:

> Illness of father. Basic revaluation.
> Basic challenge, also, to language.
> And settlement. Crisis of illness.
> Mountain. Basics. Exile and artist.

Exile he certainly was; artist he had yet to establish in the public domain. Once more he tried. From the musing and reordering came a fresh rewriting which he began after visiting his desperately ill father in January 1957. He finished the novel he now called *Border Village* on yet another hurried journey home to Pandy.

He had opened one of the Notebooks about halfway through and written, in pencil, at the top of the page:

> Joy: April 3, 1957: on my way to Pandy. You know we talked today about completing the novel. I feel I must do it now, on my way down. It is all in the clip except one page with a few lines at the top. This continues from there.

Over some 25 pages he wrote of Will's final preparation for departure for University from Pandy, and of Harry from his signalbox watching his son take the train. This was to be the end of *Border Village*. However, the tone did not seem right. The closing words of the typescript of *Border Village* remove the emotional note of the manuscript to describe Harry's routine, almost mechanical, work practice even at this breaking point:

> They were circling now, high above the station, in wider and wider sweeps. Harry rested his arms on the bar, watching them space out and draw slowly away from their circling, flying south and home. From inside the box, a bell rang: the train had reached Pont Dulas; Harry – turned, at once, from the window and went to answer it.

But in the original manuscript, preceded by the same and ultimately retained mantra which echoes in Harry's head – "When you go out first on your own. When you marry and settle. When your father dies. When you leave home" – emotion is not denied:

> Harry smiled, and turned to watch the pigeons rising. They were already above the bridge and climbing past the telephone wires. Then their circle widened slowly, and soon they were high and still circling in wider and wider sweeps. Harry looked up, resting his arms on the bar. They had spaced out more, and were flying away from those circling, level, as he looked with the blue peak of The Holy Mountain, flying south. Harry rubbed his hand over his face, and turned back into the box.

On 3 April 1957, Raymond Williams wrote END in a little pencil box underneath the above. *Border Village* was, in this form, the prototype for *Border Country* that was to follow, even if it lacked the latter's ultimate dual perspective on generational attitude and change. Readers of *Border Country* would recognise from *Border Village* near-identical themes, similarly named characters and places, whole pages of the same prose and a narrative that begins with arrival, bodies out into the dilemmas of the General Strike and ends with a departure both necessary and resented. This is still the story of railway signalman Harry Price and his wife Ellen, of their son, Will, and now of Harry's doppelgänger Morgan Rosser, socialist and entrepreneur. It is impossible to read it without a shivery sense of anticipation for the work it will yet become. Notwithstanding, it is rather more than a ghostly prior image, for it differs substantially in weight of detail and, occasionally, sharply in its intent from the ultimate transformation it would undergo in 1958.

When he incorporates the earlier version of *Border Village* into the ultimate text of *Border Country*, word and paragraph and page order move about, snatches of dialogue reappear in different contexts, and descriptive passages carry less of the freight of a social historian as they are condensed into lyrical physical description or become, in phrases, evocative of the landscape's history rather than detailed passages. Almost everywhere there is a tightening into a concise, allusive prose that leaves the motivation of his characters more enigmatically poised than any didactic settling of cause-and-effect could convey. The strongest shift of emphasis is to the character of Morgan Rosser who is, in his final and separated-out role, the novelist's solution to the problem of capturing his own father within the complexity of his father's "whole way of life". In *Border Country* Williams will imagine the contradictions by representing them in an amoeba-like character-isation of Harry Price, the signalman and Morgan Rosser, the socialist and entrepreneur; but in the first version of Rosser's character its origins and traits are made clearer and more fully explained than in their final emergence, a process from the explicit to the enigmatic which only begins in *Border Village*.

Brynllwyd had begun abruptly with the birth of a boy and the perspective of change. Settlement is dwarfed by landscape and history. This time however, in *Border Village*, we enter the village of Brynllwyd directly with Harry and Ellen, coming to work and to live. We see through their eyes a community already in existence, but one to which they will now contribute and which they will, in turn, be shaped by. The pattern of the novel is the same one he would later use for the "flashback" of Part Two of *Border Country*; it is the rhythm that is different here: he is more willing to digress on the background of other characters, related incidents or, crucially, make some events not just antecedent to the bonding effect of the disruptive crisis of the General Strike but, in themselves, partly explanatory of the local solidarity of that action.

The key figure around whom we are made to pause in this version is the widower, Morgan Rosser. It is with Rosser and his infant daughter Eira that the Prices first lodge in both novels. Only, in *Border Country*, Harry is cursorily informed that the tragically bereaved figure of Morgan is "a young chap about your own age. Come from Pontypool, his father was a ticket collector", and, a little later, that Rosser interests himself in Labour and Union politics, even travelling to Newport to participate in meetings. So, in *Border Country*, there is no surprise at Morgan's forthright stance for militant action during the General Strike of 1926, when he speaks, briefly, of "the common good", nor of Harry's occasional work as a "groundsman" for the bowling green, a position he has taken up the previous autumn. However, in *Border Village*, the issues and incidents are brought together, before the General Strike, to show how "the common good" can be attained by working together. We see a community taking on deeper formations *before* the Strike rather than merely as one of its consequences, and the making of a bowling green becomes symbol of this not an incidental to it.

Raymond Williams devotes a sub-section of some ten pages to Rosser and the bowling green immediately before the encounter with May 1926. It starts with a Rosser homily to Harry in their signal box:

> "Only the thing is," Morgan Rosser was saying, as he stood with Harry in the box, "people in a place like this have got no idea of mixing, no idea of all pulling together. Aye, certainly, if a load's too heavy, they'll get another chap to lift it with them, but only, you see, because they want it lifted for themselves, and not, as you might say, for the general good. It's like at times a colony of hermits, working away at their own stuff, staring between their toes, but the common good, what's that? They've never heard of it. It's like animals really, all for themselves."
>
> Harry hesitated, looking down.

Morgan, with his broader horizons, is too impatient to go beyond this kind of human interrelationship and how it is ambiguously expressed within these particular kinds of community. But Morgan is also shown to be right that working for the creation of a bowling green, tangible and possible, can serve a wider cause. He persists, and slowly, works his way around the various religious denominations, the stationmaster, the schoolmaster, and even the denizen of Brynllwyd House, Major Blakely. All agree to serve on the committee:

431

But Rosser, although he was not a native of the village – he came from Pontypool, where his father had been a railwayman before him, a passenger guard and eventually a ticket collector – knew well enough, from his years in Brynllwyd, the real centres of influence and action... essentially... the closely related and intermarried families of the farmers.

Rosser builds them into his cross-sectoral alliance. Whist drives and flower shows raise funds. A piece of a field is negotiated for the green's site. The public greens in Abergrwyne are studied and "good mountain-turf" contracted. Voluntary labour, bit by bit, does the rest. Harry works hard to lay the turf and is duly appointed groundsman "at six pounds a year"; mower, roller and other equipment are bought and "a shed to house them".

By April 1926, the green was in excellent condition, and ready for play. One Saturday afternoon, in bright Spring sunshine, the opening ceremony took place. Major Blakely, before bowling the first wood, paid tribute, in a short and graceful speech, to all who had contributed to making possible so happy an occasion... [but] all present would agree that without the patient efforts of Mr Rosser, they would not be there that afternoon.

The whole episode, direct forerunner of the dividing lines of the Strike, occurs on the eve of the conflict.

[Harry]... looked up at the long line of Brynllwyd – green now with the young bracken – where the turf on which he stood had been cut. Already, up there, the cleared spaces were being grown over. Down here, in the centre of the valley, the village had come together, and a new organisation had begun.

Losing this episode means that *Border Country* loses some of the richer social contextualisation that Williams presents in *Border Village*.

The former, of course, gains in other ways, not least in the deeper focus on the narrative of two adult Price men, the father and the son. As if to make up for the loss of this slower, subtle elision from harmony to dissent in *Border Country*, Raymond Williams removes the address Harry uses to Blakely in all previous versions: in *Border Country* he does not call him "Sir". This becomes all of a piece with the sharper outlines of character and attitude which frame Harry Price in *Border Country*. Through the versions his characterisation moves further and further away from both the ambiguities of Harry Williams' actual life and the ambivalence of his actions: and for that purpose he will be further decanted into the vehicle of Morgan Rosser.

In both "Border" novels Rosser arranges, as his fruit-picking and jam-making enterprise takes off after the Strike, to grow blackcurrants on Major Blakely's land and, thereby, makes a fellow signalman lose tenancy of two fields. However, it is only in *Border Village* that Blakely's opinions of Rosser are given free flow in his contemplation of what a sensible "Opposition" could be in a changing world:

> The worst thing that had come into modern politics – it was particularly noticeable in Wales – was that kind of sentimentalism which you heard from a man like "the ganger Watkins" [a "leading Labour Party man"] whenever politics were discussed. There was an emphasis, above all, on suffering, including all the suffering of the past, which was really not very relevant. Suffering needed respect, but the running of the country, and the avoidance of avoidable suffering, needed something more than this kind of emotion, which time and again seemed all such men had to offer...
> Even when the cases were real – that a woman had died poor, that a child was under-nourished, that an injured man, permanently disabled, could not afford tobacco – it was utterly disheartening to have the practical discussion which could alone help such people broken up by the sort of emotional insistence which got one nowhere... a man like Rosser... at least knew what a balance sheet looked like, and

433

knew you couldn't spend money you hadn't got.... A man like Rosser, making his own way by his own effort, had none of the resentments, the really corroding bitterness... Blakely did not so much like talking politics to him – that was not the point – but at least you could meet without tension, without embarrassment, talking the same kind of language.

For the rest, with *Border Village*, Raymond Williams returned, with more economy of effect and sureness of touch, to the burgeoning relationship between Will and Eira, another pairing of the same differences in this retelling: one who is baptised and stays, one who throws his book in the river and leaves. The crises, revisited between them all in *Border Country*, are here in *Border Village* spelled out by a writer who has, with this novel, distilled the fuller works of *Brynllwyd* and *Between Two Worlds* to another kind of essence, more allusive and yet, also, more suggestive of the need for closure. In fiction he needed to find a way of addressing Will's particular dilemma, the one he leaves him with towards the end of *Border Village*. A dilemma whose resolution was never going to be just personal.

> Everyone might see the life [of Brynllwyd] and the people here in his own way: that was the whole point. What Blakely saw, as the interesting if faintly comic life of the village people; what Morgan Rosser saw, as a narrow if infectious way of life from which he, personally, must break out, to something more revealing; what the exile might see, looking back on colour and strangeness and exaltation; what the watcher from the mountain might see, looking down at a stillness beyond persons: all these, necessarily, were different from what Harry saw – a settlement, a way he had grown to, a peace where with the first emphasis of commitment, and then with no other emphasis whatever, he knew how to live in. Yet to Will, no separate view was possible; in him, as yet, were all the responses, all the potential ways, and nothing definite could come through as his, though what came through, as a whole, was a total

image. This was the creative moment, quick and intense, in which the whole appears to be contained, yet which cannot be held, but must be shaken to pieces and only later, if at all, slowly and with a different energy regained.

There was work yet to do but Raymond Williams was sure, at last, that in his fiction and in his critical work both, he had found a voice that was appropriate to both and to their common subject. Just over two months after the first handwritten end to *Border Village*, with a typescript revised and loosely bound, he wrote to Chatto on 7 June 1957:

Dear Parsons,
I hope you won't mind my putting in the post to you the manuscript of a novel, *Border Village*, that I've recently completed. I don't know whether a new manuscript after so big a one is a mark of industry or of nuisance value but I do very much want you to see it.
It's a medium-length novel, about 80,000 words, and of an entirely different kind from the other I showed you, which was really a jeu d'esprit. With this I return to what I have always wanted to do in fiction, back into my own mainstream. It's about people and a way of life I know intimately, where the living is and always must be more important than any ideas about it.
... I've had a good many tries at this and really think at last I have got this first stage right.[29]

The late summer of 1957 in which the Williams family decamped, as had become their practice, from Hastings to Oxford, was to have seen the publication of the long awaited *Culture and Society*. It was delayed. His frustration grew. He could sense that its approach, suddenly and unexpectedly, might be central to the emerging debates of a left politics once more reaching towards intellectual enquiry. And central to that was the rumbling disquiet over the disappearance of a traditionally defined working class. That summer his own considered reflections and provoking polemics, still hidden away from public view, were gazumped by the appearance, sensational in every sense, of Richard Hoggart's *The Uses of Literacy*. Even more than Williams' work it was a book made vigorous by its hybridity and the author's intrusive personality. Both men would note, somewhat wryly, how, in later years, these two working-class intellectuals, extra-mural lecturers in English, publishing works almost simultaneously on the nature of cultural experience in an industrialised society, would find themselves wedded together as soul mates. They certainly recognised each other's worth and subsequently enjoyed a distant friendship; but soul mates they were not.

Williams' considered and generous measurement of the book came in a six-page review he wrote immediately for Bateson's autumn edition of *Essays in Criticism*.[30] He quickly connected Hoggart's "intelligent account of contemporary commercial writing" to Q.D. Leavis' *Fiction and the Reading Public* (1932) and fully acknowledged the empathetic skill with which Hoggart crossed over from critical analysis to insider sympathy with the texture of working-class life. His critique, though firmly stated, has the feel of a pulled punch. He is still in a waiting game. He can only point to the missing pieces he knows he has supplied elsewhere. Hoggart's concentration on anecdote and evidence is valuable, but if it only exposes the inadequacy of "popular culture" – itself not "working class culture" but the produced and distributed culture for the working class – it does not touch its corollary, "the coming to relative power and relative justice of your own people". Williams nods to his own future foray: "My own estimate of this difficulty [the apparent clash between "enlightened minority" and "degraded mass"] is that it is first in the field of ideas, the received formulas, that scrutiny is necessary and the approach to settlement possible."

Nor was Williams willing, in 1957, to see "working class materialism... objectively... [as anything other than] a humane ideal". Working class political "decay", for which he saw no evidence anyway, was not the product of material advancement, and he would shortly tease out his difference from Hoggart in a further article. But what, for Williams' life, serves as shadow play in these few pages is the startlingly accurate surmise that Hoggart had set out, in places, to write a novel

436

but had ended up with a hybrid form whose deep interest lay in its inadequacy to bring its insights to a point of full perception. For Williams an "autobiography" or even "a novel" would have been better than the intelligent criticism, acute sociology, personal observation and imaginative recreation which Hoggart variously employs. If Williams is on target it would be only fair to add that it is because, for himself, he had chosen an alternative separation of powers:

> I am not blaming Hoggart for this variety, but since the condition is general, I am trying to insist on the distinctions we shall all have to make. We are suffering, obviously, from the decay and disrepute of the realistic novel, which for our purposes (since we are, and know ourselves to be, individuals *within* a society) ought clearly to be revived. Sound critical work can be done; sound social observation and analysis of ideas. Yet I do not see how, in the end, this particular world of fact and feeling can be adequately mediated, except in these more traditionally imaginative terms.

This was a statement that he made knowing that its back-up, in the shape of *Border Village*, was not yet available as his fuller answer. *Border Village* was, in his mind, only a section of the roll-out of fiction he had been long assembling and its own removal in tone from the contemporary "realistic novel" was no guarantee of any kind of recognition. The personal tone of some of his comments, though clear cut, was also puzzling to contemporaries, even to friends, who had no sight or sense of the resolution he was seeking to bring about through his unrelenting, private turn to fiction. His own intuitive sense of all this would remain firm despite the acclaim that was shortly to come for his critical writings. The latter would decisively end his marginal status, both as academic teacher and as public intellectual, and success would, in turn, bring him a welcome range of new and admiring contacts. Central to this latter network was the establishment of *Universities and Left Review* as a journal and a forum.

437

The journal sprang from the roots of a diverse "Oxford left" which included a lively Labour club, a Balliol grouping of Communist Party post-graduates (most of whom, along with their mentor Christopher Hill, would leave the Party in the wake of Hungary), and a scattering of "Independents" who were temperamentally more attached to dissident Communists than to reformist Labourism. It came out in the spring of 1957, attractively produced and iconoclastic, a bridgehead between the old left communist intellectuals such as Hobsbawm and Thompson – who both wrote in the first number – and the younger generation for whom cinema, architecture, literature and, in short, a lifestyle, were not things other than political but the very bearers of political repression or liberation. The editors were the twenty-five year-old Stuart Hall, at Merton College (completing his thesis on the novels of Henry James); Charles Taylor, a twenty-seven year-old philosopher (then at All Souls but a Balliol graduate in PPE); Gabriel Pearson, twenty four and a Balliol graduate in English (who was working on Charles Dickens); and the ebullient Raphael Samuel, twenty two and a 1956 graduate in History from Balliol (subsequently researching working-class history at the LSE). The latter two were former Communist Party members and the two from overseas of the "Independent" faction within Oxford. They were intensely conscious of their generational remove from the 1930s-derived politics of those older contemporaries now in their own thirties who were so buffeted by the breaking loyalties of 1956, and thus, consciously or not, the putting down of their own more youthful ages in that very first number. At the same time, they were themselves umbilically attached to the more vibrant cultural politics of the 1930s than to the moribund wastelands of post-war intellectual endeavour, hence the nod in the title to *Left Review*, the paramount left-wing journal of the pre-war years. The pull towards cooperation with Thompson and Saville and to a merger with *The New Reasoner*, despite all the tensions involved between a "metropolitan" crowd and a "provincial" rectitude based on organisational politics, was irresistible within a few years. The merged journals would in 1960 become *New Left Review*.[31]

Raymond Williams wrote for the second number of *Universities and Left Review* in the summer of 1957[32] almost inevitably as part of a symposium on the questions around "working class culture" so disturbingly raised by Hoggart's *The Uses of Literacy*. This time he paraphrased his own arguments concerning the change of meaning of the word "culture" since the late eighteenth century, and again insisted that Hoggart's conflation of a media-drawn commercial culture with working class culture itself was a false formula which merely restated the difficulty of how things were actually made popular. At the end of the 1950s, Williams was not inclined to be daunted by the dichotomous propositions already settling into orthodoxy about "pop" culture, the popularity of "high" culture and even less so over the authenticity of "folk" culture or the loss of cultural homogeneity in working-class life. Some of that would be chewed over within academic circles for decades to come, but for Williams its bloodless taxonomy was always a distraction that led away from the detail of a lived history and the potential specificities of an undisclosed future.

In his article, politely but strongly, he reminded Hoggart why "the idea of service" amongst the liberal middle class is invariably in the service of the authority or institutions which exist, and which do not exist in order to be extended to society as a whole; whereas a working class, aghast at the notion of preparing some family members for service by educational and physical separation, looks to "continuous and co-extensive" allegiance to (local) neighbourhood and (wider) society. The clarity with which he polarised the argument and its constituent parts was undoubtedly to be clouded by the whirlpool of social change coming to Britain from the 1960s. His own hopeful admonition in 1957 to hold fast to the idea of a working class culture as the best guide for a whole society was not, however, a position he would ever abandon. Here it is, in those cracked-up days, in 1957:

> It is important to stress... basic cultural differences now, when we have in fact three offered versions of society: the "opportunity state" (bourgeois competition); welfare

capitalism (bourgeois service – the pattern of thinking of many leaders of the Labour Party); socialism (the working class idea of society as a collective democratic totality). Much of our political argument is confused, much of our controversy caused by the energy which flows into one or other of these versions from basic cultural dispositions. The political argument can be greatly deepened in quality if these things are understood. It is of course a corollary that working class life is not primarily political.... The political effect of working class life is the product of the primary affections and allegiances, in family and neighbourhood, which make up the immediate substance of this life... these are [not] to be set on one side of a line, while on the other is set the wider social product – the Labour Movement – which [Hoggart] describes as the work of a minority.... The political and industrial leadership of the working class is... not isolated, but is the articulate representation of an extension of primary values into the social fields.... It is not opposed [like other minorities] to majority values but seeks to define them in wider terms and in a different context... for the working class sees no reason... why these values should not be made the values of society as a whole....

In the late fifties... let us remember that it is only in terms of working class culture as a whole that we have the opportunity for any valuable transformation of society. There are no masses to capture, but only this mainstream to join. May it be here that the two major senses of culture – on the one hand the arts, the sciences and learning, on the other hand the whole way of life – are valuably drawn together, in a common effort at maturity.

Chapter 11

"... but I am Price from Glynmawr"

During the summer of 1957 he decided finally to become Matthew Price. This was not to be like the earlier creation of his fictional others, the boyhood familiars of his past witnessing to events. This time, as the coming crisis of his father's illness became undeniable, he found the most telling witness to the general crisis he had been analysing and observing to be the transposition into fiction of his adult self. With this decision made, he found the novel he now planned would not conform to the previous scheme. Slowly, the shape his tale now insisted upon becoming gave him, at last, the defining shape of his own fictive life. In a sense, it was only two years later with the full discovery of Matthew Price that the making of Raymond Williams, though assuredly not his own measuring, was complete.

* * * * * *

At home in Hastings, just before the teaching year for 1957-58 began, Raymond opened a Notebook and wrote "22 Oct" in the right hand corner of a page which he headed "work in hand". The list – there was always a list – began with "Novel *Matthew Price*, to write". He estimated ten weeks for completion but it was hemmed in by lesser completion rates for the plays *Koba*, *King Macbeth*, *A Dance of Life* and a flurry of new essays he had in mind, (including "What happened in 1870" for *Past and Present*, the journal established in 1952 by the Communist Historians' Group and that had become, by 1957, the British equivalent of Annales). He was already thinking his way towards a collection of essays that would, in 1959, be finished as *The Long Revolution*. This work plan, however, was to take him, "less holidays", over a thirty-two week period "to June 1958". The priorities were at the top and bottom: "Proofs *Culture and Society*" due over Christmas for January, and "*Matthew Price*" to be finished before Easter.

To say, as we may with the telescope of biographical convention to hand, that he was in the middle of his greatest creative period is to miss the inner conviction that had been, from 1956, at the core of all he did. It was this conviction that marked him out as being different from his contemporaries despite the continuing odds against any easy success and the ratchet effect of despair at the marginality of his voice in a contemporary Britain he so wished to influence. He considered, at this time, whether one of the essays for a new book might be called "Contemporary Structure of Feeling". This later became the long concluding essay "Britain in the 1960s" from *The Long Revolution* where it was published in 1961. That, too, began in the late 1950s as the Notebooks testify: phrases cluster around a fan-like diagram, whose Structure of Feeling centre ("Sof") spreads out the segments of the arc labelled "actual social experience". On an opposite page, in pencil, he described the long-term task he was contemplating and then writing over the autumn of 1957. He called it "Essays and Principles in the theory of Culture; General Studies" and wrote down, out of numerical order, its five parts as

1. Culture : a general theory
3. Naturalism : a social history
2. The Myth of 1870
5. English and the Industrial Revolution
4. Public and Private Fiction

A later hand, from the 1960s, emphatically scrawled *The Long Revolution* across the page. That phrase, his subsequent life's work, was one he had taken from *Culture and Society*. It is in the published Foreword to that book that he advises his readers how, while it had been in the press, he had been thinking of directions for further work in the field. This further work was, in 1958, to postulate "a new general theory of culture... as a theory of relations between elements in a whole way of life". It was to be about accepting the tenets of "an expanding culture" rather than regretting it, understanding its "nature and conditions" rather than restricting its reach.

The first sixteen pages of one Notebook are filled in a neat hand, one that suggests the early stages of composition rather than first thoughts, with the successive elements of definition of "work", "private life", "Individuality" and "Society", making up his compound theory of Culture. The final text of *The Long Revolution* is, of course, richer in its diet of evidence on the Popular Press, the Reading Public, Education and the "Social History" of Literary forms, but the Notebooks, revealing his workings and his data, spin outwards from dicta such as "Theories of art allow only for great art: this leads to elementary mistakes" to "When a class takes over politically, [the] culture it takes over is already made into its own (cf. C19 Russian novel). What survives is what is significant in subsequent growth." He affirmed in a truncated style why he was taking this new path for which, so readily, he would be attacked as a destroyer of the sanctities of academic compartmentalisation:

> Theory of culture is a deep response to a deep disturbance of the common life of exceptional complexity, but this is its relevance. Certain radical changes, which are still in progress, requiring total revaluation. Primary explains [sic] – as means of discovery and settlement – relationship of various elements in a whole way of life.

This was the way he had learned to work. It "bubbled up" and he tended to it until it simmered and simmered. Most of the ground work – referenced note-taking in the Bodleian in July 1958 ranging from American Speech II (1927) to Bradley Collected Papers (1928) and a host of studies of speech, language and dialect – was set out in "Personal Notes" to cover the eventual topics but, there were also notes on "Mobility" and "Labour and Culture" and "Language and Class" in various drafts, one of which was at one time headlined as a "Letter to an Unknown Reader". Then, straightforwardly from April, a new black Notebook simply starts with a page for *The Long Revolution*, the contents of which mirror almost exactly the book he would take to its final form over the autumn and winter of 1959. It sprang directly from the connections he was constantly making between everything in his sights in 1957 and 1958, and why he would famously write at the end of its Introduction, even keeping in mind all the work that would necessarily follow that: "With this book and *Culture and Society*, and with my novel *Border Country* which I believe to have, in its particular and quite different way, an essential relevance to the two general books, I have completed a body of work which I set myself to do ten years ago." Significantly then, the date actually means not the 1950 of "Ideas about Culture" but the 1949 opening up of his original exploration of "Brynllwyd". He added that this "need not interest anybody else" but thought perhaps it was "worth recording". In the draft ending of 1957, he had already written privately to "Matthew Price" to remind him that "A man's lucky if, as in your case, his life and his work have a common theme".

That last phrase was the title he now settled on for the concluding novel, crossing out *The End of Exile* with an emphatic flourish and rejecting, as alternatives, *The Power to Change* and *A Debt of Birth*. "Do not call it 'The End of Exile' " he insisted to himself in late 1957: "For what is it, then, that you are shut out from? Remember Hamlet." If the injunction seems a shade overly dramatic, it was, for all that, the rejection of endless introspection to which he was pointing. There would be no ghosts left for him to lay after 1958, only exemplars to follow whenever necessary change beckoned. The sense of something building irresistibly to a climax is the inescapable message of the notebooks, moving backwards and forwards on tides of speculation and delivery.

A future to be claimed was one that would see him introduce into his fiction for the first time a generation beyond himself and his Pandy upbringing. The orbit of Matthew Price will take in wife and children. The actual Williams children had already popped up at the front of *Culture and Society* which is dedicated to the silent observers of his work-obsessed life: "For Merryn, Ederyn, and Gwydion Madawc." Welsh credentials thereby stretched more than nominally in two directions and for the present, he acknowledged Joy Williams who had "argued the chapters with me, line by line", and was "in certain chapters... virtually the joint author". She, above all others, had overcome his doubts and worked to ensure he would be free enough to dedicate more time than most families could have envisaged as entirely warranted. There was indeed some sacrifice. He made up for it in his care and love for them but that he was seen by his family as different from other husbands and fathers, is clear. This felt difference was eventually the testimony, too, of students and colleagues, close and far from him. His personal warmth never invited intimacy. Some saw this self-containment as an unexpected rebuff. They wanted, perhaps, too much of the life of a man whose work was so entirely integrated with his personal experience that any minor lapse of behaviour, perceived or real, would become for some, a question of his entire integrity. In his own lifetime, however, there was no question but that he was tough enough to face down such facile detraction as he deliberately strode into confrontation. It was what he was seeking all along.

From 1958 he could sense alliances of support to alleviate the tenor of isolation which had surrounded much of his work since the late 1940s. He put it, almost touchingly, when, referring to CND's sudden spurt of popular growth from its foundation in 1957, he saw on the early Aldermaston marches, starting in 1958, "people... I hadn't seen in years, especially from a Communist background... people who had been separated for a decade meeting up in all sorts of ways... people... now suddenly much more in touch, including the young generation which was then emerging".[1]

For this reason he valued deeply the personal contact which the network of clubs around *Universities and Left Review* provided. Known, though not yet famed through publication, he not only gave chapter extracts to *ULR*, he willingly addressed the meetings in Oxford and in London that coalesced around an intense moment of hopefulness rather more than because of expectations of any rooted movement. The journal, to general amazement and gratification, was selling 8,000 copies across Britain. Readers would have their taste for *Culture and Society* whetted here and would soon know its coming author as a relatively senior yet somehow less official figure than the other academic socialists who addressed them in print and in person. In May 1957 Raymond Williams spoke at the vibrant ULR Club in London to over three hundred and he returned for some of their packed weekly meetings in 1958. The ULR found itself a permanent base, in the Partisan Coffee House in 7 Carlisle Street which housed the ULR offices and a heady mix of books, steam, froth and modern design. Profits from ground floor consumption were to pay for second floor production. It was the characteristic brainchild of Raphael Samuel, a dynamo of enthusiasm who was able to charm all but the most ordered – John Saville tutted ruefully over his younger friend's bankrupting ways – by his lethal combination of chaos and passion.[2] For Raymond, characteristically both very much a part of things but also slightly to one side, this was congenial company and, at last, a public platform of engagement where he could lock horns with Labour intellectuals like Richard Crossman and argue that quality of life issues were as significant an indictment of society's impoverished state as any other. For Stuart Hall: "No one expressed the fundamental and constitutive character of this argument for and within the New Left more profoundly than Raymond Williams."[3] At the Partisan discussion groups, Sunday film shows, lunch-time forums and ad hoc meetings seemed to reconstitute the pre-war atmosphere and hopes of Cambridge's Socialist Club. Eric Hobsbawm, who was inveigled into this "lunatic enterprise" despite his well-founded doubts, explained its contradictory dialectic of idealism and entrepreneurial hopelessness: "The large expensive tables and square chunky seats were designed to encourage drafting their chapters and long debates on tactics, while minimising the space for, and the rate of consumption of, income-generating customers."[4] The Coffee House advertised themselves in *ULR*, once with a picture of Joy and Raymond in the foreground in conversation with a friend. She and Joy are the ones drinking coffee. Raymond, his left elbow resting on his Notebook, looks in, not yet forty, framed by the modernity of a coming decade.

Even the recurrent round of teaching seemed to be confirming the pattern of change. For the first time, in 1958, the Delegacy's Annual Report stated flatly that the "increase in classes... has been entirely in the field of literature", and, sniffing the wind at last, that "People who regard adult education as being primarily concerned with the affairs of society need have no misgiving about this, for this intense interest in contemporary literature undoubtedly contains an important element of concern for society". That would have pleased the now veteran tutor but not at the expense of "Social Studies, including politics and economics" being "in the doldrums". Nor would another gain be happily offset by a loss: "One occupation which has once again increased its representation in classes is that of the "housewife", which now claims at 27% share... an increase to be welcomed... [but]... what must cause some concern is the decline in the proportion of men in classes". Darkly and rather myopically the Report observed that the "reason for this is obscure" and pointed to long hours and long distances, with just a glance at the institutional failure of Trades Unions to find a way to increase member participation.

Within a year Raymond Williams would be transferred to a Staff Tutor post in Oxford, bringing to an end his years as Resident Tutor in Sussex. Within a year of that, saddened by the continued rise of professional and managerial and training courses at the expense of the older dream of workers' liberal education, Williams would move to further the long revolution with which he became synonymous in the 1960s within the walls of Cambridge itself. That was part chance: the conjunction of his growing reputation and an available post, part disillusion and maybe the weariness of the itinerant tutor. It was also a part desire to engage directly and on his own terms with the central importance of "Cambridge English" to British intellectual life, for he still believed in that centrality; and, mostly it was that he could return to the University with the confidence of the man who had made himself into the measurer represented by "Matthew Price".

* * * * * *

It was not the end of exile from Cambridge that he wished to signal in the novel that was his greatest creative achievement. Nor through its crafting and writing up to the summer of 1958 did he yet see how its

447

organic shape still required a contrapuntal structure to make its ultimate feelings come through in so affecting a way. At the beginning of this final attempt he was clinging to the life rafts of previous ones. So, once more in the spring of 1958, he labelled the parts and confided them to a Notebook:

Border Village: 1920 – 1938
Our Lords the Moon and the Sun: 1938 – 45
The Grasshoppers: 1945 – 1955
The End of Exile: 1957 – 1958

What he intended for this last and soon to be renamed section, was the reintroduction in personal terms of all that he had become (or had come in a broader sense to represent) back into the world of common values which he intended his fiction to signify through the characterisation of his father. In a series of one-line jottings in a miniscule hand, almost as if they were inner confidences, he spelled it out as a disjointed puzzle:

The interaction of ideas and experience, in particular
(i) that ordinary social development, unknown by a man, is replacement of the father:
(ii) that ambiguity of attitudes (ambiguity of "replacement") to a father is known, and this reflected in social terms: attitudes, after instability, to class represented in father (the class as distinct from the father)
(a) idealisation (b) rejection

And then on, through society, neighbours, mother, son to:

(vi) intellectuals' separation of themselves (at least in phantasy). Complexity of this guilt, and the path that sections it. Of father's attitude, "that's your job". Virtue is not the work: not that "working" is better, but that the men lie [sic] equal. The future is in doing the different work.

The novel was to be 75,000 words long over twenty to twenty five episodes. He calibrated each episode to mark Morning: Afternoon:

Night. The son returns home to his dying father to be met at the station by his father's friend, Rosser. He confronts, in turn, the locations of "patch" and "village" along with the characters of his former life – Harry, Ellen, Morgan, past friends and neighbours – until at the end he leaves, as he has come, by the station which was not only his father's work place but point of both entry and departure for the son. Then, over a few more pages of notes, the tone of intent darkens into moody, enigmatic pages recalling the morphia-induced dreams of his father, giving details of the water supply that has, at last, come to Pandy, and of the threatened closure of the railway station and, perhaps, for it is hard to disentangle it, a kind of stream of consciousness from within himself – "never had the right kind of Oxonian miscellaneous mind, but that, the common theme; when you have specialised, how to bring your discipline back (is it discipline you call it; that seems right) and set it in whole. So we can talk about it. Perhaps." What is clear, from this anguish, is that he writes all this just after his father has died; when he re-casts the fictional sequence, again, it bears the title *A Common Theme* and the final return of Matthew Price ends with the exit of a funeral and the journey away to another home, another life. It had all been in the balance for such a long time.

The fine weather of the late summer of 1957 had seen Harry Williams back in his garden.[5] But only as a spectator. Gwen tended to the flowers and to her husband who seemed to grow stronger. Not strong enough to do more than contemplate an early retirement which, consulting with Jim over facts and figures and pensionable rights, he applied for in October. By the end of November the chest pains returned and so did his son: "Jim arrives home and although I am very ill, the fact of his coming helps us both.... I'm feeling better for having seen and talked to him." He was sixty-one on 30 November and on his birthday retired from the railway after forty seven years. He said he had no regrets other than that "ill health has caused it".

Before the year had ended Harry and Gwen finally saw the village, "at last", connected to the Rural District Council's water mains. Communal self-help was lessened but a community's worked-for well-being increased. Harry had always seen the connections. His son made the common water supply to the village a contentious issue for debate between the other inhabitants and the small farmers in *Brynllwyd*, where Colonel Claverley deplores the potential raising of the rates and Martin's grandfather speaks out against the lack of proper provision. That was a precise echo of a Ministry of Health enquiry held at the Parish Hall in Pandy in 1938 when the cost of a new water supply scheme, at £4,800, outraged ratepayers on the rural district council. So, as they had since before the First World War, villagers continued to receive their water from a privately owned supply which consisted of a stone intake tank at Glannant, with a line of pipes to various homes. This was the tank in *Border Country* whose muddied overflow system Harry Price deepens and lines with railway sleepers, and which he fences off with stakes to deter encroaching cattle. It was twenty years before a flow of clean uninterrupted water – with no more dependence on tarred water butts when the brook's water became a brown trickle – could be celebrated in the fiction as in the life. The small change of daily living was, as father and son agreed, the coin of greater meaning in the exchange between individual responsibilities, voluntarily taken up, and common duties, necessarily contracted for.[6]

Harry Williams opened his last diary, "The Gardener's Diary", in January 1958 and made his daily entries as usual. They were more brief but not entirely confined to noting the pain. Unexpected "spring-like" weather took him into the garden and for short walks. He paid his Club dues and registered the welcome calls of neighbours and friends. There were hours of severe pain at the end of the month. The hospital prescribed morphia. Thrombotic phlebitis was affecting his legs. They became swollen. The chest pains were "Terrible for days". Jim wrote and telephoned and on 1 March 1958 came to stay again, "and it had been lovely to see him". Following Jim's departure, Harry Williams was taken to Nevill Hall Hospital, Abergavenny, for the last time. Waking to consciousness he slashed with his biro across several days "Not properly remembered" and then, rallying slightly, made his last entries.[7] He died in Hospital on 21 March.

450

The end of that life had foreclosed the generational discussion. What Raymond had to consider now was prescribed by the finite limits that had arbitrarily called an end. His fiction needed to fix on that abrupt reality if it was to deposit the "common theme" that he felt had been emerging in lives that had been, sometimes wilfully, by themselves as well as by others, made separate. The novel shifted its stance again. It was now to be about the dominant figure of a returned "exile" who would, in often angry discussion with those left behind, find a reconciliation that also entailed moving on. The dying man, once protagonist in his pomp in *Border Village*, now moves off centre stage, his life and its purpose echoed in his son's thoughts and conversations with people from the past who prick the survivor into placing himself on a gamut between "nostalgia" and "idealisation". He wrote it down schematically once more: the arrival of Matthew Price at the station, to be met by Morgan Rosser, to be "re-introduced" to "The Patch", Matthew's wife and children, shadowy figures, pulled in by his dreams, waiting for his return from what he can no longer be to what he may not settle for. They are, at this sketchy level, the episodic entrances of the final Matthew in *Border Country* but here made linear and transparent. Raymond put aside the work for the summer, pencilling in an adjunct thought: "real points, but made in a vacuum; real issues, but in a language without breath. It is not blaming others; it is your chosen world. All going well up there? All going well? It is here, now, I must say it".[8]

More immediately he transferred the feelings gathering around his loss into the plangently personal tone of an essay he wrote that April for *Conviction*, a volume of essays edited by Norman Mackenzie of the *New Statesman*, in which there were also contributions from Richard Hoggart, Iris Murdoch, Hugh Thomas, Paul Johnson, Mervyn Jones and others committed to giving "Labour" a "new direction".[9] Raymond Williams' piece was one of the finest short essays he wrote, and this is no coincidence falling as it does between the death of his father and the publication of *Culture and Society* that autumn. The essay "Culture is Ordinary", alludes to the themes and arguments of that book but moves on to look directly at contemporary Britain and to affirm that the extension of culture (through expanding education, public subsidy of the arts and support of a press free from the dictates of advertisers, of regional provision of artistic consumption) is both vital and ordinary:

> The technical means are difficult enough, but the biggest difficulty is in accepting, deep in our minds, the values on which they depend: that the ordinary people should govern; that culture and education are ordinary; that there are no masses to save, to capture or to direct, but rather the crowded people in the course of an extraordinarily rapid and confusing expansion of their lives. A writer's job is with individual meanings, and with making these meaning common... the language changes but the voice is the same.

That is how he ended this declarative essay but he had begun it by placing himself back, on a journey, in his own country of the border, one of geographical and social frontiers, but also intellectual ones, and those between himself and his forebears. His repressed anger bursts through: "in no mood," he writes "as I walked about Cambridge, to feel glad that I had been thought deserving... no better and no worse than the people I came from... angry at my friends' talk about the ignorant masses" and he hits out at the excluding "centres of power" and notions that "contemporary culture" is "bourgeois culture". Finally, he sings in praise of what is not generally known because not felt in the experience of others:

> There is a distinct working-class way of life with its emphasis of neighbourhood, mutual obligation and common betterment, as expressed in the great working-class political and industrial institutions, [it] is in fact the best basis for any future English [sic] society. As for the arts and learning, they are... a national inheritance... available to everyone. So when the Marxists say that we are living in a dying culture, and that the masses are ignorant, I have to ask them, as I asked them then [in the 1940s], where on

earth they have lived. A dying culture, and ignorant masses, are not what I have known and see.

The later Raymond Williams, as did this one, found much of inestimable value in Marxist analysis of the relationships of power and of subservience, made and sustained by the production modes of capitalist society, but in this essay he is crushingly dismissive of any thought that the meanings of any culture (whether common or individual) can be prescribed: "they are made by living, made and remade in ways we cannot know in advance. To try to jump the future, to pretend that in some way you are the future, is strictly insane." The essay, poised between a convinced surety of thought and a teetering exploratory style, is, in this unexpected mode, his eulogy to his father, just as his novel will be an elegy for a whole way of life:

> Culture is ordinary: that is where we must start. To grow up in that country was to see the shape of a culture, and its modes of change. I could stand on the mountains and look north to the farms and the cathedral, or south to the smoke and the flare of the blast furnace making a second sunset. To grow up in that family was to see the shaping of minds: the learning of new skills, the shifting of relationships, the emergence of different language and ideas. My grandfather, a big hard labourer, wept while he spoke, finely and excitedly, at the parish meeting, of being turned out of his cottage. My father, not long before he died, spoke quietly and happily of when he had started a trade union branch and a Labour Party group in the village, and, without bitterness, of the "kept men" of the new politics. I speak a different idiom, but I think of these same things.

* * * * * *

The essay came out in October 1958 in the near wake of *Culture and Society* which Chatto and Windus issued for thirty shillings in its first big print and austere format in September. The book was, from the outset, a publishing phenomenon. It made Raymond Williams' name overnight. It ended the family's financial concerns at a stroke, its earnings eclipsing his salary. It was, in an idiom all could understand, a best-seller. It was reviewed in all the broad-sheet papers, magazines weekly and quarterly, in the provincial press and in academic journals. Almost without exception it split opinion, even in the highly favourable notices, into two sections: admiration for the long front end of essays on individual authors within the "tradition" he was now deemed to have discovered, and dismay at the uncouth, elbows and knees testament of belief. Within a few months he had read over 50,000 words of commentary on his book. He could not doubt that what had been a personal pressure had touched a general nerve. In 1979, he said that he no longer recognised the book as his own and that he would have, at that point, written it differently to the one that had come out twenty years previously; maybe, but in its own time he had confronted with that book a contemporary structure of feeling in the only way possible; that is to say, directly.

This stance is what gives the book its enduring freshness despite the occasional fusty stylistic tics of the time and the inevitable encroachment on its findings of fresh research, new ideas, different contextualisations and shifting intellectual pressure points. What comes through is the way the steady insistence of his thought puts him in the line of the thinkers he is questioning and how, at its end, he takes his own uncompromising stand. It may well lack the social historical detail which would have seen the ideas at its core put into a framework of material struggle but there is no doubt, from his incidental asides and his determined ending, that it was from within this context of struggle that he was writing.

By the end of September it had received heavy and respectful notice from *Tribune* to the *New Statesman* and the *Times Literary Supplement*. In October *The Manchester Guardian* hit what would be a constant note:

> About two thirds of this book consists of an admirably
> sympathetic exposition of the views of such as... Coleridge,

Mill, Ruskin and D H Lawrence... [on] the society in which they lived and the changes it underwent [but] the artist or the intellectual is in a relationship with the rest of society which can only be expressed in terms of "I" and "They". To maintain this is not to fall into the trap of art for art's sake. It is simply to protest against the employment of categories which are foreign to the very nature of thought or artistic creation.[10]

J.B. Priestley for the Labour *Reynold's News* did not like it either: it was overdone and too modish for the plain-spoken Yorkshireman. But it was gathering momentum, with tributes to his originality and seriousness – even if he was a little "muffled" in his thinking – by the *Daily Telegraph* and the *Sunday Times*. His publishers would have a field day plucking the best quotes from the critics of the *Observer*, *Spectator* and *The Economist*: the philosopher Stuart Hampshire; the historian Asa Briggs; the literary critic and his future Cambridge colleague, Frank Kermode; the Labour politician and intellectual gadfly, Richard Crossman; the novelist of the moment Angus Wilson. Some differed, mildly or profoundly, over his refusal of the concept of "masses" and "mob"; others doubted that equality of education could bridge the gap in "cultural standards" between people and only hoped for "better social relations"; others, like literary critic Arnold Kettle in *The Daily Worker* argued that Williams simply did not sufficiently understand how concentration on the abstraction of ideas was not enough but, nonetheless, welcomed a "Marxist contribution". Neither author nor book could have been more explicit about his disdain for abstraction in all traditions of thought but then few digested the complexities of *Culture and Society* at this first wide reading.

The Marxist historian, V.G. Kiernan, writing for *The New Reasoner*, devoted more pages to such a reading than most, but luxuriated in his own comparative depth of knowledge and delivered the standard Marxist answer of the time, one applauded by Edward Thompson, that "the great deficiency of the book is the lack of... historical fact – economic, social and political". If that seemed a harsh judgement when so much of that relevant history was yet to be written in 1958, including Thompson's own remarkable work of the early 1960s, Williams, though he may well have agreed with its thrust, would have wondered, yet again, if the attitude he struck in "Culture Is Ordinary" would ever penetrate the ideological skins of those such as Victor Kiernan, who grandly wrote of Williams' conclusion to the book ("his discursive tract for the times"):

> It is for all of us to ask whether our Welfare State with its cosy Happy Families atmosphere is supplying us with a genuine common culture or one more substitute for it, one new piece of Ersatz. Mr Williams does not gather up all the questions his enquiry raised. He leaves on one side, notably, the problem of the State, in order to concentrate on that of society and individual. His own philosophy comes out again in another dictum:
> "There are in fact no masses: there are only ways of seeing people as masses" – a difficult saying, and perhaps more an ideal for the future than a truth of past or present.

And there, perhaps, the Williams hackles that had been raised since the late 1930s would have risen again, the indignation mitigated only by the fact that the former Trinity College graduate and research Fellow, like so many others on that particular Left was, as Aneurin Bevan had once remarked of a local socialist opponent: "Strong on India. Strong on Africa... But weak on the subject of New Pits".

The reviews, short and long, kept appearing well into the spring of 1959, with notices in France, Italy, the USA, Australia and South Africa. Complexity of subject, and for some of style, was hammered home, but Williams had long known about the complexity and had decided it could not be short-circuited by more sectional definitions of "culture", nor could its importance, to his argument, be sidestepped by dilution of his broader social definitions. There was little, he decided, that he would have changed.

Of all the contemporary notices, two long review essays stand out for their precise sense of what had occurred: that of Graham Martin in *ULR* in the autumn number of 1958 and Richard Hoggart's piece in *Essays in Criticism* in April 1959. The younger man, Graham Martin, a close associate at Oxford of Stuart Hall, is more reverential, but sounds the true note of excitement at why his generation thought Williams' insights would have the impact they did indeed shortly claim. Hoggart, a near contemporary, stands aside from Williams' almost exclusive emphasis, as Hoggart saw it, on the virtues of working class experience but, with the inner understanding of each other they seemed to share, saw where Williams' drive to go forward would necessarily come from.

Graham Martin's heraldic trumpet note extended over six pages set out in three closely printed columns.[11] It was erudite and expository but, above all, it was impassioned. It claimed an understanding that other reviews had by-passed or rejected as too obscure, too demanding, too moralistic. Precisely, said Martin. What Raymond Williams is really doing in his study of these ideas about society and its culture is to show the "inadequacies of 'mind'... of 'thinking', of 'thought' to the contemporary socialist task. And the alternative is not 'feeling' but 'living': with all that implies, not only of the interpenetration of these two ways of experiencing, but, of what, only together they can express". This, he asserts, is the main business of *Culture and Society* and it is not merely a moral stress since the lived experience is Williams' key phrase. Once Martin has seen this, he can see the whole book as a challenge not only to the ideas of its readers but also to the genuine sincerity of their attachment to its demanding precepts of value, openness, change, extension of community through an expanding common culture not the atrophy of localised parochialism, its insistence that the path to a consistent empowerment is embedded within culture, that from common needs emerge real alternative courses and so an end to fantasy futures that occupy no actual ground. The peroration from within the heart of that part of a new left which was most congenial to him, takes the humanity of Williams head on; a working class valuation of human worth that comes directly out of its class experience and, by that very fact, goes beyond the damaging limits of class definition:

... the source of a positive stress, because the actual making of the unknown future "is always an exploration". We return... to an ultimate reverence not only for our own, but for every man's "lived experience", in the sharing and exploring of which we make our effort at "common understanding", at a "culture in common". The profound originality and scope of this analysis can hardly be overstated. Williams replaces the idea of "dominative" culture, good, bad or indifferent... by an idea of culture which accepts the "necessary complexity and difficulty of human affairs". As a utopian perspective it makes that vital acceptance....

[It is] a book whose full assimilation will not be soon: nor when it has been accepted in "our common understanding" will it be difficult to point to the changes that assimilation will have brought about. They are likely to go deep, and spread far. They need to.

Graham Martin's prophetic sense of the effect of *Culture and Society* was as precise as it was startling. Not even its author could have foreseen the way in which it would be such a spearhead in and eventually figure-head to the revolution of thinking and study about culture that was to come in the 1960s. Richard Hoggart sensed something else and that was where Williams had come from as a man as well as a thinker in a line of such thinkers:

There is an extraordinary sense of social change in the air today, and this has inspired a considerable amount of work by people who did not think of themselves, when they began to write, as taking part in any 'movement'. They were reacting to a common climate. We can see the results in, for example, some of the 'Angry Young Man' books, in the publications of the Institute of Community Studies, in my own *The Uses of Literacy*, in *Conviction*, in the *Universities Left Review* and in *The New Reasoner*. Here, too, *Culture and Society*'s importance can be... indicated: of all the work done on this theme during the present decade, it is the most solidly-based and intelligent.[12]

Just as Williams had expressed concerns over Hoggart taking detail for a general picture, Hoggart extended his reservations over Williams' generalities into specifics. Yet it was for Hoggart "sane and humanely" based against "narrowness", for all its driving energy of purpose. And here the spinner of stories from Yorkshire fingered the imaginative writer from Wales who twitched beneath the critical skin:

> *Culture and Society*... is an "intellectual's" book in the good sense in which we sometimes use that word. Yet what makes it quite unusually valuable is the lived-into combination of thought and feeling. This is the product not only of a mind well-equipped and well-controlled, but of one emotionally well-nourished.

Amongst all the praise and fame that came his way from the autumn of 1958 no one knew better than Raymond Williams where he wanted that emotion to take him. He wanted to show the "lived experience" and, through that alone, its meaning and he knew, as he had throughout, that only fictional reordering would let him do it. In 1958 he turned again to the shape and themes of his long-meditated fiction.

There are, in fact, two *Common Themes*, one extant as typescript fragments and the evolving other, finally re-labelled in the Notebooks, and there masquerading under the name of *Border Country*.[13] The latter is not yet the 1960 novel but, no more, and no less, than the strong hybrid he had re-grafted from *Border Village* and the first version of *Common Theme*, as he had once decisively renamed *The End of Exile*. The intention then was clear: to take Matthew Price home for rediscovery and reclamation. What seems to have happened, however, in this last fictional work-out was an iterative obsession with all that might have been, emotionally and psychologically, in order to make a life whole again. Over the autumn of 1958 with critical acclamation and reprintings of *Culture and Society* coming thick and fast after each other, he wrote himself into an imaginative cul-de-sac from which he could only retreat. In the end this was not to be about the intertwining of generational lives; it was to be about the full depicted reality of one sort of experience and the consciousness of its meaning. In the emerging Matthew Price, the academic historian who in *Border Country* would want "like a fool, to write the history of a whole people being changed", but would settle for knowing that he could "feel but not handle, touch but not grasp", he found a fiction not for his own character but for his life's distinction between the validity and typology of ways of knowing:

> To the nearest hundred, or to any usable percentage, my single figure is indifferent, but it is not only a relevant figure; without it the change can't be measured at all. The man on the bus, the man in the street, but I am Price from Glynmawr...[14]

The dedication to *Border Country*, carefully distancing itself from any traits of autobiography would read, on publication in December 1960: "I know this country, but the characters and events of the novel are imagined and are not intended to describe real people and events."[15]

But that of *A Common Theme* at the year's end in 1958, had read: "This is a country I know, and these are feelings I know, but the persons and events described exist only within the novel, and have no identity with real persons and events."[16]

To know the feelings was less of a disclaimer than his publisher required. As late as December 1959 Ian Parsons wrote to say "the main criticism that will be levelled against the book is that although it's presented as a novel it has more the 'feel' of autobiography and the development of the story is too protracted".[17] He paid little attention to Parsons' further reflections on "phrases which are very difficult to understand" because of "attempts to reproduce naturalistically the talk of inarticulate people" however "admirable" that might be. Nor did he pay attention to the publisher's equally inane view that the "flashbacks tell us little of value about Matthew's growing up as a boy". Patiently he had himself earlier expressed the view that he was "very willing to revise" since "it means too much to me to have any feeling of holding back from all necessary work".[18]

The main upshot of which was that he rewrote the "back story" of Matthew Price to introduce him, from the outset, as a university-based economic historian of eight years standing who is working on population movements into the South Wales Valleys at the onset of industrialisation. We learn he has a wife, Susan, to whom he will return at the book's end for a final ardent conversation about this turning point in his life, and two boys, Jack and Harry, named for grandfather and father, who will take life forward. In essence, they are explanation of what he has become and where he is now, but little else. The final, tauter novel of *Border Country* proceeds then without the fully tabulated emotional hinterland of Matthew Price, which he had made central to its immediate predecessor, *A Common Theme*. The loss of that fuller individual story, which Raymond Williams excised at his publisher's request, is the last instance of him writing himself out of any plot line that might proceed outside the location of Pandy/Brynllwyd/Glynmawr. What we have lost is decidedly not autobiographical fact but another species of feelings and of their expression, which lies at the heart of his biography. He cut the explanatory words because he had made the new connection:

> It was the history of the change, and he accepted the change, because his people accepted it. It was their story and he was only its voice.[19]

A Common Theme begins, not with Matthew running for a bus in London but with a train's rhythm abruptly changing as it crosses a bridge; the opening to the second section of the published *Border Country* but with changes of detail. Barry Island, not Tenby is in the compartment's faded photograph; Matthew is sweating with anxiety, and the phone call to home to inform him of his father's serious heart attack has been differently conveyed. He thinks of the network of communications:

> The lines back out of England: lines and voices. "Matthew Price", he had said curtly, when he had picked up the phone. But the name wasn't wanted (that efficiency unlearned). The number was wanted, and when he had confirmed it, he had been told to wait, the polite southern English voice echoing his own. The wait, and then suddenly

a Welsh voice: the operator at Newport, on a clear line. Back from him to the Abergrwyne operator, the same voice echoed. Back to Brynllwyd, and then a woman's voice, nervous and sudden.

A quarter past four: the call serious, evidently. Matthew listened intently to the distant voice, a Welsh voice, softened, from that valley of red earth under the Black Mountains. The border river ran from there, from Alltyrynys to Vowchurch; on the one side the Welsh voices, on the other the slow rich Herefordshire. In Brynllwyd, in his own family the voices met and mingled. Now, through the shock, Matthew heard his own voice shaping itself to the distant voice he remembered.

What follows, through various page versions in which "Sheila" becomes "Susan", is the basis of all the ultimate Matthew story on his return to Glynmawr. The conversations about class with Harry (something to live through but not to be narrowed to a sole character-isation of self) to those about ambition with Morgan Rosser (but not at the expense of a life lived in chosen settlement) highlight the picking-over-bone discursiveness that will mark out the cross-cutting of individual stories in the published *Border Country*. As soon as he completed *A Common Theme* in the autumn of 1958 he transferred its title to that ideal book of connections he had been, all along, seeking to write. The Notebooks tell the story of the interleaving of pages between *Border Village* and *Border Country*.

For the publisher there was the erasing of the difficult Welsh vowels and consonants of Brynllwyd and Abergrwyne into the reader-friendly ease of Glynmawr and Gwenton. But the melding process, even at this stage, would not prove to be as smooth as he had assumed in 1958, nor as straightforward as his memory would later have it. Quite soon, in fact, he ironed out in his mind the kinks in that process to what was some-thing other than the reality of composition. The personal chronology that he set down in his Notebooks at the time was added to – or expanded – by additional dates and facts written down later; it was in 1966 that he wrote "Autumn/Winter 58 Finish writing of *Border Country*".[20] That was a backward glance, a retrospective tidying up. It is indeed the case that the actual completion of *A Common Theme* came abruptly at the end of 1958, but *Border Country* would be a further, still alternate version made in 1959. Descriptive detail is thinned out and digressive contemplation vanishes but so, too, does the powerful and emotional charge which runs disturbingly through the marriage of Matthew and Susan Price.

Border Country of 1960 ends, in Chapter Three of Part Two, with Matthew's journey back to London, and to his wife Susan, after his father's death. *A Common Theme* of 1958, however, starts its Chapter Three with the same journey, and his uneasy observations of the eastern trajectory to Paddington and on to Matthew's sudden decision to visit Susan. This is a decision not a mere home-coming because, as we have learned early on in *A Common Theme*, they are separated and Matthew has a London flat where he lives and works. Almost sixty typescript pages give us none of the sense of closure in *Border Country* where "By measuring the distance, we come home". Instead, in passages that may have led to that measurement, since here in *A Common Theme* the father is desperately weak but not yet dead, we meet with a Matthew who has so far failed to reconcile his lost past with a newly begun future. Between him and his wife there is too much that he has left unrejected from the past for her to be willing to "take him back" in order for both to move on. She hears his words but distrusts their depth of disassociation. Matthew tells her of Eira Rosser, married (as in *Border Country*), to Dr John Evans:

> "... but then he had to go, on a call, and I was left with Eira. I could almost believe she'd arranged it; it seemed like that."
>
> "... Anyway," Susan interrupted, "you stayed. You stayed and you discussed each other's marriages."
>
> "Not just like that. I mean that was the awful part of it."
>
> "You told each other, in turn, just how your lives had gone wrong."
>
> "No," Matthew said.

"If you'd stayed together, in your own beautiful country, you'd both have been happy. You wouldn't even have had to grow up."

The possibilities of love which Matthew and Eira might have fully shared in *Border Country*, and whose continuing reverberation between the two of them in his mother's machinations Matthew so resents in the published version of 1960, is here in 1958 much more brutally explicit as Susan lays it bare:

> "How much did she want?" she asked, smiling.
> "What do you mean?" Matthew said quickly...
> "I mean what: a divorce, an affair, an odd meeting while her husband's at surgery? What?"
> "It wasn't like that," Matthew said. "You're implying it's my fault, as usual."
> "I expect she helped," Susan said. "So tell me. What?"
> "She said she had wanted my child," Matthew said, wryly.

Whatever was being used by Williams from his own past – alternative lives, different directions, his mother's abiding disaffection for Joy – and transmuted into a fiction to show graphically, through physical separation, a psychological torment far removed from the less disturbed figure of Matthew in *Border Country*, these pages are without precedent in Raymond Williams' fiction to this point. It is impossible not to believe directly in some of the anguish this fictional Matthew Price confides to his wife:

> "... What made me really angry was her keeping up a sort of alliance with my mother. Writing, visiting, passing photographs. That, after all my mother had said."
> "Yes, of course," Susan said indifferently.
> "You don't care, either way," Matthew said angrily. "You resent my even going to see this woman."
> "Which woman?" Susan asked, looking at him...
> "I went to see my father," he said slowly.
> "Yes," Susan said.

She stood with her hand on the back of a chair. She looked very tired, suddenly, and her face was much older.

"He said about his pain," Matthew said, turning away. "Like a fist gripping him, where he didn't know he was.... It was like that with me, but without his reason. It seemed, almost that I have never felt anything before."

Susan said nothing, but pushed her hand at her eyes, quickly, before looking away.

"Only then," Matthew said, "I was suddenly frightened. I felt, so deeply, the most compelling, terrible aggression. I actually wanted to hit him. To hit him, as he lay there helpless. And it came from far down, from where I was feeling I would give my whole body to save him. I did feel that. I sat on the bed, and felt the pain into me, trying to relieve him. And there, where I could feel this moving, I felt this command to hurt him."

At the conclusion of a second visit to Susan, a friendlier meeting but no more satisfactory, he leaves his house promising to "keep in touch" about his father's illness, and the "street as he walked away, was like a street of the dead". The assumption must still be that A Common Theme would have united the couple in the pain after the father's death. The way in which Raymond Williams takes such a tortuous fictional path in 1958 before in 1960 dismissing all such by-ways remains intriguing. In the 1958 version of A Common Theme/Border Country almost all of Matthew's further meditations on the relationship between a personal father and a social father, or even the notion of a man being fortunate if his life and his work are the same have their origins in discussions he has in a pub, near the British Museum and Matthew's bachelor flat, with Edward Dallas, an historian who had once taught him, and Philip Devereux, a novelist, who is about to go to live in "Crasmont" in the Black Mountains.

With this threesome, who appear together here but nowhere else, it is again the contemporary "gap in our consciousness... dangerously wide, between formal ideas and actual feelings" that is batted around in talk, which for Matthew moves too close to his own dilemmas:

[Matthew] looked away, seeing the bare church under the Holy Mountain: the church he had walked to, three times each Sunday, until at fifteen he had refused confirmation.

"What he's actually thinking about," Edward said pleasantly, "is himself and his father."

"No," Matthew said impulsively.

"... He's fortunate, essentially," Edward said to Philip. "His life and his work have a common theme."

"What theme?" Philip said.

"It's common enough," Edward said easily.

"A man as he grows must replace his father. But there are barriers to this: some necessary, some contingent."

"Why replace?" Matthew said quickly. "Why not simply succeed?"

"... Sure," Edward said. "But... What I mean about class is this... a man succeeds to his father in a personal sense.... But he succeeds to him also, in a social sense, or he may do so. In a period of exceptional mobility, like our own."

"No," Matthew said, "this isn't a period of exceptional mobility."

"People think so," Edward said. "And that's more important than the actual degree of movement."

"I don't agree. This is quite a rigid society, all the paths quite clearly defined," Matthew said. "... In the Industrial Revolution people didn't know what would happen to them, didn't know where they might finish. Now, by and large, they do. A degree of mobility has been organised, and beyond that there's nothing much."

"Look," Edward said, pointing "it's the same in effect... where there is movement at all, this crisis arises. That a man doesn't succeed to his father, but goes away in another direction. This is the actual tension... And Matthew can verify this. It's what he's thinking about it. That in a case like his a man has a personal father, but no social father. These boys leave home, go among different people, do quite different work. Instead of taking over from a father, they're out on their own."

Edward Dallas stays in the pub to drink away the afternoon. Matthew heads for the British Museum to work on his documents, to study "actual growth... its consequences, in our actual relations", as an historian who can, by so looking, "see it so clearly". What he confesses to Philip, the novelist born in Richmond who has set up home in Matthew's own country, is that he cannot see this at all when he looks through his own eyes. Then he sees only "Others, the mass, the faceless crowd" that has become "the common image". Philip suggests it is because "We value the individual... we hate crowds; we want to get away on our own", only to be told, in turn, that "we can't... if we are to stay alive". The two men who have just met and will soon part are, it seems, the most powerful elements of all Raymond Williams' dualities:

> Philip hesitated, and then spoke, looking at Matthew.
> "What you're saying, you know, leaving the abstractions aside, is that you want to go back, to go home. Then why not admit it? Why not simply go?"
> "No," Matthew said. "It has all gone too deep. Every feeling, every idea, that actually moves us, comes back, in the end, to this same thing. All we value, essentially, is the act of breaking away. Our whole effort is to distinguish ourselves, to feel separate, to get clear. We value the individual, but the individual himself is divided, by this perpetual pressure. We see not individuals, but crowds, classes, social types, categories. All our thinking and feeling is in these final terms."
> "We stick to the few we can know," Philip said.
> "And reject the others, that is the point. But we cannot reject them. The growth is common or nothing."
> "You mean about class," Philip said.
> "This is a class society, but that is only a first term. We start from the masses, the faceless crowd, and we maintain class divisions to interpret this crowd, to give us the

467

illusion of knowing others. A society without class would be more than we could bear, till we have solved this."

"And you think you can solve it?" Philip said, smiling.

"I understand it historically," Matthew said. "I'm trying to write it. But I know really, that all the work's still to do. Till it has happened in me, this movement, I can do very little."

"What, seriously, could happen?" Philip asked, bluntly. "I mean, this is an ordinary deadlock, as we live now. We cannot know all the others. We are bound, in the end to resent their pressure on us."

"We can break the image," Matthew said.

"We can change, commit ourselves, see ourselves where we are, in this actual crowd. See others in new ways by being ourselves in this way, in an actual equality of being."

* * * * * *

Raymond Williams' 1958 novel *A Common Theme* became *Border Country*, the masterpiece of his fiction, by taking away these boulders of introspection to allow his narrative of the "Patch" and also its people to flow, less hindered by the stumblestones which are also the keystones of a biographical enquiry into the making of a man's mind through the diversionary tributaries of his life. It is, after all, why he valued fiction, above all. In the novels he fashioned there would be a unifying again of the overlapping fluidity of a life and mind, since, as he had once put it, "while we may... separate out particular aspects of life and treat them as if they were self contained it is obvious that this is only how they may be studied not how they were experienced".[21] In showing that experience, Williams had to split the elemental atoms into the divisions that would allow him imaginative fission – Harry and Morgan, Matthew and Will, Jim and Raymond, and perhaps the two men who meet in these unpublished papers of *A Common Theme* and go their different, yet similar and maybe in the ultimate sense, indivisible ways, signified by the work and the life of Raymond Williams from Pandy:

They had reached the street behind the Museum, and the steps were not far ahead, where they would go in and separate.

"Well after it all," Philip said, smiling, "we arrive at the Museum."

"Yes," Matthew said and laughed.

"And you like it, you know. You like to get in there, away from the street and from people. You like to get work on your desk, papers and books, that you can draw some order from…. My own work's different."

"… There is a language between them. A common language," Matthew said quickly.

Philip smiled, and they walked on together, into the great building.

"Before the silence comes down," Philip said.

"I'm holding you to that promise. You'll come and see us when you're next in Brynllwyd."

"I'm not sure when I shall be there," Matthew said.

"But when you are, come," Philip said.

"I'll try."

Philip looked at him and smiled with affection. "And just one last thing," he said. "It isn't my business, but you're breaking yourself with this problem. Breaking yourself, and you know it can't really be solved. Why not give up, as we all do? Accept the real terms, then clear your own space and live within it."

"I tried," Matthew said. "That's part of it."

"…You've the face of a peasant," Philip said quickly, "but of a peasant turned aristocrat. I'll call you that: the reluctant aristocrat."

"Does it matter?" Matthew said, confused.

"You've been talking about looking at people," Philip said, smiling. "Now go on. Go in there. Go and draw your rents."

Matthew hesitated, and then laughed easily.

"I'll see you," he said, and moved away, raising his hand.

"This actual growth"

At this border in his life Raymond Williams wrote a Conclusion for the 1961 publication of *The Long Revolution* in which he reflected, in the personal voice to which his later readers would grow accustomed, on the intersection of experience and growth over known generations. It was a sign-post back and a direction-finder forward. He chose not to publish it. It lay unmarked amongst his papers. It appears here, then, with a serendipity I can only regard as fated. It looks to the past to find a future, as relevant now as it was then, of ever extending the possibilities and capacity for human growth.

* * * * * *

"For a boy it was different: to stand on the mountain, to watch history live in bridge and castle and furnace, and the men working in the fields below, and the home to go back to, where a future had been decided, to go out from that valley to teachers and books. Now, with a different experience, that settlement is a memory: it had to be broken to grow. For questions of fact, this authority, that discipline, to consult. For judgements, the continuous public debate, the grouping into parties and tendencies, the quick exchange and reiteration of the deciding phrase. And then to sit in the swaying train, the voices dispersed yet a few remembered, the majority of the print on its way to litter, and the city darkening as the train gathers speed, unknown people standing along bare platforms, the neon advertisement and the lighted dome of the cathedral, the noise of the diesel and the lines of lamps. There, suddenly, is a new kind of silence, and the answers fade, the deciding phrases are forgotten, the categories break. It is now the silence of midnight, when truth is said to emerge. The truth of midday, as we jerk in action, is as valid as that. The question is the same: what kind of country is this that we live in?

"If I look in one direction, I see a particular country whose past and present I feel I am beginning to understand. It is people I see first, and

470

of my own family. The long revolution has changed us, very markedly. I cannot go back beyond my grandfathers, and that, in time, is not far. 'The Greek legislator', Bagehot wrote, 'had not to combine in his polity men like the labourers of Somerset and men like Mr Grote... We have'. In my own polity, the combination is given in experience. I remember these men, both farm workers, and I cannot think or feel like Bagehot and his successors. They were of the first generation, in my family, to have votes, and I remember their descriptions of how they used them, and their shrewd and moving descriptions of men and work, in ways that leave no regret that they were neither Grote nor Bagehot. The Greek legislator in fact excluded the slaves, as beyond consideration. I have to start from the position that my own people, like the slaves, were excluded by a similar convention. I cannot play the game of wondering in what decade of the past I would have been happiest. Whether it is the high civilisation of Athens, or the mediocre civilisation of Victorian England, I start, in experience, from the position of the excluded, because that, throughout, had been the condition of my people. This alters my view of past and present, and cuts it off from the formulations of most of those who would instruct me. It was not a risk, a flirtation with Demos, when my grandfathers were given the vote. It was not an extension to the masses when they had the chance to go to school for a few years, the chance to write and read. I think, not of their lowness, but of the selfishness and indifference of those who had excluded them. Thus the long revolution, the growth of democracy and education, is to us wholly gain. It is not only the vote, the schools, the cheap papers and books. They mattered, for I saw how the vote was valued; I know how the leaving-age of eleven for my grandfathers became thirteen for my father, and for me, if not for my friends, was indefinitely extended; I have watched the local weekly, carefully read in my grandparents' cottages, supplemented by daily papers, magazines, and a few books in my father's cottage, and where I grew up in a home where seven books were owned, my children grow up with all they need. But the change has been more than this: more than an expansion in my now characteristic world of reading, education and politics. More than the vote has been the growing security at work. My father's father was turned out of his cottage in his fifties, and had to work on the roads. My mother's father, at sixty-five, had his wages docked by the precise amount of the new pension, and was given rougher work to correspond. My father's mother, bringing up eight children on fifteen shillings a week, was dying of cancer when she picked stones in the fields, at a shilling a cartload. I have too many relatives and friends, of my own generation, to be able to suppose that all this is ended, though I know that it is less. A cousin who shared my bed as a boy finds the sacks he has to load and unload, as a lorry-driver, suddenly increased in weight to two hundredweight. He accepts this, because he is a patient man, though I can see it ageing him. Not to accept it would take him at once into the world of strikes and unions, which he is not used to, and I have to think of this when I hear strikes and unions abused, by more than I want of the people I now meet and read. When my father died, after a heart-attack in his signal-box where he had been working twelve-hour shifts, I got two papers that I keep and read: a barely literate testimonial from the first farmer who employed him, at fourteen, saying he was 'a honest and trustworthy lad'; a typed letter, at the end of his railway service, arriving after he was dead, from a man in London I might meet, who could not spare a 'Mr' to a man he didn't know, but wrote 'Dear Williams', before the customary leaving phrases, as to a known inferior. This much of it persists, and because it is so, because dignity and loyalty and strength are still abused, I do not believe that the long revolution is over, but I know that gains have been made, and I honour the organizations and methods that made, defend, and seek to extend them. As I look at the improvements and changes, the human growth that is the reality of the long revolution, I see a country I love and a country that commits me. It makes sense, this history of an expanding culture and a more humane society. If the growth has been slow and uneven, still its pattern is evident. I see men of my own kind giving their lives to this effort. I see men differently bred moved by a general humanity to think of growth and to work for it. I find as much brotherhood, now, with the men I meet and read of in education, in medicine, in science as with the labourers and mechanics, of my own family and place, more harshly committed to the effort of keeping this growth going. Everything that I understand of the history of the long revolution leads me to the belief that we are still in its early stages. There, in a particular generation, is the vision and communication of a new possibility, the perception of a new human pattern. By struggle and by service an expectation is defined and eventually realised. By others, at the same time, the expectation is derided and resisted; not least, sometimes, by the men and women who would grow when the new pattern was actual. And then when after all it is realized – when it is accepted, for example, that the poor need to write – so often the ceiling that had seemed so high is there pressing on us, keeping our heads down, because we have grown to it. To break out from that, to set new expectations, is as hard as it ever was. The creative effort is always now; the earlier creations have been communicated and accepted. But the mind falls into the groove of habit: just as most radicalism is retrospective ('those were terrible injustices, there are no injustices now') so most of our thinking about growth is limited to what we have known ('everybody goes to school to fifteen'). To understand this process is to make the long revolution active. It is to see it as growth in every mind, as well as growth in the society. It is easy to think of the present as a plateau, and to give all one's energy to admiring it and looking back down the slopes we have climbed. Yet we have not climbed them; they were climbed for us, by our fathers and their fathers. I do not see, in this altered country, any permanent level. I see a pattern of growth that is still early: in education, in literacy, in relations at work, in the quality of ordinary living. I see powerful forces for growth and against it, and then it is easy to move into the language of struggle. I see also, however, in my ordinary work, a country in which there is great tolerance, goodwill and decency, often tied, it is true, to very moderate expectations, but devoted and practical, and by me deeply respected. I am used to being told, sometimes by these men, sometimes of course by the active crabbers (whom I would not like to have to convince, even in the middle of the twentieth century, that the poor need to write), that this sense of human possibility, this conviction of growth, is set too high. From many people I accept this; it cannot be proved, either way; only experience will settle it. And indeed it does not matter, if it is accepted at least that the growth is incomplete, that there is at least one more stage of the long revolution to go ('everybody will attend school till sixteen – a little later on'). This is still the country I love and am committed to, and these are men I can work with. It fits the way I see things, looking in one direction. There is the record, of this actual growth."

A Note On Sources

Detailed references to all the primary and secondary material I have used or consulted, as well as to interviews conducted and correspondence with the author can be found in the Notes to each chapter. Below I list the overall name and location of primary documentation and the books about or around Raymond Williams which I have found most useful, if only sometimes in a negative hair-pulling fashion. But I begin with the list, to 1961, of his own principal published works which I have chosen to separate by chronology of original publication date rather than by genre – a decision which readers of this book to this point will now understand.

Books by Raymond Williams to 1961

Reading and Criticism, London: Frederick Muller, 1950.
Drama from Ibsen to Eliot, London: Chatto and Windus, 1952.
Preface to Film (with Michael Orrom), London: Film Drama, 1954.
Drama in Performance, London: Muller, 1954.
Culture and Society, 1780-1950, London: Chatto and Windus, 1958.
Border Country, London: Chatto and Windus, 1960.
The Long Revolution, London: Chatto and Windus, 1961.

and see *Politics and Letters: Interviews with New Left Review,* London: Verso, 1979.

The most useful bibliographical companion to all his published work, though it now needs some updating, is the still indispensable:
Alan O'Connor, *Raymond Williams: Writing, Culture, Politics,* Oxford: Blackwell, 1989.

In order to sample his work at some length and in some guided depth, new readers in Williams could do no better than to go to:

John McIlroy and Sallie Westwood, eds. *Border Country: Raymond Williams in Adult Education,* Leicester: NIACE, 1993.

John Higgins, ed. *The Raymond Williams Reader,* Oxford: Blackwell, 2001.

Daniel Williams, ed. *Who Speaks for Wales? Nation, Culture, Identity: Raymond Williams,* Cardiff: University of Wales Press, 2003.

Primary Sources

Raymond Williams Papers	Swansea University
Chatto and Windus Files	University of Reading
BBC Written Archives	Caversham
War Diaries 21st Anti Tank Regiment	Royal Artillery P.R.O.
Papers of 21st Anti Tank Regiment	Royal Artillery Museum, Greenwich
Records of Dept. of External Studies	Bodleian Library, Oxford
Raymond Williams Collection	National Library of Wales

Books Relating to Raymond Williams

Since his death in 1988 there have been countless symposia, seminars, lectures, conferences, theses and academic articles about Williams and his legacy. There are Annual Lectures in his name under the auspices of the National Institute for Continuing Education and at the Hay-on-Wye International Literature Festival. The Raymond Williams Society supports seminars, lectures and publications in his name which build on his work, as he would have wished, with critical and challenging intent. There is every sense that this work, in all its aspects, from both explanatory and contradictory viewpoints, will continue to intrigue and inspire. The following is a more selective list of books that deal directly with either the life or work of Raymond Williams:

J.P. Ward, *Raymond Williams,* Cardiff: University of Wales Press, 1981.

Jan Gorak, *The Alien Mind of Raymond Williams,* Columbia: University of Missouri Press, 1988.

Southern Review: Literary and Interdisciplinary Essays Special Issue: Raymond Williams, Vol. 22 No. 2, July 1989. Guest Editors Bronwen Levy and Peter Otto.

Terry Eagleton, ed. *Raymond Williams: Critical Perspectives,* Cambridge: Polity Press, 1989.

Tony Pinkney, *Raymond Williams,* Bridgend: Seren, 1991.

Dennis L. Dworkin and Leslie G. Roman, eds. *Views Beyond the Border Country: Raymond Williams and Cultural Politics,* London: Routledge, 1993.

W. John Morgan and Peter Preston, eds. *Raymond Williams: Politics Education Letters,* London: Macmillan, 1993.

John Eldridge and Lizzie Eldridge, *Raymond Williams: Making Connections,* London: Routledge, 1994.

Christopher Prendergast, ed. *Cultural Materialism: On Raymond Williams,* Minneapolis: University of Minnesota Press, 1995.

Fred Inglis, *Raymond Williams,* London: Routledge, 1995.

Tom Steele, *The Emergence of Cultural Studies: Adult Education, Cultural Politics and the English Question,* London: Lawrence and Wishart, 1997.

Jeff Wallace, Rod Jones and Sophie Nield, eds. *Raymond Williams Now: Knowledge, Limits and the Future,* London: Macmillan, 1997.

John Higgins, *Raymond Williams: Literature, Marxism and Cultural Criticism,* London: Routledge, 1999.

Terry Eagleton, *The Gatekeeper: A Memoir,* London: Allen Lane, 2001.

Stephen Woodhams, *History in the Making: Raymond Williams, Edward Thompson and Radical Intellectuals 1936 – 1956,* London: Merlin, 2001.

Notes

INTRODUCTION

1 Typescript prepared for *Midcentury Authors* (New York) 1966 in Raymond Williams Papers, thereafter as RW Papers.

2 See Raymond Williams, *Politics and Letters: Interviews with New Left Review* (London: Verso, 1979), pp. 295-6 where, contemplating his "more conscious Welshness", he added that "Welsh intellectuals offer recognition of the whole range of my work, which literally none of my official English colleagues has seen a chance of making sense of".

3 Letter from Raymond Williams to Norah Smallwood, 5 Apil 1959. Chatto and Windus Files, University of Reading.

4 Raymond Williams to Ian Parsons, 2 November 1959. Chatto Files.

5 See suggested cuts in letter from Ian Parsons to Raymond Williams 7 December 1959. Chatto Files.

6 *Midcentury Authors*, op. cit. 1966.

7 See various Files of historical notes compiled by Joy Williams in RW Papers. Joy Williams (1918-91) kept the cottage in Craswall in the Black Mountains which they had bought in the early 1970s, but it was too remote for her to live in and she bought, after his death, a house in Abergavenny where she briefly lived before her death from an untreatable brain tumour in a Cardiff hospital in 1991.

8 Raymond Williams, *Loyalties* (London: Chatto and Windus, 1985), p. 293.

9 See R.W. Johnson 'Moooovement' in *London Review of Books*, 8 February 1990. Johnson, a South African political scientist then based in Oxford, never let this bone go; though in the case of Neil Kinnock who was unremittingly thought to possess neither the education nor the intellect to become Prime Minister, Johnson was at least pitch perfect about that politician's accent. And nothing else.

10 John Higgins, *Raymond Williams: Literature, Marxism and Cultural Materialism* (London: Routledge, 1999), p.9.

11 John McIlroy and Sallie Westwood (Eds.), *Border Country: Raymond Williams in Adult Education*, (Leicester: NIACE, 1993), p. 17.

12 Plaid Cymru Membership Card, 1969. RW Papers. And see Raymond Williams interview with Phil Cooke, 1984, where he says, in rather flexible mode: "In the 1960s and 1970s I felt close to the arguments being put forward by nationalists leading up and during the devolution debate [i.e. to 1979]. I even joined the Welsh party [sic] for a year or two; however, I

found it difficult to discharge my obligations living at a distance from Wales. I felt my thinking on culture and community was more reflected there than in the nationalism in Wales, especially its traditional difficulty with adhering to fully socialist principles of common ownership... I was told at the time by those inside and outside that I was idealising it, but many of its ideas remain closer to me than those of the contemporary Labour Party. I think there was just a coming together – a tendency and a movement on the ground developing against centralism". Re-printed in Daniel Williams [Ed.], *Who Speaks for Wales? Nation, Culture, Identity: Raymond Williams* (Cardiff: University of Wales Press, 2003), p. 206.

13 Interviews by Dai Smith with Joy Williams and with Stephen Heath, Patrick Parrinder, Bob Woodings, Terry Eagleton, Ian Wright and David Holbrook in October/November 1990.

14 Michael Rustin argues in 'The Long Revolution revisited' that the continued relevance of Williams' ideas lies in his "imaginative mode of understanding" which takes us beyond the notion of the working class as the incubator of social advance to the sense of the values that were attached to its aspirations being common to the potential of all citizens: "We can most valuably take from Raymond Williams the idea of a "whole way of life" as potentially subject to continuous learning and remaking over time. His conception of socialism as universal human creativity and agency based in cooperative and democratic social relationships, transcends its historical origin in the experience of industrial labour". *Soundings: A journal of politics and culture*. Issue 35 April 2007. London: Lawrence and Wishart.

15 Unpublished Ms. pages of *Border Country*. RW Papers.

1. A SETTLEMENT

1 Harry Williams Testimonials, 1913. RW Papers.

2 Raymond Williams, *Politics and Letters: Interviews with New Left Review* (London: New Left Books 1979), p. 26.

3 I am grateful to Merryn Willilams for information from her own research into her early family history.

4 Harry Williams, various First World War documents, RW Papers.

5 Loose four-page diary note of Harry Williams, 1918, RW Papers.

6 This, and the following extracts, are taken from a 1919 pocket diary kept by Harry Williams from late 1918 to December 1919. No other diary was kept, or more likely survived, until 1929. Then, with some gaps, he kept a diary intermittently until his death.

7 Raymond Williams, *Politics and Letters*, pp. 26-27.

8 Raymond Williams, *Border Country* (Cardigan: Parthian, Library of Wales Edition, 2005) pp. 36-7.

9 Raymond Williams, *People of the Black Mountains*, Vol. I (London: Chatto and Windus, 1989) p. 2.

10 David Tipper, *Stone and Steam in the Black Mountains* (Abergavenny: Blorenge Books, 1985).

11 *The Hereford Journal*, 26 July 1926.

12 Letter from Brinley Griffiths to Dai Smith, 30 October 1991.

13 Brinley Griffiths, 1991.

14 Letter from Maelor Griffiths to Dai Smith, 24 September 1991.

15 Raymond Williams, *Politics and Letters*, p. 67.

16 Letter from Ray Fawkes to Dai Smith, June 1993.

17 Charles Price in *Abergavenny in the Twentieth Century* (Abergavenny: Civic Society, International Publication, 1992) p. 106.

18 Letter from Maelor Griffiths to Dai Smith, October 1991.

19 Anna Tucker, *Abergavenny in Old Photographs* (Monmouth: Abergavenny Museum Services Publications, 1992); Anna Tucker in *Abergavenny in the Twentieth Century*; W. W. Tasker, *The Merthyr, Tredegar and Abergavenny Railway* (n.d.).

20 Raymond Williams, "Culture is Ordinary" (1958), reprinted in R. Gable (Ed.) *Resources of Hope* (London: Verso, 1989). He repeated the joke in *Politics and Letters*, p. 36. The man in question, a fellow undergraduate, and then a fellow Army Officer, was Lord Carrington.

21 Philip Lovell, untitled essay in *Abergavenny in the Twentieth Century*, p. 66.

22 Peter Coleman, untitled essay in *Abergavenny in the Twentieth Century*, p. 132.

23 Interview with ex-railwayman and local historian, Albert Lyons, by Dai Smith 1992.

24 Raymond Williams, *Politics and Letters*, p. 35.

25 *Ward Lock and Co's South Wales* (London: Ward Lock and Co's Illustrated Guide Books), pp. 44, 47.

26 *Abergavenny Chronicle,* 21 May 1926.

27 *Abergavenny Chronicle,* 7 May 1926. The Band, subsidised by the Council, was later reprimanded for their daring musical choice.

28 *Abergavenny Chronicle,* 11 June 1926.

29 "The Social Significance of 1926", originally a lecture given to Llafur: Welsh Labour History Society in 1976 on the fiftieth anniversary of the General Strike, was reprinted in R. Gable (Ed.) *Resources of Hope*.

30 Harry Williams' notepaper, headed "May 1926". RW Papers. In the published novel, and daft predecessors, he uses and quotes almost

verbatim contemporary documents cited in the pioneering work, W.H. Crook *The General Strike* (Chapel Hill: University of North Carolina, 1931). I trace his historical sources and follow his literary meanderings in detail in my "From 'Black Water' to *Border Country*: Sourcing the Textual Odyssey of Raymond Williams" in Katie Gramich (Ed.) *almanac - a yearbook of welsh writing in english: critical essays* (Parthian 2008).

31 Interview with Lew Griffiths, Pandy, 1992. This was the view shared by the Griffiths brothers, Brinley and Maelor, on reading the novel. They were adamant it was *not* the Alderman Rosser who was identified as a possible original in Fred Inglis' *Raymond Williams* (1995). Letter from Brinley Griffiths to Dai Smith, 29 Feb 1996.

32 Raymond Williams, *Politics and Letters*, p. 282.

33 Raymond Williams, "The Social Significance of 1926" (1976).

34 Raymond Williams, "The Social Significance of 1926" (1976).

2. A SCHOOLING

1 *The Hereford Journal*, June 1926. Local information.

2 H.M.I. Reports; 1903, 1913, 1938 and 1949.

3 Monmouthshire Education Committee: Admission Register; School Log Book, Pandy, 22 June 1925.

4 School Log Book, Pandy, 31 October 1900.

5 Raymond Williams, *Politics and Letters*, p. 28.

6 School Log Book, Pandy, 1 March 1921.

7 School Log Book for 1920s. Reports and notes varied in detail and length.

8 Interviews with former pupils, Bill Berglund and Violet James. Letter from Brinley Griffiths to Dai Smith, 1991. He was the first of Davies' pupils to pass the scholarship exam and wrote that pupils had a knowledge of Charles Dickens before they left school.

9 School Log Book, 1 September 1925.

10 School Log Book, 1925-29.

11 Raymond Williams, *Politics and Letters*, pp. 28-29.

12 School Log Book, Pandy, 1918.

13 Letter from Ray Fawkes to Dai Smith, 1993.

14 Interview with Sylvia Bird, neé Williams, 1989.

15 Letter from Maelor Griffiths to Dai Smith, 1991.

16 Interview with Sylvia Bird; information from Ray Fawkes, 1993.

17 School Log Book, Pandy, 11 September 1925.

18 Harry Williams' diaries, 1929-39.

19 Cymreigyddion y Fenni was The Society of Welsh Scholars of Abergavenny,

established in 1833 to promote Welsh literature, harp playing and the "native industries" of making woollens and hats. It thrived under aristocratic patronage. Long after its own local eisteddfod had ceased, the National Eisteddfod visited the town in 1913. See Chris Barber, *The Seven Hills of Abergavenny* (Abergavenny: Blorenge Books, 1992), pp. 97-98.

20 Unpublished typescript, *Border Village* pp. 195-197; 202-204. RW Papers.

21 Harry Williams' diaries 1929-39

22 Raymond Williams, untitled essay in Frederic Raphael (Ed.) *Bookmarks* (London: Quartet Books, 1975), pp. 163-5.

23 Copies can be found in RW Papers. *Macklin of the Loyals* was written by Michael Poole, a near equivalent of the "Michael Pope" which Williams would use as a journalistic by-line at Cambridge and then during the Second World War.

24 Raymond Williams, *Politics and Letters*, p. 27.

25 Ibid, pp. 24-25.

26 See *The Hereford Journal*, 1926; the plaque on the gate of St Michael's Church in Llanfihangel Crucorney; *Crucorney Church News : In Memoriam: The Rev. J.A. Hughes* (1884-1967); and interviews with Sylvia Bird, Bill Berglund and Merryn Williams.

27 Raymond Williams, *Border Country* (Library of Wales Edition), pp. 275-281.

28 I am grateful for sight of a copy of Grahame V. Nelmes "A History of King Henry VIII's Boys' Grammar School at Abergavenny: Parts I and II".

29 I am indebted to S.G. Cooper's *The Provision of Secondary Education in Abergavenny* 1902-6. Unpublished M.Ed. Thesis. University of Wales, Cardiff, 1980.

30 See *The Gobannian,* 11 January 1939.

31 Raymond Williams, "In Memory of A. L. Ralphs", *The Gobannian*, 21 (November. 1961).

32 Harold Sharpe, "Our Contributors", *The Gobannian,* 21 November 1961.

33 Wales Joint Education Committee Records: Central Welsh Board Results, 1936 and 1938. In view of his later interests, though it is not known whether he answered these particular set questions, two of the general essay topics were: "The popularity of detective novels" and "The influence of broadcasting in drama". CWB Higher Certificate Examination in English, July 1938.

34 Raymond Williams, *Politics and Letters*, p. 30.

35 Ibid.

36 There are seventeen non-consecutive pages of *Mountain Sunset* written in the red ink he used in 1939. These may be from the novel he later described

but, here, consist of widely scattered bucolic scenes, some comic and some melodramatic.

37 Ms. copy of play in Raymond Williams papers. This dates the writing as taking place in autumn 1938, with the first production in April 1939. A note diary kept by Raymond Williams gives 19 May as the date of the second performance.

38 Raymond Williams, "Two Views of Geneva", *The Gobannian* 10, January 1938. And see Peter Conradi *Iris Murdoch: A Life*, (London: Harper Collins, 2001), p.78

39 Raymond Williams, *Politics and Letters*, p. 38.

40 Raymond Williams, "Round Britain on £5", *The Gobannian* 11, (January 1939).

41 Raymond Williams, *Politics and Letters*, pp. 31-32; Harry Williams' diary, 1937.

42 Raymond Williams' notebook: Christmas Holiday Lectures in London, dated in Williams' hand as "from the 3rd to 6th, 1937" but, as his father's diary entries confirm, was actually in 1938. Clearly, the date of the new year had not yet registered with his son.

43 Raymond Williams, *Politics and Letters*, p. 32.

44 *Abergavenny Chronicle*, 27 and 30 September 1938; March 1939.

45 Letter from Maelor Griffiths to Dai Smith, 24 September 1991.

46 Raymond Williams' copy of Huxley was stamped with the fleur-de-lys insignia of King Henry VIII Grammar School and kept amongst his other books during his lifetime.

47 See the Huxley edition where the blank pages at its front had begun to fill up with his dated notes. RW Papers.

48 Raymond Williams, "Round Britain on £5".

49 Letter from Maelor Griffiths to Dai Smith, September 1991.

50 Letter from Margaret Davies to Dai Smith, 28 October 1997. See also Harry Williams' diary, April 1939.

51 Raymond Williams MS, "I Live Through the War". RW Papers.

52 Information from Maelor Griffiths who himself registered as a conscientious objector on the outbreak of the war, and was granted partial exemption: "I had to admit to myself, however, that my pacifism was born mainly out of disgust and anger at the way Chamberlain had deserted the Czechs and was of the opinion that if he could persuade him to carry on East towards the USSR he would do a deal with him. When Hitler turned towards the Low Countries and France it became quite obvious that Parliament would not be a party to that so I joined the RAF and was lucky enough to survive as a navigator."

53 Raymond Williams, *Border Country*, p. 389.

54 Harry Williams' diary, 9 October 1939.

1 Untitled novel ("Paul Ramsay") in RW Papers.

2 Raymond Williams, *Politics and Letters*, p. 32.

3 See G.M. Trevelyan, *Trinity College: A History and Guide* (Cambridge: revised edition, 1980), Trevelyan was Master of the College from 1940-51.

4 For a bemused Fred Inglis, *Raymond Williams* (1995) p. 66, any misgivings expressed by Williams about his Cambridge education was "a fit of a kind of fervour" since "he couldn't have fashioned his thought out of anywhere else".

5 Sara Payne, *Down Your Street: East Cambridge,* Vol. II (Cambridge: Pevensey Press, 1984).

6 For complementary accounts of Cambridge English in the 1920s through different biographical perspectives, see Ian McKillop, *F.R. Leavis : A Life in Criticism* (London: Allen Lane, 1995) and John Haffenden *William Empson: Among the Mandarins*, Vol. I (Oxford: Oxford University Press, 2005).

7 *Interview* with Lionel Elvin, Cambridge, 1990. Elvin (1907-2005), was the son of the General Secretary of the National Union of Clerks. He had been educated at Trinity Hall and made a Fellow there in 1930. After the War he became Principal of Ruskin College, Oxford from 1945-50 and then Head of Education at UNESCO to 1956 before taking the Chair in Education in Third World Countries at the University of London.

8 Subject to demolition and development even in the interwar years, it was completely transformed into a shopping precinct in the 1960s and 1970s. See Sara Payne, *Down Your Street*.

9 *Cambridge Varsity Post*, 15 October 1938.

10 Interview with E.J. Hobsbawm, 11 July 1991.

11 Film of the march shot by Michael Orrom survives and was used in his Channel 4 documentary *A Fragment of Memory* (1984).

12 Raymond Williams, *Politics and Letters*, p. 43.

13 Eric Hobsbawm, *Interesting Times* (London: Allen Lane, 2002), p.153.

14 H.S. Fearns, *Reading from Left to Right: One Man's Political History* (Toronto: University of Toronto Press, 1983), p. 114.

15 Paul Ramsay is shot down over Germany and is picked up, disguised as a German, by the Russians, who imprison and interrogate him. He later surfaces in Austria as Paul Bergel, using the surname of his Austrian mother who had married his Welsh railway signalman father after the First World War. He works in Austria for the Communist Party. In the fragment of the successor novel, *A Map of Treason*, he returns to England for mysterious but unspecified purposes.

16 Raymond Williams, *Politics and Letters*, p. 42.

17 Typescript of "Paul Ramsay" novel, pp. 12-13.

18 Ibid, p. 14.

19 Ibid, pp. 22-25.

20 Raymond Williams, "My Cambridge", reprinted in *What I Came to Say* (London: Hutchinson Radius, 1989), p. 8.

21 Ibid, p. 6.

22 *Cambridge University Journal*, 18 November 1939, 3 and 10 February 1940. For the quotations from Norman Mackenzie see his chapter on 1939 to 1943 in Joan Abse (Ed.), *My LSE*, (London: Robson Books, 1977).

23 *Cambridge University Journal*, 27 April 1940. See "My Cambridge", p. 8.

24 Ibid, 25 November 1939.

25 Ibid, 2 March 1940.

26 Interview with Annette Lees neé Hughes, 2 December 1990.

27 *Kelly's Directory of Devonshire* (London, 1919). Andree S.E. Winbolt, *Devon* (London: Bell and Sons, 1929) and F.L. Loveridge, *Devon* (London: Penguin Guides, 1939).

28 Margaret A. Reed, *Pilton: Its Past and People* (1977; 1985).

29 Interviews with Joy Williams, 2 and 3 April 1990. I am also indebted to Fred Dalling (1922-2001) for sight of his 1989 notes and materials on Dalling family history, and to Merryn Williams for her extensive account of Dalling family facts and lore, 2002.

30 Letter from Margaret Davies to Dai Smith, October 1997.

31 *Cambridge University Journal*, 10 February 1940.

32 Ibid, 2 March 1940.

33 Raymond Williams pencil Ms. lecture on "The Press", 17 December 1940. RW Papers.

34 Eric Hobsbawm, *Interesting Times*, p. 153.

35 Ibid, p. 154.

36 There is now a considerable literature on The Winter War but see, in particular, A.F. Upton's *Finland in Crisis, 1940-1941* (London: Faber and Faber, 1964) and *Finland 1939-1940* (London: Davis-Poynter, 1974); Jukka Nevakivi, *The Appeal that was Never Made: The Allies, Scandinavia and the Finnish Winter War, 1939-1940* (London: C. Hurst and Company 1975); D.G. Kirby, *Finland and the Twentieth Century* (London: C. Hurst and Company, 1979).
For reasons more to do with now than then, this squib of a student pamphlet (the writers were aged twenty-three and nineteen) has attracted attention and a measure of opprobrium by virtue both of its pro-Soviet apologetics and its authors' later fame. For a taste of such laments see Nick Cohen *What's Left? How Liberals Lost Their Way* (London: Fourth Estate, 2007), pp. 241-2. So,

485

in the cause of history rather than polemic, two brief quotes from rather more objective sources may help restore the blurred perspective of today by underlining how fuzzy the issues were and became from 1939 to 1941:

"Although the obduracy and unrealistic attitudes of the Finnish politicians played a part in bringing about the breakdown of talks in the autumn of 1939, the tragedy of the Winter War should more properly be seen in the light of the previous two decades of mutual distrust and failure to resolve a vital security problem. In the event, it is clear that in its determination to resist what were considered to be unjustifiable Soviet demands, even at the risk of war, the [Finnish] government echoed the feelings of the nation."

from D.G. Kirby, *Finland in the Twentieth Century*, p. 122. And Michael Futrell in his Introduction to A.F. Upton, *Finland in Crisis 1940-1941*, pp. 15-16, reflected:

"As [Upton] writes, "the struggle of this virtually unknown country had caught the imagination of the world... the Finnish war had in it something for everyone. It was David versus Goliath..." Britain and France even planned a relief expedition through Norway and Sweden... [Then]... in the summer of 1940... many people in Europe... believed that Britain had lost the war and that Germany would dominate continental Europe... Mannerheim and his colleagues... step by step approached the fateful days of June 1941 when Finland joined the German onslaught on Soviet Russia."

37 "War on the USSR?", University Socialist Club, Cambridge, 1940. Photocopy in RW Papers. In December 1939 the Russia Today Society had produced another anonymous pamphlet (possibly written by Pat Sloan) with an intended circulation of around 50,000 copies. This was *Finland: The Facts* (London, 1939). Hobsbawm and Williams would have seen this pamphlet with its detailed and often solid account of the deep, and frequently violent, social and political conflict in interwar Finland. The pamphlet's purpose, though, was to justify invasion and hail the imposed Moscow government as a democratic advance. I am grateful to Steve Woodhams and the Marx Memorial Library.

38 *Cambridge University Journal*, 11 May 1940. Aneurin Bevan, though decidedly not "anti-war" was saying the same thing, rather more eloquently, in the House of Commons. In 1942 he was already reflecting back on the social shudder caused by those early war years at home and abroad: "At the Mansion House the other day... the Prime Minister guaranteed the British Empire what we have we hold. Hon. Members dare not say that in the Rhondda Valley or on the Clyde. The British Army are not fighting for the old world. If Hon. Members opposite think we are going through this in order to keep their Malayan swamps, they are making a mistake. We can see the Conservatives

crawling out of their holes now... in 1940 and 1941 they would not have dared to say these things." Quoted in Michael Foot, *Aneurin Bevan*, Vol. I (1962: 1997 edition), pp. 182-3.

39 *Cambridge University Journal*, 27 April 1940.

40 Ibid, 18 and 25 May 1940.

41 Ibid, 25 May 1940.

42 Harry Williams' diaries, May and June 1940.

43 See Raymond Williams, *Politics and Letters*, p. 47 where he mis-remembers the magazine in which "Red Earth" was published, and "My Cambridge" p. 7.

44 Raymond Williams, "Red Earth", in *Cambridge Front*, Vol. I, Summer 1940.

45 Raymond Williams, "Mother Chapel", in *Magpie*, Trinity College Magazine, Easter 1940.

46 Harry Williams' diaries, July – September 1940.

47 See Angus Calder, *The Peoples' War, Britain 1939-45* (London: Jonathan Cape, 1969), pp. 243-47; 260-1.

48 *Cambridge University Journal*, 7 December 1940. See also CUJ, 23 and 30 November for the student Convention.

49 *Cambridge University Journal*, 16 November 1940.

50 Interview with Joy Williams, 3 April 1990; Raymond Williams, *Politics and Letters*, p. 53.

51 Raymond Williams, "Experience of the Creative Process", handwritten essay dated 11 November 1940. Two others survive, both presented to Lionel Elvin in 1939/40: "The Theory of Longinus Concerning The Sublime" and "Sonnet".

52 *Cambridge University Journal*, 7 December 1940.

53 Letter fragment, undated, from Raymond Williams to Joy Dalling, December 1940. Letter to Dai Smith from Ray Fawkes, 1993.

54 Raymond Williams Lecture on "The Press", 17 December 1940. RW Papers.

55 Harry Williams' diary, 10 January 1941. There may have been two plays but only one seems to have survived.

56 See Juliet Gardiner, *Wartime Britain 1939-45* (London: Headline, 2004), pp. 257-9.

57 Raymond Williams Ms. and typescript of play "Clear as Crystal", 1940. RW Papers.

58 Interview with Joy Williams, April 1990.

59 See "My Cambridge", pp. 8-9 and *Politics and Letters*, pp. 52-3. Also T.E.B. Howarth, *Cambridge Between Two Wars* (1978), pp. 159-60.

60 Michael Pope's "The Spoon in the Yellow River" appeared in *Cambridge University Journal*, 9 March 1940, as the "First Act of a Great New Drama";

over two columns with Lennonesque punning at the expense of the Cambridge University Mummers' "Chekhovian" production of Dennis Johnson's "The Moon and the Yellow River". Michael Pope went on, in similar vein, to contribute such free verse fun of "Lot's Wife for whom after they drew lots... they drew Lot's wife".

61 Interview with Michael Orrom, 23 October 1990. Other information from his unpublished memoir *A Fragment of Memory*, 1993. See also his *Obituary* notice by Michael Clarke in the Guardian, 17 June 1997.

62 Raymond Williams, "In Defence of Moovie" [echoing at some distance Philip Sidney's "In Defence of Poesie"], *Cambridge University Journal*, 7 December 1940.

63 Michael Orrom, *A Fragment of Memory*, p. 17.

64 See the entry on John Lehmann in Margaret Drabble (Ed.), *The Oxford Companion to English Literature* (Oxford: Oxford University Press), and Raymond Williams, *Politics and Letters*, p. 46.

65 Quotes from Michael Orrom, *A Fragment of Memory*, pp. 21-25.

66 *Cambridge University Journal*, 30 November 1940.

67 Also entitled A *Fragment of Memory*, broadcast on Channel 4.

68 Raymond Williams, *Cambridge Front*, Vol. I, No. 2, 5 March 1941. See also the Preface to *Outlook: A Selection of Cambridge Writing*, 1941. It contained verse by Arnold Rattenbury, Nicholas Moore and Alex Comfort and stories by Eric Hobsbawm ("Dopey Willey") and Maurice Craig.

69 Letter from Anne Piper to Dai Smith, 13 August 1994. Anne Piper became an activist in both the anti-nuclear and women's movements. She wrote plays, for stage and television, and eight novels.

70 Diary of Anne Richmond, April to June 1941.

71 Michael Orrom, *Fragment of Memory*, p. 30.

72 Harry Williams' diaries, 14 and 15 June 1941; interview with Joy Williams, 1990. In the English Tripos there were eighteen II:IIs that year, four Firsts and four II:Is. Muriel Bradbrook had been an examiner. *Cambridge University Reporter*, 1941.

73 Ministry of Defence Records for Lieutenant Raymond Henry Williams, P.235867 – Royal Artillery; Harry Williams' diaries, September and October 1941.

74 Major General Clarke, "Behind the Lines: The Forging of the Weapons", and Brigadier W. Swinton, "Gun versus Tank" in *Royal Artillery Commemoration Book, 1939-45*.

75 Harry Williams' diary, 8 March 1942. See also Joy Williams' Postscript to *People of the Black Mountains*, Vol. II, p. 322.

76 D. H. Macindoe, "The OCTUs: 122 OCTU" in *Royal Artillery Commemoration Book*.

77 Ibid. See also *Twentyone*, weekly newspaper of the 21st Anti-Tank Regiment, Royal Artillery, 12, 15 September 1945.

78 Interview with Annette Lees, 2 December 1990. Interview with Joy Williams, April 1990.

79 *War Diary*, 21st Anti-Tank Regiment, June to December 1942.

80 Raymond Williams, "This Time" in John Lehmann (Ed.), *New Writing and Daylight*, 1943.

81 "'Q' at Sanna's Post: And its former and subsequent history" in *Twentyone*, 4, 20 July 1945.

82 "Tank Destroyer Field Manual: Organisation and Tactics of Tank Destroyer Units", March 1942. As cited in Harry Yeide, *The Tank Killers: A History of America's World War II Tank Destroyer Force* (Staplehurst: Spellmount, 2005).

83 Jonathan Sutherland, *World War II Tanks and AFVs* (2002), pp. 56, 59.

84 "Allied Anti-tank Weapons" in Chandler & Collins (Eds.), *The D-Day Encylopaedia* (New York: Simon and Schuster, 1994).

85 Raymond Williams, Ms. of "Isn't it a Scream", RW Papers.

86 War Diary of Q Battery, 1 May 1944.

87 Raymond Williams, fragmented novel (Ms. and typescript) *Our Lords the Moon and the Sun*, RW Papers.

88 Anne Richmond's diary, 6 and 7 June 1944.

89 Interview with Michael Orrom, 1990.

4. "AN ODD ADVENTURE OR TWO"

1 Raymond Williams, *Politics and Letters*, p. 423.

2 Ibid, p. 87.

3 "Commentary", *Twentyone* 4, 20 July 1945, RW Papers.

4 *Twentyone* 16, 13 October 1945.

5 Raymond Williams, *Politics and Letters*, p. 422

6 Ibid, pp. 57–58.

7 Letter from Raymond Williams to Joy Williams, dated "Friday 24" (probably November, 1944), RW Papers.

8 Raymond Williams' personal war diary or memoir. Chapter I: "Scarborough to Bayeux", RW Papers.

9 The diary was never completed and there is a missing part of (possibly) two short chapters that would have dealt with the advance into Belgium and the liberation of Brussels.

10 Letters from Raymond to Joy Williams, 30 November 1944 and 8 February 1945.

11 Raymond Williams, *Politics and Letters*, pp. 58 and 29.

12 Raymond Williams' diary: Chapter II: "Our First Battle".

13 See Robin Neillands, *The Battle of Normandy, 1944* (London: Cassell, 2003), pp. 155–183.

14 The literature is immense but see John Keegan's classic *Six Armies in Normandy* (London: Penguin, 1982) and Max Hastings, *Overlord: D-Day and the Battle for Normandy 1944* (London: Pan, 1999). For technical detail consult Chandler and Collins [Eds.] *The D-Day Encyclopaedia*, (New York: Pan, 1994).

15 *Twentyone* 4, 20 July 1945.

16 21st Anti-Tank Regiment: Historical Notes May 1944 – May 1945, compiled in January 1946 by Major S.A. Wilson-Brown. RW Papers. Also Interview with Eddie Gibbs, wireless operator for Williams' tank.

17 Raymond Williams' diary, Chapter II: "Our First Battle".

18 Details of the movements and action of the 21st Anti-Tank Regiment, and of Q Battery within it, can be found in respective regimental and battery War Diaries, written up shortly after events had occurred.

19 Stuart Hills, *By Tank into Normandy* (London: Cassell, 2002), pp. 98–9. See also Bill Bellamy, *Troop Leader: A Tank Commander's Story* (Stroud: Sutton, 2005).

20 Interview with Eddie Gibbs, 1990.

21 Pencilled note in RW Papers.

22 Interview with Eddie Gibbs.

23 Raymond Williams, *Politics and Letters*, p. 55.

24 Raymond Williams' diary, Chapter I.

25 War Diary of Q Battery, 18 and 22 August 1944.

26 Letter from Raymond to Joy Williams, December 1944.

27 Letter from Raymond to Joy Williams, 24 February 1945.

28 Interview with Eddie Gibbs.

29 Raymond Williams' diary, Chapter III.

30 21st Anti-Tank Regiment Historical Notes, 11 July 1944.

31 John Keegan, *Six Armies in Normandy*, p. 189.

32 Robin Neillands, *The Battle of Normandy, 1944*.

33 21st Anti-Tank Regiment Historical Notes July 1944.

34 Raymond Williams, *Politics and Letters*, pp. 5 –58.

35 George G. Blackburn, *The Guns of Normandy : A Soldier's Eye View, France 1944* (London: Constable, 1995), p. xii.

36 Raymond Williams' diary, Chapter III.

37 *Twentyone* 5, 27 July 1945.

38 Raymond Williams' diary, Chapter III.

39 Ibid. See also War Diaries of Q Battery, 1 to 6 August 1944.

40 Raymond Williams' diary, Chapter V.

41 War Diary Q Battery, 16 and 17 August 1944.

42 Raymond Williams' diary, Chapter V.

43 *21st Anti-Tank Regiment Historical Notes*, 31 August to 6 September 1944; Eddie Gibbs interview.

44 Raymond Williams, *Loyalties* (London: Chatto and Windus, 1985), p. 91.

45 Raymond Williams, *Politics and Letters*, p. 45.

46 "The Traitor", pencil Ms. A red-ink note at the top of the first page reads "Get German from Eric Hobsbawm, then sub a translation".

47 See letter from Captain Ronald Felton, 11th Armoured Division, 6 September 1944 (Imperial War Museum Collection).

48 *Twentyone* 10, 1 September 1945.

49 War Diary Q Battery, 3 and 4 September 1944.

50 *Twentyone* 10, 1 September 1945.

51 "In Brussels Now", *Twentyone* 1, 29 June 1945.

52 Ibid; "Short Story of the Week" by Peter Dalling. Williams here took Joy Williams' maiden name as his pseudonym. The first part of the story is cited in Fred Inglis' *Raymond Williams* (1995) though without clear indication that it is taken from a fiction.

53 War Diary of Q Battery, 11 to 16 September 1944.

54 Raymond Williams' diary, Chapter IV.

55 Ibid.

56 Ibid, and *Twentyone* 13, 22 September 1944.

57 Max Hastings, *Armageddon: The Battle for Germany 1944–45* (London: Macmillan, 2004), pp. 56–71.

58 *Twentyone* 1, 22 September 1944.

59 Raymond Williams' diary, Chapter V.

60 Richard Holmes, "Market Garden" in his *Battlefields of the Second World War* (London: BBC, 2001). See also William F Buckingham, *Arnhem, 1944* (Stroud: Tempus, 2002).

61 War Diary of Q Battery, 19, 20 and 21 September 1944. In *The Story of the Guards Armoured Division* (1956) by Captain The Earl of Rosse and Colonel E.R. Hill the accolade was given to Raymond Williams: "The honour... to be the first British troops to fight on German soil belongs to the men of Captain R. Williams' troop of Q Battery of the 21st Anti-Tank Regiment." Yet, as both

the Battery's official War Diary and Williams' own diary confirms it was Bill Beaty with HQ troop who had reconnoitred with the Americans of 82nd Airborne and crossed into Germany. The honour is further claimed for Beaty by William Hood in his "The Gunners at Nijmegen" in *The Gunner*, 1948. In contrast, Stuart Hills' *By Tank Into Normandy* proposes that tanks of the Sherwood Rangers had been the first to cross over whilst operating with the Americans to widen the bridgehead east of Nijmegen. However, this would have been after 20 September, so the palm is likely to be that of Bill Beaty after all.

62 Raymond Williams' diary, Chapter IV.

63 Max Hastings, *Armageddon*, p. 66.

64 War Diary of Q Battery 20 and 23 September 1944.

65 Raymond Williams' "Arnhem and the War Correspondents" in *Twentyone* 14, 29 September 1945. This is precisely the later and incisively analytical view of Robin Neillands in his *The Battle for the Rhine, 1944* (London: Cassell, 2005), who exonerates the Guards Armoured Division from any actual delay in reaching Nijmegen and castigates General Gavin for not making the capture of the bridge – and hence onward swift passage to Arnhem – his first, and chief rather than belated priority.

66 Raymond Williams' diary, Chapter V.

67 This is the title (not all chapters were titled by him) of the last extant Chapter (VI) of Raymond Williams' diary.

68 Harry Williams' diary 25 December 1944.

69 Letter from Raymond to Joy Williams, n.d., probably November 1944.

70 Letter from Raymond to Joy Williams, 13 December 1944.

71 Letter from Raymond to Joy Williams, 30 December 1944.

72 Harry Williams' diary, 4 May 1945.

73 Letter from Raymond to Joy Williams, 17 January 1945.

74 Max Hastings, *Armageddon*, p. 161.

75 Letter from Raymond to Joy Williams, n.d., late December 1944.

76 Letters from Raymond to Joy Williams, n.d., October and November 1944.

77 Letter from Raymond to Joy Williams, 28 October 1944.

78 Letter from Raymond to Joy Williams, 11 January 1945.

79 Letters from Raymond to Joy Williams, 24 and 30 January, 22 February 1945.

80 Letter from Raymond to Joy Williams, 8 February 1945.

81 Raymond Williams' diary, Chapter VI.

82 War Diary of Q Battery, February and March 1945.

83 War Diary of Q Battery, 1 to 9 April 1945.

84 *21st Anti-Tank Regiment Historical Notes*, 28 April 1945.

85 Harry Williams' diary, 4 to 12 May 1945.

5. "A QUALITY BEYOND ART"

1 War Diary of 2nd Battery, 21st Anti-Tank Regiment, 2 May 1945.

2 Martin Middlebrook, *The Battle of Hamburg : The Firestorm Raid,* (London: Penguin,1980).

3 Ms. Memoir of G.C. Miller, 1945, Imperial War Museum.

4 *Twentyone*, Nos. 1 to 24, and No. 27 are extant. RW Papers.

5 Twentyone, No. 10, 1 September 1945.

6 *Twentyone*, No. 1, 29 June 1945.

7 *Twentyone*, No. 2, 6 July 1945.

8 *Twentyone*, No. 6, 3 August 1945

9 *Twentyone*, No. 4, 20 July 1945.

10 *Twentyone*, No. 5, 27 July 1945.

11 *Twentyone*, No. 2, 6 July 1945 and No. 7, 10 August 1945.

12 *Twentyone*, No. 5, 27 July 1945, No. 7 10 August 1945, and No.12, 15 September 1945.

13 *Twentyone*, No. 11, 8 September 1945.

14 Harry Williams' diary, 9 September, 18 and 19 October 1945.

15 *Twentyone*, No. 16, 13 October 1945.

16 Eric Hobsbawm was twenty-eight in 1946 and a research student at King's, Cambridge; Richard Hoggart, employed in the Extra-Mural Department at Leeds in that year was also twenty-eight, and Raymond Williams was twenty-five when he graduated that summer.
See E. Hobsbawm, *Interesting Times,* (London: Allen Lane, 2002), pp. 172-5; Richard Hoggart, *A Sort of Clowning*, (London: Chatto and Windus, 1990), pp. 73-5 and Raymond Williams *Politics and Letters* 1979 p. 61

17 *Twentyone*, No. 17, 20 October 1945.

18 Letter from Bernard Miles to Raymond Williams, not dated, RW Papers.

19 *Liberation*, a play by Raymond Williams. December 1945, RW Papers.

20 Raymond Williams, "Nijmegen Bridge", as appeared in Geoffrey Moore, (Ed.) *The Bridge*, April 1946.

21 Interview with Joy Williams, 1990.

22 *Twentyone*, No. 18, 27 October 1945.

23 Harry Williams' diary, 1945-58; records of the receipt of lengthy "interesting" letters from his son at either weekly or regular intervals until his death in 1958, but none are extant.

24 *Twentyone*, No. 18, 27 October 1945 and No. 22, 24 November 1945.

25 *Twentyone*, No. 21, 17 November 1945. This was in a letter commenting on the newspaper's growing timidity. Two pages, handwritten in red ink, began

the story of Alice, a bored young woman staring around her room, gazing in a mirror, conjuring up a 'little creature, red from head to foot' who begins to talk. Fortunately this, and his liking for red ink, stopped there.

26 *Twentyone*, No. 22, 24 November 1945 and 1st December 1945. Quintin Hogg (1907-2001) as the Conservative and pro-Munich candidate, had won a famous by-election in Oxford in 1938 against the anti-Munich all-party candidate, A.D. Lindsay, Master of Balliol. Hogg, however, voted against the Chamberlain government in 1940 in the Norway debate and, after being invalided out of war service, was a leading proponent of the Tory Reform Committee (1943) whose ideas for post-war policies were considered 'socialistic'. In 1945 he had been returned to Parliament despite the Labour landslide. Kingsley Martin (1897-1969) from a nonconformist, academic and Christian pacifist background became the first editor of the merged *New Statesman & Nation* in 1931 and guided that ailing Fabian/Liberal partnership into decades of success as the most stylish compendium of arts and politics on the dissenting but mainstream Left until he gave up the reins in 1960.

27 See Raymond Williams, *Politics and Letters* 1979, pp. 66-7; Raymond Williams' notebook, 1945/6 in R W Papers.

28 Raymond Williams' notebook, 1958, RW Papers.

29 Raymond Williams, 'Culture is Ordinary' in Norman Mackenzie (Ed.), *Conviction* (London: Macgibbon and Kee, 1958), and Raymond Williams, *Politics and Letters* 1979, p.36.

30 Harry Williams' diaries, 29 December 1945 and 1 January 1946.

31 Raymond Williams, 'My Cambridge', in *What I Came to Say*, (London: Hutchinson, 1989).

32 Harry Williams' diary, 8 August 1946. Four Firsts had been awarded – two men and two women – by the examiners Basil Willey, F.L. Lucas and Joan Bennet; with the Oxford external, V. De Sola Pinto. *Cambridge University Reporter*, 1946.

33 See Raymond Williams 'An Open Letter to W.E.A. Tutors', 1961, and *Politics and Letters* 1979, p. 64.

34 Harry Williams' diary, 16-19 August, 14 September, 1946.

35 Interview with Joy Williams, 1990; Harry Williams' diary 19, 21 September and 12, 13 October 1946.

36 See *English Story* (8th Series), Ed. Woodrow Wyatt, 1948; it was reprinted in Alun Richards (Ed.), *The New Penguin Book of Welsh Short Stories*, (London: Allen Lane, 1993).

37 See Chapter IV in Cecile Woodford, *Portrait of Sussex* (1972; 1984), and David J. Allen, *Sussex Shire County Guide* (1984; 1987).

38 Fragments of versions of this early novel, *The Art of the Actor*, can be found in RW Papers.

39 As cited from Records of the Department of External Studies, Bodleian Library, Oxford University. This topic, adult education from Oxford University and, at a tangent, Raymond Williams' participation in, learning from and influence on this work, has been studied in great depth by other scholars to whom, for this section, I am much indebted for both information and guidance. In addition to my own research in the Archives of the (now) External Studies Department and interviews conducted personally, quotation from other primary sources largely derives from their work and is duly, in place, acknowledged as such. The works I have used most are:

Lawrence Goldman, *Dons and Workers: Oxford and Adult Education since 1850* (Oxford: Oxford University Press, 1995); Roger Fieldhouse, *Adult Education and the Cold War* (Leeds: University of Leeds, 1985); Roger Fieldhouse, 'Oxford and Adult Education' and John McIlroy, 'Teacher, Critic, Explorer', in W.J. Morgan, and Peter Preston, (Eds.) *Raymond Williams: Politics, Education, Letters* (London: St Martins Press, 1993); John McIlroy, 'Border Country: Raymond Williams in Adult Education', Part 1 and Part II, in *Studies in the Education of Adults*, Vol. 22, No. 2 and Vol. 23, No. 1, 1990/1991, reprinted in the compilation of Williams' work in this field, along with further essays by the joint Editors, in John McIlroy, and Sallie Westwood (Eds.), *Border Country: Raymond Williams in Adult Education* (Leicester: NIACE, 1993).

In particular John McIlroy's quite brilliant dissection and analysis of Williams' theory and practice was thoughtfully connected to the biographical enquiries he undertook with Williams' colleagues; and I have benefited enormously from his prior and invaluable studies.

40 W.P. Baker to H.P. Smith 13 July 1946; and Frank Jacques to Smith 18 July 1946. See McIlroy *Border Country* and Fieldhouse in Morgan and Preston. Baker, later an extra-mural historian at Leeds, worked for the W.E.A. in Cambridgeshire and Jacques was Secretary of the Eastern District.

41 Roger Fieldhouse 'Oxford and Adult Education'.

42 Raymond Williams 'The Uses of Cultural Theory' in *New Left Review*, 158, 1986.

43 Lawrence Goldman, *Dons and Workers: Oxford and Adult Education since 1850*.

44 McIlroy 'Border Country'.

45 Goldman, *Dons and Workers*.

46 Richard Lewis, *Leaders and Teachers: Adult Education and The Challenge of Labour in South Wales, 1906-1940* (Cardiff: Unviersity of Wales Press), 1993.

47 Letter from Bellchambers to McIlroy, 1990. See McIlroy 'Border Country'.

48 Pickstock, in a letter to W.E. Styler, 1962, as cited by Roger Fieldhouse 'Oxford and Adult Education'.

49 Annual Reports, Oxford Delegacy for Extra Mural Studies, Year to September 1947.

50 See Annual Reports, 1947-50; and McIlroy and Westwood (Eds.), *Border Country: Raymond Williams in Adult Education*.

51 Raymond Williams 'In the Tutorial Class' in *Discussion Method: The Purpose, Nature and Application of Group Discussion* (1950).

52 Copy of 'Literature and Society since 1800', RW Papers.

6. "POLITICS AND LETTERS"

1 Raymond Williams, "The Soviet Literary Controversy in Retrospect". The Coleridgean distinction between "civilisation" and its true guardian "culture" was one Leavis had made his own, especially in *Education and the University* (1943). *Politics and Letters*, Vol. 1, Number 1, Summer 1947.

2 *Politics and Letters* (1979), p. 66.

3 Dai Smith interview with Wolf Mankowitz, November 1990.

4 *Politics and Letters* (1979), pp. 74-76.

5 Letter from Clifford Collins to Raymond Williams, 19 June (1946) in RW Papers. "Jack" is John Metcalfe who became a Director of the Critic Press.

6 Letter from Wolf Mankowitz to Raymond Williams, in RW Papers, 5 July (1946).

7 Letter from Collins to Raymond Williams, in RW Papers, 11 October (1946).

8 *Politics and Letters* (1979), p. 74.

9 Interview with Mankowitz, 1990. See also *Politics and Letters*, p. 77.

10 Letter from F.R. Leavis to Raymond Williams, 19 June 1947 in RW Papers. Williams was enquiring about the March 1935 issue to which Leavis contributed an acerbic and dissenting review essay of I.A. Richards' *Coleridge on Imagination*.

11 Interview with Mankowitz, 1990. He said he "later regretted" his attack on Thomas.

12 Editorial *Politics and Letters*, Summer 1947.

13 See, variously, *The Critic* and *Politics and Letters*, 1947/8.

14 *Politics and Letters*, Summer 1948, No. 4.

15 "Soviet Literary Controversy in Retrospect", *Politics and Letters*, Summer 1947.

16 *Politics and Letters*, Summer 1948. "The State and Popular Culture".

17 Raymond Williams, "A Dialogue on Actors", *The Critic*, Vol. 1. No. 1, spring 1947.

18 Letters to Mankowitz from Donald Wolfit, Ralph Richardson and Martin Browne; to Clifford Collins from Emlyn Williams; to Raymond Williams from Nevil Coghill and Bernard Miles. All the letters date from September 1946. RW Papers.

19 For what follows see Michael Orrom's memoir of 1994, "The New Cinema", in RW Papers.

20 Copy, undated, in RW Papers.

21 Raymond Williams, *Politics and Letters*, p. 75.

22 Raymond Williams' Preface to *Reading and Criticism* (1950).

23 Letter from Raymond Williams to Clifford Collins, 29 September 1948. RW Papers.

24 Two letters from Collins (n.ds) but probably 1949/50 thank Raymond Williams for help in finding possible work in Adult Education and from Mankowitz two friendly and chatty letters from 1949 and 1950. RW Papers.

25 Raymond Williams' four-page typescript, *Interlude*, in RW Papers. He intended incorporating this in a longer work, the early attempts at *Border Country*.

26 Raymond Williams, *Politics and Letters*, p. 77.

7. "A GOOD ACTOR STICKS TO HIS OWN LINES"

1 See Memoranda for 'October 1948' and 'February 1949' RW Papers. He had it in mind to write a play called *Timoleon*, presumably to be about the great warrior democrat (411-337BC) from the City State of Corinth, who had liberated the Greeks of Syracuse from tyrannical rule and the Carthaginian threat. Though it was not pursued it is clear why, in the late 1940s, Plutarch's account would have attracted his imagination.

2 There are three sheets, mostly in manuscript, with a list of stories for the second volume whose original title story 'Art of the Actor' gave way to 'The Claustrophile'.

3 Sixteen stories, including the very early ones slightly revised, are extant along with fragmentary pages of others and the story-section 'Black Water'.

4 This was originally 'Mr Peters goes home', 1946, and slightly different from the version quoted. See RW Papers.

5 Interview with Joy Williams, 1990.

6 Michael Orrom was peeved, over 40 years later, that he had been given no credit for this in *Politics and Letters* p. 277, where Williams simply talks of 'a fairly rare account I had found of an Englishman who had gone to the Klondike' as the basis of his 'first' novel *Ridyear*. Interview with Michael Orrom, 1990.

7 See Phil Baker's entry on Calder-Marshall (1908-1992) in the *Oxford Dictionary of National Biography* (Oxford: Oxford University Press, 2005).

8 Michael Orrom's memoir, 'The New Cinema', (1994).

9 The contemporary literature on the Gold Rush and the testing overland trips to the gold camps is extensive. The nearest title to Michael Orrom's I can find is Robert C. Kirk *Twelve Months in the Klondike*, London, 1899, but there are dozens of accounts, fact and fiction, of the hardship, despair, luck and craziness of those years in the north-west. The BBC broadcast a filmed-from-the-air account by a Canadian a year after Orrom's idea.

10 Interview with Joy Williams, 1990.

11 Typescript notes, RW Papers.

12 Typescript of early novel fragment 'Black Water', RW Papers.

13 Interview with Joy Williams.

14 Harry Williams' diaries, 1947-1950.

15 One other handwritten sheet of flimsy, from this time, was for '*Marches*, a novel by *R. W. Ridyear*', whose first section was to be 'Brynllwyd', and whose other six chapters suggested the direction of the final work, *Brynllwyd*. See early pencilled pages of extracts, schemes, ordering of pages, a sketch map, title pages. RW Papers.

16 Roger Fieldhouse, *Adult Education and the Cold War*, 1985.

17 Lawrence Goldman, *Dons and Workers*, 1995.

18 See Michael Wolfe's entry on Thomas Hodgkin in the *Oxford Dictionary of National Biography*.

19 Raymond Williams review of Robert Cumming's *The Philosophy of Jean-Paul Sartre* in *The Guardian* 29 November 1968.

20 Letter from Jack Woolford to Joy Williams, 3 February 1988. RW Papers.

21 See postcard with train times in ink. RW Papers. Information from Joy Williams.

22 See Tom Steele, *The Emergence of Cultural Studies 1945-65: Cultural Politics, Adult Education and the English Question* (London: Lawrence and Wishart, 1977), a work of exceptional lucidity and brilliant synthesis.

23 See Richard Hoggart, *A Sort of Clowning: Life and Times 1940-59* p. 126.

24 Richard Hoggart in *Adult Education*, XX, June 1948 and Raymond Williams, *Adult Education*, Vol. XXI, 1948. Extracts re-printed in McIlroy and Westwood. See also T.W. Thomas' 'Practical Criticism and the Literature Class' in *Adult Education*, Summer 1951 for a sympathetic account of Williams' book *Reading and Criticism* (1950) which, yet, counterpoints it with warnings against mechanical or abstract reading of extracts as a form of "training" and postulates, instead, "the progressively richer experience of actual literature". Tom Thomas (1917-2007), based in Swansea as a Staff Tutor, burnished a reputation as a teacher of adults which marks him out as one of the truly outstanding literature tutors of his, and Williams', generation. They, too, became friends as well as colleagues.

25 Raymond Williams, "Some Experiments in Literature Teaching", Rewley House Papers, Vol. II No. X, 1948-9.

26 Raymond Williams, 'Literature in Relation to History', Rewley House Papers, Vol. III, No. 1, 1949–50.

27 D. Butts, 'The Development of Literature Teaching in the Oxford Tutorial Class', Rewley House Papers, Vol. III, No. VII, 1958-9. In 1948 the Delegacy had 84 Tutorial Classes running overall, of which 14 were in Literature. In 1958 there were 31 Literature classes in a total of 115.

28 See Fieldhouse, 'Oxford and Adult Education' in Morgan & Preston, *Raymond Williams: Politics Education Letters*.

29 Harry Williams' diary, 9 December 1949.

30 See Asa Briggs *The History of Broadcasting in the United Kingdom: 1945-55*.

31 Letter from Raymond Williams to R.E. Keen, 21 October 1949, and from Raymond Williams to Keen, 28 December, 1949, BBC Written Archives.

32 Letters from Anna Kallin (Home Talks Dept. BBC) to Raymond Williams, 23 September 1946 and Raymond Williams to Anna Kallin, 8 October 1949; from Raymond Williams to Director of Third Programme (sending a script on 'Strindberg's Dramatic Development' for centenary of his birth in January 1949), 18 October 1948; from Raymond Williams to a producer, elaborating on the Strindberg idea, 27 November 1948; from R.E. Keen to Raymond Williams, 19 October 1949, and Raymond Williams' reply, accepting the Ibsen notion, 21 October 1949; and R.E. Keen's letter of 1 November 1949. BBC Written Archives.

33 Synopsis of proposal 'Isaac Rosenberg 1890-1918'. BBC Written Archives.

34 Letter from Keen to Raymond Williams, confirming the second Ibsen talk, 11 January 1950 and from Raymond Williams to R. E. Keen, 21 March 1950. BBC Written Archives.

35 Letter from Raymond Williams to R.E. Keen, 13 May 1950. BBC Written Archives.

36 Memorandum from R.E. Keen, 30 December 1949. BBC Written Archives.

37 Asa Briggs, *The History of Broadcasting in the United Kingdom: 1945-55*, Vol. IV, 1955.

38 R.E. Keen Memorandum, 15 June 1950. BBC Written Archives.

39 Letter from Raymond Willliams to R.E. Keen, 21 March 1950 and Keen's handwritten comments on the correspondence. BBC Written Archives.

40 R.E. Keen's memorandum on 'Practical Criticism – and Raymond Williams', 10 May 1950. BBC Written Archives.

41 Letter from R.E. Keen to Raymond Williams, 12 September 1950. BBC Written Archives.

42 Letter from Raymond Williams to R.E. Keen, 19 October 1950. BBC Written Archives.

43 Letter from R.E. Keen to Raymond Williams, 30 November 1950. BBC Written Archives.

44 A three-page fragment typescript entitled 'Three Years Hard: a comment on the Tutorial Class', that breaks off and is undated, though probably 1950/51, RW Papers.

45 Letter from Raymond Williams to Pickstock, 17 November 1950, as cited in Fieldhouse, 'Oxford and Adult Education' in Morgan and Preston, *Raymond Williams: Politics Education Letters*.

8. "THE LINE IS CROSSED"

1 Two typescript copies, one amended by hand, both undated. RW Papers.

2 Raymond Williams, *Adamson* (unpublished novel, 1951). RW Papers.

3 Michael Orrom, *The New Cinema* (typescript copy). RW Papers.

4 Letter from Wolf Mankowitz to Raymond Williams, 31 August 1950. RW Papers.

5 See Kenneth O. Morgan, *Labour in Power 1945-51* (Oxford: Oxford University Press, 1984).

6 See three pages of "Flag into Whip", RW Papers.

7 Draft openings of Raymond Williams' *Bocage*, dated 21 June 1947. RW Papers.

8 Raymond Williams' Manuscript "Black and White", not dated, RW Papers.

9 Typescript/manuscript *Our Lords The Moon and the Sun*, RW Papers.

10 Raymond Williams, *Politics and Letters*, 1979.

11 Letter from Raymond Williams to the War Office, 23 August 1950. RW Papers.

12 Letter from Raymond Williams to Under Secretary of State 29 August 1950 and reply of 1 Sept 1950; Letters of 26 August and 6 Sept from RW to Royal Artillery and War Office; to RW from Central Board for Conscientious Objectors, 28 August 1950.

13 Letter from Thomas Hodgkin to Raymond Williams, 25 April 1950.

14 Letters from War Office to Raymond Williams, 27 and 28 February 1951. RW Papers.

15 Letter from Frank Hancock to Tribunal Chairman, 27 March 1951.

16 Raymond Williams, *Politics and Letters* 1979, p. 88; Harry Williams' diary for 1950/51.

17 Raymond Williams "Application to Local Tribunal", 18 March 1951. RW Papers.

18 See judgement of Tribunal, 7 May 1951 and Notification 9 May 1951; letters from The War Office to Raymond Williams, 15 and 16 May 1951; letters from Raymond Williams to Under Secretary of State at War Office, 19 May 1951.

19 See "August 1951; Estimate of Work", RW Papers.

20 Syllabus of "What is Culture?" 1949-50, RW Papers.

21 This is written in pencil on the back of a single sheet of paper on whose other side is the start of a "story", "The Match Factory", which he incorporated in *Our Lords The Moon and Sun*. On the same side as the *Culture and Work* synopsis is a reordering of the scheme of (unpublished) *Drama from Ibsen to Eliot* which was being rewritten (see Raymond Williams' notebook) in 1949. Hence my estimated dating of this sheet to 1949, RW Papers.

22 Raymond Williams "Books for Teaching 'Culture and Environment' " in *The Use of English*, 1950, reprinted in McIlroy and Westwood.

23 See Raymond Williams' Memorandum, 26 October 1948, RW Papers.

24 Original *Bibliography*, in RW Papers.

25 Joy Williams Interview with Dai Smith, 1990.

26 See Raymond Williams "Books for Teaching", 1950.

27 Ruth Benedict, *Patterns of Culture*, (London: 1935; 1946), pp. 2, 34-36, 181-182.

28 Raymond Williams, *Politics and Letters* 1979, p.97. And see his Introduction to *Keywords* (1976) where he wrote of the 'shock of recognition' that came to him in the basement of the public library in Seaford when he casually looked up 'culture' in the OED and realised its historical connections (to art, industry and democracy) as well as its intellectual meanings.

29 See the McIlroy and Fieldhouse essays in Morgan and Preston, op. cit..

30 Memorandum August 1951, RW Papers. "Lifted Veil" is a George Eliot novella and "Mother" the film by Pudovkin.

31 Michael Orrom's typescript of "The New Cinema" 1994, RW Papers.

32 Letters in Raymond Williams File, Oxford University Archives, as cited in Fieldhouse "Oxford and Adult Education".

33 Harry Williams' diary, 16, 17, 28 February 1952.

34 For Hastings see David Thornton, *Hastings: A Living History*, (Hastings: Hastings Publishing Company, 1987); Pamela Harris, *Hastings in Old Photographs* (Gloucester: Alan Sutton, 1989).

35 Harry Williams' diary, 30 May 1954; 7, 8 January 1957.

36 "Paul Ramsay" narrative sequence and *A Map of Treason*, dated as 1952/3 in RW notebook.

37 Raymond Williams, *Culture and Society* (London: Penguin, 1958: 1961), pp. 263-4.

38 Harry Williams' diaries, 1948-58.

39 Letters from Raymond Williams to Chatto and Windus, 8 November 1950, 22 March and 5 April 1951.

40 Raymond Williams, *Drama From Ibsen to Eliot* (London: Chatto and Windus, 1952).

41 Letter from Raymond Williams to Ian Parsons (Chatto and Windus), 30 October 1951.

42 Letter from Raymond Williams to Ian Parsons, 26 November 1951.

43 Letter from John Johnson, of E.P.S. Lewin to Ian Parsons, 29 November 1951.

44 Letter from Ian Parsons to E.P.S. Lewin, 7 January 1952.

45 See Chatto and Windus Files, University of Reading: the *Times Literary Supplement* 23 January 1953 and the *New Statesman*, 3 January 1953.

46 See J.R. Williams *Tutors Bulletin of Adult Education*, June 1953; Letter from Raymond Williams appearing in *Tutors Bulletin of Adult Education*, Autumn 1953 and Williams' longer piece on 'Text and context', appearing in same publication, March 1954. All reprinted in McIlroy and Westwood, op. cit..

47 Letter from Raymond Williams to Ian Parsons, Chatto, 25 February 1953. At the typewritten letter's conclusion Williams speculated, in pen, as to the anonymous denouncer's identity and, without asking for confirmation, wrote that if he was right in that then "much that is otherwise obscure in this matter becomes clear to me".

48 Letter from Muriel Bradbrook to Dai Smith in 1993. Professor Bradbrook later became the first woman to be appointed as Professor in the English Faculty at Cambridge (1965) and was then Mistress of Girton College from 1968 to 1976. See entry by Eric Salmon in the *Oxford Dictionary of National Biography*, 2005.

9. "WHETHER IT WILL... BE THE KIND OF BOOK
YOU WOULD REALLY WISH TO PUBLISH"

1 Syllabus outline for "A Course of Study in Culture and Society"; Hastings Preparatory Tutorial Class, 1950-1, RW Papers.

2 Letter from F.R. Leavis to Raymond Williams, 1 September 1952. Leavis had waspishly added: "Where culture is concerned, the point about TSE, as I've said, is that he's a fellow countryman of Pound – at least he has never got over being one (he's still incapable, I suspect, of placing Irving Babbit)." RW Papers.

3 Raymond Williams, "The Idea of Culture" in *Essays in Criticism*, July 1953.

4 For the nature of the Journal and its relationship to *Scrutiny*, see Francis Mulhern, *The Moment of Scrutiny*, (London: Verso, 1979).

5 Letter from Raymond Williams to Ian Parsons, 3 July 1953: Chatto and Windus Archive, University of Reading.

6 Correspondence between Ian Parsons and Raymond Williams, August 1953. RW Papers and Chatto and Windus Archive.

7 Letter from Raymond Williams to Parsons, 5 October 1953. Chatto and Windus Archive.

8 Letter from Ian Parsons to Raymond Williams, 22 October 1953. RW Papers.

9 Michael Orrom "The New Cinema". Copy in RW Papers.

10 Raymond Williams "A Dance of Seeing", RW Papers.

11 Michael Orrom to Raymond Williams, 14 September 1953. RW Papers.

12 Michael Orrom and Raymond Williams, *Preface to Film*, (London: Film Drama, 1954).

13 Ibid, p. 21.

14 Raymond Williams, *Drama in Performance* (London: Muller 1954), especially pp. 13 – 14, 113 – 116, 122 – 123.

15 Michael Orrom, "The New Cinema".

16 Interview with Joy Williams, 1990.

17 Michael Orrom, "The New Cinema".

18 Raymond Williams typescript of *Legend*, RW Papers.

19 See Michael Orrom, "The New Cinema". The shooting script, with Raymond Williams' prose-poetry dialogue and "speech songs", is as *Legend*. RW Papers.

20 Raymond Williams Introduction to *Legend*, 1956, RW Papers.

21 Michael Orrom, "The New Cinema".

22 Interview with Michael Orrom, 1990.

23 Interview with Joy Williams, 1990.

24 Harry Williams' diary: June, 1956-April 1957.

25 This was written as a later entry into a Chronology of his life and work he began in one of the two notebooks he kept from 1956, RW Papers.

26 See Foreword, 1987, to the Hogarth Press Edition of *Culture and Society*, 1990.

27 See Raymond Williams "Culture is Ordinary", 1958.

28 See Eric Hobsbawm "The Historians' Group of the Communist Party" in *Rebels and Their Causes: Essays in Honour of A.L. Morton* edited by Maurice Cornforth, (London: Lawrence and Wishart, 1978).

29 Raymond Williams "Film as a Tutorial Subject", *Rewley House Papers*, summer 1953.

30 Delegacy Reports, 1952 – 3, 1954 – 5, 1955 – 6.

31 Raymond Williams, "The Teaching of Public Expression" in *The Highway*, April 1952.

32 Raymond Williams, "The Teaching of Public Expression" May 1954. *Papers in Adult Education*, No. 5. RW Papers.

33 There are four separate pages on "Language and Society", not dated in RW Papers.

34 Raymond Williams typescript of *Between Two Worlds*, 1955, RW Papers.

10. "A DECISIVE STAGE..."

1 Typewritten sheet, headed 'Winifred', dated July 1955. RW Papers.

2 Interviews with Jack Woolford and Arthur Marsh.

3 A number of short stories for children survive. RW Papers.

4 Ruth Middlemiss' written recollection (1995), of Eastbourne classes, 1953/5. I am indebted to Nicholas Treadell for this information.

5 Interview with Michael Orrom, 1990.

6 Raymond Williams' handwritten note/fragment, not dated, RW Papers.

7 Interview with Joy Williams, 1990.

8 Interview with Stuart Hall, 1990.

9 Stuart Hall, 'The "First" New Left' in *Out of Apathy: Voices of the New Left Thirty Years On* (London: Verso, 1989). See also conference papers of Oxford University Socialist Discussion Group.

10 Letter from Raymond Williams to Ian Parsons, 12 January 1956. Chatto and Windus Archive.

11 Letter from Raymond Williams to Ian Parsons, 26 March 1956.

12 Letter from Raymond Williams to Ian Parsons, 23 June 1956, from Parsons to Williams, 24 October and 3 December 1956.

13 Raymond Williams, *Politics and Letters* p. 278.

14 Raymond Williams Notebook, 10 October 1956.

15 Raymond Williams Notebook, 1956.

16 Raymond Williams, *Politics and Letters*.

17 See *The Grasshoppers*, RW Papers. Fred Inglis, *Raymond Williams* (London: Routledge, 1995), p.164, mis-identifies this as the work on which Williams told Parsons he had 'never worked so hard in my life'. Williams was referring to *Culture and Society*.

18 See Dominic Sandbrook, *Never Had It So Good: 1956-63*, (London: Little Brown, 2005), pp. 106-7.

19 John Saville 'The Twentieth Congress and the British Communist Party' in *The Socialist Register: 1976* (London: Merlin Press, 1976), p.7.

20 See especially Stephen Woodham's *History in the Making : Raymond Williams, Edward Thompson and Radical Intellectuals 1936-1956*, (London: Merlin Press, 2001), and John Saville's incisively honest *Memoirs from the Left* (London: Merlin Press, 2003).

21 Raymond Williams, *King Macbeth*, RW Papers.

22 See Raymond Williams' Foreword to 1979 Edition of *Modern Tragedy*.

23 See 'Working Class Attitudes' (transcript of conversation between Richard Hoggart and Raymond Williams on August Bank Holiday 1959), in *New Left Review*, Jan/Feb 1960 where Williams says: "I finished [*Culture and Society*] in the autumn of 1956. I was actually writing the Conclusion during the weeks of Hungary and Suez".

24 Raymond Williams single typed sheet 'Foreword', RW Papers.

25 E.P. Thompson's review of *The Long Revolution* in *New Left Review*, 1961.

26 Robert Conquest's 'Introduction' to *New Lines*, a poetry anthology showcasing Davie, Wain, Amis and others. See also Robert Hewison, *In Anger: Culture in the Cold War 1945-1960* (London: Methuen, 1981). 'On First Looking into *New Lines*' was first published in Raymond Williams' *Writing in Society*, 1984. See also the lengthier typescript pages in RW Papers.

27 *Koba* was published in 1966 in *Modern Tragedy; A Letter from the Country* became a television play in 1966. Fragments of *A Dance of Life*, 'a comedy of manners' and a full synopsis of its Acts along with a running plot line can be traced in Raymond Williams' notebooks, RW Papers.

28 The Notebooks, three for 1956 to 1961, are in RW Papers.

29 Letter from Raymond Williams to Ian Parsons, 7 June 1957, Chatto and Windus Archive.

30 Raymond Williams in *Essays in Criticism*, 7 October 1957. For Hoggart's confirmation of Williams' guesswork see 'Working Class Attitudes', *New Left Review*, 1960 where Hoggart reveals: "I had begun in 1952... thinking then of something quite simple in scope and size – a series of critical essays on popular literature. Soon I began to feel that I wanted to relate this material to the day-to-day experience of people. After this, a strange thing happened... things I'd been writing since 1946 (bits of a novel and some unconnected descriptive pieces) began to fall into place in the new book."

31 See Lin Chun, *The British New Left* (Edinburgh: Edinburgh University Press, 1993), p.15 and passim. In its first manifestation under Stuart Hall's editorship, and with Raymond Williams as a board member, *New Left Review* appeared more critical/cultural than political/theoretical and its editor as an intermediary between traditions. That did not last long. For a considered analysis of the creativity of the overall political and social thinking of the New

Left in the crucial years from 1956 to 1961, consult Michael Kenny, *The First New Left: British Intellectuals After Stalin* (London: Lawrence and Wishart, 1995).

32 Raymond Williams, 'Working Class Culture', *University Left Review*, Summer 1957.

11. "...BUT I AM PRICE FROM GLYNMAWR"

1 Raymond Williams, *Politics and Letters* (1979), p. 361.

2 See Lin Chun, *The British New Left* (1993): John Saville, *Memoirs From the Left* (2003).

3 Stuart Hall "The "First" New Left" in *Out of Apathy* (1989), p. 27.

4 Eric Hobsbawm, *Interesting Times* pp. 212-4.

5 Harry Williams' diaries, October – December 1957: January – March 1958.

6 See *Abergavenny Chronicle*, 30 September 1938.

7 Harry Williams' diary, January – March 1958.

8 Raymond Williams Notebook, R.W. Papers.

9 Raymond Williams 'Culture is Ordinary' in Norman Mackenzie (Ed.), *Conviction* 1958.

10 Anthony Hartley, *Manchester Guardian*, 7 October 1958, see review cuttings, Chatto and Windus files.

11 Graham Martin, 'A Culture in Common', ULR, Autumn 1958.

12 Richard Hoggart 'An Important Book', *Essays in Criticism*, April 1959.

13 Various pages of typescript under title *A Common Theme*, RW Papers.

14 Raymond Williams, *Border Country* p. 4.

15 Raymond Williams, Note to original edition of *Border Country*, 1960.

16 Raymond Williams, typescript note, Williams' papers.

17 Letter from Ian Parsons to Raymond Williams, 7 December 1959, Chatto and Windus files.

18 Letter from Raymond Williams to Ian Parsons, 2 November 1959.

19 See autograph changes and corrections made to typescript of *Border Country* in the collection of Raymond Williams papers (mostly proofs and typescripts) held at The National Library of Wales, Aberystwyth.

20 "Dates" in the Notebooks was written up at various times as the years passed but the first set (from 1921 to 1966) seems to have been written all at once.

21 Raymond Williams in Orrom and Williams, *Preface to Film* (1954) p. 21.

Index

Aberdare 21–2

Abergavenny 2, 23–4, 31–8, 50, 52–3, 57, 59, 60, 63, 69, 71, 385

Abergavenny Grammar School *see* King Henry VIII Grammar School

Anderson, Perry 8, 9

Arnhem 181–7

Arnold, Malcolm 369

Ballet Rambert 125–6, 130

Balliol College, Oxford 226–7, 229, 230, 234

Barnstaple 98–9, 100, 111, 134, 322

Bateson, F.W. 322, 359

Belgium 178–9

Bellchambers, Eric 232–3

Benedict, Ruth 334, 335

Berlin, Isaiah 307

Bevan, Aneurin 322, 456

Bexhill-on-Sea 304–5

Bird, Herbert 49–50

Black Mountains 2, 50, 111, 272, 386

Bradbrook, Muriel 354–7

Bridge, The 213

Briggs, Asa 307, 308, 373–4

Brighton 304–5

Browne, E. Martin 250

Brunsbüttell 199–200, 207

Brussels 179, 181, 188, 193, 205

Burton, Kay 356

Caen 151, 152, 164–5, 167, 179

Calder-Marshall, Arthur 269

Cambridge ix, x, 1, 4, 7, 10, 29, 59, 67, 77, 79, 80, 81, 82–8, 89, 93–8, 102, 111, 121–8, 130, 131, 146, 207, 216, 240, 295, 300, 447, 452

Cambridge Front 126, 128

Cambridge Review 128–129

Cambridge University Journal 103, 108, 113, 117, 121, 124

Cambridge University Socialist Club 85–6, 95, 97, 103, 105, 107, 113, 121, 123

Caudwell, Christopher 115

Caumont 167

Central Office of Information 252–3

Chatto and Windus 2, 350, 353, 362, 395, 399, 400, 453

Coghill, Neville 251

Cole G.D.H. 398

Collins, Clifford 218, 222, 232, 233, 240–5, 257, 259–60, 411

Communist Manifesto, The 72

Communist Party 85, 86, 87, 88, 103, 106–7, 111–12, 122, 229, 238, 240, 247, 248, 301, 303, 320, 341, 353, 377, 409–10, 411, 438

Communist Party Historians'
Group 302, 303, 308, 378,
409, 441
Copenhagen 205–6
Craig, Maurice 128
Cranks, John 369
Critic, The 242, 243, 245, 252

Davies, Thomas 45, 46–7, 48, 51
Day Lewis, Cecil 350
Dobb, Maurice 113
Donaldson, John 107
Dutt, Rajani Palme 112

Eagleton, Terry 5, 10
Edwards, Jimmy 107, 108
Eindhoven 182
Eliot T.S. 215, 218, 245, 250,
257, 316, 334, 349, 353
Elvin, Lionel 84–5, 232, 234
Empson, William 84, 257, 350
English Story 223
Epsom Offensive 151, 153
Essays in Criticism 322, 359
Essays in Labour History 308

Falaise 150, 168, 171, 179
Fallas, Margaret 75–6, 102–3,
131
Fawkes, Ray 31, 48–9, 57, 117
Fearns, Harry 87
Finno–Soviet War 87, 90, 103–6
First World War 16, 17–18, 34
Foot, Michael 60
Fremlin, Celia 119
Fry, Christopher 353

General Strike 37, 38–9, 41–3,
384, 386–9, 430–1

Geneva 72
Gibbs, Eddie 156, 158
Grainville-sur-Odon 154, 156,
174
Great Tradition, The 350
Great Western Railway 16, 17,
19, 26, 33, 35
Griffiths, Brinley 27
Griffiths, Maelor 28–9, 32,
70–1, 73
Griffiths, Rev. Isaac 27
Guardian, The 10, 454

Haldane, J.B.S. 86
Hall, Alan 399
Hall, Stuart 9, 398–9, 438,
446, 457
Hamburg 198, 205
Hancock, Frank 73–5, 327
Hare, David 10
Hargreaves, Sir G.P. 328
Hastings 304, 305, 336–8,
367, 377, 378, 380, 441
Heath, Stephen 10
Henderson, Hamish 107, 108
Higgins, John 7
Hill, Christopher 246, 308,
409, 438
Hobsbawm, Eric 86, 87, 96,
103, 104, 105–6, 122,
207, 308, 409–10, 438,
446
Hodgkin, Thomas 229–30, 260,
302, 303, 327
Hoggart, Richard 306, 418,
436–7, 439–40, 451,
457–9
House, Humphrey 307, 360
Howells, Kim ix

Hughes, Annette 97–8, 102, 103, 223
Hughes, Rev. J.A. 45, 46, 61
Huxley, Aldous 74, 78

Jardine, Lisa 10
Jay, Douglas 73
Jessup, Frank 302
Jesus College, Cambridge 7
Johnson, Paul 451
Johnson, R.W. 6
Jones, Mervyn 451

Keen, R.E. 311–14
Kermode, Frank 455
Kettle, Arnold 455
Kiernan, V.G. 455–6
King Hall, Stephen 73
King Henry VIII Grammar School, Abergavenny, 47, 63, 64–7
Klingender, Francis 303
Knights, L.C. 29, 219, 257

Labour Party 8, 9, 21, 37, 39, 57, 58–60, 74–5, 85, 89, 95, 112, 210, 221, 230, 322, 323, 378, 453
Larkhill 132, 133–4
Laski, Harold 95, 201
Laycock, Peter 72
League of Nations Union 65, 72
Leavis, F.R. 83, 84, 85, 115, 116, 217–9, 221, 234, 238–9, 240, 245–6, 249, 257, 314, 315, 334, 358–9, 360, 365
Left Book Club 72–3
Lehman, John 124, 135

Lindsay, A.D. 226, 229, 230
London 71–2
London School of Economics 94–7, 98, 101
Louvain 178

Mackenzie, Norman 94, 96
Mankowitz, Wolf 218, 219, 222, 231, 233, 240–6, 250, 257, 259–60, 261, 272, 322, 373, 411
Marsh, Arthur 232, 396
Martin, Graham 456–8
Martin, Kingsley 73, 86, 215
May Day Manifesto, The 9
McLean, Tony 303
Metcalfe, John 244
Middlemiss, Ruth 397
Miles, Bernard 127, 129, 208–9, 250, 251
Monmouth by-election 73–5
Moore, Nicholas 124, 127
Murdoch, Iris 72, 451
My Years in the Klondike 269

National Union of Railwaymen 22, 38
Nazi-Soviet Pact 86, 104, 111
Newcombe, H.J. 63–4, 67
New Left Review 8, 9, 438
New Reasoner, The 412, 455
New Statesman 73, 221, 353, 359, 451
New Writing and Daylight 135
Normandy 134, 138–9, 148, 149, 150, 163, 171, 172

Odon, River 151, 153, 154, 163
Operation Goodwood 164, 166

Orne, River 151–2
Orrom, Michael 87, 108, 122–4,
    126, 128, 130, 143–4, 222,
    252–3, 261–2, 269–70,
    336, 362–4, 367–72, 375,
    377, 378, 397
Orwell, George 119, 334
Outlook, 128
Oxford 338
Oxford Extra-Mural Delegacy 8,
    221–2, 226–7, 231, 301,
    379–80, 396

Pandy 17, 21, 22–31, 25, 35,
    51, 52–6, 59, 60, 117,
    130, 255, 278, 331, 339,
    246, 385, 428, 449–50
Pandy Eisteddfod 52–6
Pandy School 44–7
Parrinder, Patrick 10
Parsons, Ian 3, 350, 351–2,
    361, 362, 399–401, 435,
    460
Past and Present 308, 441
Peace Pledge Union 73, 326,
    327
People's Convention 111, 112,
    117, 119
Pickard-Cambridge, Sir Arthur
    328
Pickstock, Frank 229, 230, 233,
    302, 310, 317
Plaid Cymru 8
'Point 176' 168–71
Polhill, Vic 158, 170
Politics and Letters (journal) 244,
    245, 246, 257, 306
Pollitt, Harry 111–12
Postgate, Raymond 307

Powicke, Sir F.M. 307
Priestley, J.B. 248–9, 406–7,
    455
Pritt, D.N. 112

Quiller-Couch, Sir Arthur
    217–18

*Ragged Trousered Philanthropists,
    The* 338
Rajan, B. 244
Ralphs, Arnold L. 65–7, 257
Richards, I.A. 83–4, 316
Richardson, Ralph 250
Richmond, Anne 128–30, 143–4
Rickword, Edgell 116
Rotha, Paul 222, 252, 253,
    269, 367
Rowthorn, Bob 9

Sandbostel Concentration Camp
    198
Saville, John 409–10, 446
Scrutiny 218, 240, 245, 258,
    360
Scurfield, George 107, 124,
    125, 126, 244
Seaford 222, 225, 260, 279,
    282, 304, 305
Slater, Montagu 353
Smith, A.H. 229
Smith, John Maynard 113, 122
Stockwood, Rev. Mervyn 113
Stringer, Michael 369

Taylor, Major Dick 141, 153,
    160, 172, 325
Tawney, R.H. 227
Thompson, Denys 238, 257

Thompson, E.P. 8–9, 11, 308–9, 409–11, 418, 422–3, 438, 455

Tillyard, E.M.W. 84–5, 115, 216

Times Literary Supplement, The 353, 360

Trevelyan, G.M. 114, 115

Trojan Women, The 58–9, 288

Tutorial Classes Committee 227–9

21st Anti–Tank Regiment of the Royal Artillery 134, 137, 148, 156, 164, 171, 172, 182, 195, 199

Twentyone 180, 199, 200, 204–7, 208, 211, 323

Universities and Left Review 399, 412, 437–9, 445–6, 456

Use of English, The 333

Vire 168, 171

Vassy 168, 171

Wakefield 75

Webb, Bill 10

Williams, Ederyn 222, 267, 396, 444

Williams, Emlyn 250–1

Williams, Gladys Sylvia 49–50

Williams, Gwen 18, 19, 21, 23, 30, 31, 51–2, 58–9, 75, 79, 103, 109, 111, 134, 189, 267, 279–81, 310, 337, 346, 347, 396, 449–50

Williams Gwydion Madawc 444

Williams, Harry 12, 16–22, 26, 30, 31, 37, 39–40, 50–1, 52, 56–7, 59–60, 67, 68, 71, 75, 78, 109, 130, 131, 132, 134, 189, 281–2, 310, 337, 338, 346–8, 373, 384, 449–50 military service 17–18, 23 and General Strike 39–40 diaries 56, 67, 68, 76, 79, 109, 119, 132, 144, 206, 220–1, 279, 280–1, 337–8, 347–8, 396, 450

Williams, Herbert 18–19

Williams, Joseph 16–17

Williams, Joy ix, x, 5, 9, 11, 12, 94, 97–103, 109, 114, 117, 120, 128, 129, 130, 131, 134, 144, 189, 206, 214, 221, 267, 280, 304, 310, 334, 338, 362, 363, 370, 372–3, 374, 375, 396, 398, 444, 446

Williams, J.R. 354

Williams, Margaret 17

Williams, Merryn 134, 191, 193, 214, 267, 310, 337, 338, 396, 444

Williams, Raymond
    Welshness 1, 6–7, 8, 91–2, 231, 291–2; Marxism 1; death 4, 11; birth 25; 'Jim' 25; childhood home 29–31; passes scholarship 47; childhood 48–9; books 58–9; religion 60–1, 74; Grammar School days 65–7; applies to Cambridge 67; pacifism 73–4; joins

Communist Party 91; meets Joy Dalling 97; and cinema 121–4, 203–4; meets Michael Orrom 123; and ballet 125; and studies 130–1; enlists 131–2; military training 133–4, 139–40; commissioned 134; marries Joy 134; military service 134–7; leaves army 146, 192; wartime experiences 153–7, 189; edits *Twentyone* 199, 204–5, 207, 208; 'Michael Pope' 199–207; returns to Cambridge 207; leaves Cambridge 221; moves with Joy and family to Seaford 222–4; appointed to Extra Mural Delegacy 228; Extra Mural colleagues on 231–3; founds *Politics and Letters* and *The Critic* with Clifford Collins and Wolf Mankowitz 244–5; breaks with Clifford Collins 260–1; argument with Gwen over Joy 280; speaks on the Third Programme 311–12, 314; refuses call-up for Korean War 325–30; family move to Hastings 336–7; depression 339, 373, 375; defends himself against charge of plagiarism 355–6; film-making 362–4; breaks with Michael Orrom 371–2; female students 396–7; Notebooks 425–6, 441, 442, 443, 448; self-containment 445; father's death 450–1; *Culture and Society* published 453–4; unpublished conclusion of *The Long Revolution* 470–4

On: community 29; General Strike 42–3; school history 45; 'Scholarship Boys' 47; books in home 58; applying to Cambridge 68; being a writer 68; Douglas Jay 73; Stephen King Hall 73; politics 78–9; transition from school to Cambridge 81–2; pre-war politics 86–7; class 94; Finno-Soviet War 103–4; eve of Second World War 113–4, 118; materialist criticism 115–6; 'Modern writing' 127; military service 145, 147–8, 159–60, 161, 161–3 166–7, 169–71, 175–8, 180–1, 188; post–war rapprochement 145–6, 201–3; Arnhem 186–7; *Twentyone* 200; Harold Laski 201; pacifism 202–3, 326; British cinema 203; Denmark 205–6; Henrik Ibsen 215, 349; Cambridge English 216–7, 315; English culture 220; tutorial teaching 235–6; teaching literature 237, 306, 309, 315; culture 239, 335–6, 359, 420, 443, 452–3; Soviet literature 248; J.B. Priestley 249;

drama 249; village community 253–6; literature 258; himself 262–3; Sartre 303; Marxism 303–4; historiography 307–8; adult education 317; war 328–330; Thirties' Marxism 342–3; art and society 349–50, 360; charge of plagiarism 355–6; 'structures of feeling' 365; critical theory 366, 381; dreams 374–5; depression 375–6; *Culture and Society* 377, 418, 423; cinema and adult education 378–9; education and the working class 380; language and society 382–3; the 'masses' 419; equality 419; 'class feeling' 419–20; working class culture 420, 452–3; public service ethos 420–1; the 'ladder version of society' 421–2; *The Uses of Literacy* 436–7, 439–40; class politics 439–40; *The Long Revolution* 442, 470–4; Campaign for Nuclear Disarmament (CND) 445

Letters from RW to: Chatto and Windus 2–3, 348–9, 351, 399–400, 435; Joy Williams 147–8, 150, 189–91, 192, 193, 194; Clifford Collins 259–6

Works: *A Common Theme* 3, 459–62, 465, 468; 'A Dialogue on Actors' 249; 'A Fine Room to be Ill In' 223–4, 265; *A Map of Treason* 88–93, 340–2, 371, 427; *Adamson* 319–322, 331, 351, 352, 371, 372, 401; 'After the Game' 265–6; *Art of the Actor, The* 225–6, 265–6, 274–6, 293, 320, 331; *Between Two Worlds* 383, 384–395, 402, 426, 427; *Bocage* 323–5; *Border Country* x, 3, 12, 13–15, 48, 53, 61–2, 79, 22–3, 29, 37, 39, 40–1, 42, 80–1, 231, 276, 287, 343, 348, 384, 387, 389, 429–434, 444, 447–9, 450, 451, 459, 460–1, 462–9; *Border Village* 3, 53–6, 428–35, 437, 451, 459, 462; *Brynllwyd* 69, 264, 265, 267, 282–301, 320, 351, 383, 384, 389, 427, 434; 'Clear as Crystal' 118–120; *Communications* 382; *Country and the City, The* 6, 25; 'Culture is Ordinary' 219–20, 451–3; *Culture and Society* vii, 2, 6, 13, 217, 241, 276, 303, 332, 334, 335, 342, 344, 346, 376, 377, 401, 406, 417–23, 426, 435, 442, 444, 445, 453–9; *Drama from Ibsen to Eliot* 348, 351, 353–4; *Drama in Performance* 328, 361, 363,

365–6; *Effect of Machine on the Countryman's Work, Life and Community* 253–6; *End of Exile?, The* 427–8, 459; *English Novel from Dickens to Lawrence, The* 10; *Fight for Manod, The* 8; 'Flag into Whip' 323; 'Fragment' 267–9; 'Frontier' 126; *Grasshoppers, The* 11, 259, 383, 401–8, 427; 'Girl Who Couldn't Say Robert, The' 180; *I Live Through the War* 76–8; 'Idea of Culture, The' 359, 360–1; *Interlude* 262–3; 'Isn't it a Scream' 140–1; *Keywords* 382, 400; *King Macbeth* 412–17, 441; *Legend* 368–9, 371; 'Liberation' 208–11, 265, 323; *Long Revolution, The* ix, 2, 6, 47, 332, 335, 358, 382, 441–4, 470; *Loyalties* 5–6, 88, 172–4, 212; *Matthew Price* 441–2; *Medwyn Project, The* 331–2; 'Mr Dearman Goes Home' 266–7; *Modern Tragedy* 10; 'Mother Chapel' 110, 264; 'Mountain Sunset' 68; 'My Cambridge' 93; 'Nijmegen Bridge' 212; 'On First Looking into *New Lines*' 424–5; *Our Lords The Moon and The Sun* 142, 160, 161, 325, 331, 427; *People of the Black Mountains* 132; *Politics and Letters* x, 10, 12, 23, 86–7, 174, *Preface to Film* (with Michael Orrom) 363–4; 'Rat, The' 267; *Reading and Criticism* 215, 257–9, 264; 'Red Earth' 109–10, 118; 'Revolution in Cambridge' 216; 'Ridyear' 270–3, 319, 351; 'Sack Labourer' 128; *Second Generation* 8; *Silent Movie* 70–1; *Social Significance of 1926, The Studies in Modern Drama* 264; 'Sugar' 69, 128; 'This Time' 135–7; 'Traitor, The' 175–8; 'Understanding' 267; *Volunteers, The* 8; 'War on the USSR?' (with Eric Hobsbawm) 105–6; war diary 149, 154–6, 185, 195

Wilson–Brown, Major S.A. 160–1, 172

Winkler, R.O.C. 246

Wolfitt, Donald 250

Woodings, Bill 10

Woolford, Jack 231, 302, 304

Workers' Educational Association (W.E.A.) 66, 101, 221, 227, 228, 230, 302, 306

Wright, Ian 10

Wright, Basil 356, 369

Wyatt, Woodrow 223

Zilliacus, Konni 73, 86

Modern Wales by Parthian Books

In May 2017 Parthian Books, supported by the Rhys Davies Trust and edited by Dai Smith, launched a new series entitled Modern Wales. The series intends to look at places crucial to the development of modern Wales, such as Cardiff and Newport, as well as at the imagery and iconography which has shaped the culture and society of modern Wales. The series, in a new and distinctive livery, will include an impressive back catalogue of connected Parthian publications. The inaugural titles of the series are *To Hear the Skylark's Song* by Huw Lewis, and *Merthyr: The Crucible of Modern Wales* by Joe England. Future titles, already commissioned will include Angela John's Rocking the Boat, essays on Welsh women who pioneered the fight for equality, and Daryl Leeworthy's, *Labour Country*, a fresh and provocative look at the struggle through radical action for social democracy in Wales. In the pipeline already are new political and culturally-informed biographies of the pioneering socialist and feminist Minnie Palliser and of the great Welsh novelist, playwright and public commentator, Gwyn Thomas.

PARTHIAN

WALES: ENGLAND'S COLONY?

Martin Johnes

From the very beginnings of Wales, its people have defined themselves against their large neighbour. This book tells the fascinating story of an uneasy and unequal relationship between two nations living side-by-side.

PB / £8.99
978-1-912681-41-9

RHYS DAVIES: A WRITER'S LIFE

Meic Stephens

Rhys Davies (1901-78) was among the most dedicated, prolific and accomplished of Welsh prose writers. This is his first full biography.

'This is a delightful book, which is itself a social history in its own right, and funny.'
– The Spectator

PB / £11.99
978-1-912109-96-8

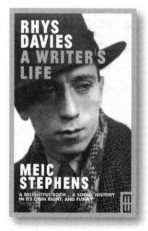

MERTHYR, THE CRUCIBLE OF MODERN WALES

Joe England

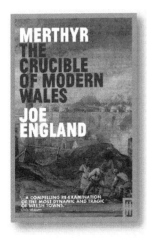

Merthyr Tydfil was the town where the future of a country was forged: a thriving, struggling surge of people, industry, democracy and ideas. This book assesses an epic history of Merthyr from 1760 to 1912 through the focus of a fresh and thoroughly convincing perspective.

PB / £18.99
978-1-913640-05-7

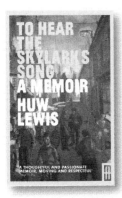

TO HEAR THE SKYLARK'S SONG

Huw Lewis

To Hear the Skylark's Song is a memoir about how Aberfan survived and eventually thrived after the terrible disaster of the 21st of October 1966.

'A thoughtful and passionate memoir, moving and respectful.'
– Tessa Hadley

PB / £8.99
978-1-912109-72-2

ROCKING THE BOAT

Angela V. John

This insightful and revealing collection of essays focuses on seven Welsh women who, in a range of imaginative ways, resisted the status quo in Wales, England and beyond during the nineteenth and twentieth centuries.

PB / £11.99
978-1-912681-44-0

TURNING THE TIDE

Angela V. John

This rich biography tells the remarkable tale of Margaret Haig Thomas (1883-1958) who became the second Viscountess Rhondda. She was a Welsh suffragette, held important posts during the First World War and survived the sinking of the *Lusitania*.

PB / £17.99
978-1-909844-72-8

BRENDA CHAMBERLAIN, ARTIST & WRITER

Jill Piercy

The first full-length biography of Brenda Chamberlain chronicles the life of an artist and writer whose work was strongly affected by the places she lived, most famously Bardsey Island and the Greek island of Hydra.

PB / £11.99
978-1-912681-06-8

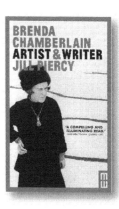

PARTHIAN Parthian Voices

A DIRTY BROTH: EARLY-TWENTIETH CENTURY WELSH PLAYS IN ENGLISH

VOLUME 1 OF TWENTIETH-CENTURY WELSH PLAYS IN ENGLISH

Edited by David Cottis

This anthology, the first in a series of three, brings together three plays from the beginnings of Welsh playwriting in English.

PB /£14.99
978-1-912681-71-6

A LADDER OF WORDS: MID-TWENTIETH CENTURY WELSH PLAYS IN ENGLISH

VOLUME 2 OF TWENTIETH-CENTURY WELSH PLAYS IN ENGLISH

Edited by David Cottis

A Ladder of Words explores the period either side of the Second World War, a time when Welsh playwrights enjoyed unprecedented commercial success.

PB / £14.99
978-1-913640-04-0

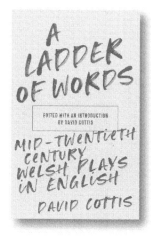

SAINTS AND LODGERS: THE POEMS OF W.H. DAVIES

Selected with an introduction by Jonathan Edwards

William Henry Davies (1871–1940) was a Welsh poet and writer. He was also a traveller and adventurer. In this collection he emerges as a poet of people, who never turns away from the suffering or the beauty of the saints and lodgers among whom he lives.

PB / £9.99
978-1-912681-34-1